THE OXFORD HANDBOOK OF

EPISTEMOLOGY

THE OXFORD HANDBOOK OF

EPISTEMOLOGY

Edited by

PAUL K. MOSER

UNIVERSITY PRESS

2002

OXFORD

UNIVERSITY PRESS

Oxford   New York

Auckland   Bangkok   Buenos Aires   Cape Town   Chennai
Dar es Salaam   Delhi   Hong Kong   Istanbul   Karachi   Kolkata
Kuala Lumpur   Madrid   Melbourne   Mexico City   Mumbai   Nairobi
São Paulo   Shanghai   Singapore   Taipei   Tokyo   Toronto

Copyright © 2002 by Oxford University Press, Inc.

Published by Oxford University Press, Inc.
198 Madison Avenue, New York, New York 10016

www.oup.com

Oxford is a registered trademark of Oxford University Press

Library of Congress Cataloging-in-Publication Data
The Oxford handbook of epistemology / edited by Paul K. Moser.
p. cm.
Includes bibliographical references and index.
ISBN 0-19-513005-7
1. Knowledge, Theory of.   I. Moser, Paul K., 1957–
BD161 096 2002
121—dc21   2001058016

1 3 5 7 9 8 6 4 2

Printed in the United States of America
on acid-free paper

In memory of

my sister, Laura Moser
August 1956–September 2001

and my father, Kenneth Moser
January 1932–July 2002

Preface

....

EPISTEMOLOGY, also known as the theory of knowledge, will flourish as long as we deem knowledge valuable. We shall, I predict, continue to value knowledge, if only for its instrumental value: it gets us through the day as well as the night. Indeed, it's hard to imagine a stable person, let alone a stable society, indifferent to the real difference between genuine knowledge and mere opinion, even mere true opinion. The study of knowledge, then, has a very bright future.

In the concept-sensitive hands of philosophers, epistemology focuses on the nature, origin, and scope of knowledge. It thus examines the defining ingredients, the sources, and the limits of knowledge. Given the central role of epistemology in the history of philosophy as well as in contemporary philosophy, epistemologists will always have work to do. Debates over the analysis of knowledge, the sources of knowledge, and the status of skepticism will alone keep the discipline of epistemology active and productive. This book presents some of the best work in contemporary epistemology by leading epistemologists. Taken together, its previously unpublished essays span the whole field of epistemology. They assess prominent positions and break new theoretical ground while avoiding undue technicality.

My own work on this book has benefited from many people and institutions. First, I thank the nineteen contributors for their fine cooperation and contributions in the face of numerous deadlines. Second, I thank Peter Ohlin, Philosophy Editor at Oxford University Press, for helpful advice and assistance on many fronts. Third, I thank my research assistant, Blaine Swen, for invaluable help in putting the book together. Finally, I thank Loyola University of Chicago for providing an excellent environment for my work on the project.

Chicago, Illinois   P. K. M.
June 2002

CONTENTS

....

Contributors

LOUISE M. ANTONY   Department of Philosophy, Ohio State University

ROBERT AUDI   Department of Philosophy, University of Nebraska, Lincoln

LAURENCE BONJOUR   Department of Philosophy, University of Washington, Seattle

ALBERT CASULLO   Department of Philosophy, University of Nebraska, Lincoln

RICHARD FELDMAN   Department of Philosophy, University of Rochester

RICHARD FOLEY   Department of Philosophy, New York University

RICHARD FUMERTON   Department of Philosophy, University of Iowa

ALVIN I. GOLDMAN   Department of Philosophy, Rutgers University

JOHN GRECO   Department of Philosophy, Fordham University

JOHN HEIL   Department of Philosophy, Davidson College

MARK KAPLAN   Department of Philosophy, Indiana University

PHILIP KITCHER   Department of Philosophy, Columbia University

PETER KLEIN   Department of Philosophy, Rutgers University

NOAH LEMOS   Department of Philosophy, De Pauw University

WILLIAM G. LYCAN   Department of Philosophy, University of North Carolina, Chapel Hill

PAUL K. MOSER   Department of Philosophy, Loyola University of Chicago

PHILIP L. QUINN   Department of Philosophy, University of Notre Dame

ROBERT K. SHOPE   Department of Philosophy, University of Massachusetts, Boston

ROY SORENSEN   Department of Philosophy, Dartmouth College

ERNEST SOSA   Department of Philosophy, Brown University and Rutgers University

THE OXFORD HANDBOOK OF

EPISTEMOLOGY

INTRODUCTION

PAUL K. MOSER

1. REPRESENTATIVE DISTINCTIONS AND DEBATES

EPISTEMOLOGY, characterized broadly, is an account of knowledge. Within the discipline of philosophy, epistemology is the study of the nature of knowledge and justification: in particular, the study of (a) the defining components, (b) the substantive conditions or sources, and (c) the limits of knowledge and justification. Categories (a)–(c) have prompted traditional philosophical controversy over the analysis of knowledge and justification, the sources of knowledge and justification (in the case, for instance, of rationalism vs. empiricism), and the status of skepticism about knowledge and justification.

Epistemologists have distinguished some species of knowledge, including: propositional knowledge (*that* something is so), nonpropositional knowledge *of* something (for instance, knowledge by acquaintance, or by direct awareness), empirical (a posteriori) propositional knowledge, nonempirical (a priori) propositional knowledge, and knowledge of how to do something. Recent epistemology has included controversies over distinctions between such species, for example, over (i) the relations between some of these species (for example, does knowledge-of reduce somehow to knowledge-that?) and (ii) the viability of some of these species (for instance, is there really such a thing as, or even a coherent notion of, a priori knowledge?).

A posteriori knowledge is widely regarded as knowledge that depends for its supporting ground on some specific sensory or perceptual content. In contrast, a priori knowledge is widely regarded as knowledge that does not depend for its supporting ground on such experiential content. The epistemological tradition stemming from Immanuel Kant proposes that the supporting ground for a priori knowledge comes solely from purely intellectual processes called "pure reason" or "pure understanding." In this tradition, knowledge of logical truths is a standard case of a priori knowledge, whereas knowledge of the existence or presence of physical objects is a standard case of a posteriori knowledge. An account of a priori knowledge should explain what the relevant purely intellectual processes are and how they contribute to nonempirical knowledge. Analogously, an account of a posteriori knowledge should explain what sensory or perceptual experience is and how it contributes to empirical knowledge. Even so, epistemologists have sought an account of propositional knowledge *in general*, that is, an account of what is common to a priori and a posteriori knowledge.

Ever since Plato's *Theaetetus*, epistemologists have tried to identify the essential, defining components of propositional knowledge. These components will yield an *analysis* of propositional knowledge. An influential traditional view, inspired by Plato and Kant among others, is that propositional knowledge has three individually necessary and jointly sufficient components: justification, truth, and belief. On this view, propositional knowledge is, by definition, justified true belief. This tripartite definition has come to be called "the standard analysis." (See the essay by Shope on this analysis.)

Knowledge is not just true belief. Some true beliefs are supported merely by lucky guesswork and thus are not knowledge. Knowledge requires that the satisfaction of its belief condition be "appropriately related" to the satisfaction of its truth condition. This is one broad way of understanding the justification condition of the standard analysis. We might say that a knower must have *adequate indication* that a known proposition is true. If we understand such adequate indication as a sort of *evidence* indicating that a proposition is true, we have adopted a prominent traditional view of the justification condition: justification as evidence. Questions about justification attract much attention in contemporary epistemology. Controversy arises over the meaning of "justification" as well as over the substantive conditions for a belief's being justified in a way appropriate to knowledge.

An ongoing controversy has emerged from this issue: Does epistemic justification, and thus knowledge, have foundations, and, if so, in what sense? The key question is whether some beliefs (a) have their epistemic justification *noninferentially* (that is, apart from evidential support from any other beliefs), and (b) supply epistemic justification for all justified beliefs that lack such noninferential justification. Traditional foundationalism, represented in different ways by, for example, Aristotle, Descartes, Bertrand Russell, C. I. Lewis, and Roderick Chisholm, offers an affirmative answer to this issue. (See the essay by Fumerton on foundationalism.)

Foundationalists diverge over the specific conditions for noninferential justification. Some identify noninferential justification with *self*-justification. Others propose that noninferential justification resides in evidential support from the nonconceptual content of nonbelief psychological states: for example, perception, sensation, or memory. Still others understand noninferential justification in terms of a belief's being "reliably produced," that is, caused and sustained by some nonbelief belief-producing process or source (for instance, perception, memory, or introspection) that tends to produce true rather than false beliefs. Such a view takes the causal source and sustainer of a belief to be crucial to its foundational justification. Contemporary foundationalists typically separate claims to noninferential, foundational justification from claims to certainty. They typically settle for a *modest* foundationalism implying that foundational beliefs need not be indubitable or infallible. This contrasts with the radical foundationalism often attributed to Descartes.

A prominent competitor against foundationalism is the coherence theory of justification, that is, epistemic coherentism. This view implies that the justification of any belief depends on that belief's having evidential support from some other belief via coherence relations such as entailment or explanatory relations. An influential contemporary version of epistemic coherentism states that evidential coherence relations among beliefs are typically explanatory relations. The general idea is that a belief is justified for you so long as it either best explains, or is best explained by, some member of the system of beliefs that has maximal explanatory power for you. Contemporary epistemic coherentism is holistic; it finds the ultimate source of justification in a *system* of interconnected beliefs or potential beliefs.

A problem for all versions of coherentism that aim to explain empirical justification is *the isolation objection*. According to this objection, coherentism entails that you can be epistemically justified in accepting an empirical proposition that is incompatible with, or at least improbable given, your total empirical evidence. The key assumption of this objection is that your total empirical evidence includes *non*conceptual sensory and perceptual content, such as pain you feel or something you seem to see. Such content is not a belief or a proposition. Epistemic coherentism, by definition, makes justification a function solely of coherence relations between propositions, such as propositions one believes or accepts. As a result, coherentism seems to isolate justification from the evidential import of the nonconceptual content of nonbelief awareness-states. Coherentists have tried to handle this problem, but no resolution enjoys wide acceptance.

Recently some epistemologists have recommended that we give up the traditional evidence condition for knowledge. They recommend that we construe the justification condition as a *causal* condition or at least replace the justification condition with a causal condition. The general idea is that you know that P if (a) you believe that P, (b) P is true, and (c) your believing that P is causally produced and sustained by the fact that makes P true. This is the basis of *the causal theory of knowing.* It admits of various characterizations of the conditions for a belief's being produced or sustained.

A causal theory owes us special treatment of our knowledge of universal propositions. Evidently, I know, for example, that all cars are manufactured ultimately by humans, but my believing that this is so seems not to be causally supported by the fact that all cars are thus manufactured. It is not clear that the latter fact causally produces *any* belief, let alone my belief that all cars are manufactured ultimately by humans. A causal theory of knowing must handle this problem.

Another problem is that causal theories typically neglect what seems to be crucial to any account of the justification condition for knowledge: the requirement that justificational support for a belief be *accessible*, in some sense, to the believer. The rough idea is that one must be able to access, or bring to awareness, the justification underlying one's beliefs. The causal origins of a belief are often very complex and inaccessible to a believer. Causal theories thus face problems from an accessibility requirement on justification. Such problems will be especially pressing for a causal theorist who aims to capture, rather than dispense with, a justification condition. *Internalism* regarding justification preserves an accessibility requirement on what confers justification, whereas epistemic *externalism* rejects this requirement. Debates over internalism and externalism abound in current epistemology, but internalists do not yet share a uniform detailed account of accessibility. (See the essays by BonJour and Sosa on such debates.)

The standard analysis of knowledge, however elaborated, faces a devastating challenge that initially gave rise to causal theories of knowledge: *the Gettier problem.* In 1963 Edmund Gettier published a highly influential challenge to the view that if you have a justified true belief that *P*, then you know that *P*. Here is one of Gettier's counterexamples to this view:

> Smith is justified in believing the false proposition that (i) Jones owns a Ford. On the basis of (i), Smith infers, and thus is justified in believing, that (ii) either Jones owns a Ford or Brown is in Barcelona. As it happens, Brown is in Barcelona, and so (ii) is true. So, although Smith is justified in believing the true proposition (ii), Smith does not know (ii).

Gettier-style counterexamples are cases where a person has justified true belief that *P* but lacks knowledge that *P*. The Gettier problem is the problem of finding a modification of, or an alternative to, the standard analysis that avoids difficulties from Gettier-style counterexamples. The controversy over the Gettier problem is highly complex and still unsettled. (See the essay by Shope for details.)

Many epistemologists take the lesson of Gettier-style counterexamples to be that propositional knowledge requires *a fourth condition*, beyond the justification, truth, and belief conditions. No specific fourth condition has received unanimous acceptance, but some proposals have become prominent. The so-called "defeasibility condition," for example, requires that justification appropriate to knowledge be "undefeated" in the sense that a specific subjunctive conditional concerning defeaters of justification be true of that justification. For instance, one defeasibility fourth condition requires of Smith's knowing that P that there be no true proposition, Q, such that if Q became justified for Smith, P would no longer be justified for Smith. So if Smith knows, on the basis of visual perception, that Mary removed books from the library, then Smith's coming to believe the true proposition that Mary's identical twin removed books from the library would not undermine the justification for Smith's belief that Mary removed the books. A different approach avoids subjunctive conditionals of that sort and contends that propositional knowledge requires justified true belief sustained by the collective totality of actual truths. This approach requires a detailed account of when justification is undermined and restored.

The Gettier problem is epistemologically important. One branch of epistemology seeks a precise understanding of the nature (for example, the essential components) of propositional knowledge. Our having a precise understanding of propositional knowledge requires our having a Gettier-proof analysis of such knowledge. Epistemologists thus need a defensible solution to the Gettier problem, however complex that solution may be.

Epistemologists have long debated the limits, or scope, of knowledge. The more limited we take the scope of knowledge to be, the more skeptical we are. Two influential types of skepticism are *knowledge-skepticism* and *justification-skepticism*. Unrestricted knowledge-skepticism states that no one knows anything, whereas unrestricted justification-skepticism offers the more extreme view that no one is even justified in believing anything. Some forms of skepticism are stronger than others. The strongest form of knowledge-skepticism states that it is *impossible* for anyone to know anything. A weaker form denies the actuality of our having knowledge, but leaves open its possibility. Many skeptics have restricted their skepticism to a particular domain of supposed knowledge: for example, knowledge of the external world, knowledge of other minds, knowledge of the past or the future, or knowledge of unperceived items. Such limited skepticism is more common than unrestricted skepticism in the history of epistemology.

Arguments supporting skepticism come in many forms. (See the essays by Klein and Heil for details.) One of the most difficult is *the Problem of the Criterion*, a version of which was stated by the sixteenth-century skeptic Michel de Montaigne:

> To adjudicate [between the true and the false] among the appearances of things, we need to have a distinguishing method; to validate this method, we need to have a justifying argument; but to validate this justifying argument, we need the very method at issue. And there we are, going round on the wheel.

This line of skeptical argument originated in ancient Greece, with epistemology itself. It forces us to face this question: How can we specify *what* we know without having specified *how* we know, and how can we specify *how* we know without having specified *what* we know? Is there any reasonable way out of this threatening circle? This is one of the most difficult epistemological problems, and a cogent epistemology must offer a defensible solution to it. Contemporary epistemology offers no widely accepted reply to this problem.

2. WHITHER UNITY?

Reflection on the state of contemporary epistemology leaves many bewildered. Just a sample of the kinds of epistemological theory now in circulation includes foundationalism, coherentism, contextualism, reliabilism, evidentialism, explanationism, pragmatism, internalism, externalism, deontologism, naturalism, and skepticism. These general positions do not all compete to explain the same epistemological phenomena. They do, however, all subsume remarkably diverse species of epistemological theory. Reliabilism, for example, now comes in many manifestations, including process reliabilism, indicator reliabilism, and virtue reliabilism. Likewise, foundationalism admits of considerable subsidiary variety, including radical foundationalism and modest foundationalism; and coherentism yields subjectivist and objectivist species, among many others. Within internalism, furthermore, we find access internalism, awareness internalism, and a host of additional intriguing species. Epistemological naturalism, too, offers taxonomic complexity, including for example eliminative, noneliminative, and pragmatic species. Is there any glimmer of hope for disciplinary unity within epistemology?

The ideal of disciplinary unity within epistemology is obscure. Two questions enable us to clarify a bit: What exactly would it take for the discipline of epistemology to be "unified"? More to the point, what does it *mean* to say that epistemology is unified? Perhaps the discipline of epistemology is unified at least in virtue of its unifying philosophical questions about the analysis, sources, and limits of human knowledge. Even so, let's consider further kinds of unity.

The first notion of unity is simple, even simplistic given the theoretical thickets of contemporary epistemology. The simple idea is that epistemology is unified if and only if all epistemologists *agree* on their theories about the analysis, sources, and limits of knowledge. Any ideal of unity using this notion, however, seems at best wishful thinking, given the turbulent history of epistemology. Expecting agreement among contemporary epistemologists is no more reasonable than ex-

pecting agreement between, say, the deductivist rationalist Descartes and the in-
ductivist empiricist Francis Bacon.

Mere agreement, in any case, is no automatic indicator of explanatory pro-
gress or even of truth. So the simple ideal is unmotivated as well as simplistic.
Clearly, the widespread disagreement in epistemology these days does not by itself
recommend relativism about truth in epistemology. Objective truth in epistemology, as elsewhere, can hide behind human disagreement. The fact that philosophers are especially skilled, even if sometimes too skilled, at fostering conceptual
diversity offers no real encouragement whatever to relativists.

The second idea of unity is that epistemology is unified if and only if all
epistemologists hold only *true* theories about the analysis, sources, and limits of
knowledge. An ideal of informative truth, and truth alone, is, we may grant, above
reproach for any discipline. Philosophers opposed to robust, realist truth as a
philosophical goal routinely fall into a kind of self-referential inconsistency, but
we cannot digress to that story here.

The problem with the ideal of truth is not that it is misguided, but rather
that we need guidelines for achieving it: in particular, guidelines that do not lead
to the bewilderment of contemporary epistemology. More specifically, we need
instruction on how pursuit of that ideal can free us from the puzzling complexity
of epistemology. The needed instruction is not supplied by that noble ideal itself.
Part of the problem is that many prominent positions within epistemology offer
different, sometimes even conflicting, guidelines for acquiring truth. So, the unity
here would be short-lived at best.

A third, more promising approach recommends a kind of *explanatory* unity.
Roughly, contemporary epistemology is unified if and only if we can correctly
explain its diversity in a way that manifests *common reasons* for epistemologists
to promote the different general positions and species of positions in circulation.
We purchase unity, according to the explanatory ideal, by *explaining*, in terms of
unifying common reasons, the kind of diversity in epistemology. The desired unity
is thus that of common rationality. In particular, I shall propose that it is the
unity of a kind of instrumental epistemic rationality. If we can secure this kind
of unity, at least, we can begin to appreciate the value of the diversity in epistemology. Our main question is, then, just this: Why is there what seems to be
unresolvable, perennial disagreement in epistemology?

a. Scientism

We might try to resolve or eliminate the disagreements of epistemology by taking
science as our ultimate epistemological authority. This would commit us to the
epistemological scientism suggested by Bertrand Russell, W. V. Quine, and others.

Quine's rejection of traditional epistemology stems from his *explanatory scientism*, the view that the sciences have a monopoly on legitimate theoretical explanation. Quine proposes that we should treat epistemology as a chapter of empirical psychology, that empirical psychology should exhaust the theoretical concerns of epistemologists. Call this proposal *eliminative naturalism* regarding epistemology. It implies that traditional epistemology is dispensable, on the ground that it is replaceable by empirical psychology. Eliminative naturalism aims for a kind of "explication" that *replaces* an inexact concept by an exact one. Aiming for such explication, eliminative naturalists introduce conceptual *substitutes* for various ordinary epistemological and psychological concepts. Quine proposes, for instance, that we *replace* our ordinary notion of justification with a behaviorist notion concerning the relation between sensation and theory.

Quine's development of Russell's scientism collapses of its own weight, from self-defeat. Eliminative naturalism regarding epistemology is not itself a thesis of the sciences, including empirical psychology. Given this objection, eliminative naturalism regarding epistemology evidently departs from Quine's own commitment to explanatory scientism. Explanatory scientism denies that there is any cognitively legitimate philosophy prior to, or independent of, the sciences (that is, any "first philosophy"), thus implying that theorists should not make philosophical claims exceeding the sciences.

Quine's own eliminative naturalism regarding epistemology seems to be an instance of philosophy prior to the sciences. Given this objection, Quine must show that his naturalized epistemology is an hypothesis of the sciences. Eliminative naturalists will have difficulty discharging this burden, because the sciences are not in the business of making sweeping claims about the status of epistemology (even if a stray individual scientist makes such claims on occasion). This may be an empirical truth about the sciences, but it is a warranted truth nonetheless, and it characterizes the sciences generally. Evidently, then, eliminative naturalism regarding epistemology, as combined with explanatory scientism, is self-defeating. A naturalist, of whatever species, should care to avoid self-defeat because the sciences do and because theoretical conflict is disadvantageous to unified explanation.

Quine might try to rescue eliminative naturalism by proposing a notion of *science* broader than that underwritten by the sciences as standardly characterized. Such a proposal would perhaps relax the implied requirement that eliminative naturalism be an hypothesis of the sciences. This, however, would land eliminative naturalists on the horns of a troublesome dilemma: either there will be a priori constraints on what counts as a science (since actual usage of "science" would not determine the broader notion), or the broader notion of science will be implausibly vague and unregulated in its employment. In the absence of any standard independent of the sciences, we certainly need an account of which of the various so-called sciences are regulative for purposes of theory formation in epistemology.

(Astrology, for example, should be out, along with parapsychology and scientology.) Such an account may very well take us beyond the sciences themselves, because it will be a metascientific account *of* the sciences and their function in regulating epistemology.

To serve the purposes of eliminative naturalism, any proposed new notion of science must exclude traditional epistemology, while including epistemological naturalism, in a way that is not ad hoc. Such a strategy for escaping self-defeat demands, in any case, a hitherto unexplicated notion of science, which is no small order. Eliminative naturalists have not defended any such strategy; nor have they otherwise resolved the problem of self-defeat. That problem concerns eliminative naturalism, and not necessarily more moderate versions of epistemological naturalism. (See the essay by Goldman for a more moderate understanding of how the sciences bear on epistemology.)

b. Pragmatism

A cousin of eliminative naturalism is *replacement pragmatism*, proposed by Richard Rorty and others. This is the twofold view that (a) the vocabulary, problems, and goals of traditional epistemology are unprofitable (not "useful") and thus in need of replacement by pragmatist successors, and (b) the main task of epistemology is to study the comparative advantages and disadvantages of the differing vocabularies from different cultures. Replacement pragmatism affirms the pointlessness and dispensability of philosophical concerns about how the world really is (and about objective truth) and recommends the central philosophical importance of what is profitable, advantageous, or useful. Since useful beliefs can be false and thereby fail to represent how the world really is, a desire for useful beliefs is not automatically a desire for beliefs that represent how the world really is. An obviously false belief can be useful to a person with certain purposes.

Replacement pragmatism implies that a proposition is acceptable to us if and only if it is *useful* to us, that is, it is useful to us to accept the proposition. (We may, if only for the sake of argument, permit pragmatists to define "useful" however they find useful.) If, however, usefulness determines acceptability in the manner implied, a proposition will be acceptable to us if and only if it is *true* (and thus *factually the case*) that the proposition is useful to us. The pragmatist's appeal to usefulness, therefore, entails something about matters of fact, or actual truth, regarding usefulness. This is a *factuality requirement* on pragmatism. It reveals that pragmatism does not—and evidently cannot—avoid considerations about the real, or factual, nature of things, about how things really are.

Replacement pragmatism invites a troublesome dilemma, one horn of which is self-defeat. Is such pragmatism supposed to offer a *true* claim about acceptability? Does it aim to characterize the *real* nature of acceptability, how acceptability *really* is? If it does, it offers a characterization illicit by its own standard. It then runs afoul of its own assumption that we should eliminate from philosophy concerns about how things really are. As a result, replacement pragmatism faces a disturbing kind of self-defeat: it does what it says *should not* be done. On the other hand, if replacement pragmatism does not offer, or even aim to offer, a characterization of the real nature of acceptability, then why should we bother with it at all if we aim to characterize acceptability regarding propositions? Given the latter aim, we should not bother with it, for it is then irrelevant, *useless* to our purpose at hand. Considerations of usefulness, always significant to pragmatism, can thus count against replacement pragmatism itself. So, a dilemma confronts replacement pragmatism: either replacement pragmatism is self-defeating, or it is irrelevant to the typical epistemologist seeking an account of acceptability. This dilemma indicates that replacement pragmatism fails to challenge traditional epistemology. Many of us will not find a self-defeating theory "useful," given our explanatory aims. Accordingly, the self-defeat of pragmatism will be decisive for us, given the very standards of replacement pragmatism.

c. Intuitionism

Many philosophers have resisted both scientism and pragmatism, looking instead to common sense or "preanalytic epistemic data" as a basis for adjudicating epistemological claims. The latter approach has attracted philosophers in the phenomenological tradition of Brentano and Husserl and philosophers in the common-sense tradition of Reid, Moore, and Chisholm. The rough idea is that we have pretheoretical access, via "intuition" or "common sense," to certain considerations about justification, and these considerations can support one epistemological view over others.

It is often left unclear what the epistemic status of the relevant preanalytic epistemic data is supposed to be. Such data, we hear, are accessed by "intuition" or by "common sense." We thus have some epistemologists talking as follows: "Intuitively (or commonsensically), justification resides in a particular case like *this*, and does not reside in a case like *that*." A statement of this sort aims to guide our formulation of a notion of justification or at least a general explanatory principle concerning justification. A simple question arises: is such a statement *self*-justifying, with no need of independent epistemic support? If so, what notion of self-justification can sanction the deliverances of intuition or common sense, but exclude spontaneous judgments no better, epistemically, than mere prejudice or guesswork?

Literal talk of self-justification invites trouble. If one statement can literally justify itself, solely in virtue of itself, then *every* statement can. Statements do not differ on their supporting themselves. Such so-called "support" is universal. A widely accepted adequacy condition on standards of justification is, however, that they not allow for the justification of *every* proposition, that they not leave us with an "anything goes" approach to justification. Literal self-justification violates this condition. Some philosophers apparently use the term "self-justification" in a *non*literal sense, but we cannot digress to this interpretive matter.

Intuitive judgments and common-sense judgments can, and sometimes do, result from special, even biased, linguistic training. Why then should we regard such judgments as *automatically* epistemically privileged? Intuitive judgments and common-sense judgments certainly can be false, as a little reflection illustrates. Such judgments, furthermore, do not always seem to be supported by the best available evidence. Consider, for instance, how various judgments of "common sense" are at odds with our best available evidence from the sciences or even from careful ordinary perception. It is unclear, then, why we should regard intuitive judgments or common-sense judgments as the basis of our standards for justification.

Common-sense theorists apparently rely on an operative *notion*, or *concept*, of justification implying that common sense is a genuine source of justification. A reliable sign of a conceptual commitment at work among common-sense theorists, particularly Moore, is that they are not genuinely open to potential counterexamples to their assumption that common sense is a genuine source of justification. A parallel point bears on advocates of intuitions and on attempts to use one's "reflective" or "considered" judgments to justify epistemic standards. Appeal to such judgments to justify statements presupposes considerations about an operative notion implying that such judgments in fact have a certain epistemic significance. An operative notion of justification enables one to deem suitable "reflection" a source of genuine *justification* and to hold that reflective judgments yield justification. Apart from the operative notion, one will lack a decisive link between reflection and justification.

The same point applies to positions that give science or pragmatic value final authority in epistemology. An operative notion of justification will enable one to deem science or pragmatic value a source of genuine *justification*. In fact, apart from the operative notion, one will lack a decisive link between science or pragmatic value and genuine justification. The conferring of justification, in terms of science or pragmatic value, will then depend crucially on an operative notion connecting science or pragmatic value with actual justification.

Our problem concerns what is ultimately authoritative in epistemology: intuitions (say, of common sense) or theory (say, scientific theory) or considerations of usefulness (as in pragmatism)? Our selection of one of these options will leave us with some kind of intuitionism, scientism, or pragmatism, and ideally our selection would not be self-defeating. How should we decide?

3. INSTRUMENTAL RATIONALITY

Any standard or strategy worthy of the title "epistemic" must have as its fundamental goal the acquisition of truth and the avoidance of error. This follows from the fact that genuine *knowledge* has truth as an essential condition and excludes error. Of course, contemporary epistemology offers numerous strategies for acquiring truth and avoiding error, including contextualist, coherentist, foundationalist, internalist, and externalist strategies. Ideally, we would be able to say convincingly that a particular strategy is more effective at acquiring truth and avoiding error than all the others, and then be done with the problem of final epistemological authority. Whatever strategy has maximal effectiveness in getting truth and blocking error would then have final epistemological authority for us. Unfortunately for us, the problem resists such quick resolution.

Skeptics can help us appreciate the problem we face. They raise *general* questions about the reliability of our cognitive sources; that is, they ask about our cognitive sources altogether, *as a whole*. In doing so, they wonder what convincing reason we have to regard those sources as reliable for acquiring truth and avoiding error. Skeptics thus would not be answered by having the reliability of one cognitive source (say, vision) checked by another cognitive source (say, touch). Any answer we give to the *general* question of the reliability of our cognitive sources will apparently rely on input from one of the very sources under question by the skeptic. Unfortunately, we cannot test the reliability of our cognitive sources without relying on them in a way that takes for granted something under dispute by skeptics.

Our offering any kind of support for the reliability of our cognitive sources will depend on our use of such cognitive sources as perception, introspection, belief, memory, testimony, intuition, and common sense. Since all such sources are under question by skeptics, with regard to reliability, our use of them cannot deliver the kind of evidence of reliability sought by skeptics. Unfortunately, we cannot assume a position independent of our own cognitive sources to deliver a test of their reliability of the sort demanded by skeptics. This is the human cognitive predicament, and no one has shown how we can escape it. Even if we have genuine knowledge, we cannot establish our claims to knowledge or reliable belief without a kind of evidential circularity. This predicament bears on skeptics too, because they cannot show without circularity that withholding judgment is the most effective means of acquiring truth and avoiding error.

Any effort to establish a set of epistemic standards as maximally reliable, or reliable at all, will meet an inescapable charge of evidential circularity. Given the generality of the skeptical challenge, we lack the resources for avoiding evidential circularity. This circularity does not preclude reliable belief or even knowledge. It rather precludes our answering global challenges in a manner free of the kind of arbitrariness characteristic of circular reasoning. The problem is not fallibilism or inductivism but question begging evidential circularity. Such circularity threatens to make reasoning in epistemology superfluous.

The best we can do, if we value epistemology, is to avail ourselves of a kind of instrumental epistemic rationality that does not pretend to escape evidential circularity. Epistemologists, by nature, offer standards that aim to secure truth while avoiding error, but some theorists wield different specific concepts of justification and different standards for discerning justification. Their common goal of acquiring truth does not yield agreement about the "best way" to acquire truth; nor does any noncircular test for effectiveness in acquiring truth. Still, there can be rationality in the face of divergence in concepts of justification and in standards for discerning justification. (See the essay by Foley on this topic.)

Different theorists can have different epistemic subgoals in using a concept of epistemic justification and can be instrumentally rational relative to their subgoals. Suppose, for example, that a theorist has the subgoal of accommodating the truth-seeking methods of the sciences in any context. In that case, a theorist might wield a concept of justification that, in keeping with the position of Russell and Quine, awards epistemic primacy to science over common sense in cases of conflict. Alternatively, suppose that a theorist has the subgoal of accommodating the deliverances of reliable group testimony in any context. In that case, a theorist might propose a contextualist concept of justification that awards epistemic primacy to group testimony over individual testimony in cases of conflict. Similarly, one might reasonably endorse internalism if one aims to evaluate truth from the standpoint of evidence accessible to the believer. On the other hand, one might reasonably endorse externalism if one has the epistemic subgoal of evaluating truth from the standpoint of cognitively relevant processes that may be inaccessible to a believer.

Instrumental epistemic rationality allows, then, for reasonable divergence in epistemic subgoals, owing to what one aims to accomplish with a specific epistemic notion or standard. We may call this view *metaepistemic instrumentalism*, for short. It enables us to explain, even explain *as rational*, epistemological divergence on the basis of a common, unifying kind of rationality: instrumental epistemic rationality. It does not follow, however, that anything goes in epistemology, for certain constraints on truth (such as the Aristotelian adequacy condition on truth identified by Tarski's schema T) will exclude a range of views. Some philosophical positions and goals will thus be beyond the pale of epistemology, at least as classically understood.

Does metaepistemic instrumentalism preclude genuine disagreement in epistemology? It certainly permits that knowledge and justification are natural kinds: that is, that they consist of causally stable properties that support explanatory and inductive inferences. Our problem is not *whether* justification is a natural kind, but rather *which* natural kind should constrain our standards in epistemology. The relativity allowed by metaepistemic instrumentalism, owing to divergence in epistemic subgoals, offers no challenge to realism about epistemic phenomena. It does not entail substantive relativism about truth, justification, or knowledge: the view that mere belief determines truth, justification, or knowledge. In addition, metaepistemic instrumentalism does not imply that all epistemological disagreements are merely semantic or otherwise less than genuine. Still, the widespread neglect of divergence in epistemic subgoals and corresponding specific epistemic notions does account for much postulating of disagreement where epistemologists are actually just talking at cross purposes. In fact, this neglect results in the common false assumption, endorsed by Rorty and other philosophical pessimists, that contemporary epistemology suffers fatal defects from its unresolvable perennial disagreements.

Metaepistemic instrumentalism enables us to explain as *rational* conceptual divergence what initially looked like unresolvable perennial disagreement. The key to such explanation is, of course, the divergence in epistemic subgoals, a divergence allowable by instrumental epistemic rationality. Recall that the human cognitive predicament blocks our eliminating, in a noncircular manner, all but our own subgoals as unreliable in achieving truth and avoiding error. It recommends the kind of epistemic tolerance allowed by metaepistemic instrumentalism, which does not pretend to deliver skeptic-resistant reasons even for instrumental epistemic rationality.

A notable epistemic subgoal shared by many epistemologists is to maximize the *explanatory* value of our belief system with regard to the world, including the position of humans in the world. Many of us thus value inference to the best available explanation as a means of acquiring informative truths and avoiding falsehoods. Dependence on instrumental epistemic rationality is not, however, peculiar to metaepistemic instrumentalism. Even skeptics are guided by their epistemic subgoals, thereby relying on instrumental epistemic rationality. In addition, many skeptical arguments owe their force to their alleged value in explaining certain epistemic phenomena, such as the nature of inferential justification in connection with the epistemic regress problem. Skeptics thus sometimes recommend their skepticism for its explanatory power, for its superiority over competing epistemological accounts. These considerations do not refute skeptics; they rather indicate the pervasive value of instrumental epistemic rationality.

Metaepistemic instrumentalism can save epistemology from skeptical worries about circularity or the mere possibility of error. It enables us reasonably to reply that, given our epistemic subgoals, skeptics are excessively risk averse. Skeptics lean heavily on the side of error-avoidance in a way that hinders, from the standpoint of common epistemic subgoals, the acquisition of explanatory truths. Skeptics, I have suggested, have not actually shown that their risk-averse strategy is the most effective means of acquiring informative truth and avoiding error. The question of how risk averse we *should* be does not demand, given metaepistemic in-

strumentalism, an answer favorable to skeptics. In the presence of varying epistemic subgoals, we can reasonably tolerate some diversity in answers to that
question.

In sum, then, we can explain, and thereby unify, the epistemological diversity
of our day. Within the tolerant confines of metaepistemic instrumentalism, we
can welcome, even as rational, much of the remarkable divergence we see in
contemporary epistemology. Some philosophers may clamor for more than instrumental epistemic rationality, but, given the human cognitive predicament, they
are well advised to spend their theoretical energy elsewhere. For the rest of us,
epistemology can proceed apace, with all its intriguing diversity and complexity.
We can now see that the diversity hides a deeper rational unity.

4. THE ESSAYS IN BRIEF

In "Conditions and Analyses of Knowing," Robert Shope examines the essential
conditions of propositional knowledge. He thus focuses on the conditions that
must be satisfied for a person to have knowledge, specifically knowledge *that
something is so*. Traditionally knowledge has been analyzed in terms of justified
true belief. Shope first addresses philosophers' disagreements concerning the truth
and belief conditions. After introducing the justification condition, he presents
counterexamples (specifically Gettier-type counterexamples) challenging the standard analysis of knowledge. These challenges have provoked several attempts to
replace or to supplement the justification condition for knowledge. Shope presents
and assesses several of these, including early causal theories, the nonaccidentality
requirement, reliable process and conditional analyses, the reliable-indicator analysis, the conclusive reasons analysis, defeasibility analyses, analyses in terms of
cognitive or intellectual virtues, and Plantinga's proper functionalism. He then
presents and defends his own account of knowledge.

In "The Sources of Knowledge," Robert Audi identifies the sources from which
we acquire knowledge or justified belief. He distinguishes what he calls the "four
standard basic sources": perception, memory, consciousness, and reason. A *basic*
source yields knowledge or justified belief without positive dependence on another
source. He distinguishes each of the above as a basic source of knowledge, with
the exception of memory. Memory, while a basic source of justification, plays a
preservative rather than a generative role in knowledge. Audi contrasts basic
sources with nonbasic sources, concentrating on testimony. After clarifying the
relationship between a source and a ground, or "what it is in virtue of which one

knows or justifiedly believes," Audi evaluates the basic sources' individual and collective autonomy as well as their vulnerability to defeasibility. He also examines the relationship of coherence to knowledge and justification, noting the distinction between a negative dependence on incoherence and a positive dependence on coherence.

In "A Priori Knowledge," Albert Casullo identifies four questions central to the contemporary discussion about a priori knowledge: (1) What is a priori knowledge? (2) Is there a priori knowledge? (3) What is the relationship between the a priori and the necessary? (4) Is there synthetic a priori knowledge? Casullo is mainly concerned with (2). He is concerned with (3) and (4) only insofar as they relate to responses to (1) and (2). He begins by offering an answer to (1) in order to put us in a position to respond to (2). Ultimately, he defines a priori knowledge as true belief with a priori justification, where a belief is a priori justified if it is nonexperientially justified. Armed with this definition, Casullo evaluates several traditional arguments for and against the existence of a priori knowledge. He concludes that no argument on either side is convincing. By arguing on a priori grounds that the opposite position is deficient, the traditional arguments reach an impasse. A successful way to defend a priori knowledge, he argues, would be to find empirical evidence that supports the existence of nonexperiential sources of justification.

In "The Sciences and Epistemology," Alvin Goldman finds that epistemology cannot be subsumed under or identified with a science. Epistemology and the sciences, according to Goldman, should remain distinct yet cooperative. He presents several examples that illustrate the relevance of science to epistemology. Drawing from work in psychology, he proposes that science can shed light on epistemic achievements by contributing to our understanding of the nature and extent of human cognitive endowments. He suggests, in addition, that psychology can also contribute to our understanding of the sources of knowledge. Finally, Goldman argues that some specific projects in epistemology can receive important contributions from psychology, economics, and sociology.

In "Conceptual Diversity in Epistemology," Richard Foley reflects on such central topics in epistemology as knowledge, warrant, rationality, and justification. He aims to distinguish such concepts in a general theory. Epistemologists have searched for that which constitutes knowledge when added to true belief. Foley calls this "warrant" and suggests that rationality and justification are not linked to knowledge by necessity. He proceeds to offer a general schema for rationality. This schema enables a distinction between "rationality" and "rationality all things considered." Foley proposes how these concepts can work together in a system that "provides the necessary materials for an approach to epistemology that is clarifying, theoretically respectable, and relevant to our actual lives."

In "Theories of Justification," Richard Fumerton offers an overview of several prominent positions on the nature of justification. He begins by isolating epistemic justification from nonepistemic justification. He also distinguishes between "having justification for a belief" and "having a justified belief," arguing that the former is conceptually more fundamental. Fumerton then addresses the possibility that justification is a normative matter, suggesting that this possibility has little to offer a concept of epistemic justification. He also critically examines more specific attempts to capture the structure and content of epistemic justification. These include traditional foundationalism and variants thereof, externalist versions of foundationalism; contextualism; coherentism; and "mixed" theories which combine aspects of coherentism and foundationalism.

In "Internalism and Externalism," Laurence BonJour suggests that the contemporary epistemological debate over internalism and externalism concerns the formulation of the justification or warrant condition in an account of knowledge. The internalist requires that for a belief to meet this condition all of the necessary elements must be cognitively accessible to the believer. The externalist, on the other hand, claims that at least some such elements do not need to be accessible to the believer. BonJour gives an overview of this dispute, beginning with internalism and then considering the main reasons offered by externalists for rejecting the more traditional epistemological approach. He investigates the externalist alternative by looking at the most popular version, *reliabilism*, and at the main objections that have been raised against reliabilism. This motivates a look at some other versions of externalism, in order to see how susceptible they are to similar objections. BonJour suggests that the opposition between the two views is less straightforward than has usually been thought. He proposes, in addition, that each of them has valuable roles to play in major epistemological issues, even though the internalist approach is more fundamental in an important way.

In "Tracking, Competence, and Knowledge," Ernest Sosa notes that in attempting to account for the conditions for knowledge, externalists have proposed that the justification condition be replaced or supplemented by the requirement that a certain modal relation obtain between a fact and a subject's belief concerning that fact. Sosa assesses attempts to identify such a relation. He focuses on an account labeled "Cartesian-tracking." This accounts for the relation in the form of two conditionals:

A.   If a person S believes a proposition $P \rightarrow P$.
B. $P \rightarrow S$ believes P.

Sosa modifies the account to make it more plausible, concluding that whereas before the modifications it was too weak to account for knowledge, with them it is too strong. He suggests that (B) be abandoned as a requirement and that (A), equipped with his modifications, can offer promising results in connection with skepticism. He argues that modified (A) coupled with the requirement that S's belief be "virtuous" can illuminate the nature of propositional knowledge.

In "Virtues in Epistemology," John Greco presents and evaluates two main notions of intellectual virtue. The first concerns Ernest Sosa's development of this concept as a disposition to grasp truth and avoid falsehood. Greco contrasts this with *moral* models of intellectual virtue that include a motivational component in their definition, namely a desire for truth. He claims, however, that if the latter were used to account for epistemic justification and knowledge, they would exclude obvious cases of knowledge. Instead, Greco offers a minimalist reliabilist account of intellectual virtue. He argues that this view, "in which the virtues are conceived as reliable cognitive abilities or powers," can be illuminating in an account of knowledge. He sets out to support this on the ground that his approach to intellectual virtue can adequately address three major problems in the theory of knowledge: Humean skepticism, the Gettier problem, and the problem of showing that knowledge is more valuable than mere true belief.

In "Mind and Knowledge," John Heil notes that our knowledge of the world depends on our nature as knowers. Many people, philosophers included, assume realism about the world toward which our beliefs are directed: that is, that the world is as it is independently of how we might take it to be. It is unclear how we could convincingly establish, in a noncircular manner, that the world is as we think it is. This suggests skepticism, and, according to Heil, realism and skepticism go hand in hand. Heil discusses the implications of such a view, particularly as they concern knowledge we seemingly have of our own states of mind. He considers the view that to calibrate ourselves as knowers we should proceed from resources "immediately available to the mind" to conclusions about the external world. He evaluates Descartes's attempt to do this and examines two other possibilities: an externalist view of mental content and an internalist approach to content.

In "Skepticism," Peter Klein divides philosophical skepticism into two basic forms. The "Academic Skeptic" proposes that we cannot have knowledge of a certain set of propositions. The "Pyrrhonian Skeptic," on the other hand, refrains from opining about whether we can have knowledge. Klein outlines two arguments for Academic Skepticism: (1) a "Cartesian-style" argument based on the claim that knowledge entails the elimination of all doubt, and (2) a "Closure Principle-style" argument based on the claim that if x entails y and S has justification for x, then S has justification for y. He evaluates both, suggesting that while there is plausible support for (2), there seems to be none for (1). Klein turns to contextualism to see if it can contribute to the discussion between one who claims that we *can* have knowledge about some epistemically interesting class of propositions and the Academic Skeptic. He outlines the background of Pyrrhonian Skepticism, pointing out that the Pyrrhonist withholds assent concerning our knowledge-bearing status because reason cannot provide an adequate basis for assent. He assesses three possible patterns of reasoning (foundationalism, coherentism, and infinitism), and concludes that the Pyrrhonist view, that reason cannot resolve matters concerning the nonevident, is vindicated.

In "Epistemological Duties," Richard Feldman uses three main questions to illuminate the topic of epistemological duties. (1) "What are our epistemological duties?" That is, what are the obligations of a believer qua believer? Is it simply our duty to form positive beliefs or to develop appropriate cognitive attitudes, which include disbelief and the suspension of judgment? Perhaps our duty is only to *try* to believe the truth. Perhaps it is more "diachronic", involving evidence gathering and other extended efforts to maximize our true beliefs and to minimize our false beliefs. After suggesting that epistemological duties pertain to the development of appropriate cognitive attitudes, Feldman asks (2) "What makes a duty epistemological?" and (3) "How do epistemological duties interact with other kinds of duties?" His pursuit of (3) contributes to his response to (2), in that he uses it to argue that a concept of distinctly epistemological duty must exclude practical and moral duties that pertain to belief and include only duties that pertain to epistemological success (the act of having reasonable or justified cognitive attitudes).

In "Scientific Knowledge," Philip Kitcher offers an approach to scientific knowledge that is more systematic than many current approaches in the epistemology of science. He challenges arguments against the *truth* of the theoretical claims of science. In addition, he attempts to discover reasons for endorsing the truth of such claims. He tries to apply current "scientific method" to this end (including confirmation theory and Bayesianism), but doubts that any context-independent method gives warrant to the theoretical claims of science. He suggests that the discovery of reasons might succeed if we ask why anyone thinks the theoretical claims we accept are true and then look for answers that reconstruct actual belief-generating processes. To this end, Kitcher presents the "homely argument" for scientific truth. It entails that when a field of science is continually applied to yield precise predictions, then it is at least approximately true. He defends this approach and offers a supplementary account that gives more attention to detail. This account includes a historical aspect (a dependence on the previous conclusions of scientists) that must answer to skeptical challenges and a social aspect (the coordination of individuals in pursuit of specific knowledge-related goals).

In "Explanation and Epistemology," William Lycan proposes that explanation and epistemology are related in at least three ways. First, "to explain something is an epistemic act, and to have something explained to you is to learn." Lycan begins his account of explanation by drawing out several paradigms for scientific explanation, but he finds it unlikely that scientific explanation will be captured by a single set of necessary and sufficient conditions. Noting, however, that scientific explanation does not exhaust an account of explanation in general, he moves on to a second way in which explanation is related to epistemology: by the idea of explanatory inference. This is the idea of proceeding from a specific explanandum to the best hypothetical explanation for that explanandum. To account for a hypothesis' being "the best," Lycan introduces "pragmatic virtues" that can increase the value of a hypothesis. This leads into a discussion of Explanationism. The third way in which explanation relates to epistemology claims that a belief can be justified if it is arrived at by explanatory inference. Lycan distinguishes four degrees of the theory, but focuses on "Weak Explanationism" (the idea that epistemic justification by explanatory inference is *possible*) and "Ferocious Explanationism" (the notion that explanatory inference is the *only* basic form of ampliative inference).

In "Decision Theory and Epistemology," Mark Kaplan finds it characteristic of orthodox Bayesians to hold that (1) for each person and each hypothesis she comprehends, there is a precise degree of confidence that person has in the truth of that proposition, and (2) no person can be counted as rational unless the degree of confidence assignment she thus harbors satisfies the axioms of the probability calculus. Many epistemologists have objected to the idea that each of us harbors a precise degree of confidence assignment. Even if we had such an assignment, the condition on a person's being rational endorsed by the orthodox Bayesian would be too demanding to be applied to beings, such as ourselves, who have limited logical/mathematical skills. In addition, in focusing exclusively on degrees of confidence, the Bayesian approach tells us nothing about the epistemic status of the doxastic states epistemologists have traditionally been concerned about— categorical beliefs. Kaplan's purpose is twofold. First, he aims to show that, as powerful as many of such criticisms are against orthodox Bayesianism, there is a credible kind of Bayesianism. Without appeal to idealization or false precision, it offers a substantive account of how the probability calculus constrains the (imprecise) opinions of actual persons and of how this account impinges on traditional epistemological concerns. Second, he aims to show how this Bayesianism finds a foundation in considerations concerning rational preference.

In "Embodiment and Epistemology," Louise Antony considers a kind of "Cartesian epistemology" according to which, so far as knowing goes, knowers could be completely disembodied, that is, pure Cartesian egos. Cartesian epistemology thus attributes little, if any, cognitive significance to a knower's embodiment. Antony examines a number of recent challenges to Cartesian epistemology, particularly challenges from feminist epistemology. She contends that we might have good reason to think that theorizing about knowledge can be influenced by features of our embodiment, even if we lack reasons to suppose that knowing itself varies relative to such features. She also argues that a masculinist bias can result in the mishandling of cognitive differences in cases where they actually exist. Antony examines a number of the ways in which the maleness of philosophy has, according to feminists, distorted epistemology. Even if a Cartesian approach offers *one* indispensable part of a comprehensive epistemology, according to Antony, we still need an epistemology that answers questions raised by our everyday, embodied lives.

In "Epistemology and Ethics," Noah Lemos suggests that moral epistemology is mainly concerned with "whether and how we can have knowledge or justified belief" about moral issues. Lemos presents and replies to several problems that arise in this connection. He addresses arguments for ethical skepticism, the view that we cannot have moral knowledge or justified belief. Assuming that we can have moral knowledge, he considers how the moral epistemologist and moral philosopher should begin their account of this knowledge. Lemos favors a particularist approach whereby we begin with instances of moral knowledge and use these to formulate and evaluate criteria for moral knowledge. He relates his approach to concerns about the nature of the epistemic justification of moral beliefs as dealt with by foundationalists and coherentists. Lemos concludes his essay by responding to arguments against particularist approaches in moral epistemology. Specifically, he addresses the claim that our moral beliefs must receive their justification from an independent moral criterion developed from nonmoral beliefs.

In "Epistemology in Philosophy of Religion," Philip Quinn focuses on the central problem of religious epistemology for monotheistic religions: the epistemic status of belief in the existence of God. His essay divides into two main sections. The first discusses arguments for God's existence. Quinn explores what epistemic conditions such arguments would have to satisfy to be successful and whether any arguments satisfy those conditions. He considers at length recent versions of the ontological and cosmological arguments, and then turns to inductive and cumulative-case arguments. The second section examines the claims of Reformed Epistemology about belief in God. It assesses Alvin Plantinga's claim that belief in God is for many theists properly basic, that is, has positive epistemic status even when it is not based on arguments or any other kind of propositional evidence. Quinn distinguishes two versions of this claim. According to the first, emphasized in Plantinga's earlier work, theistic belief is properly basic with respect to justification or rationality. Quinn gives this claim detailed critical examination. According to the second version, prominent in Plantinga's more recent work, theistic belief is properly basic with respect to warrant. Quinn addresses this version more briefly.

In "Formal Problems about Knowledge," Roy Sorensen examines epistemological issues that have logical aspects. He illustrates the hopes of the modal logicians who developed epistemic logic with Fitch's proof for unknowables and the surprise-test paradox. He considers the epistemology of proof with the help of the knower paradox. One solution to this paradox is that knowledge is not closed under deduction. Sorensen reviews the broader history of this maneuver along with the relevant-alternatives model of knowledge. This model assumes that "know" is an absolute term like "flat." Sorensen argues that epistemic absolute terms differ from extensional absolute terms by virtue of their sensitivity to the completeness of the alternatives. This asymmetry, according to Sorensen, undermines recent claims that there is a structural parallel between the supervaluational and epistemicist theories of vagueness. He also suggests that we have overestimated the ability of logical demonstration to produce knowledge.

NOTE

Many thanks to Blaine Swen for comments on this introduction and for fine help with some of the summaries in section 4.

CHAPTER 1

CONDITIONS AND ANALYSES OF KNOWING

ROBERT K. SHOPE

PHILOSOPHERS are a contentious lot, and never more so than when debating the conditions and proper analysis of knowing. Most discussion has centered on knowing that something is so ('knowing that' for short). I shall explain my own perspective after sampling the extraordinary range of existing disagreements concerning conditions of knowing that should figure in an analysis of knowing that.

THE TRUTH CONDITION

Even the seemingly innocent claim that when a subject, S, knows that h, it must be true that h (where we instantiate some complete declarative sentence for 'h') has been contested.[1] L. Jonathan Cohen points out that in appropriate contexts, saying, 'He does not know that h,' or asking, 'Does he know that h?' commits the speaker to its being true that h, and "this commitment cannot derive from an underlying entailment, because what is said is negative or interrogative in its bearing on the issue" (1992, 91). Cohen proposes that the commitment is instead due to the fact that the speech-act of saying, 'He knows that h,' normally gives the audience to understand that the speaker believes that h or accepts that h.

Cohen does not further describe the appropriate contexts that he has in mind, but I suspect that they involve what Fred Dretske (1972) calls the contribution of contrastive focusing to what is being claimed by asserting a sentence.[2] In order to rebut Cohen's challenge to the truth condition, we need to consider contrastive focusing in regard to the expression, 'He knows that h.' When it is not at issue whether h but who it is that possesses knowledge that h, we may raise the issue of whether the person in Cohen's example is among them by asking, 'Does he know that h?' But a negative answer is not simply the negation of a claim free of contrastive focusing which is made by uttering, 'S does know that h' or 'S knows that h.' It is instead the negation of a claim made by uttering the latter with a contrastive focus on whether, given those who know that h, S is among them. Or it might, depending on context, be the negation of the claim that, given that h, S knows in contrast to merely believing or accepting that h.

Accordingly, if we take a philosopher to be seeking an analysis of 'S knows that h' concerning utterances of sentences of this form which do not involve contrastive focus, we do not need to suppose that utterances of the negation of such sentences carry a commitment to its being true that h. Whether it is satisfactory to seek an analysis that is limited in this way will depend on what one wishes to construe as the nature of an analysis.[3] Philosophers have often spoken of seeking a meaning analysis, and if Dretske is right that contrastive focus affects the meaning of sentences, then some nod in the direction of enlarging the brief considerations of the preceding paragraph will be needed, even though they do not require abandoning the truth condition of knowing.

THE BELIEF CONDITION

Cohen also attacks the very common presumption that knowing is a species of believing, while criticizing an earlier objection to the belief condition advanced by Colin Radford (1966). But Cohen's critique of Radford is less than persuasive. Radford had based his objection on the following example:[4]

> Unwitting Remembrance: S sincerely tells Tom that S never learned any English history, but Tom playfully quizzes S about dates concerning it. S makes many errors and takes his answers to be mere guesses, but concerning one period gets mostly right answers. After Tom points this out, S says he now thinks he remembers having long ago studied some dates that he thinks indeed were those. (2–3)

Because Tom eventually points to S's success and S subsequently remembers having studied relevant matters and thinking it was such dates, there is reason to suppose that a memory was retained by S after the teaching which is manifested in these concluding details. Simplicity of explanation is then a reason to suppose the memory was also manifested in the earlier responses that S gave during the test.

Cohen seems to neglect these considerations when he says that we can criticize Radford by asking him to tell us more about the example, given a more specific version in which the same questions are put to S later, after S has forgotten what answers S gave to Tom. Cohen points out that there are two scenarios that Radford might describe: (1) The new answers are substantially different; (2) S keeps on giving more or less the same answers. According to Cohen, scenario (1) will provide good reason to suppose that S got the right answers initially only by a lucky fluke and thus did not know what Radford purports S knew. But Cohen then has no explanation of the final details of the original example and will need implausibly to suppose that S's seeming recollection of earlier education is a fluke. Indeed, Radford can elaborate scenario (2) so that when reminded by Tom of that earlier seeming recollection, S cannot repeat it. The plausible explanation of this version of the case will be that S's memories of the earlier lessons and their contents have finally faded to the point of being lost.[5]

Keith Lehrer (2000) maintains that the memory retention only constitutes retention of information, but not knowledge that h, because the latter requires knowing that it is correct that h. Some philosophers will protest that Lehrer's view entails that brutes and infants never know that anything is so, and will charge that Lehrer is too intellectualistic in his account because he focuses on adults who have the concepts of being correct and being true and who easily move back and forth between asserting that h and asserting that it is true/correct that h.

Sometimes Lehrer has allowed (cf. 1974) multiple senses of 'knows that,' while maintaining that the sense that applies to animals and infants is unimportant for epistemology. Yet to propose too wide a separation of senses here will not explain why intuitions are divided on Radford's example, and why the insight has not commonly emerged in discussions that some equivocation has intruded. Radford has rightly protested (1988) that those who flatly reject his categorization of such an example owe us an explanation of why intuitions have been so divided. Cohen has maintained that the example was underdescribed, but that would lead us to expect each individual to waver concerning the verdict, rather than to expect a split verdict among individuals.[6]

The account I shall eventually advocate will treat 'knows' as having a sense that expresses a broad enough category to include knowledge by brutes and infants, and will regard the type of knowing of special interest to Lehrer and to critical debate among adults as a species of such a broader category. So even if the use of 'knows' in discussing exactly that species does involve a narrower linguistic sense of the term, it is not a disconnected sense, and the difference in intuitions concerning Radford's example may be due to different presumptions about the focus of the question, 'Does S know?' with some respondents reflecting on the genus I have mentioned (and will analyze below) and others presupposing the common philosophical restriction of attention just to that species of knowing pertaining to the context of critical inquiry.

Cohen's own argument against a belief requirement for knowing (cf. 88) begins with certain insights that he credits to Descartes and to Karl Popper that a natural scientist could ideally conduct inquiries and experiments without believing the favored hypotheses the scientist employs in those inquiries. Where Popper (1972) understood 'knowledge' in a special sense as labeling, for example, theories and hypotheses that a group of scientists have made it their policy to utilize in their work, Cohen speaks of a single scientist as knowing. To be good scientists, we allow for adequate open-mindedness, and at least some members of research teams need, according to Cohen, to refrain from believing the hypotheses that they employ to be true. They need instead to accept the hypotheses, where this is a voluntary action of setting themselves to go along with the hypotheses and anything they entail, by being set to employ them as premises in predicting, explaining, and pursuing further research. Cohen proposes that having the knowledge that h implies that the scientist accepts that h and that the proposition that h deserves acceptance in the light of cognitively relevant considerations (cf. 88). Such acceptance is compatible with the scientist's realizing that a theory that h faces anomalies, or that a law that h is a simplification or idealization, and so is compatible with the scientist's disbelieving that h when nonetheless sincerely claiming to know that h (cf. 90–92). Thus, Cohen has presented what turns out to be an objection to a truth condition of knowing, provided that we treat a proposition that is a simplification or idealization as false.

But is asserting or theoretically employing a proposition recognized as a simplification or idealization putting it forth as true? If not, then perhaps the so-called truth condition of S's knowing that h may be retained when formulated as requiring that h, and if the asserting of h in the truth condition itself is similarly not taken as putting it forth as true that h.

If Cohen's view is appropriate, then it impugns Alan R. White's attempt (cf. 1982, 59–61) to fine-tune our understanding of the truth condition so that we speak of reality, not of truth, as the prime condition of knowledge.[7] My own later analysis of knowing that as a category broad enough to allow animals and infants to know will focus on the obtaining of the state of affairs expressed by the proposition that h rather than on that proposition's being true. And the state of affairs expressed by a scientist's simplification or idealization never occurs. So if utterances of the form, 'S knows that h,' do have both appropriate plural and singular subjects when we instantiate for 'h' such a simplification or idealization, then we should go along with Popper in regarding that as a different sense of 'knows that' and of 'knowledge' from the one of interest in my analysis, which Popper regards as concerning an aspect of a knowing subject.

Cohen does not dismiss the relevance of believing but incorporates it in a disjunctive requirement that S either believes that h or—in the fashion indicated above—accepts that h.[8] But philosophers are typically dissatisfied with disjunctive conditions for important phenomena.

One difficulty for Cohen's disjunction is Alan R. White's list of examples of knowledge that h prior to the beginning of any belief in that knowledge, but which turn out also to be prior to acceptance of Cohen's sort: (1) One makes a discovery but fails to recognize it; (2) One is unable to believe that one has proved what one has; (3) Hypothetically, a strange or inexplicable way of acquiring knowledge, such as clairvoyance, telepathy, intuition, suggests a correct answer to one to some question but without one's believing the answer; (4) One has been informed of something, for instance, by a teacher, but does not believe [nor accept] it (1982, 90).[9]

THE JUSTIFICATION CONDITION AND THE STANDARD ANALYSIS OF KNOWING

When S's knowing that h is treated as a state of affairs in which the truth condition and the belief/acceptance condition are satisfied in conjunction with the satisfaction of a justification condition, such an account has commonly come to be called the standard (or traditional or tripartite) analysis of knowing. It was contemplated by Plato in the Theatetus, endorsed by Kant and by a number of prominent twentieth century philosophers, including A. J. Ayer (cf. 1956, 34) and Roderick Chisholm (cf. 1957, 16).[10]

Yet philosophers have disagreed about how to construe this technical label. Taken narrowly, it means the view that S's knowing that h is a species of S's believing that h, whose differentiae, that is, characteristics that distinguish this species, are the correctness and the justifiedness of S's believing that h. From this perspective, a philosopher who rejects the belief/acceptance condition will ipso facto reject the justification condition.

Although that perspective makes it natural to speak of 'the justified, true belief analysis' of knowing, it has been recognized that a still wider understanding of the label 'the standard analysis' takes a justification condition to be independent of the belief/acceptance condition. For instance, Robert Audi (1993) points out that just as we may say to a child, 'It's justifiable for me to punish you for what you did,' or, 'I'm justified in punishing you for what you did,' and yet show mercy, so we may regard the justification condition of knowing as requiring that it be justifiable for S to believe that h—whether or not S does believe that h. The standard analysis may accordingly be phrased as follows:

S knows (that) h if and only if
h;
S believes (that) h/accepts that h; and
S is justified in believing (that)/accepting that h.

This account presents the truth condition, the belief/acceptance condition, and the justification condition indicated above as individually necessary and jointly sufficient conditions of S's knowing that h, where we substitute a full, declarative sentence for 'h' but we leave open what individuals other than adult humans are within the range of variable 'S.'

GETTIER'S COUNTEREXAMPLES AND GETTIER-TYPE EXAMPLES

In a brief, famous paper, which has provoked hundreds of responses and an ongoing debate, Edmund Gettier (1963) described the following two examples in order to argue that the standard analysis is too broad, that is, too weak to exclude some examples where S fails to know that h. (1) Coins in the Pocket: S justifiably believes about another person, Jones, the unsuspectedly false proposition that F1: 'Jones will get the job, and Jones has ten coins in his pocket.' S recognizes that this proposition entails that P1: 'The man who will get the job has ten coins in his pocket,' which S then believes on the grounds of the proposition that F1. Unsuspectedly, not only does S have ten coins in S's pocket, but it is S who is going to get the job. (2) Brown in Barcelona: S has strong evidence for a proposition, which S does not realize is false, namely, that F2: 'Jones owns a Ford.' S picks at random a city name, 'Barcelona,' and recognizes that the proposition that F2 entails that P2: 'Either Jones owns a Ford or Brown is in Barcelona.' Not having any idea of Brown's whereabouts, S proceeds to accept that P2 on the grounds of the proposition that F2.

Gettier offered no diagnosis of these examples and no formula for constructing further examples that he was prepared to regard as of the same type. But as other philosophers proceeded to offer additional examples that they regarded as importantly similar to one or another of Gettier's, the technical label, 'Gettier-type example,' sprang into use. One such example was described by Keith Lehrer (1965, 169–70):

> Mr. Nogot: Somebody in S's office, Mr. Nogot, has given S evidence, E, that completely justifies S in believing that F3: 'Mr. Nogot, who is in the office, owns a Ford.' Evidence E consists in such things as Nogot's having been relia- ble in dealings with S in the past, having just said to S that he owns a Ford, and having just shown S legal documents affirming it. From the proposition that F3, S deduces and thereby comes to believe that P3: 'Somebody in the of- fice owns a Ford.' Unsuspectedly, Nogot has been shamming and it is someone else in the office who happens to own a Ford.[11]

We shall focus on Lehrer's example because many provocative variants of it occur in the literature and because it avoids the objection that in the coins in the pocket example S's articulation of P1 may employ the phrase, 'the man who will get the job,' to refer to Jones rather than to S, so that the truth condition is not satisfied.[12]

There has been disagreement over the scope of the label, 'Gettier-type ex- ample.' Some take it to be any example where satisfaction of the three conditions of the standard analysis fails to be sufficient for S's knowing that h. Others, in- cluding myself (1983), regard Gettier as having called attention to a more special variety of counterexample, and they allow that the standard analysis might face other types of counterexamples.

COUNTEREXAMPLES CONCERNING RELEVANT ALTERNATIVES

One such example reveals the standard analysis to be too weak:

> The Barn Facsimiles: S believes that P4, 'Here is a barn,' because S sees a barn from the front while driving through an unfamiliar countryside, unaware that people there who wish to appear quite affluent have erected many papier- mâché constructions that look just like the barns in the area from the road.[13]

Ignorance arises in this case because, very roughly, S lacks the ability to dis- criminate items involved in the state of affairs of which S has knowledge from certain other relatively nearby items, whose alternative involvement would render false S's belief that h. This element is lacking in Gettier's own cases and in the Nogot case.

COUNTEREXAMPLES CONCERNING THE SOCIAL ASPECTS OF KNOWING AND UNPOSSESSED INFORMATION

Another well-known, although controversial, example that arose in the early literature provoked by Gettier's article was presented by Gilbert Harman (cf. 1968, 172):

> The Newspaper: S believes a true, bylined report in a generally reliable newspaper that P5: 'A famous civil-rights leader has been assassinated.' The report was written by a reporter who was an eyewitness. Unsuspected by S, those surrounding S do not have any idea of what to think since they have additional information consisting in later reports to the contrary, which they do not realize were due solely to a conspiracy of other eyewitnesses aimed at avoiding a racial incident.

The example, like a number of others that it in turn provoked, concerns, very roughly, evidence not possessed by S but which is available in some relevant respect. In this case, the evidence, albeit misleading, is possessed by members of the social group with which S cooperates in inquiries. This illustrates one way in which some philosophers (e.g., Sosa 1991) see knowing as relative to epistemic communities to which a knower (at least potentially) belongs, thereby challenging an egocentric focus in epistemology.

Although intuitions are divided concerning this example, those who agree with Harman that S fails to know that P5 need not regard this example as containing the same sort of detail that made Gettier's and Lehrer's counterexamples work.

THE GETTIER PROBLEM

Very few philosophers think that Gettier and Lehrer misunderstood the justification condition of the standard analysis in a way that vitiates their counterexamples.[14] 'The Gettier problem' has thus come to name the problem of finding an improvement upon the standard analysis that will avoid Gettier-type counterexamples without thereby opening the new analysis to further sorts of counterexamples. This improvement can be attempted by either (1) adding requirements to the three conditions of the standard analysis, or (2) substituting new requirements for one or more of the three conditions in the standard analysis.

Since philosophers disagree as to what species of example is labeled by 'a Gettier-type case,' they of course disagree as to what the Gettier problem is.

CHALLENGES TO THE JUSTIFICATION CONDITION

In the post-Gettier literature, various replacements or improvements upon the justification condition of the standard analysis have been explored.

Early Causal Theories

Efforts to develop causal analyses of knowing initially appeared to make the justification condition unnecessary, but had difficulty because of the causal dependence of perceptual beliefs on circumstances such as lighting conditions and S's distance from the scene in such a way as to alter verdicts concerning whether S knows. Consider the following case:

> The Beloved Speck: From wishful thinking but not reliable information S forms the true belief concerning a speck that S sees on the horizon P6: 'That is a boat bearing my approaching lover.' (Ackermann 1972, 96)

A causal analysis of knowing might deal with this example by requiring that the occurrence/obtaining of the state of affairs expressed by the proposition that h (let us henceforth symbolize this by 'the occurrence/obtaining of h*') be the cause of S's believing/accepting that h,[15] thereby entailing satisfaction of both the truth and belief conditions. In the above case, the cause of S's believing that h is likely to be regarded as S's wishful thinking, and the occurrence of h* one of the relevant background conditions.

But such a focus was seen to be too narrow. When one knows an empirical universal generalization covering all of time and space to be true, for instance that

G: 'Iron is magnetic,' the obtaining of G* is not suitably called the cause of one's believing that G. This prompted causal theorists to consider requiring that the occurrence or obtaining of h* be causally related in some other way to S's believing that h, for example (1) mention of the occurrence of h* by itself provides some causal explanation of S's believing/accepting that h; or (2) the sequence of explanations of the stream of causes and effects culminating in S's believing/accepting that h at some place includes mention of the occurrence of h*. Even if we understand suggestion (1) so that there can be different types of causal explanation, one of which involves the broad, everyday practice of selecting part of a situation as 'the cause,' it is unclear whether (1) really helps with S's knowing that G, since only some of the obtaining of G* manifests itself to one or to the investigators upon whom one depends.

In contrast, a causal analysis depending on (2) can treat the obtaining of G* as explaining those of its instances which help to cause what results eventually in one's believing that G. But (2) makes the account of knowing too broad without some further requirement, since the sequence of explanations of the sort that it mentions at least eventually utilizes, for example, the axioms of number theory, and so no matter what bizarre local causation there was of S's believing those axioms, the account confers knowledge that they hold upon S (cf. Klein 1976, 796). Even if a causal theorist is restricted to empirical knowledge, a similar objection arises. Assuming that everything today is traceable back to the Big Bang, no matter what bizarre reasons S has for believing that the Big Bang occurred, approach (2) will not show that this is a case of ignorance.

Alvin Goldman, one of the early causal theorists, acknowledged that more restrictions would have to be placed on the sort of causal connections leading to S's believing that h, as he illustrated by the following example (1967, 363):

> The Careless Typesetter: On a newspaper known to be generally reliable, a
> typesetter carelessly misprints details of a story that S misreads because of eye-
> strain in such a way as to be caused to believe the true details.

Goldman tried to deal with this case by adding the requirement that the type of causal chain leading to S's knowing that h be one such that S is able to intellectually reconstruct all of the 'important' links in it and be justified concerning the reconstruction. In so doing, Goldman retained some consideration of justification but in a vague way that makes the analysis too demanding to permit attribution of knowledge to brutes and infants.

Goldman might have attempted to avoid such overintellectualization by refraining from requiring that the right kind of causal connections for knowing involve understanding of them by the knower. Perhaps he could have required that they are what philosophers call 'nonwayward' or 'nondeviant' causal chains. There has been considerable controversy about what constitutes such nondeviance in various other contexts (e.g., concerning the performance of intentional actions;

concerning the forming of a representation of something). A detail of my own solution is that links in the chain (a) not involve 'excessive generative potential' (roughly, that it not be the case that the beginning of the link could easily have produced some other upshot than the end of the link) and (b) not involve 'excessive receptivity' (roughly, that it not be the case that the end of the link could easily have been produced by some other antecedent than the beginning of the link).[16] The above example involves both types of deviance.

Perhaps one might also show that excessive receptivity is involved in the barn facsimiles case within the causal link ending in the formation of S's percept. Yet the type of causal account under consideration ignores the social aspects of knowing and does not explain the division of intuitions concerning the newspaper case, which the account would treat as a clear case of knowing. In addition, it is unclear how the account can be adequate to cover abstract or nonempirical knowledge.

The Nonaccidentality Requirement

Peter Unger once proposed an analysis of knowing that was worded broadly enough both to hold out hopes of application to abstract knowledge and to allow the relevance of various types of causal considerations to empirical knowledge: S knows (at time t) that h if and only if it is not at all accidental (at t) that S is right about its being the case that h (1970, 48). But the vagueness of the analysis provoked very different interpretations.[17]

The suggestion might be applied to the case of Mr. Nogot by thinking of the type of accident that consists in the intersection of two previously unconnected streams of events. The stream of events that gave rise to its being true that P3: 'Someone in the office owns a Ford,' did not arise from a collection of earlier factors that included what produced S's believing that P3. In that respect it is an accident that P3 and S believes that P3.

Yet the following Gettier-type example produced by Keith Lehrer shows that this understanding of Unger's analysis makes it too weak:

> Tricky Mr. Nogot: This is like the original Nogot case except that Nogot has a compulsion to trick people into believing truths by concocting evidence that is misleading in the manner that E was misleading in that case, and Mr. Havit's owning a Ford causes Nogot to realize that P3: 'Someone in the office owns a Ford.' (1979, 76)

Lehrer's point was roughly that there is a stream of events wherein the occurrence of P3* causes tricky Mr. Nogot's cooking up the evidence which causes S's believing that P3, but S still fails to know that P3.[18]

Yet some might suppose that Unger's talk about accidentality is broad enough to cover the presence of a deviant causal chain. Perhaps excessive receptivity enters into the link that ends with tricky Mr. Nogot's forming the intention to get S to believe the truth in question. Might not Nogot be just as likely to pick some other truth to convey to S by trickery? Accordingly, I have suggested (forthcoming) an improvement upon the example in which the compulsion is highly specific to information about automotive facts regarding people in the office.

Another type of situation in which we call an event an accident is when we are calling attention to a fluke during the manifesting of the powers or suscepti-bilities of something: either (i) some part of the mechanism for the full manifes-tation of the power or susceptibility fails to obtain; or (ii) the mechanism for the manifestation of the power or susceptibility on the present type of occasion does occur but a manifestation of the power or susceptibility occurs that is considerably less likely to occur relative to the operating of the mechanism than other mani-festations. I shall eventually present an account of knowing that will entail pos-session of a representational power but, contrary to Unger, will not entail that S believes/accepts that h, for it will not entail that the power actually is manifested. Yet a full manifestation of the power in question by S's believing/accepting that h (allowing that other things may also count as a full manifestation of the power) is no fluke and does represent the occurrence of h*. In that respect, even if S is a brute or infant, it will not be accidental that S is right that h.[19]

Reliability Analyses and Conditional Analyses

Alvin Goldman's attempt to deal with the barn facsimiles example introduced a requirement that S's believing that h be produced or sustained by a 'reliable' causal process or mechanism, although not necessarily one involving the causal influence of the occurrence of the state of affairs h* (cf. 1976). Goldman restricted most of his discussion to noninferential, perceptual knowledge that h. He oversimplified by characterizing reliability partly in terms of the falsity of the following sub-junctive conditional: if S were in a relevant possible alternative situation in which it were not the case that h, then the situation would cause S to have a sense experience quite similar to the one presently actually causing or sustaining S's belief that h, which in turn would cause S to believe that h. Goldman allowed that considerations of what makes for relevance of an alternative might shift with context or perhaps with the interests of the person attributing knowledge to S. When the nearness of the barn facsimiles is taken as salient, the logical possibility that S sees one of them in rather similar circumstances becomes counterfactually relevant.

But conditionals not hedged with accompanying glosses have seldom turned out to be accurate for philosophical purposes, especially for analyzing the presence of powers or abilities (cf. Shope 1978; 1983). There are versions of the barn facsimile case that involve ignorance yet in which the above conditional is satisfied because a guardian angel is present who would block the formation of a false belief in S that h, were S to look toward a mere facsimile, for example, by blurring S's vision or by stopping S's sensory experience from causing S to believe that h. In a less fantastic variant, it might be hidden electronic machinery that is tracking S's eye motions which would have such interfering consequences.

A problem that only received Goldman's explicit attention in later stages of his research program, but which was lurking even at this point, is the Generality Problem: At what level of generality versus specificity is a given element of the analysis to be understood? Put this broadly, the problem is faced by any philosophical analysis of any topic, and failure to clarify a solution will leave an analysis vague. The problem affects our understanding of Goldman's mention of relevant alternatives. Suppose that S visually knows that P7: 'An orange balloon is floating over the horizon.' If we understand a relevant alternative situation in a quite general way so that it may include the moon's being in the direction of S's glance, we thereby leave open the continued presence of the balloon, which would block light from the moon from reaching S's eyes and would account for S's not forming a false belief that P7. Goldman points out that becoming so specific as to require that a relevant alternative situation must include the absence of the balloon would inappropriately prevent us from considering what S would believe in situations where, for instance, the balloon is at a somewhat altered distance from S. The upshot would be to incorrectly grant S knowledge that P7 when S lacks the needed discriminative ability relative to the latter situation. So Goldman makes the vague suggestion that we should only construe alternative distance-orientation-environment relations "where necessary" to involve the absence of an object about which S forms a belief that h (Goldman 1976).

Later discussion of various reliable process analyses focused on a different element because such analyses reintroduced explicit mention of the process/mechanism that causes or sustains S's believing that h and did not merely specify a simple conditional about what would happen if S were confronted with a relevant alternative. But all of these analyses face the generality problem with respect to characterizing the process leading to or sustaining belief.[20] For instance, given a very general characterization, for example, 'the process of visually experiencing an object as part of a causal generation or sustaining of a belief concerning the object,' S may be very reliable in reaching true beliefs, and so in the case of the beloved speck will turn out to know that P6. But a verdict of ignorance will instead be demanded if to the above description of the process we add that it is dominated by the influence of wishful thinking.[21] Goldman more recently suggests that cognitive science may someday identify the types of factors leading to types of beliefs (cf. Goldman 1996). But Frederick Schmitt (cf. 1990) thinks that we need to constrain epistemological type individuation by so-called folk psychology, and by how ordinary people think of types of processes involved in belief formation.

The reliance on subjunctive conditional clauses in an analysis produced trouble for Goldman in a further way. Goldman realized that even when a true belief is reached by a reliable process, a person may not know because of failing to employ other available processes, for instance, failing to draw upon additional available evidence (cf. 1985, 109). (Although it is not Goldman's illustration, some philosophers might view Harman's newspaper case in that way.) But Goldman attempts to capture this insight by requiring the truth of the subjunctive conditional, roughly, that there is no reliable process available to S which, had it been used by S in addition to the process(es) actually used, would have resulted in S's not believing that h. But suppose that S knows that P8: 'I have not during the last five minutes employed reliable process R.' For instance, R might be some reliable process of arithmetic computation. Yet had S employed this process, S would have realized it and not have believed that P8 (cf. Shope 1983, 170n).

The generality problem also affects the prospects for a reliability analysis being able to deal with Gettier-type examples. Goldman relies on considerations about relevant alternatives in order to deal with such examples. For instance, in the original Nogot case, the actual presence of people in the office who stand in legal relationships to autos which bear on whether or not the people own the vehicles is analogous to the nearby presence of barn facsimiles, and makes relevant the alternative situation in which nobody in the office owns a Ford, yet Nogot provides the same original evidence.[22]

Another of Goldman's guidelines is that the more unusual an alternative is, the less we are inclined to treat it as relevant. Apparently, this is supposed to be why S can still know that someone in the office owns a Ford in the case of Mr. Havit, which is exactly like the original case of Mr. Nogot but in which it is Mr. Havit who owns a Ford and who is not shamming when he presents the evidence to S. If we point out that S cannot discern the difference between this situation and one in which Havit's Ford has just unsuspectedly been repossessed or has been destroyed by a meteorite or runaway truck, Goldman can reply that these alternative situations are unusual.

Yet the tricky Nogot cases may appear inhospitable to this treatment. For in them we may presume that it is not unusual for someone in the office not to own a Ford, and in an alternative situation where nobody does, Mr. Nogot is set to refrain from giving S evidence that someone does. But this is a difficulty for Goldman only if S's process of belief-formation is described in enough detail to bring in numerous specific features of Mr. Nogot's intentions and motivations. The process will turn out to be unreliable if characterized at a higher level of generality, for example, as forming a belief guided by evidence that has unsuspectedly been fabricated. But a reliability theorist needs a rationale for ascending to that level of generality.

This concern is not obviated by Goldman's having eventually added to his reliability analysis by requiring not only 'local' reliability, that is, reliability in the actual context of S's believing that h, but also 'global' reliability, reliability for all or many uses of the process. For if the process is very specifically characterized, then tricky Mr. Nogot, being intelligent, careful, and hopelessly in the grips of his neurosis, will typically generate true beliefs in victims through his trickery.

The requirement of global reliability also pushed Goldman to explore various ways of characterizing what alternatives are relevant to assessing such reliability. He eventually proposed that they are the alternatives that are consistent with our general beliefs about the actual world (cf. 1986, 107). But I have pointed out (cf. 1989, 149) that we believe that there are actually very many ways in which a person could be disfigured by a mentally disturbed individual, and so Goldman's suggestion may face an insufficiently high rate of correct belief-formation in the following case of genuine knowledge:

> Fortunate Beauty: S justifiably believes the true statement that P9, 'Beauty is present,' on the basis of how Beauty looks, and has acquired a perceptual schema of her through an ordinary learning process. Yet Beauty is fortunate that no mentally disturbed individual has just recently, unsuspected by S, disfigured her in a way that would prevent S's recognizing her on the basis of her visual appearance. In many alternative ways of being disfigured so as to be unrecognized Beauty would trigger in S a false belief in the denial of P9.

Moreover, Goldman is not able to explain the divided intuitions that have been provoked by the newspaper example, since on his view S definitely fails to know because the involvement of the media makes relevant an alternative where S and those around S have the information originally described, but it is S who has the misinformation since the initial reporter for the paper was mistaken.

By not explicitly considering the manifesting of rationality during belief formation, Goldman's reliabilism has provoked the objection that it is too weak to rule out knowledge in cases (albeit possibly fictitious) of belief-formation through certain very unusual processes such as clairvoyance. Laurence BonJour (1980) describes the case of Norman's suddenly becoming able through budding, unsuspected clairvoyance to believe accurately in what city the President happens to be. BonJour holds Norman's belief to be irrational: "From his standpoint, there is apparently no way in which he *could* know the President's whereabouts" (62–63). A sufficient reason, according to BonJour, for Norman to treat his belief as an unfounded hunch and to refrain from it is the fact that "there is no way, as far as he knows or believes, for him to have obtained this information."

But Goldman may protest that BonJour in effect exposes an alternative process available to Norman, which involves reflecting seriously about whether there is the sufficient reason mentioned by BonJour, that would result in Norman's belief's not continuing.

Lehrer has constructed an analogous counterexample that does not include the above type of reason available to the subject and so is more effective as an objection: Mr. Truetemp has true beliefs once an hour as to his body temperature but no idea why he has them, since unsuspectedly a benevolent surgeon concerned with Mr. Truetemp's health problems related to body temperature has implanted a device generating such accurate beliefs via a brain probe (1996, 31–33).

Reliable Indicator Analyses

An approach that in some respects resembles the one that I shall advocate is sometimes said to treat S's believing that h (alternatively: believing it for the reasons that S does) as a reliable indicator or a reliable sign of the obtaining of h* (e.g., Armstrong 1973; for discussion see Shope 1983). This is sometimes called the thermometer model since, analogously, the height of the thermometer's mercury column may be a reliable indication of the ambient temperature's being such-and-such a degree.

The idea of x's indicating y is broad enough that it need not concern what process ends with or sustains x, but it faces a generality problem concerning the characterization of background conditions for the lawlike, probabilistic or statistical connection involved in indicating to obtain. (Compare the fact that there must be a vacuum above the mercury column in certain thermometers for the height of the column to indicate what it does.) In response, some reliability theorists have resorted to using problematic conditionals.

Conclusive Reasons Analyses

Although philosophers who defend what are called conclusive reasons analyses do not always speak of indicating, we might classify their analyses as versions of a reliable indicator view which resort to conditionals in order to characterize indicating, and which sometimes add additional requirements for knowing.

Examples of subjunctive conditional requirements that such accounts have proposed are the following or some combination of them: (1) If it were false that h then S would not believe/accept that h; (2) If S were to have the reasons S does for believing/accepting that h and it were false that h then S would not believe/accept that h; (3) There is some subset, C, of existing circumstances that are logically independent of the obtaining of h*, such that if it were false that h and C were to obtain then S would not believe/accept that h; (3') ... then S would not have the reasons S has for believing/accepting that h; (3") ... then the reasons S has for believing that h would not all be true; (4) If it were false that h and S's existing circumstances were to differ only in the ways causally or logically required by the obtaining of not-h* then S would not believe/accept that h; (4') ... then S would not have the reasons S has for believing/accepting that h; (4") ... then the reasons S has for believing that h would not all be true; (5) If it were false that h and S's existing circumstances were to differ only in the ways causally or logically required by the obtaining of not-h* and S were to employ only the belief-forming/sustaining process(es) that S did—if any—then S would not believe/accept that h.

It is puzzling how to understand any of these conditionals when it is a law of nature that h[23] or a necessary truth that h. Moreover, cases where there is potential for what philosophers and lawyers call alternative causation of S's reasons for believing that h will be counterexamples to all the above requirements, as was revealed by the following case:

> Eloise's Phone Call: As he talks on the telephone, Abelard comes to know that P10: 'Eloise is wishing me happy birthday.' He does not suspect that an actress hired by Abelard's psychiatrist to impersonate such a call was trying to get through at the same time as Eloise, and was blocked only by Eloise's having reached Abelard. (cf. Carrier 1971, 9; 1976, 242)[24]

Conditional (5) was advanced by Robert Nozick (cf. 1981), at least concerning knowledge where the truth that h is not a necessary truth. Ernest Sosa has objected (cf. 1996, 276) that typically, when S knows that h, it will be true that S knows that P12: 'S does not falsely believe that h' but even if S were falsely believing that h, S would still believe that P12.[25] This objection also shows that all the other conditional requirements listed above are too strong.

The reliability theories in question are too far removed from dealing with social aspects of knowing, which are relevant not only to the newspaper case but to the following example, which shows that analyses that rely on the above conditionals are too weak if left unsupplemented by further requirements:

> The Sports Fan's Surmise: On a quiz show, S cannot remember who achieved a certain distinction in sports but does make a correct educated guess on the basis of some fragmentary information that S can recall. (cf. Olen 1976, 151)

Hector Neri Castaneda (1980; 1989) has defended a complex conclusive reasons analysis according to which, when S knows that p, S believes some conjunction of true propositions, e, and it is a nomological truth that ceteris paribus if e then p. This truth, in turn, is relative to a true conjunction of (i) some collection, s, of propositions that express principles of world order, such as laws of nature, and (ii) some proposition, that z, about 'structural' regularities in the context which are (a) relevant to S's determining the truth or the falsity of the proposition that h and (b) such that S has a propensity to make inferences in accordance with the proposition that z (such as when inferring that p from the proposition that e). The proposition that z says that the structural circumstances are either normal or only abnormal in the respects $r_1, \ldots, r_n$. As a further condition of S's knowing that p, Castaneda requires that S believes that z.[26]

Many criticisms that I previously offered (cf. 1983) of Castaneda construed his idea of normality as a statistical one. He responded that this was not his intent and that by speaking of the normality of the situation he meant that "either there were no respects that could make that p false or doubtful or every [such] respect has been cancelled by an opposite respect, hence, has restored certainty and has defeated the falsity-making character of the former respect" (1989, 235–236). He suggested that it might be clearer to speak of the standardness than of the normality of the circumstances.

The force of the modal "could" is initially unclear in this gloss. Although one is tempted to construe it as having a nomological import, the phrase, "or doubtful" is open to interpretation as carrying an epistemic force, and seems to move in the direction of what will be called in the next section a defeasibility analysis. Yet Castaneda's contrast was with restored certainty, and he apparently means a preservation of what he called the 'guarantee' of the truth of the proposition that p, its being in that way certain to hold.

But thus construed, Castaneda's account is too weak to show why S fails to know in the tricky Mr. Nogot cases, where such a guarantee does arise from the very nature of Mr. Nogot's compulsion. I have also objected that the account fails to explain why S fails to know that P13, 'S has brain damage,' when brain damage gives S flimsy evidence that P13 (e.g., causes the seeming, but false, recollection that someone has revealed to S that P13) and where the possession of that evidence causes S to believe that P13 (cf. Shope 1983, 143n2).

Castaneda's reply to this objection was that I "do not take into account the Multiple-Species thesis" concerning knowing that (1989, 241n4). As part of that thesis, Castaneda maintains that the phrase, 'knows that', has multiple meanings, each picking out a different species of knowing that. Thus, he may be regarding the meaning that he is concerned with as different from the one that Lehrer and myself consider in regard to tricky Mr. Nogot. Indeed, Castaneda argues that in a similar fashion Lehrer and Alvin Goldman have talked past each other concerning the following well-known example introduced by Lehrer and Thomas Paxson, Jr.:

> Neurotic Grabit: S sees his acquaintance, Tom Grabit, steal a book from the library right in front of him. But unsuspected by S, Tom's mother (or father) has said that Tom was miles away at the time of the theft and has a twin brother, John, whom the parent tends to visually mistake for Tom, who was in the library at the time. Yet the parent's statement is only a neurotic lie. (cf. 1969, 228)

Epistemologists have usually followed Lehrer and Paxson in judging that S does know that P14: 'Tom Grabit stole the book.' Yet Castaneda purports (cf. 1989, 234) that Alvin Goldman reached the opposite verdict when Goldman wrote that the parent's statement "may be enough to defeat any claim" that P14 (1986, 55). But Castaneda has misunderstood the force of Goldman's "may," which concerns certain circumstances in which John's stealing the book is a relevant alternative. They are circumstances which do not contain the additional factor of the neurotic lying. So when Goldman comments that the alternative of John's stealing the book "seems to be relevant," he is only commenting on a misleading appearance to one who does not suspect the neurosis but who is aware of parents' tendency to be truthful about the whereabouts of their offspring. The proposition that Tom's parent made the statement in question is what some epistemologists call a 'misleading defeater,' roughly, something whose conjunction with S's evidence yields a basis insufficient for S's knowing yet where additional circumstances account for that not preventing S from knowing. So there is no reason to accept Castaneda's claim that Lehrer and Goldman mistakenly think that they are dealing with the same analysandum and are really explaining different meanings of 'knows that' or even revising the meaning it had for themselves previously.[27] Thus, I am unpersuaded that Castaneda and I focus on different meanings of 'knows that' in relation to tricky Mr. Nogot. Besides, such appeal to equivocation as a defense against criticism makes it too easy to resist counterexamples by multiplying meanings beyond necessity.[28]

DEFEASIBILITY ANALYSES

The need to consider the details of the demented Grabit case brings us to the threshold of defeasibility analysis of knowing that. The earliest defeasibility analyses were developed by Keith Lehrer (cf. 1965; 1970), who noticed that Gettier's two cases and a number of others that they had inspired could be handled by adding to the standard analysis a certain type of requirement as a fourth condition of S's knowing that h. One of Lehrer's proposals was to require that for any falsehood, that f, if S were to suppose for the sake of argument that not-f, then S would still be justified in believing that h. In Gettier's two examples, the relevant falsehoods that do not fit the requirement, and thus lead to a verdict of ignorance, are: 'It is Jones who will get the job' and 'Nogot does not own a Ford,' respectively. But the demented Grabit case produced a counterexample and once again a response to Gettier only began a lengthy research program.

The history of this particular line of research is too complex to summarize here.[29] For quite a while, what was in common to all proposed defeasibility conditions was a requirement of a particular truth value for some subjunctive conditional(s) about what would obtain concerning the justification of S's believing/ accepting that h if certain hypothetical circumstances were to obtain. But from a broader perspective, a defeasibility condition might be said to specify what impact is made on a certain aspect, A, of S's epistemic situation if certain hypothetical circumstances were to occur consisting in bringing A into a certain relation, R, to some proposition/propositions, D, which, unsuspected by S is/are true (and which, perhaps, is/are required to be of a specified type, T). In the above illustration from Lehrer, A is the status vis a vis being justified or not of S's believing that h,[30] R is the relation of being co-present with S's believing D, and no further requirement is made that D be of any specific type.

When a proposition impacts on A in a way proscribed by the defeasibility condition upon being in relation R to A, many philosophers say that the proposition is a 'defeater' of (or with respect to) the proposition that h. But because of examples such as demented Grabit, they try to impose a further restriction by requiring defeaters to be of some specific type, T, calling ones that are not of that type 'misleading defeaters.' When the proposed fourth condition of knowing is satisfied, so that any defeaters of the proposition that h are merely misleading defeaters, S's believing/accepting that h is typically spoken of as 'indefeasible.'

Lehrer and Peter Klein (1971; 1981; 1996) may have made the most sustained effort to perfect a defeasibility approach, resulting in quite complex accounts. Having discussed Klein at some length elsewhere (forthcoming; and cf. Plantinga 1996), I shall here focus on aspects of Lehrer's recent views.[31]

Central to Lehrer's exposition of his analysis are three technical labels. The first, 'the acceptance system of S at t', means the set of propositions true at t of the form, 'S accepts that q,' where each acceptance has the objective of obtaining truth and of avoiding falsity with respect to the content of the acceptance. 'The preference system of S at t over acceptances' means the set of propositions true at t of the form, 'S prefers accepting that q to accepting that r,' where each acceptance has the objective of obtaining truth and avoiding error with respect to the content of the acceptance. 'The reasoning system of S at t over acceptances,' means the set of propositions true at t of the form, 'S reasons from acceptance of the premises $q_1, \ldots, q_n$ to acceptance of the conclusion c,' where each inference has the objective of obtaining truth and avoiding error with respect to the content of the inference. Lehrer labels the combination of those three sets of propositions 'the evaluation system of S at t.'

Lehrer's defeasibility condition asks us to focus on what is left of S's evaluation system[32] when we delete from it every statement either of the form, 'S accepts that q,' or of the form, 'S prefers accepting that q to accepting that r,' where the proposition that q is false, and delete all members of the reasoning system of S involving unsound reasoning. Label what is left 'the ultrasystem for S.' Lehrer's defeasibility condition requires that the ultrasystem leave enough of a basis for some combination, k, of its members to relate in either of two ways to any proposition, o, (whether true or false) such that it is relative to the ultrasystem less reasonable for S to accept that h on the assumption that o is true than on the assumption that o is false: either (1) it is more reasonable relative to S's ultrasystem for S to accept that h than to accept that o, or (2) the conjunction of o and k is (i) as reasonable relative to S's ultrasystem for S to accept as o alone and (ii) not such that it is relative to S's ultrasystem less reasonable for S to accept that h on the assumption that the conjunction is true than on the assumption that the conjunction is false. In technical jargon, Lehrer calls o an 'objection' and calls satisfaction of (1) 'answering the objection,' while satisfying (2) is 'neutralizing the objection.' Thus, the defeasibility condition requires that relative to S's ultrasystem, every objection is either answered or neutralized.

The account succeeds in dealing with numerous Gettier-type cases. In Lehrer's original version of the Nogot example, where S infers that P3: 'Somebody in the office owns a Ford,' from the false intermediate conclusion that F3: 'Mr. Nogot, who is in the office, owns a Ford,' the ultrasystem will no longer include the proposition that S accepts that F3, nor the proposition that S prefers accepting that F3 to accepting that not-F3. So the ultrasystem will lack propositions rendering it at all reasonable for S to accept that P3, a prerequisite of satisfying (1) or (2).

Lehrer also applies the account to a variant where S infers that P3 from the evidence, E, without passing through the intermediate conclusion that F3. Lehrer objects that this "inference rests upon the acceptance of the false hypothetical binding the evidence to that conclusion," that is, the proposition, 'If E then Mr. Nogot owns a Ford.'[33] Lehrer notes that once the proposition that one accepts this hypothetical is purged in forming the ultrasystem, the basis is lost for reasonableness of the preference for accepting that Mr. Nogot owns a Ford over accepting that he does not, and so there is no basis left for its being more reasonable for S to accept that P3 than to accept the objection that Mr. Nogot does not own a Ford. Thus (1) is not satisfied and there are clearly no resources for satisfying (2).

But can the account deal with a variant that does not involve S's bridging the gap between evidence E to the conclusion that P3 by accepting falsehoods. In the variant, S is a highly sophisticated reasoner, whose inference to P3 is not bridged with the help of F3 but is instead bridged by acceptance of the following propositions, all of which are true: (1) 'The statements of evidence E are correct,' (2) 'E is evidence for the proposition that F3,' (3) 'The proposition that F3 entails the contingent proposition that P3,' (4) 'If E is evidence for the proposition that F3, then E is evidence for any contingent proposition entailed by the proposition that F3,' and (5) 'If both (i) the statements of evidence E are correct and (ii) if the statements of evidence E are correct then E is evidence for the proposition that P3, then P3.'

Lehrer also does not attempt to explain the conflict of intuitions concerning the newspaper case. He purports that S does not know that the assassination occurred; S's conclusion rests on accepting the proposition that the newspaper is a trustworthy source of reliable eyewitness reports about the assassination, which turns out to be false because it published the later denials (cf. 160). But in Harman's original description of the case, it was left open that it may be other news media that give such later reports—which leaves the reliability of the newspaper unscathed. Lehrer would then appear to be required to say that S does know of the assassination. But why should such a difference as to which media issue which reports make the difference between ignorance and knowledge? Moreover, it is this very variant over which intuitions have been divided.

Lehrer's account is also too strong in ruling out cases of knowledge of a sort that Risto Hilpinen (1988) has described. Hilpinen suggests that the physicist, Millikan, believed/accepted the proposition that P15: 'The charge of the electron is n.' Although that proposition is false inasmuch as later research showed the charge to be only quite close to n, Millikan's acceptance of his hypothesis could allow him to come to know various other things in his researches. It is difficult to see what basis remains in S's ultrasystem for accepting those other things, since we may presume that Millikan did not also accept the proposition, 'The charge of the electron is quite close to n,' which appears inconsistent with the proposition that P15.

VIRTUE ANALYSES

The earliest consideration in contemporary literature of whether knowing that might be analyzed in terms of cognitive or intellectual virtues was by David Braine (1971–1972).[34] But Ernest Sosa's treatment of epistemic virtues in some of the essays collected in his *Knowledge in Context* has had more influence. Linda T. Zagzebski and Abrol Fairweather (2001) regard Sosa as beginning his work on epistemic virtue from a naturalistic perspective that defines it in non-normative terms by focusing on one's arriving at true beliefs. To be sure, some philosophers construe the label, 'a virtue analysis,' so broadly as to cover any analysis that includes reference to characteristics of the knower rather than merely characteristics of believing/accepting, and they count some or all forms of reliabilism about knowing as virtue analyses. But a narrower meaning of the label may be more useful, so that a virtue analysis includes some positive normative characterization of the way in which S attains certain goals, such as believing truly, and also incorporates a mention of cognitive virtues[35] of S in that normative component. Sosa initially presented his strategy as analogous to that in moral philosophy of judging actions according to whether they result from stable virtues or dispositions which themselves make a "greater contribution of value when compared with alternatives" (1991, 189).[36]

I have interpreted (forthcoming) Sosa's position as including the following requirement: there is a field of propositions, F, such that the proposition that h is in F and there are conditions, C, such that S is in C at t (with respect to the proposition that h) and such that the first two of the following subjunctive conditionals hold because the third one does: (1) If S were to believe that h then it would be true that h; (2) If it were true that h then S would believe that h; (3) If S were in C with respect to propositions in field F and were to believe a proposition in F then that belief would be true.

Mention of conditions C and field F, of course, raises a generality problem and the question of how to prevent tricky Mr. Nogot cases from satisfying the requirement. Perhaps the latter cases are excluded by Sosa's further requirement that F is to be specified with enough generality to permit useful generalizations about the reliability of S as an informant to an epistemic community relative to which knowledge is being ascribed to S (cf. 1991, 281–284).

But I have argued (forthcoming) that such useful generalizations could arise in connection with what is nonetheless a mere rigging by external manipulators of a match between S's beliefs and the facts, so that it is important that Sosa adds yet a further requirement that the truth of (3) is due to an aspect, N, of S's "inner nature," which "adjusts" S's beliefs to facts in field F and is that "in virtue of which" the beliefs turn out to be right (cf. 1991, 191, 239, 277, 282, 284). So Sosa apparently treats a proposition ascribing a virtue to x as amounting to the statement that there are conditions K such that if x were in K then x would do A in virtue of x's inner nature.

At that point Sosa's analysis of knowing is still too weak because it can be satisfied by a belief caused by a mere capacity to acquire a cognitive virtue. Sosa himself points out that without restriction on the scope of conditions C, the latter might include the process required to get the capacity to manifest itself by the development of the virtue.[37]

It is obscure how to distinguish in a principled way the inner nature underlying a capacity to acquire a virtue from the inner nature involved in the presence of the virtue, or the inner nature involved in a process of developing a virtue from the inner nature that may need to arise during a warm-up period required for the exercise of a demanding cognitive virtue. Moreover, to add a requirement that the virtues pertinent to knowing must be the outcome of a period of maturation and development would deny any knowledge to Donald Davidson's example (1986) of Swampman, a creature who is a molecule-by-molecule duplicate of Davidson formed by lightning strikes upon organic swamp materials and thus moving and sounding like Davidson.[38]

Perhaps Sosa should accept the thesis (cf. Shope 1999) that ability/power/capacity ascriptions cannot typically be analyzed by subjunctive conditionals and avoid relying upon conditionals, as some other virtue epistemologists have done (cf. Code 1992; Kvanvig 1992; Montmarquet 1993). Sosa might try replacing reference to nature N with reference to cognitive virtues themselves, considered as powers that S manifests, for example, in the course of forming or sustaining belief/acceptance upon various occasions, some of which will also manifest still other cognitive virtues.

But even then Sosa's own account of S's knowing that h remains too weak to deal with the case described earlier concerning the extremely sophisticated reasoner. For in order to explain ignorance in Gettier-type cases such as the Nogot example, Sosa seeks to show that "you could make no connection" between the evidence E and the proposition that someone in the office owns a Ford "except by way of a falsehood" (1991, 25). It is also unclear whether Sosa is able to explain the conflict of intuitions concerning the newspaper case.

We cannot survey all virtue analyses, but since Linda T. Zagzebski has been a significant contributor to this research, we may briefly note a few concerns regarding her analysis, according to which S knows that P if and only if (1) S has a belief that P which has arisen out of some act(s) motivated by the disposition to desire the truth of beliefs; (2) each act referred to in (1) is of a type that would be/is apt to be/might be performed in S's circumstances by a person with intellectual virtues; (3) S's general attitude is such that if there were evidence against the belief that P then that evidence would lead S to reflectively consider S's evidence; (4) S has achieved the truth of the belief through/because of having the motivation referred to in (1) and having performed the type of act(s) referred to in (2); and (5) if the act(s) referred to in (2) at all involve relying upon some testimony of others in the epistemic community, then S has (also) achieved the truth of the belief that P through/because of that testimony's having been motivated by the disposition to desire the truth of beliefs and having been a type of act that would be/is apt to be/might be performed in the circumstances by a person with intellectual virtues (cf. 1996, 280–281, 295, 297).[39]

It is questionable whether requirement (1) does permit, as Zagzebski desires, knowledge on the part of animals and young children.[40] The analysis seems too weak to rule out certain tricky Mr. Nogot cases. Moreover, an example where S knows that P16: 'I lack intellectual virtue V,' appears not to fit requirement (2) because it either makes the requirement impossible to satisfy (if a person with V cannot not be in S's intellectual circumstances) or makes (2) false (if we take circumstances to concern what lies outside S's cognitive character) since a person with virtue V would not perform acts giving rise to the belief that P16.[41]

PLANTINGA'S PROPER FUNCTIONALISM

There is sometimes no positive normative content to the ascription of a function, for instance, to an instrument of torture, and so perhaps the following additional requirements for knowing that proposed by Alvin Plantinga (1993b), might not be classified as yielding a virtue analysis: (1) the cognitive faculties involved in the production of one's belief are functioning properly in an environment sufficiently similar to the one for which they were designed; (2) the portion of one's design plan covering formation of beliefs when in the latter circumstances specifies that such formation directly serves the function of forming true beliefs; (3) if those circumstances include additional beliefs or testimony, then the latter are or express beliefs also satisfying (2) (and so on, backwards through any chain of input beliefs or testimony from one person to another); and (4) there is a high statistical or objective probability that a belief produced in accordance with that portion of one's design plan in one's type of circumstances is true.

Clause (3) suffices to deal with the case of the highly sophisticated reasoner and the cases involving tricky Mr. Nogot's neurosis, but perhaps not variants of the latter where some background natural radiation causes people in the vicinity to have misleading evidence that is the sole support for a nonetheless true belief. Such tricky circumstances cases will only be ruled out if in fact the designer of us, be it God or evolution, did not include provision for them in our design plan.

I objected (1998) that the account is too weak because it permits knowledge in a variant of the Nogot case, where Mr. Nogot sincerely presents evidence E but, unsuspected by him, not only has he just lost the Ford he owned because of a meteorite strike but he has simultaneously won a Ford in a raffle.[42]

Plantinga subsequently (1999; 2000) proposed to deal with such cases by adding a further requirement concerning what he calls the mini-environment, MBE, for the exercise, E, of cognitive powers producing S's belief, B, that h. He defines MBE as the maximally specific set of circumstances obtaining when B was formed, with the exclusion of circumstances entailing that belief B is true or entailing that belief B is false. So the set does not include S's winning of the Ford in the lottery but does include the meteorite's destroying the other Ford. Plantinga then adds to his analysis of knowing that the requirement that S's mini-environment be "favorable," that is, one in which E can be "counted on" to produce a true belief. Since winning a Ford in a raffle is unusual in sincere Mr. Nogot's relevant mini-environment, the latter is not favorable and he fails to know.

But something in MBE might protect S's process of belief-formation from error. Plantinga acknowledges a variant in which mist and fog conceal barn facsimiles from S (cf. 2000, 159). So Plantinga rejects characterizing favorability by means of a conditional about what S would believe if S were to use E in MBE. Plantinga instead turns to a consideration of what he labels DMBE, defined as that portion of MBE which is the conjunction of each circumstance in MBE that is "cognitively accessible" or "detectable" by S through E. He suggests that MBE is favorable if and only if there is no state of affairs, X, included in MBE but not in DMBE such that the objective probability of B with respect to the conjunction of DMBE and X falls below a number representing a reasonably high probability, which might vary with context (2000, 160). For instance, X could be the fact that there are more barn facsimiles in the neighborhood than real barns.

Nonetheless, since S can visually detect the object that is in front of him, when S forms the true belief, 'The object that I am seeing is a barn,' DMBE will include his picking out the object in fact located on that spot and so keep the objective probability sufficiently high.

Moreover, there may be examples of knowledge where another factor, Y, outside DMBE is present such that the objective probability remains adequate with respect to the conjunction of DMBE and X and Y. Might there not be cases where X and Y are rare deviations from usual processes connecting memories with conscious recollecting but which cancel each other out so that S still has knowledge in recollecting.[43]

Perhaps Plantinga thinks that tricky Nogot cases have been ruled out by his excluding from MBE circumstances implying that B is true. For a description of Nogot's compulsion seems to have that implication. But this would not hold in a variant of the case where Nogot is instead described as having a compulsion to trick people into believing some of what Nogot does about matters concerning his officemates' car ownership, concerning which he is a highly reliable judge. So in what sense is S's mini-environment unfavorable in this sanitized tricky Nogot case?[44]

Plantinga says that Mr. Truetemp fails to know since he lacks the defeating belief, which his proper functioning requires, that he is constructed like us and none of us has the ability to directly form such accurate beliefs about body temperature (cf. 1996, 333). But this will give no way to deny knowledge in a variant where the person is little Lord Truetemp, a young child, not much learned in the ways of the world, who has not yet revealed to anyone his starting to form the beliefs in question.[45]

Objects and Knowledge

Propositional Knowledge

Philosophers frequently speak of knowing that as 'propositional knowledge.' But the emphasis on states of affairs rather than on propositions which I shall eventually employ to analyze knowing that will not require acceptance of the frequent presumption that such knowledge is partly constituted by a relationship between a knower and a proposition. Robert Stalnaker (1984) has emphasized that the fact that it is useful to employ that-phrases to label differences among mental states—for instance, believing (desiring; hoping) that the sun will rise tomorrow versus believing (desiring; hoping) that my son will rise tomorrow—is not by itself enough to show that the mental states are partly constituted by propositions and relationships to them, no more than the fact that it is useful to employ numerals to label differences among weights of objects is enough to show that weight is partly constituted by numbers and relationships to them. So whether or not we treat knowing as a mental state, it is hasty to follow some philosophers (e.g., Zagzebski and Fairweather 2001) in speaking of propositional knowledge as involving a proposition.

It is commonplace to answer a question of the form, 'What does S know?' by a that-clause of the form, 'that h.' It is harmless jargon to say that the 'content' of this knowledge is that h if all that means is that what is known is that h. But it is controversial to make the slide to the conclusion that the content is a proposition. If I ask someone to articulate a true proposition, a careful answer will not have the form 'that h' but instead simply the form 'h'. When we write out a deductive argument or articulate portions of a scientific theory, we do not do so by expressing that-clauses. But the portion of a that-clause following 'that' does express a proposition. And we do answer the question, 'What proposition is expressed?' by a phrase of the form, 'that h.' So we can speak of the content of a proposition if all that means is what proposition it is.

Knowing Objects

One may say that S knows an object, for example, Marakesh. But when one is oneself quite unfamiliar with that city, one is not ready to assert specifically what John knows about it by asserting something of the form, 'that h.' So it is tempting to think that 'S knows x,' where what is substituted for 'x' refers to an object, is to be analyzed roughly as follows: for a number of propositions about details of x, S knows those propositions to be true.

It is not unusual to resort to speaking of propositions when one is remaining noncommittal as to the details of relevant that-clauses. But in this case we produce an analysis that is too intellectualistic to cover knowers that are animals and young children, who know, for instance, their backyards, since it is controversial whether they conceive of truth in the sense of something's being true. (Moreover, not all theories of truth treat a phrase of the form, 'that it is true that h,' as semantically equivalent to one of the form, 'that h.')

This concern provides one reason for shifting our focus to a state of affairs whose occurrence or obtaining can be asserted by affirming something of the form 'h'. For instance, by affirming that Marrakesh contains mosques, we assert the occurrence of the state of affairs: Marrakesh's containing mosques. We might technically refer to the state of affairs expressed by the proposition that h, that is, the proposition that Marrakesh contains mosques, by the notation 'h*', or 'Marrakesh-contains-mosques*.' Different states of affairs concern or are about different objects, properties, or relations. My account of knowing that as a broad category will allow us to regard animals and infants as having such knowledge by speaking of them as having the power to proceed in a way that represents various states of affairs.

Knowledge by Acquaintance

Some philosophers have held that knowledge of some objects involves a 'direct' relationship called being acquainted with the object, involving experiencing aspects of the object, for example, aspects of one of one's own mental states. A. R. White rejects this view on the grounds that the experiencing may be how one comes to know, but does not constitute the knowing, and so there is no need to postulate a special sense of 'know' in such examples (cf. 1982, 41).

Yet there is a sense in which we speak of knowing an object (in the very wide philosophical sense of 'object') that does imply the experiencing of it, or aspects of it, as when the Bible says of sexual intercourse, "And he knew her." In this sense, some might maintain that even though God's omniscience entails that God knows what imperfection is like, God's perfection entails that God does not know imperfection. Again, when a formerly healthy person ages and loses general strength, we speak of the person as for the first time knowing weakness. Although we shall not be further concerned in the present discussion with this sense, it has an analogy to the one employed in our main account, which helps us to understand why it is appropriate to use 'know' in this extended sense. In the extended sense, for one to know x is for the experiencing of x to give one the power to be involved in relationships to aspects of x that represent x's having those aspects. Sexually experiencing the woman enables the man to engage in a number of interactions that, depending on details, represent the woman's body's having various intimate characteristics and her mind's having various attitudes or responses. Experiencing weakness gives the aging person the power to manifest it, frequently involuntarily, in behavior that others may point to as representing ways in which weakness gets displayed.

KNOWING AS A BROAD CATEGORY

I propose to analyze S's knowing that h—construed as a broad category—by avoiding any belief/acceptance condition, and by adding to the condition that h the following requirement, whose terminology will need some explanation:

(R)   S has the power to proceed in a way, W, such that S's proceeding in way W represents its being the case that h, that is, represents the world's or the situation's including an instance of the state of affairs h*.

Speaking of a certain sort of representing permits the requirement to be expressed succinctly.[46] This type of representing also occurs outside of knowledge contexts and is one where x can represent y even if x is not about y and not an item ordinarily called a representation.

For instance, the tree rings' being of a certain number in a cross section of a tree can represent the age of the tree in years. In explaining 'x represents y' we need to relativize this analysandum both to a contextually salient what-question concerning y, such as Q1: 'What is the age of the tree in years?' and to various contextually salient propositions being justified, for example, the proposition that the growth conditions of the tree have been normal. Relative to such details, X1, the tree rings' numbering n, representing Y1, the age of the tree in years, is analyzable, roughly, as SY1, the occurrence of a state of affairs involving Y1, having an affect in a 'nondeviant' way upon SX1, the occurrence of a state of affairs involving X1, where this relationship makes justified to at least some degree an answer to Q1 (relative to various other contextually salient propositions' being justified). Here SY1 is the occurrence for n years of a certain state of affairs concerning the tree's growth, and it has had in a 'nondeviant' way[47] some affect upon SX1, the occurrence of a state of affairs concerning the determinable: the-rings'-being-of-a-certain-number. For SY1 was the nondeviant cause of that determinable's taking the determinate form that it did. Furthermore, this causal relationship makes justified to at least some degree—relative to various other propositions' being justified, such as that the growth conditions of the tree have been normal—the following answer to Q1: 'The age of the tree is n years.'

Similarly, suppose that when S is the baby or family dog, SY2, the occurrence of certain past relationships of it to Mommy's—or Master's—coming through the door at a certain time of day, is the (nondeviant) cause of SX2, an occurrence of the creature's proceeding in a certain way, W2, say, the infant's looking toward the door—or the dog's stationing itself by the door—shortly before that time of day. Relative to other salient propositions[48] being justified, this causal relationship makes justified to at least some degree as an answer to Q2: 'What is some of the domestic situation?' the proposition that Mommy/Master will soon appear. So X2, S's proceeding in way W2, represents Y2, the impending domestic situation's including an instance of Mommy's/Master's appearing. (In such examples, S has the power spoken of in requirement (R) even before proceeding in this way, e.g., while dozing or resting at a somewhat earlier time.)

The need for a further requirement in the analysis is revealed by considering how the satisfaction of (R) explains why it is metaphorically appropriate to speak of some inanimate things as knowing, for example, to speak of the electronic door-opening equipment as knowing that something is coming up to the door. The equipment has the power to proceed in way W: exerting a force that opens the door, and X3, its proceeding in this way, represents Y3, the doorway situation's including an instance of the state of affairs of something's coming up to the door. This is because SY3, something's actually coming up to the door from, say, off the street, being nondeviantly the cause of SX3, the equipment's actually exerting a force that opens the door, justifies to at least some degree as an answer to Q3: 'What is some of the doorway situation?' the proposition that the situation includes something's coming up to the door from off the street. This is relative to other contextually salient propositions being justified, for example, concerning the function of the equipment and its being in working order.

But because such a knowledge ascription to the equipment is only metaphorical, the analysis of knowing that will need a further requirement, which is satisfied by dogs or infants but not by door-opening machinery:

(R')   S has the capacity to have a thought of an occurrence of the state of affairs h* be causally involved in S's proceeding in way W.[49]

This capacity to have reality[50] in mind when proceeding is manifested as an infant matures by the development of a corresponding power or ability. The manifesting of the latter power may then be partly involved in S's asserting that P to other inquirers. Brutes such as dogs may fail to form epistemic communities but come along as free riders to knowing, provided that they can have thoughts and the capacity mentioned in the above requirement.[51]

Thus, the requirements for knowing are indeed satisfied by Radford's case of unwitting remembrance. There S displays the power to proceed in way W4: giving the answers that were mostly accurate and later seeming to recollect having studied such matters. So X4, S's proceeding in this way, represents Y4, those having been the dates concerning the relevant historical period, because SY4, S's having actually been given lessons that included those having been the dates, was non-deviantly the cause of SX4, S's actually proceeding in way W4.[52] This causal relationship justifies to at least some degree as an answer to Q4: 'What was the historical situation during that period?' the proposition that it included most of those dates concerning the relevant matters. Such justification is relative to other propositions being justified, for example, that S's memory and communicative skills are working normally, or that what people's memories are from their having been taught lessons tends to include materials included within the lessons.[53] But the conflicting intuitions of others may instead be taking the context to be concerned with the species of S's knowing that h of special interest in most philosophical discussions.

Knowing That as a Species of the Preceding Genus

That species has been the sort which does involve, in part, S's being in some important way justified in believing or at least accepting that h, and which views S as, at least ideally, being positioned in various ways as a potential cooperating member of an epistemic community. Let us call this species discursive knowledge.[54]

A cognitive goal of great importance is developing explanations of various things, but our interest in explanation is infused with our interest in truth,[55] so that we count explanations as deficient when they contain falsehoods at various sorts of locations. A careful development of this point concerning epistemological explanations of why various factors justify various propositions yields a solution to the Gettier problem, under at least one understanding of the latter label.

To speak of justification brings into play considerations about the manifesting of rationality. Although no brief characterization of rationality is possible here, I view it (cf. 1983) as a complex interrelationship of cognitive powers and susceptibilities including ones pertaining to cooperative inquiry within epistemic communities and the pursuit of goals, quite likely evolved, and about which we can learn more through long-term empirical research.[56] To speak of the proposition that h as justified is to say that the rationality of members of a contextually relevant epistemic community would be more fully manifested in relation to ep-istemic goals by members accepting the proposition that h instead of accepting competing propositions and instead of withholding acceptance of any of these propositions. I have suggested that by taking scientific methodology as our best present guide to what it is like for rationality to be manifested, we may deal with examples of the social aspects of knowing. Indeed, it will help us to distinguish many of the examples considered above of knowledge versus ignorance.

An analysis of discursive knowledge that h will need to include not only a consideration of explanations of what makes the proposition that h justified, but also explanations of what makes the propositions in those explanations justified, and so on. In other words, the analysis will need to consider a kind of chain of explanations of justification.

This perspective may be combined with a definition of the type of chain of explanations mentioned above, which I shall call a justification-explaining chain, in order to analyze the nature of discursive knowledge as follows:

S knows ['discursively'] that h if and only if

    (i) h, and

    (ii) S believes/accepts[57] that h, and

    (iii) the proposition that h is justified, and

    (iv) S's believing/accepting that h is justified in relation to epistemic goals either through S's grasping portions of a justification-explaining chain connected to the proposition that h or indepen-dently of anything making it justified.

The technical term, 'justification-explaining chain' ('JEC' for short), which I have employed in order to abbreviate the wording of condition (iv) requires a complex definition, which fixes locations of a type where we generally wish to prohibit falsehoods when giving explanations:

By stipulation, let 'a justification-explaining chain connected to the proposi-tion that h,' mean the following:
    an ordered set of propositions such that
    (a) the first member, m_1, of the set is a true proposition of the form:

          'f_1 and that makes the proposition that h justified,'

      where the proposition that f_1 describes something sufficient to make the proposition that h justified; and
    (b) for any member, m_j, the successor of m_j is determined as follows:
      (i) there is no successor of m_j if and only if m_j is justified indepen-dently of anything making it justified;

(ii) when m_j is justified only because something makes it justified then the successor of m_j is a true proposition of the form:

'f_{j+1} and that makes m_j justified,'

where the proposition that f_{j+1} describes something sufficient to make m_j justified; and

(c) each instantiation for f_j is a disjunction of conjunctions of propositions that take any of the forms described below (allowing disjunctions and conjunctions to contain only one member):

(1) 'k_2 describes evidence for k_1,'

(2) 'k_2, and k_2 entails k_1,' where k_1 does not entail k_2,'

(3) 'k_i describes evidence for k_{i-1}, and k_{i-1} describes evidence for k_{i-2}, and . . . , and k_3 describes evidence for k_2,' where $3 \le i$,

(4) 'k_2 entails k_1,' where k_1 does not entail k_2,

(5) a form described as in any of (1) through (4) but with phrases of one or more of the following types substituting at one or more places in the description for the phrase, 'evidence for':

'good evidence for,' 'evidence of such-and-such a strength for,' 'something that justifies,' 'something that justifies to such-and-such a degree,'[58]

(6) any form other than one logically equivalent to a disjunction of conjunctions of propositions that take any of the above forms (allowing disjunctions and conjunctions to contain only one member); and

(d) for any one of k_1, k_2, . . . , k_n that is false, some member of the ordered set: m_1, . . . , entails that it is false.[59]

Deferring for the moment an explanation of what it is for S to grasp portions of such a chain, we may note that in the case of genuine knowledge involving Mr. Havit, we can suppose that a JEC might begin as follows:

(m_1)   Mr. Havit, who is in the office, owns a Ford; and that entails that P3: 'Someone in the office owns a Ford,' and (all) that makes the proposition that P3 justified.[60]

The second member of the chain, m_2, will then describe something sufficient to make m_1 a justified proposition, which will include the proposition that evidence E was given by Havit to S.

In contrast, no genuine JEC can even begin in the following, analogous fashion regarding any of the Nogot cases, except for the case of lucky Mr. Nogot:

(m_1') Mr. Nogot, who is in the office, owns a Ford; and that entails that P3: 'Someone in the office owns a Ford,' and (all) that makes the proposition that P3 justified.

This contains a falsehood at a proscribed location in all but the lucky Nogot case, since it is false that Mr. Nogot, who is in the office, owns a Ford. And there is no apparent alternative JEC in those cases that escapes such difficulties. Even in the lucky Mr. Nogot case, the second member, m_2, of a chain beginning in this fashion would contain a falsehood when maintaining that it is the evidence presented to S that makes the first conjunct of m_1' justified. What makes it justified is, instead, evidence of which S is oblivious concerning the results of the lottery draw.[61] And no alternative, genuine JEC is apparent.

What it is for S to grasp a member of the chain, for example, the proposition that K, is for S to know that K as an instance of knowing taken as a broad category. In knowing that h, S will grasp in this manner sufficient portions of such a chain to render S's believing/accepting that h justified when, roughly, it is in virtue of grasping the portions that S does that S possesses the representational power mentioned in (R).[62] This ensures that discursive knowledge is a species of the broader genus of knowing.

Application to Further Examples

Little Lord Truetemp lacks discursive knowledge as to his body temperature because he does not grasp any portion of a JEC related to the proposition that specifies the temperature. Nor does he even have knowledge as a broad category as to the temperature, since he does not manifest the power to proceed in a certain way when the implanted device makes him have a belief. We move beyond the mere susceptibility to have a belief in the case where brain damage causes S to have a seeming recollection of having been taught that P13 : 'S has brain damage,' since in this case S does proceed to accept that P13 in response to that flimsy evidence. Yet it violates the methodology for more fully manifesting rationality by members of the relevant epistemic community related to S if they accept a proposition affirming that something happened simply on the basis of someone's seeming recollection produced by brain damage. So no candidate for m_1 in this case is apparent, since it cannot contain the proposition that S's seeming recollection is part of what makes the proposition that P13 justified.[63]

In the case of the sports fan's surmise, S's proceeding to make the inference that S does on the basis of fragmentary recollections does not follow the methodological principle, adopted by members of an epistemic community for more fully manifesting rationality, to check records when in doubt before accepting something as historical fact. So if one includes in m_1 the proposition that S made this inference, such a proposition will not help to render justified the particular proposition that S surmised to be true. So S grasps no members of a genuine JEC related to the latter proposition.

In the barn facsimile case, no genuine JEC is present because the way things look to S does not render the proposition that P4: 'That is a barn,' justified. The reason, very roughly, is that it violates the methodology of the epistemic community to treat a person's accepting that h on the basis of observation when there is—so far as the epistemic community's information is concerned—significant risk of the person's failing to discriminate between the involvement of one thing in the state of affairs h* from an alternative. But, of course, this rough remark does not try to say what makes the risk significant. But at least my account is no worse off than others that face the issue of delineating relevant alternatives.

Methodological considerations about the manifesting of rationality in the acceptance of propositions while pursuing epistemic goals may help to explain the disagreement of intuitions concerning the newspaper example. Those who regard S as having knowledge of the assassination may be responding to the principle to avoid relying on testimony motivated by an intent to deceive, while those who regard S as lacking knowledge may be responding to the principle to sample widely concerning putative eyewitness testimony from sources that have been reliable. They may further be realizing that S and those around S are not in an easy position to screen for deceit in the relevant testimony by following any obvious methodological principles.[64]

Let us assume that the mental supervenes upon the material in such a way as to allow us to attribute instances of believing/accepting to the emerging Swampman, for example, the belief that P17: 'Stanford is a university in California.[65] But does he also know that P17? Perhaps we can call what is registered within him the information that P17, but even so, it is hardly a memory-trace. Nonetheless, relative to the way in which we are thinking of the example, against a background where we take the proposition to be justified that the mental supervenes on the material, and we imagine it to be a justified proposition that the exact duplication of Davidson has occurred, we can attribute to Swampman both the power to proceed in a way that represents Y17, Stanford's situation's including an instance of the state of affairs P17*, and the capacity to have a thought of P17* involved in such a way of proceeding. For Swampman is able to proceed by W17, drawing upon the registration of the information so as, for instance, to articulate the information to himself or to others upon being asked what Stanford is. Here X17, such articulation, represents Y17, because SY17, the occurrence of P17*, is non-deviantly the cause of SX17, the occurrence of such articulation, and this justifies to at least some degree the answer that P17 to the question, 'What is the situation concerning Stanford?' (relative to the justified status of the propositions mentioned above and the proposition that Donald Davidson himself justifiably accepted that P17 at the time of the duplication).

But Swampman at most knows that P17 as an example of knowing taken as a broad category. He lacks discursive knowledge that P17 because his believing/accepting that P17 fails to be justified. Another such example is one described by Stewart Cohen:

> The Sole Ponderer: S knows that P18: 'S is the only member of the epistemic community who will ever accept a proposition that mentions the proposition that q,' where the proposition that q can be any proposition whose truth makes it true that P18. (cf. 1985, 527)

The example does not involve discursive knowledge, because it occurs in a context devoid of what Lehrer calls "critical discussion and confrontation in cognitive inquiry" (1970, 9) since the truth of the proposition that P18 entails that no alternative propositions compete with it for acceptance by members of the epistemic community.

Finally, the present approach can deal with Millikan's knowledge that H (whatever is the content of the proposition that H), gained partly thanks to his having accepted that P15: 'The charge of the electron is n' (where for simplicity we ignore the relevant ranges of error). The fact that E: 'Millikan obtained the experimental data that he did in the fashion that he did' is part of what makes justified the true proposition that C: 'The proposition that P15 counts as a justified proposition relative to the scientific community of Millikan's day'. This connection is part of considerations that make justified the true proposition that T: 'The charge of the electron is reasonably/quite/significantly close to n'. One JEC connected with the proposition that H includes the proposition that T, as well as the propositions that C, that E, and the following proposition, that Q: 'The proposition that H is rationally inferable in the fashion followed by Millikan from the proposition that P15.' The JEC will mention the existence of an argument paralleling Millikan's inference to H, in which the proposition that T figures in place of the proposition that P15. Since Millikan did justifiedly accept at least the propositions that C, that E, and that Q, such a grasp of a portion of the JEC was sufficient for him to have the representational power mentioned in my analysis of his knowing that H[66], where his having accepted the proposition that H represents the obtaining of state of affairs H*.

A Symbiotic Theory of Knowing

One reason that we are willing to treat discursive knowledge as constituting a species of knowing as a broad category is that infants typically grow up to become members of epistemic communities to which ascriptions of the more complex type of knowing is relative. A second reason is that in providing an analysis of discursive knowledge, we needed to mention some states belonging to the genus, without implying that they belong to the narrower species.

Since the importance of a proposition's being justified through input from members of epistemic communities helps to explain the need for requirement (R') in the analysis of knowing as a broad category, and since the latter type of knowing is mentioned in the analysis of discursive knowledge, we may say that the analysis of the genus and the analysis of the species stand in a kind of symbiotic, but not viciously circular, relationship.[67]

NOTES

1. Philosophers generally agree that 'People used to know that the earth is flat' is merely elliptical for 'People used to think they knew that the earth is flat.'

2. Dretske points out, roughly, that 'Fred is chopping down the cherry tree' will in one context make the claim that it is Fred (in contrast to others) who is chopping down the cherry tree, in another context make the claim that the cherry tree (rather than something else) is what it is that Fred is chopping down, and in yet another context will make the claim that chopping down (rather than doing something else) is what Fred is doing to the cherry tree.

3. For more discussion of the nature of an analysis see Shope 1999 and Zagzebski 1999.

4. The example has a history of discussion too complex to summarize here. For a consideration of some of it, see Shope 1983, 180–181.

5. According to Cohen, scenario (2) provides reason to suppose that S has a disposition to feel, for example, that such-and-such a monarch reigned at such-and-such a date, although that disposition is abnormally inhibited, so that the feeling does not arise in S. And Cohen argues that the concept of believing that h is just the concept of having a disposition to feel that h. So Cohen denies that scenario (2) offers a case where S fails to believe the relevant facts. Cohen suggests that "it is because beliefs are dispositions to have certain feelings that they can vary in strength with the intensity of those feelings" (115).

Yet there is a disanalogy here with a disposition such as great fragility, which does not concern breaking more, as well as a disanalogy with a substance's strong disposition to explode, which does not concern more violence in exploding. Moreover, Cohen offers no hint of why he regards it as plausible to attribute the disposition in question to S in scenario (2). He does not think that S's voicing of answers entails the disposition, since he thinks that in order to permit attribution of beliefs to infants and animals, we do not conceptually require that belief-feelings be embodied in linguistic utterances, not even in subvocal ones (cf. 8). And even though he grants that it may be a psychological fact that most human belief-feelings are linguistically embodied, that differs from the inference from utterance to belief that Cohen makes regarding scenario (2). Nor do we find a clear indication of how to explain what inhibits the manifestation of S's supposed disposition by consulting the list of factors that Cohen offers of reasons why feelings sometimes do not occur that normally would exemplify such a disposition. The only factor on Cohen's list that might initially appear relevant to scenario (2) is that a person may "have difficulty in remembering" that h (7). But to have difficulty remembering requires that one is either trying to remember or at least wants to remember, and such details are absent from Radford's example under either scenario.

6. This problem may also arise for Lehrer's explanation of conflicting intuitions (cf. 2000, 36–37).

7. White proposes that philosophers typically have not noticed that they have drawn the conclusion that if S knows that h then it is true that h from the combination of two premises: (i) If S knows that h then h; (ii) If h then it is true that h. What follows from 'S knows that h' alone, according to White, is that h is so—that is, that h is the case (cf. 1982, 60).

8. As a persuasive example, he mentions that as flames flicker up, one's knowing the house is on fire may force itself on one's involuntary awareness but acceptance may or may not come later; again, a self-deceived person "may really know that not-p even though out of shame, say, or vanity, he continues to premise that p . . ." (99).

9. Examples that may only involve absence of belief are refusing to believe what one has proved and being unwilling to believe what one has proved. More such examples, pertinent even to the absence of acceptance, may be found on a list offered by White of how various factors can account for one's not believing that one knows that h when one does know that h and may even cease to believe that h: (5) What is known is minor and has been quite often not recalled; (6) What is known came to be known far back in childhood and can be retrieved only through hypnotism; (7) One has forgotten the circumstances in which it was learnt that h; (8) One is a witness in the shock of the moment who knows more than one thinks one does; (9) One has been subject to lengthy browbeating or cross-examination or ingenious arguments aimed at getting one to doubt that h; (10) There is intricate detail in the issue of whether h; (11) The issue of whether h has been presented in an unfamiliar guise (cf. 83–94).

Another type of challenge to a belief requirement for knowing that, at least when the requirement is combined with the presumption that knowing is a special type of believing, is that it makes sense to say things of believing that do not make sense to say of knowing. White's examples include our readiness to speak of correctly, firmly, hesitatingly, or reluctantly believing that such and such (cf. 95). For a way to reconcile such linguistic details and numerous others with a belief requirement freed from the presumption in question, see Shope 1983, 171–178.

10. Variants of the condition speak not of being justified in believing that h but of having adequate evidence, or of having the right to be sure, or of it being evident that h, or certain that h.

11. An even earlier example rather like the coins in the pocket was offered by Bertrand Russell (1948) but provoked little discussion: S has true belief as to the time by looking at a clock that, unsuspectedly, stopped twelve hours earlier. Russell did not himself comment on its being justifiable, say, because of past experience, for S to hold this belief. For possible doubt concerning such justification, see Shope 1983, 20.

12. I owe this point to Jason Kawall.

13. The example originated with Carl Ginet and was reported by Alvin Goldman (1976, 772–773).

14. Some exceptions are O. A. Johnson 1971 and 1980 and Robert Almeder 1974. For discussion, see Shope 1983 and Almeder 1992.

15. Or at least that each have a common cause, as when fire causes smoke that causes one to believe there is fire.

16. For details and a way to avoid such modal terminology, see Shope 1999.

17. For a survey and discussion of some interpretations see Shope 1983, 192ff.

18. An analogous version of Gettier's coins in the pocket example was described by George Pappas and Marshall Swain (cf. 1978, 20).

19. Indeed, adults may sometimes intentionally trick children by convenient deceptive appearances in a fashion resembling that of Lehrer's tricky Mr. Nogot, in order to more quickly and easily let a child know various things: feigning pain after a blow from the child, for instance, to let the child know that even mild blows can cause distress. But this concerns knowing as a broad category. Once adults are engaged with one another in full inquiry aiming at truth, a concern shifts to a species of this genus which, for reasons to be sketched below, excludes the tricky Nogot cases from belonging to this species.

20. D. Goldstick may have been the first to raise this issue (cf. 1972, 244).

21. A similar reversal can be made to occur by changing the level of specificity in the description of circumstances under which a process occurs, and it will not be altered simply by treating circumstances as an aspect of a process. See for example the case of the pointed to sheep in Paxson 1974.

22. And perhaps Goldman will regard the appearance of the name of cities other than Barcelona on S's list in Gettier's second example as making Brown's being in one of those other cities a relevant alternative.

23. For instance in the case of the retina-rotting drug, where an experimental drug momentarily restores sight briefly enough for S to know something by looking at his surroundings but then destroys his retinas (cf. Morton 1977, 58).

24. Another type of counterexample is when S knows that P11: 'Some of my belief's about beliefs are ones that I might not have had.' Satisfying the antecedent of any of the above conditionals guarantees that its consequent will not be satisfied, since it guarantees that S cannot but retain the belief that P11.

25. Nozick adds another conditional requirement for knowledge and speaks of S as 'tracking the truth' when both conditionals are satisfied. For discussion see Luper-Foy 1987; Shope 1984; Sosa 1996.

26. At places, Castaneda misleadingly omits the qualification, 'S's determining.' But it is needed to cover the presence of r1, the typographical error, and r2, S's eyestrain, in the case of the careless typesetter, where S fails to believe these abnormalities are present. I overlooked this in Shope 1983 and misstated the requirement that S believes that z.

27. Perhaps Castaneda would hope to explain in a similar way the contrasting intuitions that have arisen concerning the newspaper example.

28. Another argument that Castaneda offers for his multiple-species thesis presupposes the correctness of his analysis of knowing that and then points to its referring to S's believing that z. Castaneda suggests that to shift the background conditions specified within the proposition that z will be to move from a consideration of one species or type of knowing to another. But this invokes an extremely broad use of the term 'type'

and by itself does not provide motivation to posit a shift from one meaning of 'knows that' to another. Nor does it render tricky Mr. Nogot cases irrelevant as counterexamples to Castaneda's analysis.

Castaneda is comfortable with the fact that his analysis of knowing that implies that S cannot know that z in the same sense of 'know that' in which S knows that p (cf. 1980, 223). For instance, in saying, 'I know that the mechanism for picking a winner in the lottery involves such-and-such regularities and I know that last night's winning number was so-and-so,' one is supposedly shifting from one meaning of 'knows that' to another. In order to allow that young children and some brutes can have knowledge, Castaneda was led to reduce his initial requirement that S believes that z to the requirement that S at least "takes for granted" that z, where taking for granted does not require believing and can even be "inarticulable" (1989, 237). But since the proposition that z apparently concerns in part what removes nomological guarantees, it is puzzling how very young children or animals could have such a concept, and if they cannot, puzzling what taking z for granted can be for them.

Castaneda's analysis is able to deal with the case of the sports fan's surmise to the extent that he adds an additional requirement concerning methodological restrictions on forming beliefs.

29. For discussion of some of it, see Shope 1983; forthcoming.

30. But Alvin Plantinga (1996) points out that a defeasibility condition might instead focus on S's believing that h being reliably produced, or its being produced by properly functioning cognitive faculties, or its being appropriately coherent, or on still other candidates for A.

31. But for fuller clarification and illustration of them, see Lehrer's own presentation (2000).

32. For brevity, I shall henceforth suppress the temporal references.

33. This is because Lehrer distinguishes accepting that h from believing that h and treats the former as a functional state of, among other things, being prepared to infer in accordance with the assumption that h (cf. 2000, 39–41).

34. For discussion see Shope 1983, 195–196.

35. John Greco (1999) suggests that we widen this detail to include not just cognitive virtues but any normative property of S.

36. Moreover, Sosa suggests that exercising virtue pertains to accomplishing a normally desirable sort of thing (cf. 1996, 273). Sosa's frequent mention of being "right" in believing may also be taken as retaining some normative element in spite of its close tie to believing truly.

37. Sosa points out that if we take an analogous approach to all virtues, then even as a baby Chris Evert had the virtues of a tennis player (cf. 285). This is close to what I have called the problem of newly acquired abilities (cf. 1999, 64).

38. Sosa has recently (2001) endorsed the position that Swampman counts as having knowledge.

39. Since the testifier might be relying on another testifier, this last condition may more appropriately be worded by making the analysis recursive.

40. She says (cf. 1999, 108) that we can stretch the boundaries of the analysis to include children who are in the course of training to acquire cognitive virtues. But has such training begun for infants? for dogs? even for wild dogs?

41. For similar reasons, the use of conditionals may also mar Zagzebski's analyses of

justification. Perhaps she has indicated a way to avoid this concern by revising the wording of condition (2) so as to pick out the specific intellectual virtue the act manifests and requiring not merely that the act is of a type that persons with that virtue would probably do but that it is also "an act that is a mark of the behavior of persons with that virtue" (1999, 108).

42. For analogous cases see Peter Klein 1996, 105, and Richard Feldman 1996, 217–218.

43. Suppose that Plantinga were to alter his definition of favorability so that X becomes the conjunction of all factors undetectable through E. That may leave the account too weak to rule out tricky Nogot cases, where the undetectable effort to trick is conjoined with the undetectable goal of Nogot's neurosis to install some true belief. It would also make the account too weak to rule out knowledge in a case where Tom Grabit actually has an identical twin who was in the library but who abhors theft. Plantinga himself says that it is not clear whether the following case is a counterexample: one believes there is a vase in a box only because of seeing its reflection in a cleverly placed mirror (cf. 1996, 329).

44. A naturally occurring analogous case is one in which S is not fatigued but is unable to discern that she is coming down with a certain illness and that it is the illness which causes her present feelings of fatigue. On the basis of the latter evidence, she forms the true belief that rest would help her feel better. As a matter of fact, which is also undetectable by her, the illness's symptoms are always greatly mitigated by immediate rest.

45. Exactly what Plantinga thinks about this case is unclear (cf. 1996, 377n 48). He does maintain that the undesigned Swampman is not really possible and so is no counterexample (cf. 1991). But for a counterexample that Plantinga's Christian beliefs may prevent him from holding this to be impossible see Shope forthcoming.

46. For present purposes, speaking of this type of representing can be treated as using technical terminology in order to simplify expression of the analysis of knowing that. But for some reasons to regard it as characterizing one thing that we do ordinarily speak of as representing, see Shope 1999.

47. Characterized in terms of the exclusion of both excessive generative potential and excessive receptivity; see Shope 1999.

48. Including, perhaps, some concerning the basic process of operant conditioning and some concerning the tendency of owners/parents to be regular in habits concerning pets/offspring.

49. There may be reasons (cf. Shope, manuscript) for casting the resulting analysis in a recursive form.

50. Or at least h*. See note 61 concerning the possibility that h* is a normative state of affairs.

51. The relevance of a salient what-question to representing something to be the case, and derivatively to knowing something to be the case, might mislead one into accepting Alan R. White's position that to know that P is to be able to give an answer, namely, that P, which is the correct answer to a possible question (cf. 1982, pp. 119–120; and cf. E. Craig 1990). The dog and infant do manifest knowledge but not by producing it in the sense of displaying the answer to a question. Since they proceed in a way referred to in (R) as a consequence of the earlier events that I have mentioned, they might be said to have shown what some of the domestic situation is and perhaps be

said to have yielded an answer to Q2. But they still have not given an answer to a question, not even nonverbally. Hector Neri Castaneda insists (1980, 219–221), but without much supporting argument, that such brutes and infants do have questions arise in their minds and pose answers to them, and he considers possession of this power to be one kind of knowing.

52. In this example, Y4 is involved in SY4 as an intentional object. For discussion of such a detail concerning representing, see Shope 1999.

53. There are reasons (cf. Shope manuscript) for concluding that knowing as a broad category will require an analysis taking a recursive form, rather than merely including the conjunction of a truth condition with requirements (R) and (R′). Because of this, we cannot say that knowing is the representational power and cognitive capacity mentioned in those two requirements, but we can regard it as a state whose embodiment at least always partly involves their presence with respect to some states of affairs.

54. Lehrer (2001) suggests this label. Because I did not wish to become sidetracked into a consideration of whether certain normative statements, e.g., moral claims, have truth values akin to the way in which nonnormative or 'factual' statements do, in earlier discussions of the species of knowing especially pertinent to inquiry and debate within epistemic communities, I restricted attention to nonnormative propositions as instantiations for 'h' and spoke technically of the species as justified factual knowledge. But this restriction can now be avoided by the decision indicated above to articulate a so-called 'truth' condition without employing the word 'true' and phrasing the condition simply as requiring that h.

55. And in what is appropriately acceptable: see note 61.

56. For a related attitude concerning rationality, see Nozick 1993.

57. I am leaving unresolved the question of whether this detail should remain disjunctive or should speak only of acceptance, as well as leaving open whether the accounts of acceptance given by L. J. Cohen 1992 and by Lehrer 2000 are significantly different.

58. This list of substitute phrases is meant to cover all the ways in which propositions become, in the usual philosophical terminology, 'reasonable,' 'acceptable,' or 'evident.' If it does not, then further appropriate phrases should be added to the list.

59. Cf. Shope 1983, 209–211. Some may wish to regard normative statements, including ones such as, 'I know that he's a very funny man,' as true, yet to regard 'He's a very funny man' as having no truth value because there is no fact of the matter about what is humorous. Nonetheless, there are contextually varying rough standards of humor that are relative to various groups. So we could change the definition of a JEC so as to be relative to such considerations by replacing a phrase such as 'true proposition' with the phrase, 'proposition that is true or, if lacking a truth value, is appropriately acceptable,' and replacing phrases speaking of a proposition as being false with phrases speaking of a proposition that is false or, if lacking a truth value, is such that its denial is appropriately acceptable.

60. An alternative way to begin a JEC chain related to the proposition that P3 is the following (once appropriate details are filled in):

(m_1) Mr. Havit, who is in the office, has behaved in such and such a manner and has been generally reliable; and (all) that makes the proposition that P3 justified.

Another alternative is the following:

(m₁)   There is a fact that entails that someone in the office owns a Ford; and that makes the proposition that P3 justified.

61. I have suggested (1983) restricting the label, 'Gettier-type case,' to examples where the three conditions of the standard analysis are met but all apparent candidates for a JEC related to the proposition that h contain a falsehood at one of the proscribed locations and so are mere pseudochains. Roderick Chisholm 1989 also proposes to block Gettier-type examples by focussing on the role of falsehoods. For objections, see Plantinga 1993a, 63, and Shope 1998; Jason Kawall has pointed out to me that Chisholm will also not be able to admit the presence of knowledge in cases resembling Hilpinen's example about Millikan.

62. An analysis of how S's belief that h (or acceptance of the proposition that h) becomes justified through grasping in this fashion some portions of a JEC would then complete the clarification of the analysans (see Shope manuscript).

63. Paul Moser (1989) has objected to my analysis by describing the case of the hypnotized, lucky Mr. Nogot, exactly like the case of lucky Mr. Nogot, but where Nogot's behavior in the office is only the unwitting carrying out an order of a hypnotist to engage in such behavior when out of the trance. But here what S grasps is not enough to make the proposition that P3 justified, for it includes Nogot's testimony, that T, where the proposition that T fails to be justified because acceptance of it by members of the epistemic community violates the basic methodological principle to avoid trusting reports that are not issued as part of a relevant inquiry.

In none of the cases of ignorance considered thus far in this section is there even a basis for treating S as proceeding in a way that generates any degree of justification for an answer to a salient what-question, and so there is no reason even to grant S knowledge belonging to the broader category.

64. Yet there are many interesting details that need discussion concerning this case and ones that resemble it in a variety of ways (see Cohen 1986; Shope 1983; manuscript).

65. Fred Dretske's account of representing (1988) will not allow this. For discussion, see Shope 1999, 249–251.

66. Yet to show this might involve spelling out controversial details concerning how Millikan comes to accept the proposition that H so that these details link up with the justificational considerations connected with representing that pertain to satisfaction of requirement (R).

67. Also see Sosa 1991 on the relationship between what he calls animal knowledge and what he calls reflective knowledge, as well as Lehrer's contrast (2001) between what he calls primitive knowledge and discursive knowledge.

It is an advantage of an account of knowing that for it to be able to be related to an account of knowing how to do something in such a way as to help us to understand the appropriateness of employing the word 'knowing' in both contexts. For a consideration of how this may be done for the account of knowing that defended here, see Shope (forthcoming; manuscript).

REFERENCES

Ackermann, R. J. (1972). *Belief and Knowledge*. Garden City, N.Y., Doubleday.

Almeder, R. (1974). "Truth and Evidence." *Philosophical Quarterly* 24: 365–368.

———. (1992). *Blind Realism: An Essay on Human Knowledge and Natural Science*. Lanham, Md., Rowman & Littlefield.

Armstrong, D. M. (1973). *Belief, Truth, and Knowledge*. Cambridge: Cambridge University Press.

Audi, R. (1993). *The Structure of Justification*. Cambridge: Cambridge University Press.

Ayer, A. J. (1956). *The Problem of Knowledge*. Baltimore, Md.: Penguin.

BonJour, L. (1980). "Externalist Theories of Empirical Knowledge." In P. French et al., eds. 53–73.

Braine, D. (1971–1972). "The Nature of Knowledge." *Proceedings of the Aristotelian Society* 72: 41–63.

Carrier, L. S. (1971). "An Analysis of Empirical Knowledge." *Southern Journal of Philosophy* 9: 3–11.

———. (1976). "The Causal Theory of Knowledge." *Philosophia* 6: 237–257.

Castaneda, H. N. (1980). "The Theory of Questions, Epistemic Powers, and the Indexical Theory of Knowledge." In P. French et al., eds. 193–238.

———. (1989). "The Multiple Faces of Knowing: The Hierarchies of Epistemic Species." In J. W. Bender, ed., *The Current State of the Coherence Theory*. Dordrecht: Kluwer. 231–241.

Chisholm, R. M. (1989). *Theory of Knowledge*. 3d ed. Englewood Cliffs, N.J.: Prentice Hall.

Code, L. J. (1992). *An Essay on Belief and Acceptance*. Oxford: Clarendon Press.

Cohen, S. (1986). Review of *The Analysis of Knowing: A Decade of Research* by Robert K. Shope. *Philosophy and Phenomenological Research* 46: 523–528.

Craig, E. (1990). *Knowledge and the State of Nature: An Essay in Conceptual Synthesis*. Oxford: Clarendon Press.

Davidson, D. (1986). "Knowing One's Own Mind." *Proceedings and Addresses of the American Philosophical Association* 60: 441–458.

Dretske, F. (1972). "Contrastive Statements." *Philosophical Review* 81: 411–437.

Feldman, R. (1996). "Plantinga, Gettier, and Warrant." In J. L. Kvanvig, ed. 199–220.

French, P. A., T. E. Uehling, Jr., and H. K. Wettstein, eds. 1980. *Midwest Studies in Philosophy*, vol. 5: *Studies in Epistemology*. Minneapolis: University of Minnesota Press.

Gettier, E. (1963). "Is Justified True Belief Knowledge?" *Analysis* 23: 121–123; reprinted in M. Roth and L. Galis, eds.

Goldman, A. (1976). "Discrimination and Perceptual Knowledge." *Journal of Philosophy* 73: 771–791; reprinted in G. Pappas and M. Swain, eds.

———. (1985). "What Is Justified Belief?" In H. Kornblith, ed. *Naturalizing Epistemology*. Cambridge, Mass.: MIT Press. 91–113.

———. (1986). *Epistemology and Cognition*. Cambridge, Mass.: Harvard University Press.

———. (1992). *Liaison: Philosophy Meets the Cognitive and Social Sciences*. Cambridge, Mass.: MIT Press. 155–175.

Goldstick, D. (1972). "A Contribution towards the Development of the Causal Theory of Knowledge." *Australasian Journal of Philosophy* 50: 238–248.

Greco, J. (1990). "Internalism and Epistemically Responsible Belief." *Synthèse* 85: 245–277.

Grice, H. P. (1961). "The Causal Theory of Perception." *Proceedings of the Aristotelian Society* suppl. vol. 35:121–152; reprinted in R. J. Swartz, ed. 1965. *Perceiving, Sensing and Knowing.* New York: Doubleday, and in P. Grice. 1989. *Studies in the Way of Words.* Cambridge, Mass.: Harvard University Press.

Harman, G. (1968). "Knowledge, Inference, and Explanation." *American Philosophical Quarterly* 5, 164–173.

———. (1973). *Thought.* Princeton, N.J.: Princeton University Press.

Harré, R., and E. H. Madden (1975). *Causal Powers.* Oxford: Basil Blackwell.

Hilpinen, R. (1988). "Knowledge and Conditionals." In J. E. Tomberlin, ed., *Philosophical Perspectives*, vol. 2: *Epistemology.* Atascadero, Calif.: Ridgeview. 157–182.

Johnson, O. A. (1971). "Is Knowledge Definable?" *Southern Journal of Philosophy* 8: 277–286.

———. (1980). "The Standard Definition." In P. French et al., eds. 1980. 113–126.

Klein, P. (1971). "A Proposed Definition of Propositional Knowledge." *Journal of Philosophy* 68: 471–482.

———. (1976). "Knowledge, Causality, and Defeasibility." *Journal of Philosophy* 73: 792–812.

———. (1981). *Certainty: A Refutation of Scepticism.* Minneapolis, Minn.: University of Minnesota Press.

———. (1996). "Warrant, Proper Function, Reliabilism, and Defeasibility." In J. L. Kvanvig, ed. 97–130.

Kvanvig, J. L. (1992). *The Intellectual Virtues and the Life of the Mind: On the Place of the Virtues in Epistemology.* Lanham, Md: Rowman & Littlefield.

———. ed. (1996). *Warrant in Contemporary Epistemology: Essays in Honor of Plantinga's Theory of Knowledge.* Lanham, Md.: Rowman & Littlefield.

Lehrer, K. (1965). "Knowledge, Truth, and Evidence." *Analysis* 25: 168–175; reprinted in M. Roth and L. Galis, eds.

———. (1970). "The Fourth Condition for Knowledge: A Defense." *Review of Metaphysics* 24: 122–128.

———. (1974). *Knowledge.* London: Oxford University Press.

———. (1979). "The Gettier Problem and the Analysis of Knowledge." In G. Pappas, ed. *Justification and Knowledge: New Studies in Epistemology.* Boston: D. Reidel. 65–78.

———. (1996). "Proper Function versus Systematic Coherence." In J. L. Kvanvig, ed. 25–45.

———. (2000). *Theory of Knowledge.* 2d ed. Boulder: Westview Press.

———. (2001). "The Virtue of Knowledge." In L. T. Zagzebski and A. Fairweather, eds. 200–213.

Lehrer, K. and T. Paxson, Jr. (1969). "Knowledge: Undefeated Justified True Belief." *Journal of Philosophy* 66: 225–237.

Luper-Foy, S. (1987). *The Possibility of Knowledge: Nozick and His Critics.* Totowa, N.J.: Rowman & Littlefield.

Monmarquet, J. A. (1993). *Epistemic Virtue and Doxastic Responsibility.* Lanham, Md.: Rowman & Littlefield.

Morton, A. (1997). *A Guide Through the Theory of Knowledge.* Belmont, Calif.: Dickenson.

Moser, P. (1989). *Knowledge and Evidence.* Cambridge: Cambridge University Press.

Nozick, R. (1981). *Philosophical Explanations*. Cambridge, Mass.: Harvard University Press.

———. (1993). *The Nature of Rationality*. Princeton, N.J.: Princeton University Press.

Olen, J. (1976). "Is Undefeated Justified True Belief Knowledge?" *Analysis* 36: 150–152.

Pappas, G. and M. Swain. (1978). "Introduction." In G. Pappas and M. Swain, eds. 11–40.

Pappas, G., and M. Swain, eds. (1978). *Essays on Knowledge and Justification*. Ithaca, N.Y.: Cornell University Press.

Plantinga, A. (1991). "A Reply to James Taylor." *Philosophical Studies* 64: 203–217.

———. (1993a). *Warrant: The Current Debate*. New York: Oxford University Press.

———. (1993b). *Warrant and Proper Function*. New York: Oxford University Press.

———. (1996). "Respondeo." In J. L. Kvanvig, ed. 307–378.

———. (2000). *Warranted Christian Belief*. New York: Oxford University Press.

Popper, K. (1972). *Objective Knowledge: An Evolutionary Approach*. Oxford: Clarendon Press.

Radford, C. (1966). "Knowledge—by Examples." *Analysis* 27: 1–11; reprinted in M. D. Roth and L. Galis, eds.

———. (1988). "Radford Revisited." *Philosophical Quarterly* 38: 496–499.

Roth, M., and L. Galis, eds. (1970). *Knowing: Essays in the Analysis of Knowledge*. New York: Random House

Russell, B. (1948). *Human Knowledge: Its Scope and Limits*. New York: Allen and Unwin.

Schmitt, F. F. (1990). *Knowledge and Belief*. London: Routledge.

Shope, R. K. (1983). *The Analysis of Knowing: A Decade of Research*. Princeton, N.J.: Princeton University Press.

———. (1984). "Cognitive Abilities, Conditionals, and Knowledge: A Response to Nozick." *Journal of Philosophy* 81: 29–47.

———. (1989). "Justification, Reliability, and Knowledge." *Philosophia* 19: 133–154.

———. (1998). "Gettier Problems." In E. Craig, ed. *Routledge Encyclopedia of Philosophy*, vol. 4. New York: Routledge. 54–59.

———. (1999). *The Nature of Meaningfulness: Representing, Powers and Meaning*. Lanham, Md.: Rowman & Littlefield.

———. (forthcoming). "The Analysis of Knowing." In I. Niiniluoto et al., eds. *The Handbook of Epistemology*. Kluwer.

———. *Knowledge as Power*, manuscript.

Sosa, E. (1991). *Knowledge in Perspective: Selected Essays in Epistemology*. Cambridge: Cambridge University Press.

———. (1996). "Postscript to 'Proper Functionalism and Virtue Epistemology.' " In J. L. Kvanvig, ed. 271–280.

———. (2001). "For Love of Truth?" In L. Zagzebski and A. Fairweather, eds. 49–62.

Stalnaker, R. C. (1984). *Inquiry*. Cambridge, Mass.: MIT Press.

White, A. R. (1982). *The Nature of Knowledge*. Totowa, N.J.: Rowman & Littlefield.

Zagzebski, L. T. (1996). *Virtues of the Mind*. Cambridge: Cambridge University Press.

———. (1999). "What Is Knowledge?" In J. Greco and E. Sosa, eds. *The Blackwell Guide to Epistemology*. Oxford: Blackwell. 92–116.

———. (2002). "Introduction." In L. T. Zagzebski and A. Fairweather, eds. 3–14.

Zagzebski, L. T., and A. Fairweather, eds. (2000). *Virtue Epistemology: Essays on Epistemic Virtue and Responsibility*. New York: Oxford University Press.

CHAPTER 2

THE SOURCES OF KNOWLEDGE

ROBERT AUDI

KNOWLEDGE can be adequately explicated only in relation to its sources. This is in part why perception, intuition, and other generally recognized sources of knowledge have been so extensively discussed in epistemology. These and other apparent sources of knowledge are also widely considered sources of justification, and they can serve as such even if justification is not entailed by knowledge. My concern here will be primarily with sources of knowledge; but in order to bring out their epistemological importance, I will connect these sources with justification as well. I am speaking, of course, as if we may suppose that there is knowledge. Anyone who accepts some version of skepticism may simply take what is said to apply to what would be sources of knowledge or justification if there should be any knowledge or justification of the kind in question. I begin with what might be called the standard basic sources of knowledge, proceed to distinguish them from nonbasic sources and from grounds of knowledge, and, with the account of epistemic sources then before us, turn to questions of defeasibility and completeness.

I. Basic Sources of Knowledge
and Justification

If, in the history of epistemology, any sources of knowledge deserve to be called the classical basic sources, the best candidates are perception, memory, consciousness (sometimes called *introspection*), and reason (sometimes called *intuition*). Some writers have shortened the list under the heading, "experience and reason." This heading is apt insofar as it suggests that there might be some unity among the first three sources and indeed some possibility of other experiential sources; it is misleading insofar as it suggests that experience plays no role in the operation of reason as a source of knowledge. Any operation of reason that is an element in consciousness may be considered a kind of intellectual experience. The reflection or other exercise of understanding required for "reason" to serve as a source of knowledge is certainly one kind of experience.

Let us first explore what it is for a source to be basic and some of the conditions under which beliefs it yields constitute knowledge (these might be called *success conditions*). We can then consider what kind of source might be nonbasic and whether the four standard basic sources are the only basic ones.

I take it that a source of knowledge (or justification) is roughly something in the life of the knower—such as perception or reflection—that yields beliefs constituting knowledge. To call a source of knowledge (or of justification) *basic* is to say that it yields knowledge without positive dependence on the operation of some other source of knowledge (or of justification). Thus, I might perceptually know that the clock says ten by virtue of seeing its face displaying that time; and I might know by brief reflection that if two people are first cousins, they share a pair of grandparents.

It may seem that the perceptual knowledge is possible only if I remember how to read a clock and that therefore perception cannot yield knowledge independently of memory. It is true that perceptual knowledge of the kind in question depends on memory in a certain way. But consider this. A being could acquire the concepts needed for reading a clock at the very time of seeing one, and hence would not need to remember anything in order to form the belief that the clock says ten. One possibility here is the creation of a duplicate of someone like me: reading a clock would be possible at his first moment of creation. It appears, then, that although perceptual knowledge ordinarily depends in a certain way on memory, neither the *concept* of perception nor that of perceptual knowledge is *historical*. That of memory, however, is historical, at least in this sense: one cannot remember something unless one has *retained* it in memory over some period of time.

The concept of a basic source can be better understood through a different kind of example, one that brings out how even a basic source *can* yield beliefs that fail to constitute knowledge and how its success in producing knowledge may depend on what we believe through other basic sources. Suppose that I see the clock on the wall only at dusk, but still make out the hands and come to believe (correctly) that it says ten. I now turn on a bright light that shows me a system of mirrors which I remember my son has installed to deceive me in ways that amuse him. I realize that it can display a different clock with the same appearance. I now may have good reason to doubt that the clock on the wall says ten; for I realize that I would believe it did, even if I did not actually see it, but saw only the mirror image of a similar clock that does say ten. Here my would-be perceptual knowledge that the clock says ten is *defeated* by my realization that I might well be deceived. That realization, in turn, depends in part on my memory of my son's antics. We have, then, a case illustrating that, even ordinarily, I would not know the clock says ten unless there were no suitably strong "opposition" from a source different from perception. This dependence of perception on factors beyond perceptual experience, however, is what I call *negative dependence*; it does not show that perception is not a source of knowledge, but only that (at least) on occasion the source can be in some way blocked.[1]

One may now suggest that perception is not even a positively independent source because it depends on consciousness. The idea would be that one cannot perceive without being conscious; hence, perception cannot yield knowledge apart from the operation of another source of knowledge. Let us grant for the sake of argument that perception requires consciousness.[2] If it does, that is because it *is* a kind of consciousness: consciousness of an external object. We might then simply grant that perception is perceptual consciousness and treat only "internal consciousness" (consciousness of what is internal to the mind) as a source of knowledge distinct from perception. Internal consciousness, understood strictly, occurs only where the object is either internal in the way images and thoughts are (roughly phenomenal) or abstract, as in the case of concepts and (presumably) numbers. On a wider interpretation, we might have internal consciousness of dispositional mental states, such as beliefs, desires, and emotions. But even when we do, it seems to be *through* consciousness of their manifestations that we are conscious of them, as when we are conscious of anxiety through being aware of a sense of foreboding or of felt discomfort, or of unpleasant thoughts of failure, or the like.

To be sure, one might also treat consciousness as a kind of perception: external perception where the perceived object is outside the mind, internal where that is inside. But abstract objects are not "in" the mind, at least in the way thoughts and sensations are. In any case, it is preferable not to consider consciousness of these a kind of perception. One reason for this is that there is apparently a causal relation between the object of perception and whatever sensation or other mental element constitutes a perceptual response to it, and it is at least not clear that abstract entities have causal power, or at any rate the requisite kind.[3] This issue is too large to pursue here, but it may be enough to note that not all mental phenomena seem to be either perceptual in any sense or to be directed toward abstract objects. Consider daydreaming or planning. Neither need concern the abstract, nor must we suppose that there are objects in the mind having properties in their own right.[4] It would be unwise to assume that perception exhausts the activity of consciousness.

It does appear, however, that we may take perception to be a partly causal notion. If you see, hear, touch, taste, or smell something, then it affects you in some way. And if you may be said to perceive your own heartbeat or even your own anxiety, this is owing to their causing you to have some experiential impression analogous to a sense impression you might have through the five senses. Conceived in this way, perception is not a *closed concept*: it leaves room for hitherto unfamiliar kinds of experiential response to count as the mental side of perceiving an object and indeed for new or unusual kinds of objects to be perceptible.[5] This is not the place, however, to give an account of exactly what perception is. Any of the basic sources could be the subject of a deservedly long study. Let us proceed to memory as an epistemic or justificational source.

If, in speaking of perception, we are talking about a capacity to perceive, in speaking of memory we are talking about a capacity to remember. But remembering does not exhaust the operation of our memorial capacity to the extent that perceiving exhausts the operation of the perceptual capacity. There is also *recalling*, which entails but is not entailed by remembering; there is *recollecting*, which is similar to recalling but tends to imply an episode of (sometimes effortful) recall, usually of a sequence or a set of details; and there are memory *beliefs*, which may be mistaken and do not entail either remembering or even recalling. It is plausible to maintain, however, that remembering that p (where p is some arbitrarily chosen proposition) entails knowing it; and we also speak of knowing things from memory. When we do know things (wholly) in this way, it is not on the basis of other things we know. One may know a theorem from memory *and* on the basis of a simple proof from an axiom, but where one knows p wholly from memory—simply by virtue of remembering it—one does not at the time know it on the basis of knowing or believing anything else.

These points make it natural to think of memory as a basic source of knowledge. But I think it would be a mistake to claim that it is one. It *is* an epistemically *essential source*; that is, what we think of as "our knowledge," in an overall sense, would collapse if memory did not sustain it: we could know only what we could hold in consciousness at the time (at least this is so *if* what we know dispositionally at a time must be conceived as held in memory at that time, even though it is true then that if we *were* to try to bring any one of the propositions to consciousness then, we would normally have it there then[6]). By virtue of playing this role, memory is an epistemic source in an important sense. But surely one cannot know anything from memory without coming to know it through some *other* source. If we remember it and thereby know it, we *knew* it, and we must have come to know it through, say, perception or reasoning.[7]

If memory is not a basic source of knowledge, it surely *is* a basic source of justification. It is not easy to capture just how it plays this role. But consider believing that one sent a certain friend a holiday card. There is a way this belief— or at least its propositional object—can present itself to one that confers some degree of justification on the belief (I think it can confer enough to allow the belief to constitute knowledge if one is correct and there is no defeater of one's would-be knowledge, but there is no need to try to show that here). Someone might object that it is only by virtue of knowledge, though consciousness, of one's memorial images that we can be justified in such beliefs, but I very much doubt this.[8] A remembered proposition can surface in consciousness without the help of images and, often, can spontaneously surface upon the need for the proposition as an answer to a question or as a premise for an inference one sets out to make or sees to be needed.

Given the points made about memory so far, I suggest that it is an essential source of knowledge and a basic source of justification. In the former case it is *preservative*, retaining knowledge already gained; in the latter it may be *generative*, producing justification not otherwise acquired.

It is worth noting here that we may not say 'not otherwise *acquirable*'. Whatever can be known or justifiedly believed by a given person on the basis of memory can *also* be known or justifiedly believed in some other way, say through the testimony of someone else. This indicates another notion we need in understanding sources of justification and knowledge. A *basic* source of justification need not be a *unique source*, even relative to a single kind of justification (or knowledge).

If, however, memory is not a unique source, it remains true that the non-memorial source that is in principle available to one may depend, for its production of genuine knowledge, on memory or on knowledge of, or justification about, the past. If testimony is the source, for instance, the person attesting to a past event depends either on his own memory or on someone else's. If so, we might think that although memory is not a unique source for *primary* knowledge or primary justification regarding the past—where primary knowledge and justification are the kinds that do not (evidentially) depend on the knowledge or justification of anyone else—it is a unique source for *secondary* knowledge or justification *regarding the past*, as in the case in which I rely on someone's testimony about it. Perhaps, however, at the moment of his creation my duplicate could see smoke and know, by the visible facts, that there *has been* a fire. If so, then simultaneous testimony from him could give others such historical knowledge without dependence, for any of them, on (the operation of) their own memory. My duplicate would, arguably, "inherit" a capacity for induction from me, and *I* could not have acquired that capacity without relying on my memory; but he would still not actually have to rely on his own memory to know that there has been a fire. Here, then, we could have knowledge of the past that does not require the exercise of memory *by* the primary knower. Even if memory is not a unique source of any kind of knowledge or justification, the concept of such a source is significant, and it will surface again shortly.

Consciousness has already been mentioned as a basic source of knowledge. It seems clear that if any kind of experience of what is going on in the world can yield knowledge, it is introspective consciousness. Even philosophers who take pains to give skepticism its due, such as David Hume, do not deny that we have knowledge—presumably noninferential knowledge—of our own current mental life.[9] Granted, it is only consciousness of the inner world—or at least of whatever can exist "in" consciousness—that is a basic source *if* outer perception—consciousness of the external world—is not a basic source. But the inner world is a very important realm. It might include abstract objects, such as numbers and concepts, as well as sensations, thoughts, and other mental entities.

When we come to reason, there is, as with memory, a need to clarify what aspects of this general capacity are intended. Like 'memory', the term 'reason' can designate quite different things. One is reflection, another reasoning, another understanding, and still another, intuition. We reflect on a subject, reason from a premise, understand a concept or proposition, and intuit certain truths. These are only examples, and there is overlap: any of the objects in question must be understood (adequately, though not perfectly) if it is to be an object of reason, and one may need to reflect on a truth that one intuits in order to grasp its truth.

It will help to focus on a simple example, such as the logical truth that if all human beings are vulnerable and all vulnerable beings need protection, then all human beings need protection. We can reason from the "premises" (in the if-clause) to the "conclusion" (in the then-clause); but an assertive use of the if-then sentence in question need not represent giving an argument. Moreover, the proposition it expresses is not the kind that would (normally) be known by reasoning. It would normally be known by "intuition" or, in the case in which such direct apprehension of the truth does not come to a person, by reflection that indirectly yields understanding. (The *conclusion*—that all human beings need protection—may of course be known wholly by reasoning from the premises. One's knowledge of it then depends on one's knowledge of them, which will surely require reliance on a different basic source. But the proposition in question is the conditional one connecting the premises with the conclusion, and knowledge of it does not require knowledge of either the former or the latter.)

I suggest, then, that "reasoning" is not a good heading under which to capture the ratiocinative basic source we are considering, and that indeed if we distinguish reasoning from reflection of a kind that yields knowledge that *p apart from* reliance on independent premises, it is best not to use the term 'reasoning' in explicating this source. What seems fundamental about the source is that when knowledge of, or justification for believing, a proposition comes from it, it derives from an exercise of reason regarding the proposition. This may take no time beyond that required to understand a sentence expressing the proposition (which may be virtually none; nor need we assume that all consideration of propositions is linguistically mediated, as opposed to conceptual in some sense). Here it is natural to speak of intuiting. But the proposition may not be so easily understood, as (for some people) in the case of the proposition that if p entails q and q entails r, and either not-q or not-r is the case, then it is false that p. Here it is more natural to speak of reflection. In either case the source seems to operate by yielding an adequate degree of understanding of the proposition in question and thereby knowledge. It does not appear to depend (positively) on any other source and is plausibly considered basic.[10]

It also seems clear that reason is a basic source of justification. Such simple logical truths as those with the form of, 'If all As are Bs and all Bs are Cs, then all As are Cs' can be justifiedly believed, as well as known, simply on the basis of (adequately) understanding them. In at least the vast majority of the kinds of cases in which reason yields knowledge it apparently also yields justification. It can, however, yield justification without knowledge. Careful reflection can make a proposition seem highly plausible even though it later turns out to be false. If we are talking only of prima facie (hence defeasible) justification, there are many examples in logic and mathematics. Consider Russell's paradox. There seems to be a class of nonteaspoons in addition to a class of teaspoons. The latter, however, is plainly not a teaspoon, since it is a class. So, it is a nonteaspoon and hence a member of itself. The same holds for the class of nonphilosophers: being a nonphilosopher, it is a member of itself. There must then be a class of such classes—a class of all and only those classes that are not members of themselves. But there cannot be one: this class would be a member of itself if and only if it is not a member of itself. Thus, what appears, on the basis of an exercise of reason, to be true may be false.

It may be objected that it is only inferentially that one could here believe there is a class of all and only classes that are not members of themselves and that therefore it is not only on the basis of the operation of reason that one would believe this. But surely we may take reasoning to be *one* kind of such operation, particularly deductive reasoning. It is true that the *basic kind* of knowledge or justification yielded by a source of either is noninferential; there is no good reason, however, to rule that inferential cases may not be included.

To be sure, there is still the question whether inference depends on the operation of memory, in the sense that one may draw an inference from a proposition only if one *remembers* it. But surely one can hold some simple premises before one's mind and at that very time draw an inference from them. If we allow that knowledge or justification deriving from simple inferences such as those in question here need not depend on memory, we may conclude that it can be on the basis of inferential reason that the proposition in question is believed. It is a contingent matter whether such an inference *does* depend on the operation of memory. If one must write down the premises to keep track of them, it would. If, however, one can entertain the premises and conclusion together and at that time see their logical relation, it does not. The distinction between these two cases is not sharp but is often quite clear.[11]

Even regarding reason, then, we cannot say that we have an *infallible source* of knowledge: one whose every cognitive deliverance is a case of knowledge. To call a source basic is to affirm a measure of epistemic autonomy; it is not to affirm any wholesale epistemic guarantee. It is not even clear that every "deliverance" of a basic source has prima facie justification. But this is a plausible view, if (1) we take a deliverance of a source to be a belief based on it and not merely caused by it, and (2) we allow that a belief can be prima facie justified even when its justification is massively overridden. Let us suppose (1) and (2) hold. Plainly this would not entail indefeasible justification. If we suppose, then, that there would be no knowledge or justification *without* basic sources of them, we still cannot reasonably conclude that every belief those sources deliver is justified on balance or, if true, constitutes knowledge.

If we now return to the question of uniqueness, we find that, for reason, a plausible case for uniqueness is available, since some propositions, such as simple logical truths, seem (ultimately) knowable and justifiedly believable only on the basis of reason. To be sure, even simple logical truths can be known on the basis of testimony, as where someone who is logically slow first comes to know one through the testimony of a teacher. But can such truths be known or justifiedly believed without dependence on reason *somewhere* along the line? It would seem that the teacher must depend on it, or on testimony from someone who does, or who at least must rely on testimony from someone else who depends on reason, and so forth.[12] If this is right, then at least for primary knowledge and justification regarding simple logical truths, uniqueness holds.

Might we, however, make the parallel claim for perceptual and introspective cases? Could anyone (say) know the colors and feel of things if no one had perceptual knowledge? If we assume the possibility of an omnipotent and omniscient God, we might have to grant that God could know this sort of thing by virtue of (fully) knowing God's creation of things with these colors and textures. Still, wouldn't even God have to know what these properties are *like* in order to create the things in question with full knowledge of the nature of the things thus created? Suppose so. That knowledge is arguably of a phenomenal kind; if it is, the point would only show that consciousness is a unique source. Perhaps it is. If reason and consciousness are not only basic, but also the only unique sources, one can understand why both figure so crucially in the epistemology of Descartes or indeed any philosopher for whom what is accessible to conscious experience and to thought is epistemically fundamental in the far-reaching way that is implied by the combination of basicality and uniqueness.

II. TESTIMONY AS AN ESSENTIAL SOURCE

The four standard basic sources do not include testimony. At least since Thomas Reid,[13] however, there has been controversy over whether testimony belongs with these other sources or is nonbasic. There is no question of the importance of testimony. The issue is whether gaining knowledge or justification from it depends on the operation of another source.

It might seem that since to know that p on the basis of your testimony, I must perceptually know that you have attested to p, testimony-based knowledge cannot be basic. I suggest that this admittedly natural assumption is a mistake: I do not even have to believe that you have attested to p, though to be sure I must be *disposed* to believe something to this effect and may not *dis*believe it.[14] But quite apart from whether I did have to believe this, perception would have to operate for me to *receive* your testimony. Granted, your attesting to p could cause a machine to produce the belief that p (perhaps even knowledge that p) directly in me; but this would at best be a case of knowledge *due to*, not *on the basis of*, testimony. A mere cause of my knowing something is not a source of knowledge. A sudden curiosity can cause me to look up a phone number and thereby come to know it; the curiosity is not the source of my knowledge. If, by contrast, your attestation causes me to receive your testimony directly in my mind, like a message appearing in my interior monologue, I could acquire knowledge on the basis of the testimony; but this would show only that perception can be telepathic—or perhaps that there is a basic nonperceptual source of knowledge of other minds. There would still be no need for me to have my knowledge that p based (partly) on knowledge that you attested to it.[15]

With justification, it seems equally clear that apart from perceptual justification for believing something to the effect that you attested to p, I cannot acquire justification for believing it on the basis of your testimony. If, however, I am right in thinking that one need not believe, as opposed to having grounds adequate *for* knowing or justifiedly believing, that the attester gave testimony that p, then something important about testimony emerges: it *is* a source of *basic knowledge*, that is, knowledge not grounded in other knowledge (or in justified belief of some other proposition). My knowledge that p need not be inferred from any premises nor based on a belief that p was attested to. The point that testimony is a source of basic knowledge distinguishes it from other nonbasic sources of knowledge, such as inference. (Even in the case of knowledge by virtue of an inferential operation of reason, the conclusion is known or believed on the basis of a premise, hence is not basic knowledge or basically justified.) The point also helps to explain why it is natural to consider testimony a basic source of knowledge; for it is typical of such sources that they yield noninferential knowledge.

There are four further points that distinguish testimony from the basic sources. First, one cannot test the reliability of a basic source or confirm a deliverance of it without relying on that very source. With perception one must, for instance, look again; with memory one must try harder to recall or must consult other memories—and one must remember the original belief being examined, lest the target of confirmation be lost from view. With testimony, one can check reliability using any of the basic sources.

The second point has already been suggested in connection with memory. Memory is central for our knowledge at any given moment in a way testimony is not. Even if knowledge could not be acquired without the benefit of testimony given to one at least to the extent one needs in order to learn a language (a process in which what parents or others attest to is crucial to acquiring a vocabulary), once we climb that linguistic ladder we can discard it and, given normal memory, retain what we know. With the other basic sources, reason in some minimal form is indispensable to possessing any knowledge (at least in protecting us from pervasive inconsistency), and to inferential development of knowledge, which depends on deductive and inductive logic. Consciousness and perception are essential for the development of new knowledge in their domains. There is, however, no domain (except possibly that of other minds) for which continued testimony is in principle needed for increase of knowledge. Similar (but not entirely parallel) points hold for justification.

The third point is perhaps even subtler. There is a sense in which testimonially based belief passes through the will—or at least through agency: the attester must select what to attest to and in the process can also lie, in which case the belief does not constitute knowledge (and the justification the recipient may get is, in a certain way we need not pursue here, objectively defective). For the basic sources, there is no analogue of such voluntary representation of information. Indeed, testimonially based beliefs normally pass through agency twice over, since one can normally withhold belief from the proposition in a way one cannot when it is fully supported directly by experience or reason (to be sure, even in those cases there is such a thing as double support, as where someone attests to a plainly self-evident proposition one had not thought of but intuitively sees to be true on hearing it asserted).

Granted, it is a contingent matter when a person can withhold belief: some of us may be able to learn to withhold even beliefs that those speaking to us are people as opposed to robots.[16] But the normal level of control here is different from that applicable to testimony, where appraisal of credibility may always involve *both* the kinds of doubts we may have about basic sources and any we may have about the attester's response to them. To be sure, we sometimes speak of the "testimony of the senses." But this is metaphor, at least insofar as it suggests that the senses derive knowledge from another source, as attesters must eventually do, since knowledge that *p* cannot derive from an infinite or circular chain in which *no* person giving testimony that *p* knows it even in part on a nontestimonial basis.[17]

A fourth point of contrast between testimony and the standard basic sources has already been suggested. It concerns the need for grounds for the semantic interpretation of what is said on the basis of which it is taken to be *that p*. This is not a justificatory or epistemic burden intrinsic to the standard basic sources. Granted, much a priori knowledge and justification is acquired *through* consideration of linguistic expression of propositions. Still, on the most plausible account of the basis of such knowledge and justification, its object is nonlinguistic; the ground is apparently a kind of understanding of the proposition in question or, perhaps more directly, of the concepts figuring in or essential to it.

It must also be granted that a lack of semantic understanding will normally restrict the *range* propositions that are even candidates for one's a priori knowledge or justification, since one's comprehension of language will (for most of us, at least) limit the range of propositions we can get before our minds. Moreover, semantic *misunderstanding*—which is of course possible even in people of wide and deep semantic comprehension—may give us the wrong proposition or range of propositions. Nonetheless, neither of these defects need affect how good our grounds are once the right object is before us. To be sure, defeaters of knowledge or justification can come from semantically interpreted items and can afflict beliefs deriving from any of the standard sources; but none of those sources seems dependent on semantic grounds in the way that testimony is.

These contrasts between testimony and the basic sources are not meant to impugn the importance of testimony. In addition to being a source of basic knowledge, testimony is, like memory, an *essential source* of our overall knowledge. Our overall knowledge depends on it in far-reaching ways, though not perhaps as much as, and certainly not in quite the same ways as, it depends on memory. The most important thing memory and testimony have in common may be that they *transmit*, rather than *generate*, knowledge (the case with justification is different, since memory *is* a basic source of that).

As to how testimony differs from both perception and memory, there is more to say than can be said here. It is not a question of reliability; it is only a contingent matter just how reliable each is. It is not even the semantic character of the deliverances of the source; one can see a sentence (as such), as one can hear testimony—indeed, the uttered sentence may constitute someone's testimony. A crucial point made earlier bears repeating: the acquisition of knowledge or even justified belief on the basis of testimony depends on the agency of another person. Normally, the attester must not lie, or seek to deceive, in attesting to p if we are to come to know that p on the basis of the testimony. By contrast, our responses to the deliverances of the basic sources is not normally mediated by anyone else's action. Testimony may be unreliable—or otherwise unworthy of one's acceptance—both because of natural connections between the state(s) of affairs the testimony concerns *and* because of the person's exercise of agency. This is not normally so for the testimony of the senses or of memory or of reason. The point is not that the exercise of agency cannot be a "natural" phenomenon—though philosophers who think that freedom is incompatible with determinism are likely to insist that it cannot—but that the concepts of knowledge and justification apparently presuppose that if it is a natural phenomenon, it is nonetheless special.[18]

III. Sources and Grounds

To specify a source of knowledge is to indicate where it comes from, but it is also to do something more. I have already noted that to specify a mere cause of someone's knowing something is not to specify a source of the knowledge. In part this is because a source of something need not be a ground of it. As I am understanding sources of *knowledge*, and as they are generally conceived in philosophical literature, they are not just where knowledge comes from; they also provide the knower with grounds of knowledge. Grounds are what it is in virtue of which (roughly, on the basis of which) one knows or justifiedly believes. If you know that my knowledge that it is raining is perceptual, as opposed, say, to testimonial, you know not only that it comes from my perceiving something, but also that I have a perceptual ground, say a visual or auditory experience, for believing the proposition.

As this example makes clear, sources indicate the kinds of grounds to expect a person to have when the person has knowledge through that source. But the source is not itself the ground. We may of course call perception a ground of knowledge so long as we understand that so speaking of a ground does not specify just what it is. What about the converse question: Does specifying a ground of knowledge that p indicate the source of the knowledge? If the ground is experiential as opposed to propositional, then ordinarily it does. But we can speak of knowledge based on an impression that (say) a car is moving, while leaving open whether it is based on visual sensations or on inference from what one can see. It also seems possible for there to be grounds of knowledge that we cannot refer to any familiar source, as might be the case with certain religious experiences. Is this a kind of perception, or might there be a new nonperceptual source? There is probably no way to answer this in the abstract.

Suppose, however, one thought that a person could have knowledge simply implanted by virtue of a true belief's being reliably caused, where the person's brain is directly affected by a calculator and one comes to believe a truth of arithmetic that would ordinarily require calculation. If we think knowledge is possible for the *idiot savant* (the "lightning calculator"), we may count this as knowledge. If the person has no sense of any basis of the belief, such as a sense of "things adding up that way," it seems more accurate to speak of a *basis* for knowledge rather than a ground and of a cause rather than a source. But in a generic sense there is a source; and a basis is a ground in the widest sense of that term.

This is another of the many cases in which epistemologists may diverge, depending on whether they are internalists or externalists. For an internalist, if there is nothing that is in consciousness or accessible to it by reflective or introspective efforts and that can serve as justification or some kind of evidence for p, then we have at best a cause, not a ground, of knowledge. For an externalist, if the process by which the belief is produced is reliable and p is indeed true, that process itself may be said to be a ground of knowledge—or at least *to ground* it. Perhaps the externalist would agree with the internalist, however, that there is an important sense in which it is not *the subject's ground*. In any event, it seems fair to say that the dominant notions of source and ground in the philosophical literature are those in which sources supply *accessible* grounds (grounds accessible, by reflection or introspection, to the person for whom they are grounds). The four standard sources of knowledge and justification, moreover, are commonly taken to be the only basic ones.

IV. THE EPISTEMIC AUTONOMY OF THE BASIC SOURCES

A basic source of knowledge does not have a positive epistemic dependency on some other source; but it does not in general yield indefeasibly justified beliefs (if it ever does), and it can produce true beliefs whose status as would-be knowledge is undermined by some defeating factor. Each source, then, is to a significant degree subject to defeasibility. Defeat can come from a different source; hence we cannot adequately account for knowledge or justification apart from an understanding of the interconnections among the basic sources.

To what extent, then, is each basic source autonomous? To answer this we need to distinguish different kinds of autonomy. One way to focus the issue and to see the role of defeasibility in understanding the basic sources is to ask whether all the epistemic defeaters of beliefs that are well grounded in the standard basic sources (i.e., all the elements that defeat their justification or prevent their constituting knowledge) derive their defeating power from those same sources. The more general question here is whether, collectively, the standard basic sources are epistemically and justificationally *self-sufficient*, roughly self-sustaining in providing for all the knowledge-conferring and justification-conferring grounds of belief, and self-correcting, in potentially accounting for all the grounds of defeat of (would-be) knowledge and of justification. A quite similar question is whether, taken together, they are necessarily such that if a true belief enjoys adequate support from at least one of them, hence is properly evidenced, and that support is not defeated by at least one other, then the belief constitutes knowledge (or is justified on balance).

This self-sufficiency thesis has some plausibility, particularly for justification. To show whether or not it holds would take far more space than I have, but we can go some distance toward an answer by exploring the two main aspects of the question whether the standard basic sources are autonomous. First, does each source yield the knowledge or justification it does independently of confirmation of the belief in question from any other source? Call this the question of *individual autonomy*. Second, if not, then does only the entire set of basic sources meet this independence condition? This would be *collective autonomy*, a freedom from the need for confirmation by any fifth source.

There is also a kind of *negative autonomy*: invulnerability to defeat by beliefs from another source. Such defeat may occur where "seeing is believing." For instance, suppose I see a stone wall. My visual experience may yield a belief that there is one at the edge of the field, and that belief may constitute knowledge and retain justification despite a memory belief that, as of a few minutes ago, there was only a line of trees in that place. The justification that my memory belief had is thus defeated. As this example can also indicate, invulnerability to defeat from one source may be combined with vulnerability to another. If seeing a wall can yield knowledge or justification that overrides, and presumably cannot be overridden by, any provided by a memory belief of the kind in question, justification of a visual belief may be overridden by that of a tactual one. If, on a walk in the hot summer, I am justified by vision in believing that there is a water fountain before me, yet I cannot feel anything as I sweep my hands where its cool surface should be resisting them, I will neither know, nor any longer be justified in believing, that there is one there and am likely to conclude I am hallucinating.[19]

Here, at least, with respect to both justification and knowledge, touch apparently takes priority over sight.

Positively, there apparently is a measure of individual autonomy. Each source can by itself yield some justification (as well as knowledge). If, for instance, I have a perceptual impression of a piano being played, I am prima facie justified in believing that one is being played. By contrast, if I have a sufficiently vivid and steadfast memory impression of a grassy meadow where I now see a stone wall, I may have some small degree of justification for believing the spot *was* covered with grass (and the wall has appeared quickly), even if the justification of my visual belief that there is a stone wall before me cannot be overridden by that of the memory belief alone. Certainly in the normal case, justification—of some degree—from one of the four standard sources does not wait upon corroboration from other sources. The same holds for knowledge.

To be sure, one cannot be justified in believing (or know) that a lot was vacant unless one has the required concepts, such as that of vacancy; and it may be that one does not acquire concepts adequate to make justified belief possible until one has a complex group of interrelated concepts. This may imply that one gets no justification at all in isolation from justification for many related propositions. That possibility is, however, quite compatible with some grounds of one's justification being single experiences. Epistemic autonomy is consistent with conceptual dependence. We cannot believe, and hence cannot know, a proposition essentially involving concepts we do not have. But a belief might have an isolated ground without in the least being isolated conceptually or in content from other beliefs.

Regarding negative individual autonomy on the part of a source—that is, its providing justification or knowledge that is overridable only by counterevidence from the same source—plainly the four standard sources do not have it. To take a different example, the justification of a memorially justified belief that there is a wall in the field can be overridden by a perception of smooth ground there. The same perception can prevent the belief's constituting knowledge even if it is true. It may seem that reason—our rational capacity—is privileged as a source of justification. Strong rationalists might take it to possess negative individual autonomy. But surely there are some propositions, such as some in logic or mathematics, that I might justifiedly believe on the basis of reflection but, in part on the basis of sufficiently plausible testimony, can cease to be justified in believing or cease to know. Here the authority of that testimony would depend partly on perceptual and memorial factors crucial for my justifiedly accepting the credibility of the person who is its source. Thus, the overriding power of that authority does not derive from reason alone.[20]

The case for collective negative autonomy is more plausible: there is some reason to think that where a belief constitutes knowledge or is justified in virtue of support from all four sources working together, its epistemic grounding (its

grounding qua knowledge) and its justification are defeasible only through considerations arising from at least one of those very sources. If we assume that such
defeat can come only from what confers or at least admits of justification, and if
we add the highly controversial assumption that all epistemic grounding and justification of belief derive wholly from the four standard sources, we may conclude
that those sources are epistemically and justificationally self-sufficient. I make
neither assumption, but I would suggest that in fact these sources may well be
self-sufficient. For there may in fact be no other basic sources (as opposed to
causes) of knowledge or justification or of defeat.[21]

There are at least two reasons for the caution just expressed. One concerns
collective negative autonomy. The other concerns the self-sufficiency thesis, in
particular the idea that the standard basic sources are self-corrective in providing
(in principle) for all the kinds of correction needed to rectify erroneous beliefs.
Let us take these points in turn.

First, it is widely recognized that sources of unreliability in our belief-
formation processes can prevent our beliefs from constituting knowledge even if
we have no way, through the standard basic sources, of detecting the error. This
is a lesson of the Cartesian demon scenario, in which our belief-forming experiences, and even our efforts to check on the truth of our beliefs, are manipulated
so that we cannot detect certain false beliefs. But, in principle, inanimate factors
could conspire to produce the same unfortunate results. It would be a mistake,
then, to say that the basic sources are necessarily self-correcting.

Second, there is reason to think that the concept of knowledge, as opposed
to that of justification, is external in roughly this sense: knowledge is possible
without the knower's having internally accessible grounds for the belief constituting it.[22] Thus, suppose that, through the operation of a special mechanism in one's
brain, one could know what a person very near one was thinking. Such a mechanism might deliver the beliefs constituting the knowledge whenever one concen-
trates attention on the person in question in a certain way but might yield no
sense of any grounds for them; nor would there have to be any access to such
grounds. Granted, one might gain inductive evidence of one's success, but if such
knowledge is possible at all, one could presumably have it without dependence on
inductive evidence of that success. There is much controversy over whether such
externally grounded knowledge is possible; but, if it is, then the standard basic
sources are not necessarily collectively self-sufficient regarding knowledge even if
they are for justification. There can be other sources of knowledge.

For justification as opposed to knowledge, however, there is reason to think
that the four standard sources are indeed individually autonomous and, collectively, both self-sufficient and self-corrective. Each can provide grounds that can
by themselves confer justification (as well as knowledge where the belief in question is true), though defeat by counterevidence can arise from the same or a
different source and hence each lacks autonomy in the negative sense; and the

entire set of sources seems, as regards justification, to be autonomous: self-sufficient in accounting for justification (as well as for normally grounded knowledge) and, independently of any other sources, capable of accounting for defeaters of justification and, in part in that way, for correction of our beliefs. In addition, it is arguable that, at least in the case of reason and perception, there is also uniqueness, in the sense that there are kinds of knowledge and justification not possible apart from dependence on these sources. None of these properties holds for testimony, though it is like the basic sources in being both a source of direct knowledge and also epistemically essential in the ways I have described.

It has been plausibly argued, however, that one source, and perhaps *the* basic source, of justification is coherence among one's beliefs. Isn't my belief that the car was moving perhaps justified by its *coherence* with the beliefs that its orientation to the adjacent building seemed to be changing, that I recall tire sounds, and that cars are built to move? And isn't the justification of my belief that the ground where the wall stands was smooth later undermined mainly by its *incoherence* with the belief that I now see one there (one that looks quite old)? Let us explore the role of coherence in justification.

V. Coherence

Unfortunately, there is no account of coherence which we may simply presuppose. The notion is elusive, and there are highly varying accounts.[23] But this much is clear: we cannot assess the role of coherence in justification unless we distinguish the thesis that coherence is a basic source of justification from the thesis that *in*coherence can defeat justification. The power to defeat is destructive; the power to provide grounds is constructive. To see that the destructive power of incoherence does not imply that coherence has any basic constructive power, we should first note that incoherence is not the contradictory of coherence, its mere absence. It is something with a definite negative character: two beliefs that are logically and semantically irrelevant to each other, such as my beliefs that the sun is shining and that I am thinking about sources of knowledge, are neither mutually coherent nor mutually incoherent. The paradigm of incoherence is blatant logical inconsistency; positive coherence is widely taken to be far more than mutual consistency, yet far less than mutual entailment.

Clearly, that incoherence can defeat justification does not imply that coherence can create it. If it does create it (which is far from obvious), seeing this point is complicated because wherever coherence is plausibly invoked as a source of justification, there one or more of the four standard sources apparently operates in a way that provides for an explanation according to which *both* the coherence and the justification arise from the same elements responsible for well-groundedness.[24] This is best seen through cases.

Consider my belief that a leaf blower is running, grounded in hearing the usual sharp blaring sounds. This appears to be justified by the relevant auditory impressions, together with background information about what the corresponding sounds indicate. If, however, I acquired a justified belief that someone is imitatively creating the blare, my justification for believing that a leaf blower is running would be undermined by the incoherence in my belief system. Does the defeating power of incoherence imply that my original justification requires coherence among my beliefs, including the belief that no one is doing that? Does one even have that belief in such a case? It would surely not be normal to have it when there is no occasion to suspect such a thing. But suppose the belief were required. Notice how many beliefs one would need in order to achieve coherence that is of sufficient magnitude to be even a plausible candidate to generate the justification in question, for example that my hearing is normal, that there is no other machine nearby that makes the same sounds, and so on. It is not quite clear how far this must go. Do we even form that many beliefs in the normal cases in which we acquire justified beliefs of the ordinary kind in question? To think so is to fall victim to a kind of intellectualism about the mind that has afflicted coherentist theories and opposing accounts of justification alike.

A further analogy may help to show how incoherence can be a defeater of justification without its absence, or beliefs that it is absent, or justification for believing something to this effect, being a source of justification. One's job may be the source of one's income, yet a severe depression might eliminate the job. It does not follow that the absence of a depression is a source of one's income. Surely it is not. Even positive economic conditions are not a source, though one's source *depends* on them. The idea of (positive) dependence is central in understanding that of a source. It must be granted that there is a negative sense in which one's job does depend on the absence of a depression; but that dependence—a kind of vulnerability—is too negative a condition to count as a source (much less a ground) of income. For one thing, it provides no explanation of why one has the income. Similarly, we might say that one's justification negatively depends on the absence of defeaters and positively depends on one's sources. But negative dependence on incoherence does not imply positive dependence on anything in particular, including coherence, as a source, any more than an income's negative dependence on the absence of a depression implies any particular source of that income.

To be sure, nothing can serve as a source of anything without the existence of indefinitely many *enabling conditions*. Some of these are conceptual. One may, for instance, be unable to believe a proposition even when evidence for it is before one; if a child has no concept of an insurance adjuster, then seeing one examining a damaged car and talk to its owner about deductibles will not function as a source of justification for the proposition that this is an insurance adjuster. Other enabling conditions are psychological, concerning our capacities or dispositions relevant to forming beliefs. If my sensory receptors are malfunctioning, or if I do not respond to their deliverances by forming beliefs in the normal way, then I may fail to be justified in certain perceptual beliefs.

Specifying a source provides both a genetic explanation of where a thing comes from and, through supplying a ground, a contemporaneous explanation of why it is as it is; enabling conditions, by contrast, provide neither. Taken together, they explain its possibility, but not its genesis or its character. It is neither correct nor theoretically illuminating to construe the absence of the enabling conditions as part of the source or as a ground. They are indispensable, but their role should be understood in terms of the theory of defeasibility rather than the theory of sources or of positive grounds.

The importance of incoherence as a defeater of justification, then, is not a good reason to take coherence to be a source of justification. This by no means implies that justification has no relation to coherence. Indeed, at least normally, justified beliefs will cohere, in one or another intuitive sense, with other beliefs one has, typically other justified beliefs. Certainly, wherever there is justification for believing something, there at least tends to be justification for believing a number of related propositions and presumably for believing a coherent set of them. This is easily seen by reflecting on the point that a single perceptual experience provides information sufficient to justify many beliefs: that someone is blowing leaves, that there is a lawn before me, that these blaring motors should be muted, and far more.

The conception of sources of knowledge and justification that I have sketched provides a way to explain why coherence apparently accompanies justified beliefs—actual and hypothetical—namely, that both are ultimately grounded in the same basic sources. In sufficiently rich forms, coherence may, for all I have said, commonly be a *mark* of justification: an indication of its presence. The coherence conception of knowledge and justification, however, does not well explain why justification of beliefs is apparently dependent on the standard sources. Indeed, as an internal relation among beliefs, coherence may be at least as easily imagined in artificial situations where the coherence of beliefs is unconstrained by our natural tendencies. In principle, wishful thinking could yield as coherent a network of beliefs as the most studious appraisal of evidence.[25]

There is one kind of coherence that is entirely consistent with the well-groundedness conception of justification that goes with taking it to derive from basic sources in the ways I have suggested. To see this, note first that one cannot believe a proposition without having the concepts that figure essentially in it. Whereof one cannot understand, thereof one cannot believe. Moreover, concepts come, and work, in families. This point is the core of a coherence theory of conceptual function: of the acquisition of concepts and their operation, most notably in discourse, judgment, and inference. That theory—call it *conceptual coherentism*, for short—is both plausible and readily combined with the kind of view I am developing. For instance, I am not justified in believing that there is a piano before me unless I have a concept of a piano. I cannot have that unless I have many other concepts, such as the concept of an instrument, of a keyboard, of playing, of sound, of music—no one highly specific concept need be necessary, and various alternative sets will do. In part, to have a concept (of something perceptible) is (at least for remotely normal persons) to be disposed to form beliefs under appropriate sensory stimulations, say to believe a specimen of the thing to be present when one can see it and is asked if there is such a thing nearby; thus, again it is to be expected that from a single perceptual experience, many connected propositions will be justified for the perceiver.

The coherence theory of conceptual function belongs more to semantics and philosophy of mind than to epistemology. But it has profound epistemological implications. That concepts are acquired in mutual relationships may imply that justification does not arise atomistically, in one isolated belief (or desire or intention) at a time. This does not imply, however, that, once a person acquires the conceptual capacity needed to achieve justification, justification cannot derive from one source at a time. This theory of conceptual acquisition and competence is also quite consistent with the view that, far from deriving from coherence, justification, by virtue of the way it is grounded in its sources, brings coherence with it.

VI. CONCLUSION

We have seen reason to consider perception, memory, consciousness, and reason to be basic sources of justification and, except in the case of memory, of knowledge. All can yield beliefs that are both noninferential in not being based on other beliefs and noninferentially justified in not deriving their justification from being based on any other beliefs. Testimony can also yield noninferential beliefs and even what might be called basic knowledge, but it is not a basic source or knowledge or justification. Like inference, it yields knowledge and justification only given the positive cooperation of at least one of the basic sources, but because it (commonly) yields noninferential beliefs, it is closer than inference to constituting a basic source.

The basic sources yield not only knowledge and justified belief, but also co-herence. For instance, it is common for a single observation to produce a goodly number of cohering beliefs. The operation of reason—our rational capacity—tends to employ an interconnected group of concepts, such as those involving perceptible objects, psychological concepts, and logical relations, which dispose us to discover certain apparently a priori truths and to reason with and from them in ways that produce an integrated view; and memory preserves not only individual beliefs, but also our sense of some of their interconnections.

The operation of basic sources allows for defeasibility even when it yields amply justified beliefs or knowledge. Among the defeaters that can undermine would-be justification or would-be knowledge is incoherence. But it is essential to see that the pervasive possibility of defeat does not entail that each basic source has a positive dependence on any of the others, in the sense that in order to yield knowledge or justification, one source must rely on the operation of another one, or that any basic source positively depends on coherence.

At several points, I have indicated something about perception that may not apply to the other basic sources. Within very wide limits, the notion of perception is open-ended. There is no fixed a priori list of perceptual modalities. In a way the notion is schematic: definite by virtue of paradigms like sight and touch that anchor it, yet capable of being filled out by changes in our relation to the world.

Might the same be said of the notion of a basic source of knowledge or of justification? Perhaps it might. The distinction between a schematic concept being filled out over time and a change of concepts by replacement is, to be sure, not sharp. I certainly want to make room for the possibility that there are or can be basic sources of knowledge or justification not considered here. Whether we call them new basic sources or instead should say that our concepts of knowledge or justification have changed would depend in large part on how they are related to the clearly basic sources that are now essential for understanding the notions of knowledge and justification. My concern has been to clarify those in relation to their sources, especially their basic sources but also testimony and inference, which are essential though not basic sources. How those two sources extend knowledge and justification gained through the basic ones is a large problem that cannot be even be approached here.[26]

For each source of knowledge or justification, I have left room for cooperation between sources: two or more basic sources can together produce knowledge or justification, as can two or more nonbasic sources. Two or more sources from the different categories can also cooperate, as where testimony, a nonbasic source of justification, supports memory, which is a basic source of it, or where reason, by producing an inference to a proposition confirmed by memory, supports that faculty. The possibility of cooperation is matched by that of conflict. Skeptics find the latter possibility highly damaging to common-sense views of the extent of our knowledge and justification. If I have been right, it may well be that the basic sources are collectively autonomous in a way that permits adjudication of this matter. I should like to think this is so; but even if it is, on some aspects of the question the jury is still out.[27]

NOTES

1. For detailed discussion of the distinction between positive and negative epistemic dependence, see my *Epistemology* (London: Routledge, 1998), esp. chap. 7.

2. If "blind sight" is a case of perception, this may not be so (though it is arguable that the subject simply does not believe there are visual sensations or other experiential elements corresponding to perception).

3. The apparent noncausal character of abstract entities is a main reason that knowledge of them—indeed their very existence—is often considered problematic. For one kind of challenge to the causal inertness claim see Alvin Plantinga, *Warrant and Proper Function* (Oxford: Oxford University Press, 1993).

4. For introspection and consciousness, as for external perception, one can devise a plausible adverbial view, as described in chap. 1 of *Epistemology*.

5. See Fred I. Dretske, *Knowledge and the Flow of Information* (Cambridge, Mass.: MIT Press, 1981), and William Alston, *Perceiving God* (Ithaca, N.Y.: Cornell University Press, 1991), for indications of how broad the notion of perception is.

6. The need for 'if' here has been suggested already: a duplicate of me would, at the moment of creation, know dispositionally a great deal I now know from memory (not all of it, of course, because some depends on my actual history and it would have no history yet); but it is unclear how this depends on memory. Perhaps we should say that it does not depend on *remembering*—hence does not require the *operation* of memory—but does depend on *memorial capacity*, since it would not be true of me that if I needed to bring a certain item of knowledge to mind I could, unless I had sufficient memorial capacity to retain it from the moment I needed it (e.g., a phone number) to the "next" moment, at which I bring it to mind.

7. Granted, I could memorially believe *p* but not know it (having too little evidence, say) and then be told by you that *p*. But if I now know it, this is on the basis of your testimony; I don't know it from memory until I retain the knowledge and not just the belief. Believing from memory can instantaneously become knowing, but does not instantaneously become knowledge from memory.

8. For a detailed discussion of the epistemology of memory, with many references to relevant literature, see my "Memorial Justification," *Philosophical Topics* 23 (1995): 31–45.

9. See, for example, Hume's extraordinary affirmation of privileged access in the *Treatise*, cited and discussed in my *Epistemology*, chap. 3.

10. The relevant kind of understanding and the notions of a priori knowledge and justification in general are discussed in detail in chap. 4 of *Epistemology* and in my "Self-Evidence," in *Philosophical Perspectives* 13 (1999): 205–228.

11. Thus, for God or any being with infinite memorial capacity, no use of reason *essentially* depends on the exercise of memory. I might add even if the points made here

about inference and memory are mistaken, the overall point that reason may ground justification for *p* without yielding knowledge of it can be illustrated by many other cases, presumably including the proposition that some classes are members of themselves (since this embodies a type-error).

12. This point must be qualified if W. V. Quine is right in denying that there is a viable distinction between the empirical and the a priori—at least one would have to speak in terms of, say, differences in degree. For extensive criticism of Quine, see BonJour, "Against Naturalized Epistemology," *Midwest Studies in Philosophy* 19 (1994): 283–300, and for the notion of a priori justification see also my "Self-Evidence."

13. See Thomas Reid, *Essays on the Intellectual Powers of Man* (Cambridge, Mass.: MIT, 1969). For a defense of a Reidian view see C. A. J. Coady, *Testimony* (Oxford: Oxford University Press, 1992). For a contrasting account of testimony more sympathetic to a Humean perspective see Elizabeth Fricker's chapter on testimony in *Handbook of Epistemology*, ed. Ilkka Niiniluoto and Matti Sintonen (Dordrecht: Kluwer, 2002).

14. For a developed distinction between these and a case for positing fewer beliefs than most philosophers apparently do, see my "Dispositional Beliefs and Dispositions to Believe," *Nous* 28 (1994): 419–434.

15. This point may be more controversial for internalist than for externalist views, since an externalist can hold that my belief can constitute knowledge so long as it is reliably produced, even if I do not have accessible grounds for *p*, as I would if I had good inferential grounds for it. I cannot discuss the contrast between internalism and externalism in this paper. For discussion see, for example William P. Alston, *Epistemic Justification* (Ithaca, N.Y.: Cornell University Press, 1989), Paul K. Moser, *Knowledge and Evidence* (New York: Cambridge University Press, 1989), and my *Epistemology*, chap. 8.

16. I discuss the issue of voluntary control of belief and cite much relevant literature in "Doxastic Voluntarism and the Ethics of Belief," *Facta Philosophica* 1, no. 1 (1999): 87–109.

17. This point is explained and defended in my "The Place of Testimony in the Fabric of Knowledge and Justification," *American Philosophical Quarterly* 34 (1997): 404–422.

18. This point may support my view, defended in "The Place of Testimony," that to acquire justification for *p* from testimony, one needs some degree of justification for taking the attester to be credible. (I do not think one needs this to acquire prima facie justification from one of the standard basic sources.)

19. This is not to imply that just *any* tactual belief is better justified than any conflicting visual one. Matters are far more complicated, but need not be pursued in detail here.

20. This is not to deny that there may be justified beliefs of logical truths so luminous that the justification of these beliefs cannot be overridden. The point is that doxastic justification grounded in reflection can be overridden by factors that are at least not entirely a priori. That can be so even when the beliefs in question are true. For further discussion of this issue see Laurence BonJour, *In Defense of Pure Reason* (Cambridge: Cambridge University Press, 1997), and my "Self-Evidence," cited in note 10.

21. Another possibility is that there are other basic sources which are comparatively weak, so that although they may add to the justification available through the standard sources, they are not sufficient to yield belief that is justified on balance (roughly, justified to a degree ordinarily sufficient to render a true belief knowledge). On the other

hand, if they can add to justification from the standard sources, then they could render a belief that would not ordinarily defeat the justification of another belief able to do so. This would limit the self-sufficiency of the basic sources. We should surely be cautious about affirming even the de facto self-sufficiency of the sources, and I leave it open.

22. A brief treatment of externalism is provided in my *Epistemology*; for a more extensive treatment see Ernest Sosa, *Knowledge in Focus, Skepticism Resolved* (forthcoming from Princeton University Press), and chapter 8 in the present volume.

23. For two major accounts see Keith Lehrer, *Knowledge* (Oxford: Oxford University Press, 1974), and Laurence BonJour, *The Structure of Empirical Knowledge* (Cambridge, Mass.: Harvard University Press, 1985); and for much discussion see John Bender, ed., *The Current State of the Coherence Theory* (Dordrecht: Kluwer, 1989). It should be noted that in "The Dialectic of Foundationalism and Coherentism," in John Greco and Ernest Sosa, eds., *The Blackwell Guide to Epistemology* (Oxford: Blackwell, 1999), BonJour has since abandoned coherentism.

24. This is suggested and to some degree argued in my *Belief, Justification, and Knowledge* (Belmont, Calif.: Wadsworth, 1988) and *The Architecture of Reason* (Oxford: Oxford University Press, 2001).

25. If it is taken to be an internal relation among beliefs, their content does not matter, nor does their fit with experience. This sort of thing has been widely noted; see Moser, *Knowledge and Evidence*, and John Bender, *The Current State of the Coherence Theory* (Dordrecht: Kluwer, 1989), for some relevant points and many references.

26. An approach to understanding the inferential extension of justification and knowledge is developed in chap. 6 of *Epistemology*. Testimonial extension of justification and knowledge is approached in my "The Place of Testimony."

27. For helpful comments on an earlier version of this article (which derives, in part, from chap. 1 of my *Architecture of Reason* and from my paper on testimony, cited above), I heartily thank Paul Moser and Richard Swinburne.

CHAPTER 3

A PRIORI KNOWLEDGE

ALBERT CASULLO

1. INTRODUCTION

THE prominence of the a priori within traditional epistemology is largely due to the influence of Immanuel Kant. In the Introduction to the *Critique of Pure Reason*,[1] he introduces a conceptual framework that involves three distinctions: (1) the *epistemic* distinction between a priori and empirical knowledge; (2) the *metaphysical* distinction between necessary and contingent propositions; and (3) the *semantic* distinction between analytic and synthetic propositions. Within this framework, Kant poses four questions:

1. What is a priori knowledge?
2. Is there a priori knowledge?
3. What is the relationship between the a priori and the necessary?
4. Is there synthetic a priori knowledge?

These questions remain at the center of the contemporary debate.

Kant maintains that a priori knowledge is "absolutely independent of all experience."[2] This characterization is not fully perspicuous since he allows that such knowledge can depend on experience in *some* respects. For example, according to Kant, we know a priori that every alteration has its cause, despite the fact that the concept of alteration is derived from experience. Yet he is not explicit about the respect in which such knowledge must be independent of experience.

Since Kant does not offer a fully articulated analysis of the concept of a priori knowledge, he is not in a position to argue *directly* for its existence by showing that some knowledge satisfies the conditions in his analysis. Instead, he approaches the second question *indirectly* by seeking *criteria* of the a priori. Criteria provide sufficient conditions for a priori knowledge that are not included in the analysis of the concept. Kant offers two such criteria, necessity and strict universality, which he claims are inseparable from one another. Kant's primary arguments for the a priori appeal to the first. For example, he argues that since mathematical propositions are necessary and we know some mathematical propositions, it follows that we have a priori knowledge.

Kant's claim that necessity is a criterion of the a priori commits him to the following thesis about the relationship between the a priori and the necessary:

(K1)   All knowledge of necessary propositions is a priori.

He also appears to endorse

(K2)   All propositions known a priori are necessary.

Although Kant is often portrayed as holding that the categories of the a priori and the necessary are coextensive, the conjunction of (K1) and (K2) do not support that attribution, since it does not entail that all necessary propositions are known or knowable a priori. (K1) connects the third question with the second since it provides the key premise of Kant's only argument for the existence of a priori knowledge. Neither (K1) nor (K2) bears directly on the first question, since Kant does not claim that necessity is a constituent of the concept of a priori knowledge.

Kant maintains that all propositions of the form "All A are B" are either analytic or synthetic: analytic if the predicate is contained in the subject, synthetic if it is not. Utilizing this distinction, he argues that

(A1)   All knowledge of analytic propositions is a priori, and

(A2)   Some propositions known a priori are synthetic.

In support of (A2), Kant once again appeals to mathematics, arguing that the predicate terms of "$7 + 5 = 12$" and "The straight line between two points is the shortest" are not covertly contained in their respective subjects. Neither (A1) nor (A2) has a direct bearing on the first two questions since Kant does not claim that analyticity is a constituent of the concept of a priori knowledge and does not invoke either as a premise in his arguments for the existence of a priori knowledge. Kant regards (A2) as significant because it sets the stage for his primary epistemic project, which is to explain how such knowledge is possible. The project, however, presupposes that a priori knowledge of analytic propositions and a priori knowledge of synthetic propositions are fundamentally different, a presupposition Kant does not explicitly defend.

The contemporary discussion of the a priori revolves around Kant's four questions. Philip Kitcher offers an articulation of Kant's characterization of a priori knowledge.[3] He maintains that a belief is justified independently of experience only if it is indefeasible by experiential evidence. Building on the work of W. V. Quine[4] and Hilary Putnam,[5] who argue that no belief is immune to revision in light of recalcitrant experience, Kitcher concludes that mathematical knowledge is not a priori. In response, a number of theorists reject Kitcher's claim that the concept of a priori knowledge involves an indefeasibility condition and offer alternative proposals.[6]

Paul Benacerraf challenges Kant's strategy for arguing that there is a priori knowledge.[7] Benacerraf maintains that one knows a statement only if one is causally related to the entities referred to by its truth conditions and that the truth conditions of mathematical statements make reference to abstract entities. Since abstract entities cannot stand in causal relations, one cannot know mathematical statements. The tradition, however, maintains that the truth conditions of all necessary truths make reference to abstract entities.[8] Hence, Benacerraf's argument, if cogent, establishes that knowledge of necessary truths is not possible. The argument sparked a series of investigations into the general question of knowledge of abstract entities and the more specific question of the proper role of causal conditions in a plausible theory of knowledge.[9]

Saul Kripke's metaphysical and semantic results have renewed interest in Kant's account of the relationship between the a priori and the necessary.[10] Kripke forcefully argues that the concept of a priori knowledge is epistemic but the concept of necessary truth is metaphysical and, hence, one cannot assume without argument that they are coextensive. Furthermore, he maintains that there are necessary propositions known a posteriori and contingent propositions known a priori. Kripke's contentions generated a large literature addressing his particular examples as well as the more general question of the relationship between the a priori and the necessary.[11]

Kant's claim that there is synthetic a priori knowledge dominated discussion of the a priori over the past fifty years. The controversy is fueled by two related reactions to (A2). The first is due to proponents of logical empiricism who argue that only analytic propositions are knowable a priori.[12] The second is due to W. V. Quine who rejects this central tenet of logical empiricism by denying the cogency of the analytic–synthetic distinction.[13] Although Quine's conclusion is semantic, it is widely regarded as having broader implications for the existence of a priori knowledge. Theorists are reassessing both the cogency of Quine's arguments against the distinction and, more importantly, the bearing, if any, of Quine's rejection of the distinction on the question of whether there is a priori knowledge.[14]

The range of issues raised by Kant's four questions is enormous, covering most of the central areas of contemporary philosophical investigation. The focus of this essay is more limited. My goal is to address the question of whether a priori knowledge exists. Since one cannot determine whether such knowledge exists without knowing what such knowledge is, I begin by providing an analysis of the concept a priori knowledge. I utilize that analysis to show that the traditional arguments, both for and against, the a priori are not convincing. I conclude by offering an alternative strategy for defending the existence of a priori knowledge. Although the questions about the relationship between the a priori and the nonepistemic concepts of necessity and analyticity are not my primary targets, I address them insofar as they are relevant to analyzing the concept of a priori knowledge or to determining whether such knowledge exists.

2. THE CONCEPT OF A PRIORI KNOWLEDGE

There are two approaches to analyzing the concept of a priori knowledge. The first, which is *reductive*, analyzes it in terms of the concept of a priori justification. According to this approach, S knows a priori that p just in case (a) S's belief that p is justified a priori and (b) the other conditions for knowledge are satisfied. The primary target of analysis is the concept of a priori *justification*. The second, which is *nonreductive*, provides an analysis of the concept that does not include conditions involving the concept of the a priori. The primary target of analysis is the concept of a priori *knowledge*.

The conditions on a priori knowledge proposed by contemporary epistemologists draw their inspiration from Kant. They fall into two broad categories: *epistemic* and *nonepistemic*. There are three types of epistemic conditions. The first imposes conditions regarding the *source* of justification; the second imposes conditions regarding the *defeasibility* of justification; and the third appeals to the *strength* of justification. Source and defeasibility conditions are inspired by Kant's characterization of a priori knowledge as independent of all experience. Strength conditions derive from Kant's frequent association of *certainty* with the a priori.[15] Two nonepistemic conditions have played a prominent role in analyses of the a priori. Some theorists include *necessity*, which Kant endorsed as a criterion of a priori knowledge, in the analysis of the concept. Others, reacting against Kant, deny that synthetic a priori knowledge is possible, and include *analyticity* in the analysis of the concept.

Analyses of the concept of a priori knowledge fall into three categories. Pure epistemic analyses include only epistemic conditions. Impure epistemic analyses include, in addition, some nonepistemic conditions. Nonepistemic analyses consist of only nonepistemic conditions. We turn first to nonepistemic analyses.[16]

2.1. Nonepistemic Analyses

Nonepistemic analyses maintain that either necessity or analyticity provides both necessary and sufficient conditions for a priori knowledge. There is a general reason for regarding them with suspicion. The analysandum in question is epistemic. It is a type of justification. An informative analysis, however, should highlight what is distinctive about such justification. An analysis in terms of necessity or analyticity highlights what is distinctive about the propositions so justified rather than the justification itself. Hence, it will fail to be informative.

Nonepistemic analyses typically involve the expression 'a priori truth' or 'a priori proposition'. This introduces a complication since these expressions do not have a fixed meaning. Many writers introduce them as shorthand for 'truth (proposition) that can be known a priori'.[17] On this usage 'a priori' remains an epistemic predicate, one whose primary application is to knowledge or justification rather than truth. Some, however, use the expression to apply primarily to truths. So, for example, Anthony Quinton maintains that

> 'A priori' means either, widely, 'non-empirical' or, narrowly, following Kant, 'necessary'.[18]

Quinton's use of the term 'non-empirical' suggests that, on his view, the primary application of 'a priori' is epistemic since 'empirical' is typically an epistemic predicate, one whose primary application is to items of knowledge or justification. But Quinton's use of 'non-empirical' is also misleading. He explicitly maintains that it is *not* an epistemic predicate:

> The idea of the empirical is a development of the contingent. It aims to explain how a statement can owe its truth to something else, what conditions the something else must satisfy if it is to confer truth on a statement.[19]

For Quinton, 'empirical' has its primary application to truth conditions or the source of truth. Although he characterizes his initial goal as a defense of the thesis that all a priori statements are analytic, he goes on to maintain that "the essential content of the thesis is that all *necessary* truths are analytic."[20] For Quinton, the narrow sense of 'a priori', 'necessary', and 'analytic' are identical in meaning.

The upshot is that the term 'a priori' is ambiguous. It is a predicate whose primary application is to either types of justification or grounds of truth. Hence, a nonepistemic analysis of the a priori can have either as its target. If its target is the latter, then the analysis is not open to my initial argument because it is not directed toward the epistemic concept. It is directed toward a metaphysical concept pertaining to truth conditions. Our concern, however, is with the analysis of the epistemic concept.

Are there nonepistemic analyses of the epistemic concept? R. G. Swinburne defends both of the following theses:

> (S1) A proposition is a priori if and only if it is necessary and can be known to be necessary.

> (S2) A proposition is a priori if and only if it is analytic and can be known to be analytic.[21]

Unlike Quinton, Swinburne maintains that the term 'a priori' has its primary application to knowledge. An a priori proposition is one that can be known a priori. Hence, it appears that he is proposing nonepistemic analyses for an epistemic concept.

Closer examination reveals that Swinburne is not proposing either (S1) or (S2) as an analysis of the concept of a priori knowledge. Instead, he endorses Kant's analysis of a priori knowledge as absolutely independent of all experience, maintaining that Kant meant by this "knowledge which comes to us through experience but is not contributed by experience."[22] Swinburne's concern, however, is with the question of how we *recognize* such knowledge. He proposes (S1) as capturing Kant's answer to this question.

The upshot here is that not every biconditional of the form:

> (AP) A proposition is a priori if and only if . . . ,

where 'a priori' is an epistemic predicate, is an analysis of the epistemic concept designated by that term. Biconditionals of this form may be proposed in response to different questions. Swinburne's question

> (Q1) How do we identify the items satisfying some analysis of a priori knowledge?

is different from the question

> (Q2) What is the analysis of a priori knowledge?

An answer to (Q1) presupposes, rather than provides, an answer to (Q2).

Apparent nonepistemic analyses of the a priori must be scrutinized along two dimensions. What is the target of the analysis? What question is being asked of the target? My target is the concept of a priori justification as opposed to the concept of a priori truth. My contention is that a nonepistemic analysis of the former cannot succeed. Since the concept is fundamentally epistemic, any satisfactory analysis must identify the salient *epistemic* feature of such justification. This contention does not entail that there are no nonepistemic features common to all and only propositions justifiable a priori. It only entails that it is not by virtue of having those features that such propositions are justifiable a priori.

The contention that an adequate analysis of the concept of a priori justification must include an epistemic condition leaves open the possibility that it also includes some nonepistemic condition. We now turn to the question of whether some nonepistemic condition is necessary for a priori justification. My focus is on conditions involving the concept of necessity since they are the most common.

2.2. Impure Epistemic Analyses

Analyses of the concept of a priori justification that include the concept of necessity fall into two categories. Some include necessity as a component of an epistemic condition. Others include it as an independent condition. Laurence BonJour offers the following version of the traditional rationalist conception of the a priori:

> a proposition is justified *a priori* when and only when the believer is able, either directly or via some series of individually evident steps, to intuitively 'see' or apprehend that its truth is an invariant feature of all possible worlds, that there is no possible world in which it is false.[23]

The conception consists of a single condition with two components: the source of a priori justification, intuitive apprehension, and the content of such apprehensions, necessary truths.

Assessing the implications of the analysis is tricky since it involves a metaphorical use of the term 'see'. Taken literally, the locution 'S sees that p' (for example, that there is a rabbit in the garden) entails 'S believes that p'.[24] Assuming that the metaphorical use of 'see' preserves the logical features of the literal, 'S intuitively "sees" that p is true in all possible worlds' entails 'S believes that p is true in all possible worlds'. Hence, on the traditional rationalist conception, 'S's belief that p is justified a priori' entails 'S believes that necessarily p'.

The conception faces three objections. The first is due to *conceptual deficiency*. Many, including some mathematicians, are not conversant with the metaphysical distinction between necessary and contingent propositions. Consider a mathematician, S, who believes a theorem T on the basis of a generally accepted proof. S's belief that T is justified. Suppose that S lacks the concept of necessity and, as a consequence, does not believe that necessarily T. It is implausible to maintain that S's belief that T is not justified a priori merely because S lacks a concept that is not even a constituent of the content of S's belief.

The first objection can be avoided by weakening the conception to require that S believe that necessarily p *provided that* S possesses the concept of necessity. Two objections remain. The first is due to *modal scepticism*. Among philosophers conversant with the concept of necessary truth, some deny (let us suppose, erroneously) its cogency. As a consequence, they avoid modal beliefs, such as that necessarily 2 + 2 = 4. But it is implausible to maintain that none of their mathematical beliefs is justified a priori solely on the grounds that they have an erroneous metaphysical belief. Second, the conception is open to a *regress*. Suppose that S believes that necessarily p. Must S's belief that necessarily p be justified or not? If not, then it is hard to see why it is a necessary condition for the a priori justification of S's belief that p. If so, then presumably its justification must be a priori. But, in order for its justification to be a priori, S must see that necessarily p is true in all possible worlds which, in turn, requires believing that necessarily necessarily p. But now a regress threatens since we can once again ask the question: Must S's belief that necessarily necessarily p be justified or not?

R. M. Chisholm provides an analysis of the a priori in which necessity is offered as an independent necessary condition. Consider the following definitions:

D1   h is an axiom = Df   h is necessarily such [that] (i) it is true and (ii) for every S, if S accepts h, then h is certain for S.[25]

D2   h is *axiomatic* for S = Df   (i) h is an axiom and (ii) S accepts h.[26]

D3   h is known *a priori* by S = Df There is an *e* such that (i) *e* is axiomatic for S, (ii) the proposition, *e* implies *h*, is axiomatic for S, and (iii) S accepts *h*.[27]

A priori knowledge is restricted to axioms and their axiomatic consequences. In order to be an axiom, a proposition must satisfy two *independent* conditions: it must be necessarily true and certain for everyone who accepts it. These conditions are independent for neither entails the other. Since axioms are necessary truths and axiomatic consequences of axioms follow necessarily from axioms, all a priori knowledge is of necessary truths.

What support does Chisholm offer for his analysis? He opens his discussion of the a priori with the following remarks:

> There are propositions that are necessarily true and such that, once one understands them, one *sees* that they are true. Such propositions have traditionally been called *a priori*. Leibniz remarks, "You will find a hundred places in which the scholastic philosophers have said that these propositions are evident, from their terms, as soon as they are understood."[28]

This passage involves two claims: (1) some propositions have both the meta-physical property of being necessarily true and the epistemic property of being such that if one understands them, then one *sees* that they are true; and (2) such propositions have traditionally been called a priori. The key question, however, is not addressed. In virtue of which feature are they a priori? The quote from Leibniz, which invokes the authority of the scholastics, mentions only the second. There is no mention of the metaphysical property. Hence, if Chisholm's case is based on historical precedent, his analysis should be in terms of the epistemic property alone.

Chisholm's inclusion of the metaphysical condition in the analysis is not only unmotivated but also has undesirable consequences. First, either the analysis is incomplete or precludes the possibility of *false* a priori justified beliefs. D3 provides an analysis of a priori knowledge. If Chisholm's conditions on a priori *knowledge* are also conditions on a priori *justification*, then a priori justification guarantees truth. If they are not, then his account of the a priori is incomplete. Second, the analysis rules out by stipulation the possibility of a priori knowledge of contingent truths. Yet Kripke and Kitcher maintain that there is such knowledge.[29] Third, the analysis precludes the possibility of a posteriori knowledge of axioms. Suppose that S accepts axiom A on the basis of testimony. Either A is certain for S or it is not. If it is, then A is axiomatic for S and S knows a priori that A. If it is not, then A is not an axiom for it fails to satisfy condition (ii) in D1.

Chisholm's analysis of axiomatic, or noninferential, a priori knowledge also includes an epistemic condition: certainty.[30] This condition leads to the implausible consequence that it is impossible that (1) S know axiomatically that $1 + 1 = 2$; (2) S know axiomatically that $7 + 5 = 12$; and (3) the former belief is *more* justified than the latter. Yet Chisholm offers no rationale for excluding the possibility of differing degrees of noninferential a priori justification. Moreover, it also entails that if S knows axiomatically that p, and S knows a posteriori that q, then the former belief is *more* justified than the latter. It is not obvious, however, that one's belief that $7 + 5 = 12$ is more justified than one's belief that one exists.

2.3. Pure Epistemic Analyses

The most common pure epistemic analyses of a priori justification are in terms of the *source* of justification. The major divide is between negative and positive analyses. The former specify sources *incompatible* with a priori justification, the latter specify sources which *provide* such justification. The most familiar negative analysis is

(N1)   S's belief that p is justified a priori if and only if S's justification for the belief that p does not depend on experience.

Critics of negative analyses maintain that they are not sufficiently informative.[31] At best, they specify what a priori justification is *not* rather than what it *is*. The problem can be circumvented by opting for a positive analysis having the form

> (P1)   S's belief that p is justified a priori if and only if S's belief that p is justified by φ,

where 'φ' designates some specific source of justification. For example, according to Panayot Butchvarov, it designates finding the falsehood of a belief unthinkable in any circumstances.[32] But, according to Laurence BonJour, it designates apparent rational insight into the necessary features of reality.[33]

An analysis of the concept of a priori justification that enumerates the sources of such justification is too theory dependent. One cannot reject the *source* of a priori justification proffered by such an analysis without rejecting the *existence* of a priori justification. For example, given Butchvarov's analysis, one cannot reject (as BonJour does) the claim that finding the falsehood of a belief unthinkable in any circumstances is the source of a priori justification without rejecting the existence of the a priori. On this analysis, a priori justification *is* justification based on such findings. It should, however, be possible for proponents of the a priori to disagree over the source of a priori justification without thereby disagreeing over the existence of such justification. Moreover, even if some particular version of the positive analysis is extensionally adequate, the analysis is uninformative. It tells us that φ *is* an a priori source of justification but gives no indication of *why* φ is an a priori source. It does not highlight the features by virtue of which φ qualifies as an a priori source.

There is a *general* positive analysis of the a priori that avoids the problem of theory dependence:

> (P2)   S's belief that p is justified a priori if and only if S's belief that p is justified by *some* nonexperiential source.

(P2) allows proponents of the a priori to agree that there is a priori justification despite disagreeing about its source. Furthermore, it identifies the feature of sources of justification by virtue of which they qualify as a priori.

There are also two versions of the negative analysis. (N1) conceals a critical ambiguity. The condition

> (C1)   S's justification for the belief that p does not depend on experience

does not specify the *respect* in which S's justification must be independent of experience. There are, however, two possibilities: the source of *justification* for S's belief that p and the source of potential *defeaters* for S's justification. Some maintain that (C1) is equivalent to

(C2)   S's belief that p is nonexperientially justified.

Others maintain that it is equivalent to the conjunction of (C2) and

(C3)   S's justified belief that p cannot be defeated by experience.

Patently, if S's belief that p is experientially justified then S's justification depends on experience. What can be said on behalf of (C3)? Philip Kitcher argues that

> if alternative experiences could undermine one's knowledge then there are features of one's current experience which are relevant to the knowledge, namely those features whose *absence* would change the current experience into the subversive experience.[34]

According to Kitcher, if experiential evidence can defeat S's justification for the belief that p, then S's justification depends on the *absence* of that experiential evidence.

Kitcher's contention that a priori justification is incompatible with potential experiential defeaters should be distinguished from the closely related, but stronger, condition espoused by Hilary Putnam:

> Are there *a priori* truths? In other words, are there true statements which (1) it is rational to accept . . . , and (2) which it would never subsequently be rational to reject no matter how the world turns out (epistemically) to be? More simply, are there statements whose truth we would not be justified in denying in any *epistemically* possible world?[35]

According to Putnam, S's belief that p is justified a priori only if

(C4)   S's belief that p cannot be defeated by *any* evidence.

(C4), however, is not a plausible condition on a priori justification since it entails that if S's belief that p is defeasible solely by *nonexperiential* evidence then it is *not* justified a priori. Yet, if S's belief that p is justified solely by nonexperiential evidence and is defeasible solely by nonexperiential evidence then it does not in any way depend on experience. Hence, (C4) divorces the concept of a priori justification from the core idea that such justification is independent of experience.

Since Kitcher ties (C3) to (C1), it cannot be dismissed as readily as (C4). Instead, we must distinguish two different versions of the negative analysis:

(N2)   S's belief that p is justified a priori if and only if S's belief that p is nonexperientially justified; and

(N3)   S's belief that p is justified a priori if and only if S's belief that p is non-experientially justified and cannot be defeated by experience.[36]

Since (C2) is equivalent to

(C5)   S's belief that p is justified by *some* nonexperiential source,

(N2) and (P2) are equivalent. Therefore, we are left with two analyses of a priori justification. My final goal is to argue that (N2) is the superior analysis.

2.4. An Argument for (N2)

(N3), but not (N2), is incompatible with a widely endorsed criterion of adequacy. Saul Kripke puts the point as follows:

> Something may belong in the realm of such statements that *can* be known *a priori* but still may be known by particular people on the basis of experience.[37]

Kitcher, echoing this point, maintains that

> A clearheaded apriorist should admit that people can have empirical knowledge of propositions which can be known a priori.[38]

According to the criterion of adequacy, an analysis of the concept of a priori justification should allow for the following possibility:

(CA)   S knows empirically that p and S can know a priori that p.

(N3), however, precludes this possibility.

Prior to presenting the argument, one point needs to be stressed. (N3) does *not* involve a strength condition. It does not require of a priori knowledge a degree of justification greater than that minimally required for knowledge in general. Another way of putting the same point is that (N3) does not require of a priori knowledge a degree of justification greater than that required for a posteriori knowledge. Let us state this point explicitly as the *Equality of Strength Thesis*:

(ES)   The degree of justification minimally sufficient for a priori knowledge equals the degree of justification minimally sufficient for knowledge in general.

In order to keep the point explicit in the course of the argument, let us call a belief justified to the degree minimally sufficient for knowledge, a *justified*$_k$ belief.

We now turn to the argument. Let us begin by assuming

    (A)   S knows empirically some mathematical proposition that p and S can know a priori that p.

From the left conjunct of (A), it follows that

    (1)   S's belief that p is justified$_k$ empirically.

A number of empirical sources have been alleged to justify mathematical propositions: (a) counting collections of objects, (b) reading textbooks, (c) consulting mathematicians, and (d) computer results. Let us grant that each can justify S's mathematical belief that p. Each of these sources is fallible in an important respect. The justification each confers on a belief that p is defeasible by an empirically justified *overriding* defeater: that is, by an empirically justified belief that not-p. Suppose that S's belief that p is justified by counting a collection of objects and arriving at a particular result. It is possible that S recounts the collection and arrives at a different result. If S were to do so, S's original justification would be defeated by an empirically justified overriding defeater. Suppose that S's belief that p is justified by a textbook (mathematician, computer result) that states that p. It is possible that S encounters a different textbook (mathematician, computer result) that states that not-p. In each case, if S were to do so, S's original justification would be defeated by an empirically justified overriding defeater. Hence, given the fallible character of empirical justification, it follows that

    (2)   S's empirical justification$_k$ for the belief that p is defeasible by an empirically justified belief that not-p,

where 'justification$_k$' abbreviates 'justification to the degree minimally sufficient for knowledge'.

A difficult question arises at this juncture. What are the conditions under which S's justified belief that p is defeated by S's justified belief that not-p? For our present purposes, it is sufficient to note that the conditions under which S's justified belief that not-p defeats S's justification for the belief that p is a function of the relative degree of justification each enjoys. We need not adjudicate between competing accounts of the minimal degree of justification that S's belief that not-p must enjoy in order to defeat S's justified$_k$ belief that p. Let us introduce 'd' to stand for that degree of justification, whatever it is, and call a belief justified to degree d, a *justified*$_d$ belief. We can now introduce the neutral principle:

(D*)   S's justified belief that not-p defeats (can defeat) S's justified$_k$ belief that p if and only if S's belief that not-p is at least justified$_d$ (justifiable$_d$),

where 'justified$_d$' and 'justifiable$_d$' abbreviate, respectively, 'justified to degree d' and 'justifiable to degree d'.

Returning now to the argument, the conjunction of (D*) and (2) entails

(3)   S's belief that not-p is at least justifiable$_d$ empirically.

Furthermore, the conjunction of (N3) and the right conjunct of (A) entails

(4)   It is not the case that S's nonexperiential justification$_k$ for the belief that p is defeasible by S's empirically justified belief that not-p.[39]

The conjunction of (4) and (D*) entails

(5)   It is not the case that S's belief that not-p is at least justifiable$_d$ empirically.

The conjunction of (3) and (5) is a contradiction. Hence, (N3) does not satisfy the proposed criterion of adequacy. (N2), on the other hand, does satisfy the criterion since it does not preclude the possibility of defeaters of any kind. I conclude that (N2) provides the superior analysis.

My argument against (N3) highlights an important difference between overriding and undermining defeaters.[40] It is not in general true that if S's justified belief that q defeats the justification conferred on S's belief that p by source A, it also defeats the justification conferred on S's belief that p by source B. For example, although S's justified belief that he suffers from double vision defeats the justification conferred on his belief that $2 + 2 = 4$ by the process of counting objects, it does not affect the justification conferred on that belief by intuition or testimony. More generally, undermining defeaters for S's justified belief that p are *source-sensitive*. Overriding defeaters, however, are *source-neutral*. If S's justified$_d$ belief that not-p defeats the justification$_k$ conferred on S's belief that p by source A, then it also defeats the justification$_k$ conferred on S's belief that p by *any other* source. For example, suppose that S's belief that the shopping list is on the coffee table is justified$_k$ by memory, but a subsequent perceptual experience, which justifies$_d$ her belief that the list is not on the coffee table, defeats her original justification. Had S's belief that the shopping list is on the coffee table been originally justified$_k$ by testimony, S's perceptually justified$_d$ belief that it is not on the coffee table would still have defeated her original justification.

3. ARGUMENTS SUPPORTING THE EXISTENCE OF A PRIORI KNOWLEDGE

There are three approaches to arguing in support of the a priori. The first is to offer an analysis of the concept of a priori knowledge and to argue that some knowledge satisfies the conditions in the analysis. The second is to identify criteria of the a priori and to show that some knowledge satisfies the criteria. The third is to argue that radical empiricist theories of knowledge are deficient in some respect and that the only remedy for the deficiency is to embrace the a priori.[41]

3.1. Conceptual Arguments

Hilary Putnam adopts the first strategy. He endorses a conception of a priori justification that involves an indefeasibility condition. We argued in section 2.3 that neither (C3) nor (C4) is *necessary* for a priori justification. Nevertheless, if his proposed condition is *sufficient* for such justification, it can be utilized in defense of the existence of the a priori. Hence, two questions must be addressed. Does the conception provide a set of conditions sufficient for a priori justification? Do any beliefs satisfy the proposed conditions? My primary concern is with the first question.

Putnam maintains that an a priori statement is one "we would never be *rational* to give up."[42] He goes on to argue that the Minimal Principle of Contradiction (MPC), Not every statement is both true and false, is rationally unrevisable. His argument is directed against his own earlier contentions that no statements are rationally unrevisable.[43] According to his earlier view, traditional proponents of the a priori confused the property of being a priori with the related, but different, property of being *contextually* a priori. The source of the confusion is a failure to recognize two types of grounds for rational revision. *Direct* grounds for rationally revising some belief that p consist in some observation whose content justifies the belief that not-p. *Theoretical* grounds consist in a set of observations that is better explained by a theory that does not contain the statement that p than by any theory that does contain the statement that p. A statement is contextually a priori just in case it is rationally unrevisable on direct grounds but rationally revisable on theoretical grounds. A statement is a priori just in case it is rationally unrevisable on any grounds. Traditional proponents of the a priori identified statements that are not rationally revisable on direct grounds, and believed that they are not rationally revisable on any grounds. Putnam, however, argues that the purported a priori statements are rationally revisable on theoretical grounds.

The crux of his present argument is that there are no possible theoretical grounds for rationally revising MPC. How can we rule out the possibility that some future physical theory, perhaps one that we cannot now conceive, might imply the denial of MPC but nevertheless be accepted because it explains a diverse range of phenomena, yields surprising predictions that are subsequently verified, and enhances our understanding of the world? We can do so, according to Putnam, because we know at present that such a theory will have to consist of every statement and its negation. But a theory that excludes nothing is no theory at all. Hence, there are no circumstances under which it would be rational to accept it.

Putnam's proposal is unclear in one crucial respect. He is not explicit on the question of whether a priori justified belief in logical principles, such as MPC, requires supporting evidence and, if so, the nature of that evidence. There are at least three possible readings of his proposed condition on a priori justification:

(A)   p is rationally unrevisable and S believes that p;

(B)   p is rationally unrevisable and S is justified in believing that p;

(C)   p is rationally unrevisable and S is justified in believing that p is rationally unrevisable.

(A) is not sufficient for a priori justification; it is compatible with S's having *no* justification for the belief that p. According to (A), anyone who believed that MPC for whatever reason, however whimsical, would thereby be a priori justified in believing that p (assuming that MPC is indeed rationally unrevisable). But, as we argued earlier, a priori justification for the belief that p requires nonexperiential justification for that belief.

(B) is also insufficient for a priori justification since it is compatible with S's having *experiential* justification for the belief that p. For example, suppose that Hilary looks at his hand, notes the number of fingers and, on that basis, comes to believe that the statement "My hand has five fingers" is true and that the statement is not false. Hilary is justified, on a posteriori grounds, in believing that some statement is not both true and false.

Putnam, however, rejects this contention on the following grounds:

> It might turn out that there are not five fingers on my hand. For example, my hand may have been amputated and what I'm looking at may be a plastic substitute. . . . But even if it turned out that I don't have a hand, or that my hand has only four fingers, or seven fingers, or whatever, discovering that I was wrong about the observation report would not at all shake my faith in my belief that that observation report is not both true and false.[44]

This argument is not germane. Suppose, for example, that Hilary believes on the basis of looking at his hand that the statement "My hand has five fingers" is true but, when he looks again, he discovers that his hand has only four fingers. The subsequent observation that his hand has only four fingers justifies him in believing that the statement "My hand has five fingers" is false and that the statement is not true. Hence, his faith in the belief that the original observation report is not both true and false should remain unshaken since the subsequent observation also justifies that belief. Putnam's point here may be that his recognition that no epistemically possible situation would shake his faith that MPC is true justifies his belief that MPC is true. This reading of his argument leads to (C).

(C) is not sufficient for S's belief that p to be justified a priori since (C) is compatible with S's having *experiential* justification for believing that p is rationally unrevisable. For example, a student may believe that MPC is rationally unrevisable solely on the testimony of a philosophy instructor. But, if the student's justification for believing that MPC is true is based on the justified belief that MPC is rationally unrevisable then, if the latter belief is justified a posteriori, the former is also justified a posteriori. Moreover, even if S believes that MPC is rationally unrevisable on the basis of determining the consequences of denying MPC and finding some of those consequences unacceptable, it still does not follow that S's belief that MPC is rationally unrevisable is justified a priori. There are two related problems. First, in determining the consequences of denying MPC one must employ *other* principles of logic. But, in order to be justified a priori in believing that MPC is rationally unrevisable, one must be justified a priori in believing the logical principles one utilizes in deriving the consequences of denying MPC. Putnam, however, cannot appeal to (C) to establish that the logical principles used to derive the consequences of denying MPC are themselves a priori. Such an appeal invites a regress since one must consider the consequences of denying those principles, which will require further principles of logic. Second, in order to be justified a priori in believing that MPC is rationally unrevisable, one must be justified a priori in believing a theory that excludes nothing is not a genuine theory. Putnam, however, does not address whether *methodological*, as opposed to logical, principles are justified a priori.

3.2. Criterial Arguments: Necessity

Criterial arguments have a common structure. They identify some feature of propositions that we purportedly know and allege that we cannot know a posteriori propositions having that feature, from which it follows that knowledge of such propositions must be a priori. Criterial arguments differ from conceptual arguments since they do not claim that the feature alleged to be sufficient for a priori knowledge is included in the analysis of the concept of a priori knowledge.

Kant provides the best known and most influential criterial argument. He maintains that necessity is a *criterion* of the a priori: "if we have a proposition which in being thought is thought as *necessary*, it is an *a priori* judgment; . . ."[45] This claim is based on the observation that "Experience teaches us that a thing is so and so, but not that it cannot be otherwise."[46] Kant goes on to argue that "mathematical propositions, strictly so called, are always judgments a *priori*, not empirical; because they carry with them necessity, which cannot be derived from experience."[47] Hence, he concludes, knowledge of mathematical propositions is a priori.

Kant's argument, the *Argument from Necessity*, can be presented as follows:

(1) Mathematical propositions are necessary.

(2) One cannot know a necessary proposition on the basis of experience.

(3) Therefore, one cannot know mathematical propositions on the basis of experience.

The first premise is controversial. Some question the cogency of the concept of necessary truth. Others maintain that modal sentences do not express truths or falsehoods. For our purposes, I propose to grant that (1) expresses a truth in order to address the epistemic issues that it raises.

The phrase 'know a necessary proposition' in (2) is ambiguous. Let us introduce the following distinctions:

(A) S knows the *general modal status* of p just in case S knows that p is a necessary proposition or S knows that p is a contingent proposition.

(B) S knows the *truth value* of p just in case S knows that p is true or S knows that p is false.

(C) S knows the *specific modal status* of p just in case S knows that p is necessarily true or S knows that p is necessarily false or S knows that p is contingently true or S knows that p is contingently false.

(A) and (B) are logically independent. One can know that p is a mathematical proposition and that all mathematical propositions are necessary but not know whether p is true or false. Goldbach's Conjecture provides an example. Alternatively, one can know that some mathematical proposition is true but not know whether it is a necessary or contingent truth. (C), however, is not independent of (A) and (B). One cannot know the specific modal status of a proposition unless one knows both its general modal status and its truth value.

Utilizing these distinctions, we can now see that the Argument from Necessity breaks down into two distinct arguments. The first, the *Kantian Argument*, goes as follows:

(1)   Mathematical propositions are necessary.

(2*)   One cannot know the *general modal status* of a necessary proposition on the basis of experience.

(3*)   Therefore, one cannot know the *truth value* of mathematical propositions on the basis of experience.

Kant argues in this fashion. He admits that experience can provide evidence that a thing *is* so and so, or, more perspicuously, that it is the case. What he denies is that experience can provide evidence that something *must* be the case, or, more perspicuously, that it is necessary. (2*) articulates this reading. Kant concludes, on this basis, that knowledge that $7 + 5 = 12$ (*not* knowledge that "$7 + 5 = 12$" is *necessary*) is a priori.

The Kantian Argument involves the following assumption:

(4)   If the general modal status of p is knowable only a priori, then the truth value of p is knowable only a priori.

(4), however, is false. Consider a contingent proposition such as that this cup is white. If one can know only a priori that a proposition is necessary, then one can know only a priori that a proposition is contingent. The evidence relevant to determining the latter is the same as that relevant to determining the former. For example, if I determine that "$2 + 2 = 4$" is necessary by trying to conceive of its falsehood and failing, I determine that "This cup is white" is contingent by trying to conceive of its falsehood and succeeding. But if my knowledge that "This cup is white" is contingent is a priori, it does not follow that my knowledge that this cup is white is a priori. On the contrary, it is a posteriori. Hence, (4) must be rejected.

Proponents of the argument might retreat at this point to a weaker version of (4):

(4*)   If p is a necessary proposition and if the general modal status of p is knowable only a priori, then the truth value of p is knowable only a priori.

There are, however, plausible counterexamples to (4*). If Kripke is correct about the semantics of proper names, then true identity statements involving different proper names are necessary truths.[48] Knowledge that such propositions are necessary is based on thought experiments: the inability to conceive that some object is different from itself. But knowledge that they are true is based on experience, astronomical observations in the case of Hesperus and Phosphorus. Another familiar example arises when one comes to believe, and apparently know, mathematical propositions on the basis of the testimony of a teacher or the authority of a textbook.[49]

The second version of the Argument from Necessity, the *Modal Argument,* proceeds as follows:

(1)   Mathematical propositions are necessary.

(2*)   One cannot know the *general modal status* of a necessary proposition on the basis of experience.

(3**)   Therefore, one cannot know the *general modal status* of mathematical propositions on the basis of experience.

The Modal Argument is less ambitious than the Kantian Argument and, as a consequence, is not open to the objections raised against the latter. On the other hand, it is too weak to establish that mathematical knowledge differs from scientific knowledge. If sound, it establishes that knowledge of the general modal status of both mathematical and scientific propositions is a priori and is compatible with the view that knowledge of the truth value of both is a posteriori.

Nevertheless, since it is incompatible with the more general thesis that *all* knowledge is a posteriori, the Modal Argument merits careful scrutiny. What can be said in support of (2*)? The standard move is to invoke the Kantian claim that experience can teach us only what *is* the case or its Leibnizian counterpart to the effect that experience can provide knowledge of only the *actual* world but not of other possible worlds.[50] If this claim is granted, then (2*) is plausible. But a good deal of our ordinary practical knowledge and the bulk of our scientific knowledge provide clear counterexamples to the claim. My knowledge that my pen will fall if I drop it does not provide me with information about what *is* the case, for the antecedent is contrary-to-fact. It provides me with information about some possible worlds other than the actual world. Scientific laws are not mere descriptions of the actual world. They support counterfactual conditionals and, hence, provide information beyond what is true of the actual world. In the absence of further support for premise (2*), the Modal Argument should also be rejected.

3.3. Criterial Arguments: Irrefutability

In defending the existence of a priori knowledge, Kant draws attention to the alleged necessity of mathematical propositions. Proponents of logical empiricism, who were reacting against John Stuart Mill's contention that we know mathematical propositions, such as that $3 + 2 = 5$, on the basis of inductive generalization from observed cases, draw attention to a different feature of mathematical propositions: their alleged irrefutability by experience. Carl Hempel puts the point as follows:

> consider now a simple "hypothesis" from arithmetic: 3 + 2 = 5. If this is actually an empirical generalization of past experiences, then it must be possible to state what kind of evidence would oblige us to concede the hypothesis was not generally true after all. If any disconfirming evidence for the given proposition can be thought of, the following illustration might well be typical of it: We place some microbes on a slide, putting down first three of them and then another two. Afterwards we count all the microbes to test whether in this instance 3 and 2 actually added up to 5. Suppose now that we counted 6 microbes altogether. Would we consider this as an empirical disconfirmation of the given proposition, or at least as a proof that it does not apply to microbes? Clearly not; rather, we would assume we had made a mistake in counting or that one of the microbes had split in two between the first and the second count.[51]

Since Hempel maintains that we would not regard any experiential evidence as disconfirming a mathematical proposition, he concludes that such propositions are not confirmed by experience.

Hempel's argument, the *Irrefutability Argument*, can be stated as follows:

(1)   No experiential evidence can disconfirm mathematical propositions.

(2)   If experiential evidence cannot disconfirm mathematical propositions, then it cannot confirm such propositions.

(3)   Therefore, experiential evidence cannot confirm mathematical propositions.

This argument is valid and the second premise is uncontroversial. Premise (1), however, is not obviously true. Moreover, Hempel's defense of (1) is not very strong. He considers only the weakest possible case of potential experiential disconfirming evidence.

In order to bring out this point more clearly, let us first note two familiar features of inductive practice: (a) our assessments of the degree to which a particular case confirms or disconfirms a generalization is a function of the total available evidence; and (b) apparent disconfirming cases of a generalization can always be explained away in a fashion which leaves the original hypothesis unaffected. Hempel's defense of (1) is weak in several respects. First, it does not take into account the number of apparent confirming instances of the proposition in question. Second, it involves only a single disconfirming instance of the proposition. Third, the hypotheses which are invoked to explain away the apparent disconfirming instance are not subjected to independent empirical test. In such a situation, given a background of supporting evidence for the generalization, it is reasonable to discount the disconfirming instances as apparent and to explain them away on whatever empirical grounds are most plausible.

The case against premise (1) can be considerably strengthened by revising Hempel's scenario as follows: (a) the number of disconfirming instances of the proposition is increased so that it is large relative to the number of confirming instances; and (b) the hypotheses invoked to explain away the apparent disconfirming instances are subjected to independent investigation and found to be unsupported. Let us now suppose that we have experienced a very large number of apparent disconfirming instances of the proposition that $3 + 2 = 5$ and, furthermore, that empirical investigations of the hypotheses invoked to explain away these disconfirming instances produce very little, if any, support for the hypotheses. Given these revisions, the proponent of the Irrefutability Argument can continue to endorse premise (1) only at the expense of either divorcing mathematics from its empirical applications or holding empirical beliefs which are at odds with the available evidence.

This point can be brought out more clearly by considering the following set of propositions:

(a)   The mathematical proposition that $3 + 2 = 5$ is applicable to microbes;

(b)   The empirical procedure of counting microbes provides *only apparent* disconfirming evidence for the proposition that $3 + 2 = 5$;

(c)   The results of independent empirical investigation do not support the auxiliary hypotheses introduced to explain away the disconfirming evidence as only apparent.

Although (c) does not entail not-(b), it does provide strong grounds for rejecting (b). Clearly, the proponent of the Irrefutability Argument cannot simply assert (b), for to simply assert (b) without independent support is to beg the question against the radical empiricist. But (c) establishes that the independent reasons offered in support of (b) are unfounded. Hence, (b) must be rejected. The proponent of the Irrefutability Argument, however, cannot accept both (a) and not-(b). If the disconfirming evidence provided by the procedure of counting microbes is *not* merely apparent then it is genuine. So only two alternatives remain: either (i) reject (a) and hold that mathematics is not applicable to microbes, or (ii) continue to hold (b) despite (c). Neither alternative is palatable since (i) effectively divorces mathematics from its empirical applications, while (ii) puts one in a position of holding a belief which is counter to one's available evidence. The most plausible alternative is to accept (a) and reject (b). But to reject (b) is to reject premise (1) of the Irrefutability Argument. Hence, the argument falls short of its mark.

3.4. Deficiency Arguments

Laurence BonJour offers three arguments that purport to expose deficiencies in radical empiricism. The first alleges that radical empiricism leads to scepticism. Assume that some beliefs are directly justified solely by experience. Such beliefs are "particular rather than general in their content and are confined to situations observable at specific and fairly narrowly delineated places and times."[52] Either some beliefs whose content goes beyond direct experience are justified or scepticism is true. The justification of beliefs whose content goes beyond direct experience requires inference from the directly justified beliefs. Since principles of inference are *general*, they cannot be directly justified by experience.

The next two arguments are directed toward W. V. Quine's radical empiricism. The first maintains that in order for a person to be justified in believing that p the person must be in possession of a reason for thinking that p is likely to be true. According to Quine, a system of beliefs satisfying standards such as simplicity, scope, fecundity, explanatory adequacy, and conservatism is justified. But, asks BonJour,

> What reason can be offered for thinking that a system of beliefs which is simpler, more conservative, explanatorily more adequate, etc., is thereby more likely to be true, that following such standards is at least somewhat conducive to finding the truth?[53]

There are two options. Either such a reason is a priori or it is empirical. The former is incompatible with radical empiricism. The latter is question-begging since it must ultimately appeal to some of the standards it is attempting to justify.

The final objection alleges that Quine's standards for belief revision do not impose any constraints on epistemic justification:

> After all, any such standard, since it cannot on Quinean grounds be justified or shown to be epistemically relevant independently of considerations of adjustment to experience, is itself merely one more strand (or node?) in the web, and thus equally open to revision.[54]

Hence, whenever those standards appear to dictate that some belief should be revised, such revision can be avoided by revising the standards themselves. Quine cannot respond that such revision is not justified since such a response is based either on the standards themselves, which is circular, or on some further standard, which is itself revisable.

BonJour's arguments provide a basis for preferring his moderate rationalism over its radical empiricist competitors only if the former avoids the deficiencies alleged to plague the latter. Since, as I shall now show, moderate rationalism suffers from the same deficiencies, his arguments provide no basis for preferring it over radical empiricism. The first objection alleges that since the content of experience is *particular*, experience cannot directly justify *general* principles. Moderate rationalism is open to the same objection unless it can show that the content of rational insight is not limited to particular objects. BonJour maintains that although we experience only particular objects, we apprehend properties of objects.[55] The term 'apprehend' suggests an analogy to perception, which requires causal contact with the object perceived. Properties, however, cannot stand in causal relations. BonJour maintains that the perceptual metaphor is misleading. Hence, in order to underwrite the claim that we apprehend general features of objects, he must provide a nonmetaphorical account of this alleged cognitive capacity.

BonJour proposes to explain the apprehension of properties in terms of a more general theory of how a thought can be about, or have as its content, some particular property. A thought has as its content some particular property in virtue of its *intrinsic* character rather than in virtue of some *relation*, quasi-perceptual or otherwise, to that property. For a thought to be about a particular property, say triangularity, that property must be a constituent of its intrinsic character:

> The key claim of such a view would be that it is a necessary, quasi-logical fact that a thought instantiating a complex universal involving the universal triangularity in the appropriate way . . . is about triangular *things*.[56]

BonJour's explanation falls short of its goal. His goal is to explain how a thought can have as its content some particular *property*, such as triangularity. He provides, instead, only the bare outline of an explanation of how a thought can have as its content *particular* triangular *objects*. Since he does not provide an explanation of how a thought can have as its content some *property*, he fails to provide an explanation of the apprehension of properties. Hence, moderate rationalism is open to BonJour's first objection.

The second objection turns on the claim that being epistemically justified in believing that p requires having a reason for thinking that p is likely to be true. The expression 'having a reason to think that p is likely to be true' is ambiguous. Let us distinguish two senses:

(B)   S has a *basic* reason R to believe that p if and only if S has R and R makes it likely that p is true;

(M)   S has a *meta*-reason R to believe that p if and only if S has R and S has reason to believe that R makes it likely that p is true.

Let Φ be the set of conditions that Quine maintains is sufficient for justification. Assume that belonging to a system of beliefs satisfying Φ makes it likely that p is true. If S cognitively grasps the fact that p belongs to such a system, then S has a *basic* reason to believe that p. BonJour's charge is that radical empiricism cannot offer an argument to show that such reasons are truth-conducive. Hence, the problem pertains to having a *meta*-reason to believe that p.

Does moderate rationalism fare any better on this score? Assume that having an apparent rational insight that p makes it likely that p is true. Hence, if S has an apparent rational insight that p, then S has a *basic* reason to believe that p. BonJour is now faced with the question:

> What reason can be offered for thinking that a belief based on apparent rational insight is thereby more likely to be true?

His response is that the demand for a meta-reason is question-begging because, on his account, apparent rational insight is an excellent reason, in its own right, for accepting a belief:

> [It] amounts simply and obviously to a refusal to take rational insight seriously as a basis for justification: a refusal for which the present objection can offer no further rationale, and which is thus question-begging.[57]

Radical empiricists, however, can offer a similar response to BonJour's second objection. They can maintain that his demand for a meta-reason is question-begging since it refuses to take seriously that belonging to a system of beliefs satisfying Φ is an excellent reason, in its own right, for accepting a belief. Hence, radical empiricism fares *no worse* than moderate rationalism with respect to the demand for meta-reasons.

BonJour's third objection rests on two principles:

(P1)   Beliefs justified by experience are revisable; and

(P2)   The standards for revising beliefs justified by experience are themselves justified by experience.

From these two principles it follows that

(P3)   The standards for revising beliefs justified by experience are themselves revisable.

But moderate rationalism endorses analogues of these two principles:

(P1*)   Beliefs justified by apparent rational insight are revisable; and

(P2*)   The standards for revising beliefs justified by apparent rational insight are themselves justified by apparent rational insight.

Hence, moderate rationalism is committed to

(P3*)   The standards for revising beliefs justified by apparent rational insight are themselves revisable.

The remainder of BonJour's argument applies with equal force to moderate rationalism and radical empiricism. Any attempt to block revision of the standards for belief revision either appeals to the standards themselves, which is circular, or invokes some further standard, which is itself revisable. Hence, once again, moderate rationalism fares *no better* than radical empiricism.

4. Arguments Opposing the Existence of a Priori Knowledge

Arguments against the existence of a priori knowledge fall into three broad categories. Those in the first offer an analysis of the concept of a priori knowledge and allege that no cases of knowledge satisfy the conditions in the analysis. Those in the second offer radical empiricist accounts of knowledge of propositions alleged to be knowable only a priori. Arguments in the third category maintain that a priori knowledge is incompatible with plausible constraints on an adequate theory of knowledge.

4.1. Conceptual Arguments

Hilary Putnam and Philip Kitcher provide clear examples of the first approach. Both hold that the concept of a priori justification includes an indefeasibility condition. According to Putnam, an a priori statement is one "we would never be *rational* to give up. . . ."[58] Kitcher maintains that for a process to justify beliefs a priori, it must be able to "warrant those beliefs against the background of a suitably recalcitrant experience."[59] They go on to argue that beliefs traditionally alleged to be justified a priori fail to meet the requisite indefeasibility condition. We argued that the concept of a priori justification does not include an indefeasibility condition. Hence, the fact that a belief fails to satisfy an indefeasibility condition does not *immediately* entail that it is not justified a priori. There remains, however, the possibility of a more *mediate* connection.

Let us call the general thesis that a priori justification entails rational unrevisability the *Unrevisability Thesis* (UT), and distinguish between a strong and weak version of it:

    (SUT)   Necessarily, if S's belief that p is justified a priori then S's belief that p is rationally unrevisable in light of *any* evidence; and

    (WUT) Necessarily, if S's belief that p is justified a priori then S's belief that p is rationally unrevisable in light of any *experiential* evidence.

My goal is to argue that both (SUT) and (WUT) should be rejected.

We begin by considering an example that draws out more explicitly the consequences of (SUT). Suppose that Mary is a college student who has had some training in logic. As a result, she is able to discriminate reliably between valid and invalid elementary inferences on the basis of reflective thought. Today Mary wonders whether 'p ⊃ q' entails '-p ⊃ -q'. She reflects upon the statements in question and on the basis of this reflection concludes that the former does indeed entail the latter. After she assents to this conclusion, a counterexample occurs to her. The occurrence of the counterexample results in her rejecting her former conclusion and coming to believe that 'p ⊃ q' entails '-q ⊃ -p'. The salient features of the example are as follows: (a) Mary's initial belief is based on a nonexperiential process that is reliable but not infallible; (b) a process of the *same type* leads Mary to conclude that the initial belief is mistaken and to arrive at the correct conclusion; and (c) Mary's conclusions as stated in (b) are justified beliefs. Now for some more controversial claims: (d) Mary's original belief that 'p ⊃ q' entails '-p ⊃ -q' is also *justified*; and (e) Mary's original belief is justified *a priori* despite the subsequent revision.

What can be said in favor of (d) and (e)? (d) appears to be similar in all relevant respects to the following case. Mary sees a sheet of paper on the table and on that basis forms the belief that it is square. A second, closer visual examination reveals that two of the sides are slightly longer than the other two. On this basis, Mary rejects her former belief about the shape of the paper and comes to believe that it is rectangular. Since the circumstances under which Mary perceived the page were normal and Mary is a reliable discriminator of shapes, her initial belief is justified. The fact that our discriminatory powers sometimes fail us does not entail that beliefs based on shape perception are not justified. Furthermore, if such beliefs are typically justified, we don't single out particular cases as unjustified *merely* in virtue of the fact that they are false. Some other relevant difference must be cited, such as that the perceiver was impaired or the environment was gerrymandered. Hence, the routine failure of Mary's otherwise reliable shape—discriminating ability does not entail that her belief that the paper is square is unjustified despite the fact that it is false. Similarly, the routine failure of Mary's otherwise reliable ability to discriminate valid inferences does not entail that her belief that 'p ⊃ q' entails '-p ⊃ -q' is unjustified despite the fact that it is false.

The only remaining question is whether Mary's original belief is justified a priori or a posteriori. A proponent of (SUT) must maintain that the belief is justified a posteriori *merely* in virtue of the fact that it was revised. This point can be brought out more clearly by introducing the notion of a *self-correcting process*:

> (SCP)   A process ϕ is self-correcting for S just in case, for any false belief that p, produced in S by ϕ, ϕ can also justify for S the belief that not-p.[60]

(SUT) entails

> (1)   If a process ϕ is self-correcting and justifies for S some false belief that p then ϕ does not justify a priori S's belief that p.

(1) is implausible. It is insensitive to the central question of whether the justificatory process in question is experiential or nonexperiential. Hence, to endorse (1) is to divorce the notion of a priori justification from the notion of independence from experiential evidence. It is more plausible to reject (1) on the grounds that Mary's original belief as well as the belief that led her to revise the original belief are based on nonexperiential evidence. Once we reject (1), (SUT) must also be rejected.

(WUT) avoids the primary problem with (SUT). It distinguishes between revisions based on experiential evidence as opposed to revisions based on nonexperiential evidence and maintains that only the former are incompatible with a priori justification. Nevertheless, (WUT) is also open to objection.

We again begin by considering an example. Suppose that Pat is a working logician who regularly and consistently arrives at interesting results. Pat, however, is bothered by the fact that although he is a *reliable* producer of interesting proofs, he is not an *infallible* producer of such proofs. As it turns out, he has a colleague, May, who has done pioneering work in the neurophysiological basis of cognitive processes. As a radical means to self-improvement, Pat asks May to conduct a study of his efforts at constructing proofs in order to see if she can uncover some, hopefully reversible, neurophysiological cause for his infrequent erroneous proofs. The investigation reveals that (a) a particular interference pattern is present in Pat's brain when and only when he constructs an erroneous proof; and (b) whenever Pat constructs a proof under the influence of this pattern and the pattern is subsequently eradicated by neurophysiological intervention, he is able to see the flaw in the original proof and go on to correct it. Finally, there is an accepted neurophysiological theory available which supports the hypothesis that such a pattern should cause cognitive lapses. Now suppose that Pat believes that p entails q on the basis of constructing a proof which he carefully scrutinizes and finds acceptable. Despite his careful scrutiny, the proof is flawed. He later discovers in a subsequent meeting with May that (a) she had been monitoring his brain activity at the time the proof was constructed with a remote sensor; (b) the sensor indicated that the interference pattern was present; and (c) standard tests indicated that all of the equipment was functioning properly. Pat is still unable to uncover the flaw in his proof but nevertheless concludes, on the basis of May's empirical findings, that his proof is flawed and withholds the belief that p entails q.

The salient features of the example are: (a) Pat's initial belief that p entails q is based on a process of reflective thought that is reliable but not infallible; (b) Pat's initial belief that p entails q is justified by the nonexperiential process of reflective thought; and (c) the justification which the process of reflective thought confers on his belief is subsequently defeated by the empirical evidence indicating that the interference pattern is present. (a) is uncontroversial. (b) is more controversial since it involves the claim that false beliefs can be justified a priori. This claim was defended earlier in the discussion of the Mary example. We propose to grant (c) for purposes of assessing (WUT). Finally, consider (d) Pat's initial belief that p entails q is justified *a priori* despite the later revision in light of experiential evidence. (d) appears to be a straightforward consequence of (b). Since Pat's belief is justified by a nonexperiential process, it is justified a priori. A proponent of (WUT) can resist this conclusion only by insisting that since experiential evidence defeated the justification conferred on the belief by the nonexperiential process, the belief is justified, at least in part, by experiential evidence.

The proposed defense of (WUT) invokes the following symmetry between justifying evidence and defeating evidence:

(ST)   If evidence of kind A can defeat the justification conferred on S's belief that p by evidence of kind B, then S's belief that p is justified by evidence of kind A.

(ST), however, is not very plausible. Consider, for example, introspective knowledge of one's bodily sensations such as pains and itches. Some maintain that introspective knowledge is indubitable. There are no possible grounds for doubting the truth of an introspective belief about one's bodily sensations. This claim has been challenged by the so-called EEG argument.[61] The basic idea is that although introspection presently provides our only evidence for the presence of bodily sensations, it is possible that neurophysiology will evolve to the point where electroencephalograph readings also provide such evidence. Furthermore, in suitably chosen circumstances, the EEG readings may override our introspective evidence in support of a belief regarding the presence of a bodily sensation. Our purpose here is not to evaluate the argument. Suppose we grant

(N)   Neurophysiological evidence can defeat the justification conferred on a belief about one's bodily sensations by introspection.

Clearly, it does not follow that my present justified belief that I have a mild headache is based, even in part, on neurophysiological evidence. Consequently, (ST) must be rejected. Once we reject (ST), (WUT) must also be rejected.

4.2. Empiricist Accounts

One common strategy of arguing against the existence of a priori knowledge is to consider the most prominent examples of propositions alleged to be knowable only a priori and to argue that such propositions are known empirically. Let us focus on mathematical knowledge since it has received the most attention. Empiricist accounts of mathematical knowledge can be divided into two broad categories: inductive and holistic. The leading idea of inductive theories is that *epistemically basic* mathematical propositions are directly justified by observation and inductive generalization. Nonbasic mathematical propositions are indirectly justified by virtue of their logical and explanatory relationships to the basic mathematical propositions. Holistic empiricism denies that some mathematical propositions are directly justified by observation and inductive generalization. All mathematical propositions are part of a larger explanatory theory, which includes scientific and methodological principles. Only entire theories, rather than individual propositions, are confirmed or disconfirmed by experience.

John Stuart Mill is the most prominent proponent of inductivism. In the case of mathematics, his primary concern is with the first principles, the axioms and definitions, of arithmetic and geometry. His view, succinctly stated, is that these principles are justified inductively on the basis of observation. The view faces formidable obstacles. For example, definitions do not appear to require empirical justification. Moreover, the properties connoted by some mathematical terms do not appear to be exemplified by the objects of experience. Mill maintains, however, that definitions of mathematical terms assert the existence of objects exemplifying the properties connoted by the terms in the definitions and that mathematical definitions are only approximately true of the objects of experience.[62]

Very few find Mill's account to be plausible. My goal here is not to defend it. Instead, I propose to grant its cogency in order to determine whether it can be parlayed into an argument against the a priori. If Mill is correct, it follows that all epistemically basic mathematical propositions are justified on the basis of ob-

servation and inductive generalization. Moreover, all other mathematical propositions justified on the basis of these propositions are also justified on the basis
of experience. Nevertheless, the success of the account does not establish that there
is no a priori knowledge of those mathematical propositions. To draw such a
conclusion is to overlook the possibility of *epistemic overdetermination*: the possibility that mathematical propositions are (or can be) justified both experientially
and nonexperientially.

Mill is aware of this gap in his argument and appeals to a version of the
principle of simplicity:

> Where then is the necessity for assuming that our recognition of these truths
> has a different origin from the rest of our knowledge, when its existence is per-
> fectly accounted for by supposing its origin to be the same? when the causes
> which produce belief in all other instances, exist in this instance, and in a de-
> gree of strength as much superior to what exists in other cases, as the intensity
> of the belief itself is superior?[63]

Mill maintains that there is no need to hypothesize that there is a priori knowledge
to account for our knowledge of mathematics. But the appeal to simplicity is
misguided. The goal of an epistemological theory is not to offer the *simplest*
account of our knowledge of some target set of propositions. The goal is to offer
an *accurate* account of our knowledge: one that provides a complete picture of
our cognitive resources with respect to the domain of truths in question. It is an
open question whether, given our cognitive resources, we have more than a single
source of justification for beliefs within a given domain. The assumption that, for
any given domain of human knowledge, there is only a single source of justification is without foundation. The principle of simplicity rules out overdetermination of justification. Hence, Mill's empiricism, even if cogent, cannot be
parlayed into an argument against the a priori in the absence of an argument
against epistemic overdetermination.

Holistic empiricism faces a related difficulty. The classic presentation of the
position is provided by W. V. Quine.[64] There are (at least) two ways of reading
his argument. The traditional reading is that he is providing a unitary argument
against the cogency of the analytic–synthetic distinction, which proceeds by examining a variety of alternative proposals for marking the distinction. The second,
due to Hilary Putnam, is that Quine is providing two distinct arguments in "Two
Dogmas": an (unsuccessful) argument in the first four sections, targeting the analytic–synthetic distinction, and a (successful) argument in the concluding two
sections, targeting the existence of a priori knowledge.[65]

On Putnam's reading, when Quine argues that no statement is immune to
revision in light of recalcitrant experience, he is targeting a priori knowledge. The
target of the attack is the view that there are some statements confirmed no matter
what. Putnam's claim is that the concept of a statement confirmed no matter

what is not a concept of analyticity but a concept of apriority. Quine was misled into thinking that it was a concept of analyticity because of positivist assumptions about meaning. Hence, according to Putnam, if Quine's argument is sound, it establishes that there is no a priori knowledge.

My purpose here is not exegetical. I propose to grant Putnam's reading of the structure of Quine's argument. Moreover, I propose to grant that Quine has successfully established that no statement is immune to revision. My concern is whether Quine's conclusion can be parlayed into an argument against the existence of a priori knowledge, as Putnam alleges. Clearly, that conclusion, taken by itself, is not sufficient to do so. The additional premise that a priori justification entails rational unrevisability is also necessary. But, despite Putnam's claim to the contrary, the additional premise is false.

Let us now turn to the more traditional reading of Quine's argument and, once again, concede that Quine has successfully shown that the analytic–synthetic distinction is not cogent. Does this result provide the empiricist with the resources necessary to argue that there is no a priori knowledge? Once again, this premise alone does not suffice. We argued in section 2.1 that the analysis of the concept of a priori justification does not include the concept of analyticity. Hence, there is no immediate or obvious connection between the two concepts. The possibility remains that there is some more mediate connection. But, if there is such a connection, some supporting argument must be offered to show this.

4.3. Incompatibility Arguments

Paul Benacerraf provides the classic example of an argument falling into the third category.[66] He maintains that our best theory of truth provides truth conditions for mathematical statements that refer to abstract entities and our best account of knowledge requires a causal relation between knowers and the entities referred to by the truth conditions of the statements that they know. Given that abstract entities cannot stand in causal relations, there is a tension between our best account of mathematical truth and our best account of mathematical knowledge. Since it is widely held that most, if not all, a priori knowledge is of necessary truths and that the truth conditions for such statements refer to abstract entities, Benacerraf's argument raises a more general question about the possibility of a priori knowledge.

Some dismiss the argument on the grounds that its epistemic premise, which endorses a causal condition on knowledge, rests on the generally rejected causal theory of knowledge. Benacerraf's argument, however, has proved to be more resilient than the causal theory of knowledge. Proponents of the argument maintain that the causal condition endorsed by the epistemic premise of the argument draws its support from the requirements of a naturalized epistemology rather than the causal theory of knowledge.[67]

Assessing the claim that naturalism is incompatible with knowledge of abstract entities is complicated since there are many competing versions of the view. At the risk of oversimplifying, let us identify two general varieties. The first, *scientific* naturalism, is due to W. V. Quine, who rejects the traditional epistemological project of providing an a priori, philosophical justification of scientific knowledge and offers, in its place, a vision of epistemology as a branch of science.[68] The second, *philosophical* naturalism, advocates placing naturalistic constraints on traditional philosophical projects. In the case of conceptual analysis, for example, it requires that the analysans of a concept include only naturalistically respectable concepts. We are now faced with two questions. Does either philosophical or scientific naturalism preclude the possibility of knowledge of abstract entities?

4.4. Philosophical Naturalism

If philosophical naturalism precludes knowledge of abstract entities, it is in virtue of the requirements of a more promising naturalized descendant of the causal theory. The most promising is process reliabilism. Alvin Goldman maintains that

(G)   S's believing p at t is justified if and only if
    (a) S's believing p at t is permitted by a right system of J-rules, and
    (b) this permission is not undermined by S's cognitive state at t.[69]

According to (G), any belief produced by a basic reliable psychological process satisfies (a). Such a belief is justified provided that S does not possess defeating evidence such as that the belief is false or that it is produced by an unreliable process. (G) also appears to be compatible with the possibility of justified beliefs about abstract entities, since neither (a) nor (b) involves any causal conditions. (G), however, is open to objection.

Suppose that Maud belongs to an organization whose leaders believe, on flimsy grounds, that clairvoyance is a reliable source of knowledge.[70] Furthermore, suppose that extensive empirical work has been done investigating this phenomenon, the results have been negative, and this information is *present* in Maud's epistemic community. Others are aware of the information. Newspapers, magazines, books, and television widely report the information. Moreover, Maud has *ready access* to this information. Others with whom she interacts have this information and would share it if asked. The newspapers and magazines that she sometimes reads report the information. Books and periodicals owned by the library that she frequently visits document the information. Television programs broadcast on channels that she views present the information. The leaders of the organization are aware of the negative evidence, the fact that it is widely publicized, and the fact that many of their followers have ready access to the information. As a consequence, they continually urge their followers to ignore information from outside sources on the subject. Maud adheres to their wishes and succeeds in forming very few beliefs regarding clairvoyance other than those promulgated within the organization. Now suppose that she is in fact clairvoyant, the process is reliable, and Maud forms the true belief that p via this process. Maud's belief is not justified, since the evidence she has in support of the reliability of clairvoyance is flimsy and she chooses to ignore copious evidence to the contrary. Yet her belief satisfies both (a) and (b) in (G). (b) is satisfied because Maud is not justified in believing that clairvoyance is not a reliable belief-forming process. Her belief system is too impoverished to justify that belief despite the fact that she has ready access to evidence that would support it.

(G) is vulnerable to the case of Maud because it assumes that only evidence *one possesses* is relevant to the justification of one's beliefs. It does not take into account the *social* dimension of justification. Yet, as the case of Maud indicates, one cannot ignore readily available evidence, and such evidence, even if ignored, can be relevant to the justification of one's beliefs. Hence, any plausible account of undermining evidence must take into account evidence that one does *not actually possess* but which is *present* within one's epistemic community and to which one has *ready access*. Goldman's (b) must be replaced by

> (b*)   this permission is not undermined by S's cognitive state at t or evidence present within S's epistemic community to which S has ready access at t.[71]

(b*) yields the correct result that Maud's justification is undermined by the readily accessible evidence present in her epistemic community regarding the unreliability of clairvoyance. The primary consequence of (b*) is that information within S's epistemic community regarding both the possibility and the reliability of a belief-forming process is relevant to whether that process justifies the beliefs that it produces in S. Hence, the question we must address is whether the causal inertness of abstract entities provides any basis for questioning the possibility or reliability of the processes alleged to produce beliefs about such entities.

Proponents of the a priori maintain that they have cognitive access to abstract entities via a nonexperiential process, call it *intuition*, and that the process justifies beliefs about those entities. Associated with the process are cognitive states with a unique phenomenology that its proponents recognize. The experience of such phenomenologically distinct states provides them with some reason to believe that they have cognitive access to abstract entities. But there is also contrary evidence of two kinds. First, there is controversy over the existence and reliability of intuition. Some maintain that they do not have the cognitive states in question, while others acknowledge having such states but deny that they provide cognitive access to abstract entities. Moreover, there are others who question the reliability of beliefs based upon intuition, and there have been movements within the fields of mathematics and philosophy to dispel such appeals. In the face of evidence that others do not have such experiences, proponents of the a priori must believe either that they have unique cognitive equipment, or that the others have the same equipment but that it is malfunctioning, or that the others are less reliable reporters of the facts of their cognitive lives. There is little evidence to support any of the alternatives. In the face of alleged instances of intuitive error, proponents can provide only anecdotal evidence to support the contention that the instances cited are anomalous and that the process is generally reliable.

Second, these problems are reinforced by the fact that little is known about the neurophysiological mechanisms by which intuition produces beliefs. Since we take for granted that all cognitive processes have a neurophysiological basis, the absence of supporting neurophysiological evidence heightens suspicions about the existence of the process. Moreover, the causal inertness of abstract entities insures that they play no role in generating beliefs about them. Hence, if intuition is a reliable process, its reliability cannot be explained along the same lines as the reliability of our best understood cognitive processes. But, given that the underlying causal processes are unknown, we are not in a position to offer an alternative explanation. The belief that intuition is a reliable process introduces an explanatory gap, which reinforces the concerns about the reliability of the process.

The question before us is whether the causal inertness of abstract entities poses an obstacle to satisfaction of (b*) in (G) by processes, such as intuition, that produce beliefs whose truth conditions refer to abstract entities. Beliefs produced by intuition satisfy (b*) only if there is no readily accessible evidence present within one's epistemic community that calls into question the possibility or reliability of intuition. I have argued that there is such evidence. Reaching a final determination on the matter, however, requires a more detailed investigation of two issues: the scope and quality of the evidence; and how strongly a potential defeater must be supported in order to defeat the justification conferred on a belief by virtue of its being reliably produced. This more detailed investigation goes beyond the scope of the present discussion. My primary conclusion is that, within the framework of process reliabilism, the causal inertness of abstract entities poses a *threat* to a priori justification. Although process reliabilism does not rule out the *possibility* that processes such as intuition justify beliefs whose truth conditions refer to abstract entities, the absence of an explanation of how those processes can reliably produce such beliefs generates potential defeaters for such justification.

4.5. Scientific Naturalism

The final issue that we must address is whether scientific naturalism precludes knowledge of abstract entities. Penelope Maddy provides the most articulate attempt to show that the causal inertness of such entities poses a genuine problem regarding mathematical knowledge from a Quinean naturalized perspective. The problem is not conceptual but explanatory. When mathematicians, such as R. M. Solovay, form opinions on mathematical matters, they are usually correct. Hence,

> Even if reliabilism turns out not to be the correct analysis of knowledge and justification, indeed, even if knowledge and justification themselves turn out to be dispensable notions, there will remain the problem of explaining the undeniable fact of our expert's reliability. In particular, even from a completely naturalized perspective, the Platonist still owes us an explanation of how and why Solovay's beliefs about sets are reliable indicators of the truth about sets.[72]

The causal inertness of abstract entities, alleges Maddy, is a bar to explaining the reliability of Solovay's mathematical beliefs.

From a completely naturalized perspective, science is an autonomous discipline that is not subject to philosophical demands from without. Hence, if the bar to an explanation of Solovay's reliability arises from within a completely naturalized perspective, it must arise from within science. Maddy offers the following reason for thinking that the causal inertness of mathematical entities poses an obstacle to providing a scientifically acceptable answer:

> Obviously, what we are up against here is another, less specific, version of the same vague conviction that makes the causal theory of knowledge so persuasive: in order to be dependable, the process by which I come to believe claims about xs must ultimately be responsive in some appropriate way to actual xs.[73]

The alleged bar to explaining Solovay's reliability is a causal condition on reliable belief formation:

(M)   The process by which S comes to have beliefs about xs is reliable (dependable) only if that process is appropriately responsive to xs.

If the alleged bar arises from within science, there must be evidence from some relevant branch of science that supports (M). Maddy offers three supporting considerations:

(a)   the mathematics/science analogy;

(b)   the belief that all explanations are ultimately causal;

(c)   a strong form of physicalism.

All three considerations appear to be philosophical in character. Moreover, Maddy does not attempt to dispel the appearances by offering some evidence that commitment to either (a), (b), or (c) arises from within science. She does, however, maintain that there is support for (a) from within mathematics.

According to the mathematics/science analogy, mathematics resembles natural science in two important respects:

(a1) Some mathematical beliefs are basic and noninferential;

(a2) Basic mathematical beliefs are produced by a "perceptionlike" mechanism, which is most likely casual.[74]

The support Maddy offers for the analogy from within mathematics is that

mathematicians are not apt to think that the justification for their claims waits on the activities in the physics labs. Rather, mathematicians have a whole range of justificatory practices of their own, ranging from proofs and intuitive evidence, to plausibility arguments and defences in terms of consequences.[75]

Maddy's description of mathematical practice, if taken at face value, supports (a1); it supports a conception of mathematics as an autonomous discipline with its own justificatory procedures, some of which are noninferential. The primary epistemic consequence of the description is that it undercuts Quine's holistic account of mathematical knowledge. Nothing in the description supports (a2). The only support that Maddy offers for (a2) is the opinion of one, albeit significant, mathematician: Kurt Gödel. But from the fact that one mathematician endorses (a2), it does not follow that it is supported by *mathematical practice*. Mathematicians can have opinions about issues that don't arise from within mathematics, and not all issues about mathematics arise from within mathematics. Some arise from within traditional epistemology. What needs to be shown is that Gödel is addressing a question that arises from within the practice of mathematics and that his answer is generally accepted mathematical practice.

In conclusion, scientific naturalists must provide evidence from within science that indicates that knowledge of abstract entities is problematic. Our examination of Maddy's position reveals that the supporting evidence she offers is philosophical rather than scientific. Hence, she has not provided a reason to believe that scientific naturalism cannot accommodate such knowledge.

5. TOWARD A RESOLUTION

The results of sections 3 and 4 are inconclusive. Neither proponents nor opponents of the a priori offer convincing arguments for their position. Moreover, their strategy is typically negative: each argues, primarily on a priori grounds, that the opposing position is deficient in some respect. The result is an impasse. Advancing the debate beyond this impasse requires offering supporting evidence for one of the positions that is compelling to both parties. The most promising strategy for advancing the case for the a priori is to enlist empirical support for the claim that there are nonexperiential sources of justification.[76]

This strategy recommends itself on two grounds. The first is dialectical. A case for the a priori that is based on evidence and methodological principles endorsed by radical empiricists is one that they must acknowledge by their own lights. This dialectical advantage persists even if there is some competing, noncircular, a priori argument in the wings. The second is strategic. By limiting themselves to a priori arguments, proponents of the a priori place themselves in a needlessly handicapped position. They acknowledge that we have both a priori and a posteriori justified beliefs, yet don't employ the latter when supporting their position. In the absence of some principled objection to employing a posteriori support, it is simply a mistake to overlook it.

What empirical evidence is relevant to establishing that there are nonexperiential sources of justification? Before proponents of the a priori can enlist empirical support for this claim, it must be more fully articulated. Let us call this the *Articulation Project* (AP):

> Provide (a) a generally accepted description, at least at the phenomenological level, of the cognitive states that non-inferentially justify beliefs a priori; (b) the type of beliefs they justify; and (c) the conditions under which they justify the beliefs in question.[77]

We now briefly canvass the three components of (AP).

Much of the controversy over the a priori focuses on the cognitive states alleged to justify a priori. Radical empiricists claim that they find these states puzzling or even mysterious. Proponents respond that they are familiar and offer phenomenological descriptions. Yet, if one surveys these descriptions, one finds enormous variation.

Alvin Plantinga appeals to an analogy with perception to characterize the source of a priori knowledge: "*one* way to believe *p a priori* is to see that it is true."[78] Furthermore, he alleges that

> [This 'seeing'] consists, first (I suggest), in your finding yourself utterly convinced that the proposition in question is *true*. It consists second, however, in finding yourself utterly convinced that this proposition is not only true, but *could not have been false.*[79]

According to Plantinga, the perceptual analogy can be articulated in terms of some more familiar cognitive state. Phenomenological reflection reveals that the "seeing" that underlies a priori justification is not at all mysterious. It consists in being convinced that p is necessarily true.

Plantinga is not alone in resorting to a perceptual analogy to characterize the source of a priori justification. Laurence BonJour also appeals to such an analogy in articulating his account of a priori justification. He offers the following description of rational insight, the alleged source of such justification:

> when I carefully and reflectively consider the proposition (or inference) in question, I am able simply to see or grasp or apprehend that the proposition is *necessary*, that it must be true in any possible world or situation (or alternatively that the conclusion of the inference must be true if the premises are true).[80]

Although he endorses the perceptual analogy, BonJour disagrees with Plantinga in a fundamental respect. He insists that a priori insights are apparently *irreducible*: "they are apparently incapable of being reduced to or constituted out of some constellation of discursive steps or simpler cognitive elements of some other kind."[81] The perceptual metaphor cannot be articulated in terms of some more familiar cognitive state. Plantinga, alleges BonJour, simply misrepresents the phenomenological facts.[82]

Despite their differences, BonJour and Plantinga seem to agree on one point: the cognitive state that justifies a priori the belief that p includes the belief that p. George Bealer, however, disagrees even with this point. According to Bealer, a priori justification is rooted in a priori *intuition*:

> We do not mean [by intuition] a magical power or inner voice or anything of the sort. For you to have an intuition that A is just for it to *seem* to you that A. Here 'seems' is understood, not as a cautionary or "hedging" term, but in its use as a term for a genuine kind of conscious episode. . . . Of course, this kind of seeming is *intellectual*, not sensory or introspective (or imaginative). The subject here is a priori (or rational) intuition.[83]

An intellectual seeming that p must be distinguished from a belief that p. For example, it may seem to one that the naive comprehension axiom of set theory is true although one does not believe that it is true. Conversely, there are mathematical theorems that one believes on the basis of having constructed a proof but that don't seem to be either true or false.

Ernest Sosa agrees with Bealer that an intuition that p need not involve the belief that p or, for that matter, any belief at all. Nevertheless, he suggests that such seemings might be analyzable in terms of what one *would* believe in certain circumstances:

> Seemings then, whether sensory or intellectual, might be viewed as inclinations to believe on the basis of direct experience (sensory) or understanding (intellectual) and regardless of any collateral reasoning, memory, or introspection where the objects of *intellectual* seeming also present themselves as necessary.[84]

Sosa and Bealer differ in two significant respects. First, they offer different phenomenological descriptions of seemings. Sosa maintains that an intellectual seeming that p is an inclination to believe that p based on understanding that p. Bealer insists that "intuition is a *sui generis*, irreducible, natural propositional attitude which occurs episodically."[85] Hence, Bealer agrees with BonJour that the cognitive state that justifies a priori is irreducible but disagrees with him over the character of the state. Sosa, on the other hand, agrees with Plantinga that the state is reducible to a more familiar cognitive state but disagrees with him over the character of the reducing state. Second, although both agree that there are sensory and intellectual seemings, they disagree over how those seemings differ.[86] Bealer maintains that sensory seemings and intellectual seemings are phenomenologically distinct conscious states. According to Sosa, they do not differ phenomenologically. Both involve an inclination to believe that p, but they differ in the basis of the inclination: sensory seemings are based on direct experience, while intellectual seemings are based on understanding.

Proponents of the a priori are faced with a dilemma. Either we have direct introspective access to the cognitive states that provide noninferential a priori justification or we do not. If we do, sympathetic proponents of the position should be able to agree on the correct description of those states. If we do not, then some alternative rationale must be offered to support the claim that there are such states. The lack of consensus among proponents lends support to the claim of radical empiricists that more needs to be said here.

Turning to the second component of (AP), there is also wide variation among proponents over the scope of beliefs justified a priori. These differences are not typically manifest within epistemological contexts, since the focus is on stock examples such as elementary logical or mathematical propositions, simple analytic truths, and some familiar cases of alleged synthetic a priori truths. Few proponents, however, maintain that a priori knowledge is limited to those cases. Consequently, they cannot effectively address the issue of the truth-conduciveness of the cognitive states that are alleged to justify a priori by focusing exclusively on the noncontroversial cases. Instead, they must provide a more complete specification of the range of beliefs alleged to be justified by such states. In the absence of a more complete articulation of the scope of the a priori, the crucial issue of truth-conduciveness will remain a subject of speculation, supported or rejected by bits of anecdotal evidence.

There is one issue regarding the scope of a priori justification that requires particular attention. The examples of a priori knowledge typically cited by proponents are necessary truths. But, as we stressed in section 3, we must be careful to distinguish between knowledge of the *truth value* of a necessary proposition as opposed to knowledge of its *general modal status*. A critical question arises here. What is the target of a priori justification: the general modal status of a proposition, its truth value, or both? If a priori justification extends to the truth value of propositions, two further questions arise. Are beliefs regarding the truth value of necessary propositions and beliefs regarding their general modal status justified by a single cognitive state or different cognitive states? Can one have an a priori justified belief that a contingent proposition is true?

The third component of (AP) concerns the conditions under which beliefs are justified a priori. There are two distinct sets of issues here. The first is a specification of the conditions under which beliefs are prima facie justified by the cognitive state proposed as the source of a priori justification. BonJour, for example, maintains that there are certain background conditions that must be satisfied in order for an apparent rational insight to have its justificatory force: the proposition must be considered with reasonable care, the person must have an approximate grasp of the concept of necessity, and one's reason must not be clouded by dogmatism or bias.[87] Two questions emerge. Is the list complete? Are the conditions sufficiently articulated so that it can be determined whether they are satisfied? One condition is that the cognizer have an *adequate grasp* of the concept of necessity. Does such a grasp require familiarity with the basic principles of modal logic? Does a modal sceptic lack all a priori knowledge?

The second is a specification of the conditions under which prima facie a priori justification is defeasible. Defeaters fall into two broad categories: overriding defeaters and undermining defeaters. There are two primary questions in the case of overriding defeaters. First, under what conditions, if any, do conflicts of rational insight undermine justification based on such insight? Second, can there be empirically justified overriding defeaters for beliefs justified a priori? Parallel questions arise in the case of undermining defeaters. Does a track record of conflicting beliefs or errors based on rational insight undermine justification based on such insight? Can a priori justified beliefs be defeated by empirically justified beliefs regarding the cognitive processes that underlie rational insight?

Once the main pieces of the Articulation Project are in place, the project of offering empirical supporting evidence for the a priori can be implemented. Let us call this the *Empirical Project* (EP):

> Provide (a) evidence that the cognitive states identified at the phenomenological level are associated with processes of a single type or relevantly similar types; (b) evidence that the associated processes play a role in producing or sustaining the beliefs they are alleged to justify; (c) evidence that the associated processes are truth-conducive; and (d) an explanation of how the associated processes produce the beliefs they are alleged to justify.

We now briefly canvass the four areas of investigation highlighted by (EP).[88]

The leading claim of proponents of the a priori is that sources of justification are of two significantly different types: experiential and nonexperiential. Initially, this difference is marked at the phenomenological level. Proponents identify certain phenomenologically distinct states as the source of a priori justification. The fact that the states are phenomenologically distinct, however, does not insure either that they are produced exclusively by processes of a single type or, if they are, that those processes differ significantly from experiential processes. Yet the character of the processes that produce the state is relevant to whether the state justifies a priori.

For example, suppose that intellectual seemings have a distinctive and readily identifiable phenomenological character. Moreover, suppose that a tutor teaches a child to "see" that $4 \times 4 = 16$ by utilizing techniques like those employed in the *Meno* and also teaches the child that balls roll down inclined planes by having the child perform experiments with balls and planes. Finally, suppose that the child later forgets the tutor's lessons but, as a result of them, both propositions, when considered, appear to the child to be true. It is implausible to maintain that both beliefs are justified a priori for the child. The first is justified a priori since it is based on a "rational" or nonexperiential process, but the second is justified a posteriori since it is based on a perceptual or experiential process. Hence, the fact that some cognitive states have a distinctive phenomenology, one different from those associated with familiar experiential processes such as perception, memory, or introspection, does not insure either that those states are produced by a single type of process or that the process producing them is nonexperiential.

The second area of investigation assesses the claim that beliefs alleged to be justified a priori are produced and/or sustained by processes involving the cognitive state alleged to provide such justification. If an epistemic theory is to provide an account of how our beliefs are *in fact* justified, then the processes to which the theory appeals must actually play some role in acquiring or sustaining the beliefs in question. Empirical investigation can offer support for this claim. Although a proponent of the a priori might rest content with the weaker claim that the processes in question *can* justify beliefs a priori, empirical considerations remain relevant in three ways. First, if the weaker claim involves more than an assertion of mere logical possibility, evidence is necessary to show that the cognitive processes in question can, in some more robust sense, play a role in producing or sustaining the beliefs in question. Second, the epistemic status of our *actual* beliefs regarding the subject matter in question must be addressed. Do the processes that actually produce the beliefs in question also justify those beliefs? Are our actual beliefs epistemically overdetermined or unjustified? Third, some explanation of why the nonexperiential processes are not employed by cognizers is in order. Is it because the processes can be employed only by experts? Is it because the processes are cognitively dispensable? Answers to these questions are necessary to provide an accurate picture of the role of such processes in our cognitive economy.

The third area of investigation addresses the issue of truth-conduciveness. The issue plays a dual role. If truth-conduciveness is a necessary condition for epistemic justification, as many proponents of the a priori allege,[89] or, if it is a necessary condition for a priori justification, as others allege,[90] then if one is to offer evidence in support of the claim that a particular cognitive process is a source of a priori justification, one must offer evidence in support of the claim that beliefs based on that process are likely to be true. Even those who deny that truth-conduciveness is a necessary condition for epistemic justification concede that evidence to the effect that a particular source of beliefs is error-conducive defeats the justification such a source confers on the beliefs that it produces. If one is to offer evidence in support of the claim that a particular process is a source of a priori justification, one must offer evidence in support of the claim that defeating evidence is not available that undermines the capacity of that source to justify any beliefs. The claim that a process is truth-conducive or, more minimally, that it is not error-conducive is a contingent general claim that can only be supported by empirical investigation.

Empirical investigation can play a second important role in assessing the credentials of a cognitive process. In order to assess the truth-conduciveness of a belief-forming process, one must have some approximation of the full range of beliefs that can be produced and/or sustained by the process in question. The a priori is typically introduced and defended using a narrow range of examples. Radical empiricists often attack the a priori by arguing that some of the examples, such as the principles of Euclidean geometry, have turned out to be false. Merely settling these disputes cannot either convincingly support or refute the a priori since the range of cases under consideration is so limited. Historical and psychological investigations, however, can provide a fuller picture of the range of beliefs produced by such processes.

The fourth area of empirical investigation, which focuses on explanatory considerations, offers the prospect of advancing the case for the a priori along several different fronts. First, if such investigation reveals that the cognitive processes associated with states alleged to justify a priori are of a single type or of relevantly similar types, then identification of the distinctive features of those processes might provide the basis for articulating the experiential/nonexperiential distinction. The net result would be a deeper understanding of the concept of a priori justification. Second, such investigations may provide a better understanding of how the processes in question produce true beliefs about their subject matter. This understanding, in turn, is the key to providing a noncausal-perceptual explanation of how the states in question provide cognitive access to the subject matter of the beliefs they produce and why they are truth-conducive. Third, as we achieve a better understanding of these processes, our epistemological and psychological theories become more integrated. The fact that our epistemological theory coheres well with psychological theories for which we have independent support increases the overall support for the former theory.

6. CONCLUSION

I have argued for three primary conclusions. The first is a minimal conception of a priori justification: a priori justification is nonexperiential justification. Second, the traditional arguments, based largely on a priori considerations, both for and against the existence of a priori knowledge are inconclusive. Finally, the most promising strategy for advancing the case for the a priori is to offer empirical supporting evidence for the claim that there are nonempirical sources of justification.

NOTES

Thanks to Tim Black for his careful reading of an earlier version of this essay and for his helpful comments.

1. Immanuel Kant, *Critique of Pure Reason*, trans. N. K. Smith (New York: St. Martin's Press, 1965).

2. Ibid., 43.

3. Philip Kitcher, *The Nature of Mathematical Knowledge* (New York: Oxford University Press, 1983), chap. 1.

4. W. V. Quine, "Two Dogmas of Empiricism," in *From a Logical Point of View*, 2d rev. ed. (New York: Harper and Row, 1963).

5. Hilary Putnam, " 'Two Dogmas' Revisited," in *Realism and Reason: Philosophical Papers*, vol. 3 (Cambridge: Cambridge University Press, 1983).

6. See, for example, Albert Casullo, "Revisability, Reliabilism, and A Priori Knowledge," *Philosophy and Phenomenological Research* 49 (1988): 187–213; Aron Edidin, "A Priori Knowledge for Fallibilists," *Philosophical Studies* 46 (1984): 189–197; Bob Hale, *Abstract Objects* (Oxford: Basil Blackwell, 1987), chap. 6; and Donna Summerfield, "Modest A Priori Knowledge," *Philosophy and Phenomenological Research* 51 (1991): 39–66. The articles by Casullo, Edidin, and Summerfield are reprinted in *A Priori Knowledge*, ed. Albert Casullo (Aldershot: Dartmouth, 1999). For more comprehensive bibliographies on the a priori, see Albert Casullo, "A Priori Knowledge Appraised," in *A Priori Knowledge*, ed. Casullo, and *A Priori Knowledge*, ed. Paul K. Moser (Oxford: Oxford University Press, 1987).

7. Paul Benacerraf, "Mathematical Truth," *Journal of Philosophy* 70 (1973): 661–679.

8. R. M. Chisholm, *Theory of Knowledge*, 3d ed. (Englewood Cliffs, N.J.: Prentice-Hall, 1989), 26–28, provides a cogent account of the traditional view.

9. See, for example, Albert Casullo, "Causality, Reliabilism, and Mathematical Knowledge," *Philosophy and Phenomenological Research* 52 (1992): 557–584; Hartry Field, *Realism, Mathematics and Modality* (Oxford: Blackwell, 1989); Bob Hale, "Is Platonism Epistemologically Bankrupt?," *Philosophical Review* 103 (1994): 299–324; Jerrold J. Katz, "What Mathematical Knowledge Could Be," *Mind* 104 (1995): 491–522; and Penelope

Maddy, "Mathematical Epistemology: What Is the Question?," *Monist* 67 (1984): 46–55. The four articles are reprinted in *A Priori Knowledge*, ed. Casullo.

10. Saul Kripke, "Identity and Necessity," in *Identity and Individuation*, ed. M. K. Munitz (New York: New York University Press, 1971), and *Naming and Necessity* (Cambridge, Mass.: Harvard University Press, 1980).

11. See, for example, C. Anthony Anderson, "Toward a Logic of A Priori Knowledge," *Philosophical Topics* 21 (1993): 1–20; Albert Casullo, "Kripke on the *A Priori* and the Necessary," *Analysis* 37 (1977): 152–159; Keith S. Donnellan, "The Contingent A Priori and Rigid Designators," in *Contemporary Perspectives on the Philosophy of Language*, ed. P. French et al. (Minneapolis: University of Minnesota Press, 1979); Gareth Evans, "Reference and Contingency," *Monist* 62 (1979): 161–189; Philip Kitcher, "Apriority and Necessity," *Australasian Journal of Philosophy* 58 (1980): 89–101; and R. G. Swinburne, "Analyticity, Necessity, and Apriority," *Mind* 84 (1975): 225–243. The articles by Casullo, Kitcher, and Swinburne are reprinted in *A Priori Knowledge*, ed. Moser. The article by Anderson is reprinted in *A Priori Knowledge*, ed. Casullo.

12. See, for example, Carl Hempel, "On the Nature of Mathematical Truth," in *Necessary Truth*, ed. R. C. Sleigh (Englewood Cliffs, N.J.: Prentice-Hall, 1972); and A. J. Ayer, *Language, Truth and Logic* (New York: Dover, 1952).

13. Quine, "Two Dogmas."

14. See, for example, Paul A. Boghossian, "Analyticity Reconsidered," *Nous* 30 (1996): 360–391; Laurence BonJour, "A Rationalist Manifesto," *Canadian Journal of Philosophy*, suppl. vol. 18 (1992): 53–88; M. Giaquinto, "Non-Analytic Conceptual Knowledge," *Mind* 105 (1996): 249–268; Gilbert Harman, "Analyticity Regained?," *Nous* 30 (1996): 392–400; and Putnam, " 'Two Dogmas' Revisited." The first four articles are reprinted in *A Priori Knowledge*, ed. Casullo.

15. Kant, *Critique of Pure Reason*, 42, states that "such universal modes of knowledge, which at the same time possess the character of inner necessity, must in themselves, independently of experience, be clear and certain. They are therefore entitled knowledge *a priori*."

16. For a more comprehensive discussion of analyses of the concept of a priori knowledge, see chap. 1–3 of Albert Casullo, *A Priori Justification* (New York: Oxford University Press, forthcoming).

17. See, for example, Kitcher, *The Nature of Mathematical Knowledge*, and Swinburne.

18. Anthony Quinton, "The *A Priori* and the Analytic," in *Necessary Truth*, ed. Sleigh, 90.

19. Ibid., 92.

20. Ibid., 93. The emphasis is Quinton's.

21. Swinburne, in *A Priori Knowledge*, ed. Moser, 186–187.

22. Ibid., 186.

23. Laurence BonJour, *The Structure of Empirical Knowledge* (Cambridge: Harvard University Press, 1985), 192. BonJour no longer endorses this conception.

24. See, for example, Chisholm, *Theory of Knowledge*, 41.

25. Ibid., 28.

26. Ibid.

27. Ibid., 29.

28. Ibid., 26. The quoted passage is from G. W. Leibniz, *New Essays Concerning Hu-*

man Understanding, trans. and ed. Peter Remnant and Jonathan Bennett (New York: Cambridge University Press, 1982), book IV, chap. 7.

29. Kripke, *Naming and Necessity*; and Kitcher, "Apriority and Necessity."

30. Chisholm, *Theory of Knowledge*, 12, states that "p is certain for S = Df   For every q, believing p is more justified for S than withholding q, and believing p is at least as justified for S as believing q."

31. See Panayot Butchvarov, *The Concept of Knowledge* (Evanston: Northwestern University Press, 1970), part 1, section 9; and John L. Pollock, *Knowledge and Justification* (Princeton: Princeton University Press, 1974), chap. 10.

32. Butchvarov, *Concept of Knowledge*, 93.

33. Laurence BonJour, *In Defense of Pure Reason* (Cambridge: Cambridge University Press, 1998), 106–110.

34. Kitcher, *The Nature of Mathematical Knowledge*, 89.

35. Hilary Putnam, "Analyticity and Apriority: Beyond Wittgenstein and Quine," in *Realism and Reason: Philosophical Papers*, vol. 3 (Cambridge: Cambridge University Press, 1983), 127.

36. It is commonplace to distinguish between those a priori justified beliefs that are *directly* justified and those that are *indirectly* justified by nonexperiential sources. Those that are justified indirectly are justified exclusively by other beliefs that are either directly justified by nonexperiential sources or justified exclusively by other beliefs that are directly justified by nonexperiential sources. For ease of exposition, I do not introduce the distinction into my formulations. The reader should regard it as implicit in these and subsequent formulations.

37. Kripke, *Naming and Necessity*, 35.

38. Kitcher, *The Nature of Mathematical Knowledge*, 22. The plausibility of Kitcher's criterion derives from the observation that the following argument is intuitively invalid: S knows that p. It is possible that S knows a priori that p. Therefore, S knows a priori that p.

39. I follow Kitcher, *The Nature of Mathematical Knowledge*, 22, here in assuming that the modalities collapse.

40. S's justified belief that not-p is an *overriding* defeater for S's justified belief that p. S's justified belief that S's justification for the belief that p is inadequate or defective is an *undermining* defeater for S's justified belief that p.

41. There are versions of each of these three types of argument stated in terms of *justification* rather than *knowledge*. For ease of exposition, when offering general characterizations, I offer only the version stated in terms of *knowledge*. I use the term 'radical empiricism' to designate the view that *denies* the existence of a priori knowledge, and the term 'apriorism' to designate the view that *affirms* the existence of such knowledge. Similarly, I use 'radical empiricist' to designate a person or theory endorsing radical empiricism, and 'apriorist' to designate a person or theory endorsing apriorism. For a more comprehensive discussion of the supporting arguments, see Casullo, *A Priori Justification*, chap. 4.

42. Hilary Putnam, "There Is at Least One A Priori Truth," in *Realism and Reason: Philosophical Papers*, vol. 3 (Cambridge: Cambridge University Press, 1983), 98.

43. See, for example, Hilary Putnam, "The Analytic and The Synthetic," in *Mind, Language and Reality: Philosophical Papers*, vol. 2 (Cambridge: Cambridge University Press, 1975).

44. Putnam, "There Is at Least One A Priori Truth," 106.

45. Kant, 43. Kant's claim is echoed by Bertrand Russell, *The Problems of Philosophy* (Oxford: Oxford University Press, 1971), chap. 7; and by Roderick Chisholm, *Theory of Knowledge*, 2d ed. (Englewood Cliffs, N.J.: Prentice-Hall, 1977), chap. 3.

46. Ibid.

47. Ibid., 52.

48. Saul Kripke, "Identity and Necessity," and *Naming and Necessity*.

49. Tyler Burge, "Content Preservation," *Philosophical Review* 102 (1993): 457–488, disputes this claim. Burge's article is reprinted in *A Priori Knowledge*, ed. Casullo.

50. See, for example, R. M. Chisholm, *Theory of Knowledge*, 2d ed., 37; and C. McGinn "*A Priori* and *A Posteriori* Knowledge," *Proceedings of the Aristotelian Society* 76 (1975–1976), 204. Philip Kitcher, "Apriority and Necessity," 100–101, also maintains that the plausibility of the Modal version of the Argument from Necessity depends on this claim. He goes on to reject the argument for reasons different from mine.

51. Carl Hempel, "On the Nature of Mathematical Truth," 36. A. J. Ayer, *Language, Truth and Logic*, 75–76, offers a similar argument.

52. Laurence BonJour, *In Defense of Pure Reason*, 4. For a more comprehensive discussion of BonJour's position, see Albert Casullo, "The Coherence of Empiricism," *Pacific Philosophical Quarterly* 81 (2000): 31–48.

53. Ibid., 91.

54. Ibid., 92.

55. BonJour, ibid., 162, articulates the view as follows:

A person apprehends or grasps, for example, the properties redness and greenness, and supposedly "sees" on the basis of this apprehension that they cannot be jointly instantiated. Such a picture clearly seems to presuppose that as a result of this apprehension or grasping, the properties of redness and greenness are themselves before the mind in a way that allows their natures and mutual incompatibility to be apparent.

56. Ibid., 184. The emphasis is mine.

57. Ibid., 145.

58. Hilary Putnam, "There Is at Least One A Priori Truth," 98. Putnam provides a lucid summary of his case against the a priori in " 'Two Dogmas' Revisited." For a more comprehensive discussion of the opposing arguments, see Casullo, *A Priori Justification*, chap. 5.

59. Kitcher, *The Nature of Mathematical Knowledge*, 88.

60. Self-correction comes in degrees. A weaker form can be defined as follows: for *some* false belief that p produced in S by φ, φ can also justify for S the belief that not-p. Patently, other versions, both stronger and weaker, are possible. I use the strong version in this context since it yields a more straightforward argument.

61. See, for example, D. M. Armstrong, "Is Introspective Knowledge Incorrigible?," *Philosophical Review* 72 (1963): 417–432.

62. John Stuart Mill, *A System of Logic*, ed. J. M. Robson (Toronto: University of Toronto Press, 1973), book II, chaps. V and VI.

63. Ibid., 41.

64. Quine, "Two Dogmas of Empiricism."

65. Putnam, " 'Two Dogmas' Revisited."

66. Paul Benacerraf, "Mathematical Truth," *Journal of Philosophy* 70 (1973): 661–679.

67. W. D. Hart, "Review of Mark Steiner, *Mathematical Knowledge*," *Journal of Philosophy* 74 (1977): 125–126, argues that "it is a crime against the intellect to try to mask the problem of naturalizing the epistemology of mathematics with philosophical razzle-dazzle. Superficial worries about the intellectual hygiene of causal theories of knowledge are irrelevant to and misleading from this problem, for the problem is not so much about causality as about the very possibility of natural knowledge of abstract objects."

68. W. V. Quine, "Epistemology Naturalized," in *Ontological Relativity and Other Essays* (New York: Columbia University Press, 1969).

69. Alvin Goldman, *Epistemology and Cognition* (Cambridge, Mass.: Harvard University Press, 1986), 63.

70. This is a variation of a case presented by BonJour, *The Structure of Empirical Knowledge*, 40, and discussed by Goldman, *Epistemology and Cognition*, 111–112.

71. Gilbert Harman, *Thought* (Princeton: Princeton University Press, 1973), chap. 9, and *Change in View* (Cambridge: MIT Press, 1986), chap. 5, forcefully draws attention to the importance of evidence one does not possess. Alvin Goldman, "What Is Justified Belief?" in *Justification and Knowledge*, ed. George S. Pappas (Dordrecht: Reidel, 1979), 20, acknowledges the relevance of available belief-forming processes in an earlier account of undermining evidence. This account, however, is too restrictive to handle the case of Maud, since Goldman explicitly rules out gathering new evidence from the scope of available processes.

72. Penelope Maddy, *Realism in Mathematics* (Oxford: Oxford University Press, 1990), 43.

73. Ibid., 44.

74. Ibid., 45–46.

75. Ibid., 31.

76. This proposal is more fully elaborated and defended against potential objections in Casullo, *A Priori Justification*, chap. 6.

77. Our focus here, and in the subsequent discussion, is on the sources of *noninferential*, or *basic*, a priori justification since inferential, or nonbasic, a priori justification results from applying inferential principles that are (noninferentially) justified a priori to other beliefs that are (noninferentially) justified a priori. Hence, in the final analysis, all a priori justified beliefs are ultimately justified by those sources.

78. Plantinga, *Warrant and Proper Function*, 106.

79. Ibid., 105.

80. BonJour, *In Defense of Pure Reason*, 106.

81. Ibid., 108.

82. Ibid., nn. 12 and 13.

83. George Bealer, "*A Priori* Knowledge and the Scope of Philosophy," *Philosophical Studies* 81 (1996): 123, reprinted in *A Priori Knowledge*, ed. Casullo.

84. Ernest Sosa, "Rational Intuition: Bealer on Its Nature and Epistemic Status," *Philosophical Studies* 81 (1996): 154, reprinted in *A Priori Knowledge*, ed. Casullo.

85. George Bealer, "*A Priori* Knowledge: Replies to William Lycan and Ernest Sosa," *Philosophical Studies* 81 (1996): 169, reprinted in *A Priori Knowledge*, ed. Casullo.

86. The Müller–Lyer illusion provides an example of a sensory seeming.

87. BonJour, *In Defense of Pure Reason*, 133–137. He offers two different descriptions of what occurs when a cognizer fails to satisfy a background condition for justification

by an apparent rational insight: (1) the cognizer fails to have even an apparent rational insight; and (2) the justificatory force of the apparent rational insight is defeated.

88. Alvin Goldman, "A Priori Warrant and Naturalistic Epistemology," *Philosophical Perspectives* 13 (1999): 1–28, argues that psychological studies are relevant to the existence of a priori knowledge. His focus is on whether such studies support the view that basic mathematical and logical skills are innate.

89. George Bealer, Alvin Plantinga, and Ernest Sosa endorse such a condition although there are differences in their positions. Bealer, "*A Priori* Knowledge and the Scope of Philosophy," 129, endorses a reliabilist conception of *basic sources of evidence*: "something is a basic source of evidence iff it has a certain kind of reliable tie to the truth." Plantinga, *Warrant and Proper Function*, 17, endorses a reliabilist constraint on *warrant*: "the module of the design plan governing its production must be such that it is objectively highly probable that a belief produced by cognitive faculties functioning properly according to that module (in a congenial environment) will be true or verisimilitudinous." Sosa, "Modal and Other *A Priori* Epistemology: How Can We Know What is Possible and What Impossible?," *Southern Journal of Philosophy* 38, suppl. (2000): 4, endorses a reliabilist condition on *epistemic justification*: "The epistemic justification of a belief B at a time t may thus require the production of B at t through a virtue V resident in that subject. What is required for a disposition V to be a virtue is that in normal circumstances V would yield a sufficient preponderance of true beliefs in subjects like S." Although Laurence BonJour, *In Defense of Pure Reason*, 1, rejects reliabilist accounts of epistemic justification, he does introduce truth-conduciveness into his characterization of *epistemic reasons*: "Knowledge requires instead that the belief in question be justified or rational in a way that is internally connected to the defining goal of the cognitive enterprise, that is; that there be a reason that enhances, to an appropriate degree, the chances that the belief is *true*. Justification of this distinctive, truth-conducive sort will be here referred to as *epistemic justification*."

90. The most familiar example holds that, in the case of basic (or noninferentially) justified a priori belief that p, understanding that p is sufficient to "see" that p is true.

....

CHAPTER 4

THE SCIENCES AND EPISTEMOLOGY

ALVIN I. GOLDMAN

1. EPISTEMOLOGICAL PROJECTS AND THE NATURALIZING OF EPISTEMOLOGY

....

IN the last 30 years the project of linking epistemology with the sciences has usually gone under the label "naturalistic epistemology." This stems from an influential article by W. V. Quine (1969), who proposed such a linkage and gave it the "naturalizing" label. Quine's proposed linkage was a very radical one. According to him, epistemology as traditionally conceived should be abandoned and should be replaced by a branch of psychology, part of natural science.

> [E]pistemology still goes on, though in a new setting and a clarified status. Epistemology, or something like it, simply falls into place as a chapter of psychology and hence of natural science. It studies a natural phenomenon, viz., a physical human subject. This human subject is accorded a certain experimentally controlled input—certain patterns of irradiation in assorted frequencies, for instance—and in the fullness of time the subject delivers as output a description of the three dimensional external world and its history. (1969, 82–83)

Hilary Kornblith (1985, 3) calls Quine's proposal to subsume epistemology under psychology the "replacement thesis." Under the replacement thesis, epistemology would not merely make use of scientific findings but would itself become, or be replaced by, a branch of science. This proposal has not garnered many adherents. Although Quine's formulation is frequently cited and discussed—usually in a critical vein (e.g., Kim 1988)—it is rarely endorsed. For one thing, epistemology as usually understood deals at least in part with various normative concepts. It seeks to evaluate beliefs and belief-forming methods as rational or irrational, justified or unjustified, warranted or unwarranted. These kinds of normative tasks do not appear to belong to natural science; nor do they deserve to be abandoned, or replaced. If this is right, the connection between epistemology and science must not be one of identity, or subsumption. It must be some weaker sort of linkage(s). What kinds of weaker links between epistemology and the sciences make more sense?

One possible way of relating epistemology and the sciences would take its cue from the central question of Kant's epistemology, "How is synthetic a priori knowledge possible?" Kant presupposed the possibility of a certain kind of knowledge and then explored the conditions for this possibility. His detailed proposals do not concern me here. I invoke Kant only to pinpoint the type of question he posed, that is, a sort of possibility question. More specifically, his question concerned the possibility of a certain kind of *epistemic achievement*. One important way in which science can be relevant to epistemology is by shedding light on the possibility of epistemic achievements.

Many types of conditions, of course, may be required for certain epistemic achievements to be possible. Whether or not those conditions hold may have to be determined in different ways, perhaps by *conceptual analysis*, perhaps by *metaphysical* theorizing, perhaps by *cognitive science*. I do not suggest that every possibility question relevant to epistemology should be answered by science. I only propose that *some* possibility questions relevant to epistemology may be answered with the help of science.

Let us begin by looking at types of possibility questions whose answers do not (at least not obviously) appeal to science. Consider this question: Is it possible to know that p if you know that p entails q but you do not know that q? This is, in effect, a question about the concept of knowledge. Is it a feature of the knowledge concept that knowledge is "closed" under known entailment (Dretske 1970; Nozick 1981; DeRose 1995)? Closure is a threat to the possibility of knowledge for the following reason. Let p = "I have two hands." Let q = "I am not a bodiless (and handless) brain in a vat being stimulated so that I have the same experiences as I actually have (including the apparent possession of two hands)." Clearly, p entails q; and this entailment is something that I know. So if the closure principle is correct, then in order for me to know p, I must also know q. But how could I possibly know q? To know q I would have to exclude the possibility that I am a bodiless brain in a vat. But I cannot exclude that, since if I *were* one, I would have the very same experiences I actually have. Thus, it appears that I cannot know q, and by the closure principle, it would follow that I cannot know p. By similar reasoning, almost every ordinary proposition can be shown to be un-knowable. So the closure principle threatens the possibility of knowledge. How-ever, the truth of the closure principle appears to be a conceptual question rather than a scientific one. Determining the answer may not require the use of scientific methodology.[1]

Questions requiring metaphysical answers can be found both in the history of epistemology and on the current epistemological scene. Whether knowledge of physical things is possible seems to depend on the metaphysical composition, or status, of those things. So, at least, idealists like Berkeley argued. If trees are "material" things, Berkeley argued, there would be no way we could have knowl-edge of trees, because the mind could not have access to them. But if physical objects are mind-dependent objects, then they can be known. So the possibility of knowing the physical world depends on metaphysical questions, and since these metaphysical questions are not supposed to be answered by empirical science, this point does not show the relevance of science to epistemology. Analogously, to certify the possibility of having knowledge about the past, it may be crucial to determine the metaphysical status of the past (Peacocke 1999, chap. 3). But this again does not mean that scientific results must be consulted to determine the possibility of knowledge about the past.

Are there any conditions for epistemic achievement that need to be established by science? What might science tell us that would demonstrate (or support) the possibility or impossibility of certain epistemic achievements? In general, science may need to establish that human beings have certain cognitive capacities if we are to show that certain epistemic achievements are humanly possible. Of course, this just refers to human possibility. The psychological inability of humans to reach certain epistemic attainments would not preclude such attainments for other types of agents. In the main, however, epistemology is human epistemology. Most epistemological inquiry is driven by the prospects for human knowledge (ration-ality, warrant, truth, etc.). To the extent that human epistemic attainments criti-cally depend on human cognitive endowments, those endowments are relevant to epistemology. The nature and extent of those endowments are matters to be as-certained by psychological science, specifically, by psychology or cognitive science. Hence, cognitive science is relevant to certain epistemological questions.

I have spoken of epistemic "achievements" or "attainments." What kinds of attainments are in question? The attainments that typically interest epistemologists include the following: (1) true belief, (2) justified, or warranted, belief, (3) knowl-edge, (4) rational belief, and (5) special varieties of the foregoing, for example, a priori knowledge, testimony-based justification, and so forth. Exactly what is re-quired to qualify for these attainments is among the chief questions of episte-mology. Questions of human cognitive capacities are related to questions about these attainments in a way that is typified by the following scenario. An episte-mologist sets out to identify the standard that must be met for some epistemic attainment E. She tentatively identifies standard S as appropriate to E, and then turns to the scientists to get information about relevant human capacities. She is told by science—at least by certain scientists—that human cognitive capacities are inadequate to realize standard S. She then has at least three options. One option is a skeptical conclusion: epistemic attainment E is simply not feasible for human beings (or not feasible on a regular basis, perhaps). A second option is to revise her provisional account of the standard for E. Rejecting the threatened skeptical conclusion ("surely it *is* possible for humans to attain E!"), she concludes that S is not the correct standard for E. A third option is to question the initial scientific results. Scientists commonly differ among themselves on the questions within their field. Perhaps other scientists would dispute the claim that human cognitive capacities make S unrealizable by human beings. If this competing scientific story looks better, on reflection, the epistemologist might retain both S as the appropriate standard for E and the antiskeptical conclusion (E is humanly possible).[2] Any of these upshots would certainly be important to epistemology, but they depend upon what science has to offer. Thus, epistemology should proceed *in cooperation* with science.

In the discussion that follows, sections 2 and 3 provide examples that fit the foregoing mold. Examples in later sections fit different molds. For example, classical epistemology was heavily concerned with the *sources* of knowledge, where "sources" refers to the kinds of psychological faculties responsible for knowledge. Disputes about the sources of knowledge were at the root of the disagreement between rationalists and empiricists. Contemporary cognitive science directly addresses these kinds of questions, an extended example of which is presented in section 4. In the final part of the chapter, sections 5, 6, and 7, I turn to techniques and policies that might be pursued in various social and institutional contexts for maximizing knowledge or true belief in a community. This last part of the chapter, then, deals with social epistemology. Here too it is found that certain sciences—for example, economics and sociology—can contribute to epistemological projects.

2. RATIONALITY AND HUMAN REASONING POWERS

It is generally agreed that rationality, or rational belief, is a cardinal epistemic attainment. From an epistemic point of view, it is better to have rational beliefs than irrational (or nonrational) ones. So what does it take for a belief to be rational? What is the appropriate normative standard for the rationality of a belief? A common idea is that there are rules of rationality, and a belief is rational as long as it conforms to these rules, or does not violate any of them. Where do the supposed rules come from? The standard picture (Stein 1996, 4) is that the rules come from formal subject-matters such as (classical) logic and probability theory. Two candidate rules that draw on logic are the following: "One should not adopt a belief in any proposition p if one already has other beliefs which, if p were adopted, would form a logically inconsistent set." "If one believes two propositions of the form [p] and [if p then q], then one may adopt a belief in a further proposition of the form [q]." The latter rule is adapted from the logical rule of Modus Ponens. A candidate rule that draws on probability theory might be the following: "One should not assign a higher degree of probability to the occurrence of a conjunctive event (A and B) than one assigns to the occurrence of one of its conjuncts, e.g., A." For example, one should not assign a higher degree of probability to the conjunctive weather event, "Rain and a high temperature of 85° F today," than one assigns to the weather event, "Rain today."

Some of these rules are open to immediate epistemological criticism. Consider the rule against belief inconsistency. Is it really an appropriate standard of rational belief? Suppose you start with beliefs about some earlier meteorological conditions and beliefs in some meteorological laws, which together entail that it won't be cloudy this afternoon. In the afternoon you visually consult the sky and it looks cloudy. Should you believe that it is cloudy? Adopting the belief that it is cloudy would violate the rule of noninconsistency formulated above, but nonetheless it is rational for you to believe it. In this case, it is more appropriate to abandon one of your prior beliefs (say, in a meteorological law) than to desist from adding the new belief, although the new belief is inconsistent with other things you antecedently believe. Even if it isn't clear which previous belief(s) to abandon, it may still be rational to believe that it is cloudy. An analogous point applies to the belief rule associated with *Modus Ponens*. What these cases show is that it isn't so easy to derive plausible standards of rationality from formal logic. Setting aside this worry, let me work with the example of the conjunction rule of probability theory.

Is it humanly possible to conform to this rule? Two things might be meant by this. It might mean: Is it possible to conform to this rule from time to time, or occasionally? Or it might mean: Is it possible to conform to this rule in a systematic way, not merely fortuitously or by accident? These two interpretations provide distinct standards for the rationality of belief. A weak standard would say that a belief qualifies as rational as long as that individual belief does not conflict with the rule. A stronger standard would say that a belief qualifies as rational in case it results from a mechanism, faculty, process, or procedure that renders rule compliance a regular thing. In other words, a belief is rational if and only if it is produced by a rational mechanism. A mental mechanism is rational, we may propose, if it produces cognitive behavior that not only conforms to an isolated formal rule but conforms to a bundle of such rules. Let us provisionally adopt this strong standard. The crucial question, then, becomes: Do human beings have a rational mechanism, specifically, a mechanism for complying systematically with probabilistic rules?

Many psychologists answer this question in the negative. They endorse the *heuristics and biases* approach to probabilistic reasoning, founded by Amos Tversky and Daniel Kahneman. According to this approach, people do not have generally adequate mechanisms for probabilistic reasoning. Instead, when confronted with probabilistic tasks, they use a family of heuristics whose outputs "violate statistical rules of prediction in systematic and fundamental ways" (Kahneman and Tversky 1973, 48). The chief example of such a heuristic is the *representativeness heuristic*. The representativeness heuristic is the tendency to judge the probability that an object x belongs to category C by the degree to which x is representative of, or similar to, typical members of category C. This heuristic can be illustrated with experimental material that Tversky and Kahneman (1983) used to demonstrate violation of the conjunction rule. They gave subjects the following problem:

> Linda is 31 years old, single, outspoken, and very bright. She majored in philosophy. As a student, she was deeply concerned with issues of discrimination and social justice and also participated in antinuclear demonstrations.
>
> Please rank the following statements by their probability, using 1 for the most probable and 8 for the least probable.
>
> a. Linda is a teacher in elementary school.
> b. Linda works in a bookstore and takes yoga classes.
> c. Linda is active in the feminist movement.
> d. Linda is a psychiatric social worker.
> e. Linda is a member of the League of Women Voters.
> f. Linda is a bank teller.
> g. Linda is an insurance salesperson.
> h. Linda is a bank teller and is active in the feminist movement. (1983, 296)

Almost 90 percent of the subjects ranked (h) as more probable than (f). Notice that (h) is a conjunction and (f) is one of its conjuncts. So ranking (h) as more probable than (f) violates the conjunction rule of probability theory. The example illustrates the representativeness heuristic because subjects seem to be judging the probability that Linda belongs to each category in terms of Linda's similarity to that category (given the thumbnail description of her). Because Linda is not very similar to a typical bank teller, the probability of her being a bank teller is judged to be low. Because Linda is more similar to a typical member of the category of feminist bank tellers, the probability of her being a feminist bank teller is judged to be higher. Thus, the representativeness heuristic seems to lie behind people's intuitive judgments (in this type of case), but it does not conform (systematically) to probability rules.

The power of the representativeness heuristic is further illustrated by a study devised to see if subjects would recognize the validity of the conjunction rule even if they did not apply it spontaneously. They were presented with two arguments, one appealing to the basis for the conjunction rule and one appealing to the representativeness, or resemblance, heuristic. They were asked which one they found more convincing:

> Argument 1. Linda is more likely to be a bank teller than she is to be a feminist bank teller, because every feminist bank teller is a bank teller, but some women bank tellers are not feminists, and Linda could be one of them.

> Argument 2. Linda is more likely to be a feminist bank teller than she is likely to be a bank teller, because she resembles an active feminist more than she resembles a bank teller. (1983, 299)

Sixty-five percent of the subjects chose the resemblance argument over the conjunction rule argument, demonstrating the appeal of the latter.

Further evidence of the intensive use of the representativeness heuristic—and the failure to use "correct" probabilistic considerations—comes from experiments with slightly different materials. Subjects were told that personality tests had been administered to a group of 100 engineers and lawyers. Half were told that there had been 30 engineers and 70 lawyers, the other half that there had been 70 engineers and 30 lawyers. Thumbnail descriptions of these professionals had been written, and subjects were told that they were being given one of those descriptions, allegedly chosen at random. They were then asked to indicate the probability that the person described was an engineer. A correct use of probability theory, Kahneman and Tversky argued, would utilize the "base-rate" information given in the foregoing "cover story," namely, that there had been 30 engineers and 70 lawyers, or 70 engineers and 30 lawyers. Here, now, is one of the descriptions provided, which is neutral or uninformative:

> Dick is a 30-year-old man. He is married with no children. A man of high ability and high motivation, he promises to be quite successful in his field. He is well liked by his colleagues. (1973, 242)

Both groups of subjects judged the probability that Dick is an engineer about the same, around 50 percent. Apparently, they ignored the base-rate information and only used the degree of "fit," or resemblance, between Dick and the typical engineer, where in this case that fit was negligible or inconclusive. When a profile was such as to suggest the characteristics of, say, an engineer, both groups had a marked tendency to classify it in the category of engineers, regardless of the base rate explicitly given to them. This seems to show, once again, that subjects ignore considerations that are crucial according to probability theory and instead employ considerations that can clash with probability theory. Elsewhere Tversky and Kahneman (1982) describe other judgmental heuristics with similar properties.

Based on this program of empirical research, proponents of the heuristics and biases approach often draw very pessimistic conclusions about human rationality. Some writers speak of "bleak implications" for the rationality of ordinary people (Nisbett and Borgida 1975). Others maintain that the human mind is prone to "systematic deviations from rationality" (Bazerman and Neale 1986) and is "not built to work by the rules of probability" (Gould 1992). One writer suggests that human beings are "a species that is uniformly probability-blind" (Piattelli-Palmarini 1994). Using the terms of epistemology, it might be concluded that these empirical results point to "skeptical" conclusions concerning ordinary people's capacities for probabilistic reasoning, at least in terms of their spontaneous intuitions.

Furthermore, the problems are not confined to ordinary people. Even when probability problems are presented to highly educated and well-trained personnel, they often make serious errors. For example, Casscells et al. (1978) presented the following problem to a group of faculty, staff, and fourth-year students at Harvard Medical School.

> If a test to detect disease whose prevalence is 1/1,000 has a false positive rate of
> 5%, what is the chance that a person found to have a positive result actually
> has the disease, assuming that you know nothing about the person's symptoms
> or signs?

Under the most plausible interpretation of the problem, the correct (Bayesian) answer is 2 percent. But only 18 percent of the Harvard personnel gave an answer close to 2 percent. Forty-five percent of this highly trained elite completely ignored the base-rate information and said that the answer was 95 percent.

At this juncture, the prospects of a human capacity for correct probabilistic reasoning (at least a natural capacity, or mechanism) indeed look bleak. At least that is so if one accepts the interpretations of the heuristics and biases program. However, another group of reasoning researchers present a much more optimistic picture. This group, led by Gerd Gigerenzer, Leda Cosmides, and John Tooby, hold that evolution has provided human brains with a large number of functionally dedicated computers (often called "modules") designed to solve adaptive problems endemic to our hunter-gatherer ancestors. Among these modules are mechanisms devoted to inductive reasoning, which also handle *frequency* information. "[S]ome of our inductive reasoning mechanisms do embody aspects of a calculus of probability, but they are designed to take frequency information as input and produce frequencies as output" (Cosmides and Tooby 1996, 3).

This hypothesis led Cosmides and Tooby to do experiments in which the medical diagnosis task used by Cascells et al. was transformed into a problem in which both the input and the response required were formulated in terms of frequencies. Here is an example from their study in which frequency information is salient:

> 1 out of every 1000 Americans has disease X. A test has been developed to detect when a person has disease X. Every time the test is given to a person who has the disease, the test comes out positive. But sometimes the test also comes out positive when it is given to a person who is completely healthy. Specifically, out of every 1000 people who are perfectly healthy, 50 of them test positive for the disease.
>
>   Imagine that we have assembled a random sample of 1000 Americans. They were selected by lottery. Those who conducted the lottery had no information about the health status of any of these people. Given the information above, on average, how many people who test positive for the disease will *actually* have the disease?
>   ——out of——(1996, 24)

In sharp contrast to the original experiment in which only 18 percent of subjects gave the correct response, the formulation above yielded correct answers from 76 percent of the subjects. Similar results are reported by Gigerenzer (1991, 1996; see also Gigerenzer and Hoffrage 1995; Fiedler 1988), who also stresses that frequentist versions of probabilistic reasoning problems elicit high levels of performance. Actually, Tversky and Kahneman (1983) themselves were the first to note this phenomenon in their study of the conjunction problem. When problems were formulated in a frequency format, subjects did a lot better. Tversky and Kahneman speculated that a frequency formulation may lend itself to a spatial representation, in terms of tokens or areas, which makes the relation of set inclusion—important for understanding probabilistic relationships—more salient. However, they did not interpret this fact as conducive to a more optimistic view of human capabilities for probabilistic reasoning.

Cosmides, Tooby, and Gigerenzer are considered "evolutionary psychologists." They differ from the proponents of the heuristics and biases approach not only in the empirical findings that they emphasize but also in their conception of the appropriate *standard* of rationality.[3] At least this is so in the case of Gigerenzer and his collaborators. Gigerenzer and Goldstein (1996) (also see Gigerenzer 1993; Gigerenzer et al. 1999) follow Herbert Simon in propounding a "satisficing" approach to rationality, a conception that Simon (1982) referred to as *bounded rationality*. This conception emphasizes the fact that organisms must deal with limited time, limited knowledge, and limited computational capacities. The test of a good inference mechanism, for Gigerenzer and Goldstein, is that it often draws accurate conclusions about real-world environments, and does so quickly and with little computational effort. In short, the proposed normative standard for reasoning is to be "reliable, fast, and inexpensive (frugal)." Gigerenzer and collaborators have shown—in some cases quite surprisingly—how certain fast and frugal algorithms can get correct answers at least as often as computationally more expensive competitors (such as statistical linear models). For them, this is enough to qualify such methods as normatively desirable, in other words, "rational" (although Gigerenzer and collaborators typically reserve the term "rational" for rule-based standards). Thus, we have a new proposal for a standard of rationality; and many of the methods or heuristics that fail the formal-rules criterion of rationality will pass the "reliable, fast, and frugal" criterion (Gigerenzer, Hoffrage, and Kleinbolting 1991).

It is clear, then, how empirical psychology can contribute to the question of whether—or to what extent—human cognitive capacities are able to achieve rationality. It is by no means a straightforward matter, to be sure, partly because the appropriate standards or criterion of rationality are themselves up for grabs. But even here the perspectives of empirical psychology can suggest some answers, so philosophers do not have to proceed on their own in tackling this question but can join hands with psychologists in reflecting on an appropriate criterion.

3. UNDERDETERMINATION, JUSTIFIEDNESS, AND LANGUAGE ACQUISITION

In epistemology and philosophy of science, it is often maintained as a principle of justifiedness that a person is not justified in believing some hypothesis h if there is any alternative hypothesis h' that is equally compatible with the person's evidence. However, this standard of justifiedness threatens skeptical consequences: many fewer beliefs will prove to be justified than is commonly supposed. This was the scenario that worried Descartes when he contemplated his evil demon hypothesis. How could his ordinary beliefs about the physical world be justified when there is an alternative hypothesis—viz., that an evil demon is deceiving him about the physical world—that is fully compatible with all of his perceptual evidence? An example from science concerns fitting curves to data points. Scientists tend to prefer hypotheses that represent smooth curves, but why are they justified in believing smooth-curve hypotheses rather than alternative, bumpy-curve hypotheses? Another well-known example is Nelson Goodman's (1955) "grue" paradox. Let "grue" be a predicate that applies to things that are examined up until a specified time t and are green, as well as to things that are not so examined and are blue. Now suppose that a sample of emeralds is examined before time t and all are found to be green. It is natural to assume that we are justified in believing that the next emerald to be examined (after t) will also be green. However, Goodman pointed out, it is also true that all emeralds examined through time t were grue. So why not accept the alternative hypothesis that the next emerald will be grue, which implies (since it was not examined before t) that it will be blue? Are we justified in inferring that the next emerald will be green rather than grue? The induction for green seems to be underdetermined by the evidence.

A tempting approach to all of these problems is to appeal to simplicity. In each of these cases the justified hypothesis seems to be a simpler hypothesis, whereas the alternative hypothesis seems more complex, gimmicky, exotic, or baroque. For example, the hypothesis that an evil demon is deliberately trying to deceive one about a physical world seems strange, exotic, and needlessly complex as compared with a straightforward physical-world hypothesis. Goodman's "grue" predicate seems gimmicky and unappealingly baroque. So as long as simplicity can be used in determining the justifiedness of a belief, it appears that the foregoing skeptical threats can be met. However, I shall now suggest that the science of linguistics, or psycholinguistics, calls attention to cases of evidential underdetermination that cannot be resolved by appeal to simplicity. Thus, science poses new skeptical threats, even if, in the case in question, the skepticism is more local than global.

In the process of learning a language, a child is confronted (quite unbeknownst to her) with an underdetermination problem. There are alternative hypotheses about the language she encounters that are equally compatible with her linguistic data but which she never considers. The child's neglect of the alternative hypotheses enables her to learn the language with little apparent difficulty. But is the child's—and later the adult's—body of beliefs about her language actually *justified*? If we accept the principle of "no evidential underdetermination" (i.e., evidentially underdetermined beliefs are not justified), and if we accept the dominant scientific account of the available evidence, then these linguistic beliefs are not justified. Moreover, it seems impossible for them to be justified, given the presumed principle or standard of justification. Furthermore, this skeptical threat cannot be resolved by an appeal to simplicity, because the beliefs ordinarily formed are often *less* simple than alternative hypotheses.

The background behind the present threat is Noam Chomsky's (1965) *poverty of the stimulus argument.* Chomsky argued that the "primary linguistic data" available to the language-learning child are simply too thin or impoverished to allow the learner to choose the correct hypothesis about the grammar of its language. There are too many other hypotheses that the data leave open. Nonetheless, the child does acquire that grammar. Hence, the child's mind must have some sort of innately specified assumptions about what possible grammars there might be (in any of the human languages to which a child might be exposed). In other words, the mind must place some "constraints" on the grammar, and these constraints must be used to exclude some grammatical hypotheses that are abstractly possible. Only this can explain how actual language acquisition takes place.

In the principles and parameters approach that Chomsky advocated in the 1980s (e.g., Chomsky 1986), it was assumed that certain principles and parameters constitute a universal grammar; they specify the grammatical properties that hold across all human languages.[4] In virtue of these principles, the child is instinctively directed away from hypotheses that are logically compatible with the corpus of available data but do not in fact systematically describe any humanly possible language. These innate assumptions or constraints, however, do not seem to be justified for the child. The proposition that human languages fall into certain categories rather than others is not something for which the child has any *evidence*. Hence, if the only evidence for the grammar of the particular language to which the child is exposed is the child's primary linguistic data, there are alternative hypotheses compatible with these data than the one the child accepts. Hence, according to the no-evidential-underdetermination principle, the child's choice of grammar is not justified. Consequently, virtually all of the grammatical parsings that the child (and the adult) subsequently selects for the particular sentences she encounters will also be unjustified—an epistemological disaster! Moreover, this problem cannot be solved by appeal to simplicity, because the child's (and the adult's) judgments of grammaticality or linguistic correctness are based on (tacit) principles that are *less* simple than others that are theoretically possible.

An example will be useful here, taken from Chomsky (1980, 39ff). In language acquisition, one learns to associate questions with declaratives. Corresponding to the English declarative sentence "The man is here" is the interrogative sentence "Is the man here?" Corresponding to "The man who is here is tall" is the question "Is the man who is here tall?" There is an infinite class of such pairs. Since novel cases are continually encountered, both in comprehending and producing speech, the learner must form and accept a general hypothesis about how to construct interrogatives from declaratives. Here are two hypotheses for how this should go:

H_1: process the declarative from beginning to end (left to right), word by word, until reaching the first occurrence of the words *is*, *will*, etc.; transpose this occurrence to the beginning (left), forming the associated interrogative.

H_2: same as H_1, but select the first occurrence of *is*, *will*, etc., following the first noun phrase of the declarative.

H_2 is a *structure-dependent* rule, because it requires an analysis not only into a sequence of words but also abstract phrases such as "noun phrase", which specify certain abstract structures. H_1, by contrast, is a *structure-independent* rule, because it only requires an analysis into a sequence of words. If a person adopted H_1, she would regard "Is the man who here is tall?" as the interrogative that corresponds to the declarative "The man who is here is tall." If she adopted H_2, she would regard "Is the man who is here tall?" as the interrogative that corresponds to this declarative. Obviously, learners in fact adopt H_2 rather than H_1. But since H_1 seems clearly to be *simpler* than H_2, the learner chooses the less simple hypothesis rather than the simpler one.

Chomsky proceeds to argue that the child, in making this choice, does not have empirical data, or evidence, that favors H_2 over H_1.

> Now the question that arises is this: how does a child know that H_2 is correct (nearly), while H_1 is false? It is surely not the case that he first hits on H_1 (as a neutral scientist would) and then is forced to reject it on the basis of data such as [the observed correspondence of "The man who is here is tall" and "Is the man who is here tall?"]. No child is taught the relevant facts. Children make many errors in language learning, but none such as ["Is the man who here is tall?"], prior to appropriate training or evidence. A person might go through much or all of his life without ever having been exposed to relevant evidence, but he will nevertheless unerringly employ H_2, never H_1, on the first relevant occasion (assuming that he can handle the structures at all). (1980, 40)

Although this is not uncontroversial, let us assume that Chomsky is right about this. Then the language learner does not have evidence that favors H_2 over H_1; nor is H_2 simpler than H_1. So it looks as if the ordinary speaker of English cannot be *justified* in believing that H_2 is the correct principle for interrogative formation in English. This in itself may not be so problematic, because it is not so clear that the ordinary speaker *believes* this; certainly she does not believe it explicitly. But ordinary English speakers do have an indefinitely large set of beliefs about *particular* candidate interrogatives. They believe that "Is the man who is here tall?" is the correct interrogative corresponding to "The man who is here is tall." And, if queried, they would believe that "Is the man who here is tall?" is *not* a correct interrogative. How are these beliefs by ordinary English speakers justified? If they are not so justified, that will be an epistemological debacle, especially when these examples are conjoined with many other linguistic examples. A very large class of beliefs that are ordinarily presumed to be justified will turn out not to be justified.

To avoid this threat of (local) skepticism, the epistemologist needs to identify a standard of justifiedness to handle this class of cases. It must allow beliefs to be justified even when there is evidential underdetermination, and it cannot appeal straightforwardly to some generic property of simplicity. How is this to be done? Perhaps the innateness of the constraints of universal grammar can somehow play a role in conferring justifiedness. But exactly what standard of justifiedness can do this properly, without creating new problems in other domains? This is something to which epistemologists have given very little attention. If nativist approaches to cognitive science are right, however, an enormous chunk of everyday cognition is guided by innate constraints. To save a vast quantity of everyday belief from justificational oblivion, some standard of justifiedness that appropriately accommodates innate constraints must be articulated.

4. NATIVISM AND NUMERICAL KNOWLEDGE

As I argued in section 1, historical epistemologists were heavily preoccupied with the "sources" of knowledge. By "sources" they meant the mental faculties, contents, principles, or operations that conferred, or paved the way to, knowledge. The liveliest historical debate of this sort—a debate that is still with us—is the seventeenth- and eighteenth-century debate between empiricism and rationalism, or nativism. It is not easy to disentangle rationalism and nativism. On the surface, rationalism is a thesis about the existence and importance of a priori knowledge, whereas nativism is a thesis about the *innateness* of certain faculties or ideas. Are these entirely distinct theses, or are they connected? Consider the following passage from the *Encyclopedia of Philosophy*: "The theory of innate ideas, in any of its philosophically significant forms, claims that all morally right judgment or all science, or both, rest upon or consist in a knowledge *a priori* either of (a) universal principles governing reality or (b) objects transcending sensory experience" (Nelson 1967, 166). As Fiona Cowie (1999, 8) points out, this passage draws a very intimate tie between the innate and the a priori. To me the odd feature of the passage is that it makes innateness depend upon a priori knowledge, whereas I am inclined to think that, if there is an intimate tie, it is because a priori knowledge invokes innateness (Goldman 1999a). Cowey's complaint, however, is that there is a failure to distinguish a thesis about the psychological origins of a belief from a thesis about the justification of a belief.

> The problem is that while a nativist hypothesis is, at least prima facie, a reasonable sort of response to the psychological question, "Where do beliefs arrived at a priori come from?" it is not a reasonable sort of answer to the epistemological question, "What *justifies* those a priori beliefs?" Why should the mere fact of my belief's being innate, or of its following from certain innate 'principles,' serve to justify it? (1999, 8)

On Cowie's view, nativism can provide no help to epistemology. This position may be defensible if one assumes that epistemology's sole question concerns justification, and if one assumes that the causal sources of a belief have no bearing on justifiedness.

Epistemologists need not accept these claims, however. Here are four alternative views on the role innateness might play within epistemology.

(1) One might hold that a belief's justificational status is partly a matter of its psychological origins, or sustaining factors (Goldman 1979). Depending on the specific theory of justifiedness, innateness might help satisfy the conditions of justifiedness—though not by being a premise in an argument that the believer uses.

(2) One might hold that epistemology is concerned with knowledge (in the strong sense) in addition to justifiedness, but one might deny that knowledge requires justifiedness. In place of a justification condition, one might propose, for example, that knowledge is true belief acquired (or sustained) by a reliable causal process (Goldman 1986, chap. 3), and the identification of an innate faculty with pertinent properties could explain what that reliable process is.

(3) Even if one doesn't appeal to knowledge in the strong sense, one might say that epistemology is concerned with knowledge in the weak sense of true belief. Focusing on knowledge as true belief, epistemology might want to answer the explanatory question: "How is it possible for humans to acquire true beliefs in domain D (assuming that their beliefs in D are largely true)?" A possible answer might be: "Because they have an innate faculty F with such-and-such properties." This kind of answer would not necessarily provide a (noncircular) *validation* of the claim that the beliefs in domain D *are* true, but it could rebut challenges from skeptics who claim that there is no way that such beliefs *could* systematically be true.

(4) One might hold that *part* of epistemology is directly concerned with the psychological origins of belief. This does not go as far as Quine's view that epistemology as a whole coincides with part of psychology, because it leaves room for other branches of epistemology to concern themselves with justification, rationality, and knowledge. It would, however, make nativist hypotheses fall squarely within one (purely psychological) branch of epistemology.

Let us agree, then, that the question of innateness can legitimately be placed on epistemology's agenda. The question now arises: What kinds of innate factors should be of interest to epistemologists, and what kinds of factors were of interest to historical epistemologists, for example, rationalists and empiricists? When one looks closely at the historical debate, it is hard to find clear differences among the supposed "opponents" on the question of innateness. The empiricist Locke made free appeal to various innate mental faculties, including "natural powers" for forming ideas of sense and reflection, and an inborn capacity for performing "operations of Reason" such as comparison, compounding, and abstraction (Cowie 1999, 20). Cowie proposes that the difference between empiricists and nativists (or rationalists) is that the innate faculties that empiricists posited were very *general*, for example, combinatorial faculties that operate over all ideas or concepts, whereas nativists posited special-purpose, content-specific, mechanisms. Whether or not historical nativists were focused on content-specific faculties,[5] it is clear that contemporary nativism is heavily concerned with domain specificity.

Perhaps the distinctive feature of modern nativism is precisely its postulation of domain-specific faculties, each dedicated to the processing of information about a relatively narrow domain (Fodor 1983; Hirschfeld and Gelman 1994; Cosmides and Tooby, in press). At this juncture, the debate between nativism and empiricism is definitely a debate within cognitive science. The nativist approach to cognitive architecture is supported by Chomsky, Fodor, and their followers, while an empiricist, or associationist, approach to cognitive architecture is supported by connectionists such as Rumelhart, McClelland, and Elman (Rumelhart et al. 1986; McClelland et al. 1986; Elman et al. 1996).

Let us explore an example of nativism in some detail, concerning a domain of central importance to epistemology: the knowledge of number. Cognitive scientists have assembled a very powerful case for an innate, dedicated mechanism in the domain of number. Before turning to this nativist work, however, let us briefly examine a contrasting, empiricist approach.

Somewhat like the empiricist John Stuart Mill (1970), Philip Kitcher (1983) holds that children learn simple arithmetic concepts and simple numerical facts by perceiving the results of certain activities:

> Children come to learn the meanings of 'set,' 'number,' 'addition' and to accept basic truths of arithmetic by engaging in *activities* of collecting and segregating. . . . By having [these sorts of] experiences . . . [they] learn that particular types of collective operations have particular properties: . . . for example, that if one performs the collective operation called 'making two,' then performs on different objects the collective operation called 'making three,' then performs the collective operation of combining, the total operation is an operation of 'making five.' (1983, 108)

As Kitcher tells the story, what accounts for basic understanding of arithmetic is general-purpose intelligence applied to observations of real-world activities.[6] There is no hint here of an innate, special-purpose, mental mechanism devoted to a grasp of numerical concepts or numerical facts. However, compelling psychological evidence for precisely such a mechanism is now available.

The nativist theory has been defended in a most comprehensive fashion by Stanislas Dehaene (1997, 2001), and I shall follow his presentation. Other researchers in the field may disagree with selected details, but these do not matter for present purposes. The basic claim is that the foundations of numerical cognition reside in the ability to mentally represent and manipulate numerosities (approximate cardinalities) on a mental "number line," an analogical representation of number; and this representation has a long evolutionary history and a specific neural substrate. Dehaene presents four lines of evidence for this claim: (1) there are evolutionary precursors of arithmetic in animals; (2) arithmetic competence emerges early in infants independently of other abilities, including language; (3) there is a homology between the animal and human abilities for number processing; and (4) there is a dedicated cerebral substrate, as inferred from studies of brain-lesioned patients with acquired impairments in number sense and from brain-imaging studies of calculation in normal subjects.

The evolutionary advantages of being able to detect the numerosity of collections of physical objects are obvious, so it has been proposed that evolutionary pressures must have led to the internalization of numerical representations in the brain of various animal species (Gallistel 1990). The empirical literature contains considerable evidence that animals possess the ability to discriminate numerosity and that they have elementary arithmetic abilities (Boysen and Capaldi 1993; Gallistel 1990; Gallistel and Gelman 1992). Species such as rats, pigeons, raccoons, dolphins, parrots, monkeys, and chimpanzees discriminate the numerosity of sets, including visually presented objects and sound sequences. These conclusions are based on experiments that included controls for nonnumerical variables such as spacing, size, tempo, and duration of the stimuli. At least some of these experiments required little or no training of the animals, suggesting that the numerical representation is present in naïve animals. Monkeys in the wild have the ability to compute $1 + 1$ and $2 - 1$. Animals are not limited to processing small numbers only, however. Pigeons can be trained to reliably discriminate 45 pecks from 50.

Studies have established numerical abilities in preverbal human infants. Discrimination of visual numerosity was first demonstrated in six to seven month-old infants using the technique of habituation-recovery of looking time (Starkey and Cooper 1980). Infants watched as slides with a fixed number of dots, say two, were repeatedly presented until their looking time decreased, indicating habituation. At that point, presentation of slides with a novel number of dots, say three, yielded longer looking times, indicating dishabituation and therefore discrimination of two versus three. Infants' numerosity discrimination abilities are not limited to visually detected stimuli. Newborns have been shown to discriminate two- and three-syllable words with controlled phonemic content, duration, and speech rate. Like many animal species, human infants have also been shown to perform addition and subtraction with small numerosities (Wynn 1992). These experiments indicate that infants encode scenes using a representation of the number of objects in the scene, irrespective of their exact identity or location.

To demonstrate that human arithmetic abilities have a biological basis with a long evolutionary history, it is not sufficient to demonstrate that animals and preverbal infants both have rudimentary number-processing abilities. To show phylogenetic continuity, one needs to show homologies between the animal and human abilities. Strikingly, two shared characteristics of number processing have been identified in both humans and animals: the distance effect and the size effect. The distance effect is a systematic decrease in discrimination performance as the numerical distance between the numbers decreases. Closer numbers are harder to discriminate. The size effect indicates that for equal numerical distance, performance decreases with increasing number size. It is harder to discriminate 23 and

25 than 4 and 6. The distance and size effects indicate that animals and infants seem to possess only a fuzzy representation of numbers, in which imprecision grows proportionally to the number being represented. So only very small numbers (up to about 3) can be represented accurately. These phenomena are not introspectively obvious, because we can make symbolic calculations with arbitrary accuracy. Nonetheless, studies show that when comparing Arabic digits, it is faster and easier to decide that 8 is larger than 4 than to decide that 8 is larger than 7. Even in highly trained adults, adding, multiplying, or comparing two large digits such as 8 and 9 is slower and more error-prone than performing the same operations with digits 2 and 3.

The distance and size effects suggest two conclusions. First, animals, young infants, and adult humans possess an analogical representation of numerical quantity, organized by numerical proximity and with increasing fuzziness for larger and larger numbers. Second, when presented with number words or Arabic numerals, the human brain converts these numbers internally from their symbolic format into the analogical quantity representation. This biologically determined analogical quantity representation is called "the number line."[7]

The final piece of evidence for a biological mechanism of numerical cognition is a dedicated neural substrate. A specific cerebral circuit associated with the representation and acquisition of belief about numerical quantities and relations appears to be in the intraparietal cortex of both left and right hemispheres. Lesions of the inferior parietal region of the dominant hemisphere can cause number processing impairments (Gerstmann 1940). In some cases, comprehending, producing, and calculating with numbers is globally impaired. In other cases, the deficit is selective for calculation, but allows the reading, writing, and spoken recognition and production of Arabic digits and numerals. Brain-imaging studies provide independent support for this crucial cerebral site. Several additional findings indicate that this region is specifically to the "number line." For example, the inferior parietal region is unaffected by the notation used for the numbers, suggesting that it is the site of an abstract, notation-independent level of processing (Dehaene 1996). An additional relevant fact is that the association of arithmetic with the intraparietal region is independent of culture. If arithmetic were just a cultural activity without a strong foundation in brain architecture, variation would be expected as a function of learning, education, and culture. Yet reports from research groups in many countries indicate that, in most if not all cultures, lesions causing Gerstmann-type acalculia systematically fall in the inferior parietal region.

Dehaene does not postulate that only one brain area contributes to the cerebral processing of numbers. Rather, a triple-code model of number processing is hypothesized. Numerical information can be manipulated mentally in three formats: an analogical representation of quantities involving the mental number line; a verbal format, in which numbers are represented as strings of words (e.g., 'thirty-seven'); and a visual Arabic representation, in which numbers are represented as a string of digits (e.g., '37'). Exact calculation is typically linked to a natural language code rather than the analogical number line. This is because number facts, especially multiplication tables learned by rote, are usually stored in a natural language format. Exposure to language, culture, and mathematical education leads to domains of competence such as a lexicon of number words, digits for written notation, procedures for multi-digit calculation, and so on. But these abilities need to be coordinated with the innate internal number line, and this makes the cultural acquisition of formal arithmetic a nontrivial matter.

Taken together, this is a powerful scientific case for the existence of an innate mechanism of numerical cognition. Whichever epistemological application one contemplates, among the four floated earlier in this section, the existence of such a mechanism ought to constrain epistemological theorizing. It might be wondered what the implications of this mechanism are for the ontology of number, another prominent question within the philosophy of mathematics. In the last chapter of his book *The Number Sense*, Dehaene does draw conclusions about the nature of number. These conclusions, however, are rather controversial and should be carefully separated from the psychological thesis presented in the rest of his book. All that I have argued is that the psychology should constrain the epistemology of number. How it bears on the ontological question is another matter, which cannot be treated here. I believe that the epistemological issues can be pursued while preserving a good bit of neutrality on the ontological ones (Goldman 1999a).

5. PSYCHOLOGY AND THE LAW OF EVIDENCE

In the last three sections of this chapter, I shall discuss the role of the sciences in *social epistemology*. My conception of social epistemology, presented in *Knowledge in a Social World* (Goldman 1999b), is a truth-based conception. The aim of social epistemology is to determine the impact that various social and institutional practices might have on the knowledge of relevant truths by actors in a group or community. This section looks at an example from the law of evidence. A primary aim of rules of evidence is to guide the conduct of judicial proceedings so as to maximize the percentage of accurate judgments made by triers of fact (for present purposes, juries).[8] One mechanism used by the law of evidence is to exclude certain pieces of evidence—potentially misleading or prejudicial evidence—that might be presented to fact-finders. It is often controversial, however, whether such exclusions really do promote accuracy. This is where science might prove helpful. A case in point concerns the exclusion of character evidence.

The rules in American law concerning the admissibility of character evidence are quite complex. The basic rule is that evidence of a defendant's character or trait of character is not admissible for the purpose of proving that he acted in conformity with that trait (Federal Rules of Evidence, rule 404a). In addition, evidence of other crimes is not admissible to prove the character of a defendant in order to show action in conformity with that trait (Federal Rules of Evidence, rule 404b). However, evidence of other crimes, wrongs, or acts is admissible to prove other things, for example, habit, motive, opportunity, intent, preparation, plan, or knowledge in connection with the crime(s) with which the defendant is charged. Another rule permits evidence of character in order to impeach a witness, and exceptions have been introduced for sex crime cases. In the present context, the discussion will focus on reasons for excluding character and other-crimes evidence in the basic cases, without further attention to exceptions.

The primary rationale for excluding these categories of evidence is to prevent mistakes and misuse by the trier of fact. First, there is a worry that jurors will overvalue, or overestimate, the probative force of character evidence, or other-crimes evidence, in determining whether the defendant committed the crime for which he is charged. Second, there is a worry that jurors will decide to punish the defendant for acts other than those with which he is currently charged. In everyday life, of course, most of us use character evidence with some frequency. Laypersons generally believe that there are personality differences between those who commit outrageous crimes and other people. But the exclusion rules reflect skepticism on the part of the rule makers that ordinary citizens are able to make sound inferences of this sort.

An epistemological approach to evidence law may be viewed as a special case of social epistemology. It asks how each rule of evidence, or group of rules, is likely to fare from a truth-promoting vantage-point (Goldman 1999b, chap. 9). Could the system of evidence rules be improved by deleting a given rule, by amending it, or by replacing it with something quite different? This is the question I place on the table in connection with the rule of character and other-crimes evidence. The next question is what contribution science might make in assessing the probable truth consequences of retaining, deleting, or revising a given rule. In the area of character evidence, legal scholars have heavily invoked scientific research in debate over these rules.

A number of legal scholars have affirmed the basic rule for excluding character evidence roughly on the ground that character is "bunk." That is to say, one cannot make reliable inferences based on attributions of cross-situational propensities. This position is allegedly supported by a large literature in social and personality psychology that takes issue with the lay assumption that stable, long-term behavioral dispositions can explain and/or predict conduct. A prominent view in this area of psychology is *situationalism*, which holds that people's actions are situation-specific, rather than reflecting stable dispositions constitutive of character (Milgram 1963; Mischel 1968; Darley and Batson 1973; Ross and Nisbett 1991). Situationalism is understood to run strongly counter to "common sense" about behavior. Lee Ross and Richard Nisbett write:

> [P]eople are inveterate dispositionalists. They account for past actions and out-comes, and make predictions about future actions and outcomes, in terms of the person—or more specifically, in terms of presumed personality traits or other distinctive and enduring personal dispositions. (1991, 90)

In fact, write Ross and Nisbett, "standard correlation coefficients determined in well-controlled research settings" show that "personality traits" lack substantial "explanatory and predictive power" (1991, 91). If this is right, then the danger in legal settings seems to be serious. If jurors were given evidence of character traits, they would be likely to make strong inferences from such traits to the conduct under litigation; but since situationalism teaches that character traits have little predictive or retrodictive power, these inferences are likely to be mistaken.

Recently, however, some theorists of legal evidence (Park 1998; Davies 1991) have marshaled scientific evidence against situationalism and argued that none of the psychological research debunking the evidential value of personality traits has been done on behavior pertinent to crime, especially violent crime. Roger Park (1998) begins by pointing out that one of the personality theorists most cited by legal scholars on behalf of situationalism was misinterpreted and misunderstood. Walter Mischel's book *Personality and Assessment* (1968) was frequently viewed as a broadside attack on personality itself, as an effort to replace dispositions as units of study with situations and environments. But Mischel (1984, 279) later wrote that his earlier work had only been a reaction to the practice of clinical psychologists who make strong decisions about a person's life and future based on a limited sampling of personality "signs" and "trait indicators." Mischel went on to say that he did not mean to deny that different people act differently with some consistency in different classes of situations.

Park goes on to argue that criminal violence, in particular, might be a more consistent and stable type of behavior than the kinds of traits studied by social or personality psychologists. Indeed, even studies in social psychology suggest that "aggression" has a high degree of consistency and stability. This is certainly a conclusion endorsed by criminologists. Based on extensive research, Michael Gottfredson and Travis Hirschi write: "What is not arguable is that aggressive behavior, however engendered, once established, remains remarkably stable across time, situation, and even generations within a family" (1990, 50). More generally, Park reports, scientific scholarship about crime supports the view that there are individual differences between repeat offenders and the rest of the population. Recidivism data show that someone convicted and imprisoned for a criminal offense is many times more likely to commit a similar offense than a person chosen at random. He cautions that one must distinguish between using past acts for predictive purposes and using them for retrodicti⁄e purposes. If a certain type of conduct has a very low base rate in the population, predicting that someone who did it before will do it again will often be wrong. Nobody engages in it very often. But if it is known that such an act has been performed on a particular occasion, evidence that a given person (e.g., a spouse) had performed that same act previously can be relevant to the new case.

Park also emphasizes that criminal violence is not treated in the standard controlled experiments of social psychologists. The latter typically deal with constructs like extroversion, honesty, or dependency. Milgram's well-known (1963) study that is often cited as demonstrating the power of situational factors was really a study of obedience, not of violent behavior. Park warns against the temptation to make extrapolations from *ordinary* behavior to *extreme* behavior like murder (1998, 737–738).

Whichever position is right in this dispute (and the "right" position must surely be a highly nuanced one), it is agreed that the scientific truth is highly relevant to the crafting of optimal rules for the admission or exclusion of character or other-acts evidence. Insofar as the choice of such rules can be viewed as a subject for (applied) social epistemology, the science of cross-situational propensities is crucial to this branch of social epistemology.

6. Economic Theory, Knowledge, and the Market for Speech

Continuing the exploration of social epistemology, let us consider a sort of epistemological hypothesis that historically made its appearance in the context of political theory rather than epistemology. One of the classic defenses of freedom of speech rests on the idea that free speech is the best way for society to get the truth. John Milton wrote: "Let [Truth] and Falshood grapple; who ever knew Truth put to the wors, in a free and open encounter" (1959, 561). Similarly, in the twentieth century, we find the following oft-cited dictum by Justice Holmes: "[T]he best test of truth is the power of the thought to get itself accepted in the competition of the market" (1919, 630). In other words, the free competition of the market is the best way for truth to be recognized in society. This is restated in another U.S. Supreme Court opinion: "It is the purpose of the First Amendment to preserve an uninhibited marketplace of ideas in which truth will ultimately prevail" (*Red Lion Broadcasting Co. v. FCC*, 1969, 390). I presume that what it means for truth to "prevail" is that it comes to be believed, indeed widely believed, by members of society. Using the term "knowledge" in the weak sense of "true belief," a truth prevails if many people, or the majority of people, come to know that truth. Both Holmes and the *Red Lion* court seem to hold that there is no better way for knowledge to be widely acquired than via a free market for ideas, that is, a free market for speech (the expression of ideas).

What Justice Holmes meant by the "market" seems pretty clearly to be an *economic* market. The term "marketplace" in the *Red Lion* opinion is also open to that interpretation. First Amendment scholars also conceive of the argument from truth as invoking economic ideas. For example, Frederick Schauer writes (though without endorsement): "Just as Adam Smith's 'invisible hand' will ensure that the best products emerge from free competition, so too will an invisible hand ensure that the best ideas emerge when all opinions are permitted freely to compete" (1982, 16). What we have, then, is an argument for a certain institutional arrangement that appeals to the alleged knowledge-consequences of that arrangement. Freedom of speech should be prized because it will best ensure the maximization of knowledge. This is evidently a social epistemological thesis, but what justifies or rationalizes the thesis? As formulated by Schauer, it is alleged to follow from the ideas of economic theory. Just as it is a consequence of economic theory that the best products emerge from free competition (or a free market), so it is a consequence of economic theory that the best, that is, truest, ideas will emerge under free competition of ideas, that is, under a system of unimpeded speech. More precisely, the thesis does not merely assert something about the "emergence" of ideas, where "emergence" could refer to the mere airing or floating of ideas, but it asserts that the truest ideas will win acceptance or conviction by a large segment of society. The claim is that this is a consequence of economic theory.

In invoking economic theory, we move into the territory of *science*, because economics is a social science—by some accounts, the preeminent social science. This takes us squarely into territory that illustrates the theme of this chapter: a science is being invoked to support a thesis in social epistemology. The question to be addressed next is whether the science in question really does support this thesis. Is it really a consequence of economic theory that a competitive market for speech would maximize knowledge in society?

Under close inspection, the claim that economics supports this thesis runs into trouble (Goldman and Cox 1996; Goldman 1999b, chap. 7). To fit intellectual matters squarely into the framework of economic theory, we first need to assume that some product or good is involved, and that there are producers and consumers of the product. A promising interpretation for present purposes is that a speaker's messages are products, a speaker is a producer, and hearers are consumers. But we cannot view just any hearer of a message as a consumer. Only those who accept or believe a message should qualify as consumers of it, because it is only *belief* in true messages that yields (weak) knowledge, which is what interests us here. One way to think of the thesis and its putative support by economic theory is as follows. True messages are *superior* to false messages, at least as concerns intellectual matters. So, if it were generally true that competitive markets lead to the production and consumption of superior products, this would seem to support the thesis under discussion. The general spirit of this idea can be found in popular laissez-faire thinking. There is, for example, the Darwinian idea that competition encourages "survival of the fittest," where the fittest are in some sense superior or higher-quality creatures.

However, economic theory simply does not imply that the "best" or highest-quality products will be produced and consumed under free competition, at least where "quality" refers to some predesignated character of the products, such as truth or falsity. Economic theory implies that, under competition, levels of outputs for each type of good will reach efficient levels relative to the production possibilities facing producers and relative to the preferences of consumers. But this makes no categorical prediction about which types of goods will be produced in greater quantities. So market theory does not have the implication that, under competition, messages produced and consumed will have an optimal amount of truth.

A second general problem is that economic theory only guarantees efficiency under conditions of *perfect* competition, and the economic model of perfect competition is highly idealized, incorporating assumptions that go unsatisfied both in general and in the case before us. Where these assumptions are violated, optimality does not follow from competition as a theoretical proposition. Let us consider two examples of these assumptions, the first involving "externalities" and the second involving "public goods." We shall see that these assumptions do not appear to be satisfied in the case of speech.

The activities of a producer may impose costs on people with whom the producer does not trade. For example, if a firm's manufacturing process generates air pollution as a by-product, it may impose costs on people living near the firm in terms of ill health and grime. In terms of economic efficiency, the trouble is that these "external" costs may not be taken into account when the producer makes its manufacturing decisions, because the air pollution may not directly affect it and may not affect the customers for its products. Firms will take into account only the private costs of production, not those to the whole society. But this means that overall efficiency in the system is not guaranteed by free market decisions, that is, decisions unregulated by government. The problem of externalities can be dealt with by government intervention, for example, by requiring firms to pay for emissions permits, thereby prompting them to reduce their external diseconomies in a cost-efficient way.

These ideas can be applied to the case of speech, the question of whether speech should be regulated in some manner by government or left to be regulated entirely by the free market. Consider the example of the government regulation of advertising and product labeling, activities now undertaken by the U.S. federal government that constitute departures from a purely free market for speech. Are these departures from a pure market system good or bad from the vantage-point of knowledge maximization? If the thesis under discussion were right, these departures from a pure market system should have a tendency to reduce knowledge in society. But that does not seem to be their consequence. At a minimum, the *intended* effect of restrictions and requirements by the Food and Drug Administration (FDA) on the advertising and labeling of food and drugs is to *increase* knowledge and reduce false belief by consumers. The banning of false or deceptive advertising is intended to keep consumers from getting false beliefs about these products; and the mandating of accurate labels with certain contents is intended to help consumers get true beliefs about the products. So this government "interference" is intended to have, and presumably does have, positive knowledge consequences, contrary to the thesis under discussion. This can be analogized to the case of air pollution. Untruthful statements by advertisers can be considered acts of "pollution," and the regulation of such statements by government can be seen as an attempt to reduce such pollution. Where there are externalities, pure economic theory does not imply that the free market by itself guarantees efficiency.[9]

The second "idealizing" assumption of the economist's model of perfect competition concerns "public goods." It is generally recognized that the presence of public goods can cause market failure. Private goods, like hamburgers, involve exclusivity and rivalry. If you want to eat your hamburger, you can exclude me from its benefits. Public goods, by contrast, have the properties of nonexclusivity and nonrivalry. Once an army or navy is set up, for example, people living in the country will benefit from its protection whether they have paid for it or not; there is no way to exclude them from its benefits. Nonrival goods are goods for which benefits can be provided to additional users at zero marginal social cost. One more car crossing a bridge during an off-peak period requires no additional resources, since the bridge is already there anyway.

The problem with public goods is that they encourage "free riding." If other people paid for the maintenance of an army, and if I could not be excluded from its benefits once it exists, why would I be prepared to pay for it on the open market? Thus, private markets will tend to underallocate resources to public goods. Government seems required to step in because private markets will not manage to reflect consumer preferences where there are public goods.

Now, messages in an open forum that contain truths are plausible examples of public goods. They have the property of nonexclusivity because anybody can listen in and enjoy their benefits. They have the property of nonrivalry because their benefits can be provided to additional listeners at zero marginal social cost. So there is reason to expect that a private market would tend to underallocate the resources necessary to the discovery and transmission of truth. This suggests, once again, that the general principle that knowledge is maximized when government leaves the business of speech entirely in the hands of free, that is, private, markets is incorrect.

The general point being made here is a purely negative one. It is only intended to show that economic science does not support the alleged link between speech that is totally unregulated by government and knowledge maximization. No attempt is here made to advance a positive proposal for speech policy that would maximize knowledge. As the foregoing discussion hints, however, consideration of any such positive proposals will profit from economic analysis.[10]

7. SOCIOLOGY, IDEOLOGY, AND THE DIFFUSION OF KNOWLEDGE

Are there other social sciences in addition to economics that might contribute to social epistemology? Sociology is a clear candidate. Indeed, certain traditions and approaches to sociology have already made contributions to theories of social knowledge and hold the promise of many more. It must be admitted, however, that sociological treatments of these subjects are often remote from the central interests of philosophical epistemology, especially epistemology in the analytic tradition. Part of the reason for this is that analytic philosophy has focused on the mental processes of belief formation, including introspection, perception, memory, and reasoning. Even when it has worried about interpersonal sources of knowledge, such as testimony, it has often considered this from the vantage point of the receiving agent only. Thus, not much attention has been given to such influences on belief as *classes* and *institutions*, which are the hallmarks of sociology. Nonetheless, social epistemology has every reason to consider such influences, because they are not only candidates for the causes of certain beliefs, but because they might systematically produce beliefs with certain *truth values*; and the truth values of beliefs are a natural topic for epistemology.

A classical case in point is Marx's theory of ideology, which is a sociological theory of belief systems. Here is a capsule summary of Marx's theory by Daniel Little (1991), which emphasizes these points:

> The central claim of Marx's theory of ideology can be stated in these terms. Persons within class societies typically have false and distorted beliefs about themselves and the society in which they live; these beliefs, which systematically enhance the interests of existing ruling classes, may be explained causally as the result of the working of institutions through which consciousness is shaped. . . .
> [T]he industrial democracies of the twentieth century have adopted insti-

tutions of ideological control rather than overtly repressive institutions as the chief instrument of social control. These societies feature extensive ideological institutions that beguile and mystify the oppressed, making them believe that they are not exploited after all. Through these means the exploited may be induced to fail to recognize their condition for what it is. The reality of social exploitation and control may be obscured or mystified by beliefs that existing social institutions are just, fair, divinely ordained, or inevitable. . . . The theory of ideology is therefore an empirical theory about the formation and function of consciousness within a class society. (1991, 124–125)

In more recent times, another branch of sociology has bordered on social epistemology, viz., sociology of science. Perhaps influenced in part by Marx, sociologists of science (of the Edinburgh school especially) often describe scientists as influenced by class interests, political interests, and other factors usually thought to be "external" to science. However, whereas Marx and Marxists commonly assumed that sense can be made of political beliefs being true or false—ideological influences contribute toward false ones—many sociologists of science spurn truth-values entirely. Constructivist sociologists of science, in particular, have no use for the notion that truth or falsehood can attach to scientific beliefs (Latour and Woolgar 1985; Pickering 1984). Science can be studied in terms of changes in consensus belief or consensus practices within scientific communities, but standards of scientific rationality or scientific truth understood independently of consensus are not given any credence. This makes it difficult for this kind of sociology of science to establish close contact with mainstream epistemology, which commonly does accept assumptions of this sort (Kitcher 1993; Goldman 1999b, chaps. 1, 8).

Mainstream sociology offers another paradigm for the study of belief in society, viz., the sociological study of diffusion. Diffusion refers to the spread of something within a social system, where "spread" denotes a flow or movement from a source to an adopter (Strang and Soule 1998). The diffusing item might be a behavior, a strategy, a technology, or a belief, and the process of diffusion might be contagion, mimicry, social learning, organized dissemination, and so forth. For the most part, sociologists have studied things like the diffusion of hybrid corn (Ryan and Gross 1943) or the diffusion of innovations such as the telephone or tests for tuberculosis (Hagerstrand 1967; Rogers 1995). But the diffusion of belief also falls within this agenda, at least in principle. One theoretical model for approaching belief diffusion has been pursued outside of academic sociology, namely the "selectionist" model that goes by the label *memetics*. The term "memetics" was coined by Richard Dawkins (1976), to denote the study of culture built on the principles of biological evolution. "Memes" are supposed to be replicators in the domain of culture that parallel genes, the replicators of biological evolution. Suggested examples of memes are tunes, ideas, catch-phrases, and clothes fashions. There are many problems associated with memetics, not least of which is the problem of specifying units of analysis. In the case of ideas or beliefs, this is a particularly salient problem. Assume, however, that this problem can be solved. Memetics might then be in the business of studying the processes of belief diffusion, the forces that affect the propagation of belief, selecting for certain beliefs rather than their competitors.

Empirical or theoretical modeling of belief diffusion is not yet in the ballpark of epistemology, at least not by my lights. As emphasized earlier, an enterprise begins to look epistemological when it studies not only the distribution of beliefs but the distribution of *truth-valuational* properties of beliefs. Are there conditions or processes of propagation that systematically promote the diffusion of *true* belief rather than *false* belief (or the converse)? That kind of investigation would interest a social epistemologist (Goldman 2001). This is not a project that sociologists have in fact undertaken, and perhaps they are unlikely to undertake it on their own. But it is a cooperative project that can be envisaged for social epistemology, and one that would require, or at least invite, the sorts of scientific expertise to be found within sociology and allied social sciences.

NOTES

I am grateful to Massimo Piattelli-Palmarini for a number of very valuable comments on an earlier draft of this chapter.

1. I do not myself reject the use of scientific methodology in answering questions about concepts. I am inclined to think that certain types of cognitive-scientific findings about concepts can have a definite bearing on the technique of conceptual analysis (see Goldman and Pust 1997). However, this is not a standard view; nor is it a theme to be developed here. So in the text I say, with deliberate caution or evasiveness, that answering a conceptual possibility question "may not" require the use of scientific methodology.

2. I do not mean to suggest that the prospect of resolving an epistemological dilemma may be used as a *ground* for believing one scientific interpretation of the phenomena rather than a competitor. The merits of the respective scientific views should be settled by purely scientific considerations. My only point is that the epistemologist should be alert to different scientific views, and not simply swallow the first one that comes along.

3. For an excellent review of the debate, including a discussion of both empirical findings and alternative standards, see Samuels, Stich, and Bishop (2001). Their main point is that the disputes between the competing contenders in the "rationality wars" can be made to disappear, merely by distinguishing the core claims of each view from the rhetorical flourishes. I am less confident of this prospect.

4. The current Chomskyan approach, "minimalism," replaces the principles and parameters approach, but retains its central idea. In the new theory there is a re-localization of the parameters; they are shifted to the lexicon and the phonological-

morphological component. The syntactic component remains universal. For present purposes the differences between the two approaches are unimportant. (Thanks to Massimo Piattelli-Palmarini on this point.)

5. Cowie (1999, 40–43) advances a brief for this, in connection with Descartes and Leibniz.

6. Piaget (1952) told a similar story, though with more psychological complexity. A more recent non-nativist approach to mathematics is presented by Lakoff and Nunez (2000).

7. An earlier metaphor used to explain the possibility of a simple counting device is the *accumulator* metaphor (Meck and Church 1983). An example of an accumulator, provided by Dehaene (1997, 28ff.), is an automobile odometer that keeps a record of the number of miles that have accumulated since the car was put into circulation. In its simplest version, an odometer could be a cog wheel that advances by one notch for each additional mile. This is an imperfect example because an odometer uses digital notation, not used, presumably, by the counters in animals or infants. Another illustration is a water tank that stores units of water for each object counted. However, water flow into the tank may not be perfectly constant. It may vary slightly from use to use. With such an accumulator device, there would be difficulties of representing or discriminating numbers precisely, which is exactly what is found in experiments on animals.

8. Many statements in American law support the goal of truth as a primary goal of adjudication. For example, the statement of purpose of the Federal Rules of Evidence says that the "end" of the development of the law of evidence is "that the truth may be ascertained and proceedings justly determined" (rule 102). Several Supreme Court opinions also cite the truth goal. In *Texas v. Shott* (1966) the Court said: "[t]he basic purpose of a trial is the determination of truth" (416). However, it oversimplifies matters somewhat to speak of "maximizing" the truth, since in the criminal domain errors of acquitting the guilty are weighted less heavily than errors of convicting the innocent.

9. For further discussion see Goldman and Cox (1996, 23–25).

10. The analysis of information-related activity, much of which is relevant to social epistemology, is a large part of contemporary economics. Two articles that approach issues of speech and/or truth from an economic perspective are Milgrom and Roberts (1986) and Posner (1986).

REFERENCES

Bazerman, M., and M. Neale (1986). "Heuristics in Negotiation." In H. Arkes and K. Hammond, eds., *Judgment and Decision Making: An Interdisciplinary Reader*. Cambridge: Cambridge University Press.

Boysen, S., and E. Capaldi (1993). *The Development of Numerical Competence: Animal and Human Models*. Hillsdale, N.J.: Erlbaum.

Casscells, W., A. Schoenberger, and T. Grayboys (1978). "Interpretation by Physicians of Clinical Laboratory Results." *New England Journal of Medicine* 299: 999–1000.

Chomsky, Noam (1965). *Aspects of the Theory of Syntax*. Cambridge, Mass.: MIT Press.

———. (1980). "On Cognitive Structures and Their Development: A Reply to Piaget."

In M. Piattelli-Palmarini, ed., *Language and Learning: The Debate between Jean Piaget and Noam Chomsky.* Cambridge, Mass.: Harvard University Press.

————. (1986). *Knowledge of Language: Its Nature, Origin, and Use.* New York: Praeger.

Cosmides, Leda, and John Tooby (1996). "Are Humans Good Intuitive Statisticians after All? Rethinking Some Conclusions from the Literature on Judgment under Uncertainty." *Cognition* 58: 1–73.

————. (in press). "Unraveling the Enigma of Human Intelligence: Evolutionary Psychology and the Multimodular Mind." In R. Sternberg and J. Kaufman, eds., *The Evolution of Intelligence.* Hillsdale, N.J.: Erlbaum.

Cowie, Fiona (1999). *What's Within?: Nativism Reconsidered.* New York: Oxford University Press.

Darley, J., and D. Batson (1973). "From Jerusalem to Jericho: A Study of Situational and Dispositional Variables in Helping Behavior." *Journal of Personality and Social Psychology* 27: 100–108.

Davies, S. (1991). "Evidence of Character to Prove Conduct: A Reassessment of Relevancy." *Criminal Law Bulletin* 27: 504–525.

Dawkins, Richard (1976). *The Selfish Gene.* Oxford: Oxford University Press.

Dehaene, Stanislas (1996). "The Organization of Brain Activations in Number Comparison: Event-related Potentials and the Additive-Factors Methods." *Journal of Cognitive Neuroscience* 8: 47–68.

————. (1997). *The Number Sense: How the Mind Creates Mathematics.* New York: Oxford University Press.

————. (2001). "Precis of *The Number Sense.*" *Mind and Language* 16: 16–36.

DeRose, Keith (1995). "Solving the Skeptical Problem." *Philosophical Review* 104: 1–52.

Dretske, Fred (1970). "Epistemic Operators." *Journal of Philosophy* 67: 1007–1023.

Elman, Jeffrey, Elizabeth Bates, Mark Johnson, Annette Karmiloff-Smith, Domenico Parisi, and Kim Plunkett (1996). *Rethinking Innateness: A Connectionist Perspective on Development.* Cambridge, Mass.: MIT Press.

Fiedler, K. (1988). "The Dependence of the Conjunction Fallacy on Subtle Linguistic Factors." *Psychological Research* 50: 123–129.

Fodor, Jerry (1983). *The Modularity of Mind.* Cambridge, Mass.: MIT Press.

Gallistel, C. R. (1990). *The Organization of Learning.* Cambridge, Mass.: MIT Press.

Gallistel, C. R., and Rochel Gelman (1992). "Preverbal and Verbal Counting and Computation." *Cognition* 44: 43–74.

Gerstmann, J. (1940). "Syndrome of Finger Agnosia Disorientation for Right and Left Agraphia and Acalculia." *Archives of Neurology and Psychiatry* 44: 398–408.

Gigerenzer, Gerd (1991). "How to Make Cognitive Illusions Disappear: Beyond 'Heuristics and Biases.'" *European Review of Social Psychology* 2: 83–115.

————. (1996). "On Narrow Norms and Vague Heuristics: A Reply to Kahneman and Tversky." *Psychological Review* 103: 592–596.

Gigerenzer, Gerd, and Daniel Goldstein (1996). "Reasoning the Fast and Frugal Way: Models of Bounded Rationality." *Psychological Review* 103: 650–669.

Gigerenzer, Gerd, and Ulrich Hoffrage (1995). "How to Improve Bayesian Reasoning without Instruction: Frequency Formats." *Psychological Review* 102: 684–704.

Gigerenzer, Gerd, Ulrich Hoffrage, and Heinz Kleinbolting (1991). "Probabilistic Mental Models: A Brunswickean Theory of Confidence." *Psychological Review* 98: 506–528.

Gigerenzer, Gerd, Peter Todd, and the ABC Research Group (1999). *Simple Heuristics That Make Us Smart*. New York: Oxford University Press.

Goldman, Alvin (1979). "What Is Justified Belief?" In G. Pappas, ed., *Justification and Knowledge*. Dordrecht: Reidel. Reprinted in Goldman (1992).

———. (1986). *Epistemology and Cognition*. Cambridge, Mass.: Harvard University Press.

———. (1992). *Liaisons: Philosophy Meets the Cognitive and Social Sciences*. Cambridge, Mass.: MIT Press.

———. (1999a). "A Priori Warrant and Naturalistic Epistemology." In J. Tomberlin, ed., *Philosophical Perspectives*, vol. 13, *Epistemology*. Boston: Blackwell. Reprinted in Goldman (2002).

———. (1999b). *Knowledge in a Social World*. Oxford: Oxford University Press.

———. (2001). "Social Routes to Belief and Knowledge." *The Monist* 84 (2001): 346–365. Reprinted in Goldman (2002).

———. (2002). *Pathways to Knowledge: Private and Public*. New York: Oxford University Press.

Goldman, Alvin, and James Cox (1996). "Speech, Truth, and the Free Market for Ideas." *Legal Theory* 2: 1–32.

Goldman, Alvin, and Joel Pust (1997). "Philosophical Theory and Intuitional Evidence." In M. DePaul and W. Ramsey, eds., *Rethinking Intuition: The Psychology of Intuition and Its Role in Philosophical Inquiry*. Lanham, Md.: Rowman and Littlefield. Reprinted in Goldman (2002).

Gottfredson, Michael, and Travis Hirschi (1990). *A General Theory of Crime*. Stanford: Stanford University Press.

Gould, Stephen (1992). *Bully for Brontosaurus: Further Reflections in Natural History*. London: Penguin.

Hagerstrand, T. (1967). *Innovation Diffusion as a Spatial Process*. Chicago: University of Chicago Press.

Hirschfeld, Lawrence, and Susan Gelman, eds. (1994). *Mapping the Mind: Domain Specificity in Cognition and Culture*. New York: Cambridge University Press.

Holmes, Justice (1919). *Abrams v. United States* 250 U.S. 616.

Kahneman, Daniel, and Amos Tversky (1973). "On the Psychology of Prediction." *Psychological Review* 80: 237–251.

Kim, Jaegwon (1988). "What Is 'Naturalized Epistemology'?" In J. Tomberlin, ed., *Philosophical Perspectives*, vol. 2, *Epistemology*. Atascadero, Calif.: Ridgeview.

Kitcher, Philip (1983). *The Nature of Mathematical Knowledge*. New York: Oxford University Press.

———. (1993). *The Advancement of Science*. New York: Oxford University Press.

Kornblith, Hilary (1985). "Introduction: What Is Naturalistic Epistemology?" In H. Kornblith, ed., *Naturalizing Epistemology*. Cambridge, Mass.: MIT Press.

Lakoff, George, and Rafael Nunez (2000). *Where Mathematics Comes From: How the Embodied Mind Brings Mathematics into Being*. New York: Basic.

Latour, Bruno, and Steve Woolgar (1985). *Laboratory Life: The Construction of Scientific Facts*. Princeton: Princeton University Press.

Little, Daniel (1991). *Varieties of Social Explanation*. Boulder, Colo.: Westview.

McClelland, James, David Rumelhart, and the PDP Research Group (1986). *Parallel Distributed Processing: Explorations in the Microstructures of Cognition*, vol. 2. Cambridge, Mass.: MIT Press.

Meck, W., and R. Church (1983). "A Mode Control Model of Counting and Timing Processes." *Journal of Experimental Psychology: Animal Behavior Processes* 9: 320–334.

Milgram, Stanley (1963). "Behavioral Study of Obedience." *Journal of Abnormal Psychology* 67: 371–378.

Milgrom, P., and J. Roberts (1986). "Relying on the Information of Interested Parties." *Rand Journal of Economics* 17: 18–32.

Mill, John Stuart (1970). *A System of Logic*. London: Longmans.

Milton, John. "Areopagitica, A Speech for the Liberty of Unlicensed Printing." In E. Sirluck, ed. (1959) *Complete Prose Works of John Milton*.

Mischel, Walter (1968). *Personality and Assessment*. New York: Wiley.

———. (1984). "On the Predictability of Behavior and the Structure of Personality." In R. Zucker et al., eds., *Personality and the Prediction of Behavior*. New York: Academic Press.

Nelson, J. O. (1967). "Innate Ideas." In P. Edwards, ed., *Encyclopedia of Philosophy*, vol. 2. New York: Macmillan.

Nisbett, Richard, and Eugene Borgida (1975). "Attribution and the Social Psychology of Prediction." *Journal of Personality and Social Psychology* 32: 932–943.

Nozick, Robert (1981). *Philosophical Explanations*. Cambridge, Mass.: Harvard University Press.

Park, Roger (1998). "Character at the Crossroads." *Hastings Law Journal* 49: 717–779.

Peacocke, Christopher (1999). *Being Known*. Oxford: Oxford University Press.

Piaget, Jean (1952). *The Child's Conception of Number*. London: Routledge and Kegan Paul.

Piattelli-Palmarini, Massimo (1994). *Inevitable Illusions: How Mistakes of Reason Rule Our Minds*. New York: Wiley.

Pickering, Andrew (1984). *Constructing Quarks: A Sociological History of Particle Physics*. Chicago: University of Chicago Press.

Posner, Richard (1986). "Free Speech in an Economic Perspective." *Suffolk University Law Review* 20: 1–54.

Quine, W. V. (1969). "Epistemology Naturalized." In *Ontological Relativity and Other Essays*. New York: Columbia University Press.

Red Lion Broadcasting Co. v. FCC (1969). 395 U.S. 367.

Rogers, J. (1995). *Diffusion of Innovations*, 4th ed. New York: Free Press.

Ross, Lee, and Richard Nisbett (1991). *The Person and the Situation: Perspectives of Social Psychology*. Philadelphia: Temple University Press.

Rumelhart, David, James McClelland, and the PDP Research Group (1986). *Parallel Distributed Processing: Explorations in the Microstructures of Cognition*, vol. 1. Cambridge, Mass.: MIT Press.

Ryan, B., and N. Gross (1943). "The Diffusion of Hybrid Seed Corn in Two Iowa Communities." *Rural Sociology* 8: 15–24.

Samuels, Richard, Stephen Stich, and Michael Bishop (2001). "Ending the Rationality Wars: How to Make Disputes about Human Rationality Disappear." In R. Elio, ed., *Common Sense, Reasoning and Rationality*. Vancouver Studies in Cognitive Science, vol. 11. New York: Oxford University Press.

Schauer, Frederick (1982). *Free Speech: A Philosophical Enquiry*. Cambridge: Cambridge University Press.

Simon, Herbert (1982). *Models of Bounded Rationality*. Cambridge, Mass.: MIT Press.

Starkey, P., and R. Cooper (1980). "Perception of Numbers by Human Infants," *Science* 210: 1033–1035.

Stein, Edward (1996). *Without Good Reason.* Oxford: Oxford University Press.

Strang, David, and Sarah Soule (1998). "Diffusion in Organizations and Social Movements: From Hybrid Corn to Poison Pills." *Annual Review of Sociology* 24: 265–290.

Texas v. Shott (1966). 382 U.S. 406.

Tversky, Amos, and Daniel Kahneman (1982). "Judgment under Uncertainty: Heuristics and Biases." In D. Kahneman, P. Slovic, and A. Tversky, eds., *Judgment under Uncertainty: Heuristics and Biases.* New York: Cambridge University Press.

———. (1983). "Extensional versus Intuitive Reasoning: The Conjunction Fallacy in Probability Judgment." *Psychological Review* 90: 293–315.

Wynn, K. (1992). "Addition and Subtraction in Human Infants." *Nature* 358: 749–750.

CHAPTER 5

....

CONCEPTUAL DIVERSITY IN EPISTEMOLOGY

....

RICHARD FOLEY

THE core subject matters of epistemology are the concept of knowledge and a cluster of normative concepts applying to beliefs, a cluster that includes rational, reasonable, justified, and warranted belief. Epistemologists have their disagreements about how best to understand the concept of knowledge, but their disagreements about the latter cluster of concepts are more extreme. Not only is there no generally agreed way of understanding these concepts, there is not even agreement as to whether or not they are equivalent. Some epistemologists employ them interchangeably. Other epistemologists employ only one of the above notions and avoid making use of the others. Yet other epistemologists distinguish among two or more of the notions.

Despite the centrality of these concepts for epistemology (again, along with the concept of knowledge), the fact that they are used in strikingly different ways in the literature is underappreciated, just as there is too little discussion of the desiderata that a philosophical account of these notions ought to satisfy. I hope to correct this deficiency. In what follows, I make recommendations for how to distinguish these notions; I argue that what is implicitly assumed in much of the literature to be an important desideratum for accounts of the above notions is not in fact a desideratum; I identify several desiderata that have not been adequately recognized in the literature; and, finally, I illustrate how the conceptual distinctions I recommend fit together in an interlocking system that locates these epistemological concepts within a philosophically respectable and perfectly general theory of rationality.

1. JUSTIFIED (RATIONAL, WARRANTED) BELIEF AND KNOWLEDGE

The enormous impact of Edmund Gettier's 1963 article, "Is Justified True Belief Knowledge?" was dependent on the assumption, common at the time, that knowledge could be adequately defined as justified true belief. Gettier introduced a pair of counterexamples designed to show that such a definition is not adequate, but he did not question the assumption that justification is at least one of the necessary ingredients of knowledge.

The basic idea behind Gettier's counterexamples is that one can be justified in believing a falsehood from which one deduces a truth, in which case one has a justified true belief in the latter but does not know it. Gettier's article marked the beginning of a search for a fourth condition of knowledge, one that could be added to justification, truth, and belief to produce an adequate analysis of knowledge. The search thus presupposes that justification is an indispensable component of knowledge. In particular, the presupposition is that although justification, when added to true belief, is not necessary and sufficient for knowledge, it in conjunction with some fourth condition designed to handle Gettier problems, when added to true belief, is necessary and sufficient. Various fourth conditions have been proposed, many of which are variants of the idea that knowledge requires justification that is either nondefective or indefeasible, where a justification is nondefective if (roughly) it does not justify any falsehood, and where a justification is indefeasible if (roughly) it cannot be defeated by the addition of any true statement.

However, a secondary response to Gettier's counterexamples was to wonder whether something less intellectual than justification traditionally understood is better suited for understanding knowledge. Justification is often associated with our having, or at least potentially being able to generate, an argument in defense of one's beliefs, but in many instances, for example, simple perceptual knowledge, we seem not to be able to offer anything resembling an argument in defense of what we know.

The causal theory of knowledge was an initial attempt to construct an account of knowledge that is not centered on justification. According to the causal theory, knowledge requires there to be an appropriate causal connection between the fact that makes a belief true and the person's having that belief.[1] The causal theory adequately handled the original cases described by Gettier, but it ran into other problems. Knowledge of mathematics, knowledge of general facts, and knowledge of the future were especially difficult to account for on this approach. Nevertheless, the causal theory intrigued many epistemologists, in part because it fit well with the general view of knowledge implicit in the naturalized epistemology movement, according to which knowledge is best conceived as arising "naturally" from our complex causal interactions with our environment. To require that we be able to defend that which we know is to intellectualize the concept of knowledge to an unacceptable degree. Some kinds of knowledge, especially highly theoretical knowledge, might involve our being able to produce an argument in their defense, but other kinds typically do not.

Thus, in the eyes of many philosophers, whatever the defects of the causal theory of knowledge, it at least had the virtue of shifting the focus away from questions of our being able to defend our beliefs intellectually and towards questions of our being in an appropriate causal or causal-like relation with our external environment. The philosophical task, according to this way of thinking about knowledge, is to identify the precise character of this relation. Since a simple causal relation between the fact that makes a belief true and the belief itself will not do, some other causal-like relation needs to be found.

There have been numerous proposals, but the view that has had the widest appeal is the reliability theory of knowledge. There are important differences among reliabilists, but the basic shared idea is that in order for a true belief to be an instance of knowledge, it need not be caused by the fact that makes it true, but it does have to be the product of highly reliable processes, faculties, or methods. Reliabilists then differ among themselves as to the precise kind of reliability that is required.[2]

Reliability theories of knowledge led in turn to distinctive new accounts of epistemic justification, specifically, externalist ones. Initially, reliabilism was part of a reaction against justification driven accounts of knowledge, but an assumption drawn from the literature inspired by Gettier tempted reliabilists to reconceive justification as well. The assumption is that by definition justification is that which has to be added to true belief to generate knowledge, with some fourth condition added to handle Gettier-style counterexamples. For example, Alvin Goldman, who had already argued that knowledge is reliably produced true belief, relied on the above assumption to conclude further that epistemic justification must also be essentially a matter of one's beliefs having been produced and sustained by reliable cognitive processes.[3] Because a cognitive process is reliable only if it is well suited to produce true beliefs in the external environment in which it is operating, this is an externalist account of epistemic justification. By contrast, most foundationalists and coherentists are internalists, whose accounts of epistemic justification emphasize the ability of individuals to marshal considerations in defense of their beliefs.

An enormous literature has developed on the relative advantages and disadvantages of externalism and internalism in epistemology.[4] Most of this literature presupposes that externalists and internalists are defending rival theories. However, a more interesting and charitable reading of the dispute is that they are not competitors at all. Rather, they are principally concerned with different issues.

Externalists are primarily interested in explicating knowledge, but along the way they see themselves as also offering an account of epistemic justification, because justification, they stipulate, is that which has to be added to true belief in order to get a serious candidate for knowledge. For them, it is a requirement, and not merely a desideratum, that epistemic justification be explicated in such a way that it turns out to be one of the key components of knowledge. Internalists, by contrast, are primarily interested in explicating a sense of justification that captures what is involved in having beliefs that are defensible, but along the way they see themselves as also providing the materials for an adequate account of knowledge, because they too assume that justification is by definition that which has to be added to true belief to get knowledge, with some condition added to handle Gettier problems. Nevertheless, for internalists the primary desideratum for an account of epistemic justification is that it provide an explication of internally defensible believing, and it is a secondary benefit that it also capture what has to be added to true belief in order to get a good candidate for knowledge.

There are, then, these two different ways of thinking about epistemic justification, but even so, the two have proven easy to conflate, especially since some of the most influential figures in the history of epistemology argue that having internally defensible beliefs guarantees that one also has knowledge. Descartes, for example, recommended that we believe only that which is altogether impossible to doubt, in other words, only that which is internally beyond the possibility of criticism. However, he also thought that by doing so we can be altogether assured of having knowledge.

Descartes's search for an internal procedure that would guarantee knowledge proved not to be feasible, but the lesson is not that either the internal or external aspect of the Cartesian project has to be abandoned. The lesson, rather, is that there are different, equally legitimate projects for epistemologists to pursue. One set of projects involves exploring what is required for one to put one's own intellectual house in order. Another set of projects involves exploring what is required for one to stand in a relation of knowledge to one's environment. It is not unusual for the results of both kinds of projects to be reported using the language of justification, warrant, and rationality, but the terms typically have different senses when used by externalists than when used by internalists. The externalist sense tends to be closely connected with knowledge, whereas the internalist sense tends to be closely connected with some kind of internally defensible believing.

Confusion occurs when in discussing and criticizing each other's views, epistemologists slide back and forth between these senses, sometimes using justified belief, warranted belief, or rational belief to report what has to be added to true belief to get a serious candidate for knowledge and other times to report what is involved in having beliefs that are internally defensible.

The opportunities for confusion are further exacerbated by the methodological assumption mentioned above, that the properties that make a belief justified, warranted, or rational are by definition such that when a true belief has these properties, it is a good candidate to be an instance of knowledge, with some other condition added to handle Gettier-style counterexamples. This assumption has especially unfortunate consequences for the theory of rational belief. First, it places the theory in servitude to the theory of knowledge. An account of rational belief can be deemed adequate only if it explicates rational belief in such a way that rational true beliefs, absent Gettier problems, are instances of knowledge. The assumption thus rules out a priori the possibility of one's beliefs being rational and yet so deeply mistaken that not even the occasional true ones are good candidates for knowledge. Second, in tying the theory of rational belief so closely to the theory of knowledge, the assumption has the subsidiary effect of distancing the theory of rational belief from a general theory of rationality, thus discouraging efforts to explore what the rationality of beliefs has in common with the rationality of decisions, plans, actions, strategies, and so on. Third, the assumption has the effect of divorcing questions about the rationality of beliefs from our everyday assessments of each other's opinions, which tend to emphasize whether we have been responsible in forming our beliefs rather than whether we have satisfied the prerequisites of knowledge.

Such consequences point to the need of being self-conscious about how the terms "rational belief," "justified belief," and "warranted belief" are used. I will be distinguishing the three from one another. Following the usage of Alvin Plantinga, I reserve the term "warranted belief" to refer to that which, by definition, turns true belief into a serious candidate for knowledge.[5] However, I make no such stipulation about rational beliefs and justified beliefs. I do not assume that they, when true, need be good candidates for knowledge. More generally, I make no assumption to the effect of there being a simple, necessary tie between the theories of rational and justified belief and the theory of knowledge. As the theory of knowledge and the theories of rational and justified belief are independently developed, interesting and perhaps even surprising connections among them may be revealed, but I insist on not taking it for granted at the start of the enterprise that either justified belief or rational belief is by definition a component of knowledge. Relaxing the tie between knowledge on the one hand and rational and justified belief on the other hand is potentially liberating for both sides. It frees the theory of knowledge from an overly intellectual conception of knowledge, thus smoothing the way for treatments that acknowledge that most people cannot provide adequate intellectual defenses for much of what they know. Plus, there is no need for awkward attempts to read back into the account of knowledge some duly externalized notion of justified or rational belief. Simultaneously, it creates space for the theories of rational and justified belief to be embedded in a general theory of rationality. These notions ought not be cordoned off from other notions of rationality and justifiedness, as if the conditions that make a belief rational or justified have little to do with the conditions that make a decision, strategy, action, or plan rational or justified. The way we understand the rationality and the justifiedness of beliefs ought to be of a piece with the way we understand the rationality and justifiedness of other phenomena.

2. A First Step toward a Well-integrated Theory

Rationality is best understood as a goal-oriented notion. Whether the question is one about the rationality of beliefs, decisions, intentions, plans, or strategies, what is at issue is the effective pursuit of goals. For example, questions about the rationality of a decision are in the first instance questions about how effectively the decision seems to satisfy the decision maker's goals. I say "seems" because it is too stringent to insist that the decision is rational only if it succeeds. Rational decisions can turn out badly. Likewise, it is too stringent to insist that a decision is rational only if it is probable that it will achieve the goals in question, since it may be that no one could be reasonably expected to see that the decision was likely to have unwelcome consequences. Considerations such as these suggest a general schema of rationality: A decision (or plan, action, strategy, belief) is rational for the individual if it is rational for the individual to believe that it will satisfy her goals.

An obvious drawback of this schema is that it makes reference to the notion of rational belief, thus leaving us within the circle of notions we wish to understand. I return to this problem later, showing how the circle can be escaped, but I first need to address some other questions about the schema. For instance, for a decision (plan, strategy, etc.) to be rational, must it be rational for the individual to believe that it does a better job of achieving her goals than any of the alternatives, or might something less than the very best do? As I will be using the terms, reasonability admits of degrees whereas rationality does not. In particular, reasonability varies with the strengths of one's reasons, and the rational is that which is sufficiently reasonable. Given this distinction, it is possible that several options are rational for an individual even though there are reasons to prefer some of the options to others. A decision (plan, strategy, etc.) is rational if it is rational to believe that it will do an acceptably good job of achieving the goals in question.

To say that a decision (plan, strategy, etc.) will do "an acceptably good job" of achieving the individual's goals is to say its estimated desirability is sufficiently high, where estimated desirability is a matter of what it is rational to believe about its probable effectiveness in promoting the goals and the relative value of these goals. However, context also matters. A decision (plan, strategy, and so on) is rational if its estimated desirability is acceptably high given the context, where the context is determined by the relative desirability of the alternatives and their relative accessibility. The fewer alternatives there are with greater estimated desirabilities, the more likely it is that the decision in question is rational. Moreover, if these alternatives are only marginally superior or are not easy to implement, then it is all the more likely that the decision (plan, strategy, and so on) is rational. It will be rational because it is good enough, given the context.

Assessments about the rationality of an individual's decisions (plans, strategies, etc.) are to be understood as claims about whether it is rational for the individual to believe that the decision (plan, strategy, etc.) will do an acceptably good job of achieving her goals. However, the set of goals we take into account when making such assessments can vary depending on our purposes. We are sometimes interested in evaluating what it is rational for an individual to do all things considered, and we thus take into consideration all her goals. In other contexts, we are interested in taking into consideration only a subset of her goals. For example, we may want to evaluate a decision with respect to those goals that concern the individual's economic well-being. If we judge that it is rational for the individual to believe that A would be an effective means of promoting this subset of goals, we can say that A is rational in an economic sense for her. We can say this even if, with respect to all of her goals, both economic and noneconomic, it is not rational to decide in favor of A.

Thus, the general schema of rationality can be refined: A decision (plan, strategy, etc.) is rational in sense X for an individual if it is rational for her to believe that the plan will do an acceptably good job of satisfying her goals of type X.

The distinction among different types of rationality is especially important for epistemology. When assessing the rationality of beliefs, we are typically not interested in the total constellation of the individual's goals but only those that are distinctly intellectual. For example, as a rule, in assessing whether it is rational for an individual to believe a hypothesis H, we would regard as irrelevant the prospect that she would feel more secure if she were to believe H. More notoriously, in assessing whether it might be rational for her to believe in God, we are unlikely to follow Pascal in regarding as relevant the possibility that she might increase her chances of salvation by being a theist.

Consider another example. Believing that the workmanship on American automobiles is better than that on other automobiles would presumably increase the likelihood of Smith's buying an American car and thus encourage at least in a small way the prospering of the American economy, which we can stipulate is one of her goals. Nevertheless, if we are discussing with Smith what it is rational for her to believe about the workmanship on American cars, we would ordinarily regard these potential benefits of belief as irrelevant. We might be willing to grant that the goal of promoting the American economy gives her at least a weak reason to buy American cars, but we are unlikely to take this goal into account when we are discussing what she has reasons to believe.

Examples of this sort can be multiplied indefinitely. I have a friend who is convinced there is life elsewhere in the universe, because he thinks that not all of the reported sightings of extraterrestrials can be explained away. By contrast, I do not think that these sightings are strong evidence for the existence of life elsewhere, and the two of us have had friendly arguments over the issue. But in addition, my friend has remarked more than once that his belief that there is life elsewhere in the universe has various beneficial effects upon him. He reports that it has made very long-term scientific projects seem more natural to him; it has heightened his appreciation for the diversity of life on earth; and in general it has proven an effective antidote to what he regards as his general tendency to parochialism. However, when he points out these benefits, he does so as parenthetical observations to our discussions, and it is clear that he is not offering them as reasons in defense of his belief that there is life elsewhere in the universe. Of course, it may well be that my friend is exaggerating the beneficial impact of his belief, but still, it is at least arguable that the belief does indeed produce benefits of this sort. Nevertheless, it has never occurred to either of us to regard such benefits as a reason for him (or me) to believe there is life elsewhere. But why not? Why is it that in our deliberations and discussions about what to believe we so rarely consider the pragmatic benefits of belief, even though in principle there seems nothing amiss in doing so?

Although our discussions with others and our debates with ourselves rarely take into consideration the pragmatic benefits that might accrue from belief, such benefits do nonetheless play a role in shaping what we believe. Later I discuss how pragmatic considerations can help determine the kind of investigations we conduct on a topic and, as a result, indirectly influence what we believe about the topic. But in addition, pragmatic considerations often subconsciously influence what we believe. It is a commonplace, for example, that many people have a tendency to believe that which is reassuring to them, especially when what is at issue is relevant to their self-image. They do so not because they have consciously decided that this is a good policy. On the contrary, if asked, they would reject such a policy as ill advised, but it nonetheless does seem to be a policy that many people subconsciously follow. Indeed, there is empirical evidence of their doing so. Studies of so-called "overconfidence bias" document that in a wide variety of circumstances subjects consistently overestimate their own abilities. In an enormous survey of one million high school seniors, students were asked to evaluate themselves as average, below average, or above average in leadership ability. Accurate self-assessments would be expected to result in roughly equal percentages of students in the highest and lowest categories, but the actual self-assessments were strikingly different. A full 70 percent of the students viewed themselves as being above average in leadership ability, whereas only 2 percent regarded themselves as below average. Even more remarkably, when asked to rate their ability to get along with others, virtually all the students thought they were above average, with 60 percent evaluating themselves in the top 10 percent, and 25 percent evaluating themselves in the top 1 percent. Similar studies have been conducted on adults with similar results. For example, a hugely disproportionate percentage of adult drivers rate themselves as better than average drivers. Yet another survey, with special relevance to academia, revealed that a stunning 94 percent of university professors assessed themselves as better at their jobs than their average colleagues.[6]

So, pragmatic benefits do play a significant role in determining what people believe, even if the people themselves are often unaware of this role. This is an interesting point, but in itself not especially surprising, given that people are often unaware of what motivates their behavior and opinions. What is surprising, however, and indeed even puzzling, is that in our discussions and deliberations about what it is rational to believe, the working assumption seems to be that the pragmatic benefits of belief are not even relevant to the issue of what it is rational for us to believe. At first glance, there does not seem to be a comparable assumption at work in our discussions and deliberations about what it is rational for us to do. For example, we commonly decry those who act in a narrowly self-interested way, but we pointedly do not assume that self-interested considerations are beside the point in assessing what people should do. However, in discussions about what it is rational for us to believe, we ordinarily do assume this. Indeed, we assume that even the social usefulness of a belief is beside the point.

As I say, on the face of it, this seems puzzling. What an individual believes can have significant consequences not only for the quality of her life but also for the quality of the lives of those around her. So, why shouldn't these consequences be taken into account in deliberations about what it is rational for her to believe? Yet, our intellectual practice is to regard these consequences as irrelevant to the rationality of her beliefs.

This is not a new puzzle. It is merely the most general form of the dispute over Pascal's wager. There are two main points that Pascal used his wager argument to make, one about reasons for belief generally and one about reasons for belief in God. The general point is that the pragmatic benefits of a belief can be relevant to its rationality. The second and more specific point is that the potential benefits of belief in God make it rational for us to have this belief.

Although I do not argue the issue here, I think that Pascal was mistaken about his second point.[7] However, I think he was essentially correct in saying that the pragmatic benefits of a belief can in principle be relevant to its rationality. In the sections that follow, I propose a general theory of rationality, and within the context of this theory I illustrate how the pragmatic consequences of a belief can potentially affect the rationality of our having that belief. Nevertheless, I also argue that within the framework of the general theory, it is possible to explain and defend our general intellectual practice of not taking the pragmatic benefits of a belief into account in deliberations and debates about what to believe.

3. THE EPISTEMIC GOAL

In evaluating the rationality of beliefs, epistemologists have traditionally been concerned not just with any intellectual goal but rather with a very specific goal, that of now having beliefs that are both accurate and comprehensive. This goal has two aspects, either of which could be championed more easily on its own than in tandem with the other. If the goal were only to have accurate beliefs, the strategy would be to believe only that which is maximally certain, whereas if the goal were only to have comprehensive beliefs, the strategy would be to believe as much as possible.

Note also the synchronic character of the goal. The goal is not to have accurate and comprehensive beliefs at some future time but rather to have such beliefs now. To understand the significance of characterizing the goal in this way, imagine that my prospects for having accurate and comprehensive beliefs a year from now would be enhanced by now believing something for which I lack adequate evidence. For example, suppose that P involves a more favorable assessment of my intellectual talents than the evidence warrants, but suppose also that believing P would make me more intellectually confident than I would be otherwise, which would make me a more dedicated inquirer, which in turn would enhance my long-term prospects of having accurate and comprehensive beliefs. Despite these long-term benefits, there is an important sense of rational belief, indeed the very sense that traditionally has been of the most interest to epistemologists, in which it is not rational for me now to believe P. Moreover, the point of this example is not affected by shortening the time period in which the benefits are forthcoming. It would not be rational, in this sense, for me now to believe P if we were instead to imagine that believing P would somehow improve my prospects for having accurate and comprehensive beliefs in the next few weeks, or in the next few hours, or even in the next few seconds. The precise way of making this point is to say that in such a situation, it is not rational in a purely epistemic sense for me to believe P, where this purely epistemic sense is to be understood in terms of the present tense goal of now having accurate and comprehensive beliefs.

This explication of epistemically rational beliefs in terms of the goal of now having accurate and comprehensive beliefs presupposes that goals can be concerned with current states of affairs as well as future states of affairs. However, if someone wishes to stipulate that goals by definition can be concerned only with future states of affairs, it is easy enough to devise alternative terminology. "Goal" can be replaced with "desideratum" or "value," and epistemic rationality can then be understood in terms of what it is appropriate, or fitting, to believe, insofar as it is a desideratum (that is, a valuable state of affairs) for one now to have accurate and comprehensive beliefs.

Foundationalists, coherentists, reliabilists, virtue theorists, and others propose different accounts of what properties a belief must have in order to be epistemically rational, but for my present purposes, it does not matter which of these accounts is most adequate. What does matter is that whatever precise account is given, the account should make no reference to any other notion of rationality or any related notion, such as justified, warranted, or reasonable belief. In general, this requirement is adhered to in the literature. For example, foundationalists propose understanding epistemic rationality in terms of a notion of basic belief and a set of deductive and inductive relations by which other beliefs are supported by the basic ones, and they would view it as a defect if they had to make reference to a notion of rational belief (or justified, warranted, or reasonable belief) in characterizing basicality or the support relations. Unlike foundationalists, coherentists try to provide an explication of epistemic rationality in terms of a set of deductive and probabilistic relations among beliefs and properties such as conservativeness and explanatory power, but they too would view it as a defect if their explication smuggled in any reference to a notion of rational belief or one of its cognates. It is the same for proponents of other accounts of epistemically rational belief.

This characteristic of epistemically rational belief makes it suitable to correct the principal drawback of the general schema of rationality, namely, that it leaves us within the circle of notions we wish to understand. Because an account of epistemically rational belief standardly does not and should not make use of the notion of rational belief or any of its close cognates, it provides the schema with an escape route from the circle.

In particular, with an account of epistemically rational belief in hand, the general schema of rationality can be further refined: A decision (plan, action, strategy, etc.) is rational in sense X for an individual just in case it is *epistemically rational* for the individual to believe that the decision (plan, action, strategy, etc.) will do an acceptably good job of satisfying her goals of kind X.

According to this refined schema, other kinds of rationality are understood in terms of epistemic rationality, whereas epistemic rationality does not itself presuppose any other kind of rationality. The schema thus illustrates how epistemic rationality serves as an anchor for other kinds of rationality. Moreover, the schema is perfectly general. It applies to all phenomena (decisions plans, strategies, etc.) and to all forms of rationality for these phenomena (economic rationality, rationality all things considered, and so on). Most relevant for present purposes, the rationality of belief is itself an instance of the schema. Even epistemically rational belief is an instance. For example, inserting the epistemic goal into the general schema for "goals of kind X" results in the following: Believing P is rational in an epistemic sense if it is epistemically rational for an individual to believe that believing P will acceptably contribute to the epistemic goal of her now having accurate and comprehensive beliefs.

This instantiation of the general schema is compatible with all the major theories of epistemically rational belief. Every belief that satisfies the requirements of a proposed account of epistemic rationality is also an instance of the general schema, where the relevant goal is that of now having accurate and comprehensive beliefs. For example, according to coherentists, it is epistemically rational for one to believe that believing P will acceptably contribute to the epistemic goal of one's now having accurate and comprehensive beliefs only when the proposed coherentist conditions are met with respect to the proposition P, that is, only when P coheres appropriately with one's other beliefs and hence it is epistemically rational to believe that P is true. According to foundationalists, it is epistemically rational for one to believe that believing P will acceptably contribute to the epistemic goal only when the recommended foundationalist conditions are met with respect to P and hence it is epistemically rational to believe that P is true. Similarly for other accounts of epistemic rationality. To be sure, these instantiations of the general schema are altogether safe and, hence, altogether uninformative, but for the purpose of making the point that the above schema is perfectly general, the safe, uninformative nature of these instantiations is a virtue.

4. EPISTEMIC AND NONEPISTEMIC REASONS FOR BELIEF

A decision (plan, strategy, etc.) is rational in sense X if it is epistemically rational for the individual to believe that it will do an acceptably good job of satisfying her goals of kind X. Recall, however, that X can refer to all of her goals or only a subset of them. For example, if we take into consideration only the economic goals of the individual, we can judge that the decision (plan, strategy, etc.) is rational for her in an economic sense, whereas if we take into consideration all of her goals, both economic and noneconomic, we may well conclude that the decision is not rational all things considered.

Beliefs can also be assessed in terms of a variety of goals. They can be assessed in terms of how well they promote the epistemic goal of now having accurate and comprehensive beliefs but also in terms of how well they promote the individual's total constellation of goals. If it is epistemically rational for an individual to believe that believing a proposition P would effectively promote her overall constellation of goals, then it is rational for her to believe P all things considered. There are two notions of rational belief at work here. The first is the notion of epistemic rationality, defined in terms of the purely epistemic goal, and the second is a derivative notion, defined in terms of epistemically rational belief and the total set of goals of the individual. There is nothing improper about evaluating beliefs in terms of this second notion, but in fact it is rare for us to do so. The puzzle is why this should be so.

In looking for a solution to this puzzle, the first thing to notice is that our discussions and debates concerning what it is rational to believe often take place in a context of trying to convince someone, often ourselves, to believe something. In an effort to persuade, we point out the reasons there are for believing the proposition in question. But insofar as our aim is to get someone to believe something that she does not now believe, the citing of pragmatic reasons is ordinarily ineffective. Even if we convince her that she has good pragmatic reasons to believe a proposition, this is usually not enough to generate belief. By contrast, if she becomes convinced that she has good epistemic reasons to believe the proposition, that is, reasons that indicate that the proposition in question is likely to be true, this usually is enough to prompt belief.

Beliefs are psychological states that purport to represent the world accurately. In general, beliefs that are accurate are also useful, but even so, being useful is a secondary characteristic for them. Their primary function is to represent accurately. However, pragmatic reasons for believing reverse this order. They are directed first and foremost at producing a state that is useful, not a state that accurately represents. As a result, such reasons do not normally prompt belief. At best they motivate the person to get herself into an evidential situation in which belief will be possible. Think of Pascalians who resolve to attend church regularly, surround themselves with believers, and read religious tracts in an effort to alter their outlook in such a way that belief in God will become possible for them.

Thus, insofar as our concern is to persuade someone to believe a proposition, there is a straightforward explanation as to why we are generally not interested in the pragmatic reasons she might have to believe it. The explanation is that it is normally pointless to cite them, because they are not the kind of reasons that normally generate belief. Similarly, in our own deliberations about a claim, we ordinarily do not consider what pragmatic reasons we might have for believing it, and the explanation is similar to the third person case. Deliberations concerning our pragmatic reasons for belief are ordinarily inefficacious and hence pointless. Accordingly, our general practice is to ignore them in deliberations about what to believe.

This practice is not idiosyncratic. The practices that govern the citing of reasons for intending, deciding, trying, resolving, and the like are likewise ones in which reasons that are generally inefficacious are generally ignored. For example, just as the reasons we cite for believing P are ordinarily ones that purport to show that P is true, so the reasons we cite for resolving to do X are ordinarily ones that purport to show that X is worthwhile. Nevertheless, there can be reasons for resolving to do X that do not even purport to indicate that X is worthwhile, just as there can be reasons for believing P that do not even purport to indicate that P is true. Suppose that resolving to do X will itself produce benefits, that is, will do so even if in fact you do not follow through on X. Then you have a prima facie reason to resolve to do X, and you have this reason independently of whether X is worthwhile. Nevertheless, if you and I are discussing what you ought to resolve to do, neither of us is likely to cite such reasons.

Consider deterrence strategies as a case in point. Independently of whether retaliation is in fact a good strategy, you can have a reason to form a resolution to retaliate if attacked, because such a resolution may itself help ward off attacks. Suppose, for example, that threatening to retaliate is the only effective way to deter attacks, but suppose also that your threats will be convincing only if you are in fact resolved to retaliate. If you merely act as if you are prepared to retaliate, your opponents will see through your empty threats and hence will be more likely to attack. Accordingly, you have at least a prima facie reason to resolve to retaliate, and you have this reason even if actually retaliating when attacked would result in escalating hostilities that would be counter to your best interests.[8]

In a less dramatic way, the formation of ordinary, everyday intentions, decisions, resolutions, and so on can have consequences that are independent of whether the intentions, decisions, resolutions, and so on are carried out, and if these consequences are sufficiently beneficial, they would seem to provide us with powerful reasons to form the intention, make the decision, or adopt the resolution in question. Nevertheless, our practice is not to take such reasons into account when we are deliberating about what intentions, decisions, or resolutions it would be best for us to adopt, nor do we generally take such reasons into account in arguing with others about the rationality of their intentions, decisions, and resolutions.

The puzzle is why this should be so, and the solution to this puzzle is analogous to the solution for the corresponding puzzle about belief. Becoming convinced that one has these kinds of reasons to intend (decide, resolve) to do X is ordinarily not enough to generate the intention (decision, resolution). So, insofar as we are trying to persuade someone to intend (decide, resolve) to do X, it will normally be pointless to cite such reasons. By contrast, if we convince the person that X is worthwhile, this usually is sufficient to produce the intention (decision, resolution) in question. Consider again the deterrence example. Even if you know that you can successfully ward off attack by forming a resolution to retaliate, this will normally not be sufficient to produce such a resolution, in the absence of your being convinced that retaliation actually makes sense. It may well prompt you to act as if you are going to retaliate (in hopes of fooling your enemies), but it ordinarily will not be enough to generate a genuine resolution to retaliate.

Thus, in general, the practices governing reasons are such that inefficacious reasons are usually ignored. This fact about the general practice of reason-giving helps explain why we usually do not deliberate or debate over the pragmatic reasons there might be for believing a claim.

A second, and reinforcing, explanation as to why we ordinarily do not deliberate about the pragmatic reasons for belief is that such deliberations are usually redundant. Although we can have pragmatic reasons as well as epistemic reasons for believing, ordinarily our overriding pragmatic reason with respect to our beliefs is to have and maintain an accurate and comprehensive stock of beliefs. We are continually faced with a huge variety of decisions, and because we do not know in advance in any detailed way the kinds of decisions we will need to make, we likewise do not know in advance the kind of information that will be required to make these decisions well. This might not be terribly important were it not for the fact that a large number of these decisions will need to be made quickly, without the opportunity for deliberation or investigation. In making these decisions, we will thus need to draw upon our existing stock of beliefs, and if that stock is either small or inaccurate, we increase the likelihood that our decisions will not be good ones.

So, ordinarily, the system of beliefs that is likely to do the best job of promoting our total constellation of goals is one that is both comprehensive and accurate. Only by having such beliefs are we likely to be in a position to fashion effective strategies for achieving our various goals. Since by definition beliefs that are epistemically rational for us are beliefs that are rational for us insofar as our goal is to have accurate and comprehensive beliefs, it is ordinarily rational, all things considered, that is, when all of our goals are taken into account, to believe those propositions that are also epistemically rational for us to believe. Thus, for all practical purposes, taking this phrase literally, we can usually safely ignore pragmatic reasons in our deliberations about what to believe.

To be sure, there are conceivable exceptions in which epistemic reasons and overall reasons for belief are pulled apart. If someone credibly threatens me with torture unless I come to believe P, and not merely act as if I believe, then presumably it is rational for me, all things considered, to find some way of getting myself to believe P. This is so even if believing P is clearly epistemically irrational, that is, irrational insofar as my goal is to have accurate and comprehensive beliefs. However, in the vast majority of cases, where the benefits of belief itself, regardless of accuracy, are not so powerful, there are pressures that keep what it is rational to believe all things considered, from being in conflict with what it is epistemically rational to believe. These pressures are made all the more intense by the fact that nonepistemic reasons are usually not capable of directly producing belief. So, if I am to find a way of believing a proposition P that is not epistemically rational, I may need to maneuver myself into what I would now regard as a misleading evidential situation.

For example, suppose P is the proposition that there is intelligent life elsewhere in the universe, and let us grant for sake of argument that I correctly regard the currently available evidence in favor of P as unconvincing. How would I go about getting myself to believe P? The most straightforward approach would be to commit myself to an impartial investigation in hopes of eventually uncovering good evidence of life elsewhere. But insofar as I now lack good evidence for P, I also lack good evidence for thinking that an impartial investigation will uncover evidence of its truth. Or to express the point from the other direction, if I did have good evidence for thinking that a fair investigation would reveal good evidence for the truth of P, this itself would constitute good evidence for its truth.[9]

The alternative to a thorough, impartial investigation is to plot against myself so that I eventually come to have misleading but nonetheless convincing evidence. Unfortunately, such plots are unlikely to be narrowly contained. Beliefs ordinarily cannot be revised in a piecemeal fashion. Rather, large clusters of beliefs have to be altered in order for any one to be altered. Thus, a project of deliberately worsening my evidential situation in hopes of getting myself to believe a hypothesis for which I now lack good evidence is likely to involve my changing my opinions about a large number of other propositions as well. Moreover, in order for such a project to be successful, it must hide its own tracks. A measure of self-deception will be necessary, whereby I somehow get myself to forget that I have deliberately manipulated my situation in order to garner data favoring the hypothesis. Otherwise, at the end of my manipulations, I will be aware that the evidence has been skewed in favor of the hypothesis and, hence, it won't convince me.

Although there is nothing in principle irrational about my plotting against myself in this way, the costs will usually be unacceptably high relative to the benefits of the resulting belief. After all, these plots require considerable effort, and, in addition, from my current perspective they will adversely affect the overall future accuracy of my beliefs and, hence, in all likelihood the overall effectiveness of my future decision making. So, except in those rare cases in which enormous benefits are in the offing, for example, the avoidance of torture, it will be irrational to manipulate my situation so that I can come to believe that for which I now lack adequate evidence.

Again, there is a parallel with reasons for intending, deciding, trying, resolving, and the like. I can have reasons to intend to do X that are not reasons for regarding X as worthwhile, but ordinarily such reasons will not result in my having a genuine intention to do X, in the absence of my being convinced that X is worthwhile. Still, such reasons might motivate me to engage in manipulations of my situation in hopes that I eventually would come to regard X as worthwhile, which in turn would prompt me to form the intention to do X. On the other hand, a project of this sort is itself likely to have significant costs, including a measure of self-deception. These costs help ensure that ordinarily I have reasons to intend only that which I also have reasons to do, just as analogous costs help ensure that I ordinarily have reasons to believe only that which I have epistemic reasons to think true.

The lesson is that although what it is rational for an individual to believe when all of her goals are taken into account can in principle be at odds with what it is epistemically rational for her to believe, in practice this tends not to happen.

5. Pragmatic Constraints on Inquiry

Pascal was correct in maintaining that it is in principle possible to have powerful pragmatic reasons for manipulating ourselves in such a way that we come to believe a proposition for which we currently lack good evidence. However, insofar as pragmatic considerations influence what it is rational for us to believe, it is far more common for them to do so indirectly, for example, by determining how much time and effort it is reasonable to devote to investigating a topic. Pragmatic considerations impose constraints on inquiry, but, subject to these constraints, our aim normally is to determine what beliefs are true, not what beliefs are useful.

We rarely engage in direct, Pascalian deliberations about the costs and benefits of believing a claim, but on the other hand it is not at all unusual for us to deliberate about the costs and benefits of spending additional time and resources investigating a topic. To take an everyday example, in deciding whether to buy a used car, I will want to investigate the model's history of reliability as well as the condition of the specific car, but I need to decide how thoroughly to do so. Should I merely drive the car? Should I look up the frequency of repair record for the model? Should I go over the car with a mechanic, or perhaps even more than one mechanic? Similarly, if I am interested in the issue of whether ocean fish are being over harvested, I need to decide how much effort to spend investigating the issue. Should I be content with looking at the accounts given in newspapers, or should

I take the time to read a recent piece on the issue in *Nature*, or should I go to the trouble of consulting with experts?

The reasonable answer to such questions is a function of how important the issue is to me and how likely additional effort on my part is to improve my epistemic situation. As the stakes of having accurate beliefs about an issue go up and as the chances for improving my epistemic situation go up, it becomes increasingly reasonable for me to make additional efforts. These efforts, in turn, can affect what it is epistemically rational for me to believe about the issue.

Thus, in these indirect ways, pragmatic considerations can and do exercise considerable influence over what it is epistemically rational for us to believe. Additional examples of such influence are to be found in the so-called theoretical virtues, such as simplicity, fertility, problem-solving effectiveness, and the like. Consider simplicity, for example. If the simplicity of a hypothesis is a function of such considerations as the number of entities it postulates, the number of different kinds of entities it postulates, the number of laws it postulates, and the number of variables related in these laws, it is notoriously difficult to understand why the simplicity of an hypothesis should be regarded as evidence of its truth. Simplicity looks to be a pragmatic consideration, not an epistemic consideration.

Nevertheless, even as a pragmatic consideration, simplicity can play an important role in shaping what we believe, albeit not the direct role that some have thought that it plays. If we are deliberating over the merits of two rival hypotheses and neither is terribly complex, considerations of simplicity will normally not enter into our deliberations about which of the hypotheses to believe, not even if one of the hypotheses is somewhat simpler. On the other hand, considerations of simplicity do commonly play an indirect role in our deliberations. They do so because we have only limited cognitive abilities and only a limited time to exercise these abilities. As the complexity of hypotheses increases, it requires increasingly sophisticated abilities and increasing amounts of time and energy to gather evidence about them, test them, and deliberate about them. Indeed, if a hypothesis is complex enough, it may not even be possible for us to understand it. So, it won't be a candidate for belief. It will be filtered out automatically. But even among those hypotheses that in principle we are able to understand, some are so complex that it would be impractical for us to take them seriously. It would take far too much time to deliberate about them, much less to use them in making predictions and in constructing other hypotheses. Thus, they would be of little value to us even if they were true. So, they too will be filtered out. We do not take them seriously. We simply ignore them.

In other words, our intellectual practices are such that although the simplicity of a hypothesis is rarely cited as a direct reason to believe that a hypothesis is true, considerations of simplicity do nonetheless enter into our deliberations in a more subtle and indirect way. They have a filtering function. They limit the number of hypotheses we take seriously.

Or, more positively, the simplicity of a hypothesis can sometimes give us a reason to commit ourselves to a hypothesis (as opposed to believing it), where committing ourselves to it involves, among other things, using it to design experiments and to construct other hypotheses. But in such cases, the effect of considerations of simplicity on what it is rational for us to believe is once again indirect. The hope is that committing ourselves to the hypothesis will eventually generate sufficient evidence either for its truth or for the truth of a successor hypothesis, that is, evidence sufficient for belief and not merely commitment.

Moreover, this is a model for the way in which pragmatic considerations in general affect the rationality of our beliefs. It is rare for them to do so in the crass way that Pascal's wager envisions, but it is not at all unusual for them to shape our investigative and deliberative practices. They help determine the degree of time and effort it is reasonable to devote to having accurate beliefs about a topic, and they likewise help determine which hypotheses we take seriously. But within these intellectual practices, we ordinarily regard it as irrelevant whether or not belief in a hypothesis would be useful. The internal rules of our practices concerning belief tell us to be concerned only with the truth (or approximate truth) of hypotheses even though the practices themselves are thoroughly shaped by our needs, interests, abilities, and other such pragmatic considerations.

6. JUSTIFIED BELIEF AS RESPONSIBLE BELIEF

The concept of epistemically rational belief is too idealized to be directly relevant to the everyday assessments we make, and need to make, of each other's beliefs. Epistemic rationality is concerned with a very specific goal, that of now having accurate and comprehensive beliefs, whereas in reality all of us have many goals, which place constraints on how much time and effort it is reasonable to devote to having accurate and comprehensive beliefs. On the other hand, the idealized character of epistemic rationality does make it suitable to serve as a theoretical anchor for derivative notions that are less idealized and, hence, potentially more relevant to our everyday intellectual concerns.

The catch is that the most straightforward way of introducing a derivative notion of rational belief is too crude to be of much relevance for our everyday intellectual concerns. According to the general schema, it is rational all things considered (that is, when all of the individual's goals are taken into account) for an individual to believe P if it is epistemically rational for her to believe that the overall effects of believing P are sufficiently beneficial. I have been pointing out, however, that it is rare for epistemically rational belief and rational belief all things considered to come apart. There are powerful pressures that keep the two from being in conflict with one another in all but unusual circumstances. On the other hand, I have also been arguing that pragmatic considerations do nonetheless influence our beliefs. It is just that they do so indirectly, for example, by determining how much time and effort it is reasonable to devote to investigating an issue. Moreover, the everyday assessments we make of each other's beliefs reflect this influence. So, if an epistemology is to be relevant to these everyday assessments, it will have to find correspondingly indirect ways of introducing pragmatic considerations into the assessments of beliefs.

A first step toward fashioning such an epistemology is to notice that our everyday evaluations of each other's beliefs tend to be reason-saturated. We are interested, for example, in whether someone has been *reasonably* thorough in gathering evidence and *reasonably* careful and reflective in evaluating this evidence, or whether she has instead been *unreasonably* sloppy or selective in gathering evidence or *unreasonably* hasty in drawing conclusions from the evidence. The standards of reasonability and unreasonability at work in these everyday assessments are realistic ones, reflecting the fact that we all have nonintellectual interests, goals, and needs that impose limitations on how much time and effort it is reasonable to spend on gathering evidence and deliberating about a topic.

Only a notion that is sensitive to such questions of resource allocation is capable of capturing the spirit of these everyday evaluations. Indeed, since we evaluate beliefs in a variety of contexts for a variety of purposes, perhaps several notions will be needed. Still, at least many of our ordinary evaluations can be understood in terms of a notion that I call "justified belief." My use of this term departs from the uses commonly found in the current literature, where the term tends to be used schizophrenically, sometimes referring to the properties that when added to a true belief produce a good candidate for knowledge, and sometimes referring to the properties that a belief must have in order to be internally defensible insofar as the goal is to have accurate and comprehensive beliefs. By contrast, I distinguish justified belief from both warranted belief and epistemically rational belief. I reserve the term "warranted" to refer to the properties that turn a true belief into a serious candidate for knowledge, and reserve "epistemically rational" to refer to the properties that make a belief internally defensible insofar as the goal is now to have accurate and comprehensive belief. And, as I use the term "justified," a belief is justified if one has been responsible in acquiring (and retaining) it.

This use of "justified belief," although at odds with the way the term is used in contemporary epistemology, has the considerable advantage of being closely aligned with ordinary, everyday uses of "justified" to assess conduct. We are prepared to say that someone's conduct in a difficult situation is justified if we think she has responded in a responsible way to the situation in all of its complexity, where this in turn, very roughly, is a matter of her reasonably balancing the various demands of the situation. In an analogous manner, an individual's beliefs about a topic are justified if they are responsible ones for her to have given her situation in all of its complexity, where this in turn, very roughly, is a matter of her reasonably balancing the importance of having accurate beliefs about the topic against other demands on her time and energy.

The reference to achieving a "reasonable balance" leaves us within the circle of terms we want to understand, but the general schema of rationality, in conjunction with the notion of epistemically rational belief, can be used to convert this rough characterization into a theoretically respectable one.

Specifically, an individual justifiably believes a proposition P if her treatment of P has been rational all things considered. According to the general schema, her treatment of P has been rational all things considered if it is epistemically rational for her to believe that her procedures with respect to P have been acceptable, that is, acceptable given the limitations on her time and capacities and given all of her goals. Thus, if the individual has an epistemically rational belief that she has spent an acceptable amount of time and energy in gathering evidence about P and evaluating this evidence and has used acceptable procedures in gathering and processing this evidence, she is justified in having this belief.

The concept of justified belief, unlike the concept of warranted belief, is not definitionally tied to the concept of knowledge. Nor is the concept of justified belief idealized in the way that the concept of epistemically rational belief is. Built into the concept of justified belief is an acknowledgment that our nonepistemic goals impose constraints on how much time and effort it is reasonable to expend on intellectual pursuits. Given the relative unimportance of some topics, the scarcity of time, and the pressing nature of many of our nonepistemic ends, it would be inappropriate to spend very much time or effort gathering information about these topics and thinking about them.

For example, we usually do not spend appreciable time or effort deliberating about our ordinary perceptual beliefs. We believe that there is a table in front of us because we are looking at it. There is no need for deliberation. Indeed, most of our beliefs are formed in an unthinking way, and in general this is an acceptable way to proceed. Unless there are concrete reasons for suspicion, it is wasteful to spend time deliberating about what we are inclined to believe spontaneously. It is better to keep ourselves on a kind of automatic pilot and to make adjustments only when problems manifest themselves.

Even though it is an acceptable general policy not to resist what we are inclined to believe spontaneously, it is also important to be responsive when there are warning signs that our standard repertoire of intellectual faculties, practices, and skills is not serving us well. But this truism does not detract from the fact that even seemingly simple intellectual projects make use of a large number of faculties, intellectual habits, and opinions, most of which we must rely on without much thought. The bulk of our intellectual proceedings must be conducted in a largely automatic fashion. Only a fraction of our intellectual methods, practices, and faculties, and only a fraction of the opinions they generate, can be subject to scrutiny. The challenge is to identify that which is the most deserving of our attention. Each new situation presents us with new intellectual challenges, if only because we will want to know the best way to react to the situation. We are thus swamped with potential intellectual projects, but relative to the total constellation of our goals, some of these projects are more important. Similarly, relative to limitations on our time, some are more pressing than others. These are the ones worthy of attention.

Some topics are such that is not especially important for us to have accurate and comprehensive beliefs about them and, as a result, we can have justified beliefs about them even if we have spent little or no time deliberating about them. Indeed, we can have justified beliefs about them even if we are in the possession of information which, had we reflected upon it, would have convinced us that what we believe is incorrect. This is one of the ways in which, as I am using the terms, justified belief and epistemically rational belief can come apart. Even if an individual has evidence that makes it epistemically irrational to believe P, she might nonetheless justifiably believe P, since, given the unimportance of the topic, it might be appropriate for her not to have taken the time and effort to sift through this evidence.

Having justified beliefs requires one to be a responsible believer, and being a responsible believer involves exercising the appropriate level of care in forming one's opinions. One's treatment of a topic should not be hasty unless the topic is so insignificant as to invite a hasty treatment. On the other hand, being a responsible believer does not require one to exercise extraordinary care either unless the issue itself is extraordinarily important. The standards that one must meet if one's beliefs are to be justified slide up or down with the significance of the issue. If nothing much hangs on an issue, there is not much of a point in going to great lengths in order to have accurate and comprehensive beliefs about it. Accordingly, the standards one must meet are low. However, when weighty issues are at stake, more is required if one is to be responsible and, hence, the standards of justified belief become correspondingly high. Indeed, they can become more stringent than those of epistemically rational belief. The more important the issue, the more important it is to reduce the risk of error. For example, if having inaccurate opinions about a given topic would put people's lives at risk, one should conduct especially thorough investigations before settling on an opinion. If one fails to do so, the resulting beliefs will not be justified even if they are epistemically rational.

In other words, just as it is possible for a belief to be justified even though it is not epistemically rational, so too the reverse is possible. A belief can be epistemically rational and yet not be justified. This is possible because epistemically rational belief does not require certainty, not even moral certainty, whereas moral certainty sometimes is required for one to be a responsible believer. To be epistemically rational, one needs to reduce the risk of error to an acceptable theoretical level, that is, acceptable insofar as one's goal is to have accurate and comprehensive beliefs, but the risks might be acceptable in this theoretical sense even if one's procedures have been unacceptably sloppy, given that people's lives are hanging in the balance. If so, the beliefs in question will not be justified, despite the fact that they are epistemically rational.

The intellectual standards it is appropriate for one to meet vary not just with the importance of the topic at issue but also with one's social role. If part of my job is to ensure that the lifeboats are in seaworthy condition, the intellectual demands upon me to have accurate beliefs about this issue are more strenuous than they would be if this were not part of my job. If my job were different, my belief that the lifeboats are seaworthy might be justified even if I have not closely inspected the boats. A cursory look might suffice. But given the duties of my job, a cursory look won't do. It would be irresponsible for me not to inspect the boats thoroughly. I need to do more and know more in order to have justified belief.

One's social role can be relevant even when the issue at hand is primarily of theoretical interest. For example, my beliefs about early hominids and the evolution of modern humans derive from treatments of the issues in popular books and articles, which describe the opinions of various authorities on human evolution. This reliance on the opinions of experts is presumably enough for me to have justified beliefs about these issues; no more can be reasonably expected of me. On the other hand, more can be reasonably expected of the authorities themselves. They are part of a community of inquirers with special intellectual responsibilities, and as a result they need to have much more detailed knowledge than I if they are to have justified beliefs about these issues.

Nonepistemic ends thus shape in an indirect way, rather than a direct Pascalian way, what it is justified for an individual to believe. They do so because the amount of time and effort it is reasonable for an individual to devote to investigating a topic is determined by how important it is for her to have accurate opinions about the topic. As the stakes increase or decrease, so too should her efforts. The notion of justified belief that I have been sketching captures this dynamic. Indeed, the standards of justified belief can even be different for a proposition and its contrary. If you are picking wild mushrooms for dinner tonight, the costs associated with your falsely believing that this mushroom is poisonous are relatively insignificant. After all, there are other mushrooms to pick and other foods to eat. On the other hand, the costs associated with falsely believing that this mushroom is nonpoisonous are much more significant. Accordingly, the standards for your justifiably believing that the mushroom is not poisonous are higher than the standards for justifiably believing that it is poisonous. More is required for you to be a responsible believer in the former case than in the latter, given that there are heavy costs associated with a false negative while only relatively light ones associated with a false positive.

An individual justifiably believes a proposition P if it is epistemically rational for her to believe that her procedures with respect to P have been acceptable given all of her goals. However, we often do not have a very good idea of how it is that we come to believe what we do. We may not remember or perhaps we never knew. Consequently, we may not be in a position to have epistemically rational opinions one way or the about whether our procedures with respect to these beliefs have been acceptable. Such beliefs are not justified, but on the other hand they need not be irresponsible either, especially in light of the fact that the bulk of our intellectual proceedings must be conducted in a largely automatic fashion. For many beliefs, perhaps even most, it is not worth paying much attention to how we arrived at them, at least not unless there are warning signs that something has gone wrong. I will say that such beliefs are nonnegligent.

More exactly, an individual nonnegligently believes a proposition P if her treatment of P has not been irrational all things considered. As is the case with the sibling concept of justified belief, the general schema of rationality can be used to spell out in a theoretically respectable way what this means: An individual's treatment of P has not been irrational if it is not epistemically rational for her to believe that her procedures with respect to P have been unacceptable all things considered, that is, unacceptable given the limitations on her time and capacities and given all of her goals. For example, if it is not epistemically rational for her to believe that she has spent an unacceptably small amount of time in gathering evidence or in evaluating this evidence, or that she has used unacceptable procedures in gathering and processing this evidence, then her belief P is nonnegligent. In this way, the standards that must be met for a belief to be nonnegligent, like the standards for justified belief, vary in accordance with such factors as the relative importance of the topic at issue, the other demands on the individual in the situation in question, and the individual's social role.

7. Conceptual Diversity in Epistemology

I have been articulating a set of conceptual distinctions for epistemology. The key concepts are those of knowledge, warranted belief, epistemically rational belief, and justified belief. Warranted belief is defined as that which when added to true belief produces knowledge in the absence of Gettier problems. By contrast, the concepts of epistemically rational belief and justified belief are at best only contingently linked with knowledge. Epistemically rational beliefs and justified beliefs, even when true, need not be good candidates for knowledge. However, these latter two concepts are embedded within a philosophically respectable and perfectly general theory of rationality, which has the result of linking them closely both with the rationality of decisions, plans, actions, strategies, etc., and with the kinds of everyday assessments we make of each other's beliefs.

At the heart of this general theory is a schema: A decision (plan, strategy, etc.) is rational in sense X for an individual if it is epistemically rational for her to believe that the decision (plan, strategy, etc.) will do an acceptably good job of satisfying her goals of type X. The schema uses the notion of epistemically rational belief to define other derivative notions of rationality. This is a theoretically respectable strategy because an adequate account of epistemically rational belief does not make use of any other notion of rationality or any of its close cognates. The notion of epistemically rational belief can thus serve as a theoretical anchor for derivative notions of rationality.

This schema is altogether general. It applies to all phenomena whose rationality is assessed, including plans, decisions, strategies, actions, beliefs, and so on; and it applies as well to all the various kinds of rationality that are used to assess these phenomena, where the different kinds of rationality are understood by reference to different kinds of goals.

Moreover, part of the significance of the general schema is that it provides a mechanism for understanding the ordinary, everyday assessments that we make of each other's beliefs. These everyday assessments tend not to focus on whether someone has fulfilled the prerequisites of knowledge. Hence, the concept of warranted belief is not directly relevant to them. Likewise, the assessments tend not to focus exclusively on what it is appropriate for someone to believe insofar as her goal is to have accurate and comprehensive beliefs. Hence, the concept of epistemically rational belief is too idealized to be directly relevant to such assessments. Instead, our everyday assessments are concerned with whether someone has been responsible in forming her beliefs, where this is a matter of such considerations as whether she has been reasonably careful, reasonably reflective, and reasonably thorough in her treatment of the topic at issue. Alternatively, we are sometimes interested in whether the individual has at least managed to avoid being irresponsible, where this is a matter of her not having been unreasonably sloppy or hasty in her treatment of the topic.

These rough characterizations of responsible and irresponsible belief refer to standards of reasonability and unreasonability, thus leaving us within the circle of concepts we want to understand, but the general schema provides a mechanism for capturing the reason-saturated character of these everyday assessments in a philosophically respectable way. In particular, an individual justifiably believes a proposition P if her overall treatment of P has been rational all things considered, where according to the general schema this is a matter of its being epistemically rational for her to believe that her procedures with respect to P have been acceptable given all of her goals. Correspondingly, an individual nonnegligently believes P if her overall treatment of P has not been irrational all things considered, where given the general schema this is a matter of its not being epistemically rational for her to believe that her procedures with respect to P have been unacceptable given all of her goals.

This interlocking system of concepts provides the necessary materials for an approach to epistemology that is clarifying, theoretically respectable, and relevant to our actual intellectual lives. The approach is clarifying in that it sharply distinguishes the project of understanding what is required to have knowledge of a topic from the project of what is required to have epistemically rational beliefs and justified beliefs about the topic. The approach is theoretically respectable in that it is based on a perfectly general schema of rationality that can be explicated without recourse to any further notion of rationality or any of its cognates. And the approach is relevant to our actual intellectual lives, because it provides a basis for introducing various derivative notions, including the notions of justified and nonnegligent belief, that capture many of the everyday concerns we have in assessing our own and each other's beliefs.

NOTES

1. See Alvin Goldman, "A Causal Theory of Knowing," *Journal of Philosophy* 64 (1967): 357–372; and D. M. Armstrong, *Belief, Truth, and Knowledge* (Cambridge: Cambridge University Press, 1973).

2. See Alvin Goldman, *Epistemology and Cognition* (Cambridge, Mass.: Harvard University Press, 1986); Fred Dretske, *Knowledge and the Flow of Information* (Cambridge, Mass.: Harvard University Press, 1981); Robert Nozick, *Philosophical Explanations* (Cambridge, Mass.: Harvard University Press, 1981); and Ernest Sosa, *Knowledge in Perspective* (Cambridge: Cambridge University Press, 1991), especially chaps. 13–16.

3. Goldman, "A Causal Theory of Knowing."

4. For a summary and discussion of the relevant issues, see William Alston, *Epistemic Justification* (Ithaca, N.Y.: Cornell University Press, 1989), especially chaps. 8 and 9. Also see Robert Audi, "Justification, Truth and Reliability," *Philosophy and Phenomenological Research* 49 (1988): 1–29; Laurence BonJour, "Externalist Theories of Empirical Knowledge," in *Midwest Studies in Philosophy*, vol. 5, ed. French, Uehling, and Wettstein (Minneapolis: University of Minnesota Press, 1980), 53–71; Richard Fumerton, "The Internalism–Externalism Controversy," in *Philosophical Perspectives*, vol. 2, ed. J. Tomberlin (Atasacadero, Calif.: Ridgeview, 1988); Alvin Goldman, "Strong and Weak Justification," in *Philosophical Perspectives*, vol. 2, ed. Tomberlin (1988); and Ernest Sosa, "Knowledge and Intellectual Virtue," in *Knowledge in Perspective*, 225–244.

5. See Alvin Plantinga, *Warrant: The Current Debate* (New York: Oxford University Press, 1993).

6. Thomas Gilovich, *How We Know What Isn't So* (New York: Macmillan, 1991), 75–87.

7. See Richard Foley, "Pragmatic Reasons for Belief," in *Gambling on God*, ed. J. Jordan (Lanham, Md.: Rowman and Littlefield, 1994), 31–46.

8. Gregory Kavka describes a similar puzzle for intentions. In Kavka's example, someone offers me a million dollars if tomorrow I form an intention to drink a toxin on the day after tomorrow. If I form the intention tomorrow, I will get the money whether or not I actually drink the toxin on the day after tomorrow. See Kavka, "The Toxin Puzzle," *Analysis* 43 (1983): 33–36.

9. See Richard Foley and Richard Fumerton, "Epistemic Indolence," *Mind* 92 (1982): 38–56.

CHAPTER 6

THEORIES OF JUSTIFICATION

RICHARD FUMERTON

THE concept of justification may be the most fundamental in epistemology. On what became the dominant view in the twentieth century, knowledge is to be understood, at least in part, through our understanding of justification. Part of the answer many offer to Plato's question in the *Theaetetus*, "What must be added to true belief in order to get knowledge?" is justification. Furthermore, on many accounts of knowledge and justification, it is tempting to conclude that the only responsibility we are competent to carry out *qua* philosophers is to conform our beliefs to what is justified. Whether or not the world cooperates so as to turn those justified beliefs into knowledge is out of our hands.

The task of explaining and evaluating theories of justification, however, is daunting. There are not only a host of different theories of justification, there are also radical differences among epistemologists concerning how they understand what it is to offer such a theory. Some epistemologists are trying to identify the properties that *constitute* having justification while others are trying to identify properties upon which justification *supervenes*. Some philosophers take the product of their analyses to be analytic truths; others claim to be engaged in some sort of empirical investigation. In addition to the fact that there are these meta-philosophical and methodological controversies lurking in the background, there are serious questions as to whether epistemologists have even agreed on the target of their analyses. Let us begin with this last question.

Epistemic vs. Nonepistemic Justification

The first distinction an epistemologist should emphasize before putting forth a theory of justification is that between *epistemic* justification and other sorts of justification. If I ask whether S's belief is justified or rational, I might be concerned, for example, with prudential justification. It seems to be a fact that a patient's believing that she will get well often increases the chances of her recovery (even if the resulting probability remains very low). In such a situation there is surely *some* sense in which the patient would be justified in having (or at least trying to get) the optimistic belief. But even if we allow that there is a sense in which the belief is justified or rational, we don't want to allow that it is *epistemically* justified or rational. Or consider the person who is becoming paralyzed by fear of death. If believing that there is an afterlife will alleviate that fear and allow the person to live a normal life, then there is again a sense in which it would be perfectly reasonable for that person to try to bring about the belief that has this effect. Prudential reasons for believing (if they exist) have something to do with the efficacy with which believing will or might achieve certain goals or ends.

There may be other nonepistemic reasons for believing or failing to believe a given proposition. It is not wildly implausible to suppose, for example, that a husband has a special *moral* obligation, and with it a moral *reason*, to believe that his wife is faithful even in the face of rather powerful *epistemic* reasons for believing otherwise. One could even imagine a kind of "*1984* culture" in which one has *legal* obligations, and legal reasons, to have certain beliefs that are, nevertheless, epistemically irrational.

Can we find a way of characterizing epistemic justification that is relatively neutral with respect to opposing analyses of the concept? As a first stab we might suggest that whatever else epistemic justification for believing some proposition is, it must make *probable* the truth of the proposition believed.[1] The patient with prudential reasons for believing in a recovery was more likely to get that recovery as a result of her beliefs, but the *prudential reasons* possessed did not increase the probability of the proposition believed—it was the belief for which the person had prudential reasons that resulted in the increased probability. Epistemic reasons make likely the truth of what is supported by those reasons, and, although it is controversial, it is tempting to suggest that the relation of making likely is not to be understood in causal terms.

Our preliminary characterization of justification as that which makes probable the truth of a proposition may not in the end be all that neutral. As we shall see in a moment, there are those who stress an alleged normative feature of epistemic justification that may call into question the conceptual primacy of probability as a key to distinguishing epistemic reasons from other sorts of reasons. Furthermore, as we shall also see, if one understands the relation of making probable in terms of a frequency conception of probability, one will inevitably beg the question with respect to certain internalist/externalist debates over the nature of justification.

Having Justification for a Belief and Having a Justified Belief

Another preliminary, but important, distinction to stress is that between having justification for a belief and having a justified belief. There seems to be a perfectly clear sense in which there may be enormously strong epistemic reasons for me to believe a given proposition even though I don't end up believing it. In such a situation we can say that there was justification for me to believe the proposition even though I didn't, of course, have a justified belief (or a belief at all) in the relevant proposition.[2] It is tempting to suppose that we can employ the concept of having justification for believing P to define what it is for a person to justifiably believe P. Specifically, one might suggest that a person justifiably believes P when that person believes P and does so *based* on justification that the person possesses. The analysis of the basing relation is a matter of much controversy. One might hope to analyze it in causal terms. If there is justification J for S to believe P, then S believes P justifiably just in case S's belief is *caused* by the fact that there is justification for him to believe P. When one presents causal analyses of any concept, however, one should immediately be on guard against counterexamples that rely on "deviant" causal chains. If I possess justification J for believing P, and that causes the hypnotist at the party to hypnotize me into believing P when I hear a doorbell ring, it is not at all clear that I have *based* the resulting belief on the justification I possess. There may be some relatively straightforward way to revise a causal account of basing to take care of such problems (by, for example, insisting that the causal connection has to be in some sense direct) but we won't explore this issue further here.

If the distinction between possessing justification and having a justified belief is legitimate, which if either of these concepts is more fundamental? If the suggestion made above were plausible, then clearly having justification would be conceptually more fundamental than having a justified belief. We are defining the latter in terms of the former. Furthermore, if we understand the basing relation in causal terms, we should beware of *philosophers* speculating about which beliefs are or are not justified. One needs empirical evidence to support a causal hypothesis, and it strikes me that philosophers are rarely in possession of the empirical evidence they would need in order to support a psychological claim about what is or is not causing a given belief. Although epistemologists have often supposed that they are trying to determine which beliefs are justified and which are not, I would suggest that if they are to restrict themselves to questions they are competent to answer, qua philosophers, they ought to concern themselves only with the question of whether there is justification for us to believe this or that proposition. Depending on one's analysis of justification, this question may itself end up being an empirical question that philosophers are not particularly competent to address, but this is an issue to which we shall return.

JUSTIFICATION AND NORMATIVITY

A surprising number of philosophers, with radically different theories of justification, seem to agree that justification is a normative concept. Unfortunately, it is not at all clear what philosophers have in mind by characterizing a concept as normative. We might begin by suggesting that normative terms are those whose meaning can be explicated using paradigm normative expressions, and we might simply list that which is paradigmatically normative. The list might be long or short depending on whether or not we think that all normative expressions can be defined in terms of a relatively few fundamental normative notions. So one might include among the paradigmatically normative such terms as "good," "ought," should," "right," "permissible," obligatory," and their opposites.

If we proceed in this fashion it seems undeniable that the concept of epistemic justification looks suspiciously like a normative concept. As Plantinga (1992) has effectively reminded us, the etymology of the word "justification" certainly suggests that we are dealing with a *value* term. And epistemologists often seem quite comfortable interchanging questions about whether or not evidence E justifies one in believing P with questions about whether or not one *should* believe P on the basis of E. In what is often taken to be an early statement of a justified true belief account of knowledge, Ayer (1956) described knowledge as true conviction where one has the *right* to be sure. So again the idea that the concept of justification is normative is at least prima facie plausible. But we must proceed cautiously. We have already seen that we must distinguish epistemic reasons from other sorts of reasons. If we can translate talk about justified belief into talk about what we ought to believe, these same considerations suggest that we must distinguish different senses of "ought." In the prudential sense of "ought," perhaps the patient ought to believe she will get better. In the moral sense of "ought," perhaps the husband ought to believe in his spouse's innocence. But the epistemologist is concerned with what one *epistemically* ought to believe, and we still need to be convinced that there is some interesting sense in which all of these different "ought" 's express normative concepts.

If we take as our paradigm of a normative "ought" the moral "ought," then I suppose the question of whether the epistemic "ought" expresses a normative concept reduces to the question of whether there are interesting connections between it and the moral "ought." The problem now is that moral philosophers have radically different views about what makes *moral* "ought" judgments normative. Some try to distinguish the normative from the nonnormative by contrasting *prescriptive* judgements with *descriptive* judgments. But if this is supposed to be the normative/nonnormative distinction, it is far from clear that the epistemologist should accept the claim that justification is a normative concept. I suspect that most epistemologists take a belief's being justified to be a *fact* that admits of description just as straightforwardly as a belief's having a certain causal history. (Indeed, on some theories of justification a belief's being justified just *is* a matter of its causal history.)

Richard Foley (1987) has suggested that we might understand epistemic justification in terms of what one ought to believe, and he goes on to understand the difference between the epistemic "ought" and other "oughts" 's as differences between species of a common genera. Crudely put, Foley's idea is that normative judgments all assess the efficacy of achieving goals or ends. There are different kinds of normative judgments concerning what we ought to do and what we ought to believe because there are different goals or ends that we are concerned to emphasize. Thus when we are talking about *morally* justified action, the relevant goal might be something like creating good and avoiding evil. When we are concerned with what *prudence* dictates, the relevant goals or ends change, perhaps to include everything that is desired intrinsically, for example. What one *legally* ought to do is a function of the extent to which an action satisfies the goal of following the law. To fit the epistemic "ought" into this framework (and thus classify usefully the kind of normativity that epistemic judgments have) all one needs to do is specify the distinctive goals or ends that define what one *epistemically* ought to believe. And the obvious candidates are the dual goals of believing what is true and avoiding belief in what is false.

Suggestive as this account might seem, it faces enormous difficulties. It must be immediately qualified to accommodate certain obvious counterexamples. Let's return to our paradigm of a nonepistemic reason, the reason the patient had for believing that she would get well. By forming the relevant belief, the patient might produce for herself a long life which she could devote to scientific and philosophical investigation, investigation that results in an enormous number of true beliefs. Despite accomplishing the goal of believing what is true, our patient (by hypothesis) had no epistemic reason for believing that she would get well. The obvious solution to this problem (one Foley suggests) is to restrict the relevant epistemic goal to that of *now* believing what is true and *now* avoiding belief in what is false. But such a revision doesn't really address the problem. Suppose there is an all powerful being who will immediately cause me to believe massive falsehood *now* unless I accept the epistemically irrational conclusion that there are mermaids. It would seem that to accomplish the goal of believing what is true and avoiding belief in what is false now I must again adopt an epistemically irrational belief.

In desperation one might try restricting the relevant epistemic goal to that of believing what is true now with respect to a given proposition. But now we are in danger of collapsing the distinction between true belief and justified belief. Trivially, the only way to accomplish the goal of believing what is true with respect to P is to believe P when P is true. The problem is that one really wants to identify the content of the epistemic "ought" with what one is *justified* in believing will accomplish the goal of now believing what is true with respect to a given proposition. But with this revision our "goal" oriented account of epistemic justification becomes pathetically circular.[3]

There are, of course, other ways to try to understand the alleged normative character of epistemic justification, but I'm not sure any are illuminating. One might suppose that when one characterizes a belief as justified one is indicating that it is not an appropriate subject for criticism. When one says of a belief that it is unjustified, one is criticizing the belief. For the view to gain even initial credibility, it would be important to distinguish the criticism of a belief from the criticism of the subject who holds the belief. It is simply false that we would always criticize a person for holding a belief we judge to be epistemically irrational. We might, for example, suppose that the person is just too stupid to be able to evaluate properly the relevant evidence and we might, as a result, seldom criticize him for the many wildly irrational beliefs he holds. But even if one makes clear that in characterizing a belief as unjustified one is criticizing the belief not the believer, I'm not sure that one can successfully argue that a person would be guilty of *contradiction* if, in the grips of some rebellious "anti-reason" movement, that person criticizes beliefs that conform to the dictates of epistemic rationality.

Once one clearly distinguishes the epistemic "ought" from others it is not in the end clear that one gets much understanding of the concept of justification from the suggestion that epistemic judgements are in some sense normative.[4]

FOUNDATIONALISM

It is tempting to think that one can leave the question of how to understand epistemic justification aside and distinguish different theories of justification in terms of how they understand the *structure* of epistemic justification. Perhaps the most famous theory of epistemic justification is *foundationalism*—the very term for the view employs a structural metaphor. But as we shall see, foundationalism is probably best understood not just as a view about the structure of justification. Properly understood, different versions of foundationalism also give an account of the *content* of epistemic judgements.

Traditional versions of foundationalism have fallen on hard times, but given the present popularity of its externalist cousins, it is still probably the received view in epistemology. Put crudely, the foundationalist believes that all justified beliefs rest ultimately on a foundation of noninferentially justified beliefs. One gets radically different versions of foundationalism depending on how the foundationalist understands noninferential justification.

A little reflection suggests that the vast majority of the propositions for which we have justification have that status only because we justifiably believe other different propositions. So, for example, I justifiably believe that Hitler killed himself, but only because I justifiably believe (among other things) that various generally reliable historical texts describe the event. Foundationalists want to contrast my inferential justification for this belief about Hitler with a kind of justification that is not *constituted*, in whole or in part, by the having of other justified beliefs. But why should we suppose that there *is* a kind of justification that is in this way different from inferential justification?

THE REGRESS ARGUMENTS FOR
FOUNDATIONALISM

Suppose I tell you as you approach your fiftieth birthday that you will shortly go insane. I offer as my evidence that you have a genetic defect that, like a time bomb, goes off at the age of 50. Naturally alarmed, you ask me what reason I have for concluding that you have the gene. I respond that it is just a hunch on my part. As soon as you discover that I have no epistemic justification at all for believing that you have the gene, you will immediately conclude that my bizarre conclusion about your impending insanity is wildly irrational. Generalizing from examples like this, one might suggest the following principle:

> To be justified in believing P on the basis of E one must be justified in believing E

Now consider another example. Suppose I claim to be justified in believing that Fred will die shortly and offer as my justification that a certain line across his palm (the infamous "lifeline") is short. Rightly skeptical you wonder this time what reason I have for believing that palm lines have anything whatsoever to do with length of life. As soon as you become satisfied that I have no justification for supposing that there is any kind of probabilistic connection between the character of this line and Fred's life, you will again reject my claim to have a justified belief about Fred's impending demise.[5] That suggests that we might expand our *Principle of Inferential Justification* (PIJ) to include a second clause:

> (PIJ) To have justification for believing P on the basis of E one must not only have (1) justification for believing E, but (2) justification for believing that E makes probable P.

The Epistemic Regress Argument

With PIJ one can present a relatively straightforward *epistemic* regress argument for foundationalism. If all justification were inferential then for someone S to have justification for believing some proposition P, S must be in a position to legitimately infer it from some other proposition E1. But E1 could justify S in believing P only if S were justified in believing E1, and if all justification were inferential, the only way for S to be justified in believing E1 would be to infer it from some other proposition E2 justifiably believed, a proposition which in turn would have to be inferred from some other proposition E3, which is justifiably believed, and so on, ad infinitum. But finite beings cannot complete an infinitely long chain of reasoning and so, if all justification were inferential, no-one would be justified in believing anything at all to any extent whatsoever. This most radical of all skepticisms is absurd (it entails that one couldn't even be justified in believing it) and so there must be a kind of justification that is not inferential, that is, there must be noninferentially justified beliefs which terminate regresses of justification.

If we accept the more controversial second clause of PIJ, the looming regresses proliferate. Not only must S above be justified in believing E1, S must also be justified in believing that E1 makes probable P, a proposition that would have to be inferred (if there are no foundations) from some other proposition F1, which would have to be inferred from F2, and so on ad infinitum. But S would also need to be justified in believing that F1 does in fact make likely that E1 makes likely P, a proposition he would need to infer from some other proposition G1, which he would need to infer from some other proposition G2. . . . And he would need to infer that G1 does indeed make likely that F1 makes likely that E1 makes likely P. . . . Without noninferential justification, it would seem that we would need to complete an infinite number of infinitely long chains of reasoning in order to be justified in believing anything!

Peter Klein (1999) has recently defended a view he calls *infinitism*. The infinitist refuses to accept the existence of noninferential justification, acknowledges that with the availability of only inferential justification, justified belief would require us to be *able* to come up with infinitely many arguments for infinitely many premises, but argues that finite beings might very well have the capacity to do just that. There is nothing absurd in the supposition that people have an infinite number of justified beliefs (most of which are not, of course, conscious at any given time). You believe justifiably that $2>1$, that $3>1$, that $4>1$, and so on, ad infinitum. While you cannot, of course, *complete* an infinitely long chain of reasoning, you might be such that you could offer an argument for every proposition you believe. And there is nothing absurd about the suggestion that your ability to do just that is necessary for each of your beliefs being justified.

There seems to be something very odd about the idea that I need arguments to support some of my beliefs, for example, the belief that I'm in pain now, or the belief that I exist now. But even if the availability of an infinite number of dispositional beliefs weakens the foundationalists' claim that without noninferential justification we inevitably face skepticism, it's not clear that the infinitist has a rejoinder to a second regress argument for foundationalism.

The Conceptual Regress Argument

The epistemic regress argument discussed above relies on the unacceptability of a vicious *epistemic* regress. But one might also argue, more fundamentally, that without a *concept* of noninferential justification, one faces a vicious conceptual regress. What precisely is our understanding of inferential justification? What makes PIJ true (with or without its controversial second clause). It is at least tempting to answer that PIJ is analytic (true by definition). Part of what it *means* to claim that someone has inferential justification for believing some proposition P is that his justification consists in his ability to infer P from some other proposition E1 that is justifiably believed. But if anything like this is a plausible analysis of the *concept* of inferential justification, we face a potentially vicious conceptual regress. Our *understanding* of inferential justification presupposes an understanding of justification. We need to introduce a concept of noninferential justification in terms of which we can then ultimately define inferential justification.

Consider an analogy. Suppose a philosopher introduces the notion of instrumental goodness (something's being good as a means). That philosopher offers the following crude analysis of what it is for something to be instrumentally good: X is instrumentally good when X leads to something Y, which is good. Even if we were to accept this analysis of instrumental goodness, it is clear that we haven't yet located the conceptual *source* of goodness. Our analysis of instrumental goodness presupposes an understanding of what it is for something to be good and ultimately presupposes an understanding of what it is for something to be intrinsically good. The conceptual regress argument for foundationalism puts forth the thesis that inferential justification stands to noninferential justification as instrumental goodness stands to intrinsic goodness.

NONINFERENTIAL JUSTIFICATION

If there is a conceptual regress argument for foundationalism, then one hasn't completed one's foundationalist account of epistemic justification until one gives an account of noninferential justification, an account that itself employs no epistemic concepts. Those who continue to insist that epistemic justification is a normative concept, who reject naturalistic accounts of value, and who further claim that fundamental normative concepts cannot be defined, might claim that an account of noninferential justification consists in an identification of the properties of a belief or a believer upon which noninferential justification supervenes (Goldman 1979). The term "supervenience" is a piece of philosophical jargon upon which many these days rely. To say that Y supervenes upon X is usually just to claim that there is some sort of necessary connection between X and Y where one can distinguish as many species of supervenience as one can distinguish kinds of necessary connections. In what follows, I'm going to discuss different accounts of noninferential justification in terms of the conditions with which the proponent of the view *identifies* having noninferential justification. If one is nervous about identity claims one can translate the views into the language of supervenience.

NONINFERENTIAL JUSTIFICATION AS INFALLIBLE BELIEF

Descartes may be the most well-known foundationalist. Although he almost never talked about justification (his concern was with knowledge), it seems clear that he embraced the idea that there is a way of knowing that does not rely on what we have called inferential justification. On the most natural interpretation of his views, Descartes identified foundational knowledge with infallible belief. Famously, Descartes found his "first" truth in knowledge of his own existence. What distinguished Descartes's belief about his own existence from other beliefs is that the mere fact that he believed that he existed entailed that he did. Shall we understand noninferential justification in Cartesian terms? Shall we say that S's belief that P is noninferentially justified at t when S's believing P at t entails that P is true?

There are relatively few Cartesian foundationalists around these days. The view is plagued with difficulties. As Lehrer (1974) and others have pointed out, it is far from clear that this concept of infallible belief has much relevance to our fundamental understanding of noninferential justification. Consider just one technical problem. Every necessary truth is trivially entailed by all propositions (P entails Q when it is impossible for P to be true while Q is false, but if it is impossible for Q to be false then it is entailed by everything). So given the above way of understanding infallible belief, all belief in necessary truth would have noninferential justification. But this just seems wrong. If I whimsically believe some proposition whose necessity is far too complicated for me to grasp, it hardly seems plausible to maintain that the belief would have noninferential justification.

Even if we can find a way of solving the above problem, most contemporary epistemologists are convinced that foundational justification restricted to what can be infallibly believed allows far too insubstantial a foundation to support the complex edifice of what we take ourselves to be justified in believing. There may be a few contingent propositions that are trivially entailed by the fact that they are believed—my belief that I exist, that I have beliefs, that I am conscious—but once we get past propositions whose very subject matter encompasses the fact that they are believed, it's hard to come up with uncontroversial examples of infallible beliefs. As Ayer (1956, 19) argued, as long as the belief that P is one state of affairs and P's being the case is an entirely different state of affairs, it's hard to see how it can be impossible for the former to occur without the latter.

INFALLIBLE JUSTIFICATION

Rather than try to identify noninferential justification with some intrinsic feature of a belief that renders the belief infallible, one might instead look for a kind of *justification* that can *accompany* a belief and eliminate the possibility of error. Let us say that S's belief that P is infallibly justified at t when S's justification for believing P at t contains as a constituent the very truth-maker for P. But how can the justification for a belief be identified with a state of affairs that includes as a constituent something that makes true the belief?

Some traditional foundationalists have held that beliefs about experiences are justified by the very experiences that are the subject matter of the beliefs. Thus, for example, it might seem initially plausible to suppose that when I am in pain, it is the pain itself that justifies me in believing that I am in pain. On such a view, the noninferential justification I have for believing that I'm in pain—the experience of pain—trivially guarantees the truth of what I believe. But such a view clearly cries out for some further account of what distinguishes the experience of pain from, say, Caesar's assassination. The above foundationalist wants to claim that while the fact that I'm in pain can justify me in believing that I'm in pain, the fact that Caesar was assassinated cannot justify my belief that Caesar was assassinated. But what is the relevant difference between the two facts that makes it implausible to claim that one is a noninferential justifier, while the other is not? It won't do to call attention to the fact that the pain is an experience of *mine*. *My* body is undergoing all sorts of changes right now, the vast majority of which don't justify me in believing that they are occurring. So we still need a principled account of what distinguishes those states of mine that can justify beliefs about them from those states of mine that cannot.

It is tempting to suppose that the foundationalist is better off appealing to some special *relation* that I have to my pain that makes it unnecessary to look to other beliefs in order to justify my belief that I'm in pain. It's not my pain that justifies me in believing that I'm in pain. It is, rather, the fact that I have a kind of *access* to my pain that no-one else has that makes my belief noninferentially justified (while others must rely on inference in order to discover that I'm in this state). The sort of access this foundationalist appeals to is not, of course, justified belief. We need an understanding of noninferential justification that does not rely on an understanding of justified belief. Bertrand Russell (1959 and 1984) contrasted *acquaintance* with properties and facts with propositional knowledge. Acquaintance is a sui generis relation that a subject bears to certain facts in virtue of which the subject gets a kind of justification for believing the propositions made true by those facts. A slightly more complicated version of the view maintains that one is noninferentially justified in believing a proposition P when one is directly acquainted with not only the fact that P but also with a relation of correspondence between the thought that P and the fact that P (where the correspondence between a thought and a fact is the essence of a thought's being true). Since acquaintance is a relation that requires the existence of its relata, there is a trivial sense in which one can't possess this sort of justification for believing a proposition while the proposition is false.[6]

The acquaintance theory might have one interesting advantage over alternative theories in that it has the potential to offer a *unified* account of noninferential justification. According to most traditional foundationalists, two of the best candidates for noninferentially justified beliefs are empirical beliefs about the current contents of one's mind and a priori beliefs about relatively straightforward necessary truths. On the acquaintance theory, both direct knowledge of necessary truths and direct knowledge of contingent truths about one's current consciousness would have the same *source* of justification—acquaintance with facts. The difference between the two kinds of knowledge is not so much a difference in the sources of the knowledge but in the contents of the knowledge. The objects of acquaintance in the case of direct knowledge of mental states are states of affairs whose occurrence is not eternal—the objects of acquaintance in the case of direct knowledge of necessary truths are eternal states of affairs.

OBJECTIONS TO TRADITIONAL FOUNDATIONALISM

In one of the most influential arguments against foundationalism, Wilfrid Sellars (1963, 131–132) argued that the idea of foundational justification as something's being "given" to one in consciousness (something's being an object of direct acquaintance) contains irreconcilable tensions. On the one hand, to ensure that something's being given does not involve any other beliefs, proponents of the view want noninferential justification to be untainted by the application of concepts. On the other hand, the whole point of foundationalism is to end a regress of justification, to give us secure foundational justification for the rest of what we justifiably infer from those foundations. But to make sense of *inferences* from our foundations, we must ensure that what is given to us in consciousness has a *truth value*. The kind of thing that has a truth value, however, involves the application of concepts. But to apply a concept is to make a judgment about class membership, and to make a judgment about class membership always involves relating the thing about which the judgment is made to other paradigm members of the class. These judgments of relevant similarity will minimally involve beliefs about the past and thus be inferential in character (assuming that we can have no "direct" access to facts about the past).

The above objection obviously relies on a host of controversial presuppositions. In order to deflect the force of the objection, a traditional acquaintance foundationalist will no doubt emphasize the following. Being directly acquainted with a fact is not, by itself, to have a justified belief in some proposition. It is only acquaintance with a fact conjoined with awareness of a thought's corresponding to a fact that constitutes having noninferential justification. There may well be all kinds of creatures who have acquaintance with facts but no justification for believing anything precisely because they lack the capacity to form thoughts. Secondly, the classical foundationalist will, or at least should, reject the suggestion that to apply a concept is to relate the thing to which one applies the concept to other entities that fall under the concept. Such a view simply invites a vicious regress of the sort that the foundationalist is trying so desperately to avoid. After all, my judgement that X is similar to Y itself involves applying the concept of similarity to the pair X/Y. In doing so am I comparing the pair X/Y to other things that are similar to each other? In fact, I can judge something to be pain without having any recollection whatsoever of any other experience that I have had.

The direct acquaintance theorist does presuppose the intelligibility of acquaintance with facts and in doing so presupposes the intelligibility of a world that has "structure" independently of any structure imposed by the mind. Certain radical versions of "antirealism" reject that commitment to a strong "correspondence" conception of truth and with it the intelligibility of a thought/world fit of which we can be directly aware.[7] While there is some plausibility to the claim that there are, in some sense, alternative conceptual frameworks that we can impose on the world, it is surely absurd to suppose that it is even in principle possible for a mind to force a structure on a literally unstructured world. There are indefinitely many ways to sort the books in a library and some are just as useful as others, but there would be no way to begin sorting books were books undifferentiated. If we couldn't take notice of differences in the world with which we are acquainted, it's not clear how we could "choose" conceptual frameworks with which to make sense of our experience.

Laurence BonJour (1985) raised another highly influential objection to all forms of classical foundationalism (an objection raised before he himself joined the ranks of the traditional foundationalists). The objection presupposed a strong form of what we might call access internalism. Put superficially, the access internalist argues that a feature of a belief or epistemic situation that makes a belief noninferentially justified must be a feature to which we have actual or potential access. Moreover, we must have access to the fact that the feature in question makes probable the truth of what we believe. So suppose some foundationalist offers an account of noninferential justification according to which a belief is noninferentially justified if it has some characteristic X (where X can stand for any sort of property including complex relational properties). BonJour then argues that the mere fact that the belief has X could not, even in principle, justify the believer in holding the belief. The believer would also need access to (justified belief that!) the belief in question has X and that beliefs of this sort (X beliefs) are likely to be true. At least one of these propositions could only be known through inference, and thus the putative noninferential justification is destroyed.

One must be careful in one's commitment to access requirements for justification lest the view become unintelligible. One can hardly expect an epistemologist to concede that any attempt to identify the conditions X that constitute justification will fail unless one supplements the account with conditions referring to actual or potential access to X. It is immediately clear that one couldn't even in principle satisfy this access internalist. If one tries to supplement X with a believer's having access to X, one simply creates a new condition Y (X plus access) which, according to the view, would itself need to be supplemented by the addition of access requirements to Y. But Y plus access (call it Z) will also be insufficient for justification—we will need to add access conditions to Z, and so on, ad infinitum. The most the access internalist could coherently assert is some sort of necessary connection between having justification and having actual or potential access to justification, where the access in question is not *constitutive* of the justification. But however one qualifies one's access requirements for justification, access internalism seems far too demanding a theory of epistemic justification. It seems to require of epistemic agents the capacity to form ever more complex justified metabeliefs about the justificatory status of beliefs below.

TRADITIONAL FOUNDATIONALISM
AND SKEPTICISM

The dissatisfaction with traditional foundationalism probably has as much to do with the threat of skepticism as with any more technical problem facing the view. If we understand noninferential justification in terms of infallible belief or acquaintance with a thought/world fit, on most versions of the traditional view there isn't much we are noninferentially justified in believing. If acquaintance is a real relation, it seems implausible, for example, to suppose that one is directly acquainted with facts about the past or the external world. The following sort of argument seems at least initially powerful:

1. It's possible that we seem to remember having done something X without having actually done it.

2. The justification we have for believing that we did X when we have a vivid "hallucinatory" memory would be the same as the justification we have for believing that we did X were we to veridically remember doing X.

3. The justification we have for believing that we did X when we have vivid "false" memory experience is not direct acquaintance with our having done X (acquaintance is a relation that requires the existence of its relata).

Therefore,

4. The justification we have for believing that we did X when we have a veridical memory experience is not direct acquaintance with our having done X.

An exactly parallel argument is available with respect to justification for believing propositions about the external world. Such justification never gets any better than the "evidence of our senses." But,

1. The justification S has for believing some proposition about the physical world when suffering a vivid hallucinatory experience is the same as the justification S has for believing that proposition were S to have a phenomenologically indistinguishable veridical experience.

2. The justification S has when hallucinating is obviously not direct acquaintance with some feature of the physical world.

Therefore,

3. The justification S has in veridical experience is not direct acquaintance with some feature of the physical world.

If the above arguments are sound (they are certainly controversial), it is not entirely clear what will be left in the foundations of empirical justification. The classic empiricist view is that we have noninferentially justified empirical beliefs only about present conscious states. But it has been more than a little difficult to figure out how one can legitimately infer the rest of what we think we are justified in believing from such a limited set of premises. The problem is particularly acute if we accept the second clause of the principle of inferential justification. Given that clause, to advance beyond the foundations of justified belief we would inevitably need to employ nondeductive reasoning and, according to PIJ, that would ultimately require us to have noninferential justification for believing propositions describing probability connections between evidence and conclusions. As long as the relation of making probable is not defined in terms of frequency, as long as making probable is construed as a kind of "quasi-logical relation" analogous to, but different from entailment, it *may* not be absurd to suppose that one can have noninferential a priori justification for believing that one set of propositions makes probable another. It is, however, an understatement to suggest that the view is problematic.[8]

There is another source of dissatisfaction with the classic empiricist's suggestion that we identify noninferentially justified beliefs with beliefs about the character of present experience. Many would argue, on phenomenological grounds, that we rarely consider propositions describing the intrinsic character of experience. In sense experience our thought is almost always directed out of ourselves and on the existence of an external reality. It requires, the argument goes, considerable effort to turn "inward" to focus on appearance rather than external reality. If most people don't even have the beliefs that the traditional view regards as the only candidates for noninferentially justified beliefs, it seems that once again one faces an unpalatable, fairly extreme, skepticism.

EXTERNALIST VERSIONS OF FOUNDATIONALISM

Contemporary externalists offer a refreshingly undemanding account of both non-inferential and inferential justification. Just about all externalists reject the second clause of the principle of inferential justification. Moreover, noninferential justification is often understood in such a way as to allow for the possibility of a much broader foundation. Consider, for example, the best known version of externalism, Goldman's reliabilism (first set forth in Goldman 1979).

The fundamental idea behind reliabilism is strikingly simple. Justified beliefs are reliably produced beliefs. Justified beliefs are worth having because justified beliefs are probably true. The view is a version of foundationalism because it allows us to distinguish two importantly different sorts of justified beliefs—those that result from belief-independent processes and those that result from belief-dependent processes. The former are beliefs that are produced by "software" of the brain that takes as its "input" stimuli other than beliefs; the latter are beliefs produced by processes that take as their input at least some other beliefs. So, for example, it is possible that we have evolved in such a way that when prompted with certain sensory input, we immediately and unreflectively reach conclusions about external objects. And we may live in a world in which beliefs produced in such a way are usually true. Crude versions of reliabilism will regard such beliefs as noninferentially justified. Many of our beliefs, of course, result, at least in part, from prior beliefs we hold. We deduce and nondeductively infer a host of propositions describing the world in which we live. Again, on the crudest version of reliabilism, these belief-dependent processes are reliable when the "output" beliefs are usually true provided that the input beliefs are true.

There are a host of questions that a reliabilist must answer in developing the details of the view. In the crude summary provided above we characterized the reliability of a belief-independent process in terms of the frequency with which its output beliefs are true. But it takes little imagination to construct counterexamples to this naive a version of the view. Temporary paranoia might cause me to form two, and only two, beliefs about the malicious intentions of my friends, both of which happen to be true. But it hardly seems plausible to suppose that this coincidence makes for a 100 percent reliable belief-forming process. Minimally, the reliabilist will turn to counterfactuals about the frequency with which output beliefs would be true were the process to produce indefinitely many of them.[9]

If we settle the question of how to define reliability, we still need to determine whether the relevant concept of reliability should be relativized to circumstances. It seems obvious that a belief-forming process might be entirely reliable in one environment, quite unreliable in another. Intuitively, even if the process nets us a majority of true beliefs, we don't want to concede that its operation in the "wrong" environment will result in justified beliefs. The obvious solution would be to define noninferential justification for a given believer in a given environment: S is noninferentially justified in believing P in C at t when S's belief that P in C at t is produced by a belief-independent process that is reliable in C at t.

While perhaps the most influential, reliabilism is only one version of the externalist alternatives to traditional foundationalism. Armstrong (1973), for example, suggests the closely related view that some beliefs are noninferentially justified (basic) when they register accurately their subject matter the way an effective thermometer registers accurately the temperature. Although he would resent the suggestion that he is offering a theory of epistemic *justification* at all, Plantinga (1993) defines a concept of warrant in terms of beliefs produced by a cognitive apparatus that is properly functioning. He has his own distinctive theistic suggestion for how to understand proper function, but invites allies to try to define the notion in naturalistic terms (for example, in terms of evolutionary history). Plantinga's view is also a version of foundationalism because he holds that properly functioning belief-producing mechanisms need not involve *inference* from justified belief.

The most striking feature of most versions of externalism is the way in which they open the door to the possibility of a vastly expanded class of noninferentially justified beliefs. According to the reliabilist, for example, it is *never impossible* for any belief to acquire noninferential justification. No matter what I believe, it is always in principle possible that the belief is produced by a reliable belief-independent process. There might be a God who unbeknownst to me causes me to believe with complete conviction a host of true propositions and never causes me to believe a proposition that is false. Such divine inspiration would be a paradigm of a reliable belief-forming process and the resulting beliefs would all be noninferentially justified. According to the reliabilist, whether or not a given belief is justified depends entirely on whether we are fortunate enough to live in a world in which our cognitive mechanisms produce in us beliefs that are largely successful in getting at the truth.

It is tempting to suppose that externalist versions of foundationalism only delay skeptical problems. Many externalists themselves seem to allow that one can legitimately worry that one has justification for believing that first-level beliefs are justified. But it is another interesting (some would argue odd) feature of views like reliabilism that there really is no greater problem securing second-level justification than there is for securing first-level justification. If, for example, beliefs about the past produced by memory result from reliable belief-independent processes, then the view implies that beliefs about the past are noninferentially justified. But if beliefs about the past are noninferentially justified then I can easily justify my belief that they are justified. All I need to do is remember that certain beliefs about the past turned out to be true when I relied on memory and employ a standard inductive argument to generalize that beliefs produced in this way are usually true. Of course the classic foundationalist will shudder at this shocking indifference to begging the question. They will protest that one cannot use memory to justify one's belief that memory is reliable! But if reliability really is the essence of justification, it's not clear why one can't study memory using memory to get justified beliefs about its reliability. The investigation into which belief-forming processes are or are not reliable seems more a task for the cognitive psychologist than for the philosopher, but then perhaps this is why some contemporary epistemologists attempt to straddle the boundary between philosophy and empirical science.

CRITICISMS OF EXTERNALIST
FOUNDATIONALISM

If classical foundationalism seemed to require too much in order for us to secure justified beliefs, externalist foundationalism strikes many as requiring too little. At least in a philosophical context, we are interested in having justification because we are interested in gaining a certain sort of *assurance* of truth. If we start to wonder whether our beliefs about external reality accurately represent that reality, it doesn't seem particularly useful to be told that we *may* have perfectly justified beliefs provided that they are produced in such a way that they usually accurately represent reality! The justification the philosopher seeks must be such that when one possesses it one's philosophical curiosity is satisfied.

If the primary dissatisfaction with externalism is the feeling that the traditional epistemological questions that have so interested philosophers have simply been redefined in such a way as to change the subject, there are also more technical objections that have been raised to the view. Perhaps the most striking involves a variation on a thought experiment used for a different purpose by Descartes. We'll illustrate the objection focusing again on reliabilism, but variations on the theme affect most externalist analyses of epistemic justification.

Consider a possible world (a kind of *Matrix* world) in which people are consistently and massively deceived with respect to external reality by a very powerful being. It seems intuitively plausible to suppose that the victims of demonic machination would have precisely the same sort of justification we have for believing (falsely as it turns out) what they do about the world around them. But by hypothesis the demon's victims' beliefs result from unreliable processes, while, we may suppose for the argument, our beliefs result from reliable processes. If the justificatory status of the demon-world beliefs is the same as those of our world, then it just seems wrong to suppose that reliability is the essence of justification. Since his original paper advocating reliabilism, Goldman himself has struggled with how to respond to the intuitive force of this (and related) objections. After flirting (1986) with the idea of identifying the relevant reliability that defines justification as reliability in "normal" worlds (roughly, worlds in which certain fundamental beliefs we have about this world are true—whether or not they are true in the actual world!), Goldman (1988) eventually acknowledges two quite distinct concepts of justification: strong (defined by a hard-core reliabilism in which we simply refuse to acknowledge that demon-world inhabitants have epistemic justification) and weak (a less demanding concept of epistemic justification roughly defined in terms of meeting "community standards").

EVIDENTIAL EXTERNALISM

If one is convinced by the externalist that the traditional foundationalist has a concept of justification so demanding that it implies the implausible conclusion that the vast majority of our beliefs are unjustified, one might develop a kind of compromise. One might retain traditional foundationalism, replete with the principle of inferential justification, as capturing a kind of *ideal* epistemic justification that philosophers seek to attain, but which most people (and most philosophers, for that matter) fail to gain. To soften the blow, one might acknowledge a less demanding concept of epistemic justification that one *might* be able to satisfy through a kind of nonpropositional analogue of inference. Suppose, for example, that many of our beliefs about the external world are *caused* by the fact that we have had and are having certain sensations (together with a host of justified background beliefs, most of which remain dispositional). Suppose further that we rarely form beliefs about the character of these sensations, have long since forgotten many of the relevant past experiences (that nevertheless still exert their causal influence), and, of course, rarely, if ever, consciously construct some argument for the ordinary beliefs and expectations we constantly form about the world around us. The facts about sensations that causally contribute to our beliefs about the world are also *truth-makers* for propositions (whether we entertain the propositions or not) and it might be the case that the conjunction of propositions made true by the causes of our belief, together with the enormous structure of propositions dispositionally believed that form our epistemic "background," do make probable (via some sort of legitimate reasoning the epistemologist struggles, usually in vain, to uncover) common-sense, everyday beliefs. Perhaps we can acknowledge a kind of "unreflective" epistemic justification that we *might* possess provided that our internal states (including dispositional beliefs and noncognitive states like sensation) satisfy the conditions described above.

Susan Haack (1993) develops a version of this view but takes a very liberal attitude with respect to what proposition we can employ as the propositional counterpart to sensation. She seems to suggest that we can take the relevant proposition describing a sensation to be one that describes it as the sensation usually produced by a certain physical object under certain conditions. Even if the skeptic allows us a less demanding concept of epistemic justification, that skeptic will no doubt balk at the suggestion that we can take evidential connections between propositions formed this way to be the truth-makers for claims about epistemic justification. One does need criteria for choosing the propositional counterparts of sensations playing their causal role, but if it is facts that are both causes and truth-makers for propositions, one can identify the relevant evidential proposition that corresponds to a sensation as the one made true by the fact about the sensation that is causally efficacious in producing the belief in whose epistemic status we are interested.

The above account might seem to be only a minor variation on the concept of epistemic justification defined by reliabilism. Whether this is so depends on how one understands evidential connections. If making probable is a kind of quasi-logical relation holding between propositions (perhaps even holding necessarily) then the concept of unreflective justification sketched above will be able to resolve the demon-world objection to reliabilism. The internal causes of belief in the demon world are, by hypothesis, the same as the internal causes of belief in "normal" worlds. The evidential propositional counterparts to the sensory states will be the same, and the justificatory status of the resulting beliefs will be the same. Of course, there *may* (relative to what we know reflectively) be no evidential connections between the propositions that form our justified background beliefs, the propositions made true by sensation, and the propositions that constitute the conclusions of our common-sense beliefs, but should that be the case, skepticism wins the day both with respect to demanding and undemanding concepts of epistemic justification.

CONTEXTUALISM

While the evidential externalist I discussed above is prepared to distinguish more and less demanding standards of justification, the *contextualist*, for example, Annis (1978), allows for standards to "float" where the requirements for justified belief are determined in part by the context of inquiry. Recent versions of the view are most often accounts of knowledge. So, for example, Lewis (1996) suggests that S knows that P when S has a true belief that P where S's evidence eliminates all relevant alternatives to P. What makes the view contextualist is that relevancy is determined by context, including such subjective factors as whether or not the believer is taking seriously the possibility of an alternative. The view is supposed to have the virtue of accommodating both common sense and skepticism—knowledge claims in ordinary contexts will remain true, while in philosophical contexts the skeptic is likely to win the day by forcing us to consider (and thus make relevant) various skeptical scenarios. An analogous view about requirements for justification might allow that one only needs justification for believing certain premises crucial to our reaching conclusions when these background beliefs come under challenge. In ordinary contexts where everyone is happy to allow the truth of our premises and the legitimacy of our reasoning, we can get justified beliefs without having to do what would be necessary were these to come under skeptical challenge.

There is, no doubt, a *grain* of truth in the contextualist's account of our ordinary, everyday assessments of justification and knowledge. In the context of assessing the justification available for accepting a scientific theory, one simply doesn't worry about the justification we have for believing in the existence of a past or an external world. We assume in the context of such a discussion that we have certain knowledge and that certain forms of reasoning are legitimate, and go on to ask whether on these assumptions, we can legitimately infer the truth of the theory in which we are interested. Philosophers themselves often raise certain objections to common sense beliefs in one philosophical context, only to assume the truth of those very beliefs in a different philosophical context.[10] Monks debating some esoteric proposition concerning the details of their theology may well take for granted the reliability of the Old Testament as a source of truth, presumably knowing full well that should they end up debating an atheist they would need to take a quite different approach.

None of this seems to provide any real support for an interesting form of contextualism, either about knowledge or justification. That we will often "bracket" one set of issues in the context of addressing another, that we will often be interested in seeing what follows from a given set of assumptions, setting aside our ability to "satisfy reason" with respect to those assumptions, is perfectly compatible with our recognizing that in the end our reasons for accepting our conclusions are never really any better than our reasons for accepting the host of background assumptions that remain in the background until we decide to focus our attention upon them.[11]

COHERENTISM

Despite the radical differences among the traditional foundationalists and their more recent externalist counterparts, members of both camps typically share a common conception of the *foundational* structure of epistemic justification—they are common allies in the fight against coherence theories of epistemic justification.

The coherence theorist rejects the foundationalist's conception of justification as *linear*. Convinced that there is no escape from the "circle of beliefs", the coherence theorist argues that we must understand the epistemic justification for a belief in terms of the way in which the proposition believed *coheres* with other propositions believed. We can distinguish pure and impure coherence theories of justification. A *pure* coherence theory takes the justification of *every* belief to be a matter of coherence. An impure theory restricts the thesis to a subclass of beliefs. BonJour (1985), for example, defended a coherence theory of epistemic justification for *empirical* beliefs only, but there is nothing in principle to prevent a coherence theorist from restricting the theory to an even more narrow subclass of beliefs.

The vast majority of philosophers who support a coherence theory of justification take the relevant beliefs with which a given justified belief must cohere to be those present in a single individual. What justifies S in believing P is that

P coheres with some set of propositions that S occurrently or dispositionally believes (or would believe were S to reflect in a certain way). What justifies *you* in believing P is P's coherence with other propositions *you* do or would believe. But while epistemic justification relativized to an *individual's* belief system is the norm for coherence theories, one finds at least some interest in what we might call a *social* coherence theory. Roughly, the idea is that what justifies S in believing P is a matter not just of what S believes, but of what others in the community believe. A very crude social coherence theory of epistemic justification might hold that S is justified in believing P only if P coheres with the propositions believed by all or most members of S's community. Because one can distinguish as many different communities as one likes, epistemic justification on this view must always be relativized to a given community. For simplicity, we will focus on the kind of coherence theories that relativize epistemic justification to an individual's belief system, but most of what we say will apply *mutatis mutandis* to other versions of the view.

Once we are clear about which beliefs a given belief must cohere with in order to be epistemically justified, we'll need more information from the coherence theorist about what constitutes coherence. Often the coherence theorist will begin by claiming that coherence must minimally involve logical consistency, but go on to concede that consistency is far too weak a requirement to constitute the mainstay of coherence. One can imagine a person with a thousand beliefs, none of which have anything to do with any of the others but where each proposition believed is consistent with the conjunction of the others. Such a belief system hardly seems a paradigm of coherence, and we would be reluctant to concede that each has epistemic justification.

In an interesting argument, Foley (1979) has argued persuasively that consistency among the propositions one believes is not even a necessary condition for the beliefs' being justified. Focusing on lottery-type situations, Foley argues that we can easily think of a set of inconsistent beliefs each of which is perfectly justified. If there are a thousand people in a lottery that I know to be fair, I can justifiably believe of each participant that he or she will lose and also justifiably believe that not all of them will lose. None of these beliefs is logically consistent with the conjunction of the rest, but each is justified. So the coherence theorist is wrong to tell us that a belief of ours is epistemically justified only if it is consistent with the rest of what we believe. A closely related problem concerns the possibility of admitting into one's belief system a necessary falsehood F. If one believes even one necessary falsehood, then none of one's beliefs will be consistent with the rest of what one believes; the conjunction of a necessary falsehood with any other proposition is itself a necessary falsehood. It seems more than a little harsh, however, to let one philosophical or mathematical error of this sort destroy the possibility of there being *any* epistemic justification for believing *any* proposition.

Coherence theorists are wary of requiring too much for the coherence of a belief system. So, for example, one might initially suppose that a model of a coherent belief system might be one in which each proposition believed is entailed by the conjunction of the rest. But one might also worry that such a requirement is far too difficult to come by. In one sense, however, the worry is misplaced. It is actually extremely easy to satisfy the requirement. Indeed, if we include dispositional beliefs, I can confidently claim to have a belief system in which each of my beliefs *is* entailed by the rest of what I believe. And the same is, or should be, true of everyone who has taken and remembers a course in elementary logic. One of the truth-functional connectives we all learned was material implication. As long as we know its truth functional definition, we know that if P is true and Q is true then it is true that P materially implies Q and true that Q materially implies P. Consequently, I assume that if we believe P and believe Q, we will also believe (at least dispositionally) that P materially implies Q and that Q materially implies P. But then for any two propositions P and Q that I happen to believe, there will be in my belief system propositions entailing each. P will be entailed by (Q and Q materially implies P) and Q will be entailed by (P and P materially implies Q). The coherence theorist will no doubt be tempted to reply that the belief in the conditionals is entirely parasitic upon the *prior* beliefs in P and Q, but once one abandons a linear conception of justification, it's not clear what sort of *epistemic* priority P and Q are supposed to have just because they may have preceded the belief that P is true if and only if Q is true.

Ironically, perhaps probabilistic connections provide a stronger "glue" for coherence than logical relations. So a coherence theorist is likely to claim that a system of beliefs increases its coherence the more the propositions believed stand in probabilistic connections with each other. Explanatory coherence theorists emphasize the importance of having a belief system in which one maximizes the number of propositions believed where one has within one's belief system propositions that can explain the propositions believed. It's difficult, however, to regard entailment as anything other than the limit of making probable, and if it is too easy to come by a belief system in which each proposition believed is entailed by the rest, it's hard to see how one can avoid the problem by emphasizing probability.

There are enough powerful arguments against coherence theories of justification that one need not turn to more problematic concerns. And some objections to a coherence theory do seem to miss the mark. So, for example, some seem to be concerned with the fact that the coherence theorist embraces a radical relativization of justification. But any plausible account of epistemic justification will acknowledge that one person S can be justified in believing P, while another R is justified in believing not-P. The traditional foundationalist will no doubt trace the difference between the justificatory status of S and R's beliefs to differences in their memories of past experiences, but it is still the case that radical relativization of justification should be embraced as much by traditional foundationalists as by coherentists.

There is, perhaps, the vague concern that a coherence theory of justification makes one's choice of what to believe far too subjective. I want to know what to believe and the coherence theorist tells me to come up with a coherent set of beliefs. But for every coherent set of propositions I entertain, I can think of another set inconsistent with the first but just as internally coherent. Won't this make the epistemic choice of what to believe implausibly arbitrary? If a theory of justification is to give one guidance, and if one were to somehow start one's deliberations about what to believe with no beliefs at all, then it would seem that the coherence theorist gives one no advice at all concerning what to believe. But we are no doubt simply *caused* to believe firmly certain propositions, and given that we find ourselves with certain beliefs and are trying to determine whether or not to hold still others, it's not clear that the coherence theorist leaves us with no guidance.

A similar response can be made to those who worry that the coherence theorist cuts us off from the world that makes true or false our beliefs. Nothing in the theory, however, precludes the possibility of our beliefs being caused by features of a belief-independent world. The *epistemological* coherence theory holds only that whatever the cause of our beliefs, their epistemic status is a function solely of coherence.[12]

Perhaps the most devastating criticism of coherence theories was, ironically, put forth by BonJour in the course of defending the view. Earlier we talked about differences between internalists and externalists. One version of internalism (we might call it *inferential* internalism) insists that evidential connections between propositions believed does nothing to secure justification for the believer unless the believer has *access* to the fact that the evidential connections hold. We can then distinguish two radically different versions of coherentism. On one version, a belief is epistemically justified provided that it forms a part of a coherent belief system. On the other, a belief is epistemically justified provided that the believer is *aware that* (has a justified belief that) the belief coheres with the rest of what is believed. The first version of coherentism seems vulnerable to devastating counterexamples. If a person believes a set of propositions that cohere wonderfully when the person has no way of discovering the inferential connections, in what sense are the beliefs justified? Suppose, for example, that I decide to believe every proposition expressed by the fourth sentence of every paragraph in a very sophisticated physics text. Through a miraculous coincidence the propositions I believe cohere wonderfully. Each is made probable by some conjunction of the others. I, however, have no clue as to what the evidential connections are. Would anyone suppose that my good fortune translates into justification?

If we embrace instead access coherentism, then coherentists face the very regress that traditional foundationalists tried so desperately to avoid. To justifiably believe that our beliefs cohere we would need to know first what we believe and second that the propositions believed stand in the appropriate evidential relations. But as coherentists we have no foundations to fall back on. We can't just give ourselves privileged access to propositions describing our own belief states. Our only access to what we believe is through a coherence we discover between our belief that we have certain beliefs and the rest of what we believe. But to discover *this* coherence we will once again be forced to discover what we believe, and so on, ad infinitum. An equally vicious regress seems to plague any attempt to discover evidential connections. To justify our belief that a given evidential connection obtains, we would need to discover coherence between our belief that the evidential connection obtains and the rest of what we believe. But discovering that coherence would require that we discover *another* coherence between our belief about coherence and the rest of what we believe, and so on, ad infinitum.

The basic problem facing access coherence theorists is simple. As pure coherence theorists they have no business giving themselves unproblematic access to any facts about the internal or external world, or the world of logical connections. If there really is a "veil" of belief, then beliefs themselves are hidden from us by metabeliefs, which are hidden from us by metametabeliefs, and so on, ad infinitum. Whenever we attempt to get anything before our consciousness we are led on an endless goose chase toward higher- and higher-level metabeliefs.

MIXED THEORIES

Susan Haack (1993), Roderick Chisholm (1989), Ernest Sosa (1991), and others have suggested that we don't need to choose between foundationalism and coherentism. We can incorporate elements of both. Haack's crossword puzzle metaphor is perhaps the most vivid illustration of the idea. In a crossword puzzle, we are given an initial clue that may lead us to a tentative conclusion about the correct entry in the puzzle. But it is only when our tentative entry "fits" with the other entries we try that we feel confident that we have the correct solution to the puzzle. According to Haack, experience provides a kind of foundational clue with respect to truth, but coherence (fit) is necessary to raise the level of initial credibility to that of epistemic justification. Sosa allows for a kind of animal knowledge resulting from reliable belief-forming processes (where reliability is relativized to internal and external circumstances) but insists that it is only when one's belief that one has animal knowledge coheres with the rest of one's beliefs that we can turn animal knowledge into reflective knowledge. Although he is one of the most prominent foundationalists, Chisholm allowed that coherence (concurrence) among propositions believed might be one way to raise the epistemic status of those beliefs (69–71).

Such views obviously need to be evaluated carefully, but it is not clear that any concept of justification purportedly captured by the mixed theory cannot be captured by a more straightforward foundationalism. If we have foundational evidence E_1 for P_1, foundational evidence E_2 for P_2, and foundational evidence E_3 for P_3, then instead of insisting that it is coherence among P_1, P_2, and P_3 that raises the epistemic justification for believing each one, why not simply claim that it is the conjunction of E_1, E_2, and E_3 that constitutes a foundational justification for believing each of P_1, P_2, and P_3, where the conjunction of evidence makes more probable P_1, for example, than E_1 does alone?

CONCLUSION

A survey of this sort can at best suggest the rich diversity of views about the nature of epistemic justification and the equally rich diversity of objections those views face. In illustrating many of these views and objections I have painted with a very broad stroke. Moreover, there are a host of interesting variations on the views I did discuss that have been defended by able philosophers one would have liked to mention in a survey of this sort. Painting with a broad stroke can still give one a useful "big" picture, and this is all I hoped to accomplish in the preceding remarks.

NOTES

1. See Cohen (1984) for a defense of the idea that a connection to truth lies at the heart of epistemic justification.

2. We often speak of having some epistemic justification for believing a proposition in contrast with having justification simpliciter. One can have some epistemic justification for believing P when the justification does not even make P more likely to be true than not—it simply increases the probability of P's being true. In what follows I'll almost always be talking about justification as "all-things-considered justification" and will use the term in such a way that one has justification for believing P only if, all things considered, the justification makes P more likely than not to be true.

3. I have argued elsewhere that our understanding of the "ought" of practical ra-

tionality and morality is in fact parasitic upon our understanding of the epistemic ought. It is implausible to understand what it is rational or moral to do in terms of the *actual* consequences that would result from alternatives. Practical and moral reasons seem to have more to do with what one is epistemically justified in believing about consequences.

4. For a more detailed discussion of this issue, see Fumerton (2001).

5. The example may not be fair. It is far from clear that anyone really accepts as legitimate an argument whose premise describes a lifeline and whose conclusion describes length of life. Such arguments may always be enthymemes. The question then becomes whether it is still plausible to claim that one cannot justifiably accept the conclusion of any argument without justifiably believing that there exists the relevant connection between premise and conclusion. I think one can make the case that it is.

6. There is, however, nothing to prevent an acquaintance theorist from allowing that one can have noninferential justification for believing P that does not entail P's truth. It may be that one can be noninferentially justified in believing P in virtue of being directly acquainted with a fact very similar to, but ultimately different from the fact that P. For an attempt to develop this view in more detail see Fumerton (1985).

7. See, for example, Goodman (1978) and Putnam (1988).

8. One of the earliest attempts to construe probability as a relation that holds necessarily between certain propositions was Keynes (1921).

9. Or, one could replace talk of frequency in defining reliability with some other notion. Goldman toys with the idea of understanding reliability in terms of an undefined notion of propensity to produce true beliefs.

10. David Hume (1888), for example, attacked relentlessly the legitimacy of inductive reasoning and the rationality of belief in an external world, only to assume both in the context of investigating the subject matter of moral judgments.

11. For a more detailed discussion of contextualism see Moser 1985, chap. 2.

12. There is also a coherence theory of *truth* that might seem a natural ally of the coherence theory of justification. The problems facing a coherence theory of justification, however, pale in comparison to those facing the coherence theory of truth. See Fumerton (2001).

REFERENCES

Annis, David (1978). "A Contextualist Theory of Epistemic Justification." *American Philosophical Quarterly* 15: 213–219.

Armstrong, David (1973). *Belief, Truth and Knowledge*. London: Cambridge University Press.

Ayer, A. J. (1956). *The Problem of Knowledge*. Edinburgh: Penguin.

BonJour, Laurence (1985). *The Structure of Empirical Knowledge*. Cambridge, Mass.: Harvard University Press.

Cohen, Stewart (1984). "Justification and Truth." *Philosophical Studies* 46: 279–296.

Chisholm, Roderick (1989). *Theory of Knowledge*, 3rd ed. Englewood Cliffs, N.J.: Prentice-Hall.

Foley, Richard (1979). "Justified Inconsistent Beliefs." *American Philosophical Quarterly* 16: 147–158.

———. (1987). *The Theory of Epistemic Rationality*. Cambridge: Harvard University Press.

Fumerton, Richard (1985). *Metaphysical and Epistemological Problems of Perception*. Lincoln: University of Nebraska Press.

———. (2001). "Epistemic Justification and Normativity." In *Knowledge, Truth and Obligation: Essays on Epistemic Responsibility and the Ethics of Belief*, ed. Matthias Steup. Oxford: Oxford University Press.

———. (2002). *Truth and Correspondence*. Boston: Rowman & Littlefield.

Goldman, Alvin (1979). "What Is Justified Belief?" In *Justification and Knowledge*, ed. George Pappas, 1–23. Dordrecht: Reidel.

———. (1986). *Epistemology and Cognition*. Cambridge: Harvard University Press.

———. (1988). "Strong and Weak Justification." In *Philosophical Perspectives* vol. 2: *Epistemology*, ed. James Tomberlin, 51–69. Atascadero, Calif.: Ridgeview.

Goodman, Nelson (1978). *Ways of World Making*. Indianapolis: Hackett.

Haack, Susan (1993). *Evidence and Inquiry*. Oxford: Blackwell.

Hume, David (1888). *A Treatise of Human Nature*, ed. L. A. Selby-Bigge. London: Oxford University Press.

Keynes, John (1921). *A Treatise on Probability*. London: Macmillan.

Klein, Peter (1999). "Human Knowledge and the Infinite Regress of Reasons." In *Philosophical Perspectives*, vol. 13, ed. James Tomberlin, 297–325.

Lehrer, Keith (1974). *Knowledge*. Oxford: Oxford University Press.

Lewis, David (1996). "Elusive Knowledge." *Australian Journal of Philosophy* 74: 4.

Moser, Paul (1985). *Empirical Justification*. Dordrecht: Reidel.

Plantinga, Alvin (1992). "Justification in the 20th Century." In *Philosophical Issues*, vol. 2: *Rationality in Epistemology*, ed. Enrique Villanueva, 43–78. Atascadero, Calif.: Ridgeview.

———. (1993). *Warrant and Proper Function*. Oxford: Oxford University Press.

Putnam, Hilary (1988). *Representation and Reality*. Cambridge, Mass.: MIT Press.

Russell, Bertrand (1959). *The Problems of Philosophy*. Oxford: Oxford University Press.

———. (1984). *Theory of Knowledge: The 1913 Manuscript*, ed. E. Eames. London: Allen and Unwin.

Sellars, Wilfrid (1963). *Science, Perception and Reality*. London: Routledge and Kegan Paul.

Sosa, Ernest (1991). *Knowledge in Perspective*. Cambridge: Cambridge University Press.

CHAPTER 7

INTERNALISM AND EXTERNALISM

LAURENCE BONJOUR

1. INTRODUCTION

ONE of the major disputes in epistemology in the last three decades or so has been that between internalist and externalist theories of justification and of knowledge. Despite the rather large amount of effort expended by the partisans to this dispute, however, it seems fair to say that there is no very clear resolution in sight—and indeed relatively little agreement about even the force of the main arguments and objections, most of which rely heavily upon intuition. My aim in the present paper is to review the large-scale structure of this dispute and eventually to suggest a resolution of sorts, though not one that either side is likely to be fully satisfied with.

What then is the main issue? The most standard formulation is in terms of the correct specification of one part of the concept of *knowledge*: is the third condition for knowledge, the justification or warrant condition that goes beyond the requirements of belief or assent and truth, properly formulated in an internalist or externalist way? In first approximation, an epistemological theory counts as *internalist* if and only if it requires that all of the elements needed for a belief to satisfy this condition must be *cognitively accessible* to the person in question; and as *externalist*, if it allows that at least some of these elements need not be thus accessible, allowing them to be *external* to the believer's cognitive perspective.

Internalists most standardly use the term "justification" or "epistemic justification" to characterize this third condition. As we will see further below, externalist views differ among themselves as to whether their proposed externalist conditions should be viewed as competing accounts of epistemic justification or instead as replacements for the internalist's justification condition.[1]

It seems reasonably clear, though this has occasionally been challenged,[2] that internalism was taken more or less entirely for granted by the main tradition of modern epistemology, stemming from Descartes's original attempt to reconstruct his knowledge on an indubitable foundation. Thus it is appropriate to begin with internalism, considering first the main contours of the view (§ 2) and then the main reasons that have been advanced by externalists for rejecting this more traditional epistemological approach (§ 3). We will then investigate the externalist alternative, beginning with a look at the most popular version, *reliabilism* (§ 4), and at the main objections that have been raised against that specific version of externalism (§ 5). This will motivate a look at some other versions of externalism, partly with an eye to seeing how susceptible they are to these or similar objections (§ 6). Finally, in light of all this, I will suggest that the opposition between the two views is in fact substantially less straightforward than has usually been thought and that each of them has a valuable role to play in relation to major epistemological issues, even though the internalist approach is still in one important way more fundamental (§ 7).

2. Internalism: Motivation and Main Features

What then does the internalist view really amount to? In what sense must the ingredients of justification be accessible to the believer, and why is such accessibility supposed to be necessary for justification?[3]

2.1. The Main Rationale

The place to begin is with a consideration of the fundamental rationale for internalism, where there are some prominent misconceptions that need to be first set aside. Accounts of internalism often emphasize one or both of the following two ideas: first, the idea that epistemic justification has to do with satisfying one's *duty* or *responsibility* as a rational creature, so that a person's beliefs are justified just to the extent that this duty or responsibility has been fulfilled in accepting them (the deontological conception of justification); and, second, the idea that the central role or point of epistemic justification is to *guide* people in deciding what to believe (the guidance conception of justification).[4] The first of these ideas—one of which I am often cited as a leading proponent—now strikes me as largely, albeit perhaps not quite entirely, a mistake. And while the second idea points in approximately the right direction, it misses the central point just enough to muddy the issues and raise spurious problems.

The central claim of the deontological conception of justification is that satisfying one's intellectual duty or responsibility in relation to the acceptance of a particular belief is both necessary and sufficient for that belief to be epistemically justified. Both of these claims are questionable, but the claim of sufficiency more obviously so. What epistemic duty requires should surely depend on the epistemic resources that are available to a person. It is certainly possible that a person's epistemic situation, the kinds of evidence and cognitive tools and methods of inquiry available to him or her, might be so dire or impoverished (as a result of either individual or cultural deficiencies) as to make it difficult or impossible to come up with strong evidence or good epistemic reasons for beliefs about many important matters. In such a situation, it is far from clear that people who accept beliefs on less than adequate evidence or reasons or perhaps even at times on none at all, while still doing the best that they can under the circumstances, are guilty of any breach of their epistemic duty or can properly be described as epistemically blameworthy or irresponsible. One's primary epistemic duty, after all, includes *both* seeking the truth and avoiding error. But to insist that people in such an unfortunate condition should accept only those few if any beliefs for which really good evidence or reasons are available, withholding judgment on everything else, is in effect to give the avoidance of error an absolute and unwarranted priority over the discovery of truth.

In fact, however, few if any internalists would regard the beliefs that such a person might accept in such a situation, beliefs for which there is little in the way of truth-conducive reasons or evidence, as being epistemically justified to any significant degree. Such a person may well be making the best of a bad epistemic situation and may be entirely epistemically unblameworthy in doing so, but the basis upon which such beliefs are accepted still fails to make it likely to any serious degree that they are true and so does not amount to epistemic justification. My suspicion, in fact, is that this is a conclusion that virtually all epistemologists of an internalist persuasion would accept, including those like myself who are frequently cited as proponents of the deontological conception. I believe that their apparent statements to the contrary were misleading, in that they were thinking only about situations of at least approximate epistemic plenty, ones in which one has reasonable access to evidence and reasons, and so does not have to accept beliefs on some weaker, less adequate basis in order to have at least some chance of finding the truth.

Cases of epistemic poverty are cases in which it seems possible to fulfill one's epistemic duty without being epistemically justified. It is less clear that there are cases in the opposite direction, cases in which one could be epistemically justified, that is, have good, truth-conductive reasons for one's beliefs, and still fail to satisfy one's epistemic duty. Whether this is possible seems to depend largely on the scope of epistemic duty, on exactly how much it requires. If one's epistemic duty includes all that it included in the recently popular idea of *epistemic virtue*,[5] then it seems possible to believe on the basis of good reasons and evidence and still be deficient in other respects: for example, to be less open-minded or intellectually creative than a full satisfaction of epistemic duty would require.

Whether or not this is so, it seems clear that epistemic justification cannot be simply *identified* with the fulfillment of epistemic duty or responsibility as the deontological conception claims. What is true is rather something substantially weaker, but still important: seeking good epistemic reasons and evidence and believing on the basis of them is, at least in situations of relative epistemic plenty, one important requirement of epistemic duty and at least arguably the most central of all. That this is so makes it easy to understand how some internalists, myself included, were led to say things that overstated the connection between the two concepts. But it remains the case that the idea of satisfying epistemic duty turns out to shed no very direct light on the nature of epistemic justification and thus is only limited help in understanding the rationale for an internalist understanding of the latter notion.

The second mistaken conception of internalist justification, the guidance conception, holds that the primary purpose of epistemic justification is to *guide* a person in deciding what to believe. I have no quarrel with the idea that epistemic justification does sometimes serve such a function and could perhaps in principle serve it on a much wider basis than it in fact does. But we rarely in fact do anything that deserves to be described as "deciding what to believe," partly but only partly because our beliefs are rarely under anything like direct voluntary control. Thus a stress on epistemic guidance seems to me to put the emphasis in the wrong place and to invite objections concerning doxastic voluntarism that are in fact only marginally relevant to the central thrust of internalism.

In fact, the central rationale for internalism, at least as I conceive it, is both more straightforward and, I think, less problematic than that which either of these conceptions would yield. It arises when I ask simply whether or not I have good reasons for thinking that my various beliefs are true, understanding this question in a global way in which all of my beliefs (and ways of arriving at beliefs) are in question. Asking this question may be a way of partially fulfilling my epistemic duty and may also help me to decide what to believe, to whatever extent this is in my power. But it has a significance that transcends either of these motivations:

to whatever extent I am concerned with finding the truth, there is in the end simply no other way to go about it than by asking what reasons I have and how good they are—or at least none that does not beg questions or rest on unsupported assumptions.

The global epistemic issue that results from asking this question is, of course, and not by accident, essentially the same as the one that plays a central role in Descartes's *Meditations*, which provided the initial impetus for the modern development of epistemology. Contrary to what has sometimes been suggested, there is, as far as I can see, nothing in any way obviously illegitimate or misconceived about the epistemic issue thus raised. Normally, of course, we content ourselves with more limited issues. Even from the first-person standpoint, as contextualists point out, we normally ask about the reasons for a limited range of beliefs in a context in which the acceptability of a wide range of others is taken for granted and not in question. But this in no way shows that we cannot legitimately and even reasonably ask the broader question, or indeed that it is not the natural outgrowth of philosophical reflection on the more limited questions that we ordinarily focus on.

One immediate upshot of this is that the "internal" of "internalism" means primarily that what is appealed to for justification must be *internal to the individual's first-person cognitive perspective*, that is, something that is unproblematically available from that perspective, *not* necessarily that it must be internal to his or her mind or person in the way that mental states are. A person's conscious mental states play the role that they standardly do in internalist conceptions of justification, I suggest, *not* simply because they are internal to him or her in the sense merely of being his or her individual states, but rather because it is arguable that some (but not all) of the properties of such states, mainly their specific content and the attitude toward that content that they reflect, are things to which the person has a first-person access that is direct and unproblematic, that is, that does not depend on other claims that would themselves have to be justified in some more indirect way. Elaborating and defending this traditional view concerning access to the content of conscious states is beyond the scope of the present paper, though I believe that it can in fact be successfully defended.[6] But the point for the moment is that internalism when properly understood gives no special status to mental states as such: if there are, for example, unconscious mental states, states whose content and other properties fail to be reliably reflected in the person's conscious states and to which he or she has thus no unproblematic first-person access, then those mental states are no more relevant to internalist justification than would be various sorts of physiological states of which the same thing was true.

The other side of this point is that, contrary to what is sometimes suggested,[7] there is *nothing at all* about the fundamental rationale for internalism that automatically limits what is available for and relevant to internalist justification to facts about conscious mental states and their properties as such. If there are facts of some other sort that are directly and unproblematically available from a person's first-person cognitive perspective, then these are equally acceptable for this purpose. Thus, to take the most important case, if some facts about logical and probabilistic relations among propositions can be directly discerned via a priori insight in a way that does not depend on claims that can only be justified indirectly, then these facts would also be available from the first-person perspective in which the global epistemological issue is raised. In fact, it seems quite clear that most or all internalists would include such a priori knowable truths as an essential part of the basis for internalist justification. (Access to the a priori of course involves having mental states, but what is thus accessed is not merely features of those states.)

2.2. The Resources for Internalist Justification

I believe that cognitive resources of both of these kinds, facts about the contents of conscious states, and facts about a priori knowable logical and probabilistic relations, are legitimately and non-question-beggingly available within the first-person cognitive perspective that defines the internalist outlook, though I cannot undertake a defense of these claims here. Perhaps a more urgent question is what else, if anything, the internalist can initially appeal to. I say "initially," because it is of course entirely compatible with internalism that if a good case can be made from the resources that are legitimately available at a given point for the likely truth or reliability of beliefs arrived at in some further way, such as by accepting testimony of various sorts, then such additional cognitive resources become on that basis entirely acceptable to the internalist. This is why the primary concern of internalists has been to identify those resources for justification that are available *before* further arguments, arguments that can only start from those initial resources, are invoked.

Is there then anything else that is legitimately available in this initial situation? One possibility is perceptual knowledge of one's immediate physical environment. Using the fairly standard taxonomy of positions, if a direct realist view of perception should turn out to be correct, then, at least on some versions, perceptual beliefs might be directly justified in a way that would satisfy the basic rationale for the internalist view. My own view, however, is that no direct realist view genuinely succeeds in achieving this result. And if, on the other hand, the correct account of perception is a representationalist or indirect realist view, then it seems to follow that what is initially available within the first-person perspective is only the representations, with any reasons for thinking that they are likely to be true or reliable depending on further arguments of some sort on the basis of what is initially available.

What about memory? Here the question is more complicated, because memory functions in different ways at different levels of our cognitive operations. It is obvious that one sort of memory must play an essential role in assembling and keeping track of the resources for an internalist justification of any beliefs that go very far beyond the initial starting point. Any argument of any complexity or even any very large collection of sensory or mental states cannot all be held in mind at once, but must be collected and juxtaposed and reviewed over a period of time, using memory—perhaps aided by more tangible sorts of record-keeping such as writing things down on paper. But contrary to what is sometimes suggested or assumed,[8] I would suggest this is in no way a fatal or even a very serious problem for an internalist account of justification. When I ask what reasons I have from my first-person perspective for my various beliefs, there is simply nothing about this question that mandates or even really suggests that the answer can take account only of what is available or accessible at a moment, and thus no reason at all for an internalist to accept such a crippling limitation. Thus it is natural and, I believe, correct to regard this most fundamental and essential sort of memory, not as an additional cognitive resource on a par with the others, but rather as the means whereby whatever cognitive resources are available from the first-person perspective are preserved and made available on an ongoing basis.[9] This is not to deny that skeptical questions can be raised about this sort of memory, as indeed they can about essentially anything. But such questions have the effect of challenging whether the person is indeed the sort of ongoing, integrated cognitive agent that could have good reasons for his or her beliefs, rather than of challenging the justification of particular beliefs. It is the latter sort of issue with which the internalist is mainly concerned.[10]

Other sorts of memory, on the other hand, for example memories of having perceived such-and-such a physical occurrence at an earlier time (assuming that perceptual beliefs are themselves justified in some way), or of having heard or read something, or just the recollection of a fact that presents itself as having been learned in some way that is itself no longer remembered, raise issues of justification on a par with others and have to be dealt with in essentially the same way. In none of these cases is the truth or reliability of the beliefs in question something that can be directly known from the first-person perspective, so that from an internalist standpoint the justification of each of them will require further reasons or arguments of some sort, starting with those resources that are more directly available.

Given this picture, the further task of epistemology is to figure out how (and whether) various kinds of further beliefs can be justified by reference to the resources initially available. This in turn leads to the familiar litany of classical epistemological problems: the problem of the external world (if this is not successfully short-circuited by direct realism), the problem of induction, the problem of other minds, the problem of testimony, and so on.

2.3. Internalism and Foundationalism

It will be obvious to many that according to the foregoing account an internalist account of justification will be essentially foundationalist in its main structure, and this might be thought to show that the account given is too narrow, since coherentist positions, for example, are also standardly regarded as versions of internalism. I believe, however, though any very extensive discussion is impossible here, that this objection is mistaken.

In rough approximation, a coherentist view holds that the epistemic justification of a belief depends entirely on the coherence of that belief with a larger system of beliefs that is itself highly coherent. But then, though most coherentist views have either ignored or sought to evade the point, such a justification will be available from the first-person cognitive perspective only if both the existence of the beliefs that make up the system and the logical or other relations among them that constitute coherence are themselves thus available—available without relying, in a way that would be clearly circular, on coherence. But this apparently means that such a coherentist position must appeal to more or less the same initial resources that were mentioned above: a grasp of the contents of one's own mental states and a grasp of a priori justifiable relations among the resulting beliefs (together with the memory required to keep track of these elements). In this way, a genuinely internalist coherentism turns out to be a version of foundationalism, not an alternative to it.[11] And I suggest that essentially the same argument could be made for any other sort of view that genuinely counts as internalist.

3. Two Main Objections to Internalism

To someone approaching the internalism–externalism debate from the standpoint of traditional epistemology, someone who was familiar with the course of epistemological discussion from the early modern period until something like 1960, the foregoing internalist picture would seem obvious and natural, and an externalist approach to epistemological issues would most likely seem simply bizarre and irrelevant. What, such a person would probably want to ask, do the sorts of considerations to which externalists appeal, for example, facts about the causal process by which a belief is generated that are unknown to the person in question (see further below), even have to do with justification or knowledge? Why should the externalist approach to epistemological questions be taken seriously? The main answers externalists offer to these sorts of questions consist of intuitively based objections to internalism, objections that attempt to show that the whole internalist approach is fundamentally untenable.

3.1. Unsophisticated Epistemic Subjects

First, there is the claim that the internalist cannot give an intuitively acceptable account of the cognitive or epistemic condition of *unsophisticated epistemic subjects*: higher animals, young children, and even relatively unsophisticated adults. Take higher animals first, as perhaps the clearest case. Consider, for example, a reasonably intelligent dog, one who understands a fairly wide range of commands, seems to have a good memory for people and places, can communicate in various ways what appear to be desires for food or play, and also seems to exhibit emotions like happiness or fear. Though this has sometimes been denied, it is very natural to attribute conscious beliefs and other conscious mental states to such an animal. But does the dog have any *reasons* for its beliefs, anything that would amount to internalist justification?

It is obviously hard to be completely sure about the answer to these questions, involving as they do a relatively difficult version of the problem of other minds. But despite the dog's intelligence, it is hard to believe that it engages in reasoning or anything very much like reasoning, and still harder to believe that it is capable of understanding arguments of the complexity that would apparently be required for the internalist justification of all but the simplest beliefs. Indeed, it is very doubtful that such an animal can even understand the basic idea of having a reason for a belief, an understanding that seems to be required for it to have a fully explicit access to any reasons at all. Thus we seem to be led pretty inexorably to the conclusion that the dog has, from an internalist standpoint, few if any justified beliefs and hence little or no knowledge. And this is a result that externalists claim to be highly implausible. Surely, they argue, the dog *knows* such things as that there is food in its bowl (as it sniffs before eating), that its owner has just come home (as it offers what appears to be an exuberant greeting), or that there is a squirrel on the other side of the quad (as it freezes and then skulks carefully in that direction). Indeed, many will allege, it is also implausible (though perhaps not quite as implausible) to deny that the dog is in some way *justified* in holding many of its beliefs, even if not in the way that an internalist view would require.

Moreover, essentially the same sort of argument can be made in relation to relatively young children and unsophisticated or cognitively limited adults. Here again, it is hard to believe that individuals in these categories are really able to understand the complicated sorts of justificatory arguments that various brands of internalism propose for beliefs about the material world or other minds or the past. (Indeed, most fully mature and capable adults have not in fact encountered such arguments or formulated them for themselves, making it hard to see how an internalist can consistently say that the beliefs of even these individuals about such matters are justified or constitute knowledge.) But surely, it is alleged, it is much more obvious that some or all of these various kinds of relatively unsophisticated individuals (and surely the mature and capable adults) do have justified beliefs and do have knowledge concerning a variety of subjects than it is that internalism is true. And thus if internalism yields such implausible results, it should be rejected.

3.2. The Threat of Skepticism

While the first objection in effect concedes, at least for the sake of the argument, that successful internalist justificatory arguments for the various sorts of beliefs that common sense regards as constituting knowledge can be in fact found, denying only that such arguments are accessible to unsophisticated subjects (and possibly even to most mature and capable ones), the second objection argues that is it is in fact far from obvious that *any* acceptable internalist justification, whether generally accessible or not, can be found for many of these beliefs. The precise application of this point will vary from one internalist view to another, but it is impossible to deny that few if any of the classical problems of epistemology alluded to earlier have been definitively solved from an internalist standpoint and that most of them have been dealt with only in ways that are pretty tentative, quite schematic, and also highly controversial. Thus after well over three centuries of internalist investigation (counting from Descartes), it remains entirely possible—and perhaps even, as many would argue, quite likely—that no adequate internalist justification can be found for many or perhaps even most of our ordinary beliefs about the world, in which case no one would have justification or knowledge concerning the matters in question if internalism is correct. But this is again, it is alleged, an extremely implausible and intuitively unacceptable result, making the internalist view that leads to it equally unacceptable.

3.3. Assessment of These Objections

It is obvious that these two objections are closely related and similar in their basic thrust. One way to put them together would be to argue that if internalism is accepted, then the vast majority of the beliefs that common sense regards as justified and as constituting knowledge will in fact be justified and constitute knowledge for at best only a few epistemologists and students of epistemology, if even for them. But this once again seems extremely implausible, and so, it is claimed, internalism must be mistaken.

The problems that these objections point to are real, and there is no simple and straightforward reply available to them from a general internalist perspective. A serious reply to the second objection in particular would require the elaboration of a specific internalist view in substantial detail, something that is obviously impossible here. But there is one issue worth emphasizing at this point. The basic externalist claim is that internalism conflicts with deep-seated common-sense intuitions concerning the scope of knowledge and also, though perhaps a bit less clearly, the scope of justification. But what exactly is the content of the intuitions in question? Is it merely that the beliefs in question constitute knowledge or are justified in some relatively unspecified senses of these terms, which might then turn out to be the ones proposed by the externalist? Or is the content of the relevant intuitions not perhaps rather that the individuals in question do have knowledge or justification in something like the senses the internalist advocates: that they have true beliefs which they have *good reasons* of some sort for thinking to be true?—in which case showing that the beliefs in question constitute knowledge or are justified in externalist senses wouldn't really help to satisfy these intuitions.[12]

4. RELIABILISM

Having had a look at internalism and its problems, I turn to a consideration of the externalist alternatives, beginning with the most widely discussed and advocated version of externalism: *reliabilism*. Reliabilist views have most standardly been formulated as accounts of epistemic justification, and it is in that form that they will be considered here. So formulated, the central idea of reliabilism is that what makes a belief epistemically justified is the cognitive *reliability* of the causal process via which it was produced, that is, the fact that the process in question leads to a high proportion of true beliefs, with the *degree* of justification depending on the degree of reliability. If the belief-producing process is reliable in this way, then (other things being equal) it will be objectively likely or probable to the same degree that the particular belief in question, having been produced in that way, is itself true. But what makes the view a version of externalism is that reliabilism does *not* require that the believer in question have any sort of cognitive access to the fact that the belief-producing process is in this way reliable in order for his or her belief to be justified. All that matters for justification is that the process in question be in fact reliable, whether or not the person in question (or indeed anyone else) believes or has even the slightest inkling that this is so, or indeed even the slightest understanding of just what specific sort of process is involved.[13]

The clearest and most plausible illustrations of reliabilism involve belief-producing processes like sensory perception. Thus suppose that a particular individual is so constituted, as a result of natural endowment and various sorts of previous training and experience, that a very high proportion of his or her visually induced beliefs about "medium-sized" material objects (tables, trees, buildings, automobiles, etc.) and the events and processes that involve them existing or occurring in his or her immediate vicinity under favorable conditions of perception are true. If this is so, then, according to the most straightforward version of reliabilism, those beliefs are highly justified.[14] The individual in question need have no belief or any other sort of awareness that the process in question is reliable, nor indeed any very specific conception of what it involves. Neither that person nor anyone else need have any very direct or easy access to the fact of reliability should the issue somehow be explicitly raised. All that matters is that the process via which such beliefs are generated is in fact, under those conditions about that sort of subject matter, highly reliable, whether or not *anyone* is aware of this at the time in question or indeed ever becomes aware of it. And this is obviously a condition that might be satisfied by any of the unsophisticated cognitive subjects considered earlier: by higher animals such as dogs, by young children, or by unsophisticated adults. When a dog comes to believe that there is a squirrel across the quad, then if its eyes are functioning in such a way that this reliability condition is satisfied (under the relevant conditions of lighting, etc.), its belief is, according to the reliabilist, justified.[15]

The reliabilist's reliable belief-producing processes are not limited, however, to processes like sensory perception in which no prior beliefs or other cognitive states are involved in any very obvious way. For example, if the process of logical or probabilistic inference from other justified (that is, reliably produced) beliefs is a *conditionally* reliable belief-producing process, one a very high proportion of whose output beliefs are true if the relevant input beliefs are true, then the beliefs that are produced by this process starting with justified input beliefs will also count as justified according to the reliabilist account.[16] Here too, however, what matters is reliability itself and not any awareness on the part of the subject that the process is reliable, nor any understanding of why a belief arrived at in this way genuinely follows from the relevant premises. Thus if children or dogs make reliable transitions of this sort with no clear or explicit awareness of why or how they are doing so, their resulting beliefs still count as justified. Of course, it *might* turn out that a more specific process that involves explicit and critical reflection on the logical relations and principles involved is even more reliable, in which case beliefs that result from a process of this more specific sort would be even more highly justified.

I will refer to the position described so far as *simple reliabilism*. It is also possible to have more complicated versions of reliabilism that are still fundamentally externalist in character: versions that add further requirements or qualifications of various sorts to attempt to ward off potential objections. The rationale for these will emerge as we consider the objections that have been raised against reliabilist views.

5. THREE MAIN OBJECTIONS TO RELIABILISM

Does simple reliabilism provide an acceptable account of epistemic justification, one that can replace internalist views and thereby avoid the objections to internalism discussed earlier? In this section, I will consider three main sorts of objections that have been offered against reliabilist views. The first two of these question, on broadly intuitive grounds, whether the satisfaction of the reliabilist condition is (i) necessary or (ii) sufficient for the justification of a belief, while the third pertains to a difficult problem that arises within the reliabilist position.

5.1. Cartesian Demon Worlds

The first objection challenges whether the satisfaction of the reliabilist condition is *necessary* for beliefs to be justified, that is, whether *only* beliefs that satisfy that condition are justified—as would have to be the case if reliabilism were successful in providing a complete account of epistemic justification.[17] Imagine a group of people who live in a world controlled by an evil demon or evil genius of the sort imagined by Descartes. The evil demon carefully controls their sensory and introspective experience, producing in them just the sorts of experiences they would have if they inhabited a particular material world containing various specific sorts of objects and processes that interact and influence each other in lawful ways, even though the world in question does not actually exist. The people in this position are, we may suppose, careful and thorough investigators. They accumulate large quantities of sensory evidence, formulate hypotheses and theories, subject their beliefs to careful experimental and observational tests, etc., and thus arrive at a fairly comprehensive set of beliefs describing the world that they seem to experience. Perhaps they even formulate cogent epistemological arguments of various sorts for the likely truth of their resulting beliefs.

Are the beliefs about their apparent world that the people in such a Cartesian demon world arrive at in these ways justified? From an intuitive standpoint, it seems hard to deny that they are. One consideration here is that their epistemic situation may, from their subjective standpoints, well be entirely indiscernible from or even superior to our own, so that if we are confident that our own beliefs are frequently justified, we should seemingly be equally confident that theirs are. But because of the pervasive influence of the evil demon, the empirical beliefs of the demon-world people that go beyond their own subjective experience[18] are mostly false (only mostly, because some very general beliefs, e.g., that there are people, are still true and some others may be true by accident) and the cognitive processes that produce those beliefs are, at least in their world, highly unreliable: their perceptual observation produces beliefs that are mostly or entirely false, and even if their further reasoning is impeccable, it begins with these false premises and so does not lead to reliable results. Thus the simple reliabilist apparently must say that their beliefs are in fact largely or entirely unjustified, a result that seems intuitively quite implausible.

How do reliabilists respond to this objection? Some simply dig in their heels, "bite the bullet," and insist that this is the correct result and that the intuitive impression to the contrary is somehow confused or misleading. But this is obviously a dangerous line for an externalist to take, since the externalist objections to internalism considered earlier rely on similar intuitions.

Other reliabilists, however, have found the claim that the demon world people are not justified in their beliefs too implausible to accept and have instead proposed modifications to the reliabilist view that are aimed at avoiding it. Perhaps the most interesting of these is the suggestion that the reliability of a cognitive process, in the sense relevant to justification, should be assessed, not necessarily in the world that the believer whose beliefs are being assessed in fact inhabits, but rather in "normal" possible worlds—that is, in possible worlds that *actually* have the features that our actual world is commonsensically believed to have. Thus if the cognitive processes employed by the victims of the evil demon would be reliable in a world of the sort that we believe ourselves to inhabit (one that thus, among other things, contains no evil demon), then those processes count as reliable in the relevant sense. And if reliability is understood in this way, then the reliabilist can agree that the beliefs of the people in the evil demon world are justified.[19]

How successful is this response? It avoids the objection in question, but only, it might be thought, at the price of rendering the reliabilist position seriously ad hoc. It is clear enough why *genuine* reliability should be thought to be cognitively valuable, whether or not it is the right basis for justification: beliefs that are arrived at in a genuinely reliable way are thereby objectively likely to be true. But why should we value what might be referred to as "normal reliability," whether or not it is correlated with genuine reliability? After all, beliefs that result from processes that possess normal reliability are not, on that basis alone, to any degree likely to be true.

A different response to the demon world example[20] involves a distinction between *weak justification* (a person being epistemically blameless and nonculpable in holding a belief) and strong justification (the belief's being formed in a reliable way that makes it likely to be true)—where it is strong justification that is required for knowledge. The suggestion is that the beliefs of the people in the demon world are *weakly justified*, but not *strongly justified*. The question is whether this really accommodates the intuition concerning the demon world case, which seems to be that the demon world people are at least as justified in their beliefs as we are in ours.

5.2. Unusual but Reliable Cognitive Faculties

The second main objection to simple reliabilism is in a way the complement of the first. Instead of imagining a situation in which the cognitive processes that we take to be reliable are in fact unreliable, it imagines one in which there is a cognitive process that is in fact highly reliable, but which we have no reason to regard as reliable and perhaps good reasons to regard as unreliable. Thus suppose that *clairvoyance*, the alleged cognitive ability to have knowledge of distant occurrences in a way that does not depend on sensory perception or other common-sensical cognitive processes, does in fact genuinely occur and involves a process of some unknown sort that is highly reliable for certain specific people under certain specific conditions (which might include a limitation to a certain range of subject matter). And suppose that some person who in fact has this ability arrives at a belief on this basis and that the requisite conditions for reliability are satisfied. Such a belief seems to satisfy the simple reliabilist's requirement for justification, but is it in fact genuinely justified?[21]

There are several different possible cases here, depending on what else is true of the person in question. Such a person might: (a) have no belief or opinion at all about the cognitive process involved or its reliability; or (b) believe, though without justification, that the belief results from a reliable process, of which he or she may or may not have any very specific conception; or (c) possess good reasons or evidence of an internalist sort that the specific belief in question is false; or (d) possess good reasons or evidence of an internalist sort that the process in question is *not* reliable, again with or without a specific conception of its character.[22] (If the person possesses good reasons of an internalist sort that the process *is* reliable, then that would of course provide a basis for an internalist justification.) Of these possibilities, it is the first that seems most favorable to reliabilism. It is hard to see how a further belief about the process that is itself unjustified can contribute to the justification of the initial belief; and it seems obvious that a belief that is held in the face of contrary reasons pertaining either to its subject matter or in the way in which it was arrived at is more suspect as regards its justification.

Imagine, then, a specific case of sort (a). Suppose that a certain person, Norman, is in fact a reliable clairvoyant with respect to the geographical whereabouts of the President of the United States. He frequently has spontaneous beliefs or hunches, which he accepts without question, concerning the location of the President on a particular day, and in fact these are always correct. But Norman pays very little attention to news reports and other sorts of information about the President and his or her whereabouts and has never made any effort to check his hunches independently. Nor does he have any real conception of how such hunches might work or any general views about the reliability of such a process. Norman's beliefs resulting from his spontaneous clairvoyant hunches seem to satisfy the simple reliabilist's requirements for justification,[23] but are they really justified? Doesn't it seem intuitively as though Norman is being thoroughly irrational in confidently accepting beliefs on this sort of basis? (One way to think about this question is to ask whether Norman would be justified in *acting* on one of these beliefs if an urgent occasion should arise in which someone needed to find the President.)[24]

Here again some reliabilists will simply dig in their heels and insist that Norman's clairvoyant beliefs are indeed justified, dismissing intuitions to the contrary as misguided. But others respond to this sort of case (and to cases of the other sorts enumerated earlier) by imposing a further requirement that amounts to a significant qualification on the reliabilist position: roughly that the believer not have immediate access to good reasons of an internalist sort for questioning either the specific belief in question or his or her own general ability to arrive at such beliefs in the way in question.[25] The way that this applies to Norman is that arguably he should have been suspicious of his beliefs about the President's whereabouts, given that he has no reason to think that he has any sort of reliable cognitive access to such information and given that people in general do not apparently possess the ability to arrive at reliable beliefs in such a way.

There are two questions that need to be asked about this sort of response. One is whether it is possible to interpret it in such a way as to handle the Norman case without also creating an analogous problem for other reliably caused beliefs, for example those resulting from visual perception, that the reliabilist does want to say are justified on that basis alone. *If* our only justification for visual beliefs is of the externalist sort (something that most internalists will deny), shouldn't we be equally suspicious of them? The second question is whether it is possible to find a clear rationale for such a further requirement that is compatible with externalism. Why should internalist reasons be relevant in this negative way if they are not required for justification in general?

A different possible reliabilist response to cases like the Norman case is a kind of analogue of the moral theory known as rule utilitarianism, according to which appeals to utility are used in justifying general moral rules but are not directly applied to the evaluation of individual actions. Analogously, a reliabilist might suggest that considerations of reliability are used in establishing a set of epistemic rules (or perhaps instead a list of cognitive or intellectual virtues and vices), with the justification of particular beliefs then being determined by appeal to the resulting rules (or list of virtues and vices), but not directly by appeal to reliability. This would allow a reliably arrived at belief to still count as unjustified (because it does not conform to the general set of epistemic rules or intellectual virtues thus arrived at)—and equally for a belief that is unreliably arrived at to still count as justified (because it does conform to those rules or virtues), as perhaps in the demon world case.[26] One problem with such a view, as indeed with rule utilitarianism, is to provide an adequate rationale for this two-level approach to justification, which seems to aim less directly at the ultimate goal of truth. A second is whether there are any clear standards for the sorts of rules or virtues and vices that are invoked by such a view, especially but not only their level of generality, that would make it plausible that any definite list would be arrived at. (This is an issue that is closely related to the third and final problem to be discussed.)

5.3. The Generality Problem

The third main objection, known as *the generality problem*, pertains to the very formulation of the reliabilist position. What the simple reliabilist says, as we have seen, is that a belief is justified if the *general* sort of cognitive process from which it results is reliable in the way indicated. But at what *level* of generality should the relevant process be characterized? Consider my present visually induced belief that there is a white cup sitting on my computer table, and consider some of the different ways in which the cognitive process from which it results might be described (assuming as a part of all of these that my eyes are functioning normally): as the visual perception of a cup under good lighting at close range; as the visual perception of a cup (under unspecified conditions and at an unspecified distance); as the visual perception of a "medium-sized physical object" (with more or less specific indications of conditions and distance); as visual perception in general (including the perception of much larger and smaller objects, again with various specifications of conditions and distance); or just as sense perception in general. And this is only a small sampling of a much larger range of possibilities. Which of these descriptions of the cognitive process in question, we must ask, is the relevant one for applying the simple reliabilist's principle of justification?

One reason that this question poses a very serious problem for reliabilists is that the proportion of true beliefs that is produced by the processes specified in these various ways seems to vary extremely widely: I am much less likely to make a mistake about cups that are perceived at close range under good conditions than I am about cups under a wider range of conditions and distances or, even more obviously, about the objects of visual perception or sense perception in general. Indeed, it seems possible to specify the process in such detail as to make the description fit only this single case, so that the process thus described would be either 100 percent reliable (if the belief is true) or 100 percent unreliable (if the belief is false)—and thus either perfectly justified or perfectly unjustified (with both of these results seeming obviously mistaken). And it also seems possible to specify the process so broadly, including perceptions under very poor conditions of objects that are much harder to identify, so as to result in a very low degree of reliability. But which of these widely varying characterizations of the process and corresponding degrees of reliability is the right one for assessing the justification of this particular belief?

Without some way of answering this question in a relatively specific and nonarbitrary way, reliabilism apparently does not amount to a definite position at all, but only a general schema for a position that there is apparently no way to make more definite. Certainly some ways of specifying the relevant process are more natural than others; but the epistemological relevance of such naturalness is questionable, and even these more natural specifications are numerous enough to have significantly differing degrees of reliability. Though reliabilists have struggled with this problem, it seems fair to say that no very satisfactory solution has yet been found.

6. SOME OTHER VERSIONS OF EXTERNALISM

In this section, I will look at two other prominent versions of externalism, which differ in important ways from simple reliabilism and the most straightforward modifications thereof, though anything like a full discussion of these views is impossible here. One main issue is whether either of them is any more successful than reliabilism in meeting or avoiding the objections just considered or others of the same general kinds. I will suggest that they are not.[27]

6.1. Nozick's "Tracking the Truth" View

Robert Nozick's version of externalism offers an account of knowledge directly, rather than of justification. The basic idea is that a person has knowledge if and only if they have a true belief that is in a certain way counterfactually related to the truth. Assuming that person S's true belief that P was arrived at via some specifiable "method" or cognitive procedure M, it constitutes knowledge if and only if the following two conditions are satisfied:

(A)   If P weren't true and S were to use M to arrive at a belief whether (or not) P, then S wouldn't believe, via M, that P.

(B)   If P were true and S were to use M to arrive at a belief whether (or not) P, then S would believe, via M, that P.[28]

Nozick describes the situation in which these two conditions are satisfied as one in which the belief in question "tracks the truth." What makes his view a version of externalism is that the person in question need have no inkling at all that these conditions are satisfied (and so no internalist reason for thinking that P is true).

Apart from the focus on knowledge rather than justification, Nozick's view differs from reliabilist views in two other ways, one of them quite obvious and the other substantially more subtle. The obvious difference is the inclusion of condition (B), which requires that the cognitive procedure in question not only be reliable in the sense of yielding a high proportion of true beliefs, but also in the distinct sense of reliably producing such beliefs whenever the claim in question is true. Thus a cognitive procedure or "method" that often fails to yield any belief even when there is a relevant truth to be found, but that almost always produces true beliefs when it produces any beliefs at all, would satisfy the main reliabilist requirement but would not satisfy condition (B). Though this issue is tangential to the main concerns of this discussion, my suggestion would be that the inclusion of this additional requirement is a mistake. It is hard to see why the results of a method that satisfies the reliabilist requirement (so that the belief in question is highly likely to be true) should fail to yield knowledge just because the method would fail to produce a definite result on other occasions.[29]

The more subtle difference concerns the formulation of condition (A). Obviously this is at least in the same general direction as the reliabilist condition, but the two are still not quite the same. If the standard reliabilist condition were formulated in a parallel way, it would amount to something like:

(R)   If S were to believe P using cognitive procedure M under the conditions that actually obtain, then P would (probably) be true.

Here "cognitive procedure M" should be understood to refer to the relevant belief-forming process via which the belief that P was actually arrived at. Intuitively, condition (R) looks at "close" possible worlds in which S arrives at a belief that P via this method or cognitive process and requires that P be true in such situations; whereas (A) looks at "close" possible worlds where P is false and requires that the method or cognitive process not yield the belief that P in those situations. Thus (R) could apparently be true and (A) false if the closest possible worlds where P is false and S believes P anyway are close enough to be relevant to (A) but still too far away to be relevant to (R), something that seems to depend on both the specific claim in question and on the "closeness" metric.[30] But how significant this difference might turn out to be is an issue that cannot be pursued further here.

How does Nozick's view fare in relation to the objections to reliabilist views discussed earlier? Because it focuses on knowledge rather than justification, the demon world objection does not apply to it in any straightforward way: while the beliefs of the demon world people seem intuitively to be justified, they plainly do not constitute knowledge. But examples such as the clairvoyance cases still seem relevant, with at most small modifications. It is easy to imagine clairvoyance cases that satisfy both conditions (A) and (B), but still intuitively do not seem to constitute knowledge because the person in question has no reason to think that the belief is true, no reason to think that these conditions hold, and so is being irrational in accepting the belief and would also be irrational to act on it. (But this result seems to me less clear than was the analogous point in relation to reliabilism, mainly because intuitions about knowledge are to my mind less clear-cut than intuitions about justification; see the further discussion of the concept of knowledge in section 7.)

In any case, with one small qualification, the generality problem seems to apply just as much to the "method" or cognitive procedure that figures in Nozick's conditions as it did to the reliabilist's cognitive processes. The qualification is that Nozick departs from a pure externalist view by individuating "methods" by appeal to the "final upshot in experience on which the method is based" (184–185). But while this may place restrictions on the range of descriptions that can reasonably be given of the "method" that is relevant to a particular belief, there will still be far more than enough to generate the same basic problem; such experiential upshots can after all themselves be described at many different levels of generality.[31]

6.2. Plantinga's Proper Function View

Alvin Plantinga's version of externalism is offered as an account of *warrant*, defined as whatever it is that distinguishes knowledge from mere true belief. He rejects the term "justification" as a label for this quality, on the ground that it is biased in favor of internalist conceptions of what is required for knowledge (and suggests in passing that something like Chisholm's term "positive epistemic status" might have been a better term for the property in question).[32]

Plantinga offers the following summary statement of his account of warrant:

> ... a belief has warrant for me only if (1) it has been produced in me by cognitive faculties that are working properly (functioning as they ought to, subject to no cognitive dysfunction) in a cognitive environment that is appropriate for my kinds of cognitive faculties, (2) the segment of the design plan governing the production of that belief is aimed at the production of true beliefs, and (3) there is a high statistical probability that a belief produced under those conditions will be true. Under those conditions, furthermore, the degree of warrant is an increasing function of degree of belief.[33]

Though the "only if" seems to suggest that the enumerated conditions are only *necessary for* "warrant," it seems clear that they are also supposed to be at least approximately sufficient.

Condition (1) is supposed to exclude not only internal malfunction, but also external manipulation by Cartesian demons and the like. Both condition (3) and implicitly condition (1) rely on the idea of a *design plan*, a set of specifications according to which human beings (and presumably other beings) are constructed. Such a design plan will delineate, among other things, the various specific faculties or "modules" that go to make up our overall cognitive apparatus, together with the aim or purpose of each. In clarifying and elaborating this idea, Plantinga relies heavily on artifacts as examples. And while he claims that the employment of the concept of proper function and the correlative concept of design does not immediately presuppose that human beings were literally designed by an intelligent being, rather than, say, by evolution, he does ultimately argue that only a theistic view can give an adequate account of these concepts.

Condition (3) reveals the close connection between Plantinga's view and the various versions of reliabilism. His claim is that embedding reliabilism within a proper function account avoids the generality problem, presumably because the question of the reliability of a cognitive process, which could be specified at many different levels of generality, is replaced by the more tractable issue of the reliability of a relatively specific set of cognitive faculties, as specified in the "design plan." But this will work only if the idea of a "design plan" and its component cognitive faculties is applicable to the believer in question in a sufficiently clear and univocal way. If, on the other hand, there are many different, equally acceptable specifications of the design plan with different correlative sets of cognitive faculties (specified at different levels of generality and perhaps differing in other ways as well), then there could well be also significantly different assessments of the statistical probability of truth for a given belief—so that Plantinga's view would also fail to give any definite answer to the issue of whether a particular belief is justified. The elusiveness of the idea of a design plan makes it difficult to say exactly how serious this problem is, but it is not one that can be easily dismissed.

Does Plantinga's view also face analogues of the other main problems with reliabilism? Like Nozick, he avoids anything very close to the demon world problem simply by eschewing any claims about justification. But it is still possible, I believe, to describe an example that shows that the satisfaction of his conditions is not necessary for knowledge. Imagine a being, call him Frank, whose cognitive faculties are entirely produced at random, perhaps via a very complicated and unlikely set of mutations, but who through sheer chance ends up with faculties that are identical to those of a normal human being. Frank might receive what would appear to be a normal education, might obtain a job in some cognitively demanding field like one of the sciences, and might eventually make, or at least appear to make, important contributions to human knowledge. All of this appears to be quite possible in the broadly logical or metaphysical sense to which Plantinga himself so frequently appeals. But since Frank's faculties were randomly produced, he apparently has no cognitive design plan, and hence his faculties could not be correctly said to be functioning properly or to be aimed at truth in the way that Plantinga's conditions (1) and (2) require. And this would mean in turn that none of the beliefs that resulted from those faculties would be "warranted" or would constitute knowledge.

But isn't this quite an implausible result? Frank might be indiscernible in every way from the rest of us as regards his cognitive functioning, might be an apparently excellent source of information or even an apparently great teacher, and would surely believe (or seem to believe) that he had "warranted" beliefs and knowledge. He might appear to satisfy every cognitive virtue to the highest possible degree. Moreover, if Plantinga is right that making good sense of the notion of proper function ultimately requires theism[34] and if God does not in fact exist, then we are all in essentially the same situation as Frank. Plantinga's apparent response to this sort of problem[35] is to suggest that Frank has simply acquired his design plan by accident, rather than via either evolution or divine creation. But this seems to dilute the idea of a design plan so far as to destroy any real difference between Plantinga's view and more standard versions of reliabilism.

Plantinga's view also seems perhaps vulnerable to counterexamples that are at least similar to the clairvoyance example involving Norman that was considered in relation to reliabilism. Thus suppose that a certain person, call him Boris, was indeed designed by God and that deep within his brain or psyche, God has implanted a very narrow and specialized module designed to guarantee that Boris will have a true belief about some monumentally important matter. To be specific, suppose that this module is so constructed that at some appropriate temporal interval before the mundane world comes to an end with the Second Coming,

Boris will be caused to believe with maximal firmness and conviction that this is about to occur. We may suppose that the belief is accompanied by no distinctive phenomenology, beyond the strong impetus to belief itself.

Now the time has come, and Boris finds himself believing that the world will soon end, and believing it as firmly as he believes that $2 + 2 = 4$ or that he is a human being. In this case, Plantinga's account of "warrant" appears to be satisfied: the faculty or module is functioning properly; there is no problem about the environment; the module in question is aimed at producing a true belief; and, we may suppose, its reliability under the existing conditions is extremely high. Moreover, Boris's belief, we are supposing, is true, and there is no Gettier-type problem. In addition, Boris's degree of warrant for this belief will apparently be maximal, thereby effectively eliminating any worry about conflicting evidence.

Does Boris then have maximally "warranted" *knowledge* that the world will soon end? I believe that he does not, basically because he has no rational basis of any sort for his claim and so seems to be thoroughly irrational in accepting it. Moreover, it would pretty plainly be irrational for Boris to *act* on this belief, for example, by selling his house to buy full-page ads proclaiming the forthcoming event or canceling his life insurance policies (as of the date of the expected occurrence). He has lots of reasons for being suspicious of beliefs of this kind and none that is apparent for trusting it. (But this once again seems to me, for reasons that will be discussed in the next section, to be a less clear result than was the analogous point about the reliabilist's account of justification.)

7. IS A CHOICE REALLY NECESSARY?

The main upshot of our discussion so far is that both internalism and externalism face serious problems, albeit of rather different sorts, problems that do not lend themselves to easy and obvious solutions. Any further consideration of the details of those problems is beyond the scope of the present essay. Instead, I want to conclude by raising a different sort of issue, one that pertains to the significance of the internalist–externalist dispute but that also has a bearing on the seriousness of these other problems: Is it really as clear as has often been thought by philosophers on both sides that internalism and externalism should be viewed as incompatible positions between which a choice has to be made? Might it not be the case that they are better viewed as different but basically complementary approaches to epistemological issues (each no doubt better suited to some issues than to others)?

What primarily suggests the latter sort of outlook is that each of these two main approaches seems to be epistemologically valuable in important though rather different ways. Each of them addresses important epistemological issues that the other is less well suited to deal with or cannot deal with at all. The basic case for the value of internalism has already been adequately indicated in the earlier discussion of the view (in section 2): internalism addresses the historically and substantively fundamental issue of first-person justification in a way that externalism by its very nature does not and cannot do, at least not in any thoroughgoing way. But what has been somewhat misleading in the discussion so far is that externalism has been presented entirely as a way of avoiding the problems that allegedly afflict internalism, but with little indication of any positive, independent motivation for the view. In fact, however, there are also many important and clearly epistemological questions and issues for which a predominantly externalist approach seems entirely appropriate and perhaps quite indispensable.

Most of these latter questions and issues fall within the confines of what Philip Kitcher has aptly labeled "the meliorative epistemological project,"[36] that is, the general project of assessing and improving the reliability of human cognitive efforts, and within the related and broader area of social epistemology. Thus, for example, if the issue arises as to whether some particular way of organizing scientific research in a specified area is likely to be successful in discovering truths of the relevant kind, the natural approach is to investigate cases in which the form of organization in question was used to see how reliable the results turned out to be, comparing it with others that differ in various ways. This would be an essentially third-person investigation, looking from the outside at the groups of investigators who employ the various forms of organization and assessing their success from that same perspective. And it might perhaps be useful, though in no obvious way essential, to describe claims that resulted from the use of a form of scientific organization that turned out to do well in this regard as justified in an externalist or, more specifically, a reliabilist sense.

Goldman, in fact, describes in some detail an investigation of a somewhat different sort that still fits comfortably within the meliorative project: a psychological investigation of the phenomenological differences (though he does not use this label) between ostensible memories of perceptions that genuinely reflect previous perceptions and those that are merely a product of imagination, with the former obviously being more reliable with respect to the truth of the resulting claims about the things that were allegedly perceived. Genuine memories of previous perceptions turn out, it is reported, to be richer in information concerning perceived properties like color and sound, richer in contextual information about the time and place in question, and more detailed, whereas the spurious memories resulting from imagination tend to be impoverished in these respects, but to contain much more information about the subjective cognitive operations of the person in question.[37] Here again we have an investigation from an essentially external, third-person perspective, one that yields results that might clearly be valuable in the assessment of the reliability of witnesses in various contexts (and that a person who was familiar with them might also apply in assessing his or her own ostensible memories). And again, these results might be formulated by saying that the memory beliefs that satisfy the criteria for reliability are justified in an externalist or reliabilist sense.

No reasonable epistemologist should have any quarrel with any of this. Such investigations are obviously legitimate and valuable, and also obviously of epistemological, though not merely epistemological, significance. Moreover, it is very hard at best to see how questions of this sort could be effectively dealt with from an exclusively internalist perspective. It is perhaps barely imaginable that answers to such questions might be in some way consequences in the long run of an ideally complete and detailed internalist epistemological account. But insisting on dealing with them in that way would inevitably mean that in any very imaginable short run, they would not be dealt with at all.

It therefore seems clear that there would be a substantial loss to epistemology if either internalism or externalism were simply abandoned. Thus we need to ask whether there are in fact any good reasons for regarding the two views as genuinely inconsistent with each other, thereby forcing such a choice.

Consider first the formulation of the supposed issue that was offered earlier, in terms of the correct specification of the concept of knowledge. Is it really so clear that there is, as this formulation presupposes, one clear and univocal concept of knowledge, in relation to which one of these views must be right and the other simply wrong? In fact, some epistemologists have suggested that there are two or more different concepts of knowledge, one or more at least predominantly externalist in character and one or more predominantly internalist. Thus Ernest Sosa distinguishes what he calls "animal knowledge" from what he calls "reflective knowledge": whereas animal knowledge arises as a direct response to stimuli of various kinds "with little or no benefit of reflection or understanding," reflective knowledge involves a wider understanding of how the belief comes about and how it is related to the fact that is its object.[38] And J. L. Mackie, in a discussion of an objection to the idea of innate knowledge, suggests that there is a whole spectrum of possible senses of 'know': at one end is a "minimal" sense, in which knowledge is merely nonaccidentally true belief (an externalist sense); at the other end, we have what Mackie calls "authoritative, autonomous, knowledge," "the knowledge of the man who himself has epistemic justification, the right to be sure" (clearly an internalist sense).[39] I do not want to endorse every aspect of Mackie's and Sosa's views on this point, nor do I think that the distinctions they have given are exactly the same. (In particular, it seems likely that Sosa's "animal knowledge" requires somewhat more than is required by Mackie's "minimal knowledge.") But it seems to me quite plausible that there is a viable distinction to be drawn along roughly these lines, and further that much of the seemingly intractable character of the internalism–externalism debate may stem from ignoring it.

What about a formulation of the issue in terms of the concept of *epistemic justification*: is the correct understanding of *this* concept internalist or externalist in character? One problem here is that epistemic justification is perhaps most standardly specified as that species of justification which is required for knowledge. But even if an alternative specification can be found, I would suggest that the specifically epistemological notion of justification is at least to a substantial extent a technical philosophical notion, one that is not as clearly present in common sense as is often assumed. And this opens the door to the possibility, again advocated by some, that there may simply be different and incommensurable concepts of epistemic justification, one or more internalist and one or more externalist in character, leaving it again unclear in what way these are competitors between which a choice has to be made.[40] I remark in passing that I still think that the intuitive objections, discussed above, that appeal to Cartesian demon worlds and to possible cases of faculties like reliable clairvoyance show at the very least that there is something unnatural and counterintuitive about an externalist concept of justification if the use of the term "justification" is supposed to connect with ordinary uses of that term and with the related ideas of rationality and reasonableness. But if the externalist is willing to disavow or at least seriously attenuate such connections, it becomes unclear what sort of objection there could be to the introduction of externalist concepts of justification such as those that might play a role in the meliorative epistemological project.

Moreover, allowing that both internalist and externalist conceptions of knowledge and of justification are intelligible and legitimate at least mitigates some of the problems discussed earlier. We can say that animals and other unsophisticated epistemic agents do have knowledge in a sense (Sosa's "animal knowledge"), while admitting that there is another sense (Sosa's "reflective knowledge") in which they do not. Perhaps the same thing should be said about Norman. We can also say that the demon world people are justified in an internalist sense, but not perhaps in one or more externalist senses. And we can offer the hope[41] that even if internalist attempts to account for our beliefs about the world apparently lead to skepticism, we may still have knowledge and perhaps be justified in other senses. Of course, this makes it all seem too easy, and the real problems do not disappear merely by introducing further concepts. But the point is that the serious epistemological issues should not depend on insisting that there can only be one acceptable concept of knowledge or of justification, and that doing so may get in the way of the most fruitful approaches to dealing with them.

My suggestion is thus that both the internalist and the externalist approaches are legitimate in relation to genuine epistemological issues and that there is no compelling reason why one has to be chosen in preference to the other. There is intellectual room for many different kinds of epistemological issues, including many that are naturally approached from the third person and that are at least largely externalist in character, together with some that are essentially internalist issues, especially relatively global issues having to do with whether one has good reasons for one's own beliefs. What is puzzling are the claims made by each side to exclusive possession of the legitimate field of epistemology—claims that we now see could be accepted only at a significant and unnecessary intellectual cost.

Having been reconciliatory to that extent, however, I want to close by insisting that there is nevertheless a clear way in which an internalist approach, in addition to being intellectually legitimate on its own, continues to have one fundamental kind of priority for epistemology as a whole. No matter how much work may be done in delineating externalist conceptions of knowledge or justification or reliability and in investigating how those apply to various kinds of beliefs or areas of investigation, there is an important way in which all such results are merely hypothetical and insecure as long as they cannot be arrived at from the resources available within a first-person epistemic perspective. If, for example, an epistemologist claims that a certain belief or set of beliefs, whether his or her own or someone else's, has been arrived at in a reliable way, but says this on the basis of cognitive processes of his or her own whose reliability is merely an external fact to which he or she has no first-person access, then the proper conclusion is merely that the belief or beliefs originally in question are reliably arrived at (and perhaps thereby are justified or constitute knowledge in externalist senses) *if* the epistemologist's own cognitive processes are reliable in the way that he or she believes them to be. And the only apparent way to arrive at a result that is not ultimately hypothetical in this way is for the reliability of at least some processes to be establishable on the basis of what the epistemologist can know directly or immediately from his or her first-person epistemic perspective.

NOTES

1. It is generally accepted by internalists that knowledge also requires the satisfaction of a fourth condition, one designed to rule out "Gettier cases" in which a belief is justified and true, but in which its truth is intuitively an accident in relation to its justification. See Edmund Gettier, "Is Justified True Belief Knowledge?" *Analysis* 23 (1963): 121–123. Externalists have sometimes claimed that their proposed third condition can also handle this problem, eliminating the need for a fourth condition; but this is, in my judgment, a mistake. For discussion, see my "Plantinga on Knowledge and Proper Function," in Jonathan Kvanvig, ed., *Warrant in Contemporary Epistemology* (Lanham, Md.: Rowman & Littlefield, 1996), together with Plantinga's reply in the same volume.

2. See, for example, Fred Schmitt, *Knowledge and Belief* (London: Routledge, 1992).

3. There are far too many versions of internalism to even begin to take account of

specific differences between different versions or to give anything like full references. Here I have focused on giving an account of the general view that is shared by many different historical and contemporary philosophers, with the paradigmatic version in recent times being perhaps that of Roderick Chisholm in *Theory of Knowledge*, 1st, 2d, and 3d eds. (Englewood Cliffs, N.J.: Prentice-Hall, 1966, 1977, 1989).

4. For an account of the rationale for internalism that fuses these two ideas, see Alvin Goldman, "Internalism Exposed," *Journal of Philosophy*, 96 (1999): 271–293.

5. As discussed, for example, by Linda Zagzebski in her book *Virtues of the Mind* (Cambridge: Cambridge University Press, 1996).

6. For a start in this direction, see my "Toward a Defense of Empirical Foundationalism," in *Resurrecting Old-Fashioned Foundationalism*, ed. Michael DePaul (Lanham, Md.: Rowman & Littlefield, 2000).

7. E.g., by Goldman in "Internalism Exposed."

8. Again, by Goldman, ibid., among many others. In this paper, Goldman also raises a number of additional objections to internalism that I have been unable to find space for in the present discussion. For a consideration of many of them, see my paper "The Indispensability of Internalism," forthcoming in a festschrift for Goldman in *Philosophical Topics*.

9. This idea derives from Tyler Burge's "Content Preservation," *Philosophical Review* 102 (1993): 457–488, esp. 462–465.

10. Indeed, I would suggest, it is a mistake to regard this most basic use of memory as giving rise to beliefs at all. When I recall an earlier sensory state or apprehended logical relation or state of mind, I do so, not by having the *belief* that the episode in question occurred, but simply by recalling *it* directly—though what is recalled in this way might, of course, itself be a belief.

11. The point about the coherentist's need for a foundationalist view of a priori justification was recognized in my own earlier version of coherentism. See my book *The Structure of Empirical Knowledge* (Cambridge, Mass.: Harvard University Press, 1985) (hereafter *SEK*), appendix A. For a discussion of why the attempt there to avoid the need for the second foundationalist element via the so-called doxastic presumption fails, see my "The Dialectic of Foundationalism and Coherentism," in *The Blackwell Guide to Epistemology*, ed. John Greco and Ernest Sosa (Oxford: Blackwell, 1999), 117–42.

12. There is also one other moderately important initial argument for externalism: the argument that externalism is to be preferred because it fits better with a *naturalistic* approach to epistemology, one, very roughly, that views epistemology (and philosophy generally) as continuous with and similar in nature to natural science. But a consideration of the issues raised by this argument is beyond the scope of the present discussion.

13. Though many others have followed his lead, by far the main proponent of reliabilism has been Alvin Goldman. See especially his "What Is Justified Belief?" in *Justification and Knowledge*, ed. George Pappas (Dordrecht: Reidel, 1979); and his book *Epistemology and Cognition* (Cambridge, Mass.: Harvard University Press, 1986). Goldman has never, however, been an advocate of mere simple reliabilism (as specified later).

14. We will look at more qualified versions later.

15. And if the degree of reliability is high enough, and the belief is true, and there are no Gettier-type problems, the dog has knowledge.

16. See Goldman, "What Is Justified Belief?"

17. This is a claim that reliabilists typically make, though it would be possible in

principle to have a quasi-reliabilist view that held that reliability was sufficient but not necessary for justification on the grounds that an internalist justification could also be sufficient.

18. I am assuming here, in order to make the main issue clearer, that the evil demon cannot deceive them about the contents of their own mental states (or about genuinely self-evident truths).

19. See Goldman, *Epistemology and Cognition*, 107, 113, for this response to the evil demon case. Goldman has since abandoned this attempted response. See his "Strong and Weak Justification," repr. in Goldman, *Liaisons* (Cambridge, Mass.: MIT Press, 1992), 135–137.

20. Offered by Goldman in "Strong and Weak Justification."

21. For a more extended discussion of this kind of objection to externalism, see *SEK*, chap. 3.

22. See *SEK*, chap. 3, for more extended discussion of these possibilities.

23. Apart from the sort of problem raised in the third objection, considered later.

24. The Norman case was presented in *SEK*, chap. 3.

25. For an example of what seems to me to amount to such a requirement, albeit not formulated in quite this way, see Goldman, "What Is Justified Belief?"

26. In his "Epistemic Folkways and Scientific Epistemology," in *Liaisons* (Cambridge, Mass.: MIT Press, 1992), Goldman at least suggests such a view. But his version of it (which includes a speculative psychological account of the intuitions in cases like the Norman case as well as those concerning the demon world example), is offered as merely a version of *descriptive epistemology*, an account of the "epistemic folkways" implicit in common sense. This is contrasted with *normative epistemology*, an account of the more adequate norms that genuine justification and knowledge must conform to. An adequate consideration of this rather complicated view is impossible within the confines of this essay.

27. One other general sort of view that will not, for reasons of space, be considered here is a hybrid internalist–externalist view, one that combines both internalist and externalist elements. For examples of such views, see Marshall Swain, *Reasons and Knowledge* (Ithaca, N.Y.: Cornell University Press, 1981); William Alston, "An Internalist Externalism," rep. *Epistemic Justification* (Ithaca, N.Y.: Cornell University Press, 1989); and, in a quite different way, Ernest Sosa, *Knowledge in Perspective* (Cambridge: Cambridge University Press, 1991). My suggestion would be that such hybrids are vulnerable to some or all of the objections that afflict the nonhybrid views.

28. Robert Nozick, *Philosophical Explanations* (Cambridge, Mass.: Harvard University Press, 1981), 179. (Further references in this section to Nozick are to the pages of this book.) Strictly speaking, the account just given is an account of what it is to know via a specific method that *P*; to know that *P* simpliciter, it is also required that the method in question would override any other method via which *S* believes that *P* (182).

29. For further discussion of this and some other points in this brief treatment of Nozick, see my paper "Nozick, Externalism, and Skepticism," in Steven Luper-Foy, ed., *The Possibility of Knowledge: Nozick and His Critics* (Totowa, N.J.: Rowman & Littlefield, 1987), 299–313.

30. The underlying point here is just that contraposition is not in general valid for counterfactual conditionals. See David Lewis, *Counterfactuals* (Cambridge, Mass.: Harvard University Press, 1973), 35.

31. A further problem with Nozick's view is that it leads, for reasons that are too complicated to be gone into here, to the denial of the principle of epistemic closure: the principle that knowledge of *P* brings with it knowledge of the known logical consequences of *P*. Nozick presents this result as a virtue of the view, but in fact it is a very serious objection to it. See the paper cited in note 28 for further discussion of this issue.

32. One consequence of this way of understanding the term is that warrant will have to include whatever is needed to avoid Gettier-type problems (see note 1). Plantinga in fact claims that his main account of warrant does this, but this claim is, in my judgment, highly questionable, making it likely that warrant will turn out to involve two relatively distinct elements, one that plays the same general role as epistemic justification and a second that does the work of avoiding Gettier-style counterexamples. For more discussion of this question, see my paper "Plantinga on Knowledge and Proper Function," in *Warrant in Contemporary Epistemology*, ed. Jonathan Kvanvig (Lanham, Md.: Rowman & Littlefield, 1996), from which the material of this section is mostly derived. See also Plantinga's reply, in the same volume, to this criticism and to some of the further problems discussed in the text.

33. Plantinga, *Warrant and Proper Function* [hereafter *WPF*] (New York: Oxford University Press, 1993), 46–47.

34. See *WPF*, chap. 11.

35. See *WPF*, pp. 29–30

36. Philip Kitcher, "The Naturalists Return," *Philosophical Review* 101 (1992): 64–65.

37. Goldman, "Internalism Exposed," 290–291.

38. Ernest Sosa, *Knowledge in Perspective* (Cambridge: Cambridge University Press, 1991), 240.

39. J. L. Mackie, *Problems from Locke* (London: Oxford University Press, 1976), 217.

40. This may also seem to count in favor of hybrid concepts of justification (or of knowledge), such as those mentioned in note 27. Perhaps so, though it seems to me that such conceptions are much more likely to inherit the problems of each of the main views than to inherit their virtues.

41. Only a hope for the reason suggested in the final paragraph.

CHAPTER 8

....

TRACKING, COMPETENCE, AND KNOWLEDGE

ERNEST SOSA

....

GIVEN a fact <f>, what is needed in order to know it? What is needed beyond believing it, B(f), or even believing it with justification, B(f) & J(f)?[1] Epistemologists have turned externalist on this question in a variety of ways, all of which deem insufficient the justification traditionally derived from experience and reason. Externalists have supplemented or replaced such justification with "external" requirements beyond the contents of the subject's mind and beyond merely logical or evidential relations among propositions. What follows will sketch and examine some varieties of that approach and will defend one in particular.

A. SIMPLEST EXTERNALISM

....

Here are two early versions of such externalism:[2]

(1) K(f) iff B(f) is causally linked with the fact <f>.[3]

(2) K(f) iff f & B(f) & the subject "tracks" the truth re <f>: i.e., both: ~f → ~B(f), and f → B(f).[4]

But each of these proves problematic. Regarding (1), there is the barns counter-example:[5] even if you are caused to believe that here is a barn by a good look in good light at the real barn before you, that is no knowledge if unknown to you it is the one true barn in fake-barn territory. As for (2), it implies that even when one does know that p one still can never know that one is not wrong in believing that p.[6]

Account (2) uses a notion of "Nozickian" tracking. A slight modification of such tracking yields a substantially different way to account for externalist intuitions. Cartesian and Nozickian tracking are both binary: each requires the satisfaction of two conditionals. And they join in requiring that $p \rightarrow B(p)$. But Nozickian N-tracking also requires that $\sim p \rightarrow \sim B(p)$, whereas Cartesian C-tracking requires rather that $B(p) \rightarrow p$. (These are not equivalent, since subjunctive conditionals do not contrapose.) C-tracking has interesting advantages: when made a necessary condition for knowledge, it does *not* entail, for example, as *does* Nozickian tracking, the following: that despite the fact that one would never be able to know *that one is not wrong to think that p* (just try tracking *that*), one might still concurrently know *that p* nevertheless (since this one still might track, despite never tracking the other).

B. DOUBTS ABOUT TRACKING

Our alternative to Nozickian tracking is "Cartesian" because it jibes with the combination of self-intimation and infallibility distinctive of Cartesian privileged access.[7] Although Cartesian tracking can thus serve to explain privileged access to one's own current mental states, it yet remains to be seen whether it can reasonably inherit the ambition of Nozickian tracking to serve as a general account of knowledge. And in fact C-tracking seems not to escape all doubts that attach to N-tracking, as is shown for example by the following two.

> *Problem.* One does not C-track that a bird flies by outside one's window, since that might too easily have happened without one's believing it (if only, for example, one had been looking in the wrong direction). But when one sees the bird flying by one does know that it is doing so, even though one does not C-track that fact.
>
> *Question.* Reliabilists view knowledge as true belief acquired or sustained through a reliable process. Does C-tracking have any advantages over such reliability as a requirement for knowledge?

In considering these matters it will help to have before us some additional examples:

1. You believe it's 3 P.M. by reading your watch. Although your (electronic) watch is normally reliable, on the present occasion someone has gained wireless control of it while determined to have it read whatever the roll of his dice might deliver. Since the dice come up 3, he allows the watch to read 3 (which entirely by coincidence is the right time), although, if the dice had not come up 3, the controller would have intervened and made the watch accord with the dice. Here the tracking requirement will explain why you do not know, but the "true belief acquired or sustained through a reliable process" may have some trouble. After all, the epistemically salient process through which I acquire my belief (reading the time off an electronic watch, etc.) is eminently reliable (though not infallible), so my belief does seem in this example to be acquired through a reliable process, despite which it fails to be knowledge.

2. A (different) controller allows a watch to work reliably for three seconds every year, and you happen to read the watch in the favored interval, but presumably you fail to know thereby.

3. A VCR-driven screen fleetingly becomes a window allowing a good view of the scene beyond. If you are under the impression that it is a window all the while, giving you access to the scene beyond, do you know when it does fleetingly become one? Suppose, conversely, that the VCR were turned on for an instant and a scene were put randomly on the window/screen by the VCR for that randomly selected instant, where the scene on the screen just happened to match the jerkily changing scene beyond (say you're in a train traversing rapidly changing terrain). Here again, "taking at face value what you seem to see through the window" seems in general a reliable method (the present instant being randomly selected as the one instant ever when the VCR is attached and turned on). Intuitively you do not know about the scene beyond, despite the perfect accuracy of your beliefs.

If you share these intuitions, here are some possible ways to explain them: (i) with early Goldman, through a requirement that the relevant belief must derive causally from the truth of its content (from the scene beyond, in our example), (ii) through a Nozickian requirement that the belief must N-track the truth of its content,[8] or (iii) through a requirement that the belief must C-track the truth of its content. Even if, of these, C-tracking does the best job, is it a good enough job?

C. Animal Knowledge and
Dependent Tracking

Animal knowledge requires a belief that is "apt," so that one gets it right not by accident but by tracking the truth, in this sense:

> *Tracking.* One tracks the truth, *outright*, in believing that p IFF one would believe that p iff it were so that p: i.e., would believe that p if it were so that p, and only if it were so.[9]

If suitably constituted and environed you might also have an ability to track over a certain range when appropriately related to facts in that range. Good eyesight can relate you to a facing surface's color and shape (when it is not too far, well enough lit, unoccluded, etc.) in such a way that for any relevant proposition <p> about the color or shape of the surface, you would believe <p> iff it were so that p.[10] Often there is more than one way to track a truth: you might hear the bells toll, for example, without seeing them, or you might see them toll without hearing them.

If I see that a bird flies by, but only because I happen to look out the window, which I might easily not have done, do I then put myself in a condition where the bird would now be flying by iff I believed it? Obviously not; too easily might I have been looking in the wrong direction. Even when I am looking in the right direction, so long as I might too easily have looked in another direction, it remains too easily possible that the bird has flown by without my seeing it; in which case I *do* know as I look out the window something that I do *not* track: that the bird flies by. Outright tracking therefore cannot be a necessary condition for knowing.

It might be thought that we avoid our problem through strategic relativizing. Thus the knower *would* believe that p if <p> were a fact to which he was suitably related. The relevant relation for the bird watcher, for example, might be that of looking in a certain direction with an unobstructed line of sight, etc.[11] That sort of requirement apparently disposes of Russell's example of a clock that has been stopped exactly 24 hours. *Relative to its being stopped*, it is false that one *would* acquire true beliefs by reading that clock, but relative to its working, it would of course be a source of truth.

So we might introduce a concept of dependent tracking by stages as follows. First would come a kind of relativized conditional:

> *Relative to <r>, it would be so that p iff it were so that q*

defined as follows:

<r&p> would be so only if <q> were so, and <r&q> would be so only if <p> were so.

In terms of this we could then define more complex conceptions of tracking:

Relativized tracking. One tracks the truth, *relative to a fact* <r>, in believing <p> IFF relative to fact <r>, one would believe <p> iff it were so that p.

Dependent tracking. One tracks the truth, *dependently on a fact* <r>, in believing <p> IFF (a) one does not track the truth outright in so believing, but (b) one does track the truth relative to fact *r* in so believing.

What if a clock is working only by accident? Suppose the evil demon at random intervals sets it to the right time and allows it to work for three seconds. The 3-second intervals when the clock works are rare, however, occurring perhaps once a week. Within them the clock would yield true belief but no knowledge, surely, and hence no sufficient warrant.

Another example. From a darkened room one looks through a window onto a scene beyond. The window occasionally becomes an opaque screen, however, on which a VCR puts a show nearly always unrelated to the scene beyond. Just once by chance the show matches the scene outside. Anyone who mistakes the screen for a transparent window can hardly know in just that instant through beliefs just then miraculously true. What now if instead of the screening's matching the scene, the VCR/screen is randomly disabled for an instant, allowing one a view through the now transparent window? Hours of illusion could hardly frame both sides of an instant of knowledge, even if they did so seamlessly, *especially* if they did so seamlessly.

The subjects who rely on the clock or on the VCR/window are denied knowledge because they fail to know responsively enough when to believe, when to disbelieve, and when to withhold judgment. They would too easily be misled, would too easily believe incorrectly in too many similar situations that they would not discern appropriately. The clock gazer would be misled too easily about the time, as would the subject in the darkened room about the scene beyond.

Contrast with these unfortunates the perceiver who happens to see the bird's flight. She too gets it right only by accident, but this does not preclude knowledge. Why not? Because she is attuned to the factors whose combined presence favors her knowing. If that combination were missing, the subject would responsively withhold her assent. Here the unfortunates are different: the clock gazer would continue to trust the clock even when it was stopped, which too easily might have happened; the perceiver through the accidentally transparent window would still believe even with the window turned into a VCR-controlled screen, which again too easily might have happened.

Favored subjects enjoy a sensitivity to what puts them in touch with the truth, unlike the unfortunates. Favored subjects not only track dependently on a relevant combination of factors; in addition, they believe as they do guided by those factors specifically, which is not true of the unfortunates. Believing the clock when it happens miraculously to be running is not guided by the factor, among others, of the clock's running, nor is the belief from the darkened room guided by the factor, among others, of the subject's access through the fleetingly transparent window. On the contrary, in believing as they do these subjects are not responding to the factors that by luck aid their tracking, for what guides their believing is not the real presence of those factors—including the transparency of the window, or the working of the clock—but only their *appearing* to be present. The subjects believe as they do guided by the appearance of a transparent window before them, or a working clock (in combination with other factors). However, in the circumstances they do *not* track the truth *dependently* on such appearances. In each case too easily might the appearances have remained, and with them the belief, even when the belief was false. So the subjects do not track dependently on the appearances, although it is the appearances that guide their believing. As for factor combinations dependently on which they *do* track, none guides their believing. This divergence between the factors dependently on which they track and the factors that guide their believing helps explain why they fail to know, or so I am suggesting. To track through a virtue by believing that p one must thereby track the truth either outright or else dependently on factors that also in combination guide one's believing.

D. SOURCES AND THEIR DELIVERANCES

Traditionally our knowledge is said to have "sources" such as perception, memory, and inference. Epistemic sources are said to issue "deliverances" that we may or may not accept. Our senses may issue the deliverance about two adjacent lines that one is longer, for example, a deliverance rejected by those in the know about the Müller–Lyer illusion.

A deliverance of <p> to a subject S is a "saying" that p witnessed by S. Different sources correlate with different ways in which it may be said that p. Someone may say it literally, of course, in person or in writing, and S may hear it or read it. If we can believe our eyes or ears, moreover, it's because they tell us things. We experience visually or aurally as if p. Normally we accept such deliverances of our senses, unless we detect something untoward. When someone or something tells us that p, we normally know who or what is doing so. We can tell at least that a certain voice or a certain stretch of writing is doing so, or that we seem to *see* the bells toll, or seem rather to *hear* them toll. And so on.

Deliverances thus conceived make up a realm of the ostensible: ostensible perceptions, ostensible memories, ostensible conclusions, ostensible intuitions, and the like. We may or may not believe our eyes or ears, we may or may not trust our senses, or our memory, or our calculations or other reasonings.

In virtue largely of a subject's constitution and positioning vis-à-vis a fact <p>, and of the subject matter or field of that fact, a deliverance to that subject will or will not track the truth as to whether p. It is largely such factors, that is to say, which determine whether or not <p> would be so delivered to S if and only if it were true. A subject in possession of the concept of a headache would ostensibly introspect that he suffered a headache if and only if he did, and this deliverance of introspection would thereby track *outright* the truth that it delivers. Unlike perception, introspection needs no medium, so it tracks unaided by any special relation between the subject and his headache, except only for the fact that it is *his* headache. In perception, by contrast, a deliverance will track only because the subject is appropriately positioned. If I ostensibly perceive that a bird flies by, this deliverance will track the truth that it delivers only dependently on my looking in the right direction. My ostensible perception of the bird's flight by my window does not track the truth (that the bird does fly by) *outright*. Admittedly, I would not ostensibly perceive thus unless a bird *was* flying by, except in then remote possibilities of illusion, hallucination, or skeptical scenario. However, a bird might easily have flown by without my ostensibly perceiving it. This is why my ostensible perception does not then track outright the truth of its content. But it does track that truth *dependently* on my looking out the window, and so on. That is to say, if while looking out the window, and so on, I ostensibly perceived that a bird was flying by, a bird would in fact be flying by; and if while I looked out the window, and so on, a bird flew by, I would in fact ostensibly perceive that this was so.

A deliverance's tracking *in virtue* of certain conditions must be distinguished from its tracking *dependently* on those conditions. Thus I may now track that there is no loud noise in my presence *in virtue* of the facts that I am not deaf, that my ears are not plugged, and so on, but not *dependently* on those facts, since my present ostensible perception of there being no such noise tracks the truth of its content *outright;* and since it does so outright it does not do so dependently. I do track that truth *in virtue* of my ears being operative: were they inoperative I would be unable to detect the presence or absence of loud noises. It may be thought that if this is so, then I cannot really be tracking outright that silence envelops me, as I must then be tracking that truth only dependently on my ears being operative. But this is not so. I can track *outright* a certain truth in virtue of the holding of a certain contingent condition, so long as the condition's absence is a remote enough possibility (in the relevant context of thought or discussion), remote enough that it *would* not in fact obtain in the circumstances, though of course *conceivably it might.*

Examples of deliverances are test results, indicator readings, eyewitness reports, media reports, perceptual appearances, and even rational intuitions and ostensible conclusions. Contents are delivered by each such source. Acceptance of a deliverance *as such,* that is, based on the reason that it is such a deliverance, constitutes knowledge only if the source is in that instance trustworthy and its deliverance accepted with appropriate guidance. The deliverance must track the truth, and one must be so attuned to the trustworthiness of its source that one would accept its deliverances as such (for the reason that they are such deliverances) only if they did track the truth.

It would not be enough to require that source X's deliverances merely guide S to believe the contents thus delivered. It must be required rather that X's deliverances guide S to accept those deliverances *as such.* S must accept the contents thus delivered as such, and this accepting must be guided by the deliverances (and guided also by the factors dependently on which those deliverances track). Reason: What the absence of the deliverance would properly take away is its content's being accepted for the reason that it is thus delivered, on the basis of the deliverance; after all, that content itself might then be a deliverance of some other source, in which case it would not be renounced merely because the first deliverance was rejected. Moreover, if a source delivers a deliverance but that source is now untrustworthy, then, if appropriately responsive to its untrustworthiness, S will now modify his attitudes accordingly. How so? Not necessarily through no longer assenting to the deliverances of that source. For, again, what that source delivers may concurrently be delivered by a source known to S to be perfectly trustworthy, in which case S would hardly give up believing the content delivered just in virtue of being responsive to how untrustworthy the earlier source is in the circumstances. What such responsiveness will affect is rather S's attitude to that untrustworthy source's deliverances *as such:* that is, S will no longer assent to that source's deliverance, say <p>, *as a deliverance of that source.* S will no longer accept <p> *for the reason that it is a deliverance of that source, i.e., on that causal basis.* S will no longer be guided to accept those deliverances at face value, i.e., as deliverances of that source. (Your eyesight might fade while your hearing remains good; and you might then respond accordingly.)

As for the notion of "guiding," this will here be understood as nothing more than the converse of "basing": Factor F "guides" belief B if and only if belief B is "based" on F (perhaps in combination with other factors).

Again, deliverances are not beliefs or acceptances, as when perception delivers that one of the Müller–Lyer lines is longer than the other despite the fact that all things considered one has no temptation to accept that deliverance and believe accordingly. Any competence to discriminate a trustworthy source of deliverances and to be guided by its deliverances is an intellectual virtue (or has a virtue as its basis in the constitution of that subject's mind).

That sketches the tracking-through-virtue view in a way that applies naturally to the examples before us.[12] The bird-watcher may now be seen to be favored over the unfortunates (the accidental clock-gazer and the observer through the fleetingly transparent VCR/window) in the following respect. In all three cases the subject accepts a deliverance as such, but only the fortunate subject accepts it with proper guidance. In accepting that deliverance she accepts a truth tracker. She would accept the deliverances of that source only were they trustworthy truth-trackers. Not so for the unfortunates: the accidental clock-gazer, or the observer graced by fleeting transparency. Deliverances accepted by these unfortunates fail to track the truth of their contents outright. What is more, they fail also to track the truth of their contents dependently on factors that guide the subject's acceptance of them. Again, one might of course know something through accepting a deliverance that tracks *not* outright but dependently on a certain condition. If one accepts such a deliverance guided by the holding of the relevant condition, one might still thereby know the truth of the content accepted. Thus a clock that is working for brief seconds might still track relative to its ticking (given that the determined controller starts it ticking only while resetting it to the right time and would not easily act otherwise). The subject who accepts its deliverances guided (at least in part) by its ticking might learn thereby what time it is, even if one who believes the clock without hearing it tick would not share that knowledge. The difference is that the clock then tracks the time dependently on its ticking. Therefore the subject who accepts its deliverances guided by its ticking can know thereby. However, the subject who is *not* guided by its ticking, may not know through accepting the clock's reading, and would not know thereby unless the clock's readings do track dependently on some other factor that does guide the subject.

The subject who knows of the bird's flight accepts a deliverance that tracks the truth of its content either outright or else dependently on a condition that guides his acceptance, but the subject who reads the accidentally working clock fails to know thereby, because the deliverance he accepts tracks the truth of its content *neither* outright *nor* dependently on any condition which then guides him. And the same goes for the subject who accepts his ostensible perceptions when accidentally allowed a true view through the fleetingly transparent window.

A deliverance enables knowledge, then, only if it tracks the truth either outright or else dependently on a condition by which one is guided. One then knows through accepting that deliverance as such, that is, for the reason that it is such a deliverance, guided in part by the holding of that condition.

E. KNOWLEDGE AND COMPETENCE

Cartesian tracking, $B(p) \leftrightarrow p$, is composed of two conditions:

Safety $B(p) \rightarrow p$
Receptivity $p \rightarrow B(p)$

We have considered requiring such tracking for knowledge. Upon closer consideration, safety remains a plausible requirement, but we need a closer look at receptivity.

We have seen why it is wrong to require *outright* tracking. The more plausible requirement is *dependent* tracking, tracking dependently on a fact that also guides one's belief. Such tracking dependently on a fact $<q>$ entails that one's belief is *safe* dependently on $<q>$:

$[q \& B(p) \rightarrow p]$ but not-$[B(p) \rightarrow p]$

and also that one's belief is *receptive* dependently on q:

$[q \& p \rightarrow B(p)]$ but not-$[p \rightarrow B(p)]$.

We thus face the following question. If a belief $B(p)$ does not track *outright*, does it then amount to knowledge only if it is guided by a factor dependently on which it is not only *safe* but also *receptive*? That is to say, does K(p) then require that $B(p)$ be at once guided by, and receptive dependently on, some fact $<q>$: that is to say, is it required that

if not-$[p \rightarrow B(p)]$, then for some $<q>$, $[q \& p \rightarrow B(p)]$, while B(p) is guided by $<q>$?

Take the subject who looks out the window. Does her knowledge of the bird's flight require that her belief be at once guided by and receptive dependently on some fact $<q>$? Presumably that fact $<q>$ would involve her looking out the window in good light while nothing occludes the bird's path, etc.

Might a belief not be safe, however, and constitute knowledge, without being receptive, not even dependently on any fact that guides it? Take the belief that there is a bird before one. And suppose one to be stably (modally stably) so constituted (good enough eyesight, in possession of the concept of a bird, able to tell a bird by sight, etc.) and stably (modally stably) so circumstanced (good light, no occlusion, alert enough, etc.) that one's belief that there is a bird before one is indeed safe: one would not easily have that belief without being right. Compatibly, might it not yet be false that one's belief is "receptive" to that fact? Might not a bird too easily be there without one's believing it? For example, a small bird might perhaps perch quietly in the garden before one, making it hard to discern. No fact might then guide one's belief that before one there is a bird while one's belief is receptive dependently on that fact.

One can know that one faces a bird when one sees a large pelican on the lawn in plain daylight even if there might easily have been a solitary bird before one unseen, a small robin perched in the shade, in which case it is false that one would have believed that one faced a bird. *Prima facie*, then, it seems unnecessary that one's belief be receptive; one might perhaps know through believing safely even if one does *not* believe receptively. But what might have tempted advocates of tracking to impose a stronger requirement? Why might it be thought that safety must be supplemented with receptivity, as a necessary condition for knowledge?

Here is an argument. Belief of high epistemic quality is belief that is not only true but manifests good command of the subject matter and full competence on its questions, and especially on the very question at issue, the question, let us say, whether p. What might such command and competence require? Consider this proposal.

> S is *fully competent* re the question whether p *if and only if* S is so constituted and positioned relative to that question that not easily would S thus fail to believe correctly on that question: i.e., (a) not easily would S believe that p while so constituted and positioned without it being so that p, and not easily would it be so that p while S was so constituted and positioned without S believing it; and (b) not easily would S disbelieve that p while so constituted and positioned without it being false that p, and not easily would it be false that p while S was so constituted and positioned without S disbelieving that p.

It may now be argued that someone can really know that p, can have the best knowledge that p, only if his belief that p manifests full competence on the question whether p. Knowledge manifesting only partial competence is a lesser grade of knowledge. How plausible is that? Despite its initial plausibility, we have seen how implausible this turns out to be: plain knowledge, as ordinarily understood, should not be confused with fully competent believing. The subject who knows there's a bird before him when he sees a pelican in plain daylight need not be so positioned that there *would* not be a bird there without his noticing it. He might fail to notice a robin perched quietly in the shade before him, which would not affect his ability to know that there is a bird before him by seeing a pelican in plain view.

Our theory of Cartesian tracking, outright or dependent, is hence more plausibly an account of full *competence* on the question whether p, than of *knowledge* that p.[13]

Perhaps it is our knowledge of necessary truths that will be thought to require receptivity and not only safety of belief? After all, any belief in a necessary truth will be automatically as safe as could be. Not easily will one hold such a belief while it is false, since not *possibly* could one hold it while it was false. When such a belief fails to be knowledge, it may be concluded, the reason must be that it fails to be receptive. Just the fact that a truth is necessary will not make us receptive to it: it may easily be false that $p \rightarrow B(p)$ even if it is a necessary truth that p.

That is indeed tempting, but its attraction pales when we recall how implausible it is to require receptivity for knowledge of simple empirical truths such as the fact that there is a bird before one in the garden. Fortunately there is an alternative, more promising way to explain how we can fail to know in believing something that is true with apodictic necessity. For we can use the fact that a belief might be safe without being virtuous, while requiring beliefs to be *both* safe *and* virtuous in order to qualify as knowledge. What then beyond safety is required for virtuous belief?

F. Deliverances and Indications

Our sort of unary requirement, going *from* a psychological state with a certain content *to* the truth of that content, may also be used to define a desirable cognitive status for states other than belief. For example, it seems attractive for "deliverances," which may now be viewed as "indications" when they satisfy our unary requirement. Thus a deliverance/indication I(p) may be said to "indicate" outright that p IFF $I(p) \rightarrow p$; and to indicate that p "dependently on condition C" IFF both C obtains and $C\&I(p) \rightarrow p$, while it is not so that $I(p) \rightarrow p$. (A "deliverance," an instance of delivering, is a state of affairs wherein something seems to oneself to be so—a more or less complex state that may feature intellectual as well as sensory content.)

The foregoing enables us more adequately to take account of externalist intuitions through appeal, not to C-tracking, but to "indication," as follows.

S knows that p on the basis of an indication I(p) only if either (a) I(p) indicates the truth outright and S accepts that indication as such outright, or (b) for some condition C, I(p) indicates the truth dependently on C, and S accepts that indication as such not outright but *guided* by C (so that S accepts the indication as such *on the basis* of C).[14]

How is this affected by the problems for tracking? For example, how does this "indication" account fare with regard to our problems (in section B above) for Cartesian tracking? And how is it affected by the following?

1. Consider the propositional form $x + y = z$, where x, y, and z are all two-digit numbers (in the usual formulations. And suppose that S believes and would believe any proposition he takes to be of form F, simply because it is such a proposition. Some of these propositions will be true: the proposition that $22 + 22 = 44$, for example; call it P1. Consider S's belief of P1. S has an inclination to believe it, and does appear to have an indication, namely F(P1), of the truth of P1. After all, it *is* true and true outright that $F(P1) \to P1$. S accepts that indication, guided by the fact that the proposition accepted is of form F. So the effective indication is F(P1), where P1 is presented as a proposition of form F. This indication/deliverance (to S) does, again, apparently indicate the truth. Moreover, S does accept that indication/deliverance *as such*, that is, for the reason that it is such an indication/deliverance. Why then is it that S fails to know P1, if *that* is how he acquires and sustains his belief?

2. On my way to the elevator I release a trash bag down the chute from my high-rise condo. Presumably I know my bag will soon be in the basement, and I know in the elevator that the bag is already there. But what if it were not there? That presumably would be because it was snagged somehow in the chute on the way down (an incredibly rare occurrence), or through some such happenstance. But none such could affect my belief as I descend in the elevator, so I would still believe that the bag was in the basement. My belief is not sensitive, therefore, but constitutes knowledge anyhow, and can correctly be said to do so. Such "backtracking" conditionals create problems for the "sensitivity" requirement that S knows that p only if S would not believe that p if it were false.[15] By contrast, the "indications" account, in terms of an indication/fact conditional: $I(p) \to p$, seems unaffected.

G. Skepticism and Relevant Alternatives

We are considering what modal relation must obtain between a fact and a belief in order for this belief to constitute knowledge of that fact. And we have discussed the bearing on our question of the following principle:

> In order to know a fact P one must exclude (rule out, know to be false) every alternative that one knows to be incompatible with *that fact*.

Consider now a strengthening of that principle, which we may call the "principle of exclusion":

> PE   In order to know a fact P one must exclude (rule out, know to be false) every alternative that one knows to be incompatible with *one's knowing that fact*.

This principle, which already figured earlier in our discussion, also seems plausible on its face. What is more, it follows directly from simple principles that are hard to deny, or so I have argued elsewhere.[16] So let us briefly explore the bearing of this strengthened principle on the questions before us.

We turn accordingly to a more general conception of "alternatives": when you believe <p>, such an alternative <a> is a condition within which you would not know that p. This is a broader sense in that every alternative in the earlier sense is an alternative in the new sense, but not vice versa. If <a> is incompatible with <p> then <a> is a condition within which you would not know that p, but <a> can also be incompatible with your knowing that p without being incompatible with <p>. Here now are some relevant examples, some involving alternatives in the narrower sense, some only in the broader sense.

1.   You see a small yellow bird and thereby believe you see a goldfinch. But it could just as easily be a canary, which is then an alternative, A1.

2.   You see a striped equine and thereby believe you see a zebra. But stripes could be painted on a mule so it would look the same, which makes this an alternative, A2.

3.   You ostensibly see a hand and accept that at face value. But if the conditions of perception were abnormal (hallucinogenics, wax museum, bad lighting, etc.) then you would not know in believing that you see a

hand. So the conditions' being thus abnormal constitutes an alternative, A3.

4. You ostensibly see a hand and accept that at face value. But if it were a dream you would not know that you see a hand. So its being a dream is an alternative, A4.

5. You ostensibly see a hand and accept that at face value. But if you were a demon victim or an envatted brain (etc.) you would not know. So your being in such a skeptical scenario is an alternative, A5.

6. You ostensibly see a sphere and accept that at face value. But if it were a cube it would not be a sphere, and you would not know it to be a sphere you see. So its being a cube is an alternative, A6.

You might defend your belief in case 6 by saying that the very experience indicating to you that you see a sphere indicates also that it's a noncube. And someone might argue: "If it were a cube it would look different, so I can know through my experience that it's a sphere, not a cube, since my experience *would* reveal the difference." Unfortunately, this would revert to a criterion of *sensitivity* already found problematic, as our experience would *not* thus reveal the difference between one's being or not being in familiar skeptical scenarios, nor would it even reveal whether or not one is wrong in thinking that p, etc. If we are to defend your case-6 belief in a conditionals-theoretic way, therefore, we should look to the requirement of safety, not that of sensitivity. Our belief that the item is a noncube (and the corresponding visual indication guiding that belief) is indeed found to be not only sensitive but also safe; as is the belief that no demon is fooling us into thinking that it's a sphere and not a cube; and as is the simpler belief that we are not wrong in thinking it to be a sphere and not a cube. So far so good.

Consider cases 1 and 2. Advocates of safety say that if you think you see a goldfinch, or a zebra, then you know only if your belief is safe: that is, it must be that you would so believe only if your belief were true. What if alternative A1, or A2, is pressed on you? Would you offer a response analogous to the safety-inspired response in case 6? Are the corresponding beliefs in the three cases relevantly alike? Is our belief that it's a sphere and not a cube relevantly like the belief that it's a goldfinch and not a canary, and like the belief that it's a zebra and not a striped mule? In respect of sensitivity there are bound to be important differences: if it were a cube and not a sphere, then one's visual experience would be different; but if it were a canary and not a goldfinch, or if it were a striped mule and not a zebra, then (by hypothesis) our experience would still be the same. In order to deal with this, without having to grant that we can't know it's a goldfinch when we see one outside, or a zebra when we see one at the zoo, the sensitivity theorist sometimes invokes the difference between relevant and irrelevant alternatives. He does not require us to rule out that it's a canary we see, or a striped mule, even though we still would *not* believe it to be a canary even if it were a canary, and not a goldfinch; and would not believe the equine to be a striped mule even if it were a striped mule, and not a zebra. Obviously, in the case as imagined, we are not in a position to rule out with sensitivity the alternative that it's a canary we face, nor, in the other case, that it's a striped mule. The appeal to relevance is designed to exempt us from having to rule out precisely *such* alternatives, which are viewed as *irrelevant*. And the same goes for the more radical alternatives of the skeptics, as in cases 4 and 5. Some sensitivity theorists also adopt a linguistic contextualism which puts aside the question of who can know what and in what conditions, in order to concentrate rather on when it is correct to *say* that some-one "knows." And this is thought to be powerfully affected by what alternatives are somehow salient in the context of attribution.

The safety theorist has no need of that linguistic recourse. Nor does he even need the distinction between the relevant and the irrelevant. He will point out rather about case 6 that even if it were a cube it *might conceivably* look like a sphere. In the right circumstances it *might* look like a sphere despite being a cube. So we are depending rather on a condition that if it were a cube then it *would in fact* look like a cube and not like a sphere. The corresponding safety requirement is then that if it looked like a sphere it *would in fact* be a sphere and not a cube (even if it might *conceivably* look like a sphere and yet be a cube). Put another way, the safety requirement is satisfied so long as not easily would it then look like a sphere while failing to be one (given the actual setup).[17]

Similar reasoning may be seen to deliver analogous results about our other cases, 3–5.

H. Knowledge and Virtue

Knowledge requires nonaccidentally true belief; this casts some light on what knowledge is, but light dimmed by the imprecision in our notion of an accident, which itself needs explaining in the final analysis. More adequate is the notion of dependent tracking. Compare the belief that this is a ripe tomato, believed of a ripe tomato amidst a bushelful of wax replicas. Arguably, this belief *does* track the truth, dependently on the circumstance of one's focusing just on that one tomato. That is to say, if one focused just on that one tomato *while* believing that the tomato one sees is a ripe tomato, then one *would* be right in so believing. And if one focused just on that one tomato *while* it was a ripe tomato, then one *would* believe it to be ripe. But one is still right only by accident, in some relevant sense or respect. Each of the items in that top layer is believed by me to be a ripe tomato, but I am right only in this one case, which my perspective does not distinguish in any relevant respect.

Suppose I fancy myself a connoisseur of tomato ripeness, but suffer from a rare form of color blindness that precludes my discerning nearly any shade of red except that displayed by this particular tomato. Therefore my judgments of tomato ripeness are in general apt to be right with no better than even chance. But when it's the particular (and rare) shade of red now displayed, then I am nearly infallible. Oblivious to my affliction, I issue judgments of tomato ripeness with abandon over a wide spectrum of shades of red. If, unknown to me, the variety of tomato involved always ripens with this shade of red, my belief that this tomato is ripe *is* then in step with the truth. Nevertheless, in some relevant sense or respect I am right only by accident. The problem is that I am not adequately guided by the conditions on which my tracking of ripeness is dependent. I still issue my verdicts of ripeness even when those conditions are absent. In this respect I am like Magoo in his perceptual judgments, which he does not restrict to the very narrow bounds within which they are reliable.

Compare a basketball held at time t by someone S at the top of an incline. It is true, let us suppose, that if that basketball were released, it would roll down the incline. And this is true for reasons of two sorts: because of factors pertaining to the intrinsic makeup of the basketball at that time, for example, that it is then rigidly round; and because of factors extrinsic to it, for example, because it is not glued to the top of the incline, because it is in a gravitational field, and so on. Moreover, the truth of the conditional might be dependent on factors of two sorts: the external and the internal. While cradled in S's hands, the ball's internal pressure may hover at the limit above which, if released it would explode upon contact with the incline, rather than rolling down. So it may be true that if it were then released it would roll dependently on its condition at that time t, since its being in just that internal condition is too precarious a matter for it to be the case outright that it would roll if released. Alternatively, the incline may be in a moment of calm at t, even though at (t-minus-epsilon) and at (t-plus-epsilon) it is swept by winds that would blow it away rather than allowing it to roll down. So conditions of two sorts may be involved in the truth of a conditional such as: *if the ball were released it would roll down the incline,* in such a way that this conditional is true not outright but only dependently on the holding of those conditions; some such conditions are "internal," while others are "external."

Virtues are internal conditions that enable an entity to attain desirable ends (of the entity or of its users) relative to certain circumstances, conditions in virtue of which it is true that the entity *would* succeed in those circumstances. So a condition may be a virtue relative to one end-circumstance pair <E, C> while it is not a virtue relative to another <E′, C′>. Of course, the context of thought or discussion may set the relevant ends and circumstances well enough that they need not be mentioned specifically, in which case we may and do speak of virtues without qualification. But ambiguity always threatens, especially when we consider alternative possibilities: do we then retain the relativization to our actual ends and circumstances, or do we shift to our ends and circumstances in the supposed possible situation? Here lies a source of ambiguity.

There are virtues of two sorts: those included in one's fundamental nature, resident in one's innate capacities and aptitudes; and those part of one's "second nature," one's character pliable at least to some degree, at some remove. Of these, some derive from blind habituation subject to very limited rational control, maybe from one's earliest upbringing. Nevertheless, much in the normal development of one's character, moral and intellectual, derives from one's own rational control. The acts, practical or theoretical, that issue from such components of one's character, from one's rational second nature, are under one's motivational control, at least to some extent, at some remove. These acts reflect on one's character, moral or intellectual, and specifically on those components of one's character for which one is at least in part responsible. With regard to such acts and the character they reveal, one is subject to suasion, and thus a proper participant in rational deliberative dialogue, and especially subject to praise and blame.

I. Sources, Virtues, and Habits of Thought

When one believes that here is a hand, one believes one's eyes, one believes that things are as they appear, that if it looks somehow, then that is really how it is. This goes beyond just trusting one's eyesight on the appearance of a hand specifically; it involves, rather, visual appearances more generally, and sensory appearances even more generally. One believes that, absent specific signs to the contrary, reality fits how it appears in one's experience, that if it seems experientially a certain way, that is how it really is. Of course one rarely formulates any such belief in words, even in the very general way just suggested. Nearly all one's beliefs normally remain unformulated, and plenty of beliefs influence our thought and action with no benefit of formulation. I can believe and even know that someone looks somehow, has a certain facial appearance, even if I could not come close to capturing in words the full content of my belief. Easily formulable beliefs might be held, moreover, without ever being formulated. Here I mean not just deep beliefs that surface under couch analysis, but also more common ones revealed through the subject's conduct, either physical or intellectual. Thus one might believe to be G whatever one believes to be F, which might be no accident: at the time in question one might be such that one *would* believe a thing to be G upon believing it to be F. This jibes with one's holding an implicit belief that if something is F then it is (likely to be) G. Such beliefs can operate subterraneanly, even if not so deeply buried that only persistent analysis would uncover them. Some biases and prejudices, for example, are more easily uncovered than are their more Freudian underworld mates. One is shown to believe that F's are or tend to be G's through one's persistent tendency to attribute G-ness to what one takes to be F. A belief that people of a certain sort are ipso facto inferior is betrayed through one's persistent attribution of inferiority to whoever one takes to be of that sort. Even if one denies the generalization when it is formulated explicitly, and one is deemed sincere to the extent that one is not *consciously* lying, one's protestations might still be dismissed in the light of the evidence.

Freudian beliefs, biases and prejudices, beliefs about how people look and react, about how dishes taste, about how a song goes, and so on, operate in the background, unformulated, but guide our more particular beliefs and choices as we navigate an ordinary day. Despite being unformulated and, often, unreasoned, and certainly not *consciously* reasoned, such beliefs can vary significantly in their degree of epistemic justification. Some biases are *just* biases, formed on inadequate evidence or none at all. We are all familiar with irrational mechanisms that fix beliefs without justification. Some ways of acquiring a belief are not defective or inadequate, however, despite involving no reasoning from epistemically prior premises. Nor can we require that all beliefs whatever must be acquired through appeal to prior premises. That way lies vicious regress, and a very simple and direct route to the deepest skepticism. So there must be ways to acquire epistemically justified beliefs without reaching them as conclusions from premises known with epistemic priority.

If that is so, might not beliefs acquired perceptually attain epistemic justification precisely by being so acquired? Such beliefs might be "directly" justified, in the sense of acquiring justification, but *not* through a process of reasoning that leads to their acceptance as a conclusion.

Suppose we agree that there is some sort of "implicit inference" when we believe our eyes, some sort of processing that begins with how things seem experientially and ends with a corresponding belief about our surroundings. In that case, we might think of the processing as an inference from an implicit belief with the content that, absent any sign to the contrary, things would normally be pretty much as they seemed. Alternatively, we might think of it as just a "habit" of thought that has us believe things to be a certain way whenever they appear that way and there is no apparent sign to the contrary. Either way an issue of "justification" arises, surely. Can anything really substantive be seen to turn on how we choose to frame the issue? Either we shall face a question of the justification of such a habit, or we shall face an issue of the justification of an implicit belief. And in neither case is there much hope that we shall be able to explain the epistemic justification involved through appeal to the subject's abductive or inductive or analogical reasoning.[18]

In a broad sense, the issue of epistemic justification that arises in either case is that of what makes it *epistemically* right (or good or valuable or desirable or reasonable or of positive value) for us to be a certain way, whether that way is a belief or a "habit." In either case we are contingently a certain way (either through our nature or through our second nature), a way that seems epistemically evaluable. We may explain why it seems thus evaluable if we consider that the way we are, whether by hosting a certain belief or by hosting a certain "habit," is a way that bears on the "health" of one's intellectual life, on what sorts of beliefs we have and will acquire, correct ones or erroneous ones, and systematically so, given a fixed environment. Even Magoo may thus be seen to have "justified" beliefs, so long as the epistemic value of the relevant habits is to be assessed relative to the species, and not relative to the individual. (We abstract in any case from whatever other values may be promoted in the life of Magoo and others.)

Moreover, beliefs depend for their epistemic quality on how they are ingrained or sustained, even when they are part of our nature, or our second nature, perhaps in a way that reflects some even deeper character of oneself or of one's community. Since we are interested in keeping track of these, we evaluate beliefs and habits by reference to the sources that yield them and the virtue of these sources. Suppose I acquire the habit of inferring in accordance with a rule that if one gets wet and cold one will catch cold, and manage to make many true predictions that way. Suppose further that those better positioned have the best of reasons to think that getting cold and wet has nothing to do with it. Suppose finally that I acquire my habit of thought just insensibly, over the years, so that it becomes second nature to me, through the influence of grownups who are quite unreliable. Do my true predictions amount to knowledge? A habit thus acquired, through the insensible social pressure of an unreliable community, can neither constitute nor yield any knowledge or "epistemically justified" belief. Nor can it make much difference whether the generalization that corresponds to the habit ("when one gets cold and wet one tends to catch cold") is actually true or not. (If it turns out that there is after all a previously undetected but real connection, this would not show that by relying on the habit I acquired knowledge denied to the rest of us by appropriate rational scruples.)

Are the only habits of inference that can be fundamentally justified those that people have tried to codify in a logical organon, for example, a set of rules of inference, deductive or inductive? That seems a mistake, for several reasons: first, because there is no such simple set of rules; what one is justified in believing is too holistic and context dependent a matter to be codified in any formal system.

Here the Duhem/Quine considerations bear, as does Goodman's gruesome tale. It also seems a mistake, secondly, because following such rules (were there such rules, which probably there are not) could issue at best a very limited yield of justified belief, nor would it help much to give ourselves data restricted just to the character of our sensory experience, and so on. And it seems a mistake, finally, because there is no apparent reason why the so-called inductive habits would enjoy any special status superior to that of believing our eyes in conditions that seem normal, etc.

As we work our way back to the sources of our good habits, and to the sources of the sources, and so on, we shall eventually reach a set of ingrained ways not acquired or sustained by sources outside the set. And the question will remain: why are we characterized by that set of ingrained ways, when, presumably, we could have been at least somewhat different. Is it good that we are that way? Are we that way only by accident? These are reminiscent of the issues in the free will controversy. Positions open up in epistemology that are familiar from the free will controversy; proper philosophical coherence and integration will no doubt require that our philosophy of freedom and autonomy be in harmony with our philosophy of knowledge. Right, virtuous action will require conditions of freedom and autonomy likely to be matched by conditions demanded of belief nonaccidentally enough correct to count as epistemically justified and indeed as knowledge.[19]

NOTES

This chapter builds in part on, but goes for the most part beyond, the account in my "How Must Knowledge Be Modally Related to What Is Known?" in the festschrift for Sydney Shoemaker, *Philosophical Topics* (1999).

1. Here and in what follows, subject and time designations will be suppressed, so that, for example, 'B(p)' is meant to represent belief that p by subject S at time t; similarly for 'K(p)', 'J(p)', and, later, 'I(p)'.

2. Approach (1) was once Alvin Goldman's, approach (2) Robert Nozick's.

3. Where the linkage can be of either of two sorts: fact-causing-belief or fact-and-belief-both-sharing-a-cause.

4. This is a first approximation; a fuller account appeals also to the "method" used to acquire or sustain the belief. But our critique would seem to apply also to the more elaborate account. (Here 'p→q' will be short for 'it would not be so that p without it being so that q'; or we might stipulate that in our usage it amounts to 'that p *subjunctively implies* that q'; the idea is that its being so that p offers some guarantee, even if not an absolute guarantee, that it is also the case that q. The guarantee is as weak as that offered by the truth of "If I should next release this pencil (held aloft and unsupported, etc., in an actual speech context), then it would fall." A comment by Carl Ginet stimulated this improved English formulation for the arrow conditional p→q.)

5. Cited by Goldman himself.

6. Try plugging the propositional form *that one is not wrong in believing that p* in the right side of (b).

7 .This has been lucidly explained and developed by Sydney Shoemaker in recent work. See part I of his *The First Person Perspective and Other Essays* (Cambridge: Cambridge University Press, 1996), especially chap. 3, "First Person Access."

8. However, these are not the views that Goldman and Nozick respectively settle on in the end.

9. This is Cartesian tracking, not the Nozickian tracking which requires, not that one would believe that p only if it were so that p, but rather that if it were not so that p then one would not believe it. It is defended in my "Postscript to 'Proper Functionalism and Virtue Epistemology'," in *Warrant in Contemporary Epistemology*, ed. J. Kvanvig (Lanham, Md.: Rowman & Littlefield, 1996), 271–280.

10. Here and in what follows '<p>' abbreviates 'the proposition that p'.

11. Compare Plantinga's requiring for the warrant of a belief B that it have been formed by an exercise E of cognitive powers (or intellectual virtues) in a mini-environment MBE *favorable* for that exercise, that is, one such that if S were to form a belief by way of E *in MBE*, S would form a true belief. See his "Warrant and Accidentally True Belief," *Analysis* 57 (1997): 140–145; 144.

12. I do not deny that the view might still be improved through further development, and I will return to it elsewhere.

13. This account of competence is found useful in my discussion of normative objectivity, "Objectivity Without Absolutes," *Fact and Value: Essays on Ethics and Metaphysics for Judith Jarvis Thomson* (Cambridge, Mass.: MIT Press, 2001).

14. To qualify as not only necessary but also sufficient, our condition would need to be modified so as to require that the guiding indication be "fundamental" for that subject at that time: that is, not based on a deeper, more general indication. (Also we would need to take into account the requirement that one's belief be so guided *virtuously;* and considerations of perspective must also be given their due.)

15. This sort of problem is also presented by Jonathan Vogel in "Tracking, Closure, and Inductive Knowledge," in *The Possibility of Knowledge*, ed. S. Luper-Foy (Lanham, Md.: Rowman & Littlefield, 1987), and is endorsed by Stewart Cohen in his "Contextualist Solutions to Epistemological Problems: Skepticism, Gettier, and the Lottery," *Australasian Journal of Philosophy* 76 (1998): 289–306.

16. "How to Resolve the Pyrrhonian Problematic: A Lesson from Descartes," *Philosophical Studies* 85 (1997): 229–249.

17. Concerning the zebra we should distinguish between a case where the animal seen might too easily be a striped mule: where, for example, that zoo might too easily, and maybe does already, display striped mules instead of zebras. In such a situation clearly one does *not* know it to be really a zebra one sees. The safety requirement explains this through the fact that even if it looked like a zebra, and one believed accordingly, it might too easily be not a zebra but a striped mule. So far so good. But what if the zoo in question is incorruptible and would never descend to such deceit. Now the safety requirement seems satisfied, and we are able to say that one knows it to be a zebra one sees. Or, at least one can say that *as far as the safety requirement is concerned.* The safety requirement is after all just a necessary condition. So the mere fact that a belief satisfies that requirement does not commit us to counting it a case of knowledge.

On the contrary, whether or not one knows in such a case will plausibly depend also on why it is that one believes as one does. And here one must look to the "habit" of thought that leads from the perceived look to the corresponding classification. Why does one base one's belief that it's a zebra on that look?

18. Here is C. S. Peirce: "That which determines us, from given premisses, to draw one inference rather than another, is some habit of mind, whether it be constitutional or acquired. The habit is good or otherwise, according as it produces true conclusions from true premisses or not; and an inference is regarded as valid or not, without reference to the truth or falsity of its conclusion specially, but according as the habit which determines it is such as to produce true conclusions in general or not. The particular habit of mind which governs this or that inference may be formulated in a proposition whose truth depends on the validity of the inferences which the habit determines; and such a formula is called a *guiding principle* of inference" (*Collected Papers* 5, para. 265).

19. The way in which and the extent to which beliefs are not actions should not constitute an insurmountable obstacle to our exploiting the analogy between justified (right, reasonable) action and justified (right, reasonable) belief.

CHAPTER 9

VIRTUES IN EPISTEMOLOGY

JOHN GRECO

WHAT is a virtue in epistemology? In the broadest sense, a virtue is an excellence of some kind. In epistemology, the relevant kind of excellence will be "intellectual." But then what is an intellectual virtue? Some philosophers have understood intellectual virtues to be broad cognitive abilities or powers. On this view, intellectual virtues are innate faculties or acquired habits that enable a person to arrive at truth and avoid error in some relevant field. For example, Aristotle defined "intuitive reason" as the ability to grasp first principles and "science" as the ability to demonstrate further truths from these.[1] Some contemporary authors add accurate perception, reliable memory, and various kinds of good reasoning to the list of intellectual virtues. These authors follow Aristotle in the notion that intellectual virtues are cognitive abilities or powers, but they loosen the requirements for what count as such.[2]

Other authors have understood the intellectual virtues quite differently, however. On their view intellectual virtues are more like personality traits than cognitive abilities or powers. For example, intellectual courage is a trait of mind that allows one to persevere in one's ideas. Intellectual open-mindedness is a trait of mind that allows one to be receptive to the ideas of others. Among these authors, however, there is disagreement about why such personality traits count as virtues. Some think it is because they are truth-conducive, increasing one's chances of arriving at true beliefs while avoiding false beliefs.[3] Others think that such traits are virtues independently of their connection to truth—they would be virtues even if they were not truth-conducive at all.[4]

Who is right about the nature of the intellectual virtues? One might think that this is a matter of semantics—that different authors have simply decided to use the term "intellectual virtue" in different ways. In the essay that follows I will argue that there is some truth to this analysis. However, it is not the whole truth. This is because epistemologists invoke the notion of an intellectual virtue for specific reasons, in the context of addressing specific problems in epistemology. In effect, they make claims that understanding the intellectual virtues in a certain way allows us to solve those problems. And of course claims like that are substantive, not merely terminological. In part I of this essay I will review some recent history of epistemology, focussing on ways in which the intellectual virtues have been invoked to solve specific epistemological problems. The purpose of this part is to give a sense of the contemporary landscape that has emerged, and to clarify some of the disagreements among those who invoke the virtues in epistemology. In part II, I will explore some epistemological problems in greater detail. The purpose of this part is to defend a particular approach in virtue epistemology by displaying its power in addressing these problems.

PART I. HISTORY AND LANDSCAPE

1. Sosa's Virtue Perspectivism

The intellectual virtues made their contemporary debut in a series of papers by Ernest Sosa.[5] In those papers Sosa is primarily concerned with two problems in the theory of knowledge. The first is the debate between foundationalism and coherentism. The second is a series of objections that have been raised against reliabilism.

a. *Foundationalism and Coherentism*

Foundationalism and coherentism are positions regarding the structure of knowledge. According to foundationalism, knowledge is like a pyramid: a solid foundation of knowledge grounds the entire structure, providing the support required by knowledge at the higher levels. According to coherentism, knowledge is like a raft: different parts of the structure are tied together via relations of mutual support, with no part of the whole playing a more fundamental role than do others.[6] Let us use the term "epistemic justification" to name whatever property it is that turns mere true belief into knowledge. We may then define "pure coherentism" as holding that only coherence contributes to epistemic justification, and we may define "pure foundationalism" as holding that coherence does not contribute to epistemic justification at all. In the papers that introduce the notion of an intellectual virtue, Sosa argues that neither pure coherentism nor pure foundationalism can be right.

Against pure coherentism is the well-known objection that there can be highly coherent belief-systems that are nevertheless largely divorced from reality. But then coherence cannot be the only thing that matters for epistemic justification. Sosa presses this basic point in various ways. For one, consider the victim of Descartes's evil demon. By hypothesis, the victim's beliefs are as coherent as our own. That is, they are members of a coherent system of beliefs, tied together by a great number and variety of logical and quasi-logical relations. Suppose that by chance some few of those beliefs are also true. Surely they do not amount to knowledge, although both true and coherent.[7]

Another way that Sosa argues the point is to highlight the importance of experience for epistemic justification. Consider that any human being will have perceptual beliefs with few connections to other beliefs in her total belief system. For example, my perceptual belief that there is a bird outside my window has few logical relations to other beliefs that I have. But then one can generate counter-examples to pure coherentism by means of the following recipe. First, replace my belief that there is a bird outside my window with the belief that there is a squirrel outside my window. Second, make whatever few other changes are necessary to preserve coherence. For example, replace my belief that I seem to see a bird with the belief that I seem to see a squirrel. Clearly, the overall coherence of the new belief system will be about the same as that of the first. This is because coherence is entirely a function of relations among beliefs, and those relations are about the same in the two systems. But it seems wrong that the new belief about the squirrel is as well justified as the old belief about the bird, for my sensory experience is still such that I seem to see a bird and do not seem to see a squirrel. Again, coherence cannot be the only thing that contributes to epistemic justification.[8]

However, there is an equally daunting problem for pure foundationalism, although the way to see it is less direct. Consider how foundationalism might account for my knowledge that there is a bird outside the window. Since the knowledge in question is perceptual, it is plausible to say that it is grounded in sensory experience. Specifically, it is plausible to say that my belief that there is a bird outside the window is epistemically justified because it is grounded in a visual experience of a particular phenomenal quality. What is more, this explains the difference in epistemic status between my belief about the bird and the belief about the squirrel above. In the latter case, there is no grounding in sensory experience of a relevant sort. But here a problem lurks. Consider the foundationalist epistemic principle invoked above, that is, that a particular sort of sensory experience, with a particular phenomenal quality, justifies the belief that there is a bird outside the window. Is this to be understood as a fundamental principle about epistemic justification, or is it to be understood as an instance of some more general principle? If we say the former, then there would seem to be an infinite number of such principles, with no hope for unity among them. In effect, we would be committed to saying that such principles, in all their number and variety, merely state brute facts about epistemic justification. This is hardly a satisfying position. The more attractive view is that such principles are derived. But then there is more work to be done. Something more fundamental about epistemic justification remains to be explained.

This is where the notion of an intellectual virtue is useful, Sosa argues. Virtues in general are excellences of some kind; more specifically, they are innate or acquired dispositions to achieve some end. Intellectual virtues, Sosa argues, will be dispositions to achieve the intellectual ends of grasping truths and avoiding falsehoods. This notion of an intellectual virtue can be used to give a general account of epistemic justification as follows:

> A belief B(p) is epistemically justified for a person S (i.e. justified in the sense required for knowledge) if and only if B(p) is produced by one or more intellectual virtues of S.

This account of justification, Sosa argues, allows us to explain the unifying ground of the foundationalist's epistemic principles regarding perceptual beliefs. Specifically, such principles describe various intellectually virtuous dispositions. Thus human beings are gifted with perceptual powers or abilities; that is, dispositions to reliably form beliefs about the environment on the basis of sensory inputs of various modalities. Such abilities are relative to circumstances and environment, but they are abilities nonetheless. The foundationalist's epistemic principles relating perceptual beliefs to their experiential grounds can now be understood as describing or explicating these various abilities.[9]

And the payoff does not end there. For it is possible to give similar accounts of other sources of justification traditionally recognized by foundationalism. Because they are reliable, such faculties as memory, introspection, and logical intuition count as intellectual virtues and therefore give rise to epistemic justification for their respective products. In a similar fashion, various kinds of deductive and inductive reasoning reliably take one from true belief to further true belief, and hence count as virtues in their own right. By defining epistemic justification in terms of intellectual virtue, Sosa argues, we get a unified account of all the sources of justification traditionally recognized by foundationalism.[10]

Once the foundationalist makes this move, however, pure foundationalism becomes untenable. We said that perception, memory, and the like are sources of epistemic justification because they are intellectual virtues. But now coherence has an equal claim to be an intellectual virtue, and hence an equal claim to be a source of epistemic justification. The intellectual virtues were characterized as cognitive abilities or powers; as dispositions that reliably give rise to true belief under relevant circumstances and in a relevant environment. We may now think of coherence—or more exactly, coherence-seeking reason—as just such a power. In our world, in normal circumstances, coherence-seeking reason is also a reliable source of true belief and hence a source of epistemic justification.[11]

Finally, Sosa argues, we are now in a position to recognize two kinds of knowledge. First, there is "animal knowledge," enjoyed by any being whose true beliefs are the products of intellectual virtue. But second, there is "reflective knowledge," which further requires a coherent perspective on one's beliefs and their sources in intellectual virtue. We may also label the latter kind of knowledge "human knowledge," recognizing that the relevant sort of reflective coherence is a distinctively human virtue. More exactly,

S has animal knowledge regarding p only if
1. p is true, and
2. S's belief B(p) is produced by one or more intellectual virtues of S.

S has reflective knowledge regarding p only if
1. p is true,
2. S's belief B(p) is produced by one or more intellectual virtues of S, and
3. S has a true perspective on B(p) as being produced by one or more intellectual virtues, where such perspective is itself produced by an intellectual virtue of S.[12]

b. *Reliabilism*

Let us define generic reliabilism as follows.

A belief B(p) is epistemically justified for S if and only if B(p) is the outcome of a sufficiently reliable cognitive process, i.e., a process that is sufficiently truth-conducive.[13]

Generic reliabilism is a powerful view. For one, it accounts for a wide range of our pretheoretical intuitions regarding which beliefs have epistemic justification. Thus reliabilism explains why beliefs caused by perception, memory, introspection, logical intuition, and sound reasoning are epistemically justified, and it explains why beliefs caused by hallucination, wishful thinking, hasty generalization, and other unreliable processes are not. The view also provides a powerful resource against well-known skeptical arguments. For example, a variety of skeptical arguments trade on the assumption that our cognitive faculties must be vindicated as reliable in order to count as sources of epistemic justification. Because it seems impossible to provide such vindication in a noncircular way, a broad skeptical conclusion threatens. Generic reliabilism cuts off this kind of skeptical reasoning at its roots, with the idea that epistemic justification requires de facto reliability rather than vindicated reliability: the difference between knowledge and mere opinion is that the former is grounded in cognitive processes that are in fact reliable in this world.[14]

The view is powerful, but subject to a variety of problems. One of these is that reliability seems insufficient for epistemic justification. To see why, consider the following case. Suppose that S suffers from a rare sort of brain lesion, one effect of which is to cause the victim to believe that he has a brain lesion. However, S has no evidence that he has such a condition, and even has evidence against it. We can imagine, for example, that he has just been given a clean bill of health by competent neurologists. It seems clear that S's belief that he has a brain lesion is unjustified, although (by hypothesis) it has been caused by a highly reliable cognitive process.[15]

The foregoing case seems to show that reliability is not sufficient for epistemic justification. A second case seems to show that reliability is not necessary for epistemic justification. Consider again Descartes's victim of an evil demon. We said that, by hypothesis, the victim's belief system is as coherent as our own. We may now add that the victim bases her beliefs on her experience as we do, and reasons to new beliefs as we do. Clearly, the victim's beliefs cannot amount to knowledge, since she is the victim of massive deception. But still, it seems wrong to say that her beliefs are not justified at all. Let us follow Sosa and call this "the new evil demon problem" for reliabilism. According to simple reliabilism, epistemic justification is entirely a matter of reliability. But the demon victim's beliefs are not reliably formed. The problem for reliabilism is to explain why the victim's beliefs are nevertheless justified.[16]

Sosa argues that both of the above problems can be solved by invoking the notion of an intellectual virtue. Consider the case of the epistemically serendipitous brain lesion. What the case shows is that not all reliable cognitive processes give rise to epistemic justification. On the contrary, the reliabilist must place some kind of restriction on the kind of processes that do so. Sosa's suggestion is that the relevant processes are those which are grounded in the knower's intellectual virtues, that is, her cognitive abilities or powers. Since the belief about the brain lesion does not arise in this way, making this move allows the reliabilist to deny that the belief is epistemically justified.[17]

Now consider the new evil demon problem. Clearly the beliefs of the demon victim are not reliably formed and therefore lack something important for knowledge. But notice that there are two ways that a belief can fail by way of reliability. One way is that something goes wrong "from the skin inward." For example, the subject might fail to respond appropriately to her sensory experience, or might fail to reason appropriately from her beliefs. Another way to go wrong, however, is "from the skin outward." Perhaps there is no flaw to be found downstream from experience and belief, but one's cognitive faculties are simply not fitted for one's environment. It is this second way that the demon victim fails. Internally speaking, she is in as good working order as we are. Externally speaking, however, her epistemic condition is a disaster. But then there is a straightforward sense in which even the victim's beliefs are internally justified, Sosa argues. Namely, they are beliefs that result from intellectual virtues.

We saw earlier that Sosa endorses the following account of epistemic justification.

> A belief B(p) is epistemically justified for a person S if and only if B(p) is produced by one or more intellectual virtues of S.

According to Sosa, we need only add that whether a cognitive faculty counts as a virtue is relative to an environment. The victim's perception and reasoning powers are not reliable in her demon environment and hence are not virtues relative to her world. But those same faculties are reliable, and therefore do count as virtues, relative to the actual world. Accordingly, we have a sense in which the demon victim's beliefs are internally justified although not reliably formed. In fact, Sosa argues, they are internally justified in every respect relevant for animal knowledge.[18]

Finally, it is possible to define a further kind of internal justification associated with reflective knowledge. Remember that reflective knowledge requires a perspective on one's beliefs and their sources in intellectual virtue. The victim of a deceiving demon might also enjoy such a perspective, together with the broad coherence that this entails. This perspective and coherence provides the basis for a further kind of internal justification, Sosa argues.[19]

2. Moral Models of Intellectual Virtue

According to Sosa, an intellectual virtue is a reliable cognitive ability or power. Coherence-seeking reason is thus an intellectual virtue if reliable, but so are perception, memory, and introspection. Other philosophers have argued against this characterization of the intellectual virtues, however. For example, James Montmarquet's account differs from Sosa's in at least three major respects.[20]

First, cognitive powers such as perception and reason do not count as intellectual virtues at all according to Montmarquet. Rather, on his view the virtues are conceived as personality traits, or qualities of character, such as intellectual courage and intellectual carefulness. In this way the intellectual virtues are analogous to the moral virtues, such as moral temperance and moral courage.

Second, Montmarquet argues that it is a mistake to characterize the intellectual virtues as reliable, or truth-conducive. This is because we can conceive of possible worlds, such as Descartes's demon world, where the beliefs of intellectually virtuous persons are almost entirely false. But traits such as intellectual courage and intellectual carefulness would remain virtues even in such a world, Montmarquet argues. Likewise, we can conceive of worlds where intellectual laziness and carelessness reliably produce true beliefs. But again, traits like laziness and carelessness would remain vices even in such worlds. Therefore, Montmarquet concludes, the intellectual virtues can not be defined in terms of their reliability. Montmarquet's alternative is to define the virtues in terms of a desire for truth. According to this model, the intellectual virtues are those personality traits that a person who desires the truth would want to have.

Finally, on Montmarquet's view the exercise and nonexercise of the intellectual virtues are under our control and are therefore appropriate objects of praise and blame. When one faces a truck approaching at high speed, one cannot help but perceive accordingly. However, one can control whether one takes a new idea seriously, or considers a line of argument carefully. Hence we have a third way in which Montmarquet's account of the intellectual virtues departs from Sosa's.

It is clear that Montmarquet's account of the intellectual virtues has affinities with Aristotle's account of the moral virtues. Hence Montmarquet thinks of the intellectual virtues as personality traits or qualities, he emphasizes the importance of proper motivation, and he holds that the exercise of the virtues is under our control. A philosopher who follows Aristotle's model of the moral virtues even more closely is Linda Zagzebski. In fact, Zagzebski criticizes Aristotle for maintaining a strong distinction between the intellectual and moral virtues, arguing that the former are best understood as a subset of the latter.[21]

According to Zagzebski, all virtues are acquired traits of character that involve both a motivational component and a reliable success component. Hence, all moral virtues involve a general motivation to achieve the good and are reliably successful in doing so. All intellectual virtues involve a general motivation to achieve true belief and are reliably successful in doing so. But since the true is a component of the good, Zagzebski argues, intellectual virtues can be understood as a subset of the moral virtues. In addition to their general motivation and reliability, each virtue can be defined in terms of its specific or characteristic motivational structure. For example, moral courage is the virtue according to which a person is motivated to risk danger when something of value is at stake and is reliably successful at doing so. Benevolence is the virtue according to which a person is motivated to bring about the well-being of others and is reliably successful at doing so. Likewise, intellectual courage is the virtue according to which a person is motivated to persevere in her own ideas and is reliably successful at doing so.[22]

One advantage of understanding the intellectual virtues this way, Zagzebski argues, is that it allows the following account of knowledge. First, Zagzebski defines an "act of intellectual virtue."

> An act of intellectual virtue A is an act that arises from the motivational component of A, is something a person with virtue A would (probably) do in the circumstances, is successful in achieving the end of the A motivation, and is such that the agent acquires a true belief through these features of the act.[23]

We may then define knowledge as follows:

S has knowledge regarding p if and only if
1. p is true, and
2. S's true belief B(p) arises out of acts of intellectual virtue.

Since the truth condition is redundant in the above definition, we may say alternatively:

S has knowledge regarding p if and only if S's believing p arises out of acts of intellectual virtue.[24]

Even more so than Montmarquet, Zagzebski adopts Aristotle's account of the moral virtues as her model for understanding the intellectual virtues. Thus on her account (a) the intellectual virtues are understood as acquired traits of character, (b) their acquisition is partly under our control, (c) both their possession and exercise are appropriate objects of moral praise, and (d) both their lack and non-exercise can be appropriate objects of moral blame. It is noteworthy that Zagzebski's account departs from Sosa's on all of these points. Thus for Sosa the intellectual virtues are cognitive abilities rather than character traits, they need not be acquired, and their acquisition and use need not be under one's control. On Sosa's account, the possession and exercise of the intellectual virtues are grounds for praise, but this need not be praise of a moral sort. Hence we praise people for their keen perception and sound reasoning, but this is more like praise for an athlete's prowess than for a hero's courage.

On the face of things, therefore, there would seem to be a significant disagreement over the nature of the intellectual virtues. But at this point it might be suggested that the issue is merely terminological. What Zagzebski means by a virtue is something close to what Aristotle means by a moral virtue, and therefore natural cognitive powers such as perception and memory do not count as virtues on her meaning of the term. Sosa has adopted a different sense of the term, however, according to which anything that has a function has virtues. In this sense, a virtue is a characteristic excellence of some sort, and reliable perception and reliable memory qualify as intellectual excellences. But to see this as a terminological dispute obscures a substantive one. This comes out if we recall that both Sosa and Zagzebski offer accounts of knowledge in terms of their respective notions of intellectual virtue. The substantive question is now this: Which account of the intellectual virtues better serves this purpose? Sosa also invokes the intellectual virtues to address the dispute between foundationalism and coherentism over the structure of knowledge. Here we may ask again: Which notion of the intellectual virtues is best suited for this purpose?

Once the question regarding the nature of the intellectual virtues is framed this way, however, it seems clear that Zagzebski's account is too strong. Consider first the idea that knowledge arises out of acts of intellectual virtue. On Zagzebski's account, this means that knowledge must manifest dispositions that both (a) involve a certain motivational structure, and (b) involve relevant kinds of voluntary control. But neither of these requirements seems necessary for knowledge.

Consider a case of simple perceptual knowledge: You are crossing the street in good light, you look to your left, and you see that a large truck is moving quickly toward you. It would seem that you know that there is a truck moving toward you independently of any control, either over the ability to perceive such things in general, or over this particular exercise of that ability. Neither is it required that one have a motivation to be open-minded, careful, or the like. On the contrary, it would seem that you know that there is a truck coming toward you even if you are motivated *not* to be open-minded, careful, or the like.

In reply to this sort of objection, one might suggest that Zagzebski's conditions for perceptual knowledge do not require either the relevant kind of control or the relevant kind of motivation. This is because her definition of knowledge does not require that one actually possess intellectual virtues in her sense. Rather, knowledge requires only an *act* of intellectual virtue, and that is defined in terms of what an intellectually virtuous person *would* do in similar circumstances. Since intellectually virtuous persons form their perceptual beliefs without voluntary control and without Zagzebski-type motivations, Zagzebski's account of knowledge does not require either of these.[25]

The appropriate reply to this objection depends on how we are to interpret the locution "something a person with virtue A would (probably) do in the circumstances" in Zagzebski's definition of an act of intellectual virtue. If we interpret this locution strongly, so that it implies intellectually virtuous control and motivation, then Zagzebski's definition of knowledge does require these. This is the natural interpretation, since Zagzebski thinks that moral credit requires these, and that knowers deserve moral credit for their knowledge. But suppose we interpret the locution so that acts of intellectual virtue do not require virtuous control or motivation. In that case, it may be true that someone with perceptual knowledge does "something a person with virtue would do" in the circumstances. But now that "something a person with virtue would do" will not be something the virtuous person does *qua* virtuous person. In other words, Zagzebki-type intellectual virtues will be doing no work in the resulting definition of knowledge, and so knowledge will no longer be defined in terms of Zagzebski-type intellectual virtues.

Similar considerations show that Zagzebski's account of the intellectual virtues is ill suited for addressing the dispute between foundationalism and coherentism. In that context, Sosa invoked the notion of an intellectual virtue to (a) give a unified account of traditional foundationalist sources of epistemic justification, and (b) explain how coherence can be a source of epistemic justification as well. We have already seen that Zagzebski's notion of an intellectual virtue is too strong to yield an adequate account of perceptual knowledge. For the same reasons, it is also too strong to yield an adequate account of other sources of foundational knowledge, such as memory, introspection, and logical intuition. Perhaps this is especially clear in the case of logical intuition. Consider a mathematical genius who never engages in Zagzebski-type acts of intellectual virtue. For example, he never engages in acts that would be considered fair-minded, open-minded, careful, or thorough. However, suppose that despite this the person is highly reliable in relevant domains, and even outperforms other, more open-minded, fair-minded, careful and thorough mathematicians. It seems clear that such a person does not lack knowledge for lack of Zagzebski-type virtuous acts.[26]

We may conclude that the accounts of intellectual virtue defended by Zagzebski and Montmarquet are ill suited to address either the nature of knowledge or the dispute between foundationalism and coherentism over the structure of knowledge. An account of the intellectual virtues modeled on Aristotle's account of the moral virtues is too strong for these purposes. That is not to say, however, that the moral model is not apt for other purposes. Montmarquet sees this clearly when he rejects the idea that he is giving an account of epistemic justification, or the kind of justification required for knowledge. Rather, he uses the notion of an intellectual virtue to give an account of "doxastic responsibility," or the kind of responsibility for belief that can ground moral responsibility for actions. Often enough, the morally outrageous actions of tyrants, racists, and terrorists seem perfectly reasonable, even necessary, in the context of their distorted belief system. In order to find their actions blameworthy, it would seem that we have to find their beliefs blameworthy as well. An account of the intellectual virtues based on a moral model provides what we are looking for, Montmarquet argues. Such an account allows a plausible sense in which justified (and unjustified) beliefs are under a person's control, and therefore allows a way to view such beliefs as appropriate objects of moral blame and praise.

We have seen that Montmarquet's notion of an intellectual virtue is not intended to address traditional epistemological concerns about the nature and structure of knowledge. In fact, a number of authors who adopt a moral model for the intellectual virtues indicate that they are interested in problems that fall outside the scope of traditional epistemological inquiry. For example, Lorraine Code sets out to explore our "responsibility as knowers," and is concerned to emphasize the social, moral, and political importance of our cognitive practices. A major focus of Code's inquiry is the ways in which our intellectual and moral responsibilities are intertwined and interdependent. It is no surprise, therefore, that Code adopts a notion of intellectual virtue that emphasizes agency and that can ground evaluations in terms of intellectual responsibility.[27] Vrinda Dalmiya is another author who adopts a moral model of intellectual virtue that is well suited for her purposes. Dalmiya argues that knowledge of other selves requires intellectual virtues centered on the activity of caring. In effect, to know another self requires a morally significant relationship—an interactive process that involves empathy and trust, as well as important moral choices. Here again, a notion of intellectual virtue that allows relevant kinds of agency and responsibility is appropriate for the purposes at hand.[28]

It seems clear that an account of the intellectual virtues modeled on Aristotle's account of the moral virtues is apt for addressing a variety of epistemological concerns. It is a mistake, however, to generalize from such concerns to an account of knowledge per se. As we have seen, the moral model is ill suited for that purpose, since it results in an account of knowledge that is too strong.

3. Wisdom and Understanding

Perhaps another place where the moral model is useful is in accounts of "higher grade" epistemic achievements such as wisdom and understanding. According to Zagzebski, wisdom has clear moral dimensions. Thus wisdom unifies the knowledge of the wise person, but also her desires and values. This is why it is impossible for wisdom to be misused, she argues, and why it is incoherent to talk of a person who is wise but immoral. Also, wisdom is achieved only through extensive life experience and hence takes time to acquire. Therefore, Zagzebski argues, wisdom is best understood on a moral model of the intellectual virtues, either because it is such a virtue itself, or because it is the product of such virtues.[29] This seems plausible, especially if we mean wisdom to include practical wisdom, or wisdom regarding how one ought to live. But again, it would be a mistake to generalize from an account of wisdom to an account of knowledge per se. I suggest that Zagzebski's account of wisdom is plausible precisely because we think that wisdom is harder to achieve than knowledge. The stronger conditions implied by Zagzebski's account therefore seem more appropriate here than in a general account of knowledge.

I have argued that Zagzebski's position benefits from a distinction between knowledge and wisdom. By maintaining this distinction, it is possible to resist putting conditions on knowledge per se that are appropriate only for knowledge of a higher grade. In a similar fashion, Sosa's position benefits from a distinction between knowledge and understanding.[30] To see how this is so, it is useful to notice a tension in Sosa's thinking.

Recall that Sosa makes a distinction between animal knowledge and reflective knowledge. One has animal knowledge so long as one's true belief has its source in a reliable cognitive faculty. One has reflective knowledge only if one's first-order belief also fits into a coherent perspective, which perspective must include a belief that one's first-order belief has its reliable source. Sometimes Sosa writes as if animal knowledge is real knowledge, while reflective knowledge amounts to a higher achievement still.[31] In other places Sosa's evaluation of animal knowledge is less enthusiastic; he calls it "servomechanic" and "mere animal" knowledge and in one place suggests that the label is "metaphorical."[32] Either way, however, it is clear that Sosa thinks animal knowledge is of a lesser kind than reflective knowledge.

The tension is now this: as we saw above, Sosa holds that the virtue of coherence is its reliability. Like perception, memory, and introspection, reason-seeking coherence makes its contribution to epistemic justification and knowledge because it is reliable. But then why should reflective knowledge be of a higher kind than animal knowledge? If the difference between animal and reflective knowledge is a coherent perspective, and if the value of coherence is its reliability, it would seem that the distinction between animal knowledge and reflective knowledge is at most a difference in degree rather than in kind. Moreover, we have no good reason to think that a person with reflective knowledge will always be more reliable than a person with only animal knowledge. It seems clearly possible, that is, that the cognitive virtues of a person without an epistemic perspective could be more reliable than the cognitive virtues of a person with it. But then reflective knowledge is not necessarily higher than animal knowledge, even in degree.

Here is a different problem for Sosa's view. Suppose we take what seems to be Sosa's considered position, which is that human knowledge is reflective knowledge. On this view a broad skepticism threatens, because it seems clear that in the typical case most people lack the required epistemic perspective. That is, in the typical case most people lack beliefs about the source of their first-order belief, and whether that source is reliable. For example, in most cases where I have a belief that there is a bird outside my window, I do not have further beliefs about the source of that belief, or about the reliability of that source. Sosa's response to this kind of objection is to stress that the required epistemic perspective need only be implicit. Thus he writes,

> [A person judging shapes on a screen] is justified well enough in taking it that, in his circumstances, what looks to have a certain shape does have that shape. He implicitly trusts that connection, as is revealed by his inferential 'habit' of moving from experiencing the look to believing the seen object to have the corresponding shape. So the 'belief' involved is a highly implicit belief, manifested chiefly in such a 'habit'. . . . [33]

But it is important to maintain a distinction between (a) implicit beliefs and (b) habits or dispositions for forming beliefs. One reason we need the distinction is because often there are such dispositions where there are no such beliefs. For example, simple pattern recognition in perception involves dispositions of amazing subtlety and complexity—that is, dispositions to go from perceptual cues to beliefs about external stimuli.[34] But it is highly implausible to attribute *beliefs* about such perceptual cues, and about their connections to external stimuli, to perceivers. It is implausible to attribute such beliefs to adult perceivers, not to mention small children and animals. But all perceivers, small children and animals included, have the relevant dispositions to form perceptual beliefs.

Moreover, there is a second reason for Sosa to insist on the distinction between implicit beliefs and dispositions for forming beliefs. For without it, his distinction between animal knowledge and reflective knowledge collapses. Recall that even animal knowledge requires a source in reliable cognitive abilities or powers; that is, it requires a source in intellectual virtues. But the virtues required for animal knowledge just are dispositions for forming beliefs. If we identify such dispositions with a perspective on one's beliefs, then there will be no difference between animal and reflective knowledge. Therefore, Sosa's position seems to result in skepticism regarding reflective knowledge. In order to maintain a distinction between animal and reflective knowledge at all, we must understand one's epistemic perspective to involve beliefs about one's first-order beliefs and their sources, and not just dispositions for forming first-order beliefs. But then it is implausible that human beings typically have an epistemic perspective, and therefore implausible that human beings typically have reflective knowledge.

In the preceding paragraphs we have identified two problems for Sosa's position. First, Sosa's distinction between animal and reflective knowledge seems unmotivated, given his claim that the virtue of coherence is its reliability. If that claim is correct, then there is no good reason for thinking that reflective knowledge is of a higher kind than animal knowledge, or that the two belong to significantly different kinds at all. Second, if we do maintain the distinction, then the result seems to be a broad skepticism with respect to reflective (or human) knowledge. This is because most human beings fail to have the required epistemic perspective. Both these problems can be solved, however, if we recognize two plausible claims: (a) that there is a distinction in kind between knowledge and understanding, and (b) that coherence has a distinctive value through its contribution to understanding. The first problem is solved because this allows us to make a principled distinction between nonreflective knowledge and reflective knowledge: in virtue of its greater coherence through an epistemic perspective, reflective knowledge involves a kind of understanding that nonreflective knowledge lacks. The second problem is solved because this allows us to drop the requirement of an epistemic perspective for human knowledge: nonreflective knowledge is real knowledge, and even real human knowledge. Reflective knowledge is of a higher grade and of a rarer sort, involving a special kind of understanding. On this view we still get a skeptical conclusion regarding reflective knowledge, since it will still be the case that few human beings have the kind of perspective that reflective knowledge requires. But the sting is taken out of this conclusion if we recognize that it is a special kind of understanding, rather than knowledge per se, that people so often lack. We never thought that such understanding was widespread in the first place, and so a skeptical conclusion in this regard is just what we would expect.[35]

In effect, I am making the same diagnosis of Sosa's account of knowledge as I did of Zagzebski's, and I am suggesting the same solution. In both cases I have argued that the requirements they put on knowledge are too strong, and that therefore their accounts have unattractive skeptical results. And in both cases the solution is to distinguish between knowledge per se and some epistemic value of a higher grade. This allows us to weaken the requirements on knowledge so as to make it generally attainable, and at the same time to recognize the intellectual virtues that Zagzebski and Sosa want to emphasize.

However, one question remains: Why should the special kind of understanding involved in an epistemic perspective constitute a distinctive epistemic value? Granting that understanding is a distinctive epistemic value over and above knowledge per se, and granting that coherence contributes to that distinctive value, why should the particular sort of understanding involved in an epistemic perspective constitute a distinctive epistemic value all of its own? Consider that understanding has traditionally been understood in terms of knowledge of causes. Thus understanding involves knowledge of why things exist, how they work, and how they are related. This is why it is plausible that coherence contributes to understanding: coherence in general, and especially explanatory coherence, contributes to a grasp of exactly these matters. But then why should reflective knowledge, or understanding regarding the sources of one's first-order beliefs, be considered a distinctive kind of understanding, with its own distinctive epistemic value? Why should it be different from understanding about how humans came to exist, or what causes plants to grow, or how the mind is related to the body? Obviously, reflective knowledge is distinctive by virtue of its subject matter—it concerns one's first-order beliefs and their source in reliable cognitive faculties. But the relevant question concerns why reflective knowledge is distinctive *epistemically*: Why should reflective knowledge be of a different *epistemic* kind than coherent understanding regarding other things?

It seems to me that there is no good answer to this question. On the contrary, the above considerations show that reflective knowledge is not a distinctive epistemic kind at all. The important distinction is not between animal knowledge and reflective knowledge, but between knowledge per se and understanding per se.

PART II. A VIRTUE ACCOUNT OF KNOWLEDGE

In part I, we saw that different virtue theorists defend different, seemingly incompatible accounts of the intellectual virtues. In this context I argued for an irenic conclusion: that different kinds of intellectual virtue or excellence are best suited to address different issues in epistemology. In particular, I argued (1) that a minimalist notion of the intellectual virtues, in which the virtues are conceived as reliable cognitive abilities or powers, is best suited for an account of knowledge; and (2) that stronger notions of the intellectual virtues are best suited to address a range of other issues.

In part II, I will pursue the idea that a minimalist, reliabilist notion of the intellectual virtues is useful for constructing an account of knowledge. I will do so by addressing three important issues for a theory of knowledge: the challenge of skepticism, Gettier problems, and the problem of explaining why knowledge is more valuable than mere true belief. By defining knowledge in terms of the intellectual virtues so conceived, it is possible to adequately address all three of these issues. But first it will be helpful to make some general comments about virtue, epistemic justification, and knowledge.

1. Agent Reliabilism

Recall generic reliabilism and the conditions it lays down for epistemic justification:

> A belief B(p) is epistemically justified if and only if B(p) is the outcome of a sufficiently reliable cognitive process.

We saw that these conditions are too weak, as is demonstrated by the case of the epistemically serendipitous brain lesion. The lesson to be learned from that case is that not all reliable cognitive processes give rise to epistemic justification and knowledge. Such considerations gave rise to an account in terms of intellectual virtue.

> A belief B(p) is epistemically justified for a person S if and only if B(p) is produced by one or more intellectual virtues of S; i.e., by one or more of S's cognitive abilities or powers.

Here the key is to make the cognitive agent the seat of reliability, thereby moving from generic reliabilism to agent reliabilism. By restricting the relevant processes to those grounded in the knower's abilities or powers, we effectively disallow strange and fleeting processes, including brain lesions and the like, from giving rise to epistemic justification.

Recall also that this way of thinking allows an account of internal justification, or the kind of justification enjoyed even by the victim of Descartes's evil demon. Thus Sosa suggested:

> A belief B(p) is epistemically justified for S relative to environment E if and only if B(p) is produced by one or more cognitive dispositions that are intellectual virtues in E.

Notice that on this account the beliefs of the demon's victim are as justified as ours, so long as we relativize to the same environment. This kind of justification is "internal" because it is entirely a function of factors "from the skin inward," or better, "from the mind inward." This is insured by relativizing justification to external environments.

Finally, it is possible to define a sense of subjective justification, or a sense in which a belief is justified from the knower's own point of view. We have already seen that knowledge must be reliably formed. Many have had the intuition that, in addition to this, a knower must be aware that her belief is reliably formed. One way to cash out such awareness is to require an epistemic perspective on the relevant belief, but I have argued that an account in these terms is too strong for a requirement on knowledge. Nevertheless, a kind of awareness of reliability is manifested in the very dispositions that constitute one's cognitive abilities: the fact that a person interprets experience one way rather than another, or draws one inference rather than another, manifests an awareness of sorts that some relevant evidence is a reliable indication of some relevant truth. Or at least this is so if the person is trying to form her beliefs accurately in the first place—if the person is in the normal mode of trying to believe what is true, as opposed to what is convenient, or comforting, or politically correct. We may use these considerations to define a sense of subjective justification that is not too strong to be a requirement on knowledge.

> A belief B(p) is subjectively justified for S if and only if B(p) is produced by cognitive dispositions that S manifests when S is motivated to believe what is true.

In cases of knowledge such dispositions will also be virtues, since they will be objectively reliable in addition to being well motivated. But even in cases where

S is not reliable, she may nevertheless have justified beliefs in this sense, since her believing may nevertheless manifest well-motivated dispositions.

Since the notion of intellectual virtue employed in the above definitions is relatively weak, the account of epistemic justification and knowledge that results is relatively weak as well: there is no strong motivation condition, no control condition, and no condition requiring an epistemic perspective. In the sections that follow, I will argue that this minimalist approach is just what is needed in a theory of knowledge.

2. Skepticism

A number of skeptical arguments have been prominent in the theory of knowledge. These arguments constitute philosophical problems in the following sense: they begin from premises that seem eminently plausible and proceed by seemingly valid reasoning to conclusions that are outrageously implausible. On this view, skeptical arguments present a theoretical problem rather than a practical problem. The task for a theory of knowledge is to identify some mistake in the skeptical argument and to replace it with something more adequate. Two of the most difficult of these problems come from Hume. The first concerns our knowledge of unobserved matters of fact. The second concerns our knowledge of empirical facts in general.

a. Skepticism about Unobserved Matters of Fact

According to Hume's first argument, we can know nothing about the world that we do not currently observe. For example, I can't know that my next sip of coffee will taste like coffee, or even that my cat will not sprout wings and fly away.

Here is how Hume's reasoning goes. First, he points out that everything we believe about unobserved matters of fact depends on our previous observations. Thus I believe that coffee tastes a certain way because I have tasted coffee before, and I believe that cats do not have wings or fly because I have had previous dealings with cats. But such beliefs depend on an additional assumption as well, Hume argues. For my observations about coffee and cats are relevant only if I assume that things such as coffee and cats act in regular ways. In other words, I must assume that my previous observations of things give some indication of their future behavior. But how is that assumption to be justified? Hume argues that it cannot be, and that therefore all our beliefs about unobserved matters of fact are themselves unjustified.

Well, why can't the assumption be justified? Hume's answer is straightforward: the assumption is itself a belief about unobserved matters of fact, so any attempt to justify it must fall into circular reasoning. Consider that I can justify my assumption that things act in regular ways only by relying on previous observations—I have observed that they do. But these observations of past regular behavior are relevant for establishing the persistence of regular behavior only if I assume the very thing I am trying to establish—that things behave in regular ways!

Hume's argument can be put more formally as follows.

1. All our beliefs about unobserved matters of fact depend for their evidence on (a) previous observations, and (b) the assumption (A1) that observed cases are a reliable indication of unobserved cases; that things behave (and will continue to behave) in regular ways.

2. But (A1) is itself a belief about an unobserved matter of fact.

3. Therefore, assumption (A1) depends for its evidence on (A1). (1,2)

4. Circular reasoning does not give rise to justification.

5. Therefore, (A1) is unjustified. (3,4)

6. All our beliefs about unobserved matters of fact depend for their evidence on an unjustified assumption. (1,5)

7. Beliefs that depend for their evidence on an unjustified assumption are themselves unjustified

8. Therefore, none of our beliefs about unobserved matters of fact are justified. (6,7)

b. *Skepticism about the World*

Here is another argument from Hume, one which concerns all our knowledge of matters of fact about the world, whether observed or unobserved. The argument belongs to a family of skeptical arguments, all of which claim (a) that our knowledge of the world depends on how things appear through the senses, and (b) that there is no good inference from the way things appear to the way things actually are. Here is the argument put formally.

1. All of our beliefs about the world depend, at least in part, on the way things appear to us via the senses.

2. The nature of this dependency is broadly evidential—the fact that things in the world appear a certain way is often our reason for thinking that they are that way.

3. Therefore, if I am to know how things in the world actually are, it must be via some good inference from how things appear to me. (1,2)

4.   But there is no good inference from the way things appear to the way things are.

5.   Therefore, I cannot know how things in the world actually are. (3,4)

This argument is a powerful one. Premises (1) and (2) say only that our beliefs about the world depend for their evidence on the way things appear to us. That seems undeniable. Premise (4) is the only remaining independent premise, and there are excellent reasons for accepting it. One reason mirrors the first argument from Hume above. Specifically, our beliefs about the world depend for their evidence on (a) sensory appearances, but also (b) an assumption (A2) that the way things appear is a reliable indication of the way things are. But assumption (A2) is itself a belief about the world, so any attempt to justify it would depend on that very assumption. Hence there can be no noncircular inference from sensory appearances to reality.

Here is a second reason in favor of premise (4). Even if a noncircular inference from appearances to reality were possible in principle, no such inference would be psychologically plausible. In other words, it would not be plausible that such an inference is actually used when we form beliefs about objects on the basis of sensory appearances. This is because an inference takes us from belief to belief, but we do not typically have beliefs about appearances. In the typical case, we form our beliefs about objects in the world without forming beliefs about appearances at all, much less inferring beliefs about the world from beliefs about appearances.

c. Where the Skeptical Arguments Go Wrong

Notice that the two skeptical arguments from Hume cannot be dismissed on the usual grounds. For example, neither argument demands certainty for knowledge, nor does either depend on a controversial metaphysics. On the contrary, the various premises of Hume's arguments are consistent with innocent assumptions about the standards for knowledge, the ontology of appearances, the relationship between mind and world, and the like.[36] The real problem is that circular reasoning cannot give rise to knowledge, and our reasoning about things in the world, whether observed or unobserved, seems to be circular. Once again, the task for a theory of knowledge is to identify the mistake in the arguments. *Something* in the arguments is not innocent, and an adequate theory of knowledge should explain what that it is.

Agent reliabilism provides such explanations. Consider first Hume's argument concerning our beliefs about unobserved matters of fact. That argument begins with the claim that all such beliefs depend on an assumption: that observed cases are a reliable indication of unobserved cases. Another way to put Hume's claim is as follows: that our evidence for unobserved matters of fact must always contain some such assumption among its premises. But why does Hume think that? I suggest that Hume's claim is based on a widespread but mistaken assumption about knowledge and evidence. Namely, that there must be a necessary relation between an item of knowledge and the evidence that grounds it. In cases of deductive knowledge the relation will be logical. But even inductive knowledge, Hume thinks, must involve some quasi-logical relation. That is why our evidence for beliefs about unobserved matters of fact needs a premise about observed cases being a reliable indication of unobserved cases: it is only through some such premise that a quasi-logical relation, this time a probability relation, is established.

Agent reliabilism allows a straightforward diagnosis of this line of reasoning: It is a mistake to think that there must be a necessary relation between evidence and knowledge. On the contrary, knowledge requires evidence that is *in fact* reliable, as opposed to evidence that is necessarily reliable. More exactly, knowledge requires that the knower be in fact reliable in the way that she forms her beliefs on the basis of her evidence. But if that is right, then Hume is wrong to think that our beliefs about unobserved matters of fact depend on assumption (A1) for their evidence.

Agent reliabilism also explains where Hume's second skeptical argument goes wrong. That argument begins with the claim that beliefs about the world depend on the way things appear for their evidence, and it concludes from this that knowledge of the world requires a good inference from appearances to reality. But this line of reasoning depends on an implicit assumption: that sensory appearances ground beliefs about the world by means of an *inference*. This assumption is mistaken, however, and agent reliabilism explains why.

Let us define an inference as a movement from premise-beliefs to a conclusion-belief on the basis of their contents and according to a general rule. According to agent reliabilism, this is one way that a belief can be evidentially grounded, since using a good inference-rule is one way that a belief can be reliably formed. But that is not the only way that an evidential relation can be manifested—not every movement in thought constitutes an inference from premise-beliefs to a conclusion-belief according to a general rule. For example, the movement from sensory appearances to belief does not. When one forms a perceptual belief about the world, it is not the case that one first forms a belief about how things appear, and then infers that the way things appear is probably the way things are. Rather, the process is more direct than that. In a typical case of perception, one reliably moves from appearances to reality without so much as a thought about the appearances themselves, and without doing anything like following a rule of inference. Put simply, our perceptual powers are not reasoning powers.

It might be objected that the present point is merely a verbal one: I have rejected the assumption that the evidence of sensory appearances is inferential, but only by employing a restricted sense of "inference." But this objection misses

a more substantive point, namely that not all movements in thought can be evaluated by the criteria governing inferences in the narrower sense defined above. In
particular, to ask whether there is a good inference from sensory appearances to
reality misunderstands the way that sensory appearances function as evidence for
our beliefs about the world. This is the mistake that Hume's second argument
makes, and agent reliabilism explains why it is a mistake.

3. Gettier Problems

According to agent reliabilism, knowledge is true belief produced by the intellectual virtues of the believer, where intellectual virtues are understood to be reliable
cognitive abilities or powers. This account of knowledge explains a wide range of
our pretheoretical intuitions regarding which cases do and do not count as knowledge. For example, the account continues to have the advantages of reliabilism: it
explains why beliefs resulting from perception, memory, introspection, logical
intuition, and sound reasoning typically count as knowledge, and it explains why
beliefs resulting from hallucination, wishful thinking, and other unreliable processes do not. Moreover, the account handles cases that have been deemed problematic for generic reliabilism, such as the case of the serendipitous brain lesion,
and the case described in the new evil demon problem. Nevertheless, more needs
to be said in light of certain other cases. Specifically, in this section I will argue
that agent reliabilism has the resources to address a wide range of Gettier problems.

In 1963, Edmund Gettier wrote a short paper purporting to show that knowledge is not true justified belief. His argument proceeded by way of two counterexamples, each of which seemed to show that a belief could be both true and
justified and yet not amount to knowledge. Here are two examples that are in the
spirit of Gettier's originals.

> Case 1: On the basis of excellent reasons, S believes that her co-worker Mr.
> Nogot owns a Ford: Nogot testifies that he owns a Ford, and this is con-
> firmed by S's own relevant observations. From this S infers that someone in
> her office owns a Ford. As it turns out, S's evidence is misleading and No-
> got does not in fact own a Ford. However, another person in S's office, Mr.
> Havit, does own a Ford, although S has no reason for believing this.[37]

> Case 2: Walking down the road, S seems to see a sheep in the field and
> on this basis believes that there is a sheep in the field. However, due to an
> unusual trick of light, S has mistaken a dog for a sheep, and so what she
> sees is not a sheep at all. Nevertheless, unsuspected by S, there *is* a sheep in
> another part of the field.[38]

In both of these cases the relevant belief seems justified, at least in senses of justification that emphasize the internal or the subjective, and in both cases the relevant belief is true. Yet in neither case would we be inclined to judge that the person in question has knowledge.

These examples show that internal and/or subjective justification is not sufficient for knowledge. Put another way, they show that knowledge requires some stronger relation between belief and truth. From the perspective of a virtue theory, there is a natural way to think of this stronger relation. For it is natural to distinguish between (a) achieving some end by luck or accident, and (b) achieving the end through the exercise of one's abilities (or virtues). This suggests the following difference between Gettier cases and cases of knowledge. In Gettier cases, S believes the truth, but only by accident. In cases of knowledge, however, it is no accident that S believes the truth. Rather, in cases of knowledge S believes the truth as the result of her own cognitive abilities—her believing the truth can be credited to her rather than to dumb luck or blind chance.

This suggestion is on the right track, but more needs to be said. Here is why. I said that the difference between Gettier cases and cases of knowledge is that in the latter, but not the former, it is to S's credit that she believes the truth. Put another way, in cases of knowledge S is responsible for believing the truth, because she believes it as the result of her own cognitive abilities. But in the Gettier cases above, S does exercise her cognitive abilities, and this is partly why she believes the truth. Hence it is not clear that Gettier cases and cases of knowledge can be distinguished as I have suggested—it is not clear why it is appropriate to credit S with true belief in cases of knowledge and to deny credit in Gettier cases. Again, more needs to be said.[39]

The first thing to note is that attributions of credit imply attributions of causal responsibility. As I suggested above, to give S credit for her true belief is to say that she "is responsible" for her believing the truth—that her believing the truth "is the result" of her own abilities or virtues. This is in fact a general phenomenon. According to Aristotle, actions deserving moral credit "proceed from a firm and unchangeable character."[40] When we give credit for an athletic feat, we imply that it is the result of athletic ability, as opposed to good luck, or cheating, or a hapless opponent. In all such cases, an attribution of credit implies an attribution of causal responsibility for the action in question—it implies that the cause of the action is relevant abilities (or virtues) in the actor.

The second thing to note is that attributions of causal responsibility display an interesting pragmatics. Specifically, when we say that Y occurs because X occurs, or that Y's occurring is due to X's occurring, we mark out X's occurring as a particularly important or salient part of the causal story behind Y's occurring. For example, to say that the fire occurred because of the explosion is not to say that the explosion caused the fire all by itself. Rather, it is to say that the explosion is a particularly important part, perhaps the most important part, of the whole story. Or to change the example: to say that the fire occurred because of S's negligence is not to say that S's negligence caused the fire all by itself. Rather, it is to say that S's negligence is a particularly salient part, perhaps the most salient part, of the set of relevant factors that caused the fire.

What determines salience? Any number of things might, but two kinds of consideration are particularly important for present purposes. First, salience is often determined by what is *abnormal* in the case. For example, we will say that sparks caused the fire if the presence of sparks in the area is not normal. That explanation misfires, however, if we are trying to explain the cause of a fire in a welding shop, where sparks are flying all the time. Second, salience is often determined by our *interests and purposes*. If the thing to be explained is smoke coming from the engine, for example, we will look for the part that needs to be replaced. Here it is perfectly appropriate to say that the cause of the smoke is the malfunctioning carburetor, although clearly a faulty carburetor cannot cause smoke all by itself.

And now the important point is this: Since attributions of credit imply attributions of causal responsibility, the former inherit the pragmatics of the latter. Specifically, to say that S's believing the truth is to her credit is to say that S's cognitive abilities, her intellectual virtues, are an important part of the causal story regarding how S came to believe the truth. It is to say that S's cognitive abilities are a particularly salient part, perhaps the most salient part, of the total set of relevant causal factors.

We may now return to the diagnosis of Gettier problems that was suggested earlier. There I said that in Gettier cases S believes the truth, but it is only by accident that she does so. This was opposed to cases of knowledge, where it is to S's credit that she believes the truth, because she does so as the result of her own cognitive abilities. However, this diagnosis led to the following question: Why is it appropriate to credit S with true belief in cases of knowledge, but not in the two Gettier cases above, given that in all these cases S's abilities are part of the causal story regarding how S came to have a true belief? We now have an answer to that question: In cases of knowledge, but not in Gettier cases, S's abilities are a *salient* part of the causal story regarding how S came to have a true belief. It is plausible, in fact, that our cognitive abilities have a kind of "default" salience, owing to our interests and purposes as information-sharing beings. In Gettier cases, however, this default salience is trumped by something abnormal in the case. For example, someone in the office owns a Ford, but it is not the person who S thinks it is. There is a sheep in the field, but it is not in the place that S is looking. In these cases it is only good luck that S ends up with a true belief, which is to say that S's believing the truth cannot be attributed to her abilities.

These considerations suggest the following account of knowledge.

S has knowledge regarding p if and only if

1. S's belief B(p) is *subjectively* justified in the following sense: B(p) is produced by cognitive dispositions that S manifests when S is motivated to believe what is true.

2. S's belief B(p) is *objectively* justified in the following sense: B(p) is produced by one or more intellectual virtues of S, i.e. by one or more of S's cognitive abilities or powers, and

3. S believes the truth regarding p *because* S believes p out of intellectual virtue. Alternatively: The intellectual virtues that result in S's believing the truth regarding p are an important necessary part of the total set of causal factors that give rise to S's believing the truth regarding p.

If we stipulate that intellectual virtues involve a motivation to believe the truth, we may collapse the above account as follows.

S has knowledge regarding p if and only if S believes the truth regarding p *because* S believes p out of intellectual virtue.[41]

4. The Value Problem

In recent work Linda Zagzebski has called attention to the value problem for knowledge.[42] An adequate account of knowledge, she points out, ought to explain why knowledge is more valuable than mere true belief. The account of knowledge presented above readily suggests an answer to that problem.

Recall Aristotle's distinction between (a) achieving some end by luck or accident, and (b) achieving the end through the exercise of one's abilities (or virtues). It is only the latter kind of action, Aristotle argues, that is both intrinsically valuable and constitutive of human flourishing. "Human good," he writes, "turns out to be activity of soul exhibiting excellence."[43] In this discussion Aristotle is clearly concerned with intellectual virtue as well as moral virtue: his position is that the successful exercise of one's intellectual virtues is both intrinsically good and constitutive of human flourishing.

If this is correct then there is a clear difference in value between knowledge and mere true belief. In cases of knowledge, we achieve the truth through the exercise of our own cognitive abilities or powers, which are a kind of intellectual virtue. Moreover, we can extend the point to include other kinds of intellectual virtue as well. It is plausible, for example, that the successful exercise of intellectual courage is also intrinsically good and constitutive of the best intellectual life. And of course there is a long tradition that says the same about wisdom and the same about understanding. On the view I am suggesting, there are a plurality of intellectual virtues, and their successful exercise gives rise to a plurality of epistemic goods. The best intellectual life—intellectual flourishing, so to speak—is rich with all of these.

NOTES

I am indebted to many people for their comments on earlier versions of this material, including Robert Audi, Stephen Grimm, and Wayne Riggs. I would especially like to thank Ernest Sosa and Linda Zagzebski for many discussions on relevant topics.

In section II.2 I draw on material from *Putting Skeptics in Their Place* (New York: Cambridge University Press, 2000) and from "Agent Reliabilism," *Philosophical Perspectives*, vol. 13, *Epistemology* (1999).

In section II.3 I draw on material from "Knowledge as Credit for True Belief," in *Intellectual Virtue: Perspectives from Ethics and Epistemology*, ed. Michael DePaul and Linda Zagzebski, (Oxford: Oxford University Press, 2002).

1. Aristotle, *Nicomachean Ethics*, book VI.

2. For example, see Ernest Sosa, *Knowledge in Perspective* (Cambridge: Cambridge University Press, 1991); Alvin Goldman, "Epistemic Folkways and Scientific Epistemology," in his *Liaisons: Philosophy Meets the Cognitive and Social Sciences* (Cambridge, Mass.: MIT Press, 1992); and John Greco, "Virtues and Vices of Virtue Epistemology," *Canadian Journal of Philosophy* 23 (1993).

3. For example, see Linda Zagzebski, *Virtues of the Mind* (Cambridge: Cambridge University Press, 1996).

4. For example, see James Montmarquet, "Epistemic Virtue," *Mind* 96 (1987): 482–497; and James Montmarquet, *Epistemic Virtue and Doxastic Responsibility* (Lanham, Md.: Rowman & Littlefield, 1993).

5. See especially "The Raft and the Pyramid: Coherence versus Foundations in the Theory of Knowledge," *Midwest Studies in Philosophy*, vol. 5 (1980); "Epistemology Today: A Perspective in Retrospect," *Philosophical Studies* 40 (1981); "The Coherence of Virtue and the Virtue of Coherence: Justification in Epistemology," *Synthese* 64 (1985); and "Knowledge and Intellectual Virtue," *The Monist* 68 (1985), all reprinted in Sosa, *Knowledge in Perspective*. See also "Reliabilism and Intellectual Virtue" and "Intellectual Virtue in Perspective," both in *Knowledge in Perspective*. Below all page numbers for these works correspond to *Knowledge in Perspective*.

6. See especially "The Raft and the Pyramid."

7. See for example "The Foundations of Foundationalism," 157–158.

8. This argument is developed in "The Raft and the Pyramid," 184–186.

9. See "The Raft and the Pyramid," 186–189.

10. See "Epistemology Today" and "The Coherence of Virtue and the Virtue of Coherence."

11. See especially "The Coherence of Virtue and the Virtue of Coherence."

12. See especially "Knowledge and Intellectual Virtue" and "Intellectual Virtue in Perspective." At present I characterize the two kinds of knowledge in terms of necessary conditions only. This is because Sosa thinks that other conditions are necessary to make

the set sufficient. I discuss further conditions on knowledge in part II of this essay, in the section on Gettier problems.

13. See, for example, David Armstrong, *Belief, Truth and Knowledge* (Cambridge: Cambridge University Press, 1973); Fred Dretske, "Conclusive Reasons," *Australasian Journal of Philosophy* 49 (1971): 1–22; and Alvin Goldman, "What Is Justified Belief" in *Justification and Knowledge*, ed. George Pappas (Dordrecht: Reidel, 1979).

14. For more on the relation between skepticism and reliabilism, see part II of this essay.

15. This example is due to Alvin Plantinga, *Warrant: The Current Debate* (Oxford: Oxford University Press, 1993), 199.

16. This problem is due to Keith Lehrer and Stewart Cohen, "Justification, Truth and Coherence," *Synthese* 55 (1983): 191–208.

17. See "Proper Functionalism and Virtue Epistemology," *Nous* 27 (1993): 51–65. Relevant sections of this paper are reprinted as "Three Forms of Virtue Epistemology," in *Knowledge, Belief and Character*, ed. Guy Axtell (Lanham, Md.: Rowman & Littlefield, 2000).

18. Sosa develops these ideas in "Reliabilism and Intellectual Virtue" and "Intellectual Virtue in Perspective." See also "Goldman's Reliabilism and Virtue Epistemology," forthcoming in *Philosophical Topics*.

19. See especially "Intellectual Virtue in Perspective."

20. See "Epistemic Virtue" and *Epistemic Virtue and Doxastic Responsibility*.

21. *Virtues of the Mind*, especially 137–158.

22. *Virtues of the Mind*, especially 165–197.

23. *Virtues of the Mind*, 270.

24. *Virtues of the Mind*, especially 264–273.

25. A suggestion along these lines can be found in *Virtues of the Mind*, 273–283.

26. Zagzebski's response to this kind of example is that we cannot attribute knowledge to the mathematical genius without finding out more about her psychology. Her own description of how she comes to "know" is important, Zagzebski argues. "If she can say nothing at all about it, she is no different from the *idiot savant* and she does not have knowledge." See her "Responses," *Philosophy and Phenomenological Research* 60 (2000): 208–209. However, this reply seems off the mark on two counts. First, nothing in Zagzebski's account requires that one can explain, or give a description of, how one knows. Therefore, requiring the mathematical genius to do so adds something new to the conditions for knowledge that Zagzebski has previously defended. Second, and more important, such a requirement would be too strong. Thus few people can give an adequate account of how they come to have perceptual knowledge—for example, that there is a table in the room. And many people, including many epistemologists, get it all wrong when they try. But this does not prevent people from having perceptual knowledge.

27. See Lorraine Code, "Toward a 'Responsibilist' Epistemology," *Philosophy and Phenomenological Research* 44 (1984) and *Epistemic Responsibility* (Hanover: University Press of New England and Brown University Press, 1987).

28. See Vrinda Dalmiya, "Knowing People," in *Knowledge, Truth and Duty: Essays on Epistemic Justification, Responsibility and Virtue*, ed. Matthias Steup (New York: Oxford University Press, 2001).

29. *Virtues of the Mind*, 22–23.

30. So argues Stephen Grimm in "Ernest Sosa, Knowledge and Understanding," *Philosophical Studies* 106 (2001). In the next two paragraphs I am indebted to Grimm's paper.

31. For example, "This is not to deny that there is a kind of 'knowledge,' properly so called, that falls short in respect of broad coherence—'animal knowledge,' as we might call it. It is rather only to affirm that beyond 'animal knowledge' we humans, especially those of us who are philosophical or at least reflective, aspire to a higher knowledge." From "Perspectives in Virtue Epistemology: A Response to Dancy and BonJour," *Philosophical Studies* 78 (1995), 233, reprinted in Axtell (2000). See also "How to Resolve the Pyrrhonian Problematic: A Lesson from Descartes," *Philosophical Studies* 85 (1997), where Sosa endorses Descartes's distinction between unreflective *cognitio* and reflective *scientia*.

32. For example, "How then can one rule out its turning out that just *any* true belief of one's own is automatically justified? To my mind the key is the requirement that the field F and the circumstances C must be accessible within one's epistemic perspective. (Note that this requires considering servomechanic and animal so-called 'knowledge' a lesser grade of knowledge, or perhaps viewing the attribution of "knowledge" to such beings as metaphorical, unless we are willing to admit them as beings endowed with their own epistemic perspectives.)" From "Intellectual Virtue in Perspective," 274–275.

33. "Virtue Perspectivism: A Response to Foley and Fumerton," *Philosophical Issues*, vol. 5, *Truth and Rationality* (1994), 44–45. Sosa is responding to an objection from Richard Foley, "The Epistemology of Sosa," in the same volume.

34. See for example J. Hochberg, *Perception* (Englewood Cliffs, N.J.: Prentice Hall, 1978).

35. Richard Fumerton makes a similar point in "Achieving Epistemic Ascent," in *Sosa and His Critics*, ed. John Greco (Oxford: Blackwell, 2003).

36. I defend this claim at length in *Putting Skeptics in Their Place*. See especially chap. 4.

37. The example is from Keith Lehrer, "Knowledge, Truth and Evidence," *Analysis* 25 (1965): 168–175.

38. The example is slightly revised from Roderick Chisholm, *Theory of Knowledge*, 2d ed. (Englewood Cliffs, N.J.: Prentice-Hall, 1977), p. 105.

39. The remarks that follow are indebted to Joel Feinberg's insightful discussions of moral blame. See his "Problematic Responsibility in Law and Morals," "Action and Responsibility," and "Causing Voluntary Actions," all collected in *Doing and Deserving: Essays in the Theory of Responsibility* (Princeton: Princeton University Press, 1970).

40. *Nicomachean Ethics*, II.4. Feinberg argues that all attributions of moral responsibility imply that the action in question proceeds from character. This is probably too strong, since a person can be appropriately blamed for action out of character. Nevertheless, there is a special sort of moral responsibility, with which Aristotle is concerned, that does imply this. See *Doing and Deserving*, 126.

41. A number of authors have defended the idea that, in cases of knowledge, one believes the truth because one believes out of intellectual virtue. See Ernest Sosa, "Beyond Skepticism, to the Best of Our Knowledge," *Mind* 97 (1988): 153–188, and *Knowledge in Perspective*; Linda Zagzebski, *Virtues of the Mind*, and "What Is Knowledge?" in *The Blackwell Guide to Epistemology*, ed. John Greco and Ernest Sosa (Oxford: Blackwell

Publishers, 1999); and Wayne Riggs, "Reliability and the Value of Knowledge," *Philosophy and Phenomenological Research*, forthcoming.

42. Zagzebski raises the problem in *Virtues of the Mind*, 300–302, and in a more extended way in "From Reliabilism to Virtue Epistemology," *Proceedings of the Twentieth World Congress of Philosophy*, vol. 5, *Epistemology* (1999). This paper is reprinted in expanded form in Axtell (2000). For further discussion of the value problem from a virtue perspective, see Zagzebski, "The Search for the Source of Epistemic Good," in Greco (2003); Sosa, "The Place of Truth in Epistemology," in DePaul and Zagzebski (2002); and Wayne Riggs, "Reliability and the Value of Knowledge." See also chapter 8 by Sosa in this volume.

43. *Nicomachean Ethics*, I.7.

CHAPTER 10

MIND AND KNOWLEDGE

JOHN HEIL

OUR knowledge of the world is conditioned by our nature as knowers. What we can know depends in equal measure on what there is to be known—the world—and on our makeup as potential knowers. This suggests that we can hope to understand the limits and scope of human knowledge only if we have a clear appreciation of our own nature. Knowers are instruments that register how things stand. What an instrument registers depends on its makeup and deployment. Before we can confidently rely on an instrument, we must see that it is calibrated. We can calibrate an instrument only if we have a grasp of how the instrument works.

All this seems straightforward, even platitudinous. What are the implications for the possibility of knowledge of the world around us? When you set out to calibrate an instrument, you do not rely on that very instrument. You might calibrate a fuel gauge by comparing its readings to the fuel level in a particular tank. It would be pointless first to use the gauge to determine the amount of fuel in the tank, then check to see whether the gauge registers this amount. That would be like checking the accuracy of an item in the newspaper by buying a second copy (Wittgenstein 1953/1961, § 265). Instead you first determine in some other way—by eyesight, for instance—the amount of fuel in the tank. The gauge's readings can then be compared against this independently ascertained value. More generally, the process of calibrating an instrument requires that you have independent access to information as to how things stand in the domain within which the instrument is meant to function. You are then in a position to use this information to assess the accuracy of the instrument's output.

What of the human instrument? If you set out to assess the reliability of your

beliefs concerning how things stand in the world, you are in no position to compare those beliefs directly to the world: you measure beliefs about the world
against other beliefs about the world. This is akin to relying on the readings of
our fuel gauge to determine the gauge's reliability. It looks as though if we are to
calibrate ourselves as knowers, we must do so somehow "from the inside out." It
is by no means clear that this is a coherent possibility.

Descartes is famous for making this point salient. Commitment to a mind-
independent world brings with it a weighty epistemological burden. If we set
out to establish that we in fact possess knowledge of the world, we shall have
to do so in some way that does not involve our having independent knowledge
of that world. This amounts to a requirement that attempts to establish that we
have knowledge not be *epistemically circular*.[1] An argument is epistemically circular if its conclusion is presupposed in the supposition that its premises are justified. Suppose, for instance, you set out to justify your use of a Ouija Board to predict the future. You appeal to the Ouija Board, and the Ouija Board pronounces
the predictions it has made true. Here, your using the Ouija Board to assess its
own reliability presupposes just what is at issue. The worry is that we must all
be in this position when it comes to our knowledge of a mind-independent
world.

You might try appealing to the testimony of others. Even if you are not in a
position to compare your beliefs to the world, I am: I can check what you believe
against the facts and thereby ascertain your reliability. Then, provided you have
reason to trust me, you could use my assessment as evidence that you are reliable.
This is not quite right. What you compare are your beliefs against my beliefs
about the world. You are justified in accepting my word only if you are justified
in taking me to be reliable. Your belief that I am reliable, however, must be based
on something more than my say so. An independent assessment of my reliability
on your part presupposes your own reliability, however, and this is just what is
at issue. The situation resembles one in which you seek to calibrate a fuel gauge
by appealing to a second gauge of the same design. Unless you have independent
evidence that the second gauge is accurate, you are not entitled to accept its
outputs at face value. Once you see the point, you can see that an analogous
problem will arise for any attempt to ascertain the accuracy of our beliefs by
measuring them against the world.[2]

Let us be clear about what is at issue here. The apparent impossibility of
producing an epistemically noncircular demonstration that your beliefs about
goings-on in the world around you are true poses no immediate challenge to the
possibility of knowledge or justified belief. You have knowledge that something is
so, or you believe this justifiably, just in case certain conditions are satisfied. You
have knowledge (or believe justifiably) quite independently of any beliefs (justified
or not) you might have about these conditions.[3] For just this reason, you can have
knowledge (or believe justifiably) that you have knowledge (or believe justifiably)

provided your belief to this effect satisfies the pertinent conditions. The threat of epistemic circularity is not a threat to the possibility of knowledge or justified belief; it is not even a threat to our knowing (or believing justifiably) that we know (or believe justifiably). The threat, rather, is to our being able to produce a satisfying demonstration of the hypothesis that we have knowledge or believe justifiably.

Let me elaborate on this point. The philosophical literature is full of accounts of knowledge and justified belief. Let us suppose, for the sake of argument, that knowledge is justified true belief: you know something just in case you believe it, your belief is justified, and your belief is true.[4] Now the question arises: what is it for a belief to be justified? Suppose that a belief possesses knowledge-level justification just in case it possesses a property, ϕ. ϕ might be the property of being self-evident, or the property of being reliably caused, or the property of cohering with the agent's other beliefs. Take your pick.

> (J)   S's belief that p is justified just in case S's belief that p possesses ϕ. (If S's belief that p possesses ϕ and p is true, S knows that p.)

Note that (J) does not require that, in order to be justified, you must establish, or even recognize, that you are justified. You will satisfy (J), and so believe justifiably that p, provided your belief that p possesses ϕ. Your satisfying (J) does not depend on your recognizing or establishing that your belief satisfies (J). Nor does your belief's satisfying (J) depend on your recognizing that your belief possesses ϕ, much less your recognizing that ϕ is justificatory. My use of "recognize" here disguises an important point. Anyone moved to add such conditions would want to require that you not merely *believe* you are justified, or that your belief possesses ϕ, or that ϕ is warrant-bestowing. Merely believing is not enough: you would need at the very least to believe *justifiably*.[5] Adding this requirement to (J), however, yields a vicious regress of belief.

To see the point, suppose we add to (J) the requirement that you believe that p justifiably only if you believe justifiably that your belief that p possesses ϕ.

> (J*)   S's belief that p is justified just in case (i) S's belief that p possesses ϕ; (ii) S believes justifiably that S's belief that p possesses ϕ.

The second conjunct of (J*) requires that, in addition to the belief that p, S harbors a distinct belief that satisfies (J*). Call this additional belief the belief that p^*. In order for the belief that p^* to be justified, however, in order for this belief to satisfy clause (ii), S must believe justifiably that p^* possesses ϕ. This implies that S has an additional belief, the belief that p^{**}. Because S's belief that p^{**} must itself be justified, S will need a further belief . . . , and so on. Whatever you take φ to be, you will land in a regress if you include an epistemic component among the requirements for justification.

It is worth recalling that, in the *Meditations*, Descartes does not make this mistake.[6] Descartes requires only that a belief *be* self-evident (or "clear and distinct") for it to be justified, not that a believer recognize the belief to be self-evident. Your belief, on such a conception, can *be* justified even if you are not in a position to establish that it is justified—or indeed that any belief is justified. This of course does not rule out your being able to establish that your belief is justified (or that every self-evident belief is justified). It merely forbears making the warrant of your belief depend on your believing justifiably or establishing that your belief is justified.

Descartes provides an a priori argument—based on the proof of a nondeceiving God—to the conclusion that self-evident beliefs are warranted. Prior to proving God's existence and veracity, Descartes can entertain endless justified beliefs. Once in possession of this proof, however, Descartes is in a position to establish that any self-evident belief (indeed any belief inferable from self-evident beliefs via self-evident steps) must be justified. Even if this proof were mistaken, Descartes would still be justified in believing self-evident propositions, provided only that self-evidence suffices for justification.

Suppose, for a moment, that Descartes is right, that you believe that *p*, and that your belief that *p* is self-evident. Your belief that *p* is justified. Now suppose that, in addition to believing that *p*, you believe that your belief is justified: your belief that your belief that *p* is justified is itself self-evident. (Note that your believing that your belief that *p* is justified is not the same as believing that *p* is self-evident or that self-evident beliefs are justified; you might believe that a belief is justified while altogether lacking the concept of, hence a capacity to form beliefs concerning, self-evidence.) You are thereby justified in believing that your belief that *p* is justified. Your being justified in believing that *p* does not depend on this further belief, but it is entirely compatible with it.[7] If all these beliefs are true, then (as we are supposing) you know that *p* and you know that you know that *p*.

Savvy readers will have noticed that (J) is an "externalist" principle, not in the sense that it invokes factors external to the agent, but in the sense that its satisfaction does not depend on the satisfaction of an epistemic condition of the sort added to yield (J*). Any account of knowledge or justification that is to avoid a vicious regress (and thus prove unsatisfiable by finite agents) must be externalist in this sense. This is worth mentioning because "reliabilist" accounts of justification, accounts according to which a belief's possessing φ is its having been reliably produced, are sometimes regarded with suspicion because they are externalist. Reliabilism may have many defects, but this is not one of them.[8]

You might worry that this is too quick. Perhaps (J*), or something like (J*), *is* correct. If that implies that justification and knowledge are impossible for finite agents, then so be it: skeptics have long held as much. What right do we have to assume at the outset that knowledge or justified belief are humanly attainable?

The worry is misplaced. If skepticism amounted to no more than the promotion of conditions on justification that are not finitely satisfiable, then skepticism would be uninteresting. The skeptic would "win" by setting standards for knowledge impossibly high. It is scarcely news that human beings cannot do what is finitely impossible. I shall come back to the skeptic in due course. First, however, let us return to Descartes.

I have said that Descartes provides an account of justification that is externalist in the sense that it allows agents to *be* justified in holding a particular belief provided only that the belief satisfy a certain nonepistemic condition: the belief is clear and distinct, or, as I have put it, self-evident. Descartes's subsequent proof of a nondeceiving God is not required for Descartes to be justified or to have knowledge, not even for Descartes to be justified in believing (or to know) that he is justified (or knows). What function, then, does the proof of a nondeceiving God fulfill? The proof for God amounts to an attempt on Descartes's part to provide an (epistemically) noncircular argument to the conclusion that (J) *is* satisfied by finite agents. Without the proof (or some replacement proof) you could be justified in believing all sorts of things and justified in believing that you are justified in believing those things; but you would not be in a position to establish that you are justified in an epistemically noncircular way.

Think of the skeptic, not as someone who denies that we have knowledge or that we are ever justified in believing what we do, but as someone who challenges us to establish in an epistemically noncircular fashion that we are justified or that we have knowledge. Descartes aims to answer the skeptic head on by means of an a priori proof for the existence of a nondeceiving God. Were that proof successful, we should have answered the skeptical challenge.

Unfortunately, it is easy to doubt that Descartes's proof is successful. This is not because, as is often charged, the proof is circular. As James Van Cleve has made amply clear, the charge of circularity is founded on a confusion over precisely the kinds of issue under discussion.[9] In his proof for God, Descartes invokes premises that satisfy (J). The conclusion of the proof is that a nondeceiving God exists. This implies that we are justified in regarding beliefs that satisfy (J) as justified. The proof does not invoke (J), however; it does not appeal to the principle that self-evidence is justificatory. Were it to do so, the proof *would* be circular. Differently put: the proof requires that its premises satisfy (J), that its premises *be* justified, but it does not appeal to (J) as a premise. The appearance of circularity fades once this distinction is made.

You might remain unconvinced. The proof is supposed to validate the self-evidence criterion by establishing that a belief's being self-evident suffices for its being true: a connection between self-evidence and truth follows from the existence of a nondeceiving God. But in so doing, the proof appeals to self-evident premises: Descartes relies on self-evidence to validate self-evidence, and this appears circular. This worry, too, is founded on a confusion. Would the proof be improved if its premises failed to be self-evident? A sound proof includes only justified premises. A proof that beliefs satisfying a certain condition, φ, are justified is no exception. Premises deployed in such a proof *had better* satisfy φ, *whatever* you might take φ to be. In the end, Descartes's proof fails precisely *because* it includes premises that fall short of self-evidence.

Descartes's proof does not accomplish what it sets out to accomplish: to provide an epistemically noncircular a priori proof that beliefs warranted by virtue of being self-evident are true (and so constitute knowledge). This is not because the proof is circular, but because its premises fail to be self-evident and thus fall short of satisfying the standard the proof is supposed to underwrite. Still, given his aims, Descartes had the right idea. Were the proof successful, it would provide an answer to the skeptic. To be sure, it is easy to doubt that any such proof could ever be successful. No such proof could incorporate empirical premises, and it is hard to see how a proof relying exclusively on premises knowable a priori might succeed.[10]

Must we concede to the skeptic? If I am right in identifying skepticism with the view that we are in no position to provide an epistemically noncircular demonstration that our beliefs about the world are true or justified, then skepticism—or one form of skepticism—is vindicated. It is hard to see this concession as a threat, however. In fact, it appears to be an immediate consequence of our regarding the domain to which our beliefs apply as mind-independent.[11] But this is just to say that skepticism is an immediate consequence of realism: skepticism is realism seen in the mirror of epistemology (Heil 1998). Realism precludes a direct route from beliefs about the world to the world. We can defeat the skeptic by abandoning realism, but this is a cure worse than the disease.[12]

REALISM AND SELF-KNOWLEDGE

To avoid circularity, anyone hoping to follow Descartes in responding to the skeptic must proceed, as I have put it, "from the inside out." It is natural to understand this as a requirement that such a response must deploy only premises knowable a priori. But suppose we take seriously the idea that we are reasoning from the inside out: from resources immediately available to the mind (or inferable from these a priori) to a conclusion involving the external world. Resources immediately available to the mind include our thoughts, feelings, and attitudes. Descartes regards these as intrinsic states of mind. The mind scans its own intrinsic states and reasons "outward" from these.

In recent years this Cartesian doctrine has been widely attacked on the grounds that it promotes a radically misconceived picture of minds and their contents.[13] A recurrent theme in these attacks is that the contents of states of mind—what those states of mind concern—is contextually determined. Intrinsically indiscernible agents in discernible contexts can differ with respect to the contents of thoughts they entertain.

This somewhat fuzzy idea can be sharpened by means of an analogy borrowed from Wittgenstein. Imagine a picture of a smiling face. Placed in one pictorial context—a festive scene, for instance—the face expresses benign happiness; in a different context—a scene of suffering—the face expresses malevolence. What the face expresses, the face's significance, evidently is not intrinsic to it, but determined in part by its context. Externalists in the philosophy of mind extend this point to thought generally.[14] What you are thinking depends on the broader context in which your thought occurs.

Of course, not every contextual feature of an agent's context need be imagined relevant to the determination of the content of that agent's states of mind. One popular view is that agents' causal histories play an especially prominent role in fixing the content of their thoughts. This seems to be what Putnam has in mind in his much-discussed Twin Earth cases. Here on Earth, lakes, rivers, bathtubs, and ice trays are filled with water: H_2O. When you entertain a thought you would express by uttering a sentence of the form, "There is water in that tub," your thought concerns water. Now imagine an agent, exactly like you intrinsically, but living on Twin Earth, a planet exactly like Earth in all respects save one. On Twin Earth the clear, colorless, tasteless liquid that fills lakes, tubs, and ice trays is not H_2O but a distinct (though superficially similar: clear, colorless, tasteless) chemical compound, XYZ. When your Twin Earth counterpart entertains a thought the counterpart would express by uttering, "There is water in that tub," the counterpart's thought concerns, not water, but XYZ. You and your twin entertain thoughts with different contents: your thoughts concern water (not twin-water), your twin's concern twin-water (not water). You do not differ intrinsically from your twin, however.[15] It seems to follow that the contents of your thoughts (or at any rate some of your thoughts) are determined by contextual factors. If the causal theorists are right, then these factors include causal relations you bear to your surroundings.

I have no wish to defend causal theories of mind here. My aim is merely to illustrate externalist approaches to content by way of an example en route to an assessment of the epistemological implications of such views.

An immediate worry is that, if the contents of your thoughts depend on factors external to you, you could not know what you were thinking without first knowing something about these external factors.[16] Imagine you are thinking a thought you might express by uttering the sentence, "There is water in that glass." Whether this thought concerns water or twin-water depends on whether you stand in appropriate causal relations to H_2O or XYZ, respectively. The intrinsic character of the thought would be the same in either case. If the thoughts are intrinsically indiscernible, how could you be sure you were entertaining the one and not the other without first discovering whether you were causally related to H_2O or XYZ?

One response to this worry invokes the idea that any plausible account of knowledge must be externalist in the epistemic sense discussed earlier. Your belief that there is water in the glass is justified just in case it satisfies appropriate justificatory conditions. Your belief's *being* justified does not depend on your grasping these conditions, much less on your believing justifiably that they are satisfied. Imagine now that you are thinking a thought with a particular content. Your thought has this content (let us say) because you stand in some causal relation to an object at some distance from your body: you are thinking of water, perhaps, in virtue of being in a state caused by H_2O. Now suppose that you form the belief that you are thinking of water. This belief is itself a state of mind with a particular content, a content that includes the content of the thought it is about. What is required for your belief to be justified (and, assuming it is true, to constitute an instance of knowledge)?

Here is one possibility. Given a causal theory of content, your belief that you are thinking about water owes its content to whatever determines the content of the original thought: in this case, some H_2O. More generally, the content of a second-order state of mind—a thought about a thought—depends on whatever determines the content of the pertinent first-order state of mind. If that were so, the content of a second-order state would be assured of "matching" the content of its first-order counterpart. It does not matter in the least that this content is fixed by a source external to the agent. The first-order state has a particular content, and this content is included in the content of the second-order state. On a model of this kind, there is no question of inwardly examining a state, then inferring its content: the content of the first-order state is "transparent" to the second-order "introspective" state.

Consider a linguistic parallel. You say, "This is water." Your utterance (we are pretending) concerns water by virtue of your standing in a particular kind of causal relation to H_2O. This is so quite independently of your grasping this fact. Let us ask: do you know what your words mean? Well, when you say

(U)   "By 'water', I mean *water*,"

what you say is correct. Its correctness is guaranteed by the fact that whatever makes it the case that you mean *water* when you utter the word "water" will make it the case that your utterance of (U) is true.[17] You may think it implausible that the meaning of such utterances could be determined by external, causal factors. But if you grant that the meaning of utterances of "water" is externally fixed, then you seem bound to extend the same courtesy to cases like (U) in which a speaker "disquotes." Just as you would be justified in believing that by "water," you meant water, so you are justified in believing that thoughts you would express by utterances of "water" concern water.

Suppose you regard introspection on the model of inward observation: in reflecting on your own thoughts, you inwardly observe those thoughts and thereby apprehend their content. In this case, a causal account of content can still accommodate our sense that access to the contents of one's thoughts is epistemically direct. Causal relations are transitive. If the content of your thought that there is water over there is fixed by your standing in an appropriate relation to some H_2O, this might be enough to fix the content of your thought that you are thinking of water. Your second-order thought is caused by an H_2O-caused first-order thought. If you accept that the content of your first-order thought could be fixed by your standing in an appropriate causal relation to H_2O, then you ought not balk at the idea that H_2O could fix the content of your second-order thought as well.

I have been assuming a simplified externalist account of content for the sake of argument. If you accept externalism about mental content, if you think that the contents of agents' thoughts is determined by factors outside the agent, then you might extend the thesis to the contents of thoughts about thoughts. In so doing, you draw out the externalist thesis in a perfectly natural way. Suppose you imagined that, in order to ascertain the content of one of your own thoughts, you would need, first, to "observe" the thought (inwardly), and, second, to infer the thought's content, by scrutinizing its intrinsic makeup, perhaps, or by working out its cause. You would be making a move parallel to the move made by someone who thought that, in order for an agent to believe justifiably that a given belief (the agent's own or someone else's) is justified, the agent would need to believe justifiably that the belief in question satisfied some epistemic standard, ϕ. (Recall that ϕ could be being self-evident, being reliably caused, cohering with your other beliefs, or the like.) Just as a belief could be justified in virtue of possessing ϕ, so a second-order belief that some other belief is justified could be justified because the second-order belief possesses ϕ. Property ϕ need not enter into the content of either belief. Similarly, if the content of a thought is fixed by its possession of a property, ψ, this property need not enter into the content of thoughts about the thought and need not figure explicitly in any reasoning involved in ascertaining the thought's content.

Although I have taken for granted an externalist conception of content for the sake of argument—contending that externalism *per se* poses no particular threat to the possibility that we could know the contents of our own thoughts directly and without appeal to evidence as to their content-fixing properties—it is not easy to feel confident about externalism as an account of content for at least two reasons. First, externalism about content, perhaps surprisingly, shades into a kind of antirealism as to the domain concerning which first-order thoughts are directed. Second, there is good reason to think that the projective character of thought, the feature of thought encompassing its content, is grounded in non-relational features of agents. I shall address these points in turn.

For simplicity, let us suppose that the content of a thought is determined by its cause. A thought you would express by uttering a sentence of the form, "There is water in the bath," concerns water because it is caused by H_2O. As we have seen, your knowing—directly and noninferentially—the content of this thought, knowing, that is, that it concerns water, is consistent with externalism. You can know that your thought concerns water without first ascertaining that it was caused by H_2O. Suppose, however, you accept content externalism and externalism is true: thoughts' contents are determined by their causes. Now, it would seem that you could use this information to infer the existence of water (H_2O).[18] You would not be inferring the existence of water from the fact that you believe that water exists. Rather, you would be inferring the existence of water from (a) the fact that your thoughts about water concern water, together with (b) the fact that the content of a thought is determined by its cause. You seem to be in a position to establish, without the aid of empirical investigation, that water exists. If you can establish in this way that water exists, then you have the makings of a refutation of the skeptic. The skeptic holds that your thoughts could be just as they are, but the world be utterly different: think of Descartes's evil demon. Externalism about content, however, is apparently inconsistent with this possibility.

One prominent externalist, Hilary Putnam, has long insisted on this very point.[19] Putnam considers the latter-day Cartesian possibility that we might be brains in vats whose neural pathways are attached to a supercomputer programmed to feed us stimulation mimicking the stimulation we might receive from ordinary sense organs. If you are a brain in a vat, your experiences will be qualitatively indistinguishable from those of an ordinary agent. Are you deluded, then, when you entertain a thought you might express by "uttering" the sentence, "There's water in the bath"? Your "water" thoughts are not causally connected to H_2O; they are connected, instead, to an electrical pattern generated by the computer. Your "water" thoughts, then, do not concern water; they concern a certain pattern of electrical stimulation. When you say, "There is water in the bath," you "utter" a sentence that we should express in English as, "There is electrical pattern P." Would you be deluded about water? Not at all. When you entertain a thought you would express by uttering, "There is water in the bath," your thought concerns, not water, but electrical pattern P. If you are a brain in a vat, then, you do not have false thoughts about water, but true thoughts about electrical patterns generated by a supercomputer.

Imagine now that your thoughts turn to the skeptical problem. You ask: "Might I be a brain in a vat?" Assuming that the contents of your thoughts are determined by their causes, then your thoughts would concern, not brains and vats, but patterns of electrical stimulation. After a moment's consideration you announce, "I am not a brain in a vat." Are you deluded? Not at all. In entertaining a thought you would express by "uttering" the sentence, "I am not a brain in a vat," you would be entertaining a thought about patterns of electrical stimulation. And it is true that you are not a pattern of electrical stimulation!

I have argued elsewhere that, even if we accept this argument, there is still an important sense in which a brain in a vat (and, by extension, any reflective agent) could be utterly off base in what it took to be its situation (Heil 1987, 1992, chap. 5). The easiest way to appreciate this point is to imagine eavesdropping (via loud-speakers connected to the supercomputer) on a brain in a vat running through the argument and concluding, "I am not a brain in a vat." The brain has no false beliefs, perhaps, but the brain is in no position to appreciate its actual situation vis à vis vats. Any of us might worry, then, whether we are in a position analogous to that of a brain in a vat, a position that, owing to conditions on thought contents, we are in no position to consider. This strikes me as at least as good as the original skeptical worry. Let us bracket this point, however, and play along with Putnam. If we do that, then we grant that there are no transcendent truths, truths out of our reach in the way the truth about an envatted brain's situation is apparently out of its reach. This is Putnam's "internal" or "natural" realism.[20]

We have cut the ground from beneath the skeptic. Our strategy differs importantly from Descartes's, however. Descartes accepts realism and seeks to bridge the gap that realism establishes between our thoughts and the world on which those thoughts are directed. An externalist, in contrast, builds the world into our thoughts about it. In this respect, at least, there is no thought–world gap, hence no place for the skeptical challenge to take hold.

I do not say that externalism necessitates this kind of antirealism. There may be varieties of externalism that do not. It is clear, however, that many philosophers who have been attracted, for whatever reason, to externalist, anti-individualist accounts of the contents of thoughts have not adequately appreciated the apparently antirealist implications of their views. Putnam himself is a notable exception.

INTERNALISM REDUX?

Suppose I am right in placing externalism about thought contents in the antirealist camp. If you have reservations about antirealism—and here I mean antirealism about the world on which our thoughts are directed—you might want to think carefully before accepting externalist accounts of the contents of our thoughts. But what are the alternatives? Given familiar criticisms and counterexamples to internalist theories, are there viable competitors to externalism on the horizon?

Before trying to answer this question, it might be useful to distinguish two issues that are too often run together. Externalist theories of the mind frequently take advantage of externalist accounts of the semantics of natural languages. The English word "water" acquires its meaning within a community of users who are in contact with water—H_2O. A move from language to thought is made by identifying thoughts (as I have done above in trying to motivate externalism) by reference to sentences expressing those thoughts. But, even if the semantics of natural language is externalist, it need not follow that the content of thoughts is thereby determined externally. When we think in words—when we engage in what C. B. Martin calls verbal imagery—the contents of our thoughts rides piggyback on the semantics of our language[21] (see Martin 1987). But thought need not be linguistic. If that is so, and if we can envision an internalist account of the content of nonlinguistic thought, we can avoid antirealist, anti-Cartesian implications of externalism.

I shall not mount a detailed defense of this claim here, nor shall I offer a full-scale alternative to externalism about mental content. Instead, I shall sketch an internalist theory in enough detail to support my broader contention that externalism is not the only game in town. My aim is to show how the projective character of thought—its "of-ness" or "about-ness"—might stem, not from relations agents bear to their surroundings, but to agents' intrinsic features. If this is right, then we need not accept that antirealist picture according to which the mind encompasses the world on which its thoughts are directed. An externalist semantics for natural language amounts to no more (nor less) than a constraint on linguistic usage. Such a constraint packs no momentous antirealist consequences.

A SKETCH OF AN INTERNALIST ACCOUNT OF MENTAL CONTENT

It would seem a distinct possibility that the contents of states of mind owe their character to internal factors alone, factors intrinsic to agents to whom the states belong. Consider Davidson's Swampman.[22] Swampman is created when a bolt of lightning striking a swamp simultaneously vaporizes Davidson and creates a precise Davidson replica by fortuitously rearranging the particles that had made up a rotting tree stump nearby.[23]

Some philosophers—perhaps Davidson himself—have thought that, for a period of time immediately after he appears on the scene, Swampman lacks thoughts. This would be so if thought content depended on agents' causal histories and Swampman wanted the right kind of content-bestowing causal history. Of course Swampman behaves precisely as Davidson would behave and entertains "thoughts" that are intrinsically similar to Davidson's. No matter, say the causal theorists. So long as Swampman lacks appropriate causal connections to the environment, his "thoughts" are empty of content (or perhaps they simply differ in content). It cannot even be true to say that Swampman falsely *thinks* he is thinking of trees, water, and other people, although he might utter words indistinguishable from Davidson's words to this effect.

I think it more likely that Swampman, no less than Davidson, entertains thoughts in the fullest sense. The contents of these thoughts depend, not on Swampman's causal history, but on his intrinsic dispositional makeup. In this he is a precise duplicate of Davidson. His dispositional makeup would dispose Swampman to react just as Davidson would to trees, water, and people. Of course Swampman would differ from Davidson in harboring endless false beliefs: he falsely believes he wrote "Mental Events," for instance, he falsely believes that he attended Harvard, and he falsely believes he is Davidson. This, however, is a far cry from Swampman's having no thoughts at all about such matters.[24]

Thoughts depend on dispositional makeup. What are dispositions? For purposes of this discussion, I shall assume without argument that dispositions are intrinsic features of their possessors. Dispositions are conditionally characterizable, but they cannot be conditionally defined. We say a vase is fragile if it would shatter when dropped. But a vase can be fragile even if this conditional fails to hold of it. How so? Consider the following case. A fragile vase is closely observed by an angel who would cushion its fall were it dropped. The vase has a disposition, but the conditional we should naturally use to characterize it is false! Dispositions are intrinsic features of their possessors with what C. B. Martin (1997) calls "typifying manifestations." These are most naturally expressed by means of conditionals. But a disposition may be present, and conditions that ordinarily elicit its typifying manifestation be present as well, without its manifesting itself in this typifying way.[25] If an angel is on hand to cushion the vase were it to fall, the vase would not thereby cease to be fragile. Rather this manifestation of the vase's disposition to shatter would be blocked.

In general we can distinguish cases in which a disposition, though present, fails to be manifested as it typically is under conditions regarded as sufficient to elicit this manifestation, from those in which an object loses a disposition. Suppose we characterize disposition, D, as a disposition to yield M, under circumstances C (a vase's being fragile, for instance, might be for the vase to be such that it would shatter if it were dropped). Let us distinguish, then,

(A)   An object, *o*, possesses *D* under circumstances C, but *o* fails to yield *M* owing to the presence of some "blocking" disposition, D'.

(B)   An object, *o*, possesses *D*, but, owing to circumstances, comes to lose *D* prior to the onset of *M*.

An angel's cushioning the fall of a fragile vase is a case of type (A). An angel who caused a falling vase to lose the disposition to shatter (perhaps by melting it in midair) were it dropped, would be a type (B) case. In both cases, the vase (now) possesses a disposition to shatter, even though the conditional we find it natural to use in characterizing the disposition is false.[26]

Characterizing dispositions via subjunctive conditionals can be misleading in another respect. In general, dispositions require for their manifestation reciprocal disposition partners (see Martin 1997, Martin and Heil 1999). Salt is soluble in water. Salt has a disposition to dissolve when paired with water (which has a reciprocal disposition to dissolve salt). We can pick out this disposition by describing the salt as being such that, were it placed in water, it would dissolve. Suppose, for the sake of argument, a salt crystal's disposition to dissolve in water is its particular structure. (The "is" here is the is of strict identity.) This very disposition, paired with light radiation, might result in a particular pattern of absorption and reflection. Were the crystal subject to light radiation, a particular absorption/reflection pattern would result. There are two conditionals here, but only a single disposition. Think of a ball's shape. The shape of a ball disposes it to roll down an inclined plane, to make a particular kind of indentation when pressed into a lump of clay, to make a different kind of indentation when pressed into a pile of loose sawdust, to reflect light in a particular way, to reflect impact waves produced by a bat's squeak in another way, and to please a child. One disposition, many manifestations, depending on reciprocal partners. These manifestations figure in distinct conditionals, any one of which might be used to pick out the self-same intrinsic disposition.

What has any of this to do with states of mind? Consider just belief. Your harboring a particular belief, a belief that it is raining in Bendigo, for instance, might manifest itself in endless ways given endless distinct reciprocal disposition partners. It might manifest itself in your answering "Yes," to the question, "Is it raining in Bendigo?" It might manifest itself in your forming other beliefs, perhaps the belief that if you are going to Bendigo you must take an umbrella. The thesis that belief has a dispositional component is relatively uncontroversial. My suggestion, however, is that it is the dispositionality of belief that gives beliefs their "projective" character. The content of a belief—or any other "contentful" state of mind—is built into the belief via its dispositionality. The fundamental idea is simple. A salt crystal "projects" toward a particular kind of manifestation with water and so could be said to "point toward" water. Similarly, a belief about Bendigo "points toward" Bendigo by virtue of its multifarious Bendigo-related potential manifestations.

You may find the thought of a dispositional account of content unappealing.[27] I take dispositions to provide a plausible basis for "intentionality," the "of-ness" or "about-ness" of thought, but here I raise the possibility only as a vehicle to discuss the prospects for something like privileged access within an internalist framework. Thus, suppose your harboring a belief that it is raining in Bendigo is a matter of your being in a particular dispositional condition. What precisely would be involved in your recognizing yourself to have a belief with this content?

We have seen that dispositions can be designated, though not defined, by means of subjunctive conditionals. Such conditionals designate a disposition's typifying manifestations. Often it is convenient to identify a belief by reference to an utterance an agent might use to express the belief: talk of "expressing" a belief is, at bottom, just a way of talking about one kind of manifestation of the underlying disposition that constitutes the belief. Beliefs can be manifested in ways that do not include what we should ordinarily regard as typifying outward expressions. Your belief that it is raining in Bendigo, together with your perceiving that your train has arrived in Bendigo, might lead you to form a new belief: the belief that you will need your umbrella if you hope to stay dry.

Imagine, now, that prior to your arrival in Bendigo, a companion asks you whether you believe it is raining there. (Let us assume, somewhat artificially, that you regard this as a request, not for your assessment of the weather, but for a report on your beliefs about the weather.) Your belief that it is raining in Bendigo will manifest itself in your reporting that you believe it is raining. We might imagine all this transpiring inside your head. You ask yourself what you believe about the weather in Bendigo, and your belief that it is raining in Bendigo leads you to form the belief that you believe that it is raining in Bendigo. Your second-order belief is itself a manifestation of the first-order belief it concerns. The content of the original belief is grounded in its dispositionality. Possible manifestations of this include the formation of second-order beliefs. The content of these second-order beliefs inherits the content of the first-order beliefs of which they are manifestations. Of course not every manifestation of a belief is a second-order belief or even a belief. The manifestations we are considering here are *beliefs* because they are functionally on a par with other beliefs. They are second-order beliefs, beliefs *about* the belief of which they are a manifestation, because they are manifestations of that belief and they themselves include the right sort of dispositional profile.

A view of this kind accords with one component of the common-sense view: it allows for iterated "levels" of conscious awareness. You can have thoughts about your thoughts, thoughts about your thoughts about your thoughts, and so on. This does not portend a regress. You need not have thoughts about other thoughts, but, because thoughts about thoughts are common manifestations of thoughts, it is open to you to do so. It accords with common sense in another way as well. The experience of "introspecting" one's own thoughts is not the experience of observing a state or entity and working out its significance. Thoughts about thoughts unfold from the very thoughts they concern.

Imagine walking into a room and discovering a drawing on a sheet of paper taped to the wall. You might scrutinize the drawing and on that basis endeavor to work out its significance. Compare this with a drawing you make on a sheet of paper. You do not make the drawing then examine it to work out its meaning. The drawing's significance is evident to you because you drew it to have that significance. Your thoughts have the same status. You do not observe them inwardly then work out (or "read off") their significance—either by scrutinizing their intrinsic character or by ascertaining their causal ancestry. Their significance is transparent to you, not because they are wholly (or in part) inside your head, but because they are your thoughts.

What is the status of beliefs about our own thoughts? Are they warranted? Do they, when true, amount to knowledge of those thoughts, in particular, do they amount to knowledge of the content of those thoughts? Although beliefs about our own states of mind are scarcely infallible, they are paradigmatically warranted.[28] Such beliefs are, as Descartes recognized, warranted if any beliefs are.

Is there room here for the skeptic to drive his wedge? I have described skepticism (or a certain brand of skepticism) as the epistemological reflection of realism. Surely we want to be realists about states of mind of our own on which our thoughts are directed. These states of mind are mind-independent in the sense that their existing does not depend on our taking them to exist. (Berkeleyean minds and ideas are mind-independent in this sense.) This seems to open a gap between your thoughts and your thoughts about your thoughts. This is as it should be. We lack infallible "access" to our own states of mind, even when these are conscious. Epistemic privilege should not be mistaken for epistemic infallibility.

Cases in which we might be mistaken as to the character of our own thoughts are not easy to imagine. You can mistake a stick on the path in front of you for a snake: snakes and sticks of certain shapes look similar. Margarine can be mistaken for butter because margarine and butter have similar textures and tastes. It is more difficult to find cases in which one state of mind is mistaken for another.[29] The sensation produced by pressing an ice cube to the skin can be mistaken for a sensation of heat. Could you, however, mistake your thought that there is water in that container for a thought with some other content? In such a case you would be thinking that p but think that you were thinking that q.[30]

You can say that the hat is on the mat while believing you were saying the cat is on the mat. You may have intended to say that the cat is on the mat but misspoke. In that case your belief would reflect your intention, not the upshot of your intention. Could you intend to say the cat is on the mat while believing that you intend to say that the hat is on the mat? I do not say that this would be impossible, but cases of this kind are at the very least difficult to imagine. If the content of your intention is bestowed by its dispositional basis, and if thoughts about this content are manifestations of the very same dispositional basis, it will be difficult to tell a coherent story whereby the content of the latter differs markedly from the content of the former.

CONCLUDING REMARKS

Realism about a given domain implies the possibility of error about that domain, but the possibility of error need not be the same in all cases. The possibility for error when it comes to the contents of one's conscious thoughts is vanishingly small. Any account of the mind and its operation that leaves this mysterious is in serious trouble. Both externalist and internalist accounts of the contents of thoughts can cope with the knowledge we have of our own thoughts. Confusion over this topic stems in part from a misapprehension of what is required for the justification of belief (or knowledge) and what is involved in beliefs about one's own states of mind. Once we are clear on these matters, we can turn our attention to more interesting questions pertaining to the makeup of the mind.

NOTES

Jakob Hohwy provided valuable comments on a draft of this chapter. I am indebted to Davidson College for funding a research leave during 2000–2001 and to the Department of Philosophy, Monash University, for its hospitality and for supporting an invigorating philosophical environment. My greatest debt is to C. B. Martin, the most ontologically serious of the ontologically serious.

1. The remarks that follow owe an obvious debt to Alston 1993.

2. For instance by checking the pronouncements of one sensory modality against those of another modality.

3. More cautiously, your knowing or believing justifiably does not depend on your believing, believing justifiably, or knowing either conditions required for justification or that those conditions are satisfied.

4. Nothing I say depends on this point—which many regard as having been decisively refuted by Gettier (1963). If you are one of the many, replace the justification condition with whatever, in addition to truth, you take to be required for a belief to constitute an instance of knowledge.

5. If you have doubts about this, consider an agent who takes himself to be justified in believing that Seabiscuit will win the Derby on the basis of reading this in the tea leaves and believing that the tea leaves are reliable.

6. Nor do careful defenders of "coherence" accounts of justification. On such accounts a belief is justified if it coheres with an agent's other beliefs. An agent need not, in addition, believe justifiably that the belief so coheres.

7. This is precisely Descartes's situation in *Meditation* iii prior to his proof for God.

8. Reliabilism, like Cartesian self-evidence, belongs to a family of truth-linked accounts of justification and knowledge. According to Descartes, self-evidence is justificatory because self-evident beliefs must be true.

9. See Van Cleve 1979; see also Sosa 1994.

10. It is hard to think how a proof relying on a priori premises could succeed except by establishing the existence of a nondeceiving God.

11. A domain is mind-independent provided truths about the domain do not metaphysically depend on our having beliefs about those truths. Minds and their contents are mind-independent in this sense.

12. Putnam's attempt to provide a proof that we are not brains in a vat is an example of this way around skepticism. See Putnam 1981; Heil 1987.

13. See, for instance, Putnam 1975a; Burge 1979; Baker 1987; Wilson 1995.

14. Do not confuse externalism in the philosophy of mind with epistemological externalism. The former holds that the mind's contents are what they are owing to factors outside the agent. The latter promotes the far less controversial idea that conditions required for a belief's being justified cannot themselves include an epistemic component. Externalism in the philosophy of mind is sometimes called anti-individualism.

15. Your body contains water and your twin's body does not, so you cannot be precise replicas. We can pretend, however, that these intrinsic differences make no difference to the contents of your respective thoughts.

16. For early discussions of this point, see Burge 1988; Davidson 1987; Heil 1988. Owing no doubt to the popularity of externalist accounts of content, a veritable industry has grown up around the issue; for a representative sampling, see Ludlow and Martin 1998.

17. I leave aside contexts in which the sentence might be uttered with something else in mind.

18. An argument of the sort advanced here is deployed by Michael McKinsey 1991; see Heil 1992, 164–172 for one kind of response.

19. Putnam 1981, chap. 1. See also Heil 1987, 1992, chap. 5.

20. Putnam 1981, 1994. For a response to Putnam consistent with my aims here, see Van Cleve 1992. In general, philosophers who defend *kinds* of realism (internal realism, natural realism, empirical realism) do so in the course of developing antirealist theses. Internal realism, natural realism, empirical realism are no more species of realism than an alleged criminal is a kind of criminal.

21. See Martin 1987. As the Swampman case discussed below illustrates, it is far from obvious that the semantics of natural language must be externalist.

22. Davidson 1987. Swampman is standardly thought to support an externalist conception of content; I think otherwise.

23. The process whereby Swampman is created differs then from the process whereby a replica of Captain Kirk is created on the surface of planet Ork by a trans-

porter that relies on information about Captain Kirk's physical constitution in producing a replica.

24. Although I shall not push the point here, precisely the same could be said about Swampman's utterances. Swampman speaks English. A residual worry: what makes Swampman's "water" thoughts and utterances concern water and not twin-water? A Swampman replica on Twin Earth would, after all, be dispositionally indiscernible from Swampman. Here, we must take seriously the indexicality endemic to language and thought. Swampman's "water" thoughts concern the stuff in swampman's neighborhood.

25. It is important to distinguish a case in which a disposition manifests itself, but not in the way regarded as typical, from cases in which it fails to manifest itself at all.

26. These matters and many more are discussed in Martin 1996, 1997, and Martin and Heil 1999. For a reply, see Lewis 1998; see also Molnar 1999 and Bird 1999.

27. See Martin and Heil 1998 for some reasons why you should not; see also Heil 1998, chaps. 5, 6. Note that anyone sympathetic to Davidson's conception of interpretation is bound to appeal to dispositionalities. Agents satisfy interpretive schemes, not merely on the basis of what they say and do, but on what they *would* say and do. This is why Swampman's thoughts and utterances must be interpreted just as Davidson's would have been (had he survived being struck by lightning).

28. I am considering only cases in which an agent's beliefs concern the agent's current thoughts, not cases of belief about beliefs held at some earlier time and subsequently abandoned. I also exclude pathological—for instance, repressed—beliefs whose presence must be inferred by the agent.

29. The so-called propositional attitudes (beliefs, desires, intentions, and the like) include two components: (1) a "proposition" entertained and (2) an attitude toward this proposition. You could, at various times, take up different attitudes toward the same proposition. Thus, perched on the edge of a precipice, you might believe, intend, doubt, hope, fear, wish that you will fall. Cases under consideration are those in which you are wrong about the propositional component of one of your own. It may be easier to imagine cases in which you are wrong about the attitudinal component: you take yourself to fear falling from the precipice, but in fact you have a deep-seated desire to fall.

30. When I was a child, my family moved several times. At one point, I entered a new school in which one of my classmates was named Alan. I had a classmate with the same name in a different school some years earlier. For a period lasting several months, my thoughts of Alan were confused. At times it was quite unclear which Alan I was thinking of. The case resembles one in which you are transported from Twin Earth to Earth and entertain thoughts you would express by uttering "water." Neither case requires that we embrace a causal theory.

REFERENCES

Alston, William (1993). *The Reliability of Sense Perception.* Ithaca, N.Y.: Cornell University Press.

Baker, Lynne Rudder (1987). *Saving Belief: A Critique of Physicalism.* Princeton: Princeton University Press.

Bouwsma, O. K. (1949). "Descartes' Evil Genius." *Philosophical Review* 58: 141–51.

———. (1965). *Philosophical Essays*. Lincoln: University of Nebraska Press.

Burge, Tyler (1979). 'Individualism and the Mental'. *Midwest Studies in Philosophy* 4: 73–121.

———. (1988). "Individuation and Self-Knowledge." *Journal of Philosophy* 85: 649–663.

Davidson, D. (1987). "Knowing One's Own Mind." *Proceedings and Address of the American Philosophical Association* 60: 441–458.

Gettier, Edmund (1963). "Is Justified True Belief Knowledge?" *Analysis* 23: 121–23.

Heil, John. (1987). "Are We Brains in a Vat? Top Philosopher Says, 'No'." *Canadian Journal of Philosophy* 17: 427–36.

———. (1988). "Privileged Access" *Mind* 97: 238–251. Reprinted in Ludlow and Martin (1998): 129–45.

———. (1992). *The Nature of True Minds*. Cambridge: Cambridge University Press.

———. (1998). "Skepticism and Realism." *American Philosophical Quarterly* 35: 57–72.

Ludlow, Peter, and Norah Martin, eds. (1998). *Readings on Externalism and Authoritative Self-Knowledge*. Cambridge: Cambridge University Press.

McKinsey, Michael (1991). "Anti-Individualism and Privileged Access." *Analysis* 51: 9–16.

Martin, C. B. (1987). "Proto-Language." *Australasian Journal of Philosophy* 65: 277–289.

———. (1997). "On the Need for Properties: The Road to Pythagoreanism and Back." *Synthese* 112: 193–231.

Martin, C. B., and John Heil (1998). "Rules and Powers." *Philosophical Perspectives* 12: 283–312.

———. (1999). "The Ontological Turn." *Midwest Studies in Philosophy* 23: 34–60.

Molnar, George (1999). "Are Dispositions Reducible?' *Philosophical Quarterly* 49: 1–17.

Putnam, Hilary (1975a). "The Meaning of 'Meaning.' " In Keith Gunderson ed., *Language, Mind, and Knowledge* (*Minnesota Studies in the Philosophy of Science*, vol. 7), 131–193. Minneapolis: University of Minnesota Press.

———. (1975b). *Mind, Language, and Reality: Philosophical Papers*, vol. 2. Cambridge: Cambridge University Press.

———. (1981). *Reason, Truth, and History*. Cambridge: Cambridge University Press.

———. (1994). "Sense, Nonsense, and the Senses: An Inquiry into the Powers of the Human Mind." *Journal of Philosophy* 91: 445–517.

Sosa, Ernest (1994). "Philosophical Skepticism and Epistemic Circularity." *Proceedings of the Aristotelian Society* 68: 263–290.

Van Cleve, James (1979). "Foundationalism, Epistemic Principles, and the Cartesian Circle." *Philosophical Review* 88: 55–91.

———. (1992). "Semantic Supervenience and Referential Indeterminacy." *Journal of Philosophy* 89: 344–361.

Wilson, Robert (1995). *Cartesian Psychology and Physical Minds: Individualism and the Sciences of the Mind*. Cambridge: Cambridge University Press.

Wittgenstein, Ludwig (1953). *Philosophical Investigations*, trans. G. E. M. Anscombe. Oxford: Basil Blackwell.

CHAPTER 11

....

SKEPTICISM

....

PETER KLEIN

THIS essay is devoted to a discussion of the types of skepticism that have seemed most interesting to contemporary philosophers. It is divided into ten sections.

1. TWO BASIC FORMS OF PHILOSOPHICAL SKEPTICISM

....

With regard to any proposition, say p, there are just three possible propositional attitudes one can have with regard to p's truth when considering whether p is true. One can either assent to p, or assent to ~p, or withhold assenting to both p and ~p. Of course, there are other attitudes one could have towards p. For example, one could ignore p or be excited or depressed about p. But those attitudes are either ones we have when we are *not* considering whether p is true, or they are attitudes that result from our believing, denying, or withholding p.

I just spoke of "assent" and I mean to be using it to designate the pro-attitude, whatever it is, towards a proposition's truth that is required for knowing that proposition. Philosophers have differed about what that attitude is. Some take it to be a strong form of believing—something akin to being sure that p or being willing to guarantee that p.[1] Others have taken it not to be a form of belief at all because they think one can know that p without believing it, as in cases in which I might in fact remember that Queen Victoria died in 1901 but not believe that I remember it and hence might be said not to believe it all. For the purposes of this essay we need not attempt to pin down precisely the nature of the pro-attitude towards p's truth that is necessary for knowing that p. It is sufficient for our purposes to say that *assent* is that pro-attitude towards p's truth required for knowing p.

There are only three relevant possible pro-attitudes one can have toward any proposition when considering whether it is true; hence, there are just three such attitudes towards the proposition that we can have knowledge of each member of some epistemically interesting class, C, of propositions:

1. We assent that we can have knowledge of C-type propositions.
2. We assent that we cannot have knowledge of C-type propositions.
3. We withhold assent to both that we can and that we can't have such knowledge.

By an "epistemically interesting" type of proposition I mean a type such that some propositions of that type are generally thought to be known given what we ordinarily take knowledge to be. Thus, it would not be epistemically interesting if we didn't know exactly what the temperature will be a year from now. That kind of thing (a fine-grained distant future state) is not generally thought to be known given what we ordinarily take knowledge to be. But it would be interesting if we cannot know someone else's mental states, or anything about the past, or anything about the external world.

Let us call someone holding (1) an "epistemist."[2] The skepticism involved in holding (2) has gone under many names. Following the terminology suggested by Sextus, I will call it "Academic Skepticism" because it was endorsed by various members of the New Academy, especially Carneades (214–129 B.C.).[3]

The third view can be called "Pyrrhonian Skepticism" after its founder, Pyrrho, who lived about 365–275 B.C. The Pyrrhonians withheld assent to all members of the set of nonevident propositions, which includes the proposition that we do have knowledge of C-type propositions. Indeed, the Pyrrhonians often classified the Epistemists and the Academic Skeptics as "dogmatists" because they thought both types assented to a nonevident claim.[4]

Thus, *philosophical skepticism* is the view that either the attitude represented in 2 or 3 is the appropriate one. I think it is fair to say that it is Academic Skepticism that is usually meant when most contemporary philosophers write about skepticism. Thus, it is that form of skepticism which will be the primary focus of this essay.

2. ACADEMIC SKEPTICISM

A way to motivate Academic Skepticism is to trace how Descartes expanded the realm of what was doubtful (and hence from his point of view not worthy of assent) in the "First Meditation."[5] Descartes begins by noting that the senses have deceived him on some occasions and that it is never prudent to trust what has occasionally misled one. But that ground for doubting the deliverance of our senses can be neutralized because, as he points out, we seem to be able to determine when our senses are not trustworthy. To neutralize a ground for doubt, d, is to grant that d is true but conjoined with something else worthy of assent such that the conjunction no longer provides a basis for doubt. So, the proposition *that my senses have deceived me on some occasions* is not a genuine ground for doubt because, even if it were granted as true, there is a way of neutralizing its effect.

Next, Descartes considers dreaming. What if we are dreaming now? We could still have knowledge of features of the external world because there are some features shared by dream images and those "real and true" objects of which they are distorted copies. So, if we were dreaming now, we would not know what is going on about us right now, but general things such as the existence of hands are not called into doubt. And even more simple things about nature "in general" are not thereby doubtful. We still know that material objects have a spatial location, can be in motion or at rest, and can exist for a long or short period of time. So, some putative knowledge has not yet been cast into doubt because, although we might be dreaming now, there is a way to neutralize that skeptical objection.

Descartes, then, proposes a ground for doubt to which he "certainly has no reply." He puts it this way:

> In whatever way [it is supposed] that I have arrived at the state of being that I have reached—whether [it is attributed] to fate or to accident, or [made] out that it is by a continual succession of antecedents, or by some other method— since to err and deceive oneself is a defect, it is clear that the greater will be the probability of my being so imperfect as to deceive myself ever, as is the Author of my being to whom [is assigned] my origin the less powerful.[6]

In other words, at this point in the *Meditations*, since he lacks an argument for the claim that whatever is causally responsible for his "state of being" is capable of making it such that to err would be unnatural, assenting to propositions arrived at by his "state of being" is not appropriate. Thus, Descartes believes that he has identified a ground for doubting all of his supposed former knowledge by locating a proposition which, if true, would (by itself) defeat the justification he has for C-type propositions and which is such that (1) he does not (at least at this point in the *Meditations*) have a way to reject it and such that (2) he has no legitimate way to neutralize its effect.

Put another way, Descartes apparently thinks that something is worthy of assent only if it is immune to genuine doubt. And something, d, is a *ground for genuine doubt* of p for S *iff*:

4) d added to S's beliefs makes assenting to p no longer adequately justified;

5) S is neither justified in rejecting d nor has a way to neutralize d.[7]

The final step is to say that some proposition is not worthy of assent if there are genuine grounds for doubting it. In more contemporary terminology, the ground for doubt proposed by Descartes can be put like this:

U: My epistemic equipment is untrustworthy.

The *Cartesian-style Argument for Academic Skepticism* can be stated as:

CS1. If I can know C-type propositions, then I can eliminate all genuine grounds for doubting them.

CS2. U is a genuine ground for doubt that I cannot eliminate.

Therefore, I can not know C-type propositions.

Note that this Cartesian-style argument does not easily lend itself to the objection that the skeptic is contradicting herself in some way by proposing that there is an argument that shows that she fails to know because her epistemic equipment is untrustworthy while at the same time trusting her epistemic equipment to provide that very argument. She is considering the possibility that U is true and claiming that she cannot eliminate U. Thus she is neither holding contradictory beliefs nor is her practice somehow incompatible with her beliefs as it would be, for example, if she believed that M was the only good method of arriving at true beliefs and used some method other than M to arrive at the belief that X was the only good method.

The Cartesian-style argument for Academic Skepticism should be compared with what many contemporary philosophers take to be the canonical argument for Academic Skepticism that employs the Closure Principle (CP). Letting "h" stand for a C-type proposition, for example, Moore's famous "here's a hand" and letting "sk" stand for "I am in a switched-world in which there are no hands, but it appears just as though there were hands," we can state the canonical *CP-style argument for Academic Skepticism* as follows:

CP1. If I am justified in believing that h, then I am justified in believing that ∼sk.

CP2. I am not justified in believing that ~sk.

Therefore, I am not justified in believing that h.

This argument appeals to a form of the Closure Principle in CP1. Letting "Jsx" stand for "S is justified in having some pro-attitude, J, regarding x," that principle can be stated as:

CP: For all propositions, (x,y), if x entails y, and Jsx, then Jsy.[8]

One important point to note about CP is that it does not necessarily appeal to a very stringent notion of justification. Suppose that (positive) justification comes in degrees, where the lowest degree is something like mere plausibility and the highest degree is absolute certainty. CP could be recast as follows:

CP*:   For all propositions, (x,y), if x entails y, and Jsx to degree$_u$, then Jsy to degree$_v$ (where $v \geq u$)

The point is that the when the Academic Skeptic employs CP, she need not be employing a very stringent notion of justification. Indeed, a "very low standards" CP-style skeptic could hold that knowledge requires only positive justification to a very low degree.

Another *apparent* difference between the CP-style and the Cartesian-style argument is that the latter but not the former concerns knowledge. But that is an insignificant difference since the debate about the merits of skepticism takes place within the evidentialist account of knowledge. The issue is whether we have adequate reasons for any C-type proposition. Thus, since knowledge is taken to entail adequately justified assent, "knowledge" could be replaced by "adequately justified assent" in the Cartesian-style argument.

Let us return to the central difference between Cartesian and CP-style arguments and state the epistemic principle, which we can call the "Eliminate All Doubt Principle," that apparently lies behind the Cartesian-style argument:

EAD: (x,d)(if d provides a basis for genuine doubt that x, then, if assenting to x is adequately justified for S, then S is adequately justified in eliminating d.)

EAD requires that we eliminate any genuine grounds for doubt and those include more than mere contraries. In addition, recall that, according to the Cartesian, to be adequately justified in eliminating d as a ground for doubt for x, either S is adequately justified in denying d (assenting to d) or S is adequately justified in assenting to some neutralizing proposition, n, such that adding (n & d) to S's beliefs fails to make it the case that x is no longer adequately justified.[9] Thus, since every contrary of some proposition is a potential genuine ground for doubt, EAD entails CP but CP does not entail EAD.[10] To see that, consider any contrary, say c, of a proposition, say h. The proposition, c, would be a potential genuine ground for doubting h since if c were added to S's beliefs, h would no longer be adequately justified, because S's beliefs would then contain a proposition, c, that entailed the denial of h. Furthermore, the only way S could eliminate c as a ground for doubt would be by denying it, since nothing could neutralize it. Thus, EAD has the consequence that *if S is justified in assenting to h, then S is justified in denying every contrary of h.* But that is just an instance of CP, since (by hypothesis) h entails ~c. That CP does not entail EAD should be clear since there are grounds for doubting h that are not contraries of h. For example, the proposition, U, considered above is a grounds for doubting h, but h and U could both be true.

Thus, there are two basic forms of Academic Skepticism: the Cartesian-style that employs EAD and the CP-style that employs CP. Since the CP-style skeptic employs the weaker epistemic principle, we will begin by focusing on that form of skepticism. Any criticisms of it are likely to redound to the stronger form.

3. THE ARGUMENT FOR ACADEMIC SKEPTICISM BASED ON THE CLOSURE PRINCIPLE

There *appear* to be only three ways that one can respond to the CP-style skeptical argument: deny at least one premise, deny that the argument is valid, or reluctantly accept the conclusion. I say "appear" because I will suggest later that there is a fourth alternative. The second alternative—denying the validity of the argument—is equivalent to embracing an extremely severe form of skepticism because it would involve denying that *modus tollens* is a valid form of inference. And since it is easy to transform any *modus tollens* argument into one employing disjunctive syllogism (by the equivalence of a hypothetical statement to a disjunctive one with the negation of the antecedent as one of the disjuncts), either that equivalence or disjunctive syllogism would have to be rejected. Similarly, *modus ponens* or contraposition would have to be rejected. Hence, if this alternative were chosen, reasoning would come to a complete standstill. That, presumably, is why no one has ever seriously considered this alternative.

So, if we are not to embrace the conclusion of the CP-style argument, it *appears* that we must reject either CP1 or CP2. Let us examine each.

Consideration of CP1

Let us begin by examining closure. The issue is: Does closure hold for justified belief? Closure certainly does hold for some properties, for example, truth. If p is true and it strictly implies q, then q is true. It just as clearly does not hold for other properties. If p is a belief of mine, and p strictly implies q, it does not follow that q is a belief of mine. For I might fail to see the implication or I simply might be epistemically perverse or I might be "wired" incorrectly (from birth or as the result of an injury).

What about justified belief? As it is stated above, CP (or CP*) is clearly false. Every necessary truth is entailed by every proposition. But one surely does not want to claim that S is justified in believing *every* necessary truth whenever S has *any* justified belief. In addition, some entailments might be beyond S's capacity to grasp. Finally, there might even be some contingent propositions that are beyond S's capacity to grasp which are entailed by some propositions that S does, indeed, grasp. And it might be thought that S is not entitled to believe anything that S cannot grasp.

But CP can easily be repaired. We can stipulate that the domain of the propositions in the generalization of CP includes only contingent propositions that are within S's capacity to grasp and that the entailment is "obvious" to S. The skeptic can agree to those restrictions because the skeptical scenarios are posited in such a way as to render it obvious that our ordinary beliefs are false in those scenarios, and it is taken to be a contingent claim that S is in the actual circumstances as described in the antecedent.

There is one other required clarification of the restricted version of CP. "Justified belief" is ambiguous. It could be used to refer to a species of actually held beliefs—namely, those actually held beliefs of S that are justified. Or it could refer to propositions that S is entitled to hold—regardless of whether S does indeed hold them. If CP is to be acceptable, "justified belief" must be used so as to mean the latter for a reason already cited, that is, belief does not transmit through entailment.

We are now in a position to ask: Does the restricted form of closure hold regarding what we are *entitled* to believe—even if we don't, in fact, believe it? There appears to be a perfectly general argument for the restricted version. Let p entail q, and *let us suppose* that S is entitled to believe that p iff S has (nonoverridden) grounds that make p sufficiently likely to be true:[11]

1. If S is entitled to believe that p, then S has (nonoverridden) grounds that make p sufficiently likely to be true. [by the supposition]
2. If S has (nonoverridden) grounds that make p sufficiently likely to be true, then S has (nonoverridden) grounds making q sufficiently likely to be true. [because p entails q]
3. If S is entitled to believe that p, then S has (nonoverridden) grounds making q sufficiently likely to be true. [from 1,2]
4. If S has (nonoverridden) grounds making q sufficiently likely to be true, then S is entitled to believe that q. [by the supposition]
5. Therefore, if S is entitled to believe that p, S is entitled to believe that q. [from 2,3]

The supposition mentioned above seems plausible given that the debate over the merits of Academic Skepticism employs an evidentialist (as opposed to an externalist) account of justification. Premise 2 is key; and in spite of the fact that the probabilities (whether subjective or objective) transmit through entailment, it has been challenged. Fred Dretske and others have produced cases in which they believe CP fails and fails precisely because Premise 2 is false.[12]

Dretske writes:

[S]omething's being a zebra implies that it is not a mule ... cleverly disguised by the zoo authorities to look like a zebra. Do you know that these animals are not mules cleverly disguised? If you are tempted to say "Yes" to this question, think a moment about what reasons you have, what evidence you can produce in favor of this claim. The evidence you *had* for thinking them zebras has been effectively neutralized, since it does not count toward their *not* being mules cleverly disguised to look like zebras.[13]

Dretske is speaking of "knowledge" rather than beliefs to which one is entitled, but that seems irrelevant since the issue concerns the supposed lack of a sufficient source of evidence or reasons for the claim that the animal is not a cleverly disguised mule. In other words, Dretske grants that S has (nonoverridden) grounds that make it sufficiently likely that the animals are zebras, but he holds that S does not have (nonoverridden) grounds making it sufficiently likely that the animals are not cleverly disguised mules because S's evidence for the former has been "effectively neutralized."

Let us grant that S's evidence for the claim that they are zebras can not be used to show that they are not cleverly disguised mules. Would that require giving up the argument for CP? I do not think so. To see that, recall that Premise 2 claimed merely that whenever S had (nonoverridden) grounds that make p sufficiently likely to be true, then S has (nonoverridden) grounds for making q sufficiently likely to be true. It did *not* require that it be the very same grounds in both cases. Dretske's purported counterexample seems to require that CP implies that the adequate source of evidence is the same for both propositions. Thus, letting "xRy" mean that x provides an adequate evidence for y, the counterexample depends upon assuming that if closure holds between p and q, then the evidence "path" must look like this:

Pattern 1   . . . Rp

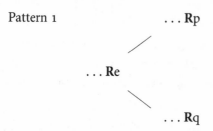

. . . Re

. . . Rq

Evidence paths specify what propositions serve as good enough reasons, *ceteris paribus,* for believing other propositions. Dretske is supposing that the very same evidence, e, that I have for p must be adequate for q whenever p entails q.

No doubt this constraint sometimes correctly portrays the relevant evidential relationships when some proposition, p, entails some other proposition, q. For example, suppose I have adequate evidence for the claim that Anne has two brothers, then it would seem that the very same evidence would be adequate for believing that Anne has at least one brother. The defender of CP, and more particularly the Academic Skeptic, could point out that closure need not require that type of evidence path in all cases in which one proposition entails another.

There are two other possibilities for instantiating closure that are captured by Premise 2 that can be depicted as follows:

Pattern 2   . . . ReRp . . . Rq

Pattern 3   . . . Re (where e includes q) Rp

In Pattern 2 cases there is some adequate evidence, e, for p; and p, itself, is the adequate evidence for q, since p strictly implies q. For example, if I have adequate evidence for believing that 2 is a prime number, I can use that proposition as an adequate reason for believing that there is at least one even prime. Indeed, consider any belief arrived at as a result of deductive inference. In such a case, we legitimately infer the entailed proposition from the conjunction of the premises that entails it. The plausibility of the famous Gettier cases depends upon Pattern 2 type cases in which closure holds. Gettier says:

> . . . for any proposition p, if S is justified in believing p, and p entails q, and S deduces q from p and accepts q as a result of this deduction, then S is justified in believing q.[14]

In Pattern 3 cases the order of the evidence is reversed because q serves as part of the evidence for p. For example, I am justified in believing that water is present if I am justified in believing that there is present a clear, odorless, watery-tasting and watery-looking fluid at standard temperature and pressure. This pattern is typical of abductive inferences. In addition, there are cases in which some contraries of h need to be eliminated prior to h's being justified. For example, in the zebra-in-the-zoo case, if I had some reason to think that the animals were cleverly disguised mules, then it could be argued that such a contrary would need to be eliminated *before* I would be justified in believing that the animals were zebras.

The crucial point for the discussion here is that granting that there is no Pattern 1 type evidence path available to S in the zebra-in-the-zoo case does not require relinquishing premise 2 in the general argument for CP. The reason is simply that CP does not entail that there is pattern 1 type evidence available in every case in which p entails q. Indeed, it could be suggested that the animals looking like zebras in a pen marked "zebras" is, *ceteris paribus*, adequate evidence to justify the claim that they are zebras; and once S is entitled to believe that the animals are zebras, S can, using the principle stated by Gettier, justifiably deduce that they are not cleverly disguised mules. That is, S can employ an evidence path like that depicted in Pattern 2.[15] Hence, the counterexamples to closure appear to fail.

In addition to the purported counterexamples to closure, there are some general theories of knowledge in which closure fails that should be examined. Robert Nozick's account of knowledge is the best such example. Roughly, his account is this:

S knows that p *iff*:

1. S believes p;
2. p is true;
3. If p were true, S would believe p;
4. If p were not true, S would not believe p.

This account is often referred to as a tracking account of knowledge since when S knows that p, S's beliefs track p.[16]

There is one important clarification of conditions 3 and 4 discussed by Nozick, namely, that the method by which S acquires the belief must be held constant from the actual world to the possible world. A doting grandmother might know that her grandchild is not a thief on the basis of very good evidence, but she would still believe that he wasn't a thief, even if he were, because she loves him. So, we must require that the grandmother use the same method in both the actual and the near possible worlds, for otherwise condition 4 would exclude cases of knowledge.

This is not the place to provide a full examination of Nozick's account of knowledge.[17] What is crucial for our discussion is that it is easy to see that Closure will fail for knowledge in just the kind of case that the Academic Skeptic is putting forward because of condition 4. Suppose S knows that there is a chair before her. Would she know that she is not in a skeptical scenario in which it merely appears that there is a chair? If the fourth condition were true, she would not know that because if she were in such a scenario, she would be fooled into thinking that she wasn't. Thus, either condition 4 is too strong or CP fails.

There are some reasons for thinking that condition 4 is too strong. Consider a relatively simple case in which S seems to have knowledge but condition 4 does not obtain. S looks at a thermometer that is displaying the temperature as 72 degrees. The thermometer is working perfectly and S comes to believe that the temperature is 72 degrees by reading the thermometer and coming to believe what it says. But if the temperature were not 72, suppose that something affected the thermometer in a way that made it read 72, so that by employing the same method (looking at the thermometer and coming to believe what it read) S would still believe that it was 72. (One could imagine all kinds of circumstances that would have that causal result. A comical one: Imagine a lizard that is now sleeping on the thermometer that would stir were the temperature to rises, thus dislodging a small rock that hits the thermometer breaking the mercury column in a way that makes the thermometer still read 72.)

Or consider this case in the literature: You put a glass of ice-cold lemonade on a picnic table in your backyard. You go inside and get a telephone call from a friend and talk for half an hour. When you hang up you remember that you had left the ice-cold lemonade outside exposed to the hot sun and come to believe that it isn't ice-cold anymore. It would seem that you could know that, even if in some near world a friend of yours who just happened to be walking by noticed the glass and, happening to have a cooler full of ice with him, put the glass of lemonade in the cooler to keep it ice-cold for you. Thus, if the lemonade were still ice-cold, you would believe that it wasn't.[18]

The moral of these cases seems to be that S can know that p even if there are some near possible worlds in which p is false but S still believes that p (employing the same method of belief formation). Perhaps what is required for knowledge is that the method work in this world—exactly as it is—even if the method would fail were there to be some slight variation in the actual world.

Further Clarification of Closure

In order to clarify CP further, it would be useful to contrast it with a stronger principle. I have already pointed out that in some cases some contraries of h need to be eliminated before h becomes justified. Suppose that the skeptic requires that all contraries to h be eliminated before h is justified. That is *much* stronger than CP because CP is compatible with Pattern 1 and Pattern 2 type evidential relationships; and in neither is every contrary to h eliminated prior to h.

If that requirement were accepted, there is a really easy route to Academic Skepticism. Consider any two contraries, c_1 and c_2. In order to be justified in believing c_1, S would first have to eliminate c_2. And in order to be justified in believing that c_2, S would first have to eliminate c_1. So, of course, S could never either be justified in believing c_1 or be justified in believing c_2. So, there would be a too quick and too dirty argument for skepticism, because, in so far as skepticism remains an interesting philosophical position, the skeptic cannot depart so outrageously from our ordinary epistemic practices.

Note that even EAD, although requiring that we be able to reject or neutralize every ground for doubt, does not require that we do that *before* we are justified in believing an hypothesis. Indeed, EAD allows for the possibility that we could use h, itself, or something that h justifies, as the basis for rejecting or neutralizing some grounds for doubt.

Consideration of CP2

Now, with those clarifications of CP (and EAD) in mind, we can turn to CP2. It claims that we are not justified in denying the skeptical hypothesis—in other words that we are not justified in believing that we are not being deceived. Is that premise true?

It is tempting to say "yes." After all, the skeptical scenarios are developed in such a way that it is supposed that we *could not* tell that we were being deceived. For example, we are asked to consider that there is an Evil Genius "so powerful" that it could (1) make me believe that there were hands when there were none and (2) make it such that I *could* not detect the illusion. But we must be very careful here. The skeptic cannot require that in order for S to know (or be justified in assenting to) something, say x, that if x were false, she would not still assent to x. We have just seen (while examining Nozick's account of knowledge) that this requirement is too strong. So the mere fact that there could be skeptical scenarios in which S still believes that she is not in such a scenario cannot provide the skeptic with a basis for thinking that she fails to know that she is not (actually) in a skeptical scenario. But even *more important*, were that a requirement of knowledge (or justification), then we have seen that closure would fail and, consequently, the basis for the first premise in the CP-style argument for Academic Skepticism would be forfeited.[19]

In addition, we have also seen that if CP is true, and it did seem to be true, then there is one evidence pattern between entailing and entailed propositions that might prove useful to the epistemist at this point in the discussion. If S could be justified in believing some proposition that entailed the denial of the skeptical hypothesis, then S could be justified in denying that hypothesis by employing evidence Pattern 2. Indeed, as G.E. Moore suggested, what is to prevent the epistemist from claiming that S is justified in denying that she is in a skeptical scenario because S is justified in believing that she has hands and CP is true?[20] A plausible answer to Moore seems to be something like this: The issue that is under dispute is whether S is justified in assenting to (or knows that) she has hands. Thus, the epistemist cannot reject CP2 by assuming the denial of the conclusion of the skeptical argument. All well and good. But the same sauce covers the gander, and the skeptic cannot claim as the reason for CP2 that *since* S is not justified in believing that she has hands, she cannot avail herself of that as her reason for being justified in believing that she is not in a skeptical scenario.

So, what reason can the skeptic give for CP2? I do not know of one that is both consistent with the defense of CP and that does not beg the question. That is not to say that CP2 is false. Far from it. Perhaps it is true. The issue is whether we are justified in accepting or rejecting it. It seems that in order to accept CP2 and CP, the skeptic would have to assert that S is not justified in believing that she has hands because evidence Pattern 2 depicts one way in which S could be justified in denying the skeptical scenario.[21]

I had mentioned earlier that there seemed to be only three responses available when confronting the CP-style argument for Academic Skepticism: accept the conclusion, reject one or both of the premises, or deny the validity of the argument. The fourth alternative is simply to point out that given the required defense of CP1, there appears to be no good argument for CP2.

Of course, there is the possibility that there is also no good argument to the conclusion that we do have knowledge of C-type propositions. Some might think that the Academic Skeptic wins in such a standoff. But recall that what distinguishes the Academic Skeptic from the Pyrrhonian Skeptic is that only the Academic Skeptic assents to the claim that we can not have knowledge. The Pyrrhonian Skeptic withholds judgment regarding whether we can have knowledge. And in a standoff, the Pyrrhonian would seem to have the appropriate attitude.

Before turning briefly to Pyrrhonism, there are a couple of loose ends that should be tied up. First, I want to briefly discuss EAD-style skepticism, and second, I want to look at one quite popular diagnosis of the CP-style argument in order to see whether it correctly portrays the dispute between the Academic Skeptic and the Epistemist.

4. Cartesian(EAD)-Style Arguments for Academic Skepticism

Mercifully, this section can be brief because we can apply the lessons learned in the discussion of CP-style arguments to an evaluation of EAD-style arguments. First, it should be clear that the general argument for CP cannot be used as a model for a general argument for EAD. The argument for CP depended crucially on the fact that h entailed ~sk. (That is what provided the basis for premise 2 in the general argument for CP.) As we saw, the negation of a genuine ground for doubt need not be entailed by h. So, the skeptic has a much harder task of motivating EAD.

But let us grant that some argument could be provided that makes EAD plausible. The same dialectical issues that we have considered in discussing potential counterexamples to CP will recur regarding EAD. Reconsider the zebra-in-the-zoo case. This time instead of the (contrary) proposition "the animals (I am seeing) are cleverly disguised mules," consider the proposition "there are cleverly disguised mules within my perceptual field," which according to EAD would have to be rejected or neutralized. If the evidence I had for believing that the animals were zebras wasn't adequate to deny the former, it is certainly not adequate for denying the latter. So the EAD skeptic will have to appeal to the analogs of Pattern 2 and Pattern 3 type cases in order to save the principle from a Dretske-like counterexample. Thus, this skeptic would be in the same dialectical situation as the CP-style skeptic because she must provide a basis for thinking that the second premise in her argument is compatible with a defense of EAD against Dretske-like objections that does not beg the question or appeal to a requirement that all grounds for doubt must be eliminated prior to a proposition being justified.

To sum up: The EAD skeptic is in a worse dialectical position than the CP skeptic. Whatever problems are associated with CP skepticism transfer to EAD skepticism and, in addition, there appears to be no plausible general argument for EAD, while there was one for CP.

5. Contextualism and Academic Skepticism

Contextualists have developed a variety of sophisticated approaches to Academic Skepticism, but what they all share is the view that the truth of sentences attributing or denying knowledge or the possession of adequate evidence to someone will vary according to some features of the context.[22] For example, one context can be such that someone, S, must satisfy relatively high standards of evidence in order to have knowledge or beliefs worthy of assent, and hence can truly be said to lack knowledge on the basis of evidence, e. While in another context, lower standards apply so that with the very same evidence, e, S can have knowledge. Just as my height could be such that in one context I'm tall and in another I'm not tall even though I remain the same height, my evidence could be such that in one context I have knowledge based upon that evidence and in another I do not have knowledge based upon the same evidence. "S knows that p" and "S does not know that p" can both be true because the truth value of each utterance depends in part upon the standards appropriate to the context in which the sentences are uttered.[23] So, in the ordinary context, S might have a justified belief because it is not required that the skeptical hypothesis be eliminated first, whereas in the more demanding "skeptical context" S would not be justified because S has not yet eliminated the skeptical hypothesis.

There are two questions to ask: Is this version of contextualism about knowledge or justified belief true? And will its truth shed light on Academic Skepticism?

In answering the first question, it could be argued that such a version of contextualism with regard to the attribution of virtually *any* property is true. Suppose that Mr. Lax says that Sam is happy. We discover that Lax is using "happy" to mean that a person is happy just in case he/she has had more happy moments than unhappy moments during a lifetime. Mr. Stringent demurs. For him, a person is happy only if he/she hardly ever experiences an unhappy moment.

Who is right about whether or not Sam is happy? Contextualists would say that they both are. But it is crucial to note that, given that each person recognizes that the other is applying different standards, Mr. Lax and Mr. Stringent can agree that, *given what Lax means*, Sam is happy and that, *given what Stringent means*, Sam is not happy.

The predicates "having knowledge," "having adequate evidence," "being justified," and the like, seem to me to be like most other predicates in this respect: Within a wide but nonarbitrary range of standards, speakers can legitimately demand that S have more or less of the relevant evidence for p before they will agree that "S knows that p" or "S has adequate evidence for p." So, the answer to the first question about the truth of contextualism seems to be: Contextualism about knowledge attributions is true. It is just one instance of the general truth that standards for the application of a term vary within a wide but nonarbitrary range according to the context of application.

Let us turn to the second and *much* more philosophically interesting question: Does the truth of this version of contextualism shed any light on Academic Skepticism? If it did, then the correct way to diagnose the dispute between the skeptic and the epistemist would be to note that the epistemist is using a lax standard and the skeptic a more stringent one. Having one's ordinary cake is compatible with eating one's skeptical cake, because in the ordinary context we do have knowledge, but as standards rise to those demanded by the skeptics, we do not have knowledge.

In response, it could plausibly be objected that this is *not* the proper diagnosis of the disagreement between the skeptic and the epistemist. The view that we are considering holds that in the skeptical context, S must first eliminate the skeptical hypothesis, but that in the ordinary context, S's epistemic burden is much more relaxed. Thus, there would be no genuine dispute between the skeptic and the epistemist—just as there is no real disagreement between Mr. Lax and Mr. Stringent about Sam's happiness.

That would be an elegant "solution" were the epistemist and the skeptic to agree that it is all a matter of whose standards one is employing. But is that right? What the skeptic claims is that we don't know what we ordinarily claim to know. We don't know C-type propositions. It's our ordinary knowledge claims that are false. If the skeptic were merely claiming that on *her* standards we don't know, the skeptic's claims—like those of Mr. Stringent—can be granted and then promptly ignored because nothing that we formerly believed that we knew turns out to be not known. The scope of our knowledge or justified beliefs in the ordinary context is left intact.

Thus, the parallel with the case of Sam's putative happiness seems to break down. In that case, Mr. Stringent would grant that Mr. Lax was correct *given what Lax meant by "happy."* But the skeptic will not grant that the epistemist is correct. The skeptic reasons that the epistemist doesn't know that h, *even given what the epistemist means by "know."* Both the epistemist and the skeptic accept CP, but the skeptic thinks that there *cannot* be any evidence for ~sk. Thus, h could not be known no matter whose standards apply.

The issue seems to boil down to this: In the ordinary context is it true—as the Academic Skeptic claims—that in order to know that there are hands, we must first eliminate the skeptical hypothesis? The epistemist might argue as follows: Suppose we are looking at Dretske's zebras and someone asks, "Do you know that those are not cleverly disguised aliens from a recently discovered planet outside our solar system? Or that they are not newly invented super-robots? Or that they are not members of the lost tribe of Israel who have been hiding out from the Assyrians disguised as zebras since the eighth century B.C. (They've had lots of time to perfect the disguise!)" Of course those are far-fetched; and even if someone advancing those alternatives happens to believe them, there appears to be no reason why one should have to rise to the bait and eliminate those alternatives prior to being justified in believing that the animals are zebras. And isn't the skeptical hypothesis—that we are not in the actual world but rather in one which just seems identical to it—just as far-fetched?

Now a contextualist might object as follows: This portrayal of contextualism is too restricted. The context not only establishes more or less stringent standards for knowledge or the possession of adequate evidence, but also establishes what is to count as a relevant alternative that must be eliminated prior to the acceptance of h. For example, the contextualist could claim that the skeptic can make the skeptical hypothesis relevant by doing something—perhaps merely mentioning it in a serious tone of voice.

The epistemist can reply to this objection by granting that although the skeptic can *try* to expand the set of relevant evidence, she will not always succeed. In Dretske's zebra-in-the zoo case, if there really were some evidence, however slight, for the claim that the animals are painted mules, then Mr. Stringent could legitimately require that S rule out that possibility prior to truly claiming that he knows that the animals are zebras. In parallel fashion, if there really were some evidence, however slight, that there is an evil genius making it merely appear that there are hands, then, and only then, could the skeptic legitimately require that S eliminate that possibility prior to being justified in believing that there are hands.

In other words, the epistemist will claim that the range of relevant alternatives is bounded by those propositions for which there is some, even minimal, evidence. It is a context-invariant feature of knowledge attributions that the relevant evidence does not include the denial of contraries for which there is no evidence whatsoever. The issue, according to the epistemist, is whether our ordinary knowledge claims are true—not whether they would be true in some context with requirements more stringent that those that are ordinarily applied.

6. PYRRHONIAN SKEPTICISM

As mentioned at the beginning of this essay, what distinguishes Pyrrhonian Skepticism from Academic Skepticism is that the former does not deny that we can have knowledge. For to deny something is merely to assent to its negation and the Pyrrhonian refrains from assenting to every "nonevident" proposition. Now, of course, a primary question concerns the scope of the nonevident.[24] But to try to resolve that is not the purpose of this essay. For our discussion I think we can suppose that a sufficient condition for some proposition being nonevident obtains whenever there can legitimately be disagreement about it. And, taking the cue from our discussion about Academic Skepticism, we can also stipulate that there can be legitimate disagreement about some proposition if there is some evidence for it and some evidence against it. So, the question is whether the proposition *S can have knowledge that there are hands* can be the subject of legitimate disagreement.

Putting the matter that way makes the answer obvious. There are arguments for Academic Skepticism which have some plausibility, and some plausible objections to those arguments which support the Epistemist's view. Plausible arguments for something constitute some evidence for it. So, we can safely conjecture that it is not evident that we have knowledge. The primary question then becomes this: What prompted the Pyrrhonian to withhold assent to all nonevident propositions?

The Pyrrhonians would practice what they called the "modes." Like piano exercises for the fingers that would result in semiautomatic responses to the printed notes on a sheet of music, the modes were mental exercises that would result in semiautomatic responses to claims being made by the dogmatists—those who assent to the nonevident. When the results of perception were introduced to settle a nonevident matter—say the actual color of an object (as opposed to how it appeared to someone), they would point out some or all of the following:[25]

1. Members of *different* species of animals probably perceived colors quite differently because their eyes are constructed differently.
2. Members of the *same* species would have different perceptions of the color depending upon such things as the condition of their eyes, the nature of the medium of perception (varying light conditions for example), and the order in which objects were perceived.

Being reminded of the relativity of perception could incline a person to refrain from assenting to judgements of perception, when those judgements were about the "real" properties of the objects. Now, perhaps a careful analysis of what is meant by "real" properties coupled with a Cartesian-like answer to some of the doubts raised earlier in the *Meditations* would suffice to respond to the Pyrrhonian concerning the relativity of our senses. For example, if we took the "real" color of objects to be that property of the object, whatever it is, that produces perceptions of a certain sort under "normal" circumstances, and if we could distinguish (as Descartes suggested) normal from abnormal circumstances, then we might have a basis for resisting the Pyrrhonian modes concerning perception. But be that as it may, whether we can have knowledge of C-type propositions is not a matter that is potentially resolvable by appeal to our senses. It will only be resolved if either the Epistemist or the Academic Skeptic has a compelling argument. Thus, the question here is whether reasoning can settle matters.

Perhaps the most influential passage in the corpus of the Pyrrhonian literature, the "Five Modes of Agrippa" in Sextus Empiricus's *Outlines of Pyrrhonism*, seeks to answer that question. Although the chapter title mentions five modes, two of them repeat those found elsewhere and are similar to the ones just discussed concerning perception. They are the modes of discrepancy and relativity and these two modes are important here because they provide the background for understanding the description of the three modes concerning reasoning. Specifically, it is presumed that the relevant object of inquiry is subject to legitimate dispute and that reasoning is employed to resolve the dispute. The issue before us then is whether reasoning can legitimately lead to assent. Sextus writes:

> The Mode based upon regress *ad infinitum* is that whereby we assert that the thing adduced as a proof of the matter proposed needs a further proof, and this again another, and so on *ad infinitum*, so that the consequence is suspension [of assent], as we possess no starting-point for our argument. ... We have the Mode based upon hypothesis when the Dogmatists, being forced to recede *ad infinitum*, take as their starting-point something which they do not establish but claim to assume as granted simply and without demonstration. The Mode of circular reasoning is the form used when the proof itself which ought to establish the matter of inquiry requires confirmation derived from the matter; in this case, being unable to assume either in order to establish the other, we suspend judgement about both.[26]

It is important to keep in mind that the modes were practices meant to discourage and, perhaps, reform the dogmatists who did assent to matters that were still the subject of legitimate dispute. These modes were designed not to undermine the utility of reasoning. Indeed, the Greek for "skeptic" is closely related to the verb "σκέπτομαι," which means "inquire." Thus, calling oneself a Pyrrhonian Skeptic did not imply a disregard for inquiry or reasoning. The modes were designed to dissuade a dogmatist from *assenting* on the basis of reasoning. They were not designed to inhibit reasoning.

Suppose that the dogmatist assents to something, say p, on the basis of a reason, say r. What the modes prescribe are ways of dealing with the dogmatist. Either one forces the dogmatist into an apparently never ending regress, or forces the dogmatist to beg the question, or forces the dogmatist to assert something arbitrarily.

As the quotation from Sextus suggests, the modes are based upon the claim that there are three possible patterns which any instance of reasoning can take. I will call the first pattern "infinitism." Today we commonly refer to the second account as "foundationalism." Finally, I will refer to the third possibility as "coherentism."

The so-called regress problem can be stated briefly in this way: There are only three possible patterns of reasoning. Either the process of producing reasons stops at a purported foundational proposition or it doesn't. If it does, then the reasoner is employing a foundationalist pattern. If it doesn't, then either the reasoning is circular, or it is infinite and nonrepeating. There are no other significant possibilities.[27] Thus, if none of these forms of reasoning can properly lead to assent, then no form can.

So, we must look briefly at the reasons that a Pyrrhonian might have for

thinking that infinitism, foundationalism, and coherentism are inherently incapable of providing an adequate basis for assent.[28]

7. FOUNDATIONALISM

Foundationalism comes in many forms. But all forms hold that the set of propositions can be partitioned into basic or nonbasic propositions. *Basic propositions*
have some autonomous bit of warrant that does not depend (at all) upon the
warrant of any other proposition.[29] *Nonbasic* propositions depend (directly or indirectly) upon basic propositions for all of their warrant.

The Pyrrhonian holds, I think, that a foundationalist cannot rationally practice
his foundationalism because it inevitably leads to arbitrariness, that is, asserting a
proposition which can legitimately be questioned but is, nevertheless, asserted
without being so scrutinized. It is important to remember that the Pyrrhonian is
not (and cannot consistently be) assenting to the claim that foundationalism is
false. A Pyrrhonian employing this mode would be attempting to show the epistemist that her so-called foundational proposition stands in need of further support.

Suppose that an inquirer, say Fred D'Foundationalist, has given some reasons
for his beliefs. Fred offers q (where q could be a conjunction) for his belief that
p, and he offers r (which could also be a conjunction) as his reason for q. Etc.
Now, being a foundationalist, Fred finally offers some basic proposition, say b, as
his reason for the immediately preceding belief. Sally D'Pyrrhonian asks Fred why
he believes that b is true. Sally adds the "is true" to make certain that Fred realizes
that she is not asking what causes Fred to believe that b. She wants to know why
Fred thinks that b is true. Now, Fred could respond by giving some reason for
thinking that b is true even if b is basic, because basic propositions could have
some nonautonomous warrant that depends upon the warrant of other propositions. But that is merely a delaying tactic since Fred is not a coherentist. In other
words, he might be able to appeal to the conjunction of some other basic propositions and the nonbasic propositions that they warrant as a reason for thinking
that b is true. But, Sally D'Pyrrhonian will ask whether he has any reason that
does not appeal to another member in the set of basic propositions for thinking
that each member in the set is true. If he says that he has none, then he is a closet
coherentist. Being a foundationalist, he must think that there is some warrant that
each basic proposition has that does not depend upon the warrant possessed by
any other proposition.

The crucial point to note here is that Sally can grant that the proposition has autonomous warrant but continue to press the issue, because she can ask Fred whether the possession of autonomous warrant is at all truth conducive. That is, she can ask whether a proposition with autonomous warrant is, *ipso facto*, at all likely to be true. If Fred says "yes," then the regress will have continued. For he has this reason for thinking that b is true: "b has autonomous warrant and propositions with autonomous warrant are somewhat likely to be true." If he says "no," then Sally can point out that he is being arbitrary, since she has asked why he thinks b is true and he has not been able to provide an answer.

Let us look at an example. Often it is held that first-person introspective reports are basic because they have some "privileged" status. My basic reason for thinking that there is an "external" object of a certain sort is that I am having an experience of a certain sort. Now, what Sally should ask is this: "Why do you think you are having an experience of that sort?" Or, again, to emphasize that she is not asking for an explanation of the etiology of Fred's belief that he is having an experience of that sort, she could ask: "Why do you think that the proposition 'I am having an experience of a certain sort' is true?"

The dilemma is that either Fred has a reason for thinking that proposition is true or he doesn't. If he does, then the regress has not stopped—*in practice*. If he doesn't, then he is being arbitrary—*in practice.*

Once again, it is crucial to recall that Pyrrhonians are *not* claiming that foundationalism is false. They could grant that some propositions do have autonomous warrant which is truth-conducive and that all other propositions depend for some of their warrant upon those basic propositions. What lies at the heart of their view is that there is a deep irrationality in being a practicing self-conscious foundationalist. The question to Fred can be put this way: On the assumption that you can not appeal to any other proposition, do you have any reason for thinking that b is true? Fred not only won't have any such reason for thinking b is true, given that constraint, he *can not* have one (if he remains true to his foundationalism). Arbitrariness seems inevitable. Of course, foundationalists typically realize this and, in order to avoid arbitrariness, tell some story (for example, about privileged access) that, if true, would provide a reason for thinking basic propositions are at least somewhat likely to be true. But then, the regress of reasons has continued.

8. COHERENTISM

At its base, coherentism holds that there are no propositions with autonomous warrant. But it is important to note that coherentism comes in two forms. What

I choose to call the "warrant-transfer form" responds to the regress problem by suggesting that the propositions are arranged in a circle and that warrant is transferred within the circle—just as basketball players standing in a circle pass the ball from one player to another.[30] I could, for example, reason that it rained last night by calling forth my belief that there is water on the grass, and I could reason that there is water (as opposed to some other liquid, say glycerin, that looks like water) on the grass by calling forth my belief that it rained last night.

Long ago, Aristotle pointed out that this process of reasoning could not resolve matters. As he put it: This is a "simple way of proving anything."[31] The propositions in the circle might be mutually probability enhancing, but the point is that we could just as well have circular reasoning to the conclusion that it did not rain last night because the liquid is not water and the liquid is not water because it did not rain last night. In this fashion anything could be justified—too simply! It is ultimately arbitrary which set of mutually probability enhancing propositions we believe because there is no basis for preferring one over the other.

The warrant-transfer coherentist could reply to this objection by claiming that there is some property, P, possessed by the propositions in one of the two competing circles that is not present in the other and the presence of that property makes the propositions in one and only one of the circles worthy of assent. For example, in one and only one of the circles are there propositions that we actually believe, or perhaps believe spontaneously.[32] But, then, it seems clear that the warrant-transfer coherentist has adopted a form of foundationalism, since he is now claiming that all and only the propositions in circles with P have some autonomous bit of warrant. And, all that we have said about the dilemma facing the foundationalist transfers immediately. Is the possession of P truth-conducive or not? If it is . . . You can see how that would go.

So much for the warrant-transfer version of coherentism. The second form of coherentism, what we can call the "warrant-emergent form" does not imagine the circle as consisting of propositions that transfer their warrant from one proposition to another. Rather, warrant for each proposition in the circle obtains because they are mutually probability enhancing. Coherence itself is the property in virtue of which each member of the set of propositions has warrant. Warrant emerges all at once, so to speak, from the weblike structure of the set of propositions. The coherentist can then argue that the fact that the propositions cohere provides each of them with some *prima facie* credibility.

This might initially seem to be a more plausible view since it avoids the circularity charge. But, aside from the fact that there are, again, just too many competing circles that are coherent, the coherentist has, once again, embraced foundationalism. The coherentist is now explicitly assigning some initial positive warrant to all of the individual propositions in a set of coherent propositions that does not depend upon the warrant of any other proposition in the set. In other words, he is assigning to them what we have called the autonomous bit of warrant and, once again, the dilemma facing the foundationalist returns.

9. INFINITISM

The third mode is designed to show the dogmatist that if he assents to some C-type proposition, p, and if he keeps providing new answers to the question "What reason do you have for x?" he will not have resolved whether p is true. For there is always another reason, one that has not already been employed, that needs to be given for a belief. A self-conscious infinitist would recognize that he should not assent to the proposition that he knows that p because he has not yet seen whether he can provide the required infinite set of nonrepeating reasons. Of course, since he also doesn't know whether there is such an infinite set of reasons available, he should not assent to the proposition that he doesn't know C-type propositions. Again, withholding seems to be the apt attitude.

As far as I can tell, infinitism has never been seriously considered as a model of reasoning suitable for the dogmatic epistemist. Some philosophers have argued that beliefs are infinitely revisable because they can always be overridden, but that is not what is essential to infinitism.[33] What is essential is the claim that reasons for a belief, p, must be infinite and nonrepeating if S knows that p. Since it is clear that such a process can never be completed, dogmatic epistemists could not endorse infinitism. (I should note, parenthetically, that this does *not* imply that infinitism is an inappropriate model for the Pyrrhonian Skeptic or that it cannot be practiced rationally.[34])

10. (VERY) SHORT ASSESSMENT OF PYRRHONISM

It appears that the Pyrrhonist is correct that no process of reasoning is such that it can resolve matters concerning what is nonevident. Thus, withholding assent about whether we can or can not have knowledge of C-type propositions seems plausible. Is that a surprising result? I should think many foundationalists and coherentists will find it so.

NOTES

I wish to thank Anne Ashbaugh for her help with this essay.

1. For discussions of the relationships between belief and knowledge see Peter Unger, *Ignorance: A Case for Scepticism* (Oxford: Oxford University Press, 1975), 63; Norman Malcolm, *Knowledge and Certainty* (Englewood Cliffs, N.J.: Prentice-Hall, 1963), 58–72; Colin Radford, "Knowledge—By Example," *Analysis* 27 (1966): 1–11; and Keith Lehrer, *Theory of Knowledge* (Boulder, Colo.: Westview, 2000), 124–125.

2. There is no readily available term. A natural one would be "cognitivist," but that term already has a very specific application in ethics.

3. Sextus Empiricus, *Outlines of Pyrrhonism*, trans. R. G. Bury (Cambridge, Mass.: Harvard University Press, 1967), I, 226–230.

4. Ibid., I, 226.

5. For a contrasting discussion of the same issue, see Barry Stroud, *The Significance of Philosophical Scepticism* (Oxford: Clarendon, 1984), chap. 1.

6. Descartes, *Meditations on First Philosophy*, in *Philosophical Works of Descartes*, ed. Elizabeth Haldane and G. R. T. Ross (New York: Dover, 1931), I, 147.

7. In the "First Meditation," Descartes does not suggest a potential ground for doubt that he rejects unless, perhaps, that he is mad (insane). He asks whether he could be mad, like people who imagine that they are kings when they are poor, or that they are clothed when they are naked, or that they are pumpkins or made of glass. His answer is, "But they are mad, and I should not be any the less insane were I to follow examples so extravagant" (145). That is a puzzling response. Is the evil genius hypothesis less "extravagant?" Or from his point of view, is the possibility that his creator was something other than a perfect god any less extravagant? Nevertheless, he at least seems to be giving reasons for rejecting that grounds for doubt. Of course, later in the *Meditations* he rejects the claim that his maker might have been less than perfect.

For an interesting discussion of rejecting or neutralizing the skeptic's objections, see Lehrer, *Theory of Knowledge*, 131–136.

8. In the Argument from Closure, x: h and y: ~sk, and sk: ~h & in the switched world it appears that h.

9. For the sake of clarity, it is important to point out that the restoring proposition could itself have genuine grounds for doubt, so that even if (r & d) did not reduce the warrant for x, [(r&d) & d¹] could defeat the justification for x since d¹ would defeat the restoring effect of r. But then, (d & d¹) would be a new ground for doubt. So, we need not include this epicycle.

10. Two propositions, {x, y}, are contraries just in case x entails ~y, but ~x does not entail y. Here are some examples: The ball is red all over, the ball is yellow all over; X is an aunt, X is an uncle. More to the point, h and sk are contraries since h entails ~sk, but ~h does not entail sk. For example, it could be the case that there is no hand

before me and I am not in a switched-world (or it doesn't appear that there is a hand before me).

11. The probability could be either subjective or objective. The reason for including "nonoverridden" in the supposition is that it would not be sufficient for S to be entitled to believe something if S only had good enough grounds to render a proposition sufficiently likely to be true because S might also have counterevidence that overrides those positive grounds.

12. Robert Audi, *Belief, Justification and Knowledge* (Belmont, Calif.: Wadsworth, 1988), 77.

13. Fred Dretske, "Epistemic Operators," *Journal of Philosophy* 67 (1970): 1015–1016.

14. Edmund Gettier, "Is Knowledge True Justified Belief?" *Analysis* 23 (1963): 122. For the sake of employing consistent terminology, I have changed "P" to "p" and "Q" to "q."

15. I have argued for that in *Certainty: A Refutation of Scepticism* (Minneapolis: University of Minnesota Press, 1981); "Skepticism and Closure: Why the Evil Genius Argument Fails," *Philosophical Topics* 23, no. 1 (1995), 213–236; and "Contextualism and the Real Nature of Academic Skepticism," *Philosophical Issues* 10 (2000): 108–116.

16. Robert Nozick, *Philosophical Explanations* (Cambridge, Mass.: Harvard University Press, 1981), 172–187.

17. For a full discussion of Nozick's account of knowledge, see Steven Luper-Foy, *The Possibility of Knowledge* (Totowa, N.J.: Rowman & Littlefield, 1987).

18. Jonathan Vogel, "Tracking, Closure and Inductive Knowledge," in Luper-Foy, *The Possibility of Knowledge*, 206.

19. It is crucial to note that the truth of CP does not depend upon the antecedent being fulfilled.

20. G. E. Moore, "Certainty," *Philosophical Papers* (New York: Collier, 1962), 242.

21. The claim here is not that the evidential relationship between h and ~sk is such that S must use Pattern 2. The claim is merely that such a path is available.

22. Much of the material in this section incorporates material from my article "Contextualism and the Real Nature of Academic Skepticism."

23. This is essentially the view put forth by Stewart Cohen in "Knowledge, Context and Social Standards," *Synthese* 73 (1987): 3–26, and his "How to Be a Fallibilist," *Philosophical Perspectives* 2 (1988): 91–123; David Lewis in "Elusive Knowledge," *Australasian Journal of Philosophy* 74 (1996): 549–567; and Keith DeRose in "Solving the Skeptical Problem," *Philosophical Review* 104 (1995): 1–52, and his "Contextualism and Knowledge Attributions," *Philosophy and Phenomenological Research* 52 (1992): 913–929.

24. This issue is fully discussed in Myles Burnyeat and Michael Frede, *The Original Sceptics: A Controversy* (Indianapolis: Hackett, 1997).

25. Sextus Empiricus, *Outlines of Pyrrhonism*, I, 40–128.

26. Ibid., 166–169.

27. Strictly speaking, there is a fourth possibility, namely that there are foundational propositions *and* that there are an infinite number of propositions between the foundational one and the one for which reasons are initially being sought. Interestingly, such a hybrid view might be indistinguishable in practice from infinitism and hence not subject to the "foundationalist's dilemma" to be discussed later. Thus, I think for our purposes we can treat this as a form of infinitism.

28. These are my own glosses on what I take to be the best arguments. I do not claim that the Pyrrhonians gave these very arguments.

29. I put it that way in order to make clear that foundationalism can embrace some-aspects of coherentism. Propositions with only minimal justification can mount up, so to speak, by gaining extra credibility. Thus, the definition of foundationalism includes both weak and strong foundationalism as characterized by Laurence BonJour in "Can Empirical Knowledge Have a Foundation?"

30. For further discussion of these two forms of coherentism, see Ernest Sosa's "The Raft and the Pyramid," *Midwest Studies in Philosophy* 5 (1980): 3–25, and Laurence Bon-Jour "Can Empirical Knowledge Have a Foundation?"

31. Aristotle, *Posterior Analytics*, I, iii, 73a5.

32. This is the suggestion put forward by Laurence BonJour in *The Structure of Empirical Knowledge* (Cambridge, Mass.: Harvard University Press, 1985).

33. See Charles Sanders Peirce, "Questions Concerning Certain Faculties Claimed for Man," *Collected Papers of Charles Sanders Peirce*, ed. Charles Hartshorne and Paul Weiss (Cambridge, Mass.: Belknap, 1965), vol. 5, bk. 2, 152–153.

34. Indeed, I think infinitism is the right "solution" to the regress problem and have so argued in "Human Knowledge and the Infinite Regress of Reasons," *Philosophical Perspectives*, vol. 13, ed. J. Tomberlin (1999), 297–325; "Why Not Infinitism?" in *Epistemology: Proceedings of the Twentieth World Congress in Philosophy*, ed. Richard Cobb-Stevens (2000), vol. 5, 199–208; and "How a Pyrrhonian Skeptic Might Respond to Academic Skepticism" in *The Skeptics: Contemporary Essays*, ed. Steven Luper (Burlington, Vt.: Ashgate, forthcoming). It is crucial to note that infinitism, if it is a solution, is a nondogmatic one, and the issue under consideration here is whether infinitism (or foundationalism or coherentism) can provide the dogmatist with a model that can lead to resolving matters.

CHAPTER 12

....

EPISTEMOLOGICAL
DUTIES

....

RICHARD FELDMAN

THE idea that people have epistemological or intellectual duties and requirements is widely accepted. Consider the following passage from John Locke:

> Faith is nothing but a firm assent of the mind: which if it be regulated, as is our duty, cannot be afforded to anything, but upon good reason; and so cannot be opposite to it. He that believes, without having any reason for believing, may be in love with his own fancies; but neither seeks truth as he ought, nor pays the obedience due his maker, who would have him use those discerning faculties he has given him, to keep him out of mistake and error. He that does not do this to the best of his power, however he sometimes lights on truth, is in the right but by chance; and I know not whether the luckiness of the accident will excuse the irregularity of his proceeding. This at least is certain, that he must be accountable for whatever mistakes he runs into: whereas he that makes use of the light and faculties God has given him, and seeks sincerely to discover truth, by those helps and abilities he has, may have this satisfaction in doing his duty as a rational creature, that though he should miss truth, he will not miss the reward of it. For he governs his assent right, and places it as he should, who in any case or matter whatsoever, believes or disbelieves, according as reason directs him. He that does otherwise, transgresses against his own light, and misuses those faculties, which were given him.[1]

It is reasonable to extract from this passage several ideas about what our duties as believers are. Locke says, first, that we have duty to "regulate our faith." His more specific idea is that it is our duty to put our faith in things only "upon good reason." The person who does as he should "believes or disbelieves as reason directs him." Thus, we are to regulate our faith as reason directs us, presumably by making proper use of reasons. If we take reasons to be the same as evidence, Locke's view is that our duty is to believe as our evidence indicates. A slightly different idea is also present in this passage. Locke says that we have a duty to "seek the truth." The difference between the duty to believe as reason directs and the duty to seek the truth will become apparent shortly.

In the widely discussed essay, "The Ethics of Belief," William K. Clifford sounds a similar theme. Clifford more explicitly than Locke links our duties to following our evidence. He writes: "It is wrong always, everywhere, and for any-one, to believe anything upon insufficient evidence."[2] A central example in the essay, concerning a shipowner who sends a ship to sea without properly investi-gating its seaworthiness, appears in a section entitled "The Duty of Inquiry." In the course of his discussion, Clifford frames some of his points in terms of the duties we all have to regulate our beliefs properly. In a passage that will not win him any political correctness awards, Clifford writes:

> It is not only the leader of men, statesmen, philosopher, or poet, that owes this bounden duty to mankind. Every rustic who delivers in the village alehouse his slow, infrequent sentences, may help to kill or keep alive the fatal superstitions which clog his race. Every hard-worked wife of an artisan may transmit to her children beliefs which shall knit society together, or rend it in pieces. No sim-plicity of mind, no obscurity of station, can escape the universal duty of ques-tioning all that we believe.[3]

Clifford seems to be endorsing something very similar to the first of the ideas found in the passage from Locke: a duty to believe as one's evidence dictates. But rather than explain this as a duty to God, Clifford says that it is a "duty to mankind." In his view, the well-being of society depends on our doing our duties as believers!

William James, in his famous essay "The Will to Believe," disputes Clifford's central claims. James's contention is that, for at least a certain class of proposi-tions, practical considerations can make belief proper even in the absence of ev-idence. He too frames part of his discussion in terms of our duties:

> There are two ways of looking at our duty in the matter of opinion,—ways entirely different, and yet ways about whose difference the theory of knowledge seems hitherto to have shown very little concern. *We must know the truth*; and *we must avoid error*,—these are our first and great commandments as would-be knowers; but they are not two ways of stating an identical commandment, they are two separable laws.[4]

This sounds similar to the second idea from the passage from Locke: our duty is to seek the truth. But James says that our duty is to *know* the truth. As we shall see, this detail makes a difference.

The idea that we have duties as believers is also prominent in the writings of some influential contemporary epistemologists, most notably Roderick Chisholm. Chisholm's specific claims varied over the years, but the central idea is illustrated by his remarks in the second edition of his *Theory of Knowledge*:

> Let us consider the concept of what might be called an "intellectual requirement." We may assume that every person is subject to a purely intellectual requirement—that of trying his best to bring it about that for every proposition *h* that he considers, he accepts *h* if and only if *h* is true. One might say that it is the person's responsibility or duty *qua* intellectual being. (But as a requirement it is only a *prima facie* duty; it may be, and usually is, overridden by other, nonintellectual requirements, and it may be fulfilled more or less adequately.)[5]

This passage from Chisholm introduces two ideas that will be important in this paper. Chisholm says that our duty is to *try* to believe all and only the truths among the propositions we consider. He does not say that it is our duty actually to believe the truths. The reason for this may have to do with the apparent involuntariness of belief. This complicates the discussion of epistemological duties significantly. Chisholm also says this epistemological (or intellectual) requirement can be overridden by others. His thought is that moral or prudential duties can outweigh epistemological duties. This also complicates the discussion.

In a recent paper, "The Epistemic Duty to Seek More Evidence," Richard J. Hall and Charles R. Johnson argue that you have an epistemic duty to seek more evidence about every proposition about which you are not certain.[6] This brings out another issue that will be important here, namely the difference between a duty merely to follow the evidence one already has and a duty that involves actions such as getting additional evidence.

These passages, and many others similar to them, provoke a variety of questions about epistemological duties. These questions will be the focus of this chapter.

1. What are our epistemological duties?

Some of the passages quoted above concern the idea that our epistemological duty is to believe as our evidence dictates. Chisholm says that out duty is to try to believe truths. But other writers suggest that our duties involve other activities, such as gathering evidence properly, seeking out a large quantity of evidence, and so on. I will defend the idea suggested by the words of Locke and Clifford that our epistemological duty is to believe as the evidence we have dictates.

2. What makes a duty *epistemological*?

Some of the quotations with which we began suggest that certain duties or obligations are *epistemological* (or *epistemic*) duties or obligations. Epistemological duties apparently differ from other sorts of duties, such as moral duties. This raises a question about what makes a particular duty an epistemological duty. My suggestion will be that a duty is epistemological if it is one we must carry out in order to be rational believers.

3. How do epistemological duties interact with other kinds of duties?

Chisholm, in the passage previously quoted, says that our intellectual duty to try to believe truths is usually overridden by other nonintellectual duties. The picture this suggests is that there are various kinds of duties, intellectual (or epistemological) duties being one such kind. These various duties can compete with one another, with one duty winning out. This picture raises numerous questions about what the other duties are and how the conflicts among the various duties are to be resolved. I will not discuss the resolution of such conflicts here, but I will make use of the possibility of conflicts in order to provide support for my answer to (2).

I. Duties and Requirements

Before turning to the questions just posed about epistemological duties, it will be helpful to say a little to clarify the idea of duties generally. What follows is far from a complete account, but it will at least provide some guidelines for the discussion that follows.

I will speak interchangeably of duties, requirements, and obligations. Although there may be reasons to find differences among these ideas, I believe that those differences will not be important here.

The Cambridge Dictionary of Philosophy defines a duty as follows: "What a person is obligated or required to do. Duties can be moral, legal, parental, occupational, etc."[7] On this usage, a certain potential bit of behavior has the property of being a duty (or being dutiful or obligatory or required) for a person. It does not, of course, follow that the person actually performed the required behavior: duties can go unfulfilled.

There are several points about this that warrant comment.

First, to say that a person has a duty to do a certain thing is to say something more than that it would be nice, or beneficial, or a good idea for the person to do that thing. It would be nice for me to say "good morning" to my neighbors when I see them as I leave for work, but few would say that I have a duty to be neighborly. My overall well-being might be improved slightly if I got a little more sleep, but it seems wrong to say that I have a duty to do so. Given the weather forecast, it probably is a good idea to mow the lawn today rather than put it off for another day. Still, presumably, I have no duty to mow the lawn. Something stronger than this must be present for there to be a duty.

Second, to say that a person has a duty to do a certain thing is to say some-thing weaker than that it is the overall best thing the person could do. Some duties are merely *prima facie* duties, and they can be outweighed by other duties. Thus, to say that a person has a duty to do a certain thing does not imply that the person does not have other duties that preclude doing that thing. Chisholm's remarks imply that epistemological duties can be outweighed by other non-epistemological duties. But conflicts between duties need not be limited to cases where the duties are of different kinds. For example, a person might have con-flicting *prima facie* moral duties.

Third, it is no easy task to say which behaviors rise to the level of duties. Consider a range of things that it would typically be good for a college teacher to do. Some of them are merely desirable: using examples that are apt to be of interest to students; telling jokes only if they are at least slightly amusing. Others seem more reasonably designated as duties: grading in a fair and consistent man-ner; giving assignments that are clear and reasonable. It is far from clear that the boundary between what is in some sense good or desirable and what is required is precise.

Fourth, trying to understand the source or basis of duties is also a source of difficulty. Some of the things that we term duties may have their basis in the explicit rules of an institution. If your university has a policy mandating that every faculty member have office hours every week, then perhaps each faculty member has a duty to do so. Legal duties have their source in the law. But other things that are often identified as duties seem not to arise from any institutional source. We might call these "natural" duties. Some would say that a parent has natural duties to care for his or her children. Epistemological duties would seem to lack any contractual or institutional source. We have not signed contracts that impose on us duties to form beliefs in any particular ways. There are no laws that impose epistemological duties on us. If we have any such duties, they arise in some other way.

One possibility, suggested by Hall and Johnson, is that we acquire duties by adopting certain goals or ends. They write: "If you accept a goal G, and action A is the best way of achieving G, then there is a sense in which you ought to do A or in which it would be rational for you to do A. We shall say that A is a *duty* relative to G."[8]

This account makes duties easier to come by than many philosophers would like. If a lecturer has the goal of getting her students to learn the course material, and using timely examples is the best way for her to do that, then, given Hall and Johnson's proposal, she has a duty (relative to that goal) to use timely examples. If I have the goal of having a well-manicured lawn, then, given their proposal, I have a duty to mow my lawn today. This proposal seems not to distinguish be-tween duties and lesser goods that best contribute toward desired ends. Of course, it is possible for them to deny that there is a distinction between duties and lesser goods and to say that there is a very weak *prima facie* duty in cases in which others would say that the behavior in question is merely the best way to achieve a desired end. It is difficult to see any decisive way to argue about this.

A different account, and one that I will rely on here, is that things of certain kinds, simply in virtue of being of that kind, have certain duties. Thus, for example, simply in virtue of being a parent, one has a duty to care for one's child. This is a parental duty. One has the duty even if one lacks the corresponding goals or desires. The law might also impose on parents a duty to care for their children. Hence, one could have both a legal and a parental duty to care for one's children. This approach leaves room to distinguish between behaviors that are merely desirable and those that are required. A parent who desires the well-being of his child may have a duty to provide basic care, but there can be things that best achieve this goal that are still not required. Unfortunately, nothing in the account as stated explains why some things are *prima facie* required and some are merely desirable. This will be left unexplained.

Although it would be good if more were said in general about duties, these remarks will suffice for present purposes.

II. EPISTEMOLOGICAL DUTIES, BROAD AND NARROW

There are several importantly different views about the sorts of epistemological duties we have. They can be arranged in a sort of hierarchy, starting with the conception that limits epistemological duties to duties to believe specific propositions and extends to conceptions that include various other kinds of behaviors associated with belief.

A. Duties to Believe

Some of the passages with which we began suggest that our epistemological duties are to have or avoid beliefs of certain sorts. One can take Clifford to be saying that you have a duty not to believe something if you have insufficient evidence for it. In his example of the shipowner who sent his ship to sea without adequate evidence of its safety, it is his belief in its safety to which Clifford objected. One might also object to his sending the ship out, and no doubt Clifford would object to that as well. But Clifford makes clear that it is the belief itself that is objectionable.[9]

The two crucial features of this view about epistemological duties are that it makes believing itself the dutiful thing and that it makes evidential support the key determinant of which beliefs one ought to have. It is possible to detach these two ideas. Thus, one could agree that our duties are to have or not have certain beliefs, but deny that evidential considerations determine which ones we ought to have or avoid. However, for present purposes the important thing is the nature of the sorts of things we have an epistemological duty to do. Not much will turn on the evidentialist aspect of the view. In any case, the first view about epistemological duties is:

> ED1.   We have an epistemological duty to believe all and only the propositions that are supported by the evidence we have.

There are minor modifications of (ED1) worth mentioning. For one thing, we should expand the dutiful attitudes to more than just belief. The general duty is to have the attitude that is supported by one's evidence—belief, disbelief, or suspension of judgment (or suitable degree of belief). And one might limit the propositions about which one has a duty to have the proper attitude to those that one considers. Thus,

> ED2.   For any proposition p, time t, and person S, if S considers p at t, then S has a duty to have the attitude toward p that fits the evidence S has at t concerning p.

(ED2) has an implication worth highlighting. It implies that we have a duty to believe what is supported by our evidence as well as a duty to withhold belief from what is not supported by our evidence. Locke and Clifford both focus on failures to fulfill the second duty. They say less about the first. Locke mentions the person "in love with his own fancies" who believes without good reason. Clifford mentions our duty to question "all that we believe." His famous saying mentions only the crime of believing without good evidence. But they could have also highlighted cases in which people fail to believe when they do have good reason. This is also a serious problem. Indeed, one could imagine Clifford modifying his case so that it is about a person who fails to believe that his ship is dangerous while having good evidence for so believing. (ED2) is clearly in the spirit of their remarks.

Many writers find it objectionable to suppose that there could be a duty to believe anything.[10] The reason for this is that we can have a duty to do a certain thing only if that thing is behavior that we can control. But our beliefs are not under our control, at least not in the relevant way. Hence, according to this argument, we can't have duties to believe or not believe things. I will not take up this issue in any detail here. For now, it is worth noting that not everyone accepts the premise that belief is not voluntary. The quotation from Locke surely suggests a kind of doxastic voluntarism, and other recent writers have defended that thesis.[11] Elsewhere I have argued that there can be duties (or obligations) to believe things even if belief is not voluntary, just as there can be parental duties or legal duties that one cannot carry out.[12] I will proceed on the assumption that this objection to there being epistemological duties to believe fails.

B. Duties to Try to Believe

Philosophers who think that belief is not voluntary and not a proper subject for duties or requirements can nevertheless contend that there are epistemological duties. These duties would concern related behavior that is under our control. Philosophers who defend (ED2) can agree that there are these additional duties as well.

In the first edition of his influential *Theory of Knowledge*, Chisholm considers the possibility that we have duties to believe propositions. He says that we can have duties to believe propositions only if beliefs are actions. He then asks, "But are beliefs actions, or possible actions, that are within anyone's power?"[13] He does not directly answer this question, but does describe the issue raised here as a difficulty for the view under consideration. This suggests that he thought that it was doubtful that beliefs were actions within our power and thus doubtful that we had duties to believe. At the comparable point in the second edition of *Theory of Knowledge* Chisholm says that each person is subject to the intellectual requirement noted earlier, namely "trying his best to bring it about that for every proposition h that he considers, he accepts h if and only if h is true."[14]

One can take Chisholm to be suggesting that we have an intellectual requirement to try to give ourselves a general disposition to believe all and only the truths among the propositions we consider. One might fulfill this obligation by cultivating the proper habits of mind, or perhaps by enrolling in critical thinking courses. It might even be that believing specific false propositions could lead to an overall increase in the balance of truths among our beliefs. However, it is clear that this is not what Chisholm had in mind. He never mentions behavior of this sort when speaking of intellectual obligations. He does say that in a specific situation our intellectual requirement might be better fulfilled by believing a proposition than by disbelieving it. This suggests that what we are to try to do is not cultivate certain habits of mind, but rather believe or disbelieve specific propositions. Thus, Chisholm's idea is:

ED3.   For any proposition p, time t, and person S, if S considers p at t, then S has a duty to try to bring it about that S believes p if and only p is true.

The implications of Chisholm's proposal may not differ significantly from those of (ED2), given that he might plausibly contend that the best way to try to believe truths is to follow one's evidence. Thus, we need not dwell on the differences between them.

It is difficult to see, however, exactly how (ED3) is supposed to improve upon (ED2) if doxastic voluntarism is a worry. If believing is not under our control, it is less than clear what we would do in order to *try* to form a belief. The proposal suggests that we can engage in a sort of mental effort, trying to coax ourselves into a particular belief. But the suggestion is, I believe, inaccurate. I, at least, would not know what to do. There are, of course, things we can do to try to get ourselves to believe particular propositions over an extended period of time, and we can try to cultivate certain habits of thought. However, as noted, this is not what Chisholm had in mind.

C. Duties to Gather Evidence

Another view that adds to or replaces the epistemological duties implied by (ED2) holds that we have epistemological duties to gather the evidence we need to have informed beliefs. Indeed, one could think that this is really the duty that Clifford's shipowner failed to fulfill. He should have gathered the evidence necessary to find out about the seaworthiness of his ship. Failing to gather that evidence was an intellectual sin. Sending the ship out without doing that was a moral sin.

In "The Epistemic Duty to Seek More Evidence," Richard J. Hall and Charles R. Johnson argue for an extensive duty to seek evidence. They assume, for the purposes of their paper, that our epistemic goal is to believe all and only true propositions. They argue that given this goal, for each proposition about which we are uncertain we have a *prima facie* duty to seek more evidence concerning it. They realize that this puts quite a burden on us, and we obviously cannot fulfill all these duties. They concede that these duties are rather weak, and they are often overridden by other factors.

Our specific formulation of Hall and Johnson's view, then, is this:

ED4.   For any proposition p, time t, and person S, if p is less than certain for S at t, then S has a *prima facie* duty at t to gather additional evidence concerning p.[15]

The key feature of (ED4) for present purposes is that it makes our duties evidence gathering, rather than simply believing as one's actual evidence dictates. It therefore does not raise the questions about doxastic voluntarism that (ED2) raises.

Hall and Johnson derive (ED4) from the premise that our epistemological goal is to believe all and only truths. They also use the principle, quoted above, according to which we have a duty to do those things that will best achieve the goals we have accepted. Of course, their conclusion only follows if it is limited to people who have "accepted" the goal of believing all and only truths. It is questionable that many people have done anything that amounts to accepting this goal. Nevertheless, as they say, it is widely asserted that something along these lines is our, or the, epistemological end or goal, whether people have explicitly signed on to it or not. And advocates of this would likely say that, as an intellectual being—one who is engaged in the activity of forming beliefs about the world— one automatically has the relevant duties. So their argument seems not to make the duties as widespread as many would like, unless they can plausibly add a premise saying that we all do have the goal of believing all and only truths.[16]

In any case, Hall and Johnson's derivation of their epistemological duties from their principle about the source of duties depends on the assumption that seeking new evidence is the best way to get true beliefs. And that is in general a sensible idea. However, there are cases in which one knows that seeking new evidence will be fruitless. There is not much point in looking for additional evidence if one knows that any such evidence is irretrievably lost. In such cases, it is not true that seeking more evidence is the best way to achieve the goal. Thus, what is supported by their principle is, at best, a somewhat modified version of their claim.

There are possible variants of (ED4) worth mentioning. (ED4) requires gathering evidence about all propositions that are less than certain. Some alternatives place more modest demands on us. For example, one could say that there is no need to seek more evidence when a proposition is justified, rather than using the high standard of certainty.[17] Another possibility is to hold that whether we ought to gather more evidence concerning a proposition varies with the importance of the proposition. Much turns on the seaworthiness of Clifford's shipowner's ship. He should have a lot of evidence about that. Less turns on whether the paint is peeling in one of the cabins, so there is no need for him to gather evidence about that proposition. One can imagine variations on (ED4) that make the duty to gather additional evidence depend upon the likelihood of actually finding that evidence. Another such factor might be the likelihood of that additional evidence conflicting with the evidence one already has.[18]

The differences between (ED4) and the various alternatives just mentioned are not crucial for present purposes. What is important about (ED4), and what distinguishes it from (ED2) and (ED3), is that (ED4) makes epistemological duties involve external behavior that occurs over an extended period of time. They are diachronic rather than synchronic duties. The previous proposals held that the central question behind epistemological inquiry was "What should I believe (or try to believe) now, given the situation I am in?" Clifford's shipowner lacked evidence for his belief, so it was wrong for him to believe as he did in the situation he was actually in. Chisholm's conception of our intellectual requirements has them yield implications about what one should believe, or try to believe, given the actual circumstances. In contrast, Hall and Johnson's view implies that our epistemological duty is to carry out a possibly extended search for more evidence. Their stated view does not say what attitude one should have toward the proposition in question in the meantime.

D. Other Epistemological Duties

If people do have diachronic epistemological duties, and these are duties that derive from the goal of believing all and only truths, then it would seem that they may well have a large number of other epistemological duties that will help them achieve this end. These other duties need not be restricted to matters of gathering evidence. There are many things we can do that will increase our chances of getting true beliefs and avoiding false ones. Perhaps eating well and getting enough sleep will help. Perhaps getting enough exercise keeps our minds sharp, or taking gingko supplements is beneficial. We might spell out this idea as follows:

> ED5.   Each person has an epistemological duty to behave in ways that will maximize that person's number of true beliefs and minimize that person's number of false beliefs.

There are, once again, possible variants on the idea. One could require behavior that maximizes the variety of true beliefs or their significance rather than their number. As before, these variations on the theme are not central for present purposes. The key feature here is that epistemological duties are, on (ED5), expanded to include behaviors that will have long-term effects on the character of beliefs. In contrast, (ED2)–(ED4) focused only on specific beliefs. Even (ED4), which introduced evidence gathering, formulated a duty that had to do with each specific proposition. In contrast, (ED5) allows for duties to engage in long-term self-improvement programs as well as duties of the sort implied by the previous formulation.

We have, then, a range of views about what our epistemological duties are. The narrowest conception is that epistemological duties are synchronic duties to have particular cognitive attitudes. A broader conception is that they are diachronic duties to acquire evidence relevant to propositions that are less than certain. A still broader conception is that they are duties to engage in behavior that will make us effective and efficient thinkers. It is possible that we have epistemological duties of all kinds. These views need not be formulated so as to preclude the others. This can be seen by considering Clifford's shipowner again. We might say that he has an epistemological obligation to suspend judgment about the seaworthiness of his ship, given the evidence he actually has. But we might say that he also has an epistemological obligation to get additional evidence about that topic. And, if he has a tendency to form unjustified beliefs, we might say that he has an epistemological duty to undertake measures that will yield general cognitive improvement.

I think, however, that (ED2) best characterizes our epistemological duties, and that the duties described by (ED4) and (ED5) are best seen as nonepistemological. I can not offer anything resembling a decisive argument for this view. However, I think that some modest support for my view emerges from consideration of what makes a duty epistemological and of what counts as epistemological success.

III. Distinguishing Epistemological Duties from Other Duties

If there are epistemological duties, it is natural to ask what makes a particular duty epistemological. One possibility is that epistemological duties can be distinguished from other duties on the basis of the sort of behavior involved. Epistemology, it is sometimes said, has to do with the regulation of belief. Epistemological duties, it might be thought, are duties that pertain to the formation, retention, or modification of beliefs. This can be understood in a way that is compatible with any of the views described in section II. They all concern themselves either with believing or other cognitive attitudes themselves or with behavior that is importantly related to these attitudes. A narrow conception of epistemological duties is that they are specifically duties to believe or hold some other cognitive attitude:

1. Any duty to believe (or disbelieve, or withhold belief) in a proposition is an epistemological duty.

A broader idea, suggested above, is:

2. Any duty importantly related to believing or other cognitive attitudes is
   an epistemological duty.

The key feature of (1) and (2) is that epistemological duties are identified by the
sort of behavior they are a duty to perform. A requirement is epistemological if
it is a requirement to have a particular cognitive attitude or is related to the
formation or retention of cognitive attitudes in an appropriate way.

The phrase "importantly related" in (2) is admittedly obscure. Almost any
requirement connects to belief in some way. If parents are required to treat their
children in particular ways, then fulfilling their requirements will most likely lead
them to have beliefs about how they have behaved. But this connection to beliefs
does not make the parental duty epistemological, according to (2). The duty is
not "importantly" related to cognitive attitudes. In contrast, a duty to collect
evidence is supposed to be importantly connected to belief formation and
therefore does count as epistemological.

Both (1) and (2) do not cohere well with an idea common among writers on
this topic, the idea that epistemological duties can conflict with, and at times be
outweighed by, nonepistemological duties. Assume that two (*prima facie*) duties
conflict for a person at a time when the person has both duties at the time, the
person is able to fulfill each duty at the time, but the person is not able to fulfill
both duties at the time. It might be better to make the duties relative to circumstances rather than times, but that detail will not be crucial here. The idea is
illustrated by a simple example. If I have a duty to go visit certain relatives today
and also have a duty to finish writing a paper, and each is such that I could do
one but cannot do both, then these two duties conflict. This is consistent with
the fact that there are possible circumstances in which I could write the paper
while visiting the relatives or somehow manage to do both. The two duties conflict
if, in the actual circumstances, I can do each but I cannot do both.

Suppose one has an epistemological duty to believe a certain proposition or
to gather evidence about it. Any duty that explicitly conflicts with this will be a
duty not to believe that proposition or not to gather evidence about it. But, by
(1) and (2), these conflicting duties will also be epistemological duties. But then
cases like this turn out not to be cases in which epistemological duties conflict
with nonepistemological duties.

It is possible to conjure up cases in which there is an epistemological duty to
believe something at a particular time and a duty to do something else at that
time. If forming the belief somehow rules out performing the other dutiful behavior, there will be a conflict. Cases of the sort in question are odd, since forming
a belief rarely precludes performing some unrelated external behavior. One possible example of the sort under discussion is as follows. Suppose a firefighter is
reading a book about his favorite hobby, gardening. He learns some facts that
make believing some conclusion about the care for roses epistemologically re-

quired. But at the very time these facts are brought to his attention, the fire alarm goes off and he ought to go fight the fire. Since the duty to fight the fire is not a duty to believe or not believe something, and, we may grant, not importantly related to believing, neither (1) nor (2) counts this as an epistemological duty. We can assume that it is a moral duty, or perhaps a duty arising from the firefighter's occupation. Suppose that he can not both go fight the fire and simultaneously form his new belief about the care for roses. We might say that the firefighter has an epistemological duty to believe the newly established conclusion, but a moral duty to go fight the fire. Under the circumstances, he can not do both. So these two duties conflict. There is in this case a conflict between an epistemological duty and a moral duty. It is even easier to see that a moral duty like this one can conflict with a duty to gather evidence. Thus, (1) and (2) do not entirely rule out conflicts of this sort.

Still, those who think that there can be conflicts between epistemological and other duties have something entirely different in mind. What they have in mind are cases in which epistemological considerations demand believing something (or collecting evidence, or doing something else to improve one's cognitive situation) and moral or other considerations demand not believing that thing (or not gathering evidence about it). They are thinking that there can be cases in which moral or prudential considerations require one cognitive attitude or behavior while epistemological considerations require a different attitude. It's not that the circumstances make believing incompatible with the morally or prudentially required behavior. Rather, morality or prudence directly dictates different cognitive attitudes. For example, prudence may require believing something when evidential considerations make that belief appear to be a bad one from an epistemological point of view. Or, epistemological considerations demand searching for more evidence while prudential considerations demand letting the matter go. Or epistemological considerations might demand studying reasoning while one's moral requirement is to refrain from that.

Chisholm describes some examples that may be useful in the present setting. He writes:

> For example, a man may have the duty to believe that the members of his family are honest or faithful without in fact knowing that they are. Or a sick man, who has various unfulfilled obligations, may have the duty to accept certain propositions if, by accepting them, he can make himself well and useful once again.[19]

These examples can be used in the present context as follows. Suppose we say that the first man has an epistemological duty to suspend judgment about the honesty and faithfulness of the members of his family, given the overall neutrality of his information about the topic. But, we may suppose, he has a familial or moral duty to give them the benefit of the doubt and believe that they are honest and faithful. And when Chisholm says in the passage just quoted that the person has the duty to have the belief, he is in effect saying that the latter duty outweighs the former. This is a case in which the epistemological duty is in fact overridden by other duties.

The second example is similar. Here the patient has no evidence supporting certain propositions, perhaps propositions such as the proposition that he will recover. But believing that he will recover may at least increase his chances of recovering, and, given his unfulfilled commitments, this is what he has a duty to do. So his epistemological duty to disbelieve that he will recover is overridden by his nonepistemological duty to believe that he will recover so that he can meet his other obligations.

If requirements count as epistemological simply in virtue of what they are requirements to do, then these examples can not be examples of conflict between epistemological requirements and other kinds of requirements. They are, instead, conflicts between two different epistemological requirements. While this might not be a conclusive consideration against this way of identifying which duties are epistemological, it does count against it.

There is intuitive support for this conclusion. In Chisholm's examples it seems clear that there is a conflict between epistemological and nonepistemological considerations. From an epistemological perspective, the thing for the person to do is not believe that the family is honest and not believe that he will recover. But moral and prudential considerations point in different directions.

The conclusion to draw for now is that (1) and (2) do not tell us what makes a duty an epistemological duty. It may be that epistemological duties always have to do with belief formation, but not all duties that concern belief formation are epistemological. Practical and moral considerations can pertain to beliefs as well.

A better way to identify which duties are epistemological is in terms of the duties associated with epistemological ends, goals, or success. Chisholm speaks of one's duties "*qua* intellectual being." Hall and Johnson say that our epistemic duties are the ones that best fulfill our epistemic goals.[20] We can avoid some puzzles about whether these goals are consciously adopted by people or whether they somehow automatically have them, by speaking instead of epistemological success. If there is such a thing as epistemological success—doing well epistemologically—then our duties can be understood in terms of it. I will discuss in section IV what counts as success as an intellectual being, as the idea is used here. But the general idea of what counts as an epistemological duty is:

3. Epistemological duties are duties that one must carry out in order to be successful from an intellectual (or epistemological) perspective.

While (3) is not terribly informative, it is not entirely devoid of helpful content. Intellectual, or epistemological, success has to do with something like acquisition of true belief, or rational belief, or knowledge. (Which of these one picks makes a big difference.) But intellectual success differs from other kinds of success, such as financial success or reproductive success. And this suggests that conclusions about epistemological duties, and perhaps other epistemological evaluations, ought not be based on considerations having to do with success in these other areas. Thus, the fact that particular beliefs or cognitive mechanisms have some kind of evolutionary advantage does not show that they are epistemically meritorious. And if there are beliefs that are absolutely essential to our survival, it does not follow that we have an epistemological duty to believe those things. Similarly, the fact that a belief has considerable moral value, perhaps enough to make it morally required, has no bearing on whether having that belief contributes to epistemological success. So (3) does a better job than (1) or (2) in segregating epistemological considerations from others. And it more readily allows for the kinds of conflicts in duties that Chisholm describes.

IV. EPISTEMOLOGICAL SUCCESS AND EPISTEMOLOGICAL GOALS

If (3) is correct, then epistemological duties can best be understood in terms of epistemological success. But what is that? In general, if there are goals associated with an activity, then success in that area consists in achieving that goal. If the goals of investing are to make money, then success consists in investing in ways that do make money. Epistemological success is thus the achievement of epistemological goals or ends. So, if our epistemological goal is to achieve certain things, then we are epistemologically successful if we do so.

Hall and Johnson begin their paper with the following remark:

> From Eve on down the generations nearly everyone has held that there are epistemic goals worth some risk or effort to pursue. Following James' admonition to know the truth and avoid error, many recent epistemologists have formulated the overall epistemic goal as believing all and only true propositions.[21]

They go on to cite several recent philosophers (myself included) who fit this tradition. It is indeed true that the idea that our twin epistemological goals are to believe truths and to avoid error is a kind of philosophical commonplace. Both goals are obviously important, since we could achieve one by believing everything and achieve the other by believing nothing. So it is balancing them out in a proper way that has struck many as crucial.

We can formulate this idea as follows:

T.   Epistemological success consists in maximizing one's true beliefs and min-
       imizing one's false beliefs.

There are possible modifications of this worth mentioning. One could add considerations about the kinds of propositions one believes, adding greater value for
believing "important" propositions than for believing trivial propositions. But I
will not discuss such variations here.

(T) has two odd consequences, both suggested by the passage from Locke
quoted at the beginning of this essay. For one thing, if the goal is to believe truths,
then a person who stumbles into the truth through a blunder or confusion has
achieved epistemological success. For example, suppose a person acquires strong
evidence against a proposition he has long defended in public. Out of stubbornness, the person retains the old belief. And suppose that, contrary to the new
evidence, the old belief is in fact true. If the goal is simply truth, he's achieved
the goal and is, in this case at least, an epistemological success. But, as Locke said
of a person who does not reason as he ought, "however he sometimes lights on
truth, is in the right but by chance; and I know not whether the luckiness of the
accident will excuse the irregularity of his proceeding." Locke here questions
whether luckily getting to the truth "excuses" the improper way of getting there.
Setting aside questions of excuses, the idea here seems to be that the person who
reasons badly and stumbles onto a truth is not believing as he ought, is not
achieving epistemological success.

Furthermore, if we achieve epistemic success by believing truths, then a person
is an epistemological failure when she carefully and correctly follows completely
reasonable procedures yet unfortunately falls into error. Recall this section of the
passage from Locke:

> he that makes use of the light and faculties God has given him, and seeks sin-
> cerely to discover truth, by those helps and abilities he has, may have this satis-
> faction in doing his duty as a rational creature, that though he should miss
> truth, he will not miss the reward of it.

A sensible application of Locke's claim here is that the person who does follow
the evidence, even if doing so happens to lead to a false belief, nevertheless does
"not miss the reward" of doing his epistemological duties. That is, such a person
achieves epistemological success.

Hall and Johnson make a distinction between "objective" and "subjective"
evaluations of beliefs and believers.[22] One might say that the person who unreasonably stumbles into the truth is epistemologically successful from an objective
perspective and that a person who follows all the rules but gets a false belief is
unsuccessful from an objective perspective. One might issue the opposite evaluations from a subjective perspective. However, this strikes me as an unattractive

and implausible position. Imagine a person who makes an unreasonable and un-reliable inference that happens to lead to a true belief on a particular occasion. It might be fortunate that he's got this true belief, but I see nothing epistemolog-ically meritorious about it. Nor can I see anything epistemologically dutiful about it. No doubt these considerations are less than decisive. Those who are unconvin-ced should take what follows to be a discussion of the kind of subjective evaluation Hall and Johnson mention.

Hall and Johnson say, correctly, that (T) is often taken to be a way to spell out James's famous remark about our duties. What is striking about (T) as a formulation of James's idea is that (T) is importantly different from what James said. He wrote: "We must know the truth; and we must avoid error—these are our first and great commandments as would be knowers."[23] This suggests a goal of having *knowledge*, and this makes a significant difference.

K.   Epistemological success consists in having knowledge.

Given that knowledge implies truth, one will achieve success only by having true beliefs. But not all true beliefs will qualify. Only those that are justified, or reliably formed, or satisfy whatever else it takes to have knowledge will qualify. Those who believe truths as a result of "irregular" proceedings will not achieve success. So (K) seems to me to be superior to (T). This view, combined with (3), yields the idea that one's epistemic duties are the duties one must carry out in order to get knowledge.

However, (K) also has some consequences that seem implausible to me. The second of the two points from Locke discussed in connection with (T) also applies to (K). The person who follows his evidence, or follows reliable methods, in the cases in which they lead him astray, is doing just what he should. If there are epistemological duties in these cases, he's doing them. He enjoys the rewards—epistemological success—of his believing, even though he lacks knowledge.

Furthermore, there are situations in which there are proper ways to proceed epistemologically even if one cannot obtain knowledge. For example, in cases in which one's evidence is counterbalanced, the proper thing to do—the dutiful thing—is to suspend judgment. But that is not a way to get knowledge. The person who suspends judgments in such cases is an epistemological success.

These considerations suggests a third view about epistemological success:

J.   Epistemological success consists in having reasonable or justified cognitive attitudes.

According to (J), when one's situation is one in which believing a particular proposition is the reasonable attitude, then to be an epistemological success is to believe that proposition. But if the reasonable thing is to disbelieve it or suspend judgment about it, then to be a success is to have the appropriate one of those attitudes. Combined with (3), the implication is that our epistemological duties are the duties we must carry out in order to have justified beliefs.[24]

(J) provides a basis for preferring (ED2), the account of our epistemic duties that makes our duties be about which attitudes we have, not about evidence gathering and other belief-related behavior. If success amounts to having justified attitudes, then the attitudes that are justified at a time are determined by the evidence one has, or perhaps the reliable methods then available, or whatever factors determine justification. In any case, by acquiring more evidence, one will (or might) change what's justified. But then what will be required is adjusting one's attitudes to that new evidence. Changing one's evidence will not be a way to make one's beliefs better justified. It is not a way to greater epistemic success.[25]

This point deserves emphasis. On the current view, in any given situation there is a set of attitudes that are justified or reasonable. A person who has those attitudes is completely successful from an epistemological perspective. If one's evidence concerning p is neutral and one suspends judgment about p, then one is a success. If one then gets some evidence in favor of p, and comes to believe p, one is not thereby more justified in one's cognitive states. One is not doing a better job epistemically. In each case one is simply having the justified attitude. If (J) is correct, then epistemic success comes from having the proper attitudes, not from getting more evidence. Given (3), it follows that one's duties are the things one must do to achieve success. And this would seem to be having the right attitudes, not such things as evidence gathering and the like.

There may be some things that will help one do a better job of having the attitudes that are justified. For example, enrolling in critical thinking courses may help. But this is a sort of indirect way of getting the proper attitudes. Perhaps one could plausibly describe that sort of thing as what's desirable without being required.

Undoubtedly some critics of this view will say that one has a positive obligation to go out and get the evidence one needs in order to have justified beliefs about the world. It is not good enough simply to adjust one's attitudes to the possibly limited evidence one has. There may be something right about this. But this undermines my thesis only if the obligation in question is an epistemological obligation. The conjunction of (3) and (J) implies that it isn't. Of course, critics will find this to be reason to reject the conjunction of (3) and (J) rather than accept my conclusion. But I think that I can provide some modest support for my view. I turn to that in the next section.

V. Epistemological Duties and Duties to Learn Truths

Earlier we examined Chisholm's examples in which one's intellectual duties were overridden by moral or prudential duties. If these conflict cases are as described, then there are nonepistemological considerations that can affect duties to believe propositions. There can be moral reasons and prudential reasons for belief, and perhaps in some cases these reasons can be sufficient to establish *prima facie* duties.[26] Analogous moral considerations can establish *prima facie* duties to gather evidence regarding propositions. If someone is locked in the vault and will run out of oxygen unless it is opened soon, and I have a way to gather evidence about the combination, then I have a moral duty to get that evidence. And, I would say, Clifford's shipowner had a moral duty to get evidence about the seaworthiness of his ship.

There are many examples relevantly like these. That is, there are cases in which moral considerations require that one gather evidence about a proposition in order to find out if it is true and then act accordingly. If believing appropriately is necessary for so acting, then perhaps it is morally obligatory to believe appropriately. We need not resort to extreme cases involving people locked in vaults. If your children are hungry, you may therefore have a duty to find out where some food is. If you have an appointment, you may have a duty to find out how to get to the designated meeting place. There are, then, numerous cases in which there are moral obligations to gather evidence, form beliefs, and act accordingly. But in these cases the duty to gather evidence does not result from any general intellectual requirement to know things or to believe truths. They result from specific moral requirements for action.

As noted in section II, one might say that these duties are epistemological duties simply because they are duties related to belief formation. And while that may not be decisively refutable, it does undermine the intuitively plausible idea that there are cases in which epistemological duties conflict with nonepistemological duties. Given this, in the familiar cases just discussed in which there are duties to gather evidence, the duties in question are moral or prudential duties, not epistemological duties. And, it seems to me, in all cases in which there is such a duty, it has a nonepistemological source. There are some cases in which a person cares deeply about something, and has strong prudential reasons to find out about it. There are other cases in which something of moral significance turns on a person acting suitably, and the person has a moral duty to find out how to act.

There are cases in which there are no moral, prudential, or other nonepistemological requirements to find out about something. Suppose, for example, a penny falls out of my pocket and lands on the floor. I suspend judgment about which side it landed on. Unless I'm curious about this, or something else turns on it, I do not see that I have a duty of any sort to find out the truth about this. I'm doing a good job, epistemologically, by suspending judgment about this. It's fine to leave that matter where it lies.

I have no argument for the conclusion that I have no duty to gather evidence in such cases. I simply am unable to see why I do have one, even a weak *prima facie* duty. The considerations from Locke seem to me to be exactly right. I have a duty to use my faculties properly. In this case, suspending judgment is the thing to do. And Clifford's admonitions also simply show that I ought to suspend judgment. They provide no basis for thinking that I have a duty to look at the penny to get evidence about its position.

One might find epistemological duties to gather evidence when the propositions in question are more significant. Again, it seems to me, where there are reasons to gather evidence, they are nonepistemological or else there is no duty to gather evidence at all. We may have moral or prudential duties to learn about topics involving our health or important political issues. Philosophers and other academicians may have duties arising out of their positions to learn about the latest information in their fields. These are highly intellectual matters, but the duties arise not from some general intellectual requirement we all have, but out of moral or prudential considerations. Thus, where there are duties to gather evidence, they are not epistemological duties.

VII. CONCLUSION

There is, then, at least a coherent position based on (3) and (J). According to (3), one's epistemological duties are what is required for epistemological success. According to (J), epistemological success amounts to having justified cognitive attitudes. In my view, that amounts to following one's evidence, but I have not defended that particular view about justification here. What we epistemologically ought to do, whenever we consider a proposition, is to have the attitude that is justified for us. To do so is the extent of our purely epistemological duties. This is what (ED2) said. We may sometimes have other duties that bear on our beliefs. For example, we may sometimes have a duty to get evidence about a topic. But such duties always have a nonepistemological source. Where there are no nonepistemological reasons to get evidence about a proposition, there is no duty at all to get evidence about it. And we may sometimes have nonepistemological duties to believe or disbelieve particular propositions. But our epistemological duty is, as (ED2) implies, simply to have justified beliefs.

NOTES

1. Locke, *An Essay Concerning Human Understanding*, ed. A. C. Fraser (New York: Dover, 1959), IV, xvii, 24, 413–414. I was led to this passage by Alvin Plantinga, who cites it in *Warrant: The Current Debate* (Oxford: Oxford University Press, 1993), 13.

2. W. K. Clifford, "The Ethics of Belief," originally printed in *Contemporary Review* (1877), reprinted in Clifford's *Lectures and Essays* (London: Macmillan, 1879), 183.

3. Ibid., 180.

4. William James, "The Will to Believe," in *The Will to Believe and Other Essays in Popular Philosophy* (New York: McKay, 1911), 17.

5. Roderick Chisholm, *Theory of Knowledge*, 2nd ed. (Englewood Cliffs, N.J.: Prentice-Hall, 1977), 14. Parenthetical remark in the original.

6. Richard J. Hall and Charles R. Johnson, "The Epistemic Duty to Seek More Evidence," *American Philosophical Quarterly* 35 (1998): 129–140.

7. *The Cambridge Dictionary of Philosophy*, 2nd ed., ed. Robert Audi (Cambridge: Cambridge University Press, 1999). Entry by Bruce Russell.

8. Hall and Johnson, "The Epistemic Duty to Seek More Evidence," 129.

9. It may well be that Clifford thought that believing on insufficient evidence was a violation of a moral duty rather than an epistemological duty. Or, better, it may be that he didn't think in terms of this distinction. For discussion see Susan Haack " 'The Ethics of Belief' Reconsidered," in *The Philosophy of Roderick M. Chisholm*, ed. Lewis Hahn (LaSalle, Ill.: Open Court, 1997), 129–144.

10. For discussion, see William Alston, "The Deontological Conception of Epistemic Justification," *Philosophical Perspectives* 2 (1988): 257–299. I have discussed this topic in "Voluntary Belief and Epistemic Evaluation," in *Knowledge, Truth, and Duty*, ed. Matthias Steup (Oxford: Oxford University Press, 2001), 77–92.

11. See Matthias Steup, "Doxastic Voluntarism and Epistemic Deontology," *Acta Analytica* 15 (2000): 25–56, and Carl Ginet, "Deciding to Believe," in *Knowledge, Truth, and Duty*, 63–76.

12. "The Ethics of Belief," *Philosophy and Phenomenological Research* 60 (2000): 667–695, and "Epistemic Obligations," *Philosophical Perspectives* 2 (1988): 235–256.

13. Roderick Chisholm, *Theory of Knowledge* (Englewood Cliffs, N.J.: Prentice-Hall, 1966), 12.

14. Ibid., 14.

15. Presumably, if ~p is certain for S, then p is less than certain. But Hall and Johnson would not want people to have a duty to look for evidence about p in such cases. There are simple modifications of (ED4) to get around this.

16. They explicitly say that everyone is an epistemic agent (137) and that everyone has the duty to seek more evidence. It is not clear to me that they mean to endorse the view that everyone has the goal of believing all and only truths.

17. Hall and Johnson reject that idea in note 10.

18. There is a puzzling issue regarding what one can reasonably think about what the evidence one doesn't have will reveal. Suppose you have modest evidence supporting P. You know that there is additional evidence available. If you have specific information about what that additional evidence indicates about P, then you rationally should take account of that fact already. If you have no additional information about what the unexamined evidence says about P, then it's less clear what you should think. Clearly, it would be unreasonable to think that P is less likely to be true simply because there is additional evidence. But it would also be unreasonable to think that the unexamined evidence would be neutral about P. After all, that fact in itself might give you reason to modify your belief in the probability of P. So maybe it's best to think that it will support P to the same extent your current evidence does. But then it's hard to see why there is any reason to look at it.

19. Chisholm, *Theory of Knowledge*, 12–13.

20. Hall and Johnson, "The Epistemic Duty to Seek More Evidence," 130.

21. Ibid., 129.

22. Ibid.

23. James, *The Will to Believe and Other Essays in Popular Philosophy*, 17.

24. I have nothing helpful to say about what distinguishes our epistemological duties from things that are merely desirable or good epistemologically.

25. There are some cases in which getting evidence can make one have better justified beliefs. Suppose Steady Stew believes p and will continue to believe p no matter what happens. That belief is now unjustified. If he were to get additional evidence, as it turns out, that evidence would establish the truth of p. In that case, Stew's belief in p would become justified. But it is extremely odd to think that he had some sort of obligation to get this evidence in order to render justified the originally unjustified belief he had.

26. This discussion leaves a variety of questions unanswered. One such question concerns the resolution of conflicts between epistemological and nonepistemological duties. Suppose one has an epistemological duty to believe a proposition and a nonepistemological duty to disbelieve it. What should one do? What is one's overriding duty? In "The Ethics of Belief," I defend the view that there is no answer to these questions, or more precisely, that there are no sensible questions asked.

CHAPTER 13

SCIENTIFIC KNOWLEDGE

PHILIP KITCHER

1. Epistemology Incognito

ALMOST everybody seems to agree that the sciences constitute the richest and most extensive body of human knowledge, and scientists routinely talk of "what we now know." Within the philosophy of science, however, there is little explicit discussion of scientific knowledge. This apparent puzzle is easily resolved by recognizing that much epistemology is done under cover by philosophers of science: discussions of scientific realism, of methods of discovery, and particularly of confirmation theory take up important parts of a theory of scientific knowledge.

Nevertheless, I think that this piecemeal practice of epistemology isn't fully satisfactory. Our understanding of scientific knowledge would benefit, I suggest, if the topic were pursued more systematically and if the perspectives of contemporary epistemology were reflected in discussions of the sciences. My aim in this essay is to offer a more systematic approach, and I hope it will reveal how certain important questions have been slighted.

Knowledge, as every beginning philosophy student learns, is a species of true belief. The differentiating marks of the species are, of course, matters of controversy. Older traditions identified knowledge with justified true belief, but, in the wake of familiar puzzles, this simple proposal has become hard to sustain. On the account I favor, for someone to know a proposition requires that the proposition be true, that the person believe it, and that the state of belief be produced by a reliable process (see Goldman 1986). That account suggests two general kinds of issues about scientific knowledge, the first concerned with the truth of the claims of the various sciences, and the second focused on the processes that generate and sustain the beliefs of scientists. I shall begin with debates about truth.

2. Controversies about Truth and Realism

Many of the things scientists know are quite mundane. The bench chemist knows that when particular reactants are mixed together the containing vessel will become quite hot (that's why the gloves are there), and the field geologist knows that there's a dip in the strata in the local railway cutting. If there is a specific worry about the truth of these claims, then it applies as well to matters that ordinary people think they know. A problem peculiar to the scientific case only arises because it's natural to celebrate much more ambitious kinds of scientific knowledge. Scientists, and those who read books and articles about developments in the sciences, often claim to know about the properties of recondite entities— genes, tectonic plates, black holes, neutrinos, and so forth. Sometimes they see a whole body of theory as a piece of scientific knowledge.

In the history of reflection on the sciences, these claims to knowledge have frequently come under fire, and, for the moment, I'm going to concentrate on attacks that deny that the statements allegedly known are true. One important line of criticism has based the denial on the grounds that the statements in question lack truth value; the other has offered an argument for thinking that those statements are false.

In the middle decades of the twentieth century, philosophers of science believed that there was an important distinction between two kinds of vocabulary. *Observational* terms were learnable through elementary kinds of experience: a child can garner the meaning of 'blue' by being shown swatches of color and told which ones count as blue. So, it was claimed, there's no difficulty in understanding how we're able to talk about observable things, events, and processes. Theoretical science, however, doesn't confine itself to this sort of vocabulary: biologists use 'gene', chemists use 'molecule', and quantum physicists use 'ψ-function'. However these usages develop, it can't be through confrontation with the entities the terms are alleged to denote. Central to logical empiricist philosophy of science was the enterprise of providing an account of how the meanings of the terms could be fixed, and, for those who doubted that the venture could be satisfactorily completed, a natural conclusion was that the sentences in which these terms figure were rightly understood as formulas lacking truth-values, deployed in a formal calculus that yielded genuinely meaningful (that is observational) statements (Carnap 1962, Scheffler 1963).

Behind the problem of the meaning of theoretical terms lay the ambitious attempt of the logical positivists to overcome the shortcomings of traditional philosophy. Convinced of the distinction between fruitful science and sterile metaphysics, Carnap, Ayer, and others sought a criterion of meaningfulness that would separate the writings of (for example) Heidegger from those of (for example) Einstein (for a classic review of their efforts, see Hempel 1965, chap. 4). Armed with the resources of mathematical logic (developed by Frege, Russell, and Hilbert), they offered various precise formulations of the criterion, only to discover that their proposals either admitted the metaphysics they hoped to exclude or debarred parts of the sciences they admired. By the 1940s the quest for a precise standard of meaningfulness seemed hopeless, and, as Hempel's classic essays document, the issue had shifted to one of deciding when it is legitimate to accept a body of statements as collectively meaningful.

Carnap's own pioneering investigations of the possibilities for fixing the meaning of dispositional terms had already made apparent how difficult it would be to provide anything like a definition of the theoretical terms routinely deployed by scientists (Carnap 1962). One common response to these difficulties was to allow that the terms were "partially interpreted" (a difficult notion that was understood in rather different ways by different writers); that response allowed for the possibility that theoretical science could count as true. An alternative, favored by many, avoided the difficulties of partial interpretation by a resolute instrumentalism: instead of thinking of theoretical science as a body of truths, we can conceive of it as an uninterpreted calculus, deployed to forge connections among statements about observables. According to the latter view, there is, strictly speaking, no scientific knowledge of genes, molecules, or quantum events.

The debate between these perspectives (the classic realism/instrumentalism controversy) was resolved in the early 1960s through an important insight of Hilary Putnam (Putnam 1962). Putnam pointed out that the original posing of the problem conflated two distinctions that ought to be kept apart. Classical logical empiricism supposed that observational terms (terms learnable through confrontations with observables) referred to (or contained within their extensions) only observables; and, by the same token, that theoretical terms (terms not learnable through confrontation with observables) referred (if they referred at all) to unobservables. A division among terms was supposed to match exactly a distinction among things. Although Putnam questioned both aspects of the match, the more crucial point lay in recognizing the possibility that a term learnable through the ostension of macroscopic objects might also refer to unobservables. So, for example, the term 'part of' may pick out a relation between entities, including both examples that may be observed and examples that are unobservable; thus we can formulate a classic definition of 'atom' as "a part of matter that has no parts." In Putnam's own well-chosen example, even children learn to talk about "people too little to see."

After Putnam's insight, it was no longer possible to maintain a general thesis to the effect that all statements of theoretical science lack truth values, and, in particular, it no longer seemed plausible to hold that the sentences of theoretical genetics or atomic chemistry lacked truth values. It does not follow that all theoretical vocabulary can be introduced using "broad spectrum" terms (terms whose extensions contain both observables and unobservables), or that logical empiricism was wrong about the language of all theories; parts of the language of quantum mechanics, for example, may fit the classical interpretation. Moreover, even though one antirealist argument had been blunted, a realist treatment of theoretical science faced further challenges.

The second critique of the view that our theoretical claims are true came from reflections on the history of science. Increased understanding of the sciences of the past convinced many historians and philosophers that there have been a vast number of cases in which a theory has been perceived as extremely successful only to be discarded later. Thomas Kuhn's famous monograph (Kuhn 1962) introduced one version of the argument: as we survey the sequence of theories about space and time, from Aristotle through Newton and his successors to Einstein (and beyond) we find "no discernible pattern of ontological development"; there is every reason to think that, just as our predecessors failed to arrive at correct views about the universe, so do we. Larry Laudan focused the antirealist complaint even more sharply (Laudan 1981). Drawing up a list of past theories that had once enjoyed considerable success—the humoral theory of medicine, catastrophist geology, subtle fluid theories of heat and electricity, the wave theory of light, phlogiston chemistry, and so forth—Laudan argued that we have every reason to think that our own predicament is similar and that our current theories, for all their successes, are false.

An important part of both versions of the argument is an implicit holism. We are invited to think of whole theories as the proper objects of knowledge, and thus, because the theory, taken as a whole, turns out to be false, we have the basis for a "pessimistic induction." It doesn't follow from the fact that a past theory isn't completely true that every part of that theory is false. If we think of individual pieces of scientific knowledge—of past astronomers who calculated the gravitational attraction on comets, theorists in optics who explained interference patterns in terms of the propagation of light waves, chemists who recognized the composition of water—it's hard not to endorse as correct a large percentage of the important theoretical claims made by the practitioners of the past, even in the antirealist's preferred examples. Where this isn't possible, as with the humoral theory of disease, an alternative strategy recommends itself; after all, medieval medicine was not exactly striking in its successes.

But there's an important objection. Antirealists will accuse their opponents of misappropriating individual statements from past theories and distorting their meaning by making them conform to current conceptions. Consider the idea that nineteenth-century optical theorists managed to make a lot of true claims about the propagation of light waves, and that these claims figured in explanations of optical phenomena (like diffraction, polarization, and interference) that are still accepted and, indeed, figure in contemporary physics textbooks. That idea depends on supposing that the nineteenth-century use of 'light wave' refers to whatever current physicists pick out by the term. Maybe we should doubt the supposition. For, in the language of nineteenth-century physics, 'light wave' is defined in terms of transmission through an all-pervading ether, sometimes even in terms of jostlings of molecules of the ether, and, since there is no such ether, 'light wave' in nineteenth-century optical usage doesn't refer to anything; consequently, although some of the statements written down by nineteenth-century physicists may look like sentences in current textbooks, they don't mean the same, and turn out to be either meaningless or false.

This objection marks the return of holism, this time in the theory of meaning, and in a form that we should resist. Virtually all nineteenth-century theorists believed in an all-pervading ether that provided a medium for the propagation of light waves. They also had other beliefs about light waves, including beliefs about the mathematical laws of propagation and beliefs about the presence of light waves in particular experimental situations. To vindicate the holist complaint, we have to hold that the reference of 'light wave' is always fixed by a set of descriptions that includes the invocation of an ether as a medium of light transmission. But this should strike us as absurd. For it means that the tokens of 'light wave' produced by Fresnel and his successors always fail to refer, even when those tokens are produced in response to experimental situations that reveal interference patterns. These unlucky optical theorists are not to be allowed to talk about the light that they are observing: if they chart the bands of brightness and darkness, explain them in terms of the mathematics of wave propagation, without making any explicit reference to a medium of propagation, the meaning holist insists that such reference is implicitly there, reducing their claims to falsehood or meaninglessness. Far more compelling, I suggest, is an interpretation that supposes the scientists to be talking about the propagation of the light they see, to be proposing that the process is governed by mathematical equations that they write down, and that the observed patterns come about because the observed propagation is governed in this way (Kitcher 1993, 144–149). So understood, our predecessors come out recognizing the truth (at least by our current lights).

If the realist approach I've outlined is applied to the allegedly problematic examples from the history of science, we arrive at a different judgment from that commended by antirealists as the basis for pessimism. Although parts of the theoretical sciences of the past have turned out to be false, even in cases in which the theories in question appeared to be highly successful, many parts of previous successful theories can be retained as true. There's no basis for a generalization that all the theoretical claims we make are likely to be false. At worst we should conclude that not all of what we believe is true. Maybe our attitude to theoretical science, in the areas where it seems to be most successful, should be like that of the author who, scrutinizing her sentences one by one concludes that each is correct, but, conscious of her own fallibility, knows that there's probably a mistake somewhere. If that's so, we shouldn't base rejection of theoretical scientific knowledge on the grounds that the tenets of our theories are not true.

3. THE SEARCH FOR METHOD

To defend our scientific knowledge, one clearly needs to do more than turn back arguments of the types just canvassed. Showing that an opponent has failed to demonstrate that a proposition isn't true doesn't amount to a serious case for its truth; and, we should recall, knowledge requires more than true belief. So an explanation of the intuitive idea that we have scientific knowledge requires significantly more work. Fortunately, however, what might appear to be two distinct tasks—arguing for the truth of scientific claims and showing how our beliefs are produced in a way that makes them knowledge and not mere true belief—seem to reduce to one. For the means we use to make a case for truth will simultaneously serve to display the knowledge-generating process.

Everyone who has read a high-school science text knows how the story is supposed to go. Scientific knowledge is based on observation and/or experiment; from statements knowable on the basis of observation, scientists reason to their conclusions using a body of strategies that can be collected under the title "scientific method." This picture of scientific knowledge has a long history, with prominent elaboration of it in the early modern period in the writings of Bacon and Descartes (influential writers with rather different views about method). Before the twentieth century, it was popular to think of scientific method as an instrument of discovery, but, in the heyday of logical empiricism, that conception came under severe scrutiny. Reichenbach, Hempel, and Popper distinguished between a "context of discovery" and a "context of justification," arguing that there were no methods that would lead scientists to the initial formulation of new hypotheses, but that, once proposed, possibly as a result of a variety of factors including imagination and luck, those hypotheses were subject to methodical check. In their treatments, scientific method reduced to the logic of confirmation.

During the past decades several authors have questioned this dismissal of the context of discovery as philosophically uninteresting. They have taken the picture of scientists generating hypotheses by serendipity or flights of fancy as a poor representation of the complex processes through which novel hypotheses emerge. Some philosophers have analyzed historical episodes of discovery with the intent to show how complex such episodes are and to identify the kinds of reasoning that occur at various stages. Others have taken up the logical empiricist challenge more directly, by trying to provide algorithms for discovery (Spirtes *et.al.* 2001, Kelly 1994).

For our purposes, however, the main issue concerns the existence of methods of generating or supporting beliefs in scientific hypotheses, whether or not the hypotheses were first formulated as a result of those methods. The most ambitious way to try to resolve that issue would be to specify a precise formal account of the conditions under which arbitrary hypotheses are supported by statements taken to be acceptable on the basis of observation. To undertake that project would be to continue the pioneering work of Carnap, Reichenbach, and Hempel on confirmation.

Logical empiricism, inspired by the successes of Frege, Russell, and Hilbert in the formalization of mathematical reasoning, yearned for a logic of confirmation. Carnap (1963) saw clearly that an analogue of the explication of the notion of logical consequence might focus on the qualitative concept of confirmation (specifying the conditions under which a statement e confirms a hypothesis h), or on the comparative concept of confirmation (specifying the conditions under which e provides greater confirmation for h than e' does for h'), or on the degree of confirmation (specifying the degree to which e confirms h). Superficially, the problem of qualitative confirmation appears easiest and that of degree of confirmation the hardest (the intermediate comparative problem has been ignored). Hempel's disclosure of the "paradoxes of confirmation" revealed, however, that appearances may be deceptive (Hempel 1965, chapters 1 and 2).

Two kinds of statements have seemed particularly important as potential occupants of the role of h: generalizations—(paradigmatically, statements of the logical form "$(x)(Ax \supset Bx)$")—and hypotheses containing some of the special theoretical vocabulary of the sciences. Hempel's account of qualitative confirmation focused on the first. A natural suggestion is that generalizations are confirmed by their instances; thus a statement of the form Aa & Ba would confirm $(x)(Ax \supset Bx)$. Hempel pointed out that a plausible principle of confirmation is that, if h and h' are logically equivalent, then e confirms h if and only if e confirms h'. To accept that principle, together with the intuitive account of instance confirmation, would yield famous peculiar consequences; since $(x)(Ax \supset Bx)$ is logically equivalent to $(x)(-Bx \supset -Ax)$, and since-Bb &-Ab confirms the latter,-Bb &-Ab confirms the former; in the famous example, the observation of a white shoe confirms the hypothesis that all ravens are black.

Hempel also demonstrated that other apparently attractive conditions could not be combined on pain of trivialization. A natural thought is that if e confirms h and h' is a logical consequence of h, then e confirms h'; another natural thought is that if e is a logical consequence of h, then e confirms h (the principle of hypothetico-deductivism, asserting that hypotheses are confirmed by generating consequences that can be observed to be true). Suppose, then, that e is a logical consequence of h; plainly e is a logical consequence of h & h'; hence e confirms h & h'; h' is a logical consequence of h & h'; therefore e confirms h'. This conclusion is disturbing, since h' can be chosen arbitrarily.

Hempel's own solution to the difficulties he raised avoided the trivialization of hypothetico-deductivism but endorsed the apparently paradoxical consequence that hypotheses ostensibly about ravens can be confirmed by observations of non-black non-ravens. His proposal was that e confirms h just in case e entails each sentence in a set, the development of h with respect to e, consisting in the instances of h with respect to the names that occur in e; thus, if e is Aa & Ba & Ab & Bb, and h is $(x)(Ax \supset Bx)$, the development of h with respect to e is {Aa $\supset$ Ba, Ab $\supset$ Bb}. Plainly, qualitative confirmation, so construed, requires that the hypothesis contain only language that occurs in the evidence statement. Hempel's account won't resolve questions about how the statements we use to report observations or experimental results confirm theoretical hypotheses couched in special language.

Clark Glymour (1980) has shown how to extend the Hempelian approach to address the problem. He generalizes the approach by allowing some parts of the theory to be used in conjunction with evidence statements to derive instances of other theoretical claims. The resultant account of evidence and testing, bootstrap confirmation, has many virtues—including an ability to explain when theories are more or less severely tested—but it has generated a cottage industry of counterexamples and proposals for revision. We still lack a convincing account of qualitative confirmation.

Many philosophers would insist that the root of the trouble is that the qualitative problem is really harder than its quantitative counterpart. Consider the paradox of the ravens. From early discussants such as Janina Hosiasson-Lindenbaum to the present, philosophers have diagnosed the trouble as lying in the fact that, although observations of white shoes really do confirm hypotheses about the color of ravens, the degree to which they do so is truly tiny. Suppose that we approach the problem using the concepts of probability theory, declaring that qualitative confirmation is to be understood as follows:

(*) e confirms h iff. $Pr(h/e) > Pr(e)$ [or $Pr(h/e\&B) > Pr(h/B)$].

If h is "All ravens are black", e is a report of a black raven and e' is a report of a white shoe, then we can allow that $Pr(h/e) > Pr(h)$, and that $Pr(h/e') > Pr(h)$—

i.e., that both statements confirm the hypothesis. But we can dissolve the paradox by noting that Pr(h/e)-Pr(h) $>>$ Pr(h/e')-Pr(h).

From the 1940s to the 1960s, Carnap pursued the enterprise of using probabilistic notions to define the degree to which a hypothesis is confirmed by a body of evidence. Perhaps because he was gripped by the example of deductive logic, he explored formal languages of a restricted kind—languages whose resources were plainly inadequate for the expression of the hypotheses of the mature sciences—attempting to specify a function c(h,e) that would assign each pair of statements in the language a real number in the interval [0,1]. In arguing that any such function must satisfy the axioms of probability theory, Carnap offered a conclusion that has continued to dominate contemporary work in confirmation theory, but, as his venture proceeded, it became ever more evident both that choices among a vast set of functions were hard to defend on rational grounds and that this difficulty would become ever more severe if the linguistic resources were extended to allow the formulation of hypotheses in even the simpler parts of the sciences.

Carnap's successors have embraced the framework of probability theory more directly, abandoning the attempt to find a logic of confirmation as he understood it (Horwich 1980, Howson and Urbach 1989, Earman 1992). Instead of thinking of a person as simply accepting some statements, rejecting others, and being in doubt about yet others, contemporary Bayesians propose that an ideally rational subject has a complete probability function defined on the language she uses. As evidence comes in, this probability function is updated by conditionalization. So if the subject comes to accept e as certain, she moves from the old probability function Pr to the new probability function Pr*, where, for any statement S

$$Pr^*(S) = Pr(S/e).$$

Plainly, this accords with the probabilistic approach to qualitative confirmation delineated in (*) above. Given that the result of making an observation or performing an experiment may not be to produce certainty about any statement expressible in the language—indeed Bayesians may have systematic reasons for objecting to the idea that observation could induce certainty—it's necessary to embellish the simple formula with something a bit more complicated. A natural proposal, offered by Richard Jeffrey (1965), is that observation induces a new probability in the statement e, Pr*(e), and that this yields a new complete probability function according to the equation

$$Pr^*(S) = Pr^*(e)Pr(S/e) + (1-Pr^*(e))Pr(S/-e).$$

(Alternatives have been offered by others; see, for example, Field 1978.)

Bayesianism has obvious virtues. It offers a fully precise analysis of the impact of evidence on scientific claims without either the restrictions to simple languages or the reliance on apparently arbitrary assumptions that bedeviled Carnap's earlier efforts. Bayesians can explain many features of qualitative confirmation, including the Hempelian "paradoxes," the significance of evidence that had been antecedently improbable, and, perhaps, the importance of the variety of evidence. In standard versions of Bayesianism, however, the arbitrariness is cheerfully acknowledged rather than avoided: subjective Bayesianism allows as rational the use of any initial probability function ("prior"), demanding only that the subject's degrees of confirmation should conform to the laws of probability, should only assign extremal probabilities (0 and 1) to logical and mathematical truths, and that updating of probability functions should follow the preferred pattern of transformation, for example (*) or Jeffrey's generalization of it. This means that subjective Bayesians must treat as rational individuals who make radically counterintuitive assignments of initial probability—who declare, for example, that some standard scientific hypothesis is to be assigned probability $10^{-(10^{10^{10^{10^{10}}}})}$, or some number even more minute, such that it might not be possible to raise the probability of the hypothesis to more than $10^{-(10^{10^{10^{10^{10}}}})}$ in the entire history of human inquiry. Bayesians take much comfort in theorems showing convergence of degrees of probability for subjects who start with very different priors, but, for any set of conditions in which a pair of people come to accept the same finite body of evidence statements, and for any real number r such that $0 < r < 1$, it will often be possible to find admissible prior probabilities such that two agents who accept those probabilities will end up assigning probabilities to some chosen statement h that differ by at least r.

Bayesianism is a powerful and elegant account of how rational people might change their minds. Recall, however, that we came to the theory of confirmation with rather different interests. We wanted to understand scientific knowledge, and it seemed that we needed answers to two questions: first, can we provide good reasons for thinking that the claims of the sciences are true?; second, can we give an account of the processes through which people, most prominently scientists, generate and sustain states of true belief in the way that distinguishes such states as states of knowledge? The hope was that an account of "scientific method", or more exactly of confirmation in the sciences, might suffice for both tasks, uncovering the reasons for endorsing the truth of large parts of science and simultaneously revealing the kinds of processes that generate true beliefs in the minds of scientists. I've offered a whirlwind tour of some developments in twentieth-century philosophy of science, one that has left us in a rather unsettling position. For, as I'll now suggest, it isn't at all clear how to adapt the powerful formal approach that currently stands as the dominant position in confirmation theory to an account of scientific knowledge.

4. IDEAL SUBJECTS AND ACTUAL KNOWERS

Here's an obvious way to apply any account of scientific method to the questions that confront us. The task of explaining scientific knowledge presumably begins once we've already understood how various kinds of everyday knowledge are obtained. Paradigmatically, these will be instances of observational knowledge. Starting with the observational knowledge available to a knower, show that the method plus the evidential basis together support the truth of the main claims of the sciences. Continue by demonstrating that the method endorses as reliable (truth-conducive) the processes that sustain the knower's beliefs in these claims. The most direct way to discharge the latter task would be if the processes in question were types of reasoning that figure explicitly in the account of method.

Suppose then that we try to follow this scenario using Bayesianism as our preferred account of method. The most promising example will be to take scientists as our knowers. Consider, then, a chemist and the issue of the truth of major parts of contemporary chemistry, ranging from claims about composition, molecular structure, the nature of chemical bonds, isomers, energetics of reactions, and so forth. However dedicated, our chemist will only have observed a rather limited set of pertinent experiments, but let's idealize, attributing to her vicarious experience of all the salient experiments and observations from the history of the subject. Can we now show that, Bayesian conditionalization, applied to any prior probabilities and to the evidential basis we've assigned, will yield high probabilities for the main claims of chemical theory. Of course not. There will be prior probability assignments, according to which we can attribute final probabilities as low as we please. One might think that the priors in question are bound to be peculiar, so that we can draw the consequence that, given any "serious" assignment of initial probabilities, the conclusions we hope to vindicate would emerge with very high posterior probabilities. But there are three important difficulties with this suggestion.

In the first place (subjective—that is, orthodox), Bayesianism doesn't endorse any distinction among priors. Any assignment that satisfies its minimal conditions is rationally acceptable. It would thus be rational for a subject to assign high probability to chemical theory (that's the good news) and equally rational for a subject to assign low probability (the bad news). If our imaginary scientist has actually proceeded by Bayesian conditionalization (and it's a big 'if'), then she's rational in assigning whatever probabilities to chemical theory emerge from this process. Bayesianism doesn't offer us any advice about whether these claims are true.

Second, it's simply an article of faith that the only prior probability assignments that will fail to generate high probabilities for chemical theory are intuitively peculiar. Nobody has done the work required to explore that issue (and with good reason!). Third, there's an important gap between assigning a statement a high probability and accepting it as true. However high we set the threshold for acceptance, it will still be possible to generate difficulties—this is one of the morals of a famous paradox. For suppose we say that p is acceptable as true just in case it's assigned probability greater than r. Choose n so that $(n-1)/n$ is greater than r, and consider a fair lottery with n tickets. It's rational (we'll assume) to assign probability $1/n$ to each statement of the form "Ticket t will win the lottery," and hence to assign probability $(n-1)/n$ to the negation of that statement. So a rational subject should accept each statement of form "Ticket t will not win", and conclude that no ticket will win. Presumably, however, a rational subject will believe that some ticket will win. Although there are various proposals for addressing such difficulties, Bayesianism has not generated a convincing account of acceptance, and, without it, we can't connect its probabilistic framework with conclusions about scientific knowledge.

One obvious response to these concerns might propose dropping our everyday epistemological notions in favor of the refined perspective offered by the best theory of method (Bayesianism). What goes wrong, perhaps, is that we introduce a family of folk notions—knowledge and its relatives—into a context for which a much more precise vocabulary is available. Strictly speaking, we should abandon the rough and imprecise terminology of ordinary discussion in favor of sharper concepts and distinctions.

I think that this suggestion loses any attractions it may have when we consider the second task set above for an account of method, the task of explaining and vindicating the actual processes that generate and sustain belief. One important idealization already figured explicitly in my attempt to apply Bayesianism to our actual scientific knowledge, when I supposed that our chemist had vicarious experience of all the pertinent experiments. Yet it's also entirely clear that actual chemists don't have anything comparable to the probability functions hypothesized in Bayesian theory, that they don't update in the envisaged way, and that, in everyday practice, chemical doctrines are accepted and inscribed "on the books," to be passed on to others, not merely associated with high probabilities. The actual processes that are supposed to generate and sustain scientific knowledge are at a vast remove from the Bayesian picture of the ideal subject.

To point this out is not to suggest that Bayesianism is useless, but merely that it can't be directly applied to understanding our scientific knowledge, the scientific knowledge that scientists, and those they inform, actually have. Quite possibly, Bayesian concepts furnish a wonderful normative standard, one that we can use at a later stage of inquiries into scientific knowledge. Before we reach that point, however, we'll need an account that stays closer to the actual ways in which scientific knowledge is acquired, retained, and distributed. People don't actually accept the main claims of chemistry (or any other science) because they have approximated some Bayesian procedure. It might be useful, then, to ask why anyone thinks that the science we accept is true and to look for answers that reconstruct actual human procedures and reasoning. Once we have an answer to that question, we might then consider how to appraise what goes on, either from a Bayesian perspective or by some other standard.

5. Homely Motivations and Philosophical Worries

Many educated people believe that DNA is the genetic material in animals and plants, that DNA molecules typically take the form of a double helix, and that human beings normally have about 30,000 genes. Few of them have any direct evidence for any of these conclusions, and nobody has direct evidence for all the conclusions. Scientific knowledge is social and historical: social because those outside the scientific community take the word of textbooks, popularizations of science, newspaper reports, and so forth, and because those inside the scientific community accept an enormous amount of what their colleagues, technicians, and suppliers tell them; historical because everyone, even the most pathbreaking scientist, relies on the findings of people who are now dead, and on claims that have been passed down, sometimes from quite remote figures in distant communities. Yet there's more to scientific knowledge than our collectively depending on a long tradition. For many people, including some outside the scientific specialty, can say a bit more about why they accept the doctrines I've listed.

There's a homely argument for the truth—or at least the approximate truth—of major pieces of science. When a field of science is applied, again and again, to yield predictions and interventions that are, apparently, extremely precise, then it would seem to be miraculous that things should work so well unless the claims that are applied were approximately true. Consider the three claims from molecular genetics. With respect to the first two, both molecular biologists and outsiders know that those claims are put to work in astonishing manipulations of organisms: flies and mice are made to order, with very different properties in different tissues, bacteria are grown with DNA inserts that cause them to produce large quantities of proteins we need for medical purposes. While the third claim hasn't been deployed in the same way, we accept it because it's the product of hypotheses and techniques that have proved their success.

This homely argument has encountered important philosophical objections. One is the appeal to the history of science, already considered above. If we're to use the success of parts of science as a sign of their approximate truth, then, it seems, we have to block the concern that many previous communities, beguiled by views we now take to be wrong, could equally have claimed success. I take it that the line of response sketched above disposes of this objection, insofar as it attempts to suggest that our most successful sciences are likely to be thoroughly false. Unfortunately, that isn't enough to vindicate the idea that we're warranted, on this basis, in claiming (approximate) truth. An influential line of reasoning proposes that the methods used to support our beliefs must either be subject to direct check or must be backed by methods that do allow for direct checking (Fine 1986, Laudan 1981, van Fraassen 1980). On what basis so we assume that our successes in prediction and intervention signal the approximate truth of our theoretical claims?

The right response to this question is in the spirit of Putnam's point about the possibility of using language that can be learned in connection with observables to introduce language that picks out unobservables. The link between success—predictive and interventional success—and approximate truth of the representations that generate the success becomes apparent to us from everyday contexts. We're familiar with a number of kinds of situations in which some people advance conclusions about things hidden from them, use those conclusions to guide their behavior, and are successful to the extent that their beliefs about the hidden items are roughly right. From the bridge table, to the activity of detecting crime, from diplomacy to any number of more mundane social and economic interactions, we gain a vast amount of evidence for thinking that people are successful in coping with situations causally affected by things they can't observe to the extent that those people form approximately correct beliefs about the things in question. Of course, in such situations, the things are not in principle unobservable—others can observe them and compare the actual properties with the properties ascribed by the subjects. Once the correlation is in place, however, it can be used more broadly to warrant the inference of approximate truth from empirical success, even when the generating beliefs represent entities beyond human powers of observation.

Skeptics will balk. How can we trust the inference from success to approximate truth in cases where there's no possibility of a check? Shouldn't we be epistemically modest and not stick our necks out? These questions embody a faulty way of looking at the situation. We gain evidence for a correlation between human predictive and interventional success and the approximate truth of the representations that are put to work in the successes. Nobody would suggest that our ability to check up on the properties of the entities is a causally relevant feature of the situation, that the correlation would be profoundly affected by the presence of people who can directly detect what is going on. So there's no reason for thinking that the reliability of the connection is diminished when the entities in question lie beyond the reach of human observation. What the skeptic recommends is not so much epistemic modesty as metaphysical hubris. The world is arranged so that a method that would otherwise be reliable goes astray when applied to draw conclusions about things beyond the contingent limits of human perception.

I claim, then, that the homely argument from scientific success can provide us with a basis for believing that the claims of our most successful sciences are approximately true. It must be admitted, however, that this homely argument is blunt. If there were reasons for thinking that the apparent successes could be garnered in many other ways, by putting to work very different systems of belief and representation, then those reasons would surely override our everyday confidence. We require, therefore, a supplementary account of the ways in which scientific knowledge is generated and supported, one that will take a closer view of the details.

6. HISTORICISM AND SKEPTICISM

Philosophers are thoroughly familiar with the grand forms of skepticism. Since the early modern period, epistemology has struggled to assuage doubts about the existence of an external world, other minds, the past, and so forth. In the past decades, however, research in the history and sociology of science has issued in a newer form of skepticism, one less easily dismissed as "merely" a philosophical problem. Many scholars have emphasized the complex ways in which scientific knowledge is "shaped" (or "constructed" or "negotiated"). In effect, they have challenged philosophers to find a route to our actual current corpus of scientific beliefs that we can view, retrospectively, as entrenching doctrines by reliable processes and as avoiding arbitrary decisions. Although the challengers do not usually put things in this way, they can be read as advancing the following claim: Even if we set to one side the classical philosophical concerns about the existence of an external world, or the possibility of knowing the future on the basis of inductive generalization, there is no reason to "privilege" the system of belief we've inherited from the past; at crucial points in the history of science, our predecessors have had to resolve controversies without anything that could count as good reasons for doing so; but for historical contingencies, we'd have come to adopt a very different set of beliefs, which would have been retrospectively endorsed in much the same way (Collins 1985, Latour 1987, Shapin 1992).

There are standard ways of dodging this challenge. Many philosophers of science believe, either tacitly or explicitly, that we can stand outside the historical tradition and appeal to some combination of evidence uncontroversially available to us, in the present, and a context-independent scientific method to warrant the science we practice. I've already indicated my doubts about this proposal. To reiterate the point, let me indicate the kind of historicism I take to be unavoidable.

Consider our belief that the earth describes an elliptical orbit with the sun at one focus. An ambitious philosopher might claim that this belief was initially warranted on the basis of evidence acquired by Copernicus (and/or Kepler) and transmitted to his (their) successors. Such ambitions play into the skeptic's hands, for a well-informed student of early modern science will have little difficulty in showing how the opponents of Copernicus (and Kepler) could supply excellent reasons against their proposals. A more prudent line would be to suggest that various kinds of evidence for heliocentrism were assembled throughout the seventeenth and eighteenth centuries, culminating in the nineteenth century with the detection of stellar parallax. Thus we can turn powerful telescopes into the night sky and convince ourselves that the earth does indeed move.

Surely there is something correct about this. But it's worth reflecting on the pedigree of our knowledge. We can build such instruments, point them appropriately and rely on their deliverances because of an enormous body of work carried out by previous generations of scientists. Naïve historicism proposes that any proposition we know must have been warrantedly accepted at its point of entry into the scientific corpus (or even into scientific discussion). A more sophisticated thesis recognizes the tangled lines that lead back from our knowledge into the past, seeing that some of the things we accept are warranted because of historical events in which different doctrines were adopted on the basis of good evidence. Behind the confirmation of heliocentrism that appeals to stellar parallax, for example, we find the refinements of astronomical practice that enabled the nineteenth century to build powerful telescopes, and beyond them the subtle arguments and technical demonstrations that Galileo used to convince his contemporaries that he had devised an instrument capable of revealing the properties of the heavens. Nobody in the present—or in the recent past—has had to confront the issue of whether telescopes can disclose phenomena "beyond the moon." Instead, each generation has relied on Galileo's successful resolution of an important debate that began around 1610 and was closed by about 1615.

The version of historicism I am commending takes very seriously a much-quoted passage from Neurath: we are indeed like sailors who have to rebuild our ship on the open ocean. The dependency of individual scientists on their colleagues is becoming ever more obvious, and it should remind us of their extraordinary dependence on those who have preceded them. Once the point is appreciated, we should see that the challenge posed above is serious. Suppose that Galileo failed to offer good reasons in support of the telescope, that he won by bamboozling his contemporaries. Then our claim to knowledge is undermined. He didn't know that telescopes provide reliable knowledge of the heavens, and neither do we. Our decision to leave particular planks alone, as we tinker with the rest of the boat, will succeed only if those planks were properly placed by our predecessors. History matters.

This means that the historicist poses a genuine skeptical challenge. Can it be met? Skeptical voices from the history and sociology of science argue that it cannot. They offer three general arguments. The first denies that the canons of method beloved of traditional logical empiricist philosophy of science are adequate to resolve certain crucial episodes in the history of science. The second alleges that no set of canons can succeed because of the omnipresence of underdetermination of theory by evidence: given any body of evidence, even an ideally complete one, there will always be many scientific theories equally well supported by the data. The third suggests that decisions among rival scientific theories often (perhaps always) involve judgments about the relative priority of different values, and that these judgments can be made differently, with equally good reason, by different people. I'll consider the arguments in turn.

From the writings of Kuhn in the 1960s to contemporary versions of historicist challenges, there has been a series of debates between philosophers who hoped to show how their favorite version of the methods of scientific justification would resolve various past controversies and skeptical opponents who point out how the alleged "rational reconstruction" employs dubious assumptions or slights the complications of the episode. In appraising this long sequence of discussions, I'll be brief and dogmatic: philosophical history has been illuminating and successful to the extent that it's foregone the ambition of showing how some precise formal method has been implicit in scientific decision-making. Efforts at squeezing historical incidents into some preferred philosophical box (for example, Bayesianism) have simply invited critics to point out the untidy bits of the past that fail to fit. Far more convincing have been attempts simply to canvass the types of reasoning that played a role in ending the scientific controversies of the past, attempts that try to assimilate historical actors to our everyday judgments of reliable and reasonable procedure without leaping to theoretical claims about how such judgments are to be systematized. So, to take a celebrated example, we have a far deeper understanding of the ways in which evidence and argumentation persuaded many scientists to adopt the idea of descent with modification, in the period between 1859 and 1871, than any reconstruction drawn from philosophical theory could provide. The best response to historicist skepticism is to begin by delineating as clearly as possible the strategies of argument, without commitment to any philosophical theory of scientific method, and using this to buttress a conclusion about the similarity between the behavior of the participants in the debate and our everyday judgments of good reason.

This only paves the way for the second and third skeptical arguments I distinguished above. For the historicist skeptic will probably concede the reasonableness of what Darwin and his fellow-travelers did. The point is that others who resisted could equally be seen as reasonable. In defending that point, skeptics can appeal to underdetermination.

In the heyday of logical empiricism, when a theory was conceived as a set of axioms, preferably in a first-order language, it was easy to motivate a general argument for the underdetermination of theory by evidence. The philosophical analyst could identify a set of statements—the theorems of the theory couched solely in observational terms—that could constitute all possible evidence; it's then relatively easy to argue that there will always be theories that appear to make different claims that share all the same observational consequences. The doctrine could be illustrated by famous examples from physics. One (theories that ascribe different motions to the solar system with respect to absolute space) constitutes a case in which it seems that the theories indiscernible by the evidence are genuine rivals; another (the Heisenberg and Schrödinger pictures of quantum mechanics) is an instance in which the alleged rivals are versions of the same doctrine.

I agree that the examples are genuine, and that the difference between the two types reveals the hopelessness of finding a single general tactic of coping with underdetermination. It doesn't follow, however, that underdetermination is rampant throughout science. Once we step away from the well-known examples, cases are remarkably hard to come by. Consider, for purposes of illustration, the famous Watson–Crick hypothesis about the structure of DNA. What rival hypothesis accounts for all the evidence that supports (or could support) this piece of science? Here genuine scientific problems and possibilities fail us, and the skeptical imagination must turn philosophical. An alternative to Watson–Crick: up to 1/1/3000 the bases jut inward, thereafter they point outward; all the evidence we have (maybe all the evidence human beings could have, in some sense of 'could') is compatible with either theory. But the rival has been conjured by retreating from the ground on which historicist skepticism has proudly stood—the actual course of the history of science—to the epistemological laboratory of traditional philosophy and the grander forms of skepticism that were initially not supposed to be at issue. Historicist skepticism was exciting because it invaded the space in which philosophers play backgammon with their friends, rather than confining itself to the study in which more ethereal concerns are considered.

In short, there's no sound general argument for underdetermination, and the historicist only succeeds in creating the illusion of trouble because of philosophical devotion to an outworn formalist ideal. Once we give up the thought that scientific theories are toy formal structures whose bodies of relevant evidence can be neatly delineated, we're free to take the worrying examples as they come, to admit pragmatically that there may be some questions we can't ever settle, without supposing that all issues are like that. But, along with the form of underdetermination I've already touched on, there's another, made most visible in the course of Kuhn's study of scientific revolutions (Kuhn 1962). With respect to such episodes as the Copernican revolution and the transition from phlogiston chemistry to the "new chemistry" of Lavoisier and his colleagues, Kuhn suggested that, from the beginning of the debate to its resolution, the evidence and arguments available to both parties could, with equal reason, be taken as favoring either position. This occurred not because each contending doctrine was equally good at accounting for the same body of evidence, but because each had a different profile of problems and successes, and reasonable people might weigh the various accomplishments and difficulties differently.

Philosophical history of the type considered in connection with the first skeptical argument liberates us from Kuhn's pessimistic picture. When we look more closely at the incidents in question, carefully presenting the evidence and arguments proposed by the parties, we see that, while the controversies really do show something like Kuhnian symmetry at early stages, they evolve in ways that favor the view that finally triumphs. Consider Lavoisier against the phlogistonians. From a relatively early stage of the debate, Lavoisier convinced his opponents that combustion involves a gain in weight, and most parties thereupon conceded that combustion can't *simply* be a process in which something (phlogiston) is lost to the air. The preferred phlogistonian view thenceforward was that phlogiston is emitted and something else absorbed, with the weight gain accounted for by the relative heaviness of the latter. Instead of some debate in which phlogistonians touted the explanatory virtue of explaining why some substances are combustible (because they contain phlogiston) and Lavoisier emphasized the weight gain in combustion, there was a protracted and complex controversy, in which the rival scientists endeavored to identify the compositions of a wide range of substances, in accordance both with the constraints imposed by their different pictures of combustion and a growing body of experimental findings. Very roughly, this decade-long discussion consists in showing that there are more and more places in which phlogistonian assignments of composition are inconsistent and fewer and fewer places in which Lavoisier's preferred assignments are threatened with inconsistency. Enormous numbers of possibilities are explored, but, by the mid-1780s, it becomes extremely hard to see what resources phlogiston theory can use to specify the composition of (what we call) oxides, salts, and acids (Kitcher 1993, 272–290). The decisions of the many chemists who jump on Lavoisier's bandwagon are as reasonable—and as easy to understand—as those of the car owner who decides that the rattling in the engine block, the grinding of the gears, the need for a new alternator, the leaking oil on the garage floor, the rust under the doors, and the many short circuits mean that it's time to turn in a vehicle that has been running for fifteen years.

I claim that Kuhnian underdetermination dissolves under the perspective of philosophically informed history. A complete rebuttal to historicist skepticism would require far more of this kind of history than we yet have. To close this section, let me venture a brief explanation of why the informal canvassing of reasons and arguments might serve us better than attempts to apply formal accounts of confirmation. It's not that the efforts at formalizing method are useless; rather they reveal the microstructure of certain kinds of scientific arguments. Where they fail us is in elucidating the complicated ways in which, in the historical development of the sciences, the simple arguments to which they apply are combined to undergird judgments about the problems and prospects of programs of research. The situation is analogous to discussions of grandmaster chess. Numerous good books instruct the aspiring player in the precise details of tactics and combinations, but the literature on strategy is much more impressionistic and suggestive. Hence it's relatively easy for an intelligent beginner to learn chess tactics, but the process of understanding strategic refinements is a much lengthier—and chancier—affair. Perhaps future chess theorists will develop formal measures of strategic worth (and if they do, we can expect the task of developing expert programs that can rout humans to become far less difficult), and, by the same token, it may be that some future group of theorists of science will be able to articulate formal accounts of the ways in which individual pieces of argumentation are juxtaposed to close major scientific controversies. Historicist skeptics have seen that we currently lack any such formal accounts, and that the "tactical" considerations philosophers can analyze with precision are insufficient to explain the resolution of revolutions. They are best answered by assembling the phenomena on which a future formal account would build.

7. EPISTEMOLOGY PROCLAIMED: A SOCIOHISTORICAL ACCOUNT OF SCIENTIFIC KNOWLEDGE

Logical empiricism to the contrary, epistemology isn't exhausted by logic. The tradition of trying to do for science what Frege and Russell managed for mathematics has yielded important insights that can serve us well, both in analyzing individual reasoning by past scientists and in resolving current disputes that turn on methodological matters. What I've been suggesting is that the epistemology of science needs more, that part of what it needs is an understanding of the ways in which our present knowledge is dependent on the past and an investigation of the routes which have led our predecessors to accept ideas we now take for granted.

But the enrichment of logic by history is only a part of it. Knowledge, I suggest, is a social endeavor, and its social aspects are manifest in the sciences.

Good inquiry isn't just a matter of the conformity of individual minds to the rules of right reason, but also the coordination of individuals in pursuit of collective goals (Kitcher 1993, chap. 8). The concept of knowledge is important to us because of our interest in truth—more exactly, our interest in particular kinds of truths. To mark something out as an item of knowledge is to indicate that it can be depended on, used in practical activities or in further investigations. We should think of ourselves as having at our disposal an expanding store, to which we may occasionally contribute. Elements of the store are passed on to subsequent generations, some figuring in the education of all, others taught to those who will pursue particular specialties. Seen from this perspective, certain general epistemological questions arise.

What rules ought to govern the incorporation of new hypotheses within the store? How is the information "on the books" best made accessible to the individuals who may want to draw from it? How is the store to be monitored and possibly revised? The general form of an answer to these questions must make reference to our goals. Thus a fundamental task for the philosophical study of scientific knowledge is to articulate an account of the aims of the enterprise. Generations of philosophers of science have tacitly assumed that those goals are time- and context-independent. The simplest version is to suppose that the aim of the sciences is to deliver a complete and accurate account of nature. But that is surely too simple. The notion of a *complete* account of nature makes no more sense than that of a complete map of our globe: sciences, like maps, are inevitably selective. A better proposal would be to suggest that there are certain kinds of truths that are privileged, and that the sciences seek to elicit these "fundamental" truths. To articulate that proposal would require its champions to explain just what makes some propositions fundamental, and that, I believe, is no trivial task. Perhaps there is no way to complete it. Perhaps we have to settle for a view that sees the kinds of truths we seek as dependent on our institutions and our history. Science may be like mapmaking, endeavoring to find accurate representations of aspects of the world that answer to evolving human interests.

Assuming that this debate has been resolved and that we have an account of the aims of the sciences (one possibly relativized to time and context), we can turn to the three questions posed in the last paragraph. The most ambitious way to address them would be to try to find the optimal ways of achieving our goals. That is likely to be too much to hope for. Lacking vast amounts of relevant information (including the kinds of information we expect inquiry to provide!) we probably can't arrive at firm views about how to organize the social epistemic venture. Yet even if an epistemology of science can't deliver the ambitious answer, we may ask it to help us avoid obvious pitfalls, and perhaps to improve our current condition.

Consider some obvious potential troubles. If we require that nothing ever be entered in the store of knowledge without constant checking and rechecking in each generation, then much of the point of the social enterprise will be vitiated: to adapt Newton's famous metaphor, we are unlikely to be able to create that pyramid of giants that enables even the pygmies at the top to see a long way. On the other hand, a liberal policy for inclusion would run the risk that later generations would be constantly building on faulty ideas they inherited from their predecessors, with the consequent wastage of time and effort. Somewhere between the conservative and liberal poles lies the optimal policy, and even though we can't identify it, we can at least avoid the extremes; further, because we understand the problems of the extremes, we can interrogate our own practice, asking if small modifications (or large ones) would be more likely to guard against one of the problems.

A similar approach is desirable with respect to issues about managing of the store so as to make the information it contains accessible and about modifying of the store with time. The social organization of knowledge may place too great an emphasis on drawing connections among separate lines of inquiry (at costs of pursuing those inquiries in depth), or it may stress the transmission of specialized knowledge (losing sight of connections among different fields). Similarly epistemic traditions may be closed, brooking no challenges to pieces of "established knowledge," or relatively open, encouraging some mavericks in each generation to gain fame and fortune by successfully overturning some important part of the conventional wisdom. Just as closure would be a disaster for fallible beings like ourselves, so too complete openness would divert efforts that might better be directed towards building on what previous generations have produced.

For almost half a century, discussions of scientific knowledge have been distorted partly by the misguided thought that epistemology is a part of logic, partly by the association of historicism with skepticism. If the epistemology of science no longer goes incognito, we may find that interesting issues have been neglected, and we may be able to combine insights from rather different philosophical traditions. My sketch of a sociohistorical approach to scientific knowledge is a preliminary advertisement for one way in which that might proceed.

REFERENCES

Carnap, Rudolf (1962). "The Methodological Character of Theoretical Concepts." *Minnesota Studies in the Philosophy of Science*, vol. 1. Minneapolis: University of Minnesota Press. 38–76.

———. (1963). "The Aim of Inductive Logic," reprinted in S. Luckenbach, ed. *Probabilities, Problems, and Paradoxes*. Encino, Calif.: Dickenson.

Collins, H. M. (1985). *Changing Order*. London: Sage.

Earman, John (1992) *Bayes or Bust?* Cambridge Mass.: MIT Press.

Field, Hartry (1978). "A Note on Jeffrey Conditionalization." *Philosophy of Science* 45 (1978): 361–367.

Fine, Arthur (1986). *The Shaky Game.* Chicago: University of Chicago Press.

Glymour, Clark (1980). *Theory and Evidence.* Princeton: Princeton University Press.

Goldman, Alvin (1986) *Epistemology and Cognition.* Cambridge, Mass.: Harvard University Press.

Hempel, C. G. (1965) *Aspects of Scientific Explanation.* Glencoe, Ill.: Free Press.

Horwich, Paul (1980). *Probability and Evidence.* Cambridge: Cambridge University Press.

Howson, Colin, and Peter Urbach. (1989) *Scientific Reasoning.* La Salle, Ill.: Open Court.

Jeffrey, Richard (1965). *The Logic of Decision.* New York: McGraw-Hill.

Kelly, Kevin (1994). *The Logic of Reliable Inquiry.* New York: Oxford University Press.

Kitcher, Philip (1993). *The Advancement of Science.* New York: Oxford University Press.

Kuhn, Thomas S. (1962). *The Structure of Scientific Revolutions.* Chicago: University of Chicago Press.

Latour, Bruno (1987). *Science in Action.* Cambridge Mass.: Harvard University Press.

Laudan, Larry (1981). "A Confutation of Convergent Realism." *Philosophy of Science* 48: 19–49.

Putnam, Hilary (1962). "What Theories Are Not." Reprinted in Putnam, *Mathematics, Matter, and Method: Philosophical Papers*, vol. 1. Cambridge: Cambridge University Press, 1975. 215–227.

Scheffler, Israel (1963). *The Anatomy of Inquiry.* New York: Knopf.

Shapin, Stephen (1992). *A Social History of Truth.* Chicago: University of Chicago Press.

Spirtes, Peter, et al. (2001). *Causation, Prediction and Search.* New York: Academic.

Van Fraassen, Bas (1980). *The Scientific Image.* Oxford: Oxford University Press.

CHAPTER 14

···

EXPLANATION AND EPISTEMOLOGY

···

WILLIAM G. LYCAN

EXPLANATION and epistemology are closely related in at least three ways. First, the notion of explanation is itself an epistemic one. To explain something is an epistemic act, and to have something explained to you is to learn.

Second, there is a form of ampliative inference that has come to be called 'inference to the best explanation' or, more briefly, 'explanatory inference.' Roughly: From the fact that a certain hypothesis would explain the data at hand better than any other available hypothesis, we infer with some degree of confidence that that leading hypothesis is correct. There is no question but that this inference is often performed. Arguably, every human being performs it many times in a day, perhaps without letup.

Third, there is an epistemological thesis, sometimes called 'Explanationism,' to the effect that explanatory inference is (not only performed but) warranted and does epistemically justify the accepting of its conclusion. That thesis comes in several grades of strength, but even its lowest grade is controversial among epistemologists.

1. EXPLANATION

What is explanation? That question has been voluminously discussed, though by philosophers of science rather than by epistemologists, since the heyday of Logical Positivism. The Ur-answer of the twentieth century was Hempel and Oppenheim's (1948) Deductive-Nomological (D-N) theory, also called the 'covering law' model. According to that theory, one explains a fact or event (the 'explanandum') by showing that it followed by law of nature from a preëxisting set of circumstances or conditions. Such a showing would take the form of a deductive argument, a deduction of the explanandum from the antecedent conditions and one or more laws of nature.

To take an example of Jaegwon Kim's (1967): A room had its walls painted white. But the walls later blackened. Why did they? Explanation: (i) The paint contained lead carbonate; (ii) the gas used for lighting the room contained sulfur (evidently the example is set in a pre-electric century); (iii) lead carbonate combines with sulfur to form lead sulfide; and (iv) lead sulfide is black. (Though i–iv do not strictly entail that the walls blackened, they can be eked out: We can add that the burning of the gas *gave off* sulfur, that the sulfur diffused through the air and made contact with the paint on the wall, etc.) Initially, there was paint containing lead carbonate, and sulfur was introduced; so the laws of chemistry kicked in and blackening was the then logically inevitable result.

More generally, a D-N explanation takes the form:

$C_1, C_2, \ldots, C_k$ Antecedent conditions
$L_1, L_2, \ldots, L_r$ Laws of nature

$\therefore E$ The explanandum

—where the horizontal line and the $\therefore$ symbol mean that E has been logically deduced from the two sets of premises.

The D-N model was soon beset by counterexamples and other objections of many different types. (For a review, see Salmon 1989.) But for our purposes, the important thing to notice is that a D-N explanation exhibits what are actually several different features, each of which is individually relevant to the business of explaining.

First, a D-N explanation is a case of *subsuming*. The explanandum is collected under a generalization, given by the pertinent laws. Thus it is exhibited as part of an overall pattern.

Second, a D-N explanation shows that, given the antecedent conditions, the explanandum *was to be expected*, or could have been predicted, by anyone who knew the laws.

Third, if we assume that for X to lead by natural law to Y entails that X causes Y, a D-N explanation is a *causal* explanation. (More strongly, it presents a case of causal *necessitation*; it does not merely cite some causal factors.)

Fourth, a D-N explanation is a *complete* explanation, not in the sense of containing all imaginably relevant information, but in that of containing enough explanatory information to *entail* its explanandum. Given the antecedent conditions and the laws, it is not even conceivable that the explanandum should not have ensued.

For proponents of the D-N model, it was only natural that the foregoing four features should coincide. But one lesson of the subsequent critical literature is that they do not fully coincide in real life; there are many cases of explanation in which they come apart. Take the last feature first: Real explanations in real science almost never have it. Toy examples in Newtonian physics do, and perhaps our paint example would if thoroughly enough filled in, but quantum-mechanical, biological, geological, and certainly meteorological explanations do not. Quantum-mechanical explanations are probabilistic; and special-science explanations rest too heavily on idealizations and are too vulnerable to lower-level hardware breakdowns.

So, in particular, a causal explanation need not be 'complete' in the entailing sense. A perfectly good causal explanation can also fail to show that its explanandum was to be expected. Standard examples of this are highly improbable events whose mechanisms we can work out but only after the fact. For example, evolutionary biology can explain the emergence of a trait in a population, but could not have predicted in advance that that trait would emerge (Scriven 1959); an atomic nucleus suddenly decayed at time t and gave off an alpha particle; quantum mechanics can and does explain the particle's emission, but quantum mechanics itself entails that the emission at t was highly improbable and could not possibly have been predicted (Railton 1978). Nor need a subsumption show that its explanandum was to be expected; the nucleus in Railton's example is subsumed under a rigorous quantum-mechanical law, and thus elegantly exhibited as part of a pattern, but the law is a probabilistic law rather than a universal generalization.

And a perfectly good causal explanation can fail to subsume in the D-N sense. I can show that one event caused another without knowing any interesting general law that underlies my explanation. For example, I might work out by Mill's Methods that it was the chicken salad that must have gone bad and poisoned the stricken cafeteria patrons without having any idea what toxin did the poisoning or according to what biological laws. Conversely, a good subsumption need not be causal, as when physics relies on purely geometrical explanation (or for that matter, when geometry does). And, by the same token, we can show that a surprising event was to have been expected (had we known one or two of its antecedents in light of an inductive correlation between them and it), without having the faintest idea of how or why the antecedents led to the event.

Thus, so far we have three distinct though overlapping paradigms for scientific explanation—subsumption, showing-to-be-expected, and causal. And there are at least two more. One is the 'pragmaticist' conception associated with Scriven 1962, van Fraassen 1980 and others, of *filling a gap in understanding* by answering a 'why' question in a contextually informative way. It can readily be checked that filling a gap in understanding, being a matter of individual psychology, is conceptually independent of any of the preceding three paradigms. A fifth paradigm, sometimes touted in textbooks, is the *reduction of the unfamiliar to the familiar*. Such reduction, though it happens (as in the case of assimilating electricity to the coursing of little balls through a pipe), is somewhat unusual in science; certainly molecular genetics, general relativity, and economics do little of it. 'Scientific explanation' begins to look like a family-resemblance sort of category, comprising the distinct conceptions mentioned so far as well as perhaps others.

Certainly it comprehends a few more specialized explanatory formats as well. There is the sort of *function-analytical* explanation that pervades cognitive psychology, biology, computer science, systems theory as applied to artifacts, electrical engineering, and auto mechanics (Simon 1969, Wimsatt 1976; Cummins 1983). One explains the behavioral capacities of an organism or system by decomposing that system into subsystems and showing how the subsystems coöperate to produce the corporate output of the whole; then, for any of the subsystems, the process can be repeated at the next lower level of organization, and so on. (An automobile works—locomotes—by having a fuel reservoir, a fuel line, a carburetor, a combustion chamber, an ignition system, a transmission, and wheels that turn. If one wants to know how the carburetor works, one will be told what its parts are and how they work together to infuse oxygen into fuel; and so on.) There are the special patterns of explanation found in history and sometimes in the social sciences: We often explain people's behavior by *rationalizing* it, by showing why it was a good idea from the principals' point of view (Dray 1963, Dennett 1987). This style of explanation presupposes norms of theoretical and practical rationality; nothing of the sort appears in physics or chemistry, though such norms are not *entirely* foreign to evolutionary biology.

'Scientific explanation,' if that means explanation of any type that is regularly offered in the sciences, is motley. It is not likely to be captured by a single set of necessary and sufficient conditions.

Of course, not all explanation is scientific explanation, nor is epistemology primarily concerned with scientific explanation. Most of the explanations that ordinary people (including ordinary philosophers) provide and receive in real life are not scientific, but are couched in terms of everyday things, events, and people.

2. EXPLANATORY INFERENCE

As its name suggests, an inference to the best explanation proceeds from an explanandum or a set of data to a hypothesis that explains the data better than any available competing hypothesis would. To put it in that way sounds scientific, and indeed, the sciences do justify their theoretical posits on grounds of the posits' explanatory power. The germ theory of disease is accepted (in part) because it explains striking epidemiological facts, as well as patients' symptoms. Even more vividly, the atomic theory of matter is accepted because it explains the very remarkable generalizations of classical chemistry. Astronomical hypotheses were originally accepted only because they explained the synchronic and diachronic patterns of light observable in the night sky.

But, again, explanatory inference is hardly limited to science. A detective solves a murder case by reflecting on the various clues and constraints and arriving at the best explanation of the clues given the constraints, the story that makes the best sense of the clues. An auto mechanic diagnoses your car trouble by inferring the best explanation of the car's symptoms. It may be tempting in such cases to say that the detective or the mechanic has arrived at the 'only possible' explanation and therefore has really performed a deduction, by ruling out all the alternate possibilities (Sherlock Holmes talked explicitly in this way). But that would not be accurate. There are always many possibilities that have not been logically ruled out by the evidence but are just poor or outright fanciful explanations: The murder *might* have been committed by a very small paratrooper who landed silently in pre-dawn darkness on the garage roof and had some way of getting through the window without breaking it, etc. Or it might have been committed by invisible aliens. 'The only possible explanation' has to mean 'the only even halfway plausible explanation.'

Nor is explanatory inference limited to professional practitioners such as detectives and mechanics. We all perform it in everyday life as well. I find what appear to be droppings on my lawn and infer that an unleashed animal has been by. The last slice of pizza has unexpectedly disappeared from the refrigerator, and I infer that my daughter has stopped at home after school instead of proceeding directly to her orchestra rehearsal. Some philosophers, such as Russell (1959) and Quine (1960), argue that our constant flood of beliefs about ordinary physical objects in our environment is the result of constant explanatory inference from the ways we are appeared to.

In some but not all of the foregoing examples, the inferred explanans can be directly checked after the fact. For example, the murderer may be caught and confess; the auto mechanic may then check the relevant engine part and verify her diagnosis; I can interrogate my daughter when she gets home. But ordinarily we make the explanatory inferences with some confidence *whether or not* we then go on to check them.

Representing explanatory inference schematically:

$F_1, F_2, \ldots, F_n$ are facts in need of explanation.

Hypothesis H explains the F_i.

No available competing hypotheses would explain the F_i as well as H does.

∴ H is true.

Some commentary is required. (1) What are 'facts'? For our purposes, they are just states of affairs that, in the context, are reasonably presumed to obtain. (They do not have to be facts about any particular privileged subject-matter, such as about objects that have been 'directly observed.' Nor do they have to be known with certainty.) (2) When is a fact genuinely 'in need of' explanation? An interesting question, but let us not try to settle it here; substantive disagreements about what does or does not need explaining are rare. (3) 'Explains' in the second premise cannot, without question-begging, mean 'actually explains'; rather, it is used in the sense of 'would explain if true.' (4) Which type(s) of explaining, from among the types distinguished in section 1, sustain the present pattern of inference? Causal explanation, certainly; probably showing-to-be-expected; and probably function-analytical; but extensive discussion is needed here. (5) 'As well as' in the third premise implies an evaluative comparison; one hypothesis explains the facts *better than* another one explains them. There must therefore be criteria for ranking hypotheses in this way. And so there are; see the next section. (6) Of course the explanatory argument form is not deductively valid; the conclusion is not logically entailed by the premises. The ∴ sign should here be pronounced as 'therefore, probably,' indicating that the argument is ampliative.

The foregoing schema must be restricted in at least two ways. First, the third premise alone is not strict enough to motivate the superior hypothesis H, because H might be only barely superior to a very poor field (Lehrer 1974, 180). Suppose a strange and weird event occurs, and no faintly plausible explanation suggests itself. All we can think of is that the event was perpetrated by aliens. The hypothesis that it was caused by aliens from Venus is less implausible than the hypothesis that it was caused by aliens from outside our solar system, since it at least does not require interstellar travel. But it is not at all plausible and should not be accepted even to a small degree.

The moral is that there must be a threshold. In addition to merely outstripping its competitors, H must meet some minimum standard of credibility. (Though we must leave it open that H be antecedently improbable; obviously we do often confidently infer explanations that would have seemed highly improbable until we had seen the particular set of data they explain.)

One might think of adding that besides meeting the minimum standard, H must outstrip its nearest competitor by a considerable margin. After all, if H' is nearly as good an explanation as is H, falling just barely short, why should we then plump decisively for H? But we do not need to plump decisively for the conclusion of an explanatory inference. Like any ampliative argument form, our schema's instances warrant their conclusions to varying degrees. In the present circumstance, though we would not be warranted in accepting H in marked pref- erence to H', we would be warranted *to a very small degree* in accepting H rather than H'.

The second restriction is required by the possibility of subjects who are very unimaginative. Suppose I am especially gullible. I receive a gaudy letter in the mail telling me that I have won a money prize, and all I need to do to collect the prize and perhaps further millions is to fill out the complicated form in the en- velope and return it by mail to the Publishers' Raffle Co. to participate in their final drawing. I do this, believing that I have won a money prize and that all I need to do to collect the prize and perhaps further millions is to fill out the form; no alternate explanation of my having been sent the letter occurs to me. Or suppose I am just no good at thinking up hypotheses: I find the slice of pizza missing and I conclude wonderingly that my refrigerator is defective in such a way that it makes pizza disappear without trace. These are not reasonable infer- ences.

So we need to restrict the third premise by requiring that a reasonable range of hypotheses have at least tacitly been considered. (What range is 'reasonable' in a given context will depend both on the contextual facts and on the subject's existing beliefs and expectations.)

But now we must address the question of what makes one hypothesis a better explanation than another.

3. The Explanatory Virtues

We must consider the case in which two competing hypotheses explain or accom- modate overlapping data, and neither has been refuted by having been shown to entail something false; thus they are viable mutual competitors. How do we tell which is 'better,' that is, which should be preferred? In practice, we make such judgments on the basis of various pragmatic reasons (Quine and Ullian 1978, Thagard 1978, Harman 1986): H may be preferable because it is simpler, or because it explains more than does its competitor, or because it is more readily testable, or because it is less at odds with what we already reasonably believe, or (more likely) because of some more complex combination of such factors.

The preference for *simplicity* in particular is illustrated by the standard example of experimental scientists' practice in curve-fitting on graphs: Given a set of data points that in fact lie along a straight line, any scientist will go ahead and draw a straight line through them rather than any more complicated curve, and leave it that way unless further, refuting data should come in. This compelling smoothness of the linear hypothesis is a virtue of some sort, one that is not shared by the hypotheses respectively expressed by other curves that pass through the very same data points, such as perhaps a sine curve. Notice that there are countless many more complex curves that pass through those same points, including one that looks like a rather scrawled handwritten token of 'God defend New Zealand.'

There are many different types and respects of simplicity other than the simplicity of a mathematical function: elegance of structure; parsimony of posits and/ or of ontology; fewer principles taken as primitive; and no doubt more. It should not be suggested that 'simplicity,' even simplicity in a single respect, is easily measured, or even that it can be given a clear general characterization; see Foster and Martin 1966 and Sober 1975. And simplicity's different kinds and respects overlap and cut across each other, often conflicting; there are no set rules for resolving such conflicts.

When a theory explains more than does its competitor, especially if the added explananda are taken from a distinct range of phenomena, we speak of greater explanatory *power*; other things being equal, we prefer a hypothesis of greater power. Perhaps this is a higher-order manifestation of the drive for simplicity; it makes for greater simplicity in the overall belief system that contains the two ranges of data.

Other pragmatic virtues include:

Testability. Other things being equal, a hypothesis H will be preferred to a competitor H' if H has more readily testable implications. The verificationists were rash to hold that untestability amounted to cognitive meaninglessness, but testability is an important component of the merit of a hypothesis. Intuitively, if a hypothesis makes no testable predictions, it has little explanatory force. Suppose someone believes that the tides and the weather at sea are controlled by capricious demons who are invisible and otherwise undetectable. This subject has no further belief on the topic, and is unable to predict future weather because, he says, it all depends on the demons' whims at the time. Thus, his only available explanation of a past event is, 'The demons must have wanted it that way,' which (n.b., even if we are perfectly happy to accept the existence of demons) is not highly explanatory.

Fecundity. H will be preferred to H' if H is more fruitful in suggesting further related hypotheses, or parallel hypotheses in other areas. (Perhaps this is a higher-order form of simplicity again.)

Neatness. H will be preferred to H' if H leaves fewer messy unanswered questions behind, and especially if H does not itself raise such questions.

Conservativeness. H will be preferred to H' if H fits better with what we already believe. If this sounds dogmatic or pigheaded, notice again that, inescapably, we never even consider competing hypotheses that would strike us as grossly implausible; the detective would never so much as entertain the hypothesis that the crime was committed by invisible Venusian invaders, nor the mechanic that your car trouble is caused by an infusion of black bile or evil fairy dust. Nor should we consider such hypotheses, even if we could enumerate them all; someone who insisted on doing so would be rightly accused of wasting everyone's time. All inquiry is conducted against a background of existing beliefs, and we have no choice but to rely on some of them while modifying or abandoning others—else how could any such revisions be motivated?

Every pragmatic virtue is a matter of degree. And there is the obvious complication: Our preference for any one of the virtues always comes qualified by 'other things being equal,' and the 'other things' are the respective degrees of the other virtues. Clearly the virtues can conflict among themselves. Perhaps the most obvious tension holds between simplicity and conservativeness, since often simplification is gained only through bold overthrowing of previously accepted theory, as in the case of Copernican vs. Ptolemaic astronomy. But because of the complexity of any detailed real-world case study, there is no generally accepted policy for weighing the various degrees of the various virtues against each other in any particular inquiry. The lack of such a policy understandably has led some epistemologists to skepticism or relativism concerning theory choice based on pragmatic virtues. At the very least, it would be an Augean task to sort through the history of science and other factual inquiry, comparing cases of what we consider reasonable theory choice and trying to sift out the combinations of degrees of the various virtues that motivate our judgments of the reasonableness of those choices.

Still, in the vast majority of ordinary cases we do not much disagree on which hypotheses are better than others. Such disagreement is the exception rather than the rule, and even when there is disagreement, consensus can often be reached through discussion that makes more of the relevant factors explicit. Even in science, disagreement at the frontier presupposes a great deal of agreement on theory choices made in the past.

4. EXPLANATIONISM

The slightly barbarous label "Explanationism" was coined by James Cornman (1980). As the term shall be used here, it designates roughly the doctrine that what justifies an ampliative inference—or more generally the formation of any new belief—is that the doxastic move in question improves the subject's explanatory position overall, or as we sometimes say, the move increases the explanatory coherence of the subject's global set of beliefs. In particular, the Explanationist holds that some beliefs are indeed justified by 'inference to the best explanation' as described in the previous section. Explanationism derives from Peirce and Dewey, by way of Quine (1960) and Wilfrid Sellars (1963). But Harman (1965) was the first to articulate it and defend it against better entrenched competing epistemologies. It has since received support from Thagard (1978, 1989), Lycan (1988), and Lipton (1991).

One must distinguish between at least three grades of Explanationism; we may call them respectively 'Weak,' 'Sturdy,' and 'Ferocious.' (A fourth and higher grade will be mentioned shortly.) Weak Explanationism is only the modest claim that explanatory inference *can* epistemically justify a conclusion. (As we shall see, that claim has been vigorously disputed.)

Sturdy Explanationism adds that explanatory inference can do its justifying intrinsically, that is, without being *derived* from some other form of ampliative inference, such as probability theory, taken as more basic. (That claim is disputed by Cornman 1980 and by Keith Lehrer 1974, who argue that explanatory inference is at bottom a use of probability theory. Other theorists have tried to reduce individual explanatory virtues, such as simplicity, to probabilistic features.)

Ferocious Explanationism adds that no other form of ampliative inference is basic; all are derived from explanatory inference. (That claim is disputed by almost everyone.) Interestingly, Harman originally defended Ferocious Explanationism, ignoring the two weaker forms, by trying to exhibit various common patterns of traditional inductive inference as enthymematic instances of explanatory inference; see also Lycan (1988, chap. 9). Harman's mature explanationist view of all reasoning is given in Harman 1986. At times he seems to incline toward an even more ambitious doctrine, which we might call 'Holocaust Explanationism': the view that *all* inference and reasoning, including deductive as well as ampliative, is derived from explanatory inference. That would require reconstructing simple logical deduction in explanatory terms.

Weak Explanationism is a commonsensical view, but of course we must address objections that have been made against it, especially as they are a fortiori objections to the stronger doctrines. Sturdy Explanationism is slightly more contentious, but in the absence of any actual attempt to reduce all the pragmatic virtues to probabilistic or confirmation-theoretic notions, there is little point in considering criticisms of it that do not also apply to Weak Explanationism. (The Weak-but-not-Sturdy view has not been pursued in any detail, and in any case would be too technical to be usefully discussed here.) Following consideration of the objections to Weak, we shall then concentrate on the pros and cons of Ferocious Explanationism.

5. Two Objections to Weak Explanationism, and Replies

Van Fraassen (1980) argues that explanation—even the most rigorous causal explanation that takes place in science—is interest- and/or context- and/or understander-relative in each of a number of ways. If explanation is in the eye of the beholder, but we remain more or less realist about epistemic justification, then the former is no fit foundation for the latter.

Actually van Fraassen calls attention under this heading to what are a number of different and unrelated phenomena, of which the most pertinent are the following. (1) The nonuniqueness of causes. Van Fraassen points out (115, 125–126) that any choice of 'the' cause of an event from among all the event's contributing factors is undeniably interest-relative; the most one can find in nature is a set of causes, causal factors and conditions that combine to lead by law to the event. (Reply: Quite so. But nothing in the Explanationist program presupposes otherwise.) (2) Knowledge-relativity. Van Fraassen gives an example (125) designed to show that explanation is relative to what one knows. (Reply: Of course an explanation may be helpful or unhelpful to one depending on what one already knows. No surprise there, and nothing damaging either to anyone's theory of anything: that whether an explanation tells you anything you didn't already know depends on what you already knew is tautologous, and so irrelevant to any philosophical argument.) (3) Alleged interest-dependence of the explanans-explanandum asymmetry in particular. Van Fraassen accepts the contention, attributed to Sylvain Bromberger, that normally the height of the flagpole explains the length of its shadow rather than the other way around, and he joins Bromberger (1966) in taking this to embarrass the D-N model. But he resists the diagnostic conclusion that the asymmetry is something in nature that the concept of explanation latches onto. Rather, he says, explanation itself, a relation solely between theories and minds, is asymmetrical. The asymmetry is psychological and depends on our interests, combined, of course, with our natural expectations based on de facto regularities of nature. (Reply: Van Fraassen's key example, his romantic story of 'The Tower and the Shadow,' is unconvincing; see Kitcher and Salmon 1987.)

(4) Relativity to contrast-class. Here we come upon a phenomenon that indeed must be addressed in any discussion of explanation and epistemology. Van Fraassen reminds us (127–128, cf. Garfinkel 1981) of the familiar point that 'why' questions, and hence explanations (their answers), seem ambiguous as to focus within their complement clauses—that is, 'why' questions seem to request different explanations depending on emphasis. Van Fraassen offers the example, 'Why did Adam eat the apple?' In asking that, we normally would want to know why Adam ate the apple rather than scrupulously avoiding it as ordered by God. But different explanatory requests could be produced using nearly the same sentence by varying surface syntax or just intonation: 'Why was it Adam who ate the apple?'; 'Why was it the apple that Adam ate?'; 'Why did Adam *eat* the apple?' Requests for explanations, and hence presumably explanations themselves, are finer-grained—individuated more finely—than are explananda as expressed by ordinary unmarked propositions.

What this shows is that explanation has a built-in 'as opposed to . . . ' clause. ('Why did Adam eat it as opposed to avoiding it?' vs. 'Why did Adam as opposed to Eve eat it?' vs. 'Why did he eat the apple as opposed to the serpent, grilled?') In each case, what van Fraassen calls a contrast-class is presupposed—people who might have eaten the apple, things that Adam might have eaten, and the like. This seems a fair criticism of the original D-N model. The model would have to be modified to make the premises of a D-N explanation home in on the syntactic element of the explanandum-conclusion that signals the appropriate contrast-class. But what bearing has the relativity to contrast-class on Weak Explanationism?

Lipton (1991) offers an excellent discussion of contrast-relativity. As he describes the phenomenon '[a] contrastive . . . [explanandum] consists of a fact and a foil, and the same fact may have several different foils' (35). He neither affirms nor (strictly) denies van Fraassen's apparent assumption that all explanations are implicitly contrastive, but he gives heavy weight to the contrastive case. He argues that often it is easier to explain a contrast than to explain the uncontrasted fact alone (cf. Garfinkel 1981, 30): Lipton's preference for contemporary plays may explain why he went to see *Jumpers* last night rather than *Candide*, but that does not suffice to explain why he went to see *Jumpers*. (Though sometimes it can be the other way around; we can explain why Jones contracted paresis without being able to explain why Jones rather than Smith did.)

One might suppose that what is going on in a case of contrast-relativity is just that two *different explananda* are being considered. If so, then van Fraassen's argument would in no way damage Weak Explanationism, because the explanatory-inference schema already isolates and presupposes a single given explanandum. But Lipton (though himself an Explanationist) goes on to make a point that casts some doubt on this simple move, by arguing that there is no simple reduction of a contrastive explanation to noncontrastive (particularly truth-functional) form. In particular, one cannot reduce explaining contrastively why *P rather than Q* to explaining noncontrastively why (it is the case that) *P and not Q*, because the latter would involve explaining each conjunct, and as we saw, either conjunct might be harder to explain than was the original contrast.

Lipton's antireduction case is convincing, but notice that it does not help van Fraassen refute Weak Explanationism. For even if there is no truth-functional or other simple reduction of contrastive explananda to noncontrastive ones, we can still distinguish the contrastive explananda from each other. Van Fraassen himself even gives a helpful notation in which to do so, in terms of his contrast-classes attaching to syntactic elements of the original uncontrasted explananda. So far as has been shown, it is still entirely open to us to hold that cases of contrast-relativity are merely cases of distinct explananda, and if that is what they are, they are no threat to Weak Explanationism.

Let us then turn to a second objection to Weak Explanationism. Van Fraassen offers the following eloquent rebuke to common sense.

> Judgements of simplicity and explanatory power are [admittedly] the intuitive and natural vehicle for expressing our epistemic appraisal. What can an empiricist make of these . . . virtues which go so clearly beyond the [more narrowly evidential] ones he considers pre-eminent?
>
> There are specifically human concerns, a function of our interests and pleasures, which make some theories more valuable and appealing to us than others. Values of this sort, however, . . . cannot rationally guide our epistemic attitudes and decisions. For example, if it matters more to us to have one sort of question answered rather than another, that is no reason to think that a theory which answers more of the first sort of question is more likely to be true. (87)

Van Fraassen's second paragraph suggests two different arguments against Weak Explanationism. Each is attractive on its face.

The first argument can be put as follows. The explanatory virtues' pragmatic value are just a mixture of corner-cutting convenience—really a form of epistemic laziness—and merely aesthetic appeal. In curve-fitting, we prefer the smoothest hypothesis because the smooth curve both is easier to draw and looks prettier. But why should anyone think that convenience and prettiness count in any way toward truth? Why should a theory's being simpler than another theory make the first theory more likely to be true, to match reality? The Grecian urn's motto, that beauty and truth are one, was just Keats running romantically out of control.

Sometimes a similar worry is expressed about simplicity by asking why we should be entitled to the assumption that 'the world is simple.' But that is a fallacious reading of the explanationist appeal to a pragmatic virtue. The preference for simple theories over complex ones, is an epistemic *norm* only, not a metaphysical claim or assumption about what the world is like. Whether or not it does have justifying force as the Weak Explanationist contends, its doing so would not depend on any prior vague assumption about the structure of the world. The norm directing one to use a sharp chisel when sculpting marble does not depend on the marble's itself being 'sharp' in any sense.

Why, then, should we believe that a hypothesis' being simpler (or more fruitful or neater or whatever) make that hypothesis more likely to be true? Some philosophers have suggested that the appeal to a pragmatic virtue can justify only if one has first *shown* in some substantive way that that virtue is truth-conducive, even if one need not do that showing by invoking a sweeping metaphysical generalization about what the world is like. It seems unlikely that anyone could establish such a thing. To make an induction over the history of thought, for example, in the hope of establishing that simpler theories had a better truth-tracking record than more complicated ones, would not only be unfeasible but would require us (now) to have access to past truths independently of appeals to simplicity and the other pragmatic virtues.

Lycan (1988, 155–156) responded to that challenge in a way that can better be put as follows. Let us advert to the epistemology of epistemology. Epistemology is a study of norms, the norms governing belief and inference. Inescapably it rests on 'intuitions' about what such things are justified, reasonable, legitimate, and the like. In epistemology, as in ethical theory and for that matter in deductive logic, the intuitions in question are normative to begin with. Now, the (here meta-) epistemology appropriate to a normative subject is that of 'reflective equilibrium' as proposed by Goodman (1955) for deductive logic, used by linguists to justify rules of theoretical syntax, and developed by Rawls (1971) for ethical theory: Roughly, we begin with our instinctive normative intuitions and build an accordingly normative theory to systematize them. Mutual adjustment occurs until what Rawls calls 'narrow' reflective equilibrium is reached; then factual knowledge and perhaps also other norms are admitted to the equation, resulting in further adjustment and eventual 'wide' reflective equilibrium.

On the present view, epistemology starts with the attempt at narrow reflective equilibrium. The move to wide equilibrium will involve attending to probability theory, empirical cognitive science, and perhaps other areas. But each equilibrium is likely to respect the pragmatic virtues. For our pragmatic preferences are not merely preferences, but normative practices: We instruct our science students in the techniques of curve-fitting, epicycle elimination and the like, and science would be in a bad way if we did not. Of course, the reflective procedure might not turn out as the Weak Explanationist predicts, in which case we should reject Explanationism after all. But if the procedure does preserve and shore up Weak Explanationist intuitions, that is all the justification that can, or need, be given for the view and for the pragmatic virtues themselves. On pain of regress, some set of epistemic norms or other must be seen to be epistemologically primitive. We may be wrong in thinking that the pragmatic virtues are what occupy that role, but the primitiveness the Weak Explanationist claims for them cannot *itself* be an objection. Notice that aside from reflective equilibrium, we cannot give a (non-question-begging) justification for Modus Ponens, either, or for a syntactic rule such as Equi-NP Deletion. Certainly we cannot 'show' that either of those is truth-conducive; but there is no embarrassment in that. As Bentham said, that which is used to prove everything else cannot itself be proved.

But surely there must be some connection to truth? Yes: If our wide reflective equilibrium vindicates Weak Explanationism in the foregoing way, then the pragmatic virtues do justify. If a subject's belief is thus justified by the virtues, it is justified. But to be justified in believing that P is just to be justified in believing that it is true that P, really true that P, and as many iterations of 'true that' as one might like. Truth is not something to which we have access independently of holding justified beliefs. The demand for an independent 'connection to truth' is misguided.

The method of reflective equilibrium has been disputed in meta-epistemology, as it has been in meta-ethics; see particularly Stich (1990). If it should be discredited, then the present reply to van Fraassen fails and his challenge stands. Note, though, that we need not capitulate and try to show that the pragmatic virtues conduce directly to truth. There may be a third alternative. Stich himself advocates an open-minded, itself pragmatic methodological attitude towards theory preference and epistemic values generally.

6. A TOUGHER OBJECTION TO WEAK EXPLANATIONISM

The second argument suggested by the van Fraassen passage is one which has also been made by Ian Hacking (1982) (cf. Cartwright 1983): Truth is a relation between a theory or hypothesis and the world. But the pragmatic virtues are relations between theories and our human minds, to which relations the world seems irrelevant. The virtues have to do with the roles that hypotheses play in our private cognitive economies, not with anything external to us. They are (in Hacking's phrase) only what make our minds feel good. The point is no longer just to ask rhetorically why making our minds feel good should be taken to be a warrant of truth; it is that the virtues are positively the wrong sort of properties to be so taken.

This second argument is most compelling for the case of conservativeness. That a hypothesis fits comfortably with what we already believe makes that hypothesis pleasant and attractive to us, but hardly justifies it. To think it does justify is to assume that what we already believe is justified, merely by the fact of our believing it, and that idea strikes most philosophers as false on its face. (But see Sklar 1975 and Lycan 1988, chap. 8, countered in turn by Christensen 1994.)

Two replies may be made to the second argument. First, it falsely assimilates the pragmatic virtues to self-seeking emotive or other purely conative 'reasons' for believing things (as in Pascal's wager, or a case in which we are offered a lot of money if we can get ourselves to believe that unrestrained exploitation of the environment will be a good thing for everyone). The fact is that the virtues are genuinely cognitive and in one important sense epistemic values. (On the difference between the pragmatic values and purely conative reasons for believing, see Harman 1997.)

There is an idea, emphasized by Reliabilists but prevalent among epistemologists more generally, that 'truth is the goal of cognition,' and hence that nothing should count as cognitive unless it can be shown to be truth-conducive or at least *is* somehow directly truth-conducive. But it is fairly easy to see that truth cannot be the only epistemic value. Suppose it were. If the goal, like Descartes', is merely to avoid falsehood, then we could reach our ultimate epistemic goal simply by confining our assent to tautologies; we would still thereby believe uncountably many truths. If, instead, the idea is to believe *all* truths, the goal would be radically unreachable. Realizing those things, the truth-centered epistemologist usually alludes to a 'favorable balance of truth over error.' But 'favorable' as regards what? Some further value or interest must be consulted to judge what is 'favorable,' or the suggestion is meaningless.

Second reply to van Fraassen and Hacking: More specifically, it is hardly unreasonable to suppose with Peirce that beliefs are *for* something, and that cognition has a function. Truth cannot possibly be the only goal of cognition. There must at least be something in the way of informativeness or other usefulness, however that might be measured. Since belief is a guide to action, a belief's other pragmatic virtues may also contribute to its overall cognitive goodness.

Lycan (1988, chap. 7) argues that the way in which the pragmatic virtues do this is precisely by making cognition efficient in guiding action. They are the product of good design or 'design' by natural selection. A hyperskilled cognitive bioengineer fitting human beings for a post-Pleistocene environment would, arguably, have endowed us with the same habits of hypothesis preference as those listed in section 3 above. For example, she would have built us to prefer (other things being equal, as always) simpler hypotheses to complex ones. Simpler hypotheses are more efficient to work with. Complexities incur greater risk of error in application. And for that matter, simplicity is itself a form of efficiency, in that we want to achieve plenitude of result, in the way of data subsumed and results predicted, but with economy of means. For the same sorts of reason, the engineer would program us to seek explanatory power when other costs are low.

The engineer would not want us to load up on beliefs that have little or nothing to do with our immediate interactions with our environment, unless those beliefs play an enormous unifying, simplifying, and systematizing role. Hence, she would have us prefer more readily testable hypotheses to less testable ones.

Other things being equal, it would be more efficient for us to be able to extrapolate a type of hypothesis motivated by one subject-matter to other, not obviously related areas, so very likely the engineer would have us seek fruitfulness. It is perhaps more obvious that she would instill an aversion to messy belief systems full of deadends and paths that lead nowhere. If we think of belief systems as maps or charts, clearly a neat one will allow us to find our way around our environment more surefootedly than would a messy one. (But what if the system has been made too neat and contains inaccuracies? The recommendation of neatness methodologically assumes, here as always, that the system in question is unrefuted. Notice too that even in fact, as in real-world cartography, accuracy should not always trump neatness; some error is tolerable, even mandatory, in the interest of smooth and fast action, if the particular error is unlikely to cause much trouble.) Also, a particular belief that raises awkward questions is thereby distracting, sapping at least some time and mental energy.

Finally, the engineer would make us conservative, at least to the minimal extent of not revising our beliefs without some reason to do so. Like social change, all belief revision comes at a price, drawing on energy and resources. Arbitrary and gratuitous changes of belief, therefore, are to be avoided. If there were a habit of making such changes, the resulting instability would be inefficient if not constantly confusing.

Thus, from the design point of view, it seems to be a good thing that we cognize according to the pragmatic virtues. We would not function at all well unless we did so.

(It must be emphasized that the Darwinized Peircean view sketched in the preceding few paragraphs is not an attempt at *justifying* appeal to the pragmatic virtues in any usual epistemic sense of 'justify.' As we have seen, the Weak Explanationist maintains that although the virtues are *identified* through reflective equilibrium as basic cognitive values of ours, they are, thus, basic; there is nothing that could justify them. The function of our cognitive bioengineer story is only to rebut Hacking's charge that they are only mind candy, not cognitive in their value.)

The invoking of an idealized bioengineer as a metaphor for evolutionary design will and should raise some hackles, for it suggests the Panglossian view that our cognitive powers are optimally suited for getting us about the place, or at least that when we are in top epistemic form we will seek the pragmatic virtues for all we are worth. The first of those suggestions is plainly false, since nothing about homo sapiens is *optimally* suited for anything very interesting. The second suggestion is very likely not true either, since, once we have started to consider adaptation to our environment, there may be other cognitive features that the engineer would find useful but that can conflict with the explanatory virtues, say for special purposes. (See Stich 1985; Lycan 1988, 145–53.) If the Explanationist wants to stand by the present Peircean response to van Fraassen's and Hacking's challenge, he must block the two Panglossian suggestions. That in itself is no great feat, because they are not strictly entailed by the engineer story; but the Explanationist must block them in a principled way, showing how and why the explanatory virtues are of central cognitive value even though they are neither adaptively optimal nor even (necessarily) adaptively overriding within the cognitive system.

A further objection to the design response is that the idealizations needed to bring the engineer story into line with Explanationist epistemic norms are greater and more tendentious than is the familiar idealization of our species' selection history that affords 'designer' metaphors in biology generally (Davies 2001). Evolution by natural selection aims at reproductive fitness only, and it is hard to see how the value notions of epistemology could ultimately be reduced through any series of independently motivated idealizations to nothing but reproductive fitness. Here one does get the sense that truth would then have nothing to do with it.

Van Fraassen (1989) pursues the "mind candy" argument in more detail, and his new version(s) will have to be answered.

7. WEAK EXPLANATIONISM VS. CLASSICAL CONFIRMATION THEORY

According to a classical, purely formal confirmation theory, if two competing theories or hypotheses explain or accommodate *exactly the same* data, neither of them may be preferred to the other. For each is confirmed to the same degree, and so the two hypotheses are precisely equal in epistemic status, warrant or credibility. Yet in real life, one of the two may be preferred very strongly. It seems to opponents of Weak Explanationism that we have considerations of two different sorts: data, hard evidence, bearing a quasi-formal probabilifying or confirming relation to each of the competing hypotheses H and H', and the additional pragmatic virtues attaching differentially to H and H'. The confirming relation is commonly expressed by terms like 'likely,' 'probable,' and 'confirms' in the foregoing narrow sense; the model for it is formal inductive logic or confirmation theory based on probability theory, conceived by the Positivists as a strict analogue to deductive logic. Let us call it 'narrow confirmation.'

Following mainstream epistemology, let us also use the word 'justify' and its variants to signify overall epistemic rationality. 'Justified' will then mark out the class of beliefs it is epistemically rational to hold, and 'justification' will mean the relation between those beliefs and the evidence in virtue of which holding them is rational. The question then becomes, is justification in this general epistemic sense exhausted by narrow confirmation? Which is again to ask whether the explanatory virtues are merely practical bonbons of no specifically epistemic, truth-conducing value, or are instead genuine reasons for accepting a theory as more likely to be true than is a competitor that lacks them.

The claim that narrow confirmation does exhaust justification is what Lycan (1998) called 'the spartan view.' There it was argued that the spartan view gives rise to skeptical quandaries: van Fraassen's and others' radical skepticism about scientific unobservables; renewed evil-demon skepticism about the external world; and Goodman's 'grue paradox.' A proponent of the spartan view must either accept some skeptical thesis or take on the task of showing how a classical confirmation theory can overcome the skeptical quandaries without at least tacit appeal to the pragmatic virtues. (Lipton 1991, chap. 6, argues that the raven paradox, in addition, will yield to Explanationist treatment.) If one is persuaded and wishes to resist skepticism, it seems there are three paths: to modify classical confirmation theory in order to respect the virtues; to relegate classical confirmation theory to a confined role in inquiry, granting that justification far outruns narrow confirmation; or to abandon confirmation theory entirely as a bad job.

Roughly the first path has been taken by Glymour (1980), whose idea is to broaden the notion of 'confirmation,' so that H may be counted as 'better confirmed' than H' even though H and H' are still equally probabilified by the evidence base. If, however, one wants to demote or abandon confirmation theory entirely, one faces the daunting task of building a systematic account of the pragmatic virtues, their measurement and their comparative interaction. And to date, no theorist has taken more than a step or two in that direction.

8. Ferocious Explanationism Defended

The most obvious direct argument in favor of Ferocious Explanationism is from the presumed truth of Weak Explanationism and the lack of any promising program for reducing the pragmatic virtues to probabilistic or confirmation-theoretic notions; if explanatory inference does justify, but so far as we know the virtues are not reducible to some more familiar epistemic value, then, so far as we know, explanatory inference justifies directly, without being derived from some more basic form of ampliative inference. Reflective equilibrium may also lead to this conclusion, on top of Weak Explanationism in the first place.

More distinctively, Harman (1965, 1968) began the task of reconstructing standard inductive argument forms as enthymematic explanatory inferences. For example, from the fact that all the emeralds observed so far have been green, we inductively infer that all emeralds are green. Harman would say this is because the latter conclusion best explains the observations. Suppose it did not; suppose we are somehow independently assured that it just *happens* that all the emeralds we have observed so far have been green. Then it does not seem that we are entitled to our usual inductive inference—especially when we take into account that all the emeralds we have observed have also been grue (= green and examined before some future time t_f or blue and not examined before t_f). Explanatory considerations are needed, the Explanationist will argue, in order to justify inferring 'All emeralds are green' instead of the competing generalization, 'All emeralds are grue.'

And consider the more general form of enumerative induction:

N% of all the observed Xs have been F.

∴ Roughly N% of all Xs are F.

If we suppose that what licenses a sampling inference of this form is that its conclusion best explains its premise, we can also account for the two characteristic fallacies associated with the form. The besetting fallacies are those of *insufficient sample* and *biased sample*. The former is committed when too few Xs have been observed; the latter when we have independent reason to think that the proportion of F Xs in our sample differs from the proportion of all Xs that are F.

'Insufficient sample' is a fallacy, the Explanationist will say, because when the sample is too small, the suppressed assumption of best explanation fails. Suppose I have observed just two marbles in my entire life; one was yellow and one was blue. Those facts are hardly best explained—are probably not explained at all—by the hypothesis that 50 percent of all the marbles in the world are yellow and 50 percent are blue. At least, the latter hypothesis seems to make no prediction that if someone samples two marbles, one will be yellow and the other will be blue.

What is wrong with 'biased sample' is that when a sample is discovered to be biased, that affords precisely a *better explanation* of the distribution than is the hypothesis that the general population is distributed in that way. If only registered

Republicans are consulted in a poll designed to test public approval of George W. Bush's performance in his first year as U.S. President, the best explanation of the resulting positive rating is that Republicans tend to support Bush, who was their own candidate, not that a majority of Americans do.

One can carry the argument a good deal farther than mere enumerative induction. In an extended case study (of Semmelweis's search for the causes of childbed fever), Lipton (1991, chap. 5) shows that on the whole, Mill's Methods can be neatly integrated into and explained by a careful stepwise use of contrastive explanatory inference. Where explanatory inference diverges from the Methods, the Methods are seen to be lacking (chap. 7).

Unfortunately for the Ferocious Explanationist, there are other forms of inductive and statistical inference that are not so easily represented as enthymematic explanatory inferences. For example, Harman (1968) has tackled statistical syllogism:

N% of all Fs are G.

∴ The next observed F will be G.

But, as is argued by Lycan (1988, 184–186), his treatment is not satisfactory, and neither is the one that Lycan there proceeds to substitute for it. Here is perhaps the worst problem case (due to Joseph Tolliver): Consider a random-distribution process operating over a closed surface; say a nucleus of some kind explodes and scatters lots of particles randomly onto the inner surface of a containing hollow sphere. The particles end up distributed fairly evenly over that surface. Now, take a large subregion R of the inner surface; say, R is the 90 percent that is left when we have mentally subtracted a small wedge from the sphere. And take any one of the particles, p. By hypothesis, the vast majority of the particles landed in R, so, probably to degree .9, p did (so long as p is not known to be atypical). That inference is statistically reasonable but does not seem to be explanatory in any way at all. In particular, by hypothesis, the process is random and nothing about the particles themselves makes it true that most of them land in R.

So it seems there is at least one central and prevalent form of ampliative inference that resists the Ferocious Explanationist's efforts.

But here is a new argument for the Ferocious view, aimed at those opponents such as van Fraassen who reject explanatory inference, at least taken as primitive, but who rely confidently on some more traditional forms of inductive and statistical inference: Inductive and statistical inference rely on evidence that is in the subject's possession. The evidence concerns what has been observed. What has been observed now lies in the past, however recent. The evidence is believed on the basis of memory. But, far from accepting all or even most of the remembered evidence, why should we believe in the reality of any past at all? Why should we not instead accept a Russellian eleventh-hour-creation hypothesis, that the world, whatever it may include besides our present sensations and memory impressions, sprang fully formed into existence half a second ago, though to be sure complete with all the memory impressions and perceptions of apparent traces and records?

One cannot resolve the conflict between the hypothesis that our memories are veridical and the Russellian hypothesis by appeal to inductive or statistical argument, for it is the data premises of any such argument that are neutralized by the Russellian hypothesis. Why, then, is it reasonable for us to believe in the reality of the past at all, much less in its statistical details? It is hard to think of any answer that does not invoke explanatory considerations taken as primitive. The obvious answer is that the veridicality hypothesis heavily outweighs the Russellian hypothesis at least in simplicity, neatness, and conservativeness, though certainly the details here would be hard to settle.

9. OBJECTIONS TO FEROCIOUS EXPLANATIONISM, AND REPLIES

Keith Lehrer (1974, chap. 7) has offered several objections to the Ferocious view.

First, he says (178), there are 'completely' justified empirical beliefs (in addition to the conclusions of statistical syllogisms, noted in the previous section) whose justification depends in no way on explanatory considerations. For example, we can use the Pythagorean Theorem to infer from the respective spatial locations of a mouse and an owl that the mouse is five feet from the owl. (Reply: The Pythagorean Theorem itself is justified by the explanatory roles of the geometric principles from which it is derived. Rejoinder (179): It need not have been. A tribe constitutionally averse to explanation might have worked out the Theorem as an empirical generalization.)

Second (170–171; cf. Cornman 1980), achieving explanatory coherence is cheap. One can greatly increase the explanatory coherence of one's overall belief system by simply *throwing out data;* that is, whenever a lower-level belief resists explanation or causes trouble in conjunction with another belief, we can preserve explanatory order by just ceasing to hold that belief, rather than by adding epicycles to the system in an attempt to accommodate it. So the splendid explanatory virtue of a belief system is *in itself* no reason to accept that system. (Reply: Lehrer seems to assume either an unrealistic degree of doxastic voluntarism, or a strange absence of norms concerning what doxastic items must be respected, or both. We constantly find ourselves with *spontaneous beliefs,* most but not all produced by our sense organs, which we neither can simply choose to abandon nor would be justified in trying to do so.)

Third (181), for any hypothesis or theory held on explanatory grounds, 'there are *always* conflicting theories concerning some aspect of experience that are equally satisfactory from the standpoint of explanation,' so a rational decision between the conflicting theories would necessarily have to appeal to some entirely nonexplanatory desideratum. The obvious reply to this is to remind Lehrer that we are to infer the best *available* explanation; we are not responsible for Plato's Heaven. But presumably what he has in mind is that in principle there might be an algorithm that could be applied to a given theory and would reliably generate a competing theory with at least as much explanatory merit as the original. (Reply: Why should Lehrer or anyone else be confident that there is such an algorithm? But even if there is, conservativeness can decide in favor of the original and against the mockup. The original was already believed when the algorithm spit out its artificial competitor. Several strong rejoinders can be made here, even if we set aside Lehrer's own rejection [184] of conservativeness as an epistemic value; for further discussion, see Lycan 1988, 174–177.)

There is a further and more fundamental issue, which seems to demand further substantive work from the Ferocious Explanationist.

10. THE UNEXPLAINERS

According to any Explanationist, beliefs are justified by their ability to explain other beliefs. But explanation is asymmetric. If there is not to be an infinite regress or a vicious circle of explainings, there must be some beliefs that get explained but do not themselves explain anything else—ultimate data, if you like. Nor is this conclusion merely theoretical, for we can think of plenty of examples. To take one of George Pappas', I believe that my visual field contains little moving spots. Or imagine that you hear a loud report; your belief that you heard a report does not seem to explain anything; you just did seem to hear one. These beliefs are what Sellars (1973) and Lehrer (1974, 162) call 'explained unexplainers.' But if the unexplainers are not themselves justified, they cannot in turn justify the hypotheses that explain them, and the whole belief system is left without foundation. Yet if they are justified, they are so in some way other than by what they explain; so the Ferocious Explanationist must cave in and admit that there is nonexplanatory justification of some sort.

Actually that is not too large a capitulation for the Ferocious theorist, if it is one at all. For the Ferocious view is stated specifically in terms of ampliative inference. So it is open to the Ferocious theorist to hold that the unexplainers are all *noninferential* beliefs, and the Ferocious view simply does not apply. We might give any plausible independent account of the unexplainers' justification. We might join Chisholm (1977) in appealing to 'self-presenting' mental states, or we might go all the way against Sellars and Quine and hold out for an unrevisable sensory given. Or we might turn Reliabilist about noninferential beliefs; Reliabilism always seemed to work best for noninferential beliefs in any case.

Still, it is at least embarrassing for the Ferocious theorist to bifurcate her overall epistemology in such a way. For example, if she were to go Reliabilist about the explanatory foundation, thoroughgoing Reliabilists such as Goldman (1986) would naturally ask, why bother with the Explanationist superstructure? Why not be a Reliabilist all the way up?

The more ambitious Explanationist has at least three less bifurcatory possible moves here. One is to argue that there are not really any total unexplainers and that not all explanatory circularity is vicious; perhaps there is a virtuous circle of explanation, with lots of little individual *near*-unexplainers teaming up collectively to explain some apparently higher-level belief. Another is to maintain that the unexplainers are justified by *being explained*, and resist the charge of vicious circularity that would naturally attend that move. A third would be to appeal to one or more of the pragmatic virtues, applied at the level of the unexplainers.

Lycan (1988, chap. 8) pursues the third strategy, invoking conservativeness. Recall from the previous section that we have 'spontaneous' beliefs that merely arise in us and (normally) cannot just be abandoned. Noninferential beliefs will, at least normally, be spontaneous in that sense. Now, a spontaneous belief is a belief, and the canon of conservativeness sketched in section 3 above entails (what admittedly may seem outrageous) that the bare fact of our holding a belief renders that belief justified at least to a tiny degree. The belief may accrete further justification by being explained, indeed by being swept up into a large network of strongly cohering beliefs. Therefore, at least some noninferential beliefs will be justified, but justified solely by pragmatic virtues even though they themselves explain nothing.

Incidentally, Explanationism is often referred to as 'explanatory coherentism' and regarded as a species of coherentist epistemology, though this essay has not emphasized that theme. On it, see Harman 1986, Thagard 1989, and Lycan 1996.

11. Conclusion

Despite the commonsensical status of Weak Explanationism, there is nothing uncontroversial about Explanationism in any form. The arguments pro and con presented here only begin to illuminate the issues.

REFERENCES

Bromberger, S. (1966). "Why-Questions." In *Mind and Cosmos*, ed. R. Colodny. Pittsburgh: University of Pittsburgh Press.

Cartwright, N. (1983). *How the Laws of Physics Lie*. Oxford: Oxford University Press.

Chisholm, R. (1977). *Theory of Knowledge*, 2d ed. Englewood Cliffs, N.J.: Prentice-Hall.

Christensen, D. (1994). "Conservatism in Epistemology." *Noûs* 28: 69–89.

Cornman, J. (1980). *Skepticism, Justification, and Explanation*. Dordrecht: Reidel.

Cummins, R. (1983). *The Nature of Psychological Explanation*. Cambridge, Mass.: Bradford Books/MIT Press.

Davies, P. (2001). *Norms of Nature: Naturalism and the Nature of Functions*. Cambridge, Mass.: Bradford Books/MIT Press.

Dray, W. (1963). "The Historical Explanation of Action Reconsidered." In *Philosophy and History*, ed. S. Hook. New York: New York University Press.

Dennett, D. C. (1987). *The Intentional Stance*. Cambridge, Mass.: Bradford Books/MIT Press.

Foster, M. H., and M. L Martin, eds. (1966). *Probability, Confirmation, and Simplicity*. New York: Odyssey.

Garfinkel, A. (1981). *Forms of Explanation*. New Haven, Conn.: Yale University Press.

Glymour, C. (1980). *Theory and Evidence*. Princeton: Princeton University Press.

Goldman, A. (1986). *Epistemology and Cognition*. Cambridge, Mass.: Harvard University Press.

Goodman, N. (1955). "The New Riddle of Induction." In Goodman, *Fact, Fiction, and Forecast*. Cambridge, Mass.: Harvard University Press.

Hacking, I. (1982). "Experimentation and Scientific Realism." *Philosophical Topics* 13: 71–88.

Harman, G. (1965). "The Inference to the Best Explanation." *Philosophical Review* 74: 88–95.

———. (1968). "Enumerative Induction as Inference to the Best Explanation." *Journal of Philosophy* 64: 529–533.

———. (1986). *Change in View*. Cambridge, Mass.: MIT Press.

———. (1997). "Pragmatism and Reasons for Belief." In *Realism/Antirealism and Epistemology*, ed. C. B. Kulp. Lanham, Md.: Rowman & Littlefield. Rev. version is in G. Harman, *Reasoning, Meaning, and Mind*. Oxford: Clarendon, 1999.

Hempel, C. G., and P. Oppenheim (1948). "Studies in the Logic of Explanation." *Philosophy of Science* 15: 135–175.

Kim, J. (1967). "Explanation in Science." In *The Encyclopedia of Philosophy*, ed. P. Edwards, vol. 3. New York: Macmillan.

Kitcher, P. and W. Salmon (1987). "Van Fraassen on Explanation." *Journal of Philosophy* 84: 315–330.

Lehrer, K. (1974). *Knowledge*. Oxford: Oxford University Press.

Lipton, P. (1991). *Inference to the Best Explanation*. London: Routledge.

Lycan, W. G. (1988). *Judgement and Justification*. Cambridge: Cambridge University Press.

———. (1996). "Plantinga and Coherentisms." In *Warrant and Contemporary Epistemology*, ed. J. Kvanvig. Totowa, N.J.: Rowman & Littlefield.

———. (1998). "Theoretical/Epistemic Virtues." In *Routledge Encyclopedia of Philosophy*, ed. E. Craig. London: Routledge, 1998.

Quine, W. V. (1960). *Word and Object*. Cambridge, Mass.: MIT Press.

Quine, W. V., and J. S. Ullian (1978). *The Web of Belief*, 2d ed. New York: Random House.

Railton, P. (1978). "A Deductive-Nomological Model of Probabilistic Explanation." *Philosophy of Science* 45: 206–226.

Rawls, J. (1971). *A Theory of Justice*. Cambridge, Mass.: Harvard University Press.

Russell, B. (1959). *The Problems of Philosophy*. New York: Oxford University Press.

Salmon, W. (1989). "Four Decades of Scientific Explanation." In *Minnesota Studies in the Philosophy of Science, vol. 13, Scientific Explanation*, ed. W. Salmon and P. Kitcher. Minneapolis: University of Minnesota Press.

Scriven, M. (1962). "Explanations, Predictions, and Laws." In *Minnesota Studies in the Philosophy of Science, vol. 3, Scientific Explanation, Space, and Time*, ed. H. Feigl and G. Maxwell. Minneapolis: University of Minnesota Press.

Sellars, W. (1963). "Some Reflections on Language Games." In *Science, Perception and Reality*. London: Routledge and Kegan Paul.

———. (1973). "Givenness and Explanatory Coherence." *Journal of Philosophy* 70: 612–624.

Simon, H. (1969). "The Architecture of Complexity." In *The Sciences of the Artificial*. Cambridge, Mass.: MIT Press.

Sklar, L. (1975). "Methodological Conservatism." *Philosophical Review* 84: 374–400.

Sober, E. (1975). *Simplicity*. Oxford: Oxford University Press.

Stich, S. P. (1985). "Could Man Be an Irrational Animal? Some Notes on the Epistemology of Rationality." *Synthese* 64: 115–135.

———. (1990). *The Fragmentation of Reason*. Cambridge, Mass.: Bradford Books/MIT Press.

Thagard, P. (1978). "The Best Explanation: Criteria for Theory Choice." *Journal of Philosophy* 75: 76–92.

———. (1989). "Explanatory Coherence." *Behavioral and Brain Sciences* 12: 435–467.

Van Fraassen, B. (1980). *The Scientific Image*. Oxford: Oxford University Press.

———. (1989). *Laws and Symmetry*. Oxford: Oxford University Press.

Wimsatt, W. (1976). "Reductionism, Levels of Organization, and the Mind-Body Problem." In *Consciousness and the Brain*, ed. G. Globus, G. Maxwell, and I. Savodnik. New York: Plenum.

CHAPTER 15

DECISION THEORY AND EPISTEMOLOGY

MARK KAPLAN

I

HAS a Bayesian anything to teach an epistemologist? To judge from much of the literature in epistemology, most practitioners of the discipline think not. As typically portrayed by epistemologists, a Bayesian is someone who is committed to the following two doctrines:

(i) for each person and each hypothesis that person is capable of comprehending, there is a precise, real-valued degree of confidence that person has in the truth of that hypothesis; and

(ii) that no person can be counted as rational unless the degree of confidence assignment she thus harbors satisfies (at least) the Kolmogorov axioms of probability.[1]

The Bayesian thus portrayed cuts a figure that most epistemologists have found quite unattractive. The following five objections have figured prominently in their explanations of why they are so repelled.

1. The Psychology Objection

The Bayesian's claim that each of us harbors a precise degree of confidence assignment is simply not credible. Reflection on their own cases has convinced many epistemologists that there are a great many hypotheses (particularly hypotheses about which they have little evidence) in whose truth they do not have a precise degree of confidence. The standard Bayesian reply is that a degree of confidence is to be understood as a disposition to bet or to choose—not as a consciously felt degree of conviction—and is thus not the sort of thing whose presence can reliably be detected by reflection.[2] But this is a reply that many epistemologists have found singularly uncompelling. The extent to which it is possible to elicit from a person dispositions to bet or choose that are at odds with her felt conviction has only served to convince these epistemologists that the dispositional analysis of degrees of confidence to which Bayesians are appealing is itself in error.[3]

2. The Idealization Objection

The condition on a person's being rational that the Bayesian endorses is far too demanding. It follows from the Kolmogorov axioms of probability that every tautology receives the maximum probability, probability 1, every contradiction the minimum, 0. Thus, it follows from the Bayesian's condition on rationality that you cannot be considered rational so long as there is even one tautology in which you fail to invest the maximum degree of confidence or one contradiction in which you fail to invest the minimum. While this may be a reasonable constraint to impose on a being of limitless logical acumen, it is (many epistemologists have complained) hardly appropriate to impose on real-life human beings. Indeed, they have argued, there are circumstances in which it is rational for a real-life human being knowingly to violate this constraint.

Suppose that P is some complicated hypothesis. You have determined that P is either a tautology or a contradiction, but you haven't determined which. A friend with pretty good logical acumen tells you that she is fairly confident that P is a tautology. In such circumstances, it would seem you have no business being certain that P—no business assigning P the maximum degree of confidence. After all, your friend is neither sure that P is a tautology nor (let us suppose) perfectly reliable in her verdicts. Nor would you seem to have any business being certain that not-P—that would be to ride roughshod over the testimony of your friend. What would seem reasonable is for you to invest more confidence in P than in its negation but assign neither hypothesis an extreme degree of confidence.[4]

3. The Ignorance Objection

Even regarded as a condition on the rationality of an ideal inquirer (an inquirer who has a degree of confidence assignment, together with sufficient cognitive resources to ensure that this assignment satisfies the Kolmogorov axioms of probability), the Bayesian's condition is at odds with our epistemic intuitions about what such an inquirer should do in cases of ignorance. Imagine that you are an ideal inquirer who satisfies the Bayesian condition. Consider the following hypotheses:

(P)   Mark Kaplan was wearing brown shoes on his tenth birthday.

(Q)   There was ice-skating in Milwaukee's Cathedral Square in 1996.

If I've chosen correctly, then you haven't the slightest idea whether or not either of the two hypotheses is true. The only way you have to express your ignorance as to the truth value of P and the truth value of Q is to invest in each a degree of confidence no greater and no less than the degree of confidence you invest in its negation. You must invest in each a degree of confidence equal to ½.[5]

Now consider

(P v Q)   Either Mark Kaplan was wearing brown shoes on his tenth birthday or there was ice skating in Milwaukee's Cathedral Square in 1996.

It is a consequence of your harboring a degree of confidence assignment that satisfies the Kolmogorov axioms of the probability calculus that (letting "con(X)" represent your degree of confidence in hypothesis X)

$$\mathrm{con}(P \vee Q) = \mathrm{con}(P) + \mathrm{con}(Q) - \mathrm{con}(P \& Q),$$

where (by the definition of conditional probability)

$$\mathrm{con}(P \& Q) = \mathrm{con}(P|Q)\mathrm{con}(Q).$$

And what value will con(P|Q) have? con(P|Q) represents your degree of confidence in P given Q. This being so, con(P|Q) should be greater than con(P) just if you regard Q as a hypothesis that, if true, counts as evidence that P; it should be less than con(P) just if you regard Q as a hypothesis that, if true, counts as evidence that not-P.[6] But, if I have chosen P and Q as I hope I have, you regard Q as neither of these things: you regard Q as a hypothesis that, if true, has no evidential bearing whatsoever on P's truth. Thus, you are bound to assign con(P Q) the same value as you assign con(P): ½. This being so, conformity to the Bayesian condition on rationality will require you to arrange your degrees of confidence so that

$$\text{con}(P \lor Q) = \text{con}(P) + \text{con}(Q) - \text{con}(P)\text{con}(Q) = \tfrac{3}{4}.$$

But, some epistemologists have argued, this is a bizarre result. You are every bit as ignorant as to the truth-value of P v Q as to the truth values of its disjuncts. That the Bayesian condition would nonetheless require you to invest so great a degree of confidence in P v Q shows that the Bayesian condition on rationality is defective.[7]

4. The Theory Objection

The Bayesian condition on rationality would have an ideal inquirer treat explanatory theories as incredible. Imagine again that you are an ideal inquirer who satisfies the Bayesian condition on rationality. Consider any explanatory theory. Suppose the theory is expressible as the set of hypotheses, $\{P_1,...,P_n\}$. Your degree of confidence in the truth of the theory will be equal to your degree of confidence in the conjunction of the P_i, $\text{con}(P_1 \&..\& P_n)$. It follows from the fact that your degree of confidence assignment satisfies the Kolmogorov axioms of probability that

$$\text{con}(P_1 \&..\& P_n) = \text{con}(P_1)\text{con}(P_2|P_1)\text{con}(P_3|(P_1 \& P_2)) \ldots \text{con}(P_n|(P_1 \&..\& P_{n-1})).$$

If the theory is typical of those one encounters in the empirical sciences, the product on the right side of the foregoing equation will have a very large number of multiplicands, to a large percentage of which you will not be prepared to assign the maximum degree of confidence. If there are even 10 multiplicands in which you do not have a degree of confidence greater than 0.9, an absurdly rosy scenario, that alone will ensure that $\text{con}(P_1 \&..\& P_n)$ does not exceed 0.35. On a more realistic scenario, $\text{con}(P_1 \&..\& P_n)$ will be much lower still. Thus, some epistemologists have complained, it is impossible to see how an ideal inquirer who satisfied the Bayesian condition could possibly have the slightest interest in any scientific explanatory theory. Her satisfaction of the Bayesian condition guarantees that she will find any such theory entirely incredible.[8]

5. The Irrelevance Objection

In concentrating exclusively on the propriety of our degree of confidence assignment, the Bayesian does not contribute to our epistemological inquiries; he changes the subject. Epistemologists are interested in the propriety of *categorical* belief—the sort of thing that one either has or doesn't have, full stop. When epistemologists pursue the theory of epistemic justification, it is the epistemic justification of *categorical* beliefs that occupies their attention. When epistemologists pursue the theory of knowledge, it is the conditions under which a *categorical* belief will count as knowledge into which they are inquiring. So, even were it free of all the foregoing objections, the Bayesian's account of rational degree of confidence assignments could not hope to contribute to the inquiries that concern epistemologists. For this account simply does not say anything about the epistemic propriety of the doxastic attitudes epistemologists care about—that is, categorical beliefs.[9]

How powerful are these objections? While I think that some are more powerful than others, I think it is fair to say that, if a Bayesian is the sort of creature described at the outset, then these objections jointly provide a powerful reason not to be Bayesian. But, for all that, I am convinced that it is a mistake to conclude that Bayesianism has nothing to teach epistemologists. That is because I am convinced there is available a much more modest and sensible variant on the Orthodox Bayesian view epistemologists have so rightly seen fit to reject. What I want to do in this essay is provide a sketch of this view—a view I have called "Modest Bayesianism." I want to explain how it handles—indeed, how it is inspired by— the objections I've just rehearsed. And I want to explain why it is a doctrine of epistemological import. Addressing the latter task will provide an occasion to talk about what I think is the most disorienting, and philosophically interesting, feature of the Bayesian approach to epistemology: the way it finds in decision theory a foundation for epistemological doctrines.

II

Let me begin the sketch with Modest Bayesianism's psychology. It is, true to the name, modest. In contrast to its orthodox ancestor, which strains our credulity by assuming that actual persons have real-valued degree of confidence assignments, Modest Bayesianism assumes only that any person harbors at least some confidence-rankings: that she can, for at least some pairs of hypotheses, say in which (if either) she invests the greater confidence, in which (if either) she invests equal confidence. It is, of course, compatible with this assumption that there are some hypotheses (for example, the tautology, "Either Milwaukee is North of Chicago or it is not") in which she has a precise degree of confidence. But it is also entirely compatible with this assumption (and doubtless true of any actual person) that there are a great many pairs of hypotheses that she has not so ranked—a great many pairs of hypotheses as to whose relative credibility she is undecided—either because she hasn't gotten round to ranking them, or because she finds no grounds for ranking them one way rather than another. The Psychology Objection is no objection to Modest Bayesianism.

Nor is the Idealization Objection. The Idealization Objection shows that it is not a credible condition on the rationality of an actual person that she assign every tautology a degree of confidence equal to 1. The question is: if so, is there anything on which this requirement *can* credibly be thought to be a condition? The typical Bayesian response is to say that the requirement is a condition on the rationality of an idealized inquirer.[10] But (as many epistemologists have observed) this response is not at all satisfying. We are not idealized inquirers. This being so, it is not in the least obvious how, so construed, the requirement that tautologies be assigned the maximum degree of confidence can be of any import to *us*.[11]

Modest Bayesianism offers another response: the requirement is to be understood as a *regulative ideal*. By that I mean it is to be understood as putting forth a constraint the violation of which opens a state of opinion to rational criticism. It is to be understood as saying that your state of opinion is open to rational criticism insofar as there is a tautology to which you have failed to assign a degree of confidence equal to 1.

It is, of course, one thing to say that your state of opinion is open to criticism if it violates a certain constraint, another thing to say that *you* are open to criticism if your state of opinion violates that constraint. You can hardly be held open to criticism for violations (such as your failure to assign the maximum degree of confidence to every tautology, no matter how complicated) that are due only to your limited cognitive capacities, limited logical acumen, limited time. Nor can you reasonably be held open to criticism for a violation that you do not know how to avoid (as in the case in which you don't know whether the hypothesis is a tautology or a contradiction and, thus, don't know what degree of confidence in P—1 or 0—would avoid the violation).

Thus there is nothing in the requirement, understood as a regulative ideal, that provides grounds for calling you irrational if you fail to assign the maximum degree of confidence to a tautology you don't recognize as a tautology; or, if you fail to assign a hypothesis an extreme degree of confidence when you know it is either a tautology or a contradiction but you don't know which. The requirement that tautologies receive the maximum degree of confidence is a requirement on the cogency of opinion, not the rationality of persons.

The two are not, however, unrelated. The reason we are disinclined in the cases described above to count you as not rational is that we deem your failure to satisfy the requirement as eminently excusable: your failure is due entirely to your limited logical acumen. We would feel differently if your violation could have been avoided had you but paid the slightest attention to the form of the hypothesis before you, or if had you been the least bit careful, or if had you made even the most cursory check. This suggests that, while a wildly implausible requirement on the rationality of actual persons, the requirement that tautologies receive the maximum degree of confidence nonetheless plays an important role in our assessments of the rationality of actual persons: we will not count a person's failure to invest the maximum degree of confidence in a tautology as rational unless we deem her failure to be excusable.[12]

And, cast as a requirement on the cogency of opinion—as a requirement the violation of which opens the offending state of confidence to rational criticism—the requirement that tautologies receive the maximum degree of confidence occupies even more central a role in inquiry. The question of what constitutes a rational criticism of a state of opinion is central to the enterprise of rational inquiry—an enterprise whose aim, after all, is to determine what opinions may be sufficiently immune to rational criticism to warrant adoption. The requirement that tautologies be assigned the maximum degree of confidence offers an extremely modest, but nonetheless genuine, contribution to that enterprise.[13]

Of course, the requirement that a person harbor a degree of confidence assignment that satisfies *all* the Kolmogorov axioms of probability—of which the requirement that tautologies be assigned the maximum degree of confidence is but one—would offer a far more substantive contribution. But is it a regulative ideal we should endorse? Modest Bayesianism sees in the Ignorance Objection decisive reason why we should not. From the perspective of Modest Bayesianism, what is responsible for the unintuitive result revealed in the Ignorance Objection is that the orthodox Bayesian regulative ideal demands that, on pain of opening your state of opinion to criticism, you assign each of P and Q a precise degree of confidence. It is a regulative ideal that would have you behave towards P and Q—two hypotheses as to whose truth-value you have virtually no evidence—exactly as you would if they were hypotheses as to whose truth-value you had excellent evidence. Insofar as it would have you assign the value 0.5 to each of P and Q, the regulative ideal would have you behave toward these hypotheses just as you would were each predicting the outcome of a different toss of a coin of whose fairness you were certain.

Now, it is indeed true that, as in the coin-toss case, the evidence in the case described in the objection neither favors P nor Q over its negation. But that is because, in the case described in the objection, *you have virtually no evidence at all as to the truth values of P and Q.* If the evidence you have gives you no reason to assign either hypothesis a greater (or a lesser) degree of confidence than you assign its negation, the evidence also gives you no reason *not to* assign one or both of the hypotheses a greater (or lesser) degree of confidence than you assign its negation. The evidence gives you no reason to assign either hypothesis any particular degree of confidence rather than some other. If so, the appropriate way to respond to the case described in the Ignorance Objection—the appropriate way to respect the difference between the evidence in this case and the evidence in the coin-toss case—is to acknowledge as much and to refrain from assigning a degree of confidence to either hypothesis. But that is just to say that the Ignorance Objection describes a circumstance in which it would be wrong—even wrong for an ideal inquirer—to harbor a degree of confidence assignment. We must conclude that the orthodox Bayesian regulative ideal is not one we should want to satisfy.

What would Modest Bayesianism put in its stead? Let me approach the answer a bit indirectly. I said that Modest Bayesianism lays the blame for the unintuitive result revealed in the Ignorance Objection on the fact that the orthodox Bayesian regulative ideal demands that you harbor a degree of confidence assignment. Satisfying this demand would require you *either* to rule out (i.e., regard as inferior to at least one other) all but one degree of confidence assignment *or*, failing that, to pick one degree of confidence assignment from the ones you haven't ruled out. The complaint, then, is that orthodox Bayesianism would thus have you *either* rule out, for no good reason, any degree of confidence assignment that fails to assign the value 0.5 both to P and to Q, *or* adopt, for no good reason, one state of opinion rather than another. And the moral issued by Modest Bayesianism— that you should not assign either hypothesis any particular degree of confidence— is that (a) provided it satisfies the Kolmogorov axioms, you are simply in no position to rule out a degree of confidence assignment on the basis of what it assigns to these two hypotheses, and (b) to adopt one state of opinion rather than another for no good reason is to open that state of opinion to criticism.

How does any of this bear on the propriety of your confidence rankings? Consider the case at hand. Suppose you have taken the Modest Bayesian moral to heart. That is, suppose that we can pick any two values (identical or otherwise) from 0 through 1, and there will be a degree of confidence assignment you haven't ruled out on which P has the first value and Q has the second. Under such a circumstance you hardly seem in a position to invest more confidence in one hypothesis than the other—say, more confidence in P than in Q. After all, there are assignments you haven't ruled out on which P gets a lower value than Q. To be in a position to invest more confidence in P than in Q, you would have to have ruled out every assignment on which P gets a lower value than Q and (at the very least) not ruled out at least one on which P gets a greater value than Q.

Nor are you in any better position to be equally confident in the two hypotheses. There are, after all, myriad degree of confidence assignments you have not ruled out that, if adopted, would have you investing a greater degree of confidence in one hypothesis than you do in the other. To be in a position to be equally confident that P as you are that Q you presumably would have to have ruled out all those assignments.

But if you are neither in a position to be more confident in one hypothesis than the other, nor in a position to be equally confident in each hypothesis, you have but one alternative: indecision. In the case at hand, you should leave P unranked with respect to Q.

If this is right, then questions about the propriety of your adopting a particular confidence ranking are intimately tied to questions about the propriety of your ruling out certain degree of confidence assignments—and they are tied in such a way as to require that:

> Your state of opinion is open to rational criticism unless it is characterizable as a nonempty set W of degree of confidence assignments each of which satisfies the Kolmogorov axioms of probability and where for every hypothesis, P and Q,
>
> (i) you are just as confident that P as you are that Q only if every member of W assigns P and Q the same value;
>
> (ii) you are more confident that P than you are that Q only if every member of W assigns P at least as great a value as it assigns Q, and at least one member of W assigns P a greater value than it assigns Q; and
>
> (iii) otherwise you are undecided as to the relative credibility of P and Q.[14]

For all its modesty, this Modest Bayesian regulative ideal has some bite. It would deem your state of opinion open to criticism if you harbor a confidence ranking of hypotheses that cannot be so ranked in probability. It would also deem your state of opinion open to criticism if there is any pair of hypotheses you have left unranked whose ranking is fixed by every probability assignment compatible with your confidence ranking. Yet it is a regulative ideal that allows you to do pretty much what epistemic intuition says you should do in the case described by the Ignorance Objection. It allows you to respond to the fact that you have no evidence as to the truth values of P, Q, and (P v Q) by allowing there to be, for each of the three hypotheses, and for each real number from 0 through 1, a degree of confidence assignment you have not ruled out that assigns that hypothesis that number.

I say "pretty much" because there is one respect in which the Modest Bayesian regulative ideal would have you discriminate between P v Q and its disjuncts. There is no degree of confidence assignment compatible with the Kolmogorov axioms on which P v Q is assigned a lower value than either of its disjuncts. Thus the Modest Bayesian regulative ideal requires you to rule out all such assignments. But if you take the Modest Bayesian moral to heart—if, for every pair of real values from 0 to 1, there is an assignment you haven't ruled out on which P gets the first value and Q the second—there will be plenty of degree of confidence assignments you have not ruled out that satisfy the axioms, preserve your being exactly as confident in P given Q as you are in P, and assign P v Q a greater value than either of its disjuncts: for example, the one we imagined you harbored in the Ignorance Objection—it assigns each of P, Q, and P given Q probability ½, and P v Q probability ¾. Thus, according to the Modest Bayesian regulative ideal, you must, on pain of opening your state of opinion to rational criticism, invest more confidence in P v Q than you do in either of its disjuncts.

Now, I recognize that some epistemologists may be tempted to conclude that, in thus running afoul of the epistemic intuition that all three hypotheses ought to be treated in the same way, Modest Bayesianism's regulative ideal shows itself to be defective as well. What I want to argue now is that this would be a mistake. But to understand *why* it would be a mistake requires understanding the distinctive way in which Bayesianism approaches epistemology. At the heart of that approach is an insight into the relation between confidence and preference.

III

Suppose you are offered a free choice between two identical gambles, one a gamble on the hypothesis H and the other a gamble on the hypothesis G. That is, the prizes in the two gambles are so designed that you are indifferent between winning the one gamble and winning the other, indifferent between losing the one gamble and losing the other. You prefer, of course, winning to losing. Suppose, further, that the truth-values of H and G are not in any other way auspicious for you, and that neither their truth-values nor the desirability of the prizes that ride on their truth-values are going to be affected by which, if either, of the two gambles you prefer. Now, think about what will decide the choice for you. It is pretty clear that your preference will depend entirely on what confidence ranking (if any) you have for H and G: you will find the gamble on H preferable to the gamble on G if and only if you are more confident in the truth of H than you are in the truth of G. Thus what I will call The *Bayesian Insight*:

> Your state of confidence and preference is open to rational criticism if the following condition is not satisfied: where P and Q are any hypotheses, you prefer a gamble on P to an identical gamble on Q if and only if you are more confident that P than you are that Q.[15]

This insight into the relation between confidence and preference is surely a modest one. But, modest though it may be, it opens up a distinct approach to epistemology. It has been a traditional concern of epistemology to say, in some general way, by what principles the opinions of a rational person ought to be constrained. Epistemologists have sought such principles, and evidence for their legitimacy, in various places. Some have sought insight from the traditional sources—from reflections on the metaphysical structure of the world, from analyses of the nature of justification. Others have argued that insight is available only from the scientific study of the empirical world—from the analysis of the way actual human inquirers behave, from the findings of cognitive psychology, from the application of evolutionary biology to human cognition.

The foregoing insight suggests a different place to look. The insight tells us that, on pain of opening our states of confidence and preference to criticism, we will invest more confidence in P than in Q just if we prefer a gamble on P to an identical gamble on Q. This means that, if we can find a theory that says something general and informative about when (on pain of inviting such criticism) we ought to prefer one gamble to another, we have reason to think it will be a theory that tells us something general and informative about when (on pain of inviting such criticism) we ought to invest more confidence in one hypothesis than in another—a theory that will constitute a genuine contribution to epistemology. Bayesianism's claim is to have found just such a theory.

This is not the occasion to present a full-blown account of how to derive the regulative ideal I have touted here, and its probabilistic constraints on confidence rankings, from such a theory.[16] But, even absent such a presentation, it is not hard to see, given the Bayesian Insight, why you should invest more confidence in P v Q than you do in either of its disjuncts. Given the Bayesian Insight, you should invest more confidence in P v Q than you do in either of its disjuncts if and only if you should prefer a gamble on P v Q to an identical gamble on either of its disjuncts. And it is obvious that you should prefer such a gamble.

After all, you cannot possibly fare any better by gambling on a disjunct of P v Q rather than on the disjunction itself; any circumstance in which you would win a gamble on a disjunct is a circumstance in which you would win a gamble on the disjunction. But, for all you know, you could fare worse. You haven't the slightest idea which if either of P and Q is true. For all you know, P is true and Q is false. For all you know Q is true and P is false. If P is true and Q is false and you were to gamble on Q rather than on P v Q, you would be worse off for it. If Q is true and P is false and if you were to gamble on P rather than on P v Q, you would, again, be worse off for it. But if you cannot possibly do better by gambling on one of the disjuncts of P v Q rather than on P v Q itself, and, for all you know, you could do worse, the direction your preference should take is surely clear: you should prefer a gamble on P v Q to an identical gamble on either of its disjuncts. That is, given the Bayesian Insight, you should be more confident in the truth of P v Q than you are in the truth of either of its disjuncts.

Not everyone will be convinced. There is a worry some epistemologists have had about the Bayesian Insight and its kin—a worry about the necessary condition it would impose on your investing more confidence in P than in Q. Talk of gambling, they have complained, only makes sense when the preconditions for gambling are met—when it is possible to determine whether the gamble one is talking about has been won or lost and, thus, possible to pay off the gambler in the event she wins. That means that, even if such talk makes sense in the case at hand—even if it is possible to determine what color shoes I wore on my tenth birthday and what activities occupied Cathedral Square in 1996—it will not make sense in a great many others. Suppose that P and Q are scientific theories, for example. In that case, it makes no sense to talk of gambling on P and Q because the preconditions for gambling are not met. No one is in a position to pay off the gamble if the theory is true—because no one can ever be in a position to determine that the theory is true. Thus it is simply nonsense to require, as the Bayesian Insight does, that you invest more confidence in P than in Q only if you prefer a gamble on P to an identical gamble on Q.[17]

But notice that, while it is certainly true that the preconditions for your actually gambling on a theory are simply not met, neither are the preconditions for my having spent the second week of April 2000 in Positano. I, in fact, spent the second week of April 2000 in Milwaukee. There is nothing anyone can do to change that. Yet it still makes sense for me to prefer having spent that week in that idyllic Amalfi coast town to having spent the time in Milwaukee. But if it ever makes sense to prefer that things were otherwise than they in fact were, we must reject the view that the preconditions for the realization of a state of affairs must be met for there to be sense in speaking of your preferring that state of affairs to some other. And once we reject that view, it is hard to see anything at all problematic in supposing—even as we concede that the preconditions for gambling on theories are not met—that you, say, prefer having $100 ride on one theory to having $100 riding on another.

There is another worry, however. It is easy enough to see why, insofar as you want your confidence-rankings to be consistent with your preferences, my argument for investing more confidence in P v Q than in its disjuncts should weigh with you. But suppose that your interests are purely epistemic. Suppose that you are concerned solely with the epistemic propriety of investing more confidence in P v Q than in its disjuncts—and not at all with the ramifications this confidence-ranking has for your preferences. How, some epistemologists would ask, can the argument have any force? The fact that, say, your being equally confident in P and in P v Q commits you to an unacceptable indifference between a gamble on P and an identical gamble on P v Q may well be important from the point of view of your desire to have reasonable preferences. But it seems to provide no *epistemic* reason not to be equally confident in the two hypotheses. It seems to provide no reason why, say, a being that had no preferences at all would be mistaken in being equally confident in P and in P v Q.[18]

But does it really? Suppose that you go to the doctor because you are suffering from fatigue and loss of appetite. You are going to the doctor to initiate an inquiry that will result in your harboring a reasoned state of confidence that does not just satisfy your curiosity about what is wrong with you, but also can provide doxastic input into whatever decisions you and your doctor will have to make as to how to proceed with treatment. You do not always conduct inquiry with the purpose of arriving at a state of confidence that will do this double duty. Sometimes your inquiry is motivated solely by curiosity. But even then you expect the resulting state of confidence to be capable of doing double duty. We expect even the state of confidence produced by pure research—so often of no immediate use to any decision-making of interest—to be capable of such use.

If this is so, then the adequacy of an epistemology needs to be judged by something more than how well it answers to our intuitions about the extent to which you should consider your curiosity about the truth-value of a hypothesis to have been satisfied. An epistemology's adequacy also needs to be judged by how well it answers to our intuitions about good decision-making and, in partic- ular, the role reasoned opinion should play in good decision-making. That is, an epistemology should be judged adequate only to the extent that it places con- straints on a confidence-ranking appropriate to its double role: as curiosity- satisfier and decision-making guider.

But then the sort of argument I gave for investing more confidence in P v Q than in either of its disjuncts cannot justly be accused of turning on considerations external to the epistemic realm. On the contrary, this argument is focused squarely on a matter critical to the adequacy of an epistemology: it means to show that any epistemology that does not demand, in the circumstances described, that you invest more confidence in P v Q than in either of its disjuncts cannot but sanction an unreasonable preference—cannot but sanction an opinion unsuited to guide decision-making. It means to show that any such epistemology will fall short in a critical aspect of its own vocation.

To be sure, if we were preferenceless beings—if our opinions had no call to inform our decision-making—the argument I offered might well lose its bite. But, by the same token, if we didn't care about science, the demonstration that a given epistemological doctrine is incompatible with empirical theories' being capable of evidential support would also leave us cold. Yet no one would suggest that we can develop an adequate epistemology without concerning ourselves with how it co- heres with good scientific practice. It is no more sensible to suppose that we could develop an adequate epistemology without concerning ourselves with how it co- heres with good deliberative practice. The task facing epistemology is not to find a small set of intuitions to which it can answer and call its own. It is rather to find a way to contribute to, and cohere with, the broad story of rational human endeavors. It is, I think, a task to which the Bayesian Insight—and the Bayesian approach to epistemology that it makes possible—provides a signal contribution.

IV

Of course, the Bayesian approach to epistemology has its own charge of excessive narrowness to answer. The Irrelevance Objection charges that, in focusing exclusively on the propriety of a person's states of graded confidence, the Bayesian approach turns its back on the doxastic attitude with which epistemologists are—and have historically been—concerned: categorical belief. In so doing (the charge goes), the Bayesian approach simply does not address the inquiries that concern epistemologists most—the inquiry into the conditions under which a categorical belief is justified, the inquiry into the conditions under which a person has (a categorical belief that counts as) knowledge. The Bayesian approach simply changes the subject.

But notice that it is far from obvious why an inquiry into the propriety of states of graded confidence should be thought irrelevant to an inquiry into the propriety of categorical beliefs. True, we don't think about categorical belief exactly as we do about confidence. Whereas confidence clearly admits of degrees, we are inclined to think that either you believe a hypothesis or you don't—*tertium non datur*. But this is no obstacle to thinking that facts about the way in which you invest confidence in hypotheses translate into facts about beliefs. Consider how we think about millionaires. We hold that either you are a millionaire or you aren't, it is not a matter of degree. Yet we recognize that being a millionaire is a state of wealth, and wealth does admit of degree. We count you as a millionaire just in case you are sufficiently wealthy. It is natural to suppose that categorical belief bears a similar relation to confidence. Although either you categorically believe a hypothesis or you do not, categorical belief is a state of confidence which admits of degree. We count you as categorically believing P ("believing P" for brevity) just in case you are sufficiently confident in the truth of P.

And, if this is right, then the Bayesian approach to epistemology operates, not on the margins of epistemology, but at its center. For, if this is right, belief is just confidence in the rough. The Bayesian's inquiry into the propriety of states of confidence is simply an inquiry into beliefs under another description, and its results enjoy a secure claim to bear on our more familiar epistemological concerns.

The real problem in reconciling the Bayesian inquiry into the propriety of states of graded confidence with the traditional epistemological inquiry into the propriety of categorical beliefs is not that the former is irrelevant to the latter. Rather, it is that the Bayesian inquiry raises a fundamental challenge to the very intelligibility of the notion of categorical belief.

To see this, consider how one might make out the view that categorical belief is a state of confidence—how one might go about translating talk of categorical belief into talk about investing confidence in hypotheses. There are only two initially plausible ways to go about it.

The first is to adopt the *Certainty View* of belief, to define talk about belief as talk about maximal confidence, about certainty: to believe P is just to be certain that P. Of course, you are going to count as being maximally confident in the truth of P if and only if there is no other hypothesis in whose truth you are more confident. And, given the Bayesian Insight, that is to say that (on pain of opening your state of confidence and preference to criticism) you will be certain of the truth of P only if there is no other hypothesis—not even a tautology—on which you would prefer to gamble. But then the Certainty View commits us to maintaining that (on pain of opening our state of confidence and preference to criticism) there must be nothing we believe on whose truth we would not be as happy to gamble as we would on the truth of a tautology. Moreover (because the result of conjoining a set of hypotheses that has probability 1 must itself have probability 1), we must be certain—and as happy to bet as we would be to bet on a tautology—that *everything* we believe is true. If belief actually required a commitment of this magnitude, there could be precious little we could reasonably believe—much less than we credit ourselves with reasonably believing.

The other alternative is to think of believing a hypothesis as having an amount of confidence above a certain threshold in the truth of the hypothesis—where, for your confidence in the truth of P to be above the threshold, you needn't be certain that P, but you do need to be more confident that P than you are that not-P. But this alternative, the *Confidence Threshold View* of belief, will fare no better.

It would seem to be a fundamental fact about categorical belief that a *reductio* of a set of beliefs is a criticism of that set of beliefs—that it is a criticism of a set of beliefs that the set logically implies a contradiction. That is to say, it would seem to be a fundamental fact about categorical belief that the following principle of *Deductive Cogency* holds:

> The set of hypotheses you categorically believe is open to rational criticism if it does not satisfy the following conditions:
>
> (i) it includes all the logical consequences of that set, and
> (ii) it includes no contradiction.

But the principle of Deductive Cogency is quite incompatible with the Confidence Threshold View. Imagine yourself confronted with a fair lottery with one million tickets, only one of which will win.[19] Now consider the set of hypotheses, {not all the tickets in the lottery will lose, ticket #1 will lose, ticket #2 will lose, . . . , ticket #1,000,000 will lose}. Here is a set of a hypotheses that you cannot categorically believe without violating Deductive Cogency: the set logically implies a contradiction. Yet, by the lights of the Confidence Threshold View, it is not just a set of hypotheses you can believe without inviting any criticism; it is a set of hypotheses you will (provided any reasonable setting of the threshold) have no choice but to (because you will, by definition) believe. It is a set of hypotheses in each member of which you will have (and you would expose your confidence ranking to criticism if you didn't have) a degree of confidence equal at least to .999999—higher than any threshold we might reasonably contemplate. The moral is clear: insofar as we think that, even though you invest that much confidence in the hypotheses in the set, you invite criticism of your set of beliefs if you categorically believe all the hypotheses in the set—indeed, insofar as we think it is at least *open to you* not to categorically believe them all—we must conclude that belief is not a state of confidence above a threshold.[20]

The upshot would seem to be that neither the Certainty View nor the Confidence Threshold View of belief is correct. Talk of belief cannot be defined in terms of talk of confidence. For facts about how you invest confidence in hypotheses do not translate into facts about beliefs. Belief is not a state of confidence. One might think that the lesson to be learned is that the Irrelevance Objection has been sustained. The Irrelevance Objection claims that a Bayesian has nothing to teach an epistemologist. One might think that what we have seen is that this claim is correct: when it comes to the questions about belief and knowledge that concern epistemologists most, Bayesianism gives us no advice at all.

This charge of irrelevance, however, will not stick. The mere fact that belief is not a state of confidence does not show that Bayesianism has nothing to say about the propriety of beliefs. After all, no gamble is a state of confidence but, given the Bayesian Insight, it is clear that Bayesianism has a great deal to say about the propriety of at least some gambles. There is, however, another charge of irrelevance that *does* stick—although this charge goes in a rather different direction.

Suppose we grant that Modest Bayesianism is adequate to the domain of rational decision-making. That is, suppose we grant that (just as in orthodox decision theory) it is states of confidence (albeit in the form of confidence rankings) that provide the doxastic input into rational decision-making.[21] Then, since belief is not a state of confidence, what you believe is of absolutely no importance—an epistemology concerned with the propriety of your beliefs is of absolutely no consequence—to rational decision-making. It is to an epistemology directed at ensuring the propriety of confidence-rankings that you will have to turn for methodological insight when you want to ensure the propriety of that doxastic input. If your decision-making is going to satisfy the demands of reason, you are going to have to attend to your confidence-rankings. You are going to have to do your best to decide, for each hypothesis P on whose truth value the outcome of a decision depends, which are the hypotheses in which you invest more confidence than you invest in P, which are the ones in which you invest less. You will have to decide as best you can, and so far as reason permits, roughly how much confidence you invest in P.

But now comes a key question. Once you have done all this (once you have ranked P as best you can, once you have done what an epistemology concerned with the propriety of confidence-rankings requires you to do with P) what is now supposed to motivate us to say (what could we possibly *mean* if we say, what could we possibly be trying to find out by saying): "Fine. You have decided as best you can how confident you are in the truth of P. But do you *believe* P?"

There is, of course, a natural answer: "Why, we are motivated by a desire for a methodology to arrive—not at confidence-rankings or rational preferences—but at beliefs!"[22] But however natural it may be, this answer will not do. What we need to be told is what exactly a methodology that arrives at belief arrives *at*— what difference it makes to the way we conduct our lives (if only our lives as inquirers) *what* belief we arrive at. After all, if the best that can be said about categorical belief is that it is not a state of confidence, if the best that can be said is that it has nothing to do with decision-making or the inquiry that serves our decision-making, then it may be because categorical belief is not anything at all: categorical belief is an outmoded notion whose day has come and gone. And if that is so—if Richard Jeffrey is right in thinking (with most Bayesians) that, in crafting the Bayesian approach to epistemology, "Ramsey sucked the marrow out of the ordinary notion [of belief], and used it to nourish a more adequate view"[23]—then, once you have decided roughly how much confidence you invest in P, there is no more settling of opinion about P left for you to do.

And if this is really the state of play, then the Irrelevance Objection is, indeed, vindicated—but only in a most ironic fashion. Bayesianism indeed has nothing to contribute to the study of justified categorical belief. But that is only because there *is* nothing that answers to the expression, "categorical belief."

V

It is hard, however, not to feel that there is something left over—something we care about, something we used our old talk of categorical belief to talk about— that talk about confidence-rankings simply cannot capture. The challenge issued in the last section is to say what that something is—to show what there is in the bones of the old notion of categorical belief that Ramsey missed.

Modest Bayesianism maintains that that there is, indeed, something left over— something we have used our talk of categorical belief to talk about. Modest Bayesianism does not, however, claim that this is what our talk of categorical belief *has* always been about. The moral that Modest Bayesianism draws from the last section is that our naïve notion of categorical belief is deeply confused. There can be no question of coming up with a new definition of belief that will succeed where the Certainty and Confidence Threshold views did not. The enterprise of coming up with a definition of categorical belief that is faithful to our naïve notion of categorical belief is simply one that cannot coherently be accomplished.

The notion I will (on behalf of Modest Bayesianism) be defining below is not meant to capture, or even replace, our naïve conception of belief—only to do some of the work left over after its demise. To emphasize this fact (and to forestall misunderstandings), I will not call the thing I am defining "belief." The expression "belief" is too closely tied to the notion of confidence. It is this very tie that has brought our naïve notion of categorical belief to grief. Instead I will use a much more flexible term of art, "acceptance."

I say that it is more flexible because our ordinary practice already contains uses of "accept" that are not tied to confidence. For example, we think of our accepting P for the sake of argument as being entirely compatible with our investing any amount of confidence (including very little) in the truth of P. Thus my hope is that, if it should turn out that the thing I will be calling "accepting that P" is compatible with (say) having very little confidence that P, there will be no argument from ordinary usage to the effect that I thereby bruise intuition. If I am mistaken in that hope, then I suggest that the reader who feels her intuitions bruising replace my talk of acceptance with talk of Modest-Bayesian-acceptance or employ some other neologism of her choosing. It is the attitude I will be picking out, not the epithet I use to pick it out, that is of concern here. It is an attitude to which we devote a great deal of attention in the conduct of inquiry, an attitude that we have been using our ordinary talk of belief to talk about, an attitude that talk of confidence-rankings alone simply cannot capture. And it is an attitude by appeal to which we can make sense of our interest in powerful theories, thereby answering the Theory Objection.

The attitude I mean to pick out is one I have been displaying in the very writing of this essay. In writing this essay, I am making a set of categorical assertions. And I am making these categorical assertions—and you understand me to be making these categorical assertions—in a particular context: the context of inquiry. What is special about the context of inquiry is that the primary aim of making assertions in the context of inquiry is not to amuse or to entertain or to shock, as it is, say, in a comedic context. Insofar as we understand a person to be asserting a hypothesis P in the context of inquiry, we understand her to have passed P through a special filter. We understand her to be asserting what she does quite deliberately. That is, we understand that, among the options of asserting P, asserting the negation of P and making neither assertion, she prefers to assert P. And we understand her to have determined that, whatever else she hopes to gain by asserting P (be it fame, favorable reviews, or just a chuckle), she would still prefer to assert P (as opposed to asserting that not-P or making neither assertion) were she harboring but one aim: the aim to assert the truth (as it pertains to P).

It is this attitude toward P that I want to pick out by the expression "accepting P." That is, I want to say that a person accepts P just when she is willing to assert

P in the context of inquiry: that is, just if, faced with a decision problem wherein her sole aim was to assert the truth (as it pertains to P), where her only options were to assert that P, assert that not-P, or make neither assertion, she would prefer to assert that P.

It is an attitude to which we devote a great deal of attention in the conduct of inquiry. In this sense of "accept," it is clear that it matters a great deal to us what it is people accept. We manifest enormous interest in what people are willing to assert in the context of inquiry and in the propriety of their being willing to assert what they do. The amount of time and energy we devote to producing and scrutinizing of books, articles, and lectures testifies to our preoccupation with the practice of assertion in the context of inquiry. Moreover, in the current sense of "accept" it is clear the difference your accepting P makes to the way you engage in that practice: you will be willing to assert P in the context of inquiry if and only if you accept P.

It is an attitude we have been using our naïve talk of belief to talk about. It is fair to say that, as natural as it is to suppose that categorical belief is a state of confidence, it is equally natural to suppose that, in the context of inquiry, a person will be willing to assert P if and only if she believes P.

It is an attitude that talk of confidence-rankings alone simply cannot capture. The attitude of acceptance I have been describing cannot be defined in terms of states of confidence—and for much the same reasons our naïve notion of categorical belief could not. Acceptance cannot be defined as certainty, because we are willing (and think ourselves right to be willing) to assert in the context of inquiry hypotheses of whose truth we are not certain. And acceptance cannot be defined as a state of confidence above some lower threshold, since consistency in what we are willing to assert in the context of inquiry is something we care a great deal about. Were the attitude of acceptance I have described definable as just a state of confidence above a threshold, we would have no worry whatsoever about flatly asserting, of each ticket in a million-ticket lottery which we have flatly asserted to be fair, that this ticket will lose. But this is not something any of us is prepared to do in the context of inquiry.[24]

It is an attitude by appeal to which we can make sense of our interest in powerful theories, thereby answering the Theory Objection. Since acceptance, in the sense I have defined it, *is* dissociated from confidence, the fact that we cannot but be confident in the falsehood of any powerful theory does not rule out our accepting such a theory. Acceptance, as I have defined it, is not a state of confidence. There is nothing contradictory in the notion that we might accept—that is, be willing to assert in the context of inquiry—a theory even as we were extremely confident that it is false.

Indeed, not only is there no contradiction in this notion, the definition of acceptance actually suggests how a person could be *rational* to accept a theory at the same time as she is confident it is false. To see this, let us take a brief look at the aim to assert the truth. The truth is just an error-free, comprehensive story of the world: for every hypothesis P, it either entails P or entails not-P and it entails nothing false. This being so, the aim to assert the truth *tout court* is not one anyone can reasonably expect to achieve. But it is, nonetheless, an aim we can pursue: when we aim to assert the truth, we aim to assert as comprehensive a part of that error-free story as we can. In pursuing that aim, the desire for comprehensiveness and the desire to avoid error are bound to conflict. When we are choosing what to include in our story of the world, the choice of whether to include a stronger rather than a weaker claim will often amount, in effect, to a choice *either* to indulge our desire for comprehensiveness at the cost of increasing our risk of frustrating our desire to avoid error, *or* to override the desire for comprehensiveness to avoid increasing the risk of error. A methodology for arriving at rational acceptance (in the present sense of "acceptance") will be a methodology for negotiating trade-offs between these competing desires.[25]

Now, in the case of a substantial empirical theory, the trade-off required to include it our theory of the world is clear: a substantial empirical theory is not available except at the price of importing a high risk of error. One perfectly reasonable reaction to this situation would be to recoil from the risk of error involved in asserting such a theory and, accordingly, refrain from asserting such theories in word and print. But another perfectly reasonable reaction would be to recoil from the prospect of foregoing the assertion of such theories in word and print and, accordingly, decide that the comprehensiveness one gains in asserting a substantial empirical theory is worth the risk of error involved. There is no reason to suppose that a person who has the second reaction, as I suspect most of us do, would not be entirely rational to prefer to assert such a theory were her sole aim to assert the truth with respect to that theory—that is, no reason, on the present understanding of "accept," to suppose that it is not entirely rational for her to accept such a theory. There is no reason why the mere improbability of substantial theories need render them inappropriate objects of acceptance.

If this is right, then we have found a way, within the confines of Modest Bayesianism, to furnish a straightforward response to the Theory Objection. We are interested in powerful theories because we view them (at least insofar as they are powerful) as attractive objects of acceptance—attractive things to assert in the context of inquiry. The fact that we (rightly) regard them as improbable is no bar to our accepting them. Acceptance is not a state of confidence. In accepting them we do not thereby become confident they are true. Rather, in accepting them as true, we adopt nothing beyond a willingness to assert them in the context of inquiry.

What makes this response possible, of course, is the recognition that, to do the work we thought our naïve conception of categorical belief (construed as a state of confidence) could do on its own, we need to divide the labor between two distinct notions: a notion (acceptance) that has to do with what we are willing to assert in the context of inquiry and a notion (confidence) that has to do with our preferences amongst gambles. It is with only with respect to the former that Deductive Cogency is properly to be considered a regulative ideal; it is only with respect to the latter that the Modest Bayesian regulative ideal is properly to be considered a regulative ideal. But, distinct though they are, acceptance and confidence do not occupy entirely disjoint spheres. For, however one ultimately wants to flesh out the details of how we negotiate the trade-off between comprehensiveness and error-avoidance in deciding what to accept, this much will be true: the propriety of our assessment of the risk of error we run in accepting a given hypothesis comes to nothing more, and nothing less, than the propriety of our assessment of how confident we should be that the hypothesis is false. Thus the Bayesian's probabilistic constraint on confidence-rankings will have secure place in any account of rational acceptance.[26]

This much said, it is worth noting that this division of labor provides the materials to see our way through three puzzles that have bedeviled the theory of rational (justified) belief.

The first is the Paradox of the Lottery, a version of which I exploited in my discussion of the Confidence Threshold View. Recall that you are confronted with what you are all but certain is a fair lottery with one million tickets of which only one will win. For each ticket in the lottery you will want to have a degree of confidence roughly equal to 0.999999 in the hypothesis that this ticket will lose. In the hypothesis that not all the tickets will lose you have a degree of confidence close to 1. Despite the high degree of confidence you (rightly) invest in each of the hypotheses mentioned, it would seem that you would open your set of beliefs to criticism were you to believe them all—for they comprise an inconsistent set of hypotheses.

It is certainly a paradox so long as one thinks of belief as a state of confidence short of certainty. Reason would at one and the same time seem to (a) demand you believe of each ticket (because it demands that you be so confident of each ticket) that it will lose and (b) demand that you *not* believe, of each ticket, that it will lose (because the set of beliefs you would then harbor would be inconsistent). But divide the labor in the way I have suggested, and the air of paradox vanishes. Modest Bayesianism demands only that you be extremely confident, of each ticket, that it will lose. Properly understood, Deductive Cogency demands only that you be unwilling to assert in the context of inquiry (i.e., that you not accept), of each ticket, that it will lose. Given that acceptance is not a state of confidence, there is no contradiction in these two demands.

The second puzzle is the Paradox of the Preface.[27] Suppose you are reading through a substantial book you have written. As you read it through, you affirm, of each sentence, that you believe it to be true. That set of sentences logically implies the conjunction of all the sentences. So, Deductive Cogency requires that you believe this conjunction. But, as you reflect on how ambitious your book is and your human fallibility, you come to appreciate that the probability that all the sentences in your book are true in every detail is pretty low—it is far less probable than that there is some mistake lurking in your book. This being so, it seems only reasonable to believe that at least one of those sentences is false. But in adopting the belief that some errors *do* remain, you come to harbor a set of beliefs that implies the contradiction, "All the sentences in my book are true and at least one of them is false." And, in so doing, you violate Deductive Cogency.

What lends the Paradox of the Preface its air of paradox is (again) the naïve assumption that belief is a state of confidence above a threshold. Think of belief this way, and, when you see Deductive Cogency demanding (as it does) that you believe that everything you wrote in the book is true, you will read it as demanding that you be *confident* that everything you wrote in the book is true. And this is a requirement that, under the circumstances, will be patently incompatible with the demand Modest Bayesianism makes upon your states of confidence.

But reconstrued as governing acceptance (as defined here), Deductive Cogency's injunction to accept that everything you wrote in the book is true says nothing about your states of confidence. It says only that, in the context of inquiry, you should not shy away from asserting that everything you wrote in the book is true. Granted, you are bound to have good reason to be extremely confident that it is false that everything you wrote in the book is true. But there is no contradiction in supposing that you are willing to assert in the context of inquiry something of whose falsehood you are extremely confident.

Indeed, not only is there no contradiction in supposing this, but I have already sketched (in response to the Theory Objection) what seems to be a perfectly good reason why, in the context of inquiry, you *would* be willing to assert something of whose falsehood you are extremely confident: ambitious theories are not available at any lower price. After all, supposing your book is a good one, the conjunction of the (postprefatory) assertions it contains is just such a good, ambitious theory. And, if so, the same argument goes through: given the choice between asserting that theory true, asserting it false (i.e., that it contains some error), and asserting neither, the rational thing to do (unless you are prepared to forgo the assertion of theories in word and print) is to assert the theory true. The rational thing is for you to assert that everything you have asserted in your book is true.

Note that there is nothing immodest in your making this assertion. You are free to confess to the risk of error you have incurred in writing a book so full of content as yours. Indeed, the preface of your book, devoted as it will be to general remarks about the nature and/or genesis of your book, is an entirely appropriate place for you to admit that you are very confident that your book is not error-free. It is entirely appropriate—and compatible with the demands of Deductive Cogency—for you to admit in the preface that you have probably made some mistakes in the pages that follow and for you to exculpate from blame for such errors everyone whose help you have acknowledged. Acceptance, as defined by

Modest Bayesianism, is not a state of confidence. Thus Deductive Cogency neither prohibits your being extremely confident, nor prohibits your confessing that you are extremely confident, that your book contains some error. It only forbids you to take back in your preface what you assert in the rest of the book: it only forbids you flatly to assert that your book is in error.[28]

Another payoff of our definition of acceptance is that it provides a neat way of dealing with a third puzzle: the pessimistic induction from the history of science to the effect that no scientific theory can legitimately be believed to be true. The line of thought is this. If you look at the history of science or medicine or history (and the list goes on), what you find is that theories believed to be true at earlier times are shown to be mistaken in the light of information discovered later. We thus have excellent reason to believe that *our* theories will be found to be mistaken by the light of information that is yet to be discovered. Given this, it is hard to see how we can possibly believe our current theories. We have excellent reason to believe that they are false.[29]

Given our naïve notion of categorical belief, the puzzle is real. But in the light of the division of labor proposed by Modest Bayesianism, we have the following reply available. The pessimistic induction is this far right: the history of inquiry provides excellent inductive evidence for the hypothesis that our current theories are mistaken. That is, this history gives us excellent reason to be confident that these theories are mistaken. But to say we have excellent reason to be confident P is false is not to say that we have excellent reason not to accept P—that is, to be unwilling to assert P in the context of inquiry. On the contrary. We have already acknowledged an independent reason to be confident our ambitious theories are false. (They say so much about the world that they're likely to be mistaken in some way or another.) And we have seen how we can reconcile this with our being rational to accept them as true all the same. Accepting P doesn't *mean* being confident P is true; it means being willing to assert P in the context of inquiry. And ambitious theories aren't available for assertion except at the price of asserting something likely to be false.

Of course all this does not quite put the Irrelevance Objection to bed. Even if it be granted that contemporary epistemologists' questions about the propriety of our categorical beliefs can find proper expression (and some new, attractive answers) within the framework of Modest Bayesianism, there remains the question as to whether their questions about knowledge can likewise be accommodated. At least this much can safely be said by way of an answer.

To judge from the epistemological literature devoted to the analysis of "S knows that P," most epistemologists think of knowledge as simply being true belief that meets some sort of epistemic condition. The belief is justified, where that justification is (in some important sense) undefeated. Or, it is (in some important sense) no accident that the agent has the true belief in question. By and large, the philosophers of this persuasion hold that it is no condition on a person's knowing that P that she know, or even that she believe, that she knows that P. Knowledge, so conceived, is at a far remove from the knowledge-qua-certainty of, say, Descartes. This being so, it is hard to see how there could be anything driving contemporary analyses of "S knows that P" that would stick at the idea of substituting "accept" (as defined here) for "belief" in those analyses. That is to say, it is hard to see what there is that would stick at the idea that a person can know a proposition she regards as improbable.

VI

With this, I rest my case for a Modest Bayesianism. I have two hopes. The first is that I have by now established, at the very least, that the Bayesian approach to epistemology is a good deal more resilient than it has often been portrayed. That is, I hope I have gone some way towards making the case that (despite the precise and extremely demanding mathematical constraint on opinion for which it is widely known) the Bayesian approach can be so crafted as to accommodate, even as it places substantive constraints on, the opinions of people like us—limited in our logical and mathematical acumen, indeterminate in our opinions, and most often deprived of evidence good enough to warrant greater precision. My second hope is that I have conveyed some sense of how fertile is the idea—so central to the Bayesian approach to epistemology as I have sought to portray it—that there is important epistemological insight to be found in reflection on our preferences.[30]

NOTES

1. Where P and Q are any hypotheses, the Kolmogorov axioms hold that

(i) $prob(P) \geq 0$;
(ii) $prob(P) = 1$, when P is a tautology; and
(iii) $prob(P \vee Q) = prob(P) + prob(Q)$, when P and Q are mutually exclusive.

2. See, for example, Ellery Eells, *Rational Decision and Causality* (Cambridge: Cambridge University Press, 1982), 41ff.

3. See, for example, Alvin Goldman, *Epistemology and Cognition* (Cambridge, Mass.: Harvard University Press, 1986), 326–328.

4. See, for example, John Pollock, *Contemporary Epistemological Theories* (Totowa, N.J.: Rowman & Littlefield, 1986), 110; Alvin Plantinga, *Warrant: The Current Debate*

(Oxford: Oxford University Press, 1993), 140–141; Richard Foley, *Working without a Net* (Oxford: Oxford University Press, 1993), 158–162, 174–175.

5. For example, Harold Jeffreys, *Theory of Probability*, 3rd ed. (Oxford: Oxford University Press, 1961), 33–34, writes (the emphasis is his):

> If there is no reason to believe one hypothesis rather than another, the probabilities are equal ... *to say that the probabilities are equal is a precise way of saying that we have no good grounds for choosing between the alternatives* ... The rule that we should take them equal is not a statement of any belief about the actual composition of the world, nor is it an inference from previous experience; it is merely the formal way of expressing ignorance.

6. For a defense of this claim, see my *Decision Theory as Philosophy* (Cambridge: Cambridge University Press, 1996), 45–62. The claim is an expression of the relevance conception of evidence, which is central to Bayesian work in the theory of confirmation. See, for example, Wesley C. Salmon, "Confirmation and Relevance," in *The Concept of Evidence*, ed. Peter Achinstein (Oxford: Oxford University Press, 1973), 95–123; Paul Horwich, *Probability and Evidence* (Cambridge: Cambridge University Press, 1982).

7. See Pollock, *Contemporary Epistemological Theories*, 110–111.

8. This objection is due to Clark Glymour. See his *Theory and Evidence* (Princeton: Princeton University Press, 1980), 83–84. See, too, Richard Miller, *Fact and Method* (Princeton: Princeton University Press, 1987), 319–323.

9. See Robert Nozick, *Philosophical Explanations* (Cambridge, Mass.: Harvard University Press, 1981), 255.

10. See, for example, Paul Horwich, *Probability and Evidence*, 12, where he writes:

> More specifically, the Bayesian approach rests upon the fundamental principle:
> (B) That the degrees of belief of an ideally rational person conform to the mathematical principles of probability theory. ...

11. See, for example, Alvin Plantinga, *Warrant: The Current Debate*, 132–146.

12. Why not the stronger claim: we will count a person's degree of confidence in a tautology as rational just if either it is maximal or it is excusably not maximal? To see why not, suppose she assigns P the maximal degree of confidence on a whim: she has no reason to assign it the maximal degree of confidence but does so all the same. As it happens, P is a tautology. I doubt that we want to count her confidence as rational.

13. For a similar line of response, see Brad Armendt, "Dutch Books, Additivity and Utility Theory," *Philosophical Topics* 21 (1993): 1–20, 4.

14. This is a slight rewrite of a regulative ideal I defend in *Decision Theory as Philosophy*, 21. For discussion of how it compares to some other nonorthodox Bayesian competitors, see 23–31.

15. This expression of the Bayesian Insight has antecedents in Frank Ramsey's definition of an ethically neutral proposition; and in Leonard Savage's definition of personal probability. See Frank P. Ramsey, "Truth and Probability," in *Foundations of Mathematics and Other Logical Essays*, ed. Richard Braithwaite (London: Routledge and Kegan Paul, 1931), 156–198, and also in David H. Mellor, ed., *Philosophical Papers* (Cambridge: Cambridge University Press, 1990); see Leonard J. Savage, *The Foundations of Statistics*, 2d ed. (New York: Dover, 1972), 31.

16. I offer such an account in *Decision Theory as Philosophy*, chap. 1.

17. See, for example, Hilary Putnam, "Probability and Confirmation" in his *Philosophical Papers*, vol. 1 (Cambridge: Cambridge University Press, 1975); Ian Hacking, "Slightly More Realistic Probability," *Philosophy of Science* 34 (1967): 311–325, esp. 316.

18. See, for example, David Christensen, "Dutch-book Arguments Depragmatized: Epistemic Consistency for Paptial Believers," *Journal of Philosophy* 93 (1996): 450–479, esp. 455–456.

19. What follows is the lottery paradox, due to Henry Kyburg, *Probability and the Logic of Rational Belief* (Middletown: Wesleyan University Press, 1961), 197. It has almost without exception been deployed by philosophers to pose a puzzle about rules governing rational belief, rather than (as I am deploying it here) to pose a puzzle about the nature of belief. But see Gilbert Harman, *Thought* (Princeton: Princeton University Press, 1973), 118, where he sees in the lottery paradox reason to deny that belief can be defined in terms of degrees of confidence. It should be noted that there are many (Kyburg among them) who view the paradox as providing a reason to abandon the principle of Deductive Cogency. See, for example, Henry Kyburg, "Conjunctivitis," in *Induction, Acceptance and Rational Belief*, ed. Marshall Swain (Dordrecht: Reidel, 1970); Richard Foley, "The Epistemology of Belief and the Epistemology of Degrees of Belief," *American Philosophical Quarterly* 29 (1992): 111–124.

20. Some defenders of the Confidence Threshold view are unmoved by these considerations. It would be one thing, they respond, if the Confidence Threshold View licensed the wholesale disregard of *reductio* arguments. This would, indeed, be intolerable. But the view does no such thing. On the contrary. On the Confidence Threshold View, a *reductio* of a small number of hypotheses can constitute a very serious criticism, showing that there is no way consistent with a probabilistic constraint on confidence rankings to rank all of the hypotheses involved high enough that they will all exceed the threshold for belief. For example, a *reductio* of ten hypotheses would show that one cannot invest a degree of confidence greater than 0.9 in any one of them without being forced to invest a degree of confidence less than 0.9 in at least one other. Only *reductios* that require very large numbers of hypotheses (for example, the *reductio* that would seek to convince us that we should not believe, of every ticket in the lottery, that it will lose) lack critical bite, since it is compatible with there existing such a *reductio* that our confidence in each of the hypotheses involved exceed the threshold of belief. But, these philosophers want to say, such *reductios* lack force anyway. (This line of thought was pressed on me independently by Ruth Weintraub and Scott Sturgeon.)

But will this reply really do? Suppose that you charge me with producing a chronology of the events that preceded a serious accident. Suppose that the chronology I produce takes the following form: "At 8:00 A.M. event A occurred. After event A occurred, event B occurred. After event B occurred, event C occurred . . . After event Y occurred, event Z occurred. After event Z occurred, event A occurred." You ask me whether I concede that the x-occurred-after-y relation is transitive and not reflexive. Naturally, I do. "Then how," you ask, "can you possibly offer this as a chronology of the events leading up to the accident? Given what you have (rightly) conceded, your chronology logically implies a contradiction—namely, that there is an event (event A) that occurred after itself and no event occurred after itself."

There can be no question but that the *reductio* you have produced has critical bite:

it exposes the fundamental inadequacy of the chronology I have produced. This inadequacy is in no way mitigated by the fact that the *reductio* requires 29 hypotheses to derive its contradiction. That is, the inadequacy of my chronology is in no way mitigated by the fact that the derivability of this contradiction is compatible with my having, and being entirely warranted in having, an extremely high degree of confidence (greater than 0.96) in the truth of each of the twenty-nine hypotheses—that is, a degree of confidence great enough to qualify as a belief, by the lights of the Confidence Threshold view (and any reasonable setting of the threshold). It would in no way serve to blunt your criticism if I were to point out to you that it was compatible with your *reductio* that I am warranted in being this confident in each of the twenty-nine hypotheses. The inescapable conclusion is that the idea that only *reductios* of relatively small numbers of hypothesis have critical bite (and, thus, the principle of Deductive Cogency is too strong) simply won't wash: the difficulty the lottery case poses for the Confidence Threshold view of belief is real.

21. Think of an act as just something that, for some set of mutually exclusive and exhaustive hypotheses, designates for each hypothesis in the set a consequence that will ensue if that hypothesis is true. It is characteristic of an Orthodox Bayesian decision theory—and there is more than one variant; see Peter Fishburn, "Subjective Expected Utility: A Review of Normative Theories," *Theory and Decision* 13 (1981): 129–199—to put forward some small set of constraints on a person's preferences over acts (so construed), the violation of any one of which constraints would seem to be sufficient to open her preferences to the charge that they are not rational, and then prove that a person cannot satisfy these constraints unless her states of opinion and valuation satisfy three substantive conditions:

(i) that she harbor a precise degree of confidence assignment that conforms to the Kolmogorov axioms of the probability;

(ii) that the utility of the consequences for her—the intensity of her preference for them—be captured by a numerical utility assignment unique up to linear transformation; and

(iii) that she prefer one act to another just if the former bears greater expected utility, where the expected utility of an act is just the weighted sum of the utility of its consequences for her, the utility of each consequence weighted by her degree of confidence that the hypothesis on which the act's having the consequence depends is true.

The most influential variant on Orthodox Bayesian decision theory is to be found in Leonard Savage, *The Foundations of Statistics*. Patrick Maher presents a defense and exposition of Savage's theory in his *Betting on Theories*. See, too, Peter Fishburn, *Utility Theory for Decision Making* (New York: Wiley, 1970), chap. 14. For another theory that is particularly influential in philosophical circles, see Richard Jeffrey, *The Logic of Decision*, 2nd ed. (Chicago: University of Chicago Press, 1983).

To grant that Modest Bayesianism is adequate to the domain of rational decision-making is thus to grant that there exist a pair of conditions that stand to the second and third conditions in the way the Modest Bayesian regulative ideal stands to the first. It is to grant that properly weakened, Orthodox Bayesian decision theory can be rendered adequate. For a defense of one way of doing this, see Maher, *Betting on Theories*. For another, see my *Decision Theory as Philosophy*, chap. 1.

22. See Robert Nozick, *Philosophical Explanations* (Cambridge, Mass.: Harvard University Press, 1981), 255.

23. Richard Jeffrey, "Dracula Meets Wolfman: Acceptance vs. Partial Belief," in *Induction, Acceptance and Rational Belief*, ed. Swain, 157–85; see 172.

24. There can be small surprise that acceptance, as I have defined it, is not also definable in terms of states of confidence. In arguing earlier that categorical belief could not be a state of confidence, I was implicitly appealing to the role categorical belief plays in describing what we are willing to assert in the context of inquiry to show why the Certainty and Confidence Threshold views of belief could not be right.

25. The view that, in determining what to accept, we seek both comprehensiveness and avoidance of error, has played a central role in the work of Isaac Levi. See, for a recent example, *The Fixation of Belief and Its Undoing* (Cambridge: Cambridge University Press, 1991). But Levi holds a variant on the view, no more tenable than the Certainty View, that acceptance is a state of certainty. (For him, maximal confidence is a necessary, though not sufficient, condition of acceptance.) So, from my point of view, Levi can be said to have taken (indeed, pioneered) a correct approach to rational methodology but to have applied it to the wrong thing. More recently, Patrick Maher has also construed comprehensiveness and avoidance of error as the aims of rational acceptance; see his *Betting on Theories*. But, as I have explained in *Decision Theory as Philosophy* (110n) his account of what acceptance is does not meet the Bayesian challenge to the intelligibility of belief outlined above.

26. I do not in fact think that the negotiation is to be thought of as a direct weighing of the two (or even more than two) desiderata. Rather, I think the negotiation is reflected in the way we actually argue for the truth of the hypotheses we accept. See *Decision Theory as Philosophy*, chap. 4. For two views on which the negotiation takes the form of a decision problem with epistemic values as utilities, see Isaac Levi, *Gambling with Truth* (New York: Knopf, 1967), and Patrick Maher, *Betting on Theories*.

27. D. C. Makinson, "The Paradox of the Preface," *Analysis* 25: 205–207.

28. And there is no question that an author's flat assertion in her preface that the book is mistaken *would* be read as taking back what she says in the rest of the book. Indeed, it is not hard to anticipate that a reader's reaction would be to wonder why the author hadn't taken the time to correct the error if she is prepared flatly to assert it exists.

29. See, for example, Bas Van Fraassen, "Empiricism and the Philosophy of Science," in *Images of Science*, ed. Paul M. Churchland and Clifford A. Hooker (Chicago: University of Chicago Press, 1985), 294; Richard Miller, *Fact and Method* (Princeton: Princeton University Press, 1987), 166–167.

30. This essay offers a new motivation for (and slight revision of) the view defended in my *Decision Theory as Philosophy*. Some paragraphs have been lifted from that work and others written during the period of its gestation. I would like to thank Joan Weiner for comments on various drafts of this paper, and Scott Sturgeon, both for comments on the penultimate draft and for extensive discussion of the matters about which this essay is concerned. During some of the time I was working on this essay, I was a Senior Fellow of the American Council of Learned Societies, a Visiting Fellow of the Philosophy Programme of the School of Advanced Studies at the University of London, and a guest of the Ligurian Study Center for the Humanities and Arts in Bogliasco. All three institutions have my heartfelt thanks. I have also had the good fortune to have

read versions of this essay (and to have benefited from the response of audiences) at the University of St. Andrews, the University of Edinburgh, the 34th Annual University of Cincinnati Philosophy Colloquium, the Bled (Slovenia) Conference on Vagueness, the University of Illinois at Chicago, the Inland Northwest Philosophy Conference, and Birkbeck College London.

CHAPTER 16

EMBODIMENT AND EPISTEMOLOGY

LOUISE M. ANTONY

ANALYTIC epistemology more or less presumes that knowers are all alike. That is, to be more precise, it presumes that knowledge (and affiliated phenomena) can be identified and characterized without taking into account the kinds of properties that actually distinguish one human being from another. This goes for both intrinsic and extrinsic properties—for biological sex as well as for cultural identity. It's not that analytic epistemology denies that such factors are relevant to knowledge. It will be (or ought to be) readily conceded by analytic epistemologists that such factors as whether one is male or female, rich or poor, may have profound effects on the kinds of experiences one has, the kinds of thoughts one thinks, the opportunities one has for thinking and experiencing, and so on, so that the content of one's beliefs will vary partly as a result of these factors. So, too, will the nature and degree of one's warrant for holding one's beliefs: A woman may, for example, have both a kind and degree of warrant for the proposition that parturitional labor is painful that are (at least at present) unavailable to a man.

But none of this, it's assumed, really matters to epistemology, because none of this makes a difference to the question of what knowledge *is*. The differences we're talking about all contribute to differences in *inputs* to the cognitive machinery, differences which may well lead, after all, to differences in *outputs*; but, it will be averred, epistemology is interested in the *machinery* itself. Perhaps a man cannot have a woman's experiences, and perhaps, as a result, there are things he can never come to know that she could. Still, if he could somehow be put into her situation—if his "machine" could be provided with the same inputs she re-ceives—then he could—and would—know just what she does. For that matter, nothing about the particular way in which a knower's cognitive machinery is physically realized matters to the characterization of the machine itself—all such features are safely relegated, for the purposes of analytic epistemology, to features of "context."

So when and if analytic epistemologists ever discover what's true if and only if "S" knows that "*p*," they'll have found something that holds for any knower, no matter what they're like, or where they are situated. We might thus, following Lorraine Code, refer to work that's guided by this assumption as "*S-knows-that-p*" epistemology.[1] I'm going to refer to it, however, as "Cartesian" epistemology, the idea being that, for all this brand of epistemology cares, knowers could be completely disembodied—pure Cartesian egos. I'll refer collectively to those fea-tures from which Cartesian epistemology prescinds as a knower's "embodiment."

In this essay, I survey and discuss a variety of recent challenges to Cartesian epistemology, thus understood. My focus will be on feminist epistemology. But while feminist philosophers have been the most visible and vocal critics of Car-tesian epistemology, they are not the only ones. Psychologists like Richard Nisbett and empirically minded analytic philosophers like Stephen Stich have also raised objections, and I will have something to say about these as well. While all of these critics tend to position themselves as radical opponents of "mainstream" episte-mology,[2] I intend to show that the criticisms they make are consonant with a number of mainstream developments, particularly externalism and naturalized epistemology.

KNOWERS, KNOWING, AND THEORIES THEREOF

Let me begin by drawing a distinction between two different ways that one might criticize Cartesian epistemology. The first way would be to argue that, contrary to the defining assumption of Cartesian epistemology, embodiment *does* matter to what knowledge is, or to how knowers know. This might be the case, for example, if it turned out that there were gender differences in cognitive capacities, or if one's language determined one's conceptual repertoire, or if epistemic norms varied importantly from culture to culture. If embodiment were to turn out to affect epistemic phenomena in this way, I would say that embodiment has "ground-level" effects on epistemology. But there's a second, different way of criticizing Cartesian epistemology, and that would be to argue that embodiment matters to the way in which one *theorizes about* knowledge, so that, in particular, Cartesian epistemology reflects contingent and nonuniversal features of the embodiment of the theorists who espouse it. These sorts of effects I would call "meta-level" effects.

Appreciation of this distinction will help head off a common misconception about feminist epistemology, viz., that it is a field *premised* on the view that men and women think differently.[3] Some feminist epistemologists do believe this (although they still do not hold the very crude views often attributed to them), but many, perhaps most, do not. The prevailing view within feminist epistemology is that male dominance of the field has resulted in a distorted or incomplete picture of human knowledge *generally*. For example: many feminist epistemologists believe that men are more apt than women to endorse an epistemic norm of strict impartiality, but these same theorists also believe that such a norm is inappropriate for *any* human knower.[4] Feminist epistemologists, in other words, have been most interested in investigating the potential meta-effects of embodiment on epistemology, and considerably less interested in trying to demonstrate the existence of ground-level effects.

The reasons why feminist epistemology has this higher-level orientation has to do with the kinds of things that drew feminist attention to analytic epistemology in the first place. During the so-called second wave of feminist activism, many women within the academy began to ask pointed questions about their disciplines: why are there so few women in this field? Why have women's activities, achievements, and concerns received so little scholarly attention? Why have these questions not been asked before?[5] Probably the first thing that struck feminists looking in this way at the Western philosophical tradition was its disdain for the feminine.[6] Although women were largely ignored by the major philosophers, whenever we *were* discussed, we were denigrated. Strikingly, the insult often involved a philosopher's explicitly denying to women some characteristic that that philosopher had elsewhere held to be essential to full personhood, making us, by definition, less than human. Thus Aristotle, who defined "man" as a rational animal, claimed that women's reason was defective in that it was "without the power to be effective."[7] Locke, who thought that "man" could transcend natural power relations by means of civil agreement, still found it obvious that in case of conflict between husband and wife, "the rule . . . naturally falls to the man's share, as the abler and the stronger."[8] Rousseau, who took freedom to be the distinguishing mark of humanity, held that it followed from the different natures of men ("active and strong") and women ("passive and weak") that "woman is made to please and be dominated" by man.[9] Perhaps most notoriously of all, Kant, who made acting from apprehension of the categorical imperative the essence of moral agency, averred that "I hardly believe that the fair sex is capable of principles."[10]

This sort of thing was bad enough; but feminists in philosophy noticed that philosophical misogyny took another, more insidious form as well. Not only were women explicitly denied reason and autonomy—such charges could be met head-on and rebutted—but we were implicitly insulted by characterizations of valued faculties, traits, and processes that depended on invidious contrasts with "feminine" characteristics. Although philosophers have disagreed throughout the ages about such matters as the reliability of knowledge gained through the senses, this much is true: whenever a dichotomy is employed to explicate an epistemic distinction, the higher valued term will be the one more strongly associated with men and masculinity. For the Greeks, the distinction between form and formlessness was clearly associated with the distinction between male and female, and laid the foundation for a broad set of associations that pervades Western thought: that which is law-governed, articulated, rational, spiritual, and eternal is masculine; the feminine is unruly, formless, material, and ephemeral.[11]

Many feminists in philosophy began to suspect that this pervasive misogyny had left deep marks on the content of epistemology, and in particular, on our received views of the nature of knowing and the knower. When we reflect on the "methodology" of philosophy, this suspicion is only heightened. Philosophy's reliance on introspection and imagination, on the philosopher's "intuitions" about the "results" of "thought experiments" leaves a great deal of room for the idiosyncrasies of individual philosophers to intrude. Human beings are not, in general, fully aware of the factors that influence their thinking and are not therefore in a good position to tell, by introspection alone, whether their judgments reflect universal features of the human condition, or only contingent features of their own situation. The danger is exacerbated if there is too much homogeneity among theorists: consensus among the group will serve as a false marker of the objectivity of members' judgments, rather than being recognized for what it is—an artifact of their mutual similarity. The risk of distortion is further increased if the homogeneous group is privileged, since it is characteristic of the psychology of the privileged to think of themselves as typical or normal—the "unmarked" case of "human" (consider: what determines whether a cuisine, form of dress, or style of music counts as "ethnic"?) The tendency of the privileged to normalize themselves can result in their taking a critical stance toward difference, in case it is finally noticed: difference from oneself is treated as a deviation from the norm, and hence as a defect.[12] It seems highly plausible that some such process must have been in effect in order for philosophers to have made some trait—say reason—the defining feature of humanity, while noting almost parenthetically that women don't have any. The irony is that such philosophizing will be overtly committed to the universality of its claims—the catch is that the universe is carefully delineated so as to exclude possible counterexamples.

We can see, then, why feminists are inclined to be skeptical about Cartesian epistemology: an epistemological programme that is *premised* on the irrelevance of bodily difference may—in just that respect—reflect nonuniversal features of

the theorist's specific embodied position. This position, notice, is quite independent of anyone's position on the question whether there *exist* important cognitive
universals—feminists have mainly been concerned about the results of theorizing
from a position that fails even to consider the relevance of differences in embod-
iedness for questions about knowledge. It's valuable to note, in this context, that
Stephen Stich has been expressing quite similar concerns about the methodology
of analytic epistemology for over a decade. In "Reflective Equilibrium, Analytic
Epistemology and the Problem of Cognitive Diversity," for example, he argues
that there is every reason to think that, even if human beings' repertoire of cognitive mechanisms and strategies are biologically specified and species-wide, there
is still substantial room for epistemically important differences to arise in the ways
we seek and process information as a result of environmental variables, especially
cultural ones. The possibility of there being such differences, Stich argued,

> adds a certain urgency to one of the more venerable questions of epistemology.
> For if there are lots of different ways in which the human mind/brain can go
> about ordering and reordering its cognitive states, if different cultures could or
> do go about the business of reasoning in very different ways, *which of these
> ways should we choose?*[13]

That Stich asks this question is greatly to his credit. He goes on in this essay to
challenge the legitimacy of both philosophical analysis and reflective equilibrium,
two methodological mainstays of analytic epistemology.

Since then, data have emerged that suggest that the scenario Stich earlier
envisions as a mere possibility may be, in fact, a reality. Work by Richard Nisbett
and his associates[14] and by Weinberg, Nichols, and Stich[15] indicates that there are
significant differences by both cultural background and by socioeconomic class
(Stich's work only) in respect to both epistemic habits and epistemic intuitions.
In a wide-ranging series of experiments, Nisbett and his colleagues found that
"Westerners" (represented by individuals of European heritage raised in the United
States) and "East Asians" (individuals raised in China, Japan, or Korea or first or
second-generation East Asian immigrants to the United States) performed in systematically different ways on tasks involving attention and control, explanation
and prediction, and inference. Nisbett et al. summarize their findings in this way:

> We find East Asians to be more *holistic*, attending to the entire field and as-
> signing causality to it, making relatively little use of categories and formal logic,
> and relying on "dialectical" reasoning. Westerners are more *analytic*, paying at-
> tention primarily to the object and the categories to which it belongs and using
> rules, including formal logic, to understand its behavior.[16]

Nisbett et al. hypothesize that these cognitive differences are attributable to systematic differences in the social structures of contemporary societies predominantly influenced by the intellectual systems of ancient Greece on the one hand,

and those of ancient China on the other. Greek-influenced societies, according to them, emphasized individual power and valorized debate. Chinese-influenced societies located agency in the social collective as a whole and valorized consensus. The different social norms and patterns of behavior that resulted from these different worldviews and value sets influenced the ways in which people saw the world and reasoned about it.

Weinberg, Nichols, and Stich followed up this and other work on cultural difference with a series of studies in which individuals from either different cultural backgrounds or different socio-economic groups were presented with several stock thought-experiments from analytic epistemology—some tapping into the internalism/externalism debate, others involving various Gettier-type cases where there is some unusual disconnect between the truth of and the warrant for a given belief. The results obtained by Weinberg et al. did not pattern quite as neatly as those of Nisbett et al., but the important point for both their purposes and mine is the fact that differences did exist.[17] That analytic epistemology has presumed a uniformity of intuition among all its participants has both obscured the existence of diversity and forestalled a needed discussion about what such diversity would or ought to mean for our conception of "the knower."

The point of this section, as I said, was to distinguish criticisms of Cartesian epistemology that allege metaeffects of embodiment from those that allege ground-level effects. I hope I've succeeded in making out the claim that one might have good reason for thinking that theorizing about knowledge can be inflected by features of the theorizer's embodiment, even if one has no reason to think that knowing itself varies according to such features. But I've also argued that, in the specific case of philosophy, masculinist bias can be presumed to lead to the mistreatment of cognitive difference in case it exists. Notably, no one in either of the research groups I've been discussing offers an explanation for the presumptions of cognitive uniformity that they are concerned to challenge. I offer, for their and your consideration, these feminist speculations about the ways in which privilege, including especially masculine privilege, can inflect theorizing.

I cannot close this section without saying something, however, about the issue of gender differences in cognition. As I remarked above, feminist epistemology is too often caricatured as committed to some crude form of difference thesis—as if it were a sort of epistemological analogue of *Men Are from Mars, Women Are from Venus*. But while feminist epistemology has not in fact been much given to positing gender differences, there has developed a sizeable literature outside philosophy purporting to demonstrate the existence of gender differences in "ways of knowing." Much of the work in this vein was stimulated by Carol Gilligan's influential studies of moral reasoning. Inspired by what appeared to her to be a significant gender gap in performance on Lawrence Kohlberg's test of moral development, she produced several studies which she claimed supported the existence of a "different voice" in moral reasoning—different, that is, from the "voice" that Kohlberg had normalized as the best and highest form of moral deliberation. Gilligan claimed that her studies demonstrated the following systematic difference: while males tended to handle moral dilemmas by appeal to abstract principles, treating the problematic situations almost like algebra problems, females were more apt to reason holistically and contextually, and to attempt to understand the situation from several different points of view. The male approach Gilligan dubbed "the perspective of justice," and the female approach, "the perspective of care." Kohlberg's almost exclusive focus on the development of the justice perspective ensured that the care perspective would, inevitably, be denigrated, misidentified, or simply ignored.[18]

Subsequently, some psychologists claimed to have demonstrated the existence of differences between men and women with respect to styles of knowing in general.[19] Criticisms, however, abound. L. J. Walker, in a meta-analysis of studies using the Kohlberg scale, found no significant gender differences,[20] and a review of literature on gender differences in cognition by Mary Brabeck and Ann Larned found little support for a distinctively female way of knowing.[21] It is perhaps surprising and ironic, in light of Nisbett's data, to find so little in the way of gender effects in cognition, for Nisbett finds just the sort of differences cross-culturally that feminists predict will be found between genders, and posits very similar mechanisms to explain the differences. Nisbett himself has sometimes found small gender effects, but nothing very substantial, and small compared to the cultural effects.[22] The data on their face, therefore, suggest that the prevailing cultural ethos may swamp the differences due to gender—whether these effects are presumed to be biological or social.

FEMINIST EPISTEMOLOGY:
THE POSITIVE PROGRAMME

Supposing then, that gender has had an impact on theorizing in epistemology, we then ask: what's the nature of that impact, and what, if anything, should we do about it? To answer the latter question, we need to be a bit clearer about the ways in which gender is supposed to affect theorizing. First of all, we need to distinguish the claim that it's the *homogeneity* of the philosophizing set that has resulted in distorted theory from the claim that it's their *maleness* that's responsible. This second claim turns out to split into two, as well, but first let me say something about the first claim.

Some feminist epistemologists, most prominently Helen Longino, have argued that the problem with the maleness of philosophy—or of any field, for that matter—is not that it has been *male*, but rather that it has been homogenous. According to Longino, whenever a group of inquirers are too similar to each other, bias of some sort will likely result. The reason is, according to Longino, that if everyone believes the same thing, then that belief is substantially less likely to be subjected to dispute or to empirical test. Diversity of viewpoint and interest generates the "essential tensions" that promote the generation and testing of new ideas and that militate against premature convergence onto inadequate theories. Now one of the assumptions of Cartesian epistemology is that knowing is *individualistic*. This means, among other things, that epistemic norms, like objectivity and rationality, are applied, in the first instance, to individual knowers: it is individuals, their beliefs, and their thinking that are assessed as objective or non-objective, rational or irrational, or justified or unjustified. Longino disputes this assumption. According to her, objectivity and justification are fundamentally *social*. Objectivity is not, and could not be, according to Longino, a property of individual knowers, for knowers isolated from the productive pressures of social intercourse cannot subject their beliefs to the kinds of testing that is necessary to overcome the limitations of any single epistemic location. Objectivity is thus a social, rather than an individual norm; objectivity is a feature of a properly constituted epistemic community. Longino's view, which essentially broadens general empiricist method to cover societies instead of individuals, is called *social empiricism*.[23]

On Longino's view, it would be as bad (although bad, perhaps, in a different way) if our community of theorists were to be all female as it has been for them to be all-male, and that's because, as I've explained, it's the homogeneity that does the damage. I doubt that any feminist epistemologist would disagree that homogeneity *per se* is problematic—we are all for diversity, and on grounds similar to the ones Longino gives. But some feminist theorists think that homogeneity is not the only problem: maleness, in this case, is a problem too. So let's turn to the second claim.

It's one thing to say that gender is a parameter of variation in theorizing; it's quite another to say *how* variation by gender is related to variation in theorizing. In order to disarticulate the possibilities, let me introduce a distinction that's current, although not uncontested, within the feminist literature: *gender* vs. *biological sex*. Prescinding from subtleties and controversies, the distinction is this: *biological sex* is a physical property of an organism, involving genes, endocrinology, and morphology. The human species is largely, but not entirely dimorphic with respect to sex, and, for the most part, sex is determined genetically. *Gender* is the social significance assigned to sex; usually, but not always, biological females are assigned the gender "woman" and biological males are assigned the gender "man." The extent to which biological sex determines gender is a controversial question. It seems to be part of our system of gender roles in the United States in 2002, for example, that men fight in wars and women do not. Perhaps this fact is the predictable if not inevitable result of differences in biology between males and females that make males eager to engage in aggressive activity and females reluctant to do so; perhaps it's the result of a contingent, socially negotiated system of conventions (as is surely true for the fact that women carry purses and men do not). Either way, some mechanism is keeping the gender generalization in place, and that's enough for it to be reliably true that gender has an effect on the probability of one's fighting in a war. Let's call the first sort of mechanism—where the result is obtained without the mediation of social convention—an *essentialist* mechanism, and the second sort a *social constructivist* (or for short, *constructivist*) mechanism.[24]

Now we can distinguish constructivist vs. essentialist versions of the claim that gender affects epistemology. The essentialist version says that the biological sex of a theorist has a distinctive effect on some aspect of theorizing, independently of the theorist's experiences, education, cultural background, or social position. This might be true if, as some theorists claim, androgenization of the fetal brain causes males to be better at mathematics than females; if that's correct, then we might expect male theorists to develop more subtle mathematical theories than female theorists do. The constructivist version says that the biological sex of a theorist affects theorizing via the effects of the theorist's occupying a certain social role, which is only contingently related to the theorist's biological sex. This might be true if, as some theorists claim, boys receive more social encouragement and support for studying mathematics than girls do; if that's correct, then we would still expect male theorists to develop more subtle mathematical theories than female theorists do. Obviously, as my example shows, the brute facts about gender differences in style or content of theorizing can't decide between essentialist and constructivist hypotheses as to why these differences exist. To decide that, we need different kinds of evidence and arguments than we have surveyed so far.

One of the alleged effects of gender on theorizing in epistemology that I've already discussed is the tendency involved for philosophers, because they are all male, to either ignore or denigrate difference. The mechanism that I proposed for explaining this was constructivist. One could, I suppose, posit an essentialist mechanism, one that says that there is a biological connection between being male and being arrogant, but that is not what feminist critics have had in mind. The feminist claim is that, in male-dominated societies (and let's leave aside for the moment how societies got to be male-dominated), maleness is connected with social privilege; social privilege then produces (a certain kind of) arrogance. If that's the mechanism, then gender is relevant to theorizing *via* the effects of occupying the social role that constitutes that gender, rather than directly through the effects of having a body sexed in one way rather than another.

Some sort of constructivist account of the way in which gender affects theorizing is at the heart of almost all work in feminist epistemology; this is just another way of reiterating my earlier claim that feminists are not at all attracted to the idea that there are (as we can say now) *essential* differences between the way men and women think. Most feminist epistemologists—indeed everyone with whom I'm familiar—offer constructivist, not essentialist criticisms of Cartesian epistemology. Note, too, that Nisbett and his colleagues, and Weinberg, Nichols, and Stich also seem to favor constructivist, rather than essentialist explanations for the cultural differences they document. On the other hand, the challenge that Weinberg, Nichols, and Stich raise for the programme of (what I'm calling) Cartesian epistemology is one that must be addressed regardless of the explanation for the existence of difference. Whether it's culturally ingrained habits or differences in neural circuitry that accounts for observed differences in performance on cognitive tasks or judgments in epistemic matters, epistemology has to figure out what to say if it turns out that not all knowers are alike.

There are quite a few feminist philosophers who defend constructivist accounts of theorizing in epistemology. One important theoretical strain of this sort is *standpoint theory*. Standpoint theory is rooted in Marxist thought and adapted to feminist purposes by such theorists as Nancy Hartsock, Sandra Harding, Robin May Schott, Naomi Scheman, and bell hooks.[25] Race and feminist theorist bell hooks has developed a standpoint theory that takes account of both race and gender,[26] and Marilyn Frye has argued for a lesbian standpoint.[27] All versions of standpoint theory say this: In a socially stratified society, different social positions yield distinctive epistemic positions, and some are better than others. In particular, the epistemic position of a member of an oppressed group is, at least in principle, superior to the epistemic position of the oppressor. The reason this is so is that oppressors have a vested interest in constructing and projecting as true a story about the reasons for the stratification that rationalize and vindicate their superior positions—an ideology—which may not be (and typically is not) objectively correct. Members of the oppressed group will need, as a matter of survival, to understand this story, and even to pretend that they believe that it is true. But they, unlike their oppressors, have no *motive* for accepting the story as true. At the same time, if the oppressed individuals are members of a group whose activities are central to the actual day-to-day life of the community (workers, in the Marxist version, women in the feminist version), then they have a better chance of viewing the real workings of the social machinery, to see who actually depends on whom, and so forth. If the oppressed individuals can develop a critical awareness of their situations as members of a class within a class-stratified society, then they can be said to have achieved a privileged standpoint. (The process is the process of building "class consciousness" in traditional standpoint theory, and of "consciousness raising" in feminist standpoint theory.)

The idea that marginality can confer some epistemic privilege is one that many feminists accept, even if they are not convinced that the mechanisms posited by standpoint theorists work as smoothly and as inexorably as they are sometimes presented. Many feminist theorists have agreed that the epistemic standpoints of the marginal do offer insights that may not be available (or not easily available) to those who occupy positions of privilege, but at the same time, point out that marginality also entails certain epistemic costs: everything from reduced access to education to increased risk of psychpathology.[28] Another problem with standpoint theory from a pragmatic, political point of view is that it can seem to license either the appropriation of the experience of marginal individuals (a white woman's "borrowing" the authority of a black woman's diary, for example, to bolster her own position) or of romanticizing that experience. Besides the personal injustice done to the individual whose experience is treated in either of these ways, appropriation and romanticization negate the epistemic advantages that accrue to the standpoint of the marginal person, because, in each case, it is the epistemic position of the non-marginal person that is really in play.

There are other views, which, while not standardly classified as standpoint theories, do share with standpoint theories the idea that one's position within a complex or stratified society has systematic epistemic consequences. One of these is the view adopted by both Evelyn Fox Keller and Naomi Scheman, according to which one's position as an infant within a patriarchically structured family, creates a self-conception that has consequences for one's ultimate view of one's relation to other people and to the external world.[29] This view draws on a descendent of psychoanalytic theory, "object-relations theory." On this theory, both male and female children have to construct gender identities for themselves, and in order to do so, look to their parents for models. In a patriarchal society, however, women will be almost solely responsible for childcare (in many cases, it will be the child's mother, but if not the mother, usually some other woman). That means that girls can develop a sense of being female simply by identifying with the caregiving adult, while boys have to do it by negation—being male is *not* like whatever my female caregiver is. There are, according to Keller and Scheman, several results. Keller argues that males develop a near-pathological sense of separation from everything they experience as being outside them—an artifact of the psychic barrier they needed to draw between themselves and their female caregivers in order to forge a male identity. This leads, Keller argues, to the canonization of a notion of objectivity that actually impedes scientific investigation—better, she argues, to develop a sympathetic and symbiotic relationship with nature.[30] According to Scheman, the process of defining male by negating female means that males grow up with a powerful need to deny or to despise any trace of the feminine they find within themselves. This results in a perverse fascination with problems like skepticism, where anxieties about deception and falseness are nurtured, and a tendency to distrust faculties, like the senses and the emotions, that are associated with the female.

Another way in which the maleness of philosophy has seemed to feminists to distort epistemology has to do with the details of everyday existence for creatures like ourselves. A large part of the content of gender roles in patriarchical societies has to do with the assignment of "maintenance" work. Certain kinds of mundane work, including housework, cooking, childcare, and nursing of the sick, traditionally have fallen to women, and this is consonant with the pattern of associations that link women with the body, with material things, and with the concrete and ephemeral. The content of philosophical thinking has reflected that division, with the result that philosophical questions have been framed in an extremely abstract way, with little attention paid to the concrete instantiations of the concepts under investigation.

The Cartesian knower provides a paradigm case. The knower is conceived as without sex, certainly, indeed without a body, and without particular location. Now as I took pains to point out at the beginning of this essay, one needn't saddle Cartesian epistemologists with the view that knowers actually *are* Cartesian egoists—they needn't really believe that one doesn't need a body in order to know. But it is assumed that the details about embodiment, or the situation in which one is embodied, make no difference to the crucial phenomena and relations. We could as well be Cartesian egos—or brains in vats—justification and knowledge would be just as before.

Now to my mind, the first and most devastating challenge to this way of thinking of epistemology came from Quine (who was most assuredly male!) in his attack on the programme of rational reconstruction within epistemology. Quine's point was that any attempt to figure out how we ought to go about seeking knowledge and revising belief in light of experience—any attempt at a normative epistemology—had to begin by investigating empirically those cases in which our knowledge-seeking behavior had been successful. And one of the first things that such inquiry will bring to light is the fact that it matters very much to our knowledge-seeking that we are embodied beings, and how we are embodied. Consider: an eternal being, who had no need for nourishment or rest, would have no reason to tolerate epistemic risk, and hence no need of any kind of inductive logic. We, on the other hand, operate under tight constraints—we have to make up our minds well before the evidence is all in, or we don't live to publish our results. Given all this, the best way to develop a normative epistemology, according to Quine, is to take seriously the kinds of constraints that beings like ourselves must negotiate, and discover the strategies that enable us to succeed in coming to know what we are able to come to know.

Some feminist theorists find in this, Quine's "naturalized epistemology," a good framework for addressing the epistemological questions that are pressing for those of us interested in promoting social change, and for repairing the deficiencies in Cartesian epistemology that led to the neglect of various aspects of knowing.[31] (Quine, it should be said, never condoned this particular application of his theory.) For example, it has seemed to feminists that there is a great need for a better understanding of the social dimensions of knowing. Of course, Longino and other social empiricists address some of this need. But there are other questions as well, concerning especially our practice of giving and receiving testimony. That testimony is an essential element of human epistemic practice is an insight that emerges from a naturalized approach to knowledge, but it has been feminists who have had the most to teach us about what testimony involves. Three writers in particular, Annette Baier, Lorraine Code, and Karen Jones, have enriched our understanding of the moral and affective dimensions of epistemic engagement with other people, Baier and Jones by emphasizing the role of *trust* in testimony, and Code through her exploration of the notion of *epistemic responsibility*.[32] Alison Jaggar has long argued for the epistemic importance of emotions generally, seeking to discredit the idea that good knowing involves the absence of emotion.[33]

Another theoretical framework stimulated by the same insight about the importance of looking at knowledge as it actually occurs is the study of *situated knowledge*. Here the leading idea is that there can be no fruitful abstraction of "the knower" from the situation in which the knowing occurs, that knowledge is in fact a composite phenomenon, involving the knower and the knower's environment.[34]

The final criticism I want to explain concerns the role that science has played in the promotion and legitimation of oppressive hierarchies. Feminists and other progressives have, by now, documented numerous cases in which science has lent its authority to sexist, racist, or classist theories with little or no empirical legitimacy.[35] Understanding the mechanisms by which scientific authority is constructed, and the correlative processes by which the voices of non-experts are sometimes silenced is a large item on the agenda of any genuinely feminist epistemology. That, in fact, may be the best way to think about the effects of embodiment on epistemology—in terms of engagement and disengagement. The Cartesian attempt to treat essentially embodied agents in a disembodied way leads pretty surely to a disengaged epistemology—to a way of studying epistemology that sees knowledge only in abstract terms. I am not saying that there is no need for disengaged epistemology—indeed, I have argued strenuously that the Cartesian approach is a necessary component of any epistemological project. But it should never be forgotten that it is not all we need—that, apart from its inherent interest and beauty, philosophy is needed to answer real questions, thrown up by our ordinary, embodied lives.

NOTES

1. Lorraine Code, "Taking Subjectivity into Account," in *Feminist Epistemologies*, ed. Linda Alcoff and Elizabeth Potter (New York: Routledge, Chapman, and Hall, 1993), p. 15.

2. See, for example, Linda Alcoff and Elizabeth Potter, "Introduction: When Feminisms Intersect Epistemology," in Alcoff and Potter, *Feminist Epistemologies*, 1–4, and Stephen Stich, "Reflective Equilibrium, Analytic Epistemology and the Problem of Cognitive Diversity," *Synthese* 74 (1988): 391–413.

3. See Susan Haack, "Knowledge and Propaganda: Reflections of an Old Feminist," *Partisan Review* 4 (1993): 556–564.

4. See, for example, Evelyn Fox Keller, "Gender and Science," in *Discovering Reality: Feminist Perspectives on Epistemology, Metaphysics, Methodology, and Philosophy of Science*, ed. Sandra Harding and Merrill Hintikka (Dordrecht: Reidel 1983), 187–205.

5. This question is the topic of Sandra Harding's essay, "Why Has the Sex/Gender System Become Visible Only Now?," in Harding and Hintikka, *Discovering Reality*, 311–324.

6. Unless I explicitly say otherwise, I'll be restricting my focus to the philosophizing done in the analytic tradition, together with the antecedents of that tradition (which I refer to as "the Western tradition"). I characterize the analytic tradition historically, to be, roughly, the style of philosophizing that has dominated the English-speaking world (Australia, Canada, New Zealand, the United Kingdom, and the United States) since the early part of the twentieth century. (So, contra Rorty, I claim American pragmatism for the analytic tradition.)

I make no claims about non-Western traditions, although I would be surprised if the stories about the role of women were much different.

7. Aristotle, *Politics*, in *Philosophy of Woman*, 3rd ed., ed. Mary Mahowald (Indianapolis: Hackett, 1994), 31.

8. John Locke, *Two Treatises of Government*, in Mahowald, *Philosophy of Woman*, 72.

9. Jean-Jacques Rousseau, *The Emile*, in Mahowald, *Philosophy of Woman*, 89.

10. Immanuel Kant, "Of the Distinction of the Beautiful and the Sublime in the Interrelations of the Two Sexes," in Mahowald, *Philosophy of Woman*, 105. In fairness, I should point out that Kant immediately adds the qualification, "and I hope by that not to offend, for these are also extremely rare in the male." But one should not assume from this that Kant did not intend to assert a categorical difference between male and female powers, for he says quite explicitly: "Women will avoid the wicked not because it is unright, but because it is ugly; and virtuous actions mean to them such as are morally beautiful."

11. The whole sorry history has been documented and analyzed by Genevieve Lloyd in her important book, *The Man of Reason: "Male" and "Female" in Western Philosophy* (Minneapolis: University of Minnesota Press, 1984). See also Lynda Lange, "Woman Is Not a Rational Animal: On Aristotle's Biology of Reproduction," and Elizabeth V. Spelman, "Aristotle and the Politicization of the Soul," both in Harding and Hintikka, *Discovering Reality*, 1–15 and 17–30, respectively.

12. See Iris Young, *Justice and the Politics of Difference* (Princeton, N.J.: Princeton University Press, 1990), especially chap. 4, "The Idea of Impartiality and the Civic Public."

13. Stich, "Reflective Equilibrium," 393.

14. Richard Nisbett, Incheol Choi, Kaiping Peng, and Ara Norenzayan, "Culture and Systems of Thought: Holistic vs. Analytic Cognition," forthcoming in *Psychological Review*.

15. Jonathan Weinberg, Shaun Nichols, and Stephen Stich, "Normativity and Epistemic Intuitions," forthcoming in *Philosophical Topics*.

16. Nisbett et al., "Culture and Systems of Thought," 2.

17. Naomi Scheman anticipated the possibility that judgments about Gettier cases might be inflected by one's social position. See her "Feminist Epistemology," *Metaphilosophy* (1995): 177–189, esp. 187–189.

18. Carol Gilligan, *In a Different Voice* (Cambridge, Mass.: Harvard University Press, 1982).

19. The *locus classicus* is Mary Belenky, Blithe Clinchy, Nacny Goldberger, and Jill Tarule, *Women's Ways of Knowing: The Development of Self, Voice, and Mind* (New York: Basic, 1986).

20. L. J. Walker, "Sex Differences in the Development of Moral Reasoning: A Critical Review," *Child Development* 55: 677–691.

21. Mary M. Brabeck and Ann G. Larned, "What We Do Not Know about Women's Ways of Knowing," in *Women, Men, and Gender: Ongoing Debates* ed. Mary Roth Walsh (New Haven: Yale University Press, 1997).

22. Personal correspondence.

23. Helen Longino, *Science as Social Knowledge* (Princeton, N.J.: Princeton University Press, 1990). Other important advocates of the view that epistemic norms should be understood as applying primarily to whole communities, rather than to individuals within them, are Miriam Solomon and Elizabeth Anderson. See Solomon's *Social Empiricism* (Cambridge, Mass.: MIT Press Bradford Books, 2001) and Anderson's "Knowledge, Human Interests, and Objectivity in Feminist Epistemology," *Philosophical Topics* 23 (1995): 27–58.

24. For a more precise and detailed exposition of these and related distinctions, see Sally Haslanger, "Ontology and Social Construction," *Philosophical Topics* 23 (1995): 95–125.

25. Nancy Hartsock, "The Feminist Standpoint: Developing the Ground for a Specifically Feminist Historical Materialism," in Harding and Hintikka, *Discovering Reality*, 283–310; Sandra Harding, "Rethinking Standpoint Epistemology: 'What Is Strong Objectivity?' " In *Feminist Epistemologies*, 49–82; Robin May Schott, "Resurrecting Embodiment: Toward a Feminist Materialism," in *A Mind of One's Own: Feminist Essays on Reason and Objectivity*, ed. Louise M. Antony and Charlotte Witt (Boulder: Westview, 1993); Naomi Scheman, "Feminist Epistemology."

26. bell hooks, *Feminist Theory: From Margin to Center* (Boston: South End, 1984).

27. Marilyn Frye, "To Be and Be Seen: The Politics of Reality," in *The Politics of Reality* (Freedom, Calif.: Crossing, 1983), 152–174.

28. See, for example, Bat-Ami Bar On, "Marginality and Epistemic Privilege," in Alcoff and Potter, *Feminist Epistemologies*, 83–100.

29. Keller, "Gender and Science," and Scheman, "Feminist Epistemology."

30. See her account of Barbara McClintock's practice in *A Feeling for the Organism: The Life and Work of Barbara McClintock* (San Francisco: Freeman, 1983).

31. Jane Duran, *Toward a Feminist Epistemology* (Lanham, Md. Rowman & Littlefield, 1991); Lynne Hankinson Nelson, *Who Knows? From Quine to a Feminist Empiricism* (Philadelphia: Temple University Press, 1990); and Louise Antony, "Quine as Feminist: the Radical Import of Naturalized Epistemology," in Antony and Witt.

32. See Annette Baier, "Trust and Anti-Trust," *Ethics* 96 (1986): 231–260; Lorraine

Code, *What Can She Know? Feminist Theory and the Construction of Knowledge* (Ithaca, N.Y.: Cornell University Press, 1991); Karen Jones, "The Politics of Credibility" in *A Mind of One's Own*, 2nd ed. forthcoming.

33. Alison Jaggar, "Love and Knowledge: Emotion in Feminist Epistemology," in *Women, Knowledge, and Reality*, ed. Ann Garry and Marilyn Pearsall, 2nd ed. (New York: Routledge), 166–190.

34. Donna Haraway, "Situated Knowledges: The Science Question in Feminism and the Privilege of Partial Perspective," in *Simians, Cyborgs, and Women: The Reinvention of Nature* (New York: Routledge, 1991), and Miriam Solomon, "Situatedness and Specificity," Symposium on Situated Cognition, Eastern APA Meetings, Atlanta, December 29, 1996.

35. A very small sample: Barbara Ehrenreich and Deirdre English, *For Her Own Good: 150 Years of the Experts' Advice to Women* (New York: Doubleday, 1989); Ruth Hubbard, *The Politics of Women's Biology* (New Brunswick, N.J.: Rutgers University Press, 1992); and Leon Kamin, *The Science and Politics of IQ* (Mahwah, N.J.: Erlbaum, 1974).

CHAPTER 17

EPISTEMOLOGY AND ETHICS

NOAH LEMOS

MORAL philosophy, construed broadly, is concerned with what actions are morally right and wrong, what kinds of things are intrinsically good or bad, and what traits of character are moral virtues or vices. Whether and how we can have knowledge or justified belief about these matters is a main concern of moral epistemology. In this essay, I attempt to outline some of the main problems and solutions that arise in moral epistemology. The essay is divided into four sections. The first addresses some main arguments for ethical skepticism. The second considers some views about how one should proceed in moral epistemology and in moral philosophy. The third section deals with coherentism and foundationalism, including reliabilist foundationalism, as they pertain to the structure and source of our epistemic justification for moral and evaluative beliefs. The final section returns to the problem of how we should proceed in moral philosophy and moral epistemology, more specifically to the view that we should "get outside" our moral beliefs in order to discover and assess general moral principles and particular moral judgments. The outline of problems and the survey of solutions is by no means complete or exhaustive. More important, in many cases, the proposed solutions are at best tentative, depending upon a fuller treatment of issues beyond the scope of this essay. So, for example, whether moral foundationalism is ultimately a satisfactory stance in moral epistemology will depend upon whether foundationalism in general can be defended against various objections not considered here. As with any survey or outline, there is always a trade-off between breadth and depth of coverage. Where the mean lies, as Aristotle might say, rests with perception so I apologize in advance for blindspots. With these caveats let us turn to ethical skepticism.

ETHICAL SKEPTICISM

Whether some moral beliefs are instances of knowledge or enjoy epistemic justification is deeply debated. In addition, there is no clear consensus, even among the friends of moral knowledge, about how it is possible or what might be its source. However, this situation is not peculiar to moral beliefs. The same, of course, might be said about beliefs concerning the external world or other minds. Some philosophers have denied that we can know anything about the external world or about other minds, and among those who hold that we do have such knowledge there is no clear consensus about how we do know such things. Given our concern with moral epistemology, let us distinguish general skepticism from skepticism about some particular domain, for instance ethics, other minds, or the external world. Suppose we take general skepticism to be the view that there is no knowledge of any sort and that no belief is epistemically justified. Ethical skepticism, in contrast, is the view that there is no moral knowledge and that there are no epistemically justified moral beliefs. Of course, if general skepticism were true, then it would follow that ethical skepticism is also true. But many people attracted to ethical skepticism are not general skeptics, and ethical skepticism seems more widespread than skepticism about other domains, such as the external world and other minds. Many ethical skeptics take there to be a special problem with ethical knowledge and justification and advance a variety of considerations in support of their view. Among the most important arguments for ethical skepticism are the argument from disagreement and an argument that appeals to the explanatory requirement. Let us begin with the former.

Some ethical skeptics challenge the notion that there is any knowledge of moral truths that transcend the varied moral outlooks and attitudes of particular cultures. They do so by pointing to what appear to be deep and unresolvable moral disagreements.[1] Moral beliefs about slavery, monogamy, infanticide, and the burial of the dead have varied among cultures. In our own society there are deep disagreements over the permissibility of abortion, the death penalty, and homosexuality. Not only are such disagreements deep and pervasive, but they seem to resist resolution. According to the skeptic, the best explanation for these disagreements is that moral attitudes simply reflect differences in upbringing and socialization rather than the apprehension of objective moral truths or moral facts that transcend the attitudes of a particular culture. People hold the moral attitudes they do because of their upbringing and socialization, and not because they have apprehended objective moral truths. Often coupled with these points is the view that moral knowledge would require some reliability in judging the objective moral facts. But the lack of agreement is taken to indicate a lack of reliability about objective moral matters. Just as we would have reason to doubt the reliability of people's perceptual faculties concerning objective properties of size and shape given widespread differences in visual reports, the widespread differences of moral judgments are, the skeptic urges, a reason to doubt the reliability of people's moral judgments. If people are simply not reliable about moral matters, then there is reason to think that they lack moral knowledge.

Ethical cognitivists who defend the existence of moral knowledge make a variety of responses to this line of argument.[2] First, the claims that we are unreliable judges of objective moral truths and that there is no moral knowledge might seem plausible given some conceivable levels of moral disagreement. But it is far from clear what that level is or that we are even close to it. The argument from disagreement seems more plausible if we focus exclusively on the extent of disagreement. But the ethical cognitivist might fairly remind us of the wide extent of actual ethical agreement. He might point to such things as the United Nations Declaration of Human Rights, which is widely endorsed by the international community, and to widely held prohibitions against murder, theft, assault, and rape. He might also point to mundane moral truisms within our culture and others that we rarely formulate, but which almost all of us believe or are disposed to believe. These would include such truisms as one ought not to swerve into oncoming traffic, one ought not to run over pedestrians, and bosses ought not to disembowel their secretaries. Furthermore, he might note that some instances of moral disagreement are merely apparent, insofar as they involve applying the same general moral principles to different social circumstances. So for example the principle of maximizing utility or promoting the good of all might in the harsh environment of the Eskimo justify the practice of infanticide without justifying such a practice in a less harsh environment. Different funeral practices might reflect different customary or traditional ways of showing respect for a person while being consistent with and supported by the principle of showing respect.

In addition to pointing out areas of wide moral agreement, the ethical cognitivist might be able to explain moral disagreements in ways that do not imply that there is no moral knowledge. Instances of disagreement in perceptual cases do not tend to support the general unreliability of perception given some accounts of how perceptual error arises. The fact that perceptual reports differ under certain conditions, such as poor lighting, distance, or eye disease, does not support the view that perception is typically unreliable or that there is no perceptual knowledge. So, too, the ethical cognitivist might be able to develop an "error theory" for moral beliefs. He might, for example, point out that some moral beliefs depend on mistaken beliefs about the nonmoral facts, such as mistaken beliefs about the commands of God or gods, the consequences of actions and policies, and the nature of a person. Disagreements and mistakes about nonmoral facts can and do lead to moral disagreements and moral mistakes. But such disagreements do not imply that there is no knowledge of general moral principles or particular moral claims. He might also point out that in some cases moral disagreements can be explained by the fact that one or both parties is influenced by such things as self-interest, partiality, or partisanship. Such things can affect one's moral judgment in ways that lead to error and disagreement. What is more, the ethical cognitivist might even concede that about certain moral matters many people are indeed unreliable, without conceding a pervasive unreliability that supports moral skepticism. He might note that because one is unreliable with respect to a certain range of *nonmoral* facts it hardly follows that one is unreliable with respect to them all. The Presocratic philosopher who is an unreliable judge of various biological, astronomical, and theological facts might be highly reliable about many other nonmoral matters, such as the existence of other people, their thoughts and feelings, and the size and shape of medium-sized objects in his environment. So, too, someone not very reliable about moral matters concerning political policies of distributive justice, tax policy, health care and so on, might be quite reliable about more mundane moral matters, such as not driving on the sidewalk or veering into oncoming traffic. Unreliability about some nonmoral matters does not imply that one is unreliable about them all, and unreliability about some moral matters does not imply unreliability about them all.

The ethical cognitivist might also concede that many of our moral beliefs as well as our dispositions and habits of moral judgment are deeply influenced by our upbringing. But he might note that the same is true of many of our nonmoral beliefs and habits of judgment. Our beliefs about science, history, and geography are deeply influenced by our upbringing, and our upbringing and socialization also influence many of our dispositions to form beliefs, including whether we form them critically, on the basis of evidence, and whether we reason more or less in accord with the principles of logic. That our beliefs about science, history, and geography were acquired through training and education within our particular cultural milieu does not imply that they are not instances of knowledge. Moreover, the fact that other cultures have held different views about science, history, or geography does not imply that our views simply reflect the attitudes of our culture and that there are no objective scientific, historical, or geographical truths. At least it seems that *were* this so, then there would not be a *special* problem with ethics. Objective ethical truths would then be no worse off than objective scientific or geographical truth.

Still, the ethical skeptic holds that there is a difference between disagreements in science, for example, and ethics. The ethical skeptic holds that disagreements in science seem resolvable in a way that disagreements in ethics do not. In science, for example, there are methods and standards of evidence that can be used to settle or, at least, significantly narrow the range of disagreement. In contrast, the skeptic argues, ethical disagreements do not seem capable of such resolution. In ethics, there are many methods and standards to which one might appeal to resolve ethical disagreements. One might appeal to a version of hedonistic utilitarianism or a Kantian principle of respect for persons, to name but two. Which ethical standard is correct seems difficult to resolve, especially if each party to the dispute finds his favored principle cohering with and supported by his own moral "intuitions". One's appeal to one's own intuitions to support one's general standards and principles seems simply to beg the question against those with different intuitions and different standards.

Yet here the ethical cognitivist might note that we are being asked to compare disagreements at different levels. Isn't it the case that those committed to the same principle might be able to resolve or at least significantly narrow the scope of their ethical disagreement? Ethical disagreements do seem resolvable, or at least more nearly so, given agreements on specific moral standards. That much seems right even if there remains significant disagreement over which standards are correct.

Now when we turn to the nonmoral sphere, we find that the methods and principles of science reflect one way of ascertaining nonmoral facts. But here too there are alternative methods and principles, including such things as astrology, crystal-ball gazing, and the appeal to sacred texts. Of course appeals to these other standards fail decisively according to the standards of science, but they might well meet their own standards and in this way be "self-supporting". Suppose the crystal-ball gazer finds that his crystal ball tells him that gazing is reliable, and that the sacred text proclaims its own inerrancy. In this way, disagreements between those committed to the standards of science and those committed to these other standards might be as irresolvable as disagreements between those committed to different moral standards such as the utilitarian and the Kantian. Why then should we think, the ethical cognitivist might ask, that the irresolvability of such disputes whether in the moral or the nonmoral sphere is crucial to the question of knowledge or indicative of a special problem for ethics? If the presence of irresolvable disputes in ethics implies that there is no ethical knowledge, wouldn't the presence of irresolvable disputes in the nonmoral sphere between the scientifically minded and the devotees of a sacred text imply that there is no scientific knowledge? It is not clear, of course, that this is the lesson to be drawn from the presence of irresolvable disputes.[3] Consider a dispute with someone who denies that a contradictory proposition is false. It might be that there is no way to resolve such a dispute, since any attempt to produce an argument will, if pushed far enough, presuppose the very point at issue. Some disputes over basic logical points might simply be incapable of resolution, at least without begging the question. But that hardly shows that there is no logical knowledge, or, if that were the moral drawn, then ethics would not face a special problem. Again, science yields knowledge only if sense perception, memory, inductive and abductive inference are reliable. But it is not clear that the reliability of these sources can be shown in any non-question begging way, and there seems to be no way to resolve a dispute with the philosophical skeptic who demands such non-question-begging support. If knowledge that p requires that one be in a position to give a non-question-begging argument that one's way of forming beliefs or that one's principles of belief formation are reliable, then it is not simply our ways of forming moral beliefs that would fail this requirement. But why accept this requirement at all?

Let us turn to a second important line of argument. It holds that we have no reason to believe in moral facts because such facts never play a role in explaining our moral beliefs or observations.[4] Here we take "observation" to mean any immediate judgment or belief that is not based on conscious reasoning. According to this argument, we have reasons or evidence to believe that there are facts of a certain kind only if facts of that kind play some part in a causal explanation (or the best causal explanation) of our beliefs or observations. This argument against moral facts presupposes what is sometimes called the "explanatory requirement". There are different ways of stating the requirement, but one may put it is as follows: p is a reason to believe q only if q (or something that entails q) is part of the best explanation for p. The explanatory requirement appears to be met in many cases involving perception, and perceptual reasons seem to satisfy the explanatory requirement. For example, the fact that Mary observes that there is a table before her is a reason for Mary to believe that there is a table before her, and it seems that the fact that there is a table before her explains or is part of what explains her having this particular observation. In contrast, it is argued that we can have no reason for believing that there are moral facts, because moral facts never appear to play any causal role in explaining our moral observations and beliefs. Suppose, for example, that Jane rounds the corner to see Albert set a cat afire, and she forms the belief that Albert's action is wrong. It is argued that Jane's belief that Albert's action is wrong is not reason for her to believe that there is an objective moral fact, since we can explain her having this belief in terms of her moral training, her psychological background, and her "background moral theory". In short, we can explain why she forms that belief without appealing to the existence of an objective moral fact. That she believes his act is wrong tells us something about her moral sensibility, but it is no reason to believe that there are objective moral facts.

There are at least two lines of response to this argument. The first holds that moral facts do enter into causal explanations.[5] For example, one might claim that part of the best explanation for the occurrence of a revolution is that the distribution of goods in that society was unjust. Similarly, one might hold that Hitler's crimes are explained by the fact that he was evil. Critics of this response might urge, for example, that it was not the fact of injustice that caused the revolution, but simply the psychological fact that large numbers of people believed that the society was unjust that caused the revolution. Similarly, one might argue that Hitler's actions could be explained by various psychological facts about him, say, his beliefs that Jews are evil or his belief in the importance of racial purity. Alternatively, one might hold that the cause of the revolution was not the moral fact of injustice but the fact that wealth was concentrated in the hands of a few. Here one might point to the underlying nonmoral facts of distribution, facts "in virtue of which" the society was unjust as explaining the revolution. Defenders of the causal role of moral facts might challenge whether the availability of these alternative explanations undermines the moral explanations or shows them to be completely irrelevant.

A second line of response is to reject the explanatory requirement itself. Consider our mathematical and modal knowledge. We know that $2 + 3 = 5$ and we know that this is necessarily so. Such mathematical and modal facts do not seem to be part of a causal explanation for why we believe such things. Or take the proposition that it is impossible for anything to be red and green all over at the same time. It is far from clear that this modal claim figures into any causal explanation of why we believe it. Now, one might object that we do have indirect observational evidence for mathematical propositions. In explaining the observations that support a physical theory, scientists often appeal to mathematical principles. Since mathematics often plays a role in scientific explanations, there is indirect observational evidence of mathematics. But while this is so, it ignores the fact that our mathematical principles are not merely well-confirmed empirical generalizations. Our mathematical beliefs have a level of certainty and warrant for us greater than what could be afforded by indirect observational evidence. Many of our mathematical and modal beliefs are far more certain than any of the explanatory laws of the natural sciences. Consequently, it seems that we have some reason or evidence for accepting such propositions independently of what we observe and independently of their playing a part in the best explanation of what we observe. Again, take any observation O, for which we might think the modal fact that $2 + 3$ is necessarily 5 is part of the best explanation. It seems we could explain O by appealing to the fact that $2 + 3 = 5$ or even that 2 and 3 is usually 5. Since we could explain any observation without appealing to the modal claim, and since the best explanation would seem to be one that did not invoke the stronger modal claim, we do not have even indirect observational evidence for the modal claim. Modal facts such as 2 and 3 is necessarily 5 never seem relevant to causal explanations of our observations. That one can explain one's observations without appealing to modal facts does not suggest that one ought to be a modal skeptic. But if this is so, why should the explanatory irrelevance of moral facts to our observations be a ground of moral skepticism?[6]

We might ask whether the explanatory requirement itself figures into any causal explanations of what we observe. By its own lights, we could have a reason for believing the causal requirement only if it plays a role in a causal explanation of what we observe. But it is not at all clear that it does. If the explanatory requirement plays no role in causal explanations of what we observe, then the explanatory requirement seems self-defeating, at least insofar as its irrelevance to causal explanations of what we observe implies, by its own lights, that we have no reason for believing it to be true. Of course, the psychological fact that one accepts the explanatory requirement might explain why one believes some things as reasons and not others. The same is true, though, about the psychological fact that one accepts some moral principle. Yet neither the explanatory requirement nor the moral principle would be part of the causal explanation for our making the observations we do. But not all explanations are causal explanations. We might see the explanatory requirement as a principle that explains why some things are not *reasons*. It might explain why some things should lack the *normative* status of being a reason for believing some proposition. But moral principles, too, could have explanatory power in that way. The principle of utility might explain why some acts are not *right*. Indeed, if we take the explanatory requirement as a normative principle that tells us what conditions must be met for something to be a reason for belief, then its role in explanations seems no different from normative ethical principles. So, either the explanatory requirement is self-defeating insofar as it suggests that we have no reason to believe it or it plays an explanatory role that is no different in kind from that which moral principles might also play.[7]

Finally, we must note that many philosophers have held analyses of moral language that imply that ethical skepticism is true. Noncognitivist analyses of moral language hold that morally evaluative sentences have no truth value, that strictly speaking they are neither true nor false. If moral sentences have no truth value, then strictly speaking they cannot be objects of knowledge. If one can be epistemically justified in believing that p only if p has a truth value, then no one can be epistemically justified in accepting a moral sentence. There are two main versions of noncognitivism in ethics, *emotivism* and *prescriptivism*. Emotivism holds, in its simplest form, that our moral utterances are mere expressions of our attitudes and thus are not true or false. Thus, when one says, "Murder is wrong," one means something like "Murder! Boo!." Similarly, when one says, "Gratitude is good," one means something like "Gratitude! Hurray!." Such emotional ejaculations express the speaker's attitude but lack truth value. Prescriptivism emphasizes the action-guiding role of moral language. According to prescriptivism, when one says, "Murder is wrong," one is attempting to guide people's conduct. Moral language, on this view, is best understood in terms of imperatives. Thus, when one says, "Murder is wrong," one means something like, "Do not murder!," and when one says, "Gratitude is good," one means something like, "Show gratitude!" Many sophisticated noncognitivist analyses of moral language were developed in the twentieth century by philosophers such as A. J. Ayer, C. L. Stevenson, and R. M. Hare. Noncognitivists need not deny, and many did not deny, that moral utterances can be reasonable or justified. Hare, for example, points out that the issuing of commands can be unreasonable. It can be unreasonable to issue conflicting commands such as "Shut the door!" and "Do not shut the door!" This sort of unreasonableness is not, however, epistemic. For the noncognitivists there is no need to answer the question, "How can one know what is right or wrong?" since, on their view, such knowledge is not possible.

In spite of the popularity of noncognitivist analyses, ethical cognitivism has remained stubbornly persistent. Let us take ethical cognitivism to be the view that some ethical propositions are true or false and that some people are epistemically justified in accepting them. There are a variety of considerations against noncognitivist analyses of our ordinary use of moral language. First, we commonly take ourselves to be *asserting* something when we make a moral judgment, and the form of our judgment is typically declarative or assertive in form. In making a moral judgment the ordinary user of moral language is not merely expressing his attitude the way one expresses disgust by uttering "Ugh!" or joy by exclaiming "Hurray!" Such attitudes might accompany most moral judgments, but the ordinary user of moral language takes himself to be describing or characterizing the object of his judgment. Second, we think that some forms of moral argument are deductively valid and others aren't. Consider, for example, the following argument: (i) if stealing is wrong, then it is wrong to encourage others to steal, (ii) stealing is wrong, (iii) therefore, it is wrong to encourage others to steal. This argument seems to be deductively valid. Ordinarily, we take a valid deductive argument to be one in which the premises logically imply the conclusion. But if noncognitivism is true, then the premises of this argument have no truth value, and, if so, it is hard to see in what way they could logically imply the conclusion. Third, moral sentences can meaningfully occur as the antecedent in conditional sentences, such as (i). But it is far from clear that mere prescriptions or imperatives or the expressions of attitudes can meaningfully take the place of such antecedents. What would it mean to say, "If don't steal, then . . .", or "If boo to stealing, then . . ."? Fourth, our ordinary moral beliefs seem to reflect a commitment to ethical cognitivism. We believe that in some cases a person ought to have known that what he did was wrong, that in some cases a person should have known better than to act as he did. Similarly, we sometimes excuse a person from moral blame when we believe that she lacked the capacity to know what is right or wrong. That we accept this excuse without excusing everyone reflects the ordinary assumption that people have the capacity to know right from wrong.

In considering the plausibility of noncognitivism in ethics, we may also consider its plausibility in epistemology. Many philosophers have suggested that epistemic concepts are *evaluative* concepts. They have suggested, for example, that when we take a belief to be an instance of knowledge or justified, we are making a positive evaluation of it. Similarly, when we hold that a belief is unjustified or unreasonable we are making a negative evaluation of it. If epistemic concepts are evaluative, and if we can know that we know or that we are epistemically justified in believing various things, then it follows that we do have some evaluative knowledge. Noncognitivist analyses of epistemic concepts such as "knowledge" and "epistemic justification" have not enjoyed the same popularity as noncognitivist analyses of moral terms. A noncognitivist analysis of epistemic terms would imply that sentences such as "He knows he has hands" and "She knows her name" are not true and the sentences, "He knows that the earth is flat" and "He knows that 2 = 3" are not false. Claims to knowledge based on the silliest superstitions would not be false and claims to justification based on the best possible evidence would not be true. To many philosophers such implications seem implausible. Furthermore, given that knowing that *p* requires that *p* is true, one could never know that one knows anything. A noncognitivist analysis of epistemic concepts would rule out epistemic knowledge. Finally, the implausibility of such claims is not limited to philosophers who think we do have epistemic knowledge, for many skeptical philosophers who deny that we do know that we know do not hold that such epistemic claims lack a truth value. Many skeptics believe that claims to knowledge have a truth value, and some skeptics believe knowledge claims are simply *false*. Many philosophers would find that epistemic and ethical terms are in the same boat and that epistemic noncognitivism is not very plausible. Why should we think, they might ask, that ethical noncognitivism is any more plausible? In spite of its implausibility in the epistemic sphere, perhaps some might think noncognitivism is the right stance to take concerning both epistemic and ethical concepts. If this is so, then it would be a mistake to think that there is a special problem faced by claims of ethical knowledge that is not also faced by claims of epistemic knowledge.

PARTICULARISM AND WIDE REFLECTIVE EQUILIBRIUM

Roderick Chisholm once suggested that epistemology is concerned with two main questions. These are (A) What do we know? What is the extent of our knowledge? And (B) How do we know? What are the criteria of knowledge? Chisholm was a *particularist*, who assumed that we can pick out particular instances of knowledge independently of knowing a criterion of knowledge and then use these particular instances to formulate and assess criteria of knowledge. In other words, he held that we can begin with an answer to (A) and then work out an answer to (B). Furthermore, as a "common sense" epistemologist Chisholm took for granted that he knew many things, for example, that there are other people, that they think and have bodies, that they were alive yesterday. Moreover, he took for granted that he and others *know* that they know such things. In this respect, he took for granted that we know some *epistemic* facts and that a satisfactory epistemic theory should be adequate to our knowing such facts.

When we turn to moral epistemology, how should we proceed? If we follow Chisholm's particularism, we might hold that we can pick out various instances of moral knowledge and epistemically justified moral belief. For example, I might hold that I know or am justified in believing that I ought not to rob the bank this afternoon, that it would be wrong for me to kill my secretary now, that I ought to make my house payment next month. I might also hold that many other people know similar things. Along with such homely common-sense bits of moral knowledge, one might hold that one knows or is justified in believing various general moral and evaluative claims, such as keeping promises is a *prima facie* duty, there is a *prima facie* duty not to lie, that a life filled with wisdom, pleasure, and moral virtue is intrinsically better than one filled with ignorance, pain, and wickedness. We might hold further that not only do we know such things, but that we know that we know them. We know that they are instances of moral knowledge. And we might go on to use such bits of moral knowledge in attempting to formulate and assess criteria or theories of moral knowledge.

The moral philosopher may do something similar. The primary concern of the moral philosopher is not to find epistemological theories or criteria about knowledge or justification. But at least one concern of the moral philosopher is to discover criteria of right action. Just as the epistemologist may ask what makes a belief justified or an instance of knowledge, the moral philosopher may ask what makes an action right or a thing intrinsically good. In attempting to answer such questions, he may take an approach similar to that which Chisholm takes in epistemology. He might assume that he can pick out instances of right or wrong action, or instances of what is intrinsically good, independently of knowing a general criterion of right action or what is intrinsically good and then use such information in attempting to formulate and assess criteria of right action or value. Though the primary concern of the moral philosopher is not to formulate epistemological criteria, epistemological issues lurk about. If asked *why* take those particular claims as data, he might hold that it is reasonable to do so since he knows them or is at least epistemically justified in accepting them. He might hold that it is their having some positive epistemic status that makes it reasonable to take them as data.

The Chisholmian approach to epistemology may be viewed as a particular application of a methodological approach common in both epistemology and ethics, namely, the *method of wide reflective equilibrium*.[8] In the method of wide reflective equilibrium one begins with one's (i) particular considered judgments, (ii) beliefs about general principles, and (iii) general background theories. One then seeks to achieve a coherent balance or "equilibrium" between these various elements. In some cases, this might require abandoning or revising some of one's particular judgments in favor of, say, a general principle that seems on reflection more reasonable. In other cases, one might give up or revise the general principle in favor of the particular judgment. The epistemologist might begin with particular judgments about what he takes himself to know or to be justified in believing. He might begin, for example, with particular epistemic judgments such as, "I know I have hands" and, "Almost everyone, including myself, knows his own name." Along with such particular epistemic judgments he might begin with his belief in some general principles such as, "If a belief is formed on the basis of memory, then that belief is epistemically justified." Similarly, the moral philosopher might take as data particular moral judgments such as, "It would be wrong for me to kill my secretary now" or, "I ought to give more to charity." He may also take as data various general moral principles such as, "If an act is the breaking of a promise, then that act is *prima facie* wrong." Through the process of seeking overall coherence, the epistemologist or the moral philosopher seeks to improve his epistemic and moral beliefs, both particular and general, and to discover what makes acts right or beliefs justified.

We might contrast the method of wide reflective equilibrium with the *method of narrow reflective equilibrium.* In the latter we seek coherence only within a certain specific domain. For example, one might seek coherence merely between one's particular moral judgments and one's general moral principles, ignoring the relevance of considerations outside the domain of the moral. But in wide reflective equilibrium one does not restrict oneself to beliefs within a given domain. One seeks a harmony between one's particular judgments and general principles and whatever other considerations might strike one as relevant. Thus, in wide reflective equilibrium nothing that might seem relevant is excluded. So conceptions of the person and the functioning of social institutions as well as principles of economic theory might be brought to bear on questions about particular moral judgments and general principles. What favors the method of wide reflective equilibrium is that nothing that seems relevant is excluded.

As we have seen, Chisholm suggests that we can pick out instances of knowledge and justified belief and use such knowledge as data in formulating and assessing epistemic theories. If we follow this particularist approach in moral epistemology we will hold that we can pick out instances of moral knowledge and justified moral belief and use such instances in developing criteria or theories in moral epistemology. Similarly, the moral philosopher might assume that he can pick out instances of right action or the good and use these instances in formulating criteria of rightness and goodness.

A particularist approach assumes that we can identify instances of knowledge and right action independently of knowing a general criterion. Some critics find this view unsatisfactory. They hold that one cannot pick out particular instances of knowledge or justified belief unless one has a criterion of knowledge or justification. Similarly, one cannot pick out particular instances of right action unless one has a criterion of right action. One line of support for this view is thought to rest upon the *supervenient* character of evaluative concepts and properties. Consider, for example, the following passage by William Alston:

> In taking a belief to be justified, we are evaluating it in a certain way. And, like any evaluative property, epistemic justification is an evaluative property, the application of which is based on more fundamental properties. . . . Hence, in order for me to be justified in believing that S's belief that p is justified, I must be justified in certain other beliefs, viz., that S's belief that p possesses a certain property, Q, and that Q renders its possessor justified. (Another way of formulating this last belief is: a belief that there is a valid epistemic principle to the effect that any belief that has Q is justified.)[9]

Many philosophers hold that evaluative properties *supervene* or depend on nonevaluative properties. On this view, a thing has an evaluative property "in virtue of" its having various nonevaluative properties. Thus, if a strawberry is good, then it is good in virtue of its being sweet, juicy, worm-free, etc. As Alston suggests, this thesis of supervenience is thought to hold of all evaluative properties, including moral, aesthetic, and epistemic. Closely related to the thesis of supervenience is the view that two things cannot differ in their evaluative properties without differing in their underlying nonevaluative properties. So, if one strawberry is good and another isn't, then they must differ in their nonevaluative properties. The thesis that evaluative properties supervene on nonevaluative properties is quite plausible. But Alston suggests that justified belief that a particular thing has an evaluative property epistemically requires justified belief in a general principle that tells us on what the evaluative property supervenes. More broadly, knowledge of particular moral or epistemic facts would depend on knowledge of general moral or epistemic principles of supervenience. Granted knowledge of the general principle along with knowledge of the thing's nonevaluative properties one would be in a strong position to know that it has the evaluative property. But making justified belief in such general principles of supervenience a requirement for particular evaluative beliefs would seem to imply that very few people, if any, have any justified particular evaluative judgments. This is so simply because it seems very few people have the requisite justified beliefs in the general principles. So we might ask whether justified belief in such general principles is really necessary.

I think the answer is "no." First, we should not confuse claims about *exemplification* with claims about *application*. In assuming that evaluative properties are supervenient we assume that they are exemplified in virtue of the exemplification of nonevaluative properties. But this is different from Alston's claim that the application or attribution of an evaluative property is based on the underlying properties on which the evaluative property supervenes. That things exemplify evaluative properties in virtue of their nonevaluative properties does *not* imply that attribution or knowledge of evaluative properties must be based on attribution or knowledge of those underlying properties. Thus, the claim that knowledge of a criterion must be epistemically prior to knowledge of particular instances does not follow from the supervenient character of evaluative properties. Second, it seems plausible that there are justified attributions of other supervenient properties that do not depend on justifiedly believing in a criterion of supervenience. Many philosophers hold, for example, that mental properties supervene on physical properties such as states of the brain. But does our knowledge of our own mental properties or those of others depend on knowledge of what the mental supervenes upon? Surely not.

The requirement that one know general principles of supervenience in order to know particular evaluative facts does not follow from the supervenient nature of the evaluative. It also seems incompatible with our having knowledge of other sorts of supervenient properties, such as mental properties. Finally, it imposes too high a standard for knowledge of supervenient properties, including evaluative and moral properties. There are alternative conceptions of justification that do not impose such a requirement. Such a requirement is not imposed by coherentist or foundationalist, including reliabilist foundationalist, theories of justification and knowledge. So let us turn to consider how these views bear on the issue of justified moral belief and moral knowledge.

FOUNDATIONALISM AND COHERENTISM

Foundationalist theories of justification and knowledge hold that knowledge and justification exhibit a two-tier structure. Some instances of knowledge and justification are noninferential or foundational, while others are inferential and nonfoundational in that their positive epistemic status depends on or derives from foundational knowledge or justification. Items in the foundation are often said to be "basic" or "immediate" knowledge or basically or immediately justified. A basic or "foundational" belief is one that has some level of epistemic justification that does not derive from nor depend positively on one's other beliefs. It has some level of justification that is independent of the justification, if any, that it might derive from its logical relations to, or its cohering with, one's beliefs. There are many different forms of foundationalism. *Radical* foundationalism holds that foundational knowledge or justification must enjoy some very high and privileged epistemic status such as being certain, indubitable, infallible, or indefeasible. Radical foundationalism also holds that nonfoundational beliefs must bear some entailment relation to items in the foundation. *Modest* foundationalism does not make either of these claims. It does not insist that foundational knowledge or justification must be certain, indubitable, etc., and it does not insist that nonfoundational knowledge or justification must be entailed by items in the foundation. In other words, the positive epistemic status enjoyed by nonfoundational beliefs need not be transmitted by entailment relations to the foundation. Contemporary foundationalists tend to favor some form of modest foundationalism. Among foundationalists there are a variety of views about the source or ground of basic or immediate knowledge or justification. Among the main candidates are the following (i) self-justification, (ii) justification by nondoxastic or nonpropositional experiences, and (iii) justification by issuing from a reliable faculty, process, or "epistemic virtue".

Modest foundationalists typically hold that foundational justification is defeasible, that it can be defeated, undercut, or overridden in some cases by additional evidence or justified beliefs. So, for example, your belief that there is a red object before you can lose its justification if you acquire additional evidence that there is a red light shining on that object. What one is foundationally justified in believing can change over time as one acquires additional evidence. It is important to note, however, that foundational justification does *not* positively depend, that is, is not based on, grounds for denying that there are defeaters. Foundational justification does not depend on or require justified belief that there are no defeaters. We should say rather that foundational justification negatively depends on the absence of defeaters and on one's *not* having justified belief that there are defeaters. Critics of foundationalism sometimes overlook this important distinction.

There are a wide variety of possibilities open to moral epistemologists who favor some form of foundationalism. Some foundationalist moral epistemologists hold that some moral and evaluative propositions are instances of basic or foundational knowledge or justification. Historically prominent candidates include *prima facie* moral principles and propositions about what has intrinsic value. For example, W. D. Ross held that we had basic moral knowledge of some *prima facie* moral principles:

> That an act *qua* fulfilling a promise, or *qua* effecting a just distribution of good
> ... is *prima facie* right, is self-evident; not in the sense that it is evident from
> the beginning of our lives, or as soon as we attend to the proposition for the
> first time, but in the sense that when we have reached sufficient mental maturity and have given sufficient attention to the proposition it is evident without
> any need of proof, or of evidence beyond itself. It is evident just as a mathematical axiom, or the validity of a form of inference, is evident. ... In our confidence that these propositions are true there is involved the same confidence

in our reason that is involved in our confidence in mathematics. . . . In both cases we are dealing with propositions that cannot be proved, but just as certainly need no proof.[10]

In holding that such *prima facie* principles are self-evident and not dependent for their justification on proof, Ross holds that they are instances of foundational moral knowledge. He compares such principles to axioms of mathematics and basic principles of logic and suggests that our confidence that these principles are true involves "the same confidence in reason that is involved in our confidence in mathematics." For Ross, the apprehension of these moral principles is based on reason, and so it may be taken as a form of basic or foundational a priori knowledge or justification. A similar view was once expressed by Bertrand Russell concerning our knowledge of what is intrinsically good:

> *A priori* knowledge is not all of the same logical kind we have been hitherto considering. Perhaps the most important example of non-logical *a priori* knowledge is knowledge as to ethical value. I am not speaking of judgments as to what is useful or as to what is virtuous, for such judgments do require empirical premises; I am speaking of judgments as to the intrinsic desirability of things. . . . We judge, for example, that happiness is more desirable than misery, knowledge than ignorance, goodwill than hatred, and so on. Such judgments must, in part at least, be immediate and *a priori*. . . . In the present connexion, it is only important to realize that knowledge as to what is intrinsically of value is *a priori* in the same sense in which logic is *a priori*, namely in the sense that the truth of such knowledge can be neither proved nor disproved by experience.[11]

In this passage, Russell, like Ross, holds that we have basic or immediate ethical knowledge. Like Ross, Russell suggests that this ethical knowledge is basic a priori knowledge. Their views are a form of rationalistic foundationalism.

One unfortunate consequence of Ross's comparing *prima facie* moral principles to the axioms of mathematics and logical principles is that it suggests that the former must have the same level of high epistemic privilege such as certainty and indefeasibility that the latter have been taken to enjoy. To many, such a suggestion seems implausible. For however reasonable Ross's principles or various propositions about the intrinsically good might be, very few, if any, seem to enjoy the certainty or indefeasibility of simple mathematical or logical axioms such as $2 + 3 = 5$, or if p, then p. Yet we need not take Ross's comparison to suggest that the *prima facie* principles are certain or indefeasible. We might simply take him to be claiming that our knowledge of such principles is like them insofar as they are both basic and a priori. Of course, according to some accounts of a priori knowledge and justification, basic a priori knowledge and justification must be certain and indefeasible. But again, if this is so, then very few *prima facie* principles or substantive claims about what is intrinsically good would be basic a priori knowledge. It is open to Ross, however, to reject such accounts of a priori knowledge and justification. He might adopt modest foundationalism concerning a priori knowledge and deny that basic a priori knowledge must be certain and indefeasible. Several recent writers have urged such a view.[12] This view also has distinguished historical precedents. Russell suggested that intuitive justification comes in degrees,[13] and A. C. Ewing held that basic a priori justification need be neither certain nor indefeasible.[14] But among the clearest opponents of the view that basic a priori beliefs must be certain and indefeasible is Thomas Reid. Reid asks us to consider the case of a mathematician who, having completed a demonstration, submits it to the examination of a fellow mathematician he takes to be a competent judge. Reid writes, "Here I would ask again, Whether the verdict of his friend, according as it is favorable or unfavorable, will not greatly increase or diminish confidence in his own judgment? Most certainly it will and it ought."[15] According to Reid, the level of justification the mathematician's belief enjoys can be affected by the testimony of his friend. Even though he might have a priori grounds for accepting the conclusion, the justification these grounds confer can be diminished or defeated by the testimony of others. In the preceding example, Reid deals with the nonbasic a priori justification one has for accepting the conclusion of an argument. However, similar conclusions apply to the level of justification for noninferential a priori beliefs. Reid concedes that honest disagreement about "first principles" is possible. "A man of candour and humility will, in such a case, very naturally suspect his own judgment, so far as to be desirous to enter into a serious examination, even of what he has long held as a first principle."[16] I take Reid to hold that knowledge of such disagreements can lower the credence we ought to place in that judgment. For Reid, then, empirical or non–a priori considerations can lower or defeat the justification of some things which enjoy basic a priori justification. Of course, it isn't only empirical considerations that can lower or defeat a priori justification. Alvin Plantinga calls our attention to the various assumptions that lead to Russell's paradoxes, such as that every property has a complement, that there is a property of self-exemplification, and so on.[17] Each of these propositions has a certain degree of plausibility for us. Indeed, it is precisely because the initial assumptions seem so plausible, that each has "a ring of truth" to it, that their paradoxical implications seem so startling. Yet once we see what they imply, it is reasonable for us to reject one or more of these assumptions. Our justification for believing them is undercut or defeated by seeing what they imply.

A modest foundationalism with respect to the a priori allows us to respond to a certain sort of criticism of the view that some ethical and evaluative principles can be known a priori. One might object that such principles cannot be known a priori because many philosophers have understood them without seeing that they are true. But if we accept a modest foundationalism such criticism is not decisive. It is perfectly possible for someone to have basic a priori justification for believing p, and for others who consider p not to be justified in believing it. This is so simply because those who reject *p* might have (or merely think they have) defeating evidence not shared by those who accept *p*. We need not assume that disagreement implies that either party is not justified in her attitude toward *p* or that *p* cannot be an item of basic a priori justification for either party. Moreover, if we accept a modest foundationalism concerning the a priori, we need not hold that when two people have conflicting basically justified beliefs there is simply nothing more to say or that rational discussion must come to an end. By coming to see the implications of his views, one party might find it on balance more reasonable to give up his initial belief. Presumably, that would be so for the mathematician who sees that intuitively plausible propositions lead to Russell's paradox.

Modest foundationalism also allows us to acknowledge the importance of certain kinds of "coherence" in the justification of moral beliefs. First, if one's belief that *p* is *not* defeated by one's other evidence, then we may say that one's belief enjoys a form of coherence with one's other beliefs. This sort of coherence is a form of negative dependence consisting in the absence of defeaters and is compatible with modest foundationalism. A second, perhaps more interesting, role for coherence would be the enhancing of one's justification. If one has an a priori justification for believing *p*, the level of one's justification for believing *p* need not be very high. But the fact that one's belief that *p* coheres with other things one believes insofar as it bears certain explanatory and supporting relations to them might raise the level of justification that one's belief enjoys. Nothing in the notion of modest a priori justification or modest foundationalism in general rules out this important role for coherence.

So far we have considered forms of rationalistic foundationalism that hold that some moral principles and claims about intrinsic value enjoy basic a priori justification and that our justification for such things is rooted in reason. But we should note that there are other possibilities. One might hold that there is a moral faculty distinct from reason that yields basic knowledge and justification for these beliefs. Such a view might hold that what justifies these beliefs is not their origin in the epistemic virtue of reason, but in some other sort of reliable faculty or epistemic virtue, perhaps "conscience" or "the moral faculty." Another possibility is that some ethical or value beliefs are foundationally justified in virtue of some nondoxastic experience that accompanies one's comprehending consideration of certain states of affairs. Some philosophers have suggested that emotional experiences can play this sort of justificatory role.[18] Franz Brentano, for example, suggests that our knowledge of intrinsic value has its source in the experience of "correct" emotions of love, hate, and preference. Brentano writes, "Our knowledge of what is truly and indubitably good arises from the type of experience we have been discussing, where a love is experienced as being correct."[19] Alexius Meinong took a similar stance. He writes, "When I say, 'The sky is blue,' and then say, 'The sky is beautiful' a property is being attributed to the sky in either case. In the second case a feeling participates in the apprehension of the property, as, in the first case, an idea does."[20] Max Scheler writes, "The actual seat of the entire value-a priori (including the moral a priori) is the *value cognition* or *value-intuition* that comes to the fore in feeling, basically in love and hate.... A spirit limited to perception and thinking would be absolutely *blind* to values."[21] We might take such views to hold, roughly, that if one contemplates a certain state of affairs, *p*, and has a certain sort of positive emotional experience toward *p*, and one has no defeaters for the proposition that *p* is intrinsically good, then one is justified in believing that *p* is intrinsically good. Similarly, certain negative or "anti" emotions might be a source of justification for believing that some states of affairs are intrinsically bad. Such a broadly empirical view would locate the source of our basic knowledge of value not in reason but in our emotions. Indeed, it might be possible to combine some form of reliabilism or epistemic virtue account with such emotional experience approaches and hold that it is not just any emotion that plays this justificatory role, but rather emotions that are the products of or flow from a virtuous or properly functioning character.

The traditional candidates for basic ethical beliefs include some beliefs about what is intrinsically good and some general moral principles, including, but not limited to, principles of *prima facie* rightness and wrongness. But what about particular moral judgments, such as when I see some teenage thugs torturing a cat and judge that their actions are wrong, or my judgments that I ought to repay Smith the $5 that I owe him, or that it would be wrong for me to kill my secretary now. Can such particular judgments be epistemically basic? Here it seems that foundationalists might give different answers. We may distinguish three possibilities: (1) all particular moral beliefs depend for their justification upon justified belief in some general moral principle, (2) all particular moral beliefs depend for their justification upon justified nonmoral belief, and (3) some particular moral beliefs do not depend for their justification upon either justified belief in general moral principles or justified nonmoral beliefs. Some foundationalists will accept (1). Even if they reject Alston's view that one must be justified in believing some general principle of supervenience, they might still hold that particular moral judgments must be justified in virtue of believing some general moral principle even if this is only some *prima facie* principle. Thus, for example, in order to be justified in believing that some particular act, A, is wrong, one must be justified in believing that (i) A has F (where F is some nonmoral feature) and (ii) acts that have F are *prima facie* wrong. The belief that A is wrong need not be inferred from these other beliefs, but they constitute the subject's evidence for his moral judgment and it derives its justification from them. If this is so, then particular moral judgments are not epistemically basic. Other foundationalists might reject (1) and accept (2). They might hold, for example, that in some cases the particular moral judgment is justified in virtue of being the product of a reliable cognitive process, faculty, or epistemic virtue. They might hold that the nonmoral belief that A has F is an "input" and that the belief that A is wrong is an "output" and that the belief that A is wrong is justified in virtue of being the output of a reliable cognitive process or epistemic virtue where the subject has no defeating evidence. Here the justification of the moral belief does not depend on justified belief in a general moral principle. According to this view, belief in general moral principles is not essential for justified particular moral judgments. Still, one who takes this approach might yet hold that justified particular moral judgments depend for their justification on other beliefs, such as the nonmoral belief that A has F. So, for example, my judgment that the act of torturing the cat is wrong depends for its justification on my justified belief that the act is causing the cat pain. In this case, my belief that torturing the cat is wrong would still not be epistemically basic.

Yet, some foundationalists might go even further and accept (3), holding that some particular moral judgments do not derive their positive epistemic status from other beliefs. Such a position would treat some particular moral judgments as being analogous, for example, to various justified aesthetic judgments. Consider, for example, someone driving in the mountains who comes suddenly upon a spectacular vista and forms the belief, "That's beautiful." Here the justification of the aesthetically evaluative judgment would seem to depend upon his nondoxastic perceptual states, and not upon the subject's beliefs and even less upon his belief in some general aesthetic principle. In this sort of case, which seems fairly common among aesthetic judgments, the subject does not even form nonevaluative beliefs on which the aesthetic judgment would be based. He simply makes the aesthetically evaluative judgment on the basis of his experience. Some foundationalists would allow that something similar can occur in the moral sphere. Consider cases in which one sees the thuggish boys torturing a cat, or one sees an old woman fall on an icy sidewalk. One might hold that the judgments, "That's wrong" and "I ought to help her" are justified by being the product of a reliable cognitive faculty or epistemic virtue. In such cases, the "inputs" are not beliefs, but rather one's nondoxastic perceptual states to the effect that the cat is in pain and that the woman has fallen. In this sort of situation, the foundationalist need not deny that one might also be justified in believing that the cat is in pain or the old woman has fallen. Indeed, he might hold that the nondoxastic perceptual states that are evidence for the wrongness of the act are also evidence for the cat's being in pain or for the old woman's having fallen. Still, he would simply hold that one's justification for the moral belief does not depend for its justification on these beliefs. Foundationalists of this sort would hold that such particular moral judgments are epistemically basic.

One line of criticism directed at all these forms of foundationalism takes as a general principle that one is *not* justified in any belief that p unless one is justified in believing that the process that led to that belief is reliable or at least reliable in the circumstances that led to that belief. Thus, according to this objection, whether one's belief is rooted in reason, some distinct moral faculty, or emotional experience, one is justified in accepting beliefs on that basis only if one is justified in believing that that way of forming beliefs in those circumstances is reliable. Furthermore, the objection goes, suppose the subject does believe (i) that his way of forming moral beliefs under conditions C is reliable (very likely to produce true beliefs), and (ii) that his belief that p was formed in that way under those conditions. He will then be in a position to infer that (iii) his belief that p is very likely to be true. This objection holds, first, that if one's justification for believing that p epistemically depends on one's having these other sorts of beliefs, (i) and (ii), then one's justification for believing that p is *not* basic after all. Second, the critic might hold, if the subject is *able* in this way to infer that p is likely to be true from these others beliefs, then one's justification for believing that p is again not basic.[22]

Foundationalists make a variety of responses to this line of objection. First, many foundationalists will deny the general principle upon which the objection rests. They will deny that one is justified in believing that p only if one is justified in believing that the process that led to that belief is reliable. They will note that small children and the epistemically unsophisticated might have many justified beliefs, such as mnemonic and perceptual beliefs, without having any belief about the reliability of their faculties or their belief producing processes. Indeed, they might not even have the concepts of "reliability," "faculty," or "belief forming process." Many foundationalists will hold that the principle in question is simply too strong insofar as it would deny justified belief and knowledge to small children and the epistemically unsophisticated. Though they may hold that knowledge or justification requires that one's belief originate in a reliable faculty or process, they would not require, in addition, that one be justified in believing that one's belief have such an origin. Moreover, they might point out that some versions of the coherence theory take a similar stance. For the coherentist, roughly, one's belief that p is justified in virtue of belonging to a coherent body of beliefs, and a coherent body of beliefs need not include the belief that one's belief that p has its origin in a reliable process. Second, suppose one is epistemically sophisticated and does believe that (i) his way of forming moral beliefs under conditions C is reliable, and (ii) his moral belief that p was formed under conditions C. Would this imply that his belief that p is not basic? Many foundationalists would say no. In order for a belief to be basic it is sufficient that it have some noninferential source of justification. The mere fact that an additional supporting inference is available to the subject does not imply that his belief that p epistemically depends on such an inference, and it does not imply that there is no noninferential source. The availability of such an inference is thus compatible with one's belief that p being basic.

Foundationalist and related reliabilist theories of justification and knowledge are not the only options open to the moral cognitivist. Among moral philosophers, coherence theories have enjoyed considerable support.[23] A coherence theory of justification holds, roughly, that the only thing that confers justification on S's believing that p is the fact that S's belief that p coheres with the rest of S's beliefs. Coherence theories, so construed, hold that a belief is justified because and only because it coheres with a subject's other beliefs. There are two fundamentally important features of coherence theories. First, coherence theories deny that there are any basic or foundational beliefs. Second, coherence theories are doxastic theories of justification insofar as they maintain that one's justification is a function of one's beliefs or doxastic states. Though some foundationalists hold that basic beliefs are justified, at least in part, by being the product of a reliable belief forming process, and others hold that some basic beliefs are justified in virtue of sensory and perceptual states, coherentists deny that such things are sources of justification. Of course, this does not prevent the coherentist from holding that beliefs about one's sensations or beliefs about the reliability of one's faculties can be relevant to one's justification.

Coherentists in moral theory hold that one is justified in believing any moral proposition just in case it coheres with one's other beliefs. These other beliefs might include moral beliefs about particular cases and general moral principles, as well as nonmoral beliefs about human nature, social institutions and practices, economic principles, the consequences of actions and policies, etc. Coherence theories of justified moral belief do not require that one know or even believe general criteria of supervenience. Moreover, they do not require that one know or believe that one's belief that p is part of a coherent body of belief, and they do not require that one deduce or show how p follows from other things one believes. For the coherentist, it is sufficient for justification that one's belief that p belong to a coherent body of beliefs.

It is important to distinguish a coherence theory of justification from the method of wide reflective equilibrium. The latter, as noted above, seeks coherence between particular judgments, general principles, and various background beliefs and theories. Still, acceptance of the method of wide reflective equilibrium does not commit one to accepting a coherence theory of justification. One might value the seeking of coherence without holding that coherence is the only source of justification. So, for example, one might hold that it is reasonable for the scientist to seek explanations that cohere with his perceptual observations and still hold that his perceptual observations have some source of justification other than mere coherence, such as their being grounded in his nondoxastic perceptual experience, or their issuing from a reliable faculty of perception.

Neither a foundationalist nor a coherentist approach to justification commits one to the sort of view Alston suggests. The foundationalist may hold that some moral or evaluative beliefs are basic and do not depend on justified belief in general principles of supervenience. Similarly, the coherentist may hold that some moral beliefs are justified in virtue of their coherence with one's other beliefs, which need not include belief in general principles of supervenience. Neither view rules out the particularist approach that Chisholm and others have adopted, and neither seems incompatible with the method of wide reflective equilibrium.

Coherence theories, like foundationalist theories, face a variety of objections. Consider the following common type of objection. Consider two men, A and B, who, let us suppose, have the same beliefs. Suppose that A believes he has a headache, and let this belief cohere with the rest of his beliefs. Suppose that A believes that he is in pain, that he has recently desired aspirin, and so forth. Imagine that our other man, B, has the same body of beliefs as A so that B believes he has a headache, that he is in pain, that he has recently desired aspirin, and so on. But now let us suppose that A really does have a headache and B does not. While each man's belief that he has a headache coheres equally well with the rest of his beliefs, to many philosophers it does not seem that each man is equally justified with respect to his belief that he has a headache. They would hold that B, unlike A, is simply not justified in believing that he has a headache or, perhaps more cautiously, that A is simply more justified in his belief that he has a headache than B is. But if either of these claims is true, then A is justified in virtue of something other than the mere coherence of his beliefs, since the beliefs of A and B are *ex hypothesi* equally coherent. If A's belief is more justified, then something other than mere coherence is relevant to the justification of belief. It is often charged that coherence theories "cut justification off from the world," that they "do not allow justification to be tied down to the world." This sort of example is taken to illustrate one sense in which this is so. Coherence theories do not allow anything outside the circle of one's beliefs to count as a reason or source of justification. They treat nondoxastic states, such as sensory states and perceptual experiences and the reliability of processes such as introspection and memory as irrelevant to the justification of a subject's beliefs.

In moral philosophy similar objections have been raised against coherence theories of justification. Consider, for example, the following passage by Hare:

> The appeal to moral intuitions will never do as a basis for a moral system. It is certainly possible, as some thinkers of our own time have done, to collect the moral opinions of which they and their contemporaries feel most sure, find some relatively simple method or apparatus which can be represented, with a bit of give and take, and making plausible assumptions about the circumstances of life, as generating these opinions; and then pronounce that this is the moral system which having reflected, we must acknowledge to be the correct one. But they have absolutely no authority for this claim beyond the original convictions, for which no ground or argument was given. The 'equilibirum' that was reached is one between forces which might have been generated by prejudice, and no amount of reflection can make that a solid basis for morality. It would be possible for two mutually inconsistent systems to be defended in this way: all that this would show is that their advocates had grown up in different moral environments.[24]

In this objection, Hare seems to hold that mere coherence is not sufficient to guarantee justified or reasonable moral beliefs, for those beliefs and the resulting equilibrium might be rooted in mere prejudice. Hare's point is that someone deeply prejudiced, excessively self-interested, or badly brought up might be able to hold coherent moral views, and yet those moral beliefs might be unjustified or unreasonable. As in the previous "headache" objection, the point is that mere coherence is either not sufficient to make moral beliefs reasonable or justified or, at least, that it is not the only thing relevant to the reasonableness or justification of belief.

Of course, in the passage quoted above Hare is not merely attacking coherence theories of justification. He is also attacking coherence methods in moral philosophy, such as the method of wide reflective equilibrium. However, it seems that one might agree with Hare's criticism of coherence theories of justification without endorsing his criticism of coherence methods, such as the method of wide reflective equilibrium. This is because one might think, as noted above, that coherence methods are not committed to holding that coherence is sufficient for the justification or reasonableness of moral belief. One might hold that two sets of beliefs, both of which are in "equilibrium", might differ in their justification or reasonableness because of factors other than the mere coherence of those beliefs, for example the nondoxastic states of believers or the reliability of their belief producing processes or their epistemic virtues. Foundationalist theories would not be committed to the view that a moral view formed on the basis of prejudice or excessive self-interest has the same positive epistemic status as an equally coherent moral view that was not so formed.

FURTHER OBJECTIONS TO PARTICULARISM AND WIDE REFLECTIVE EQUILIBRIUM

Many philosophers find the method of wide reflective equilibrium and the particularist approach favored by Chisholm unsatisfactory. Quite apart from the sort of objection raised in the second section, they think that taking our ordinary moral beliefs or "intuitions" as data for discovering and assessing moral criteria to be unacceptable. Consider the following passages by Richard Brandt:

> Various facts about the genesis of our moral beliefs militate against the mere appeal to intuitions in ethics. Our normative beliefs are strongly affected by the particular cultural tradition which nurtured us, and would be different if we had been in a learning situation with different parents, teachers, or peers.

Moreover, the moral convictions of some people derive, to use the words of Peter Singer, "from discarded religious systems, from warped views of sex and bodily functions, or from customs necessary for the survival of the group in social and economic circumstances that now lie in the distant past." What we should aim to do is step outside our own tradition somehow, see it from the outside, and evaluate it separating what is only a vestige of a possibly once useful moral tradition, from what is justifiable at present. The method of intuitions in principle prohibits our doing this. It is only an internal test of coherence, what may be no more than a reshuffling of moral prejudices.[25]

Brandt's criticism is similar to that raised above by Hare. Again, Hare writes:

The intuitions that give rise to the conflict are the product of our upbringings and past experiences of decision-making. They are not self-justifying: we can always ask whether the upbringing was the best we could have, or whether the past decisions were the right ones, or even if so, whether the principles then formed should be applied to a new situation, or, if they cannot all be applied, which should be applied. To use intuition itself to answer such questions is a viciously circular procedure; if the dispositions formed by our upbringing are called into question, we cannot appeal to them to settle the question.[26]

Both Brandt and Hare object to the method of wide reflective equilibrium and the appeal to our ordinary moral beliefs or "intuitions." Brandt rejects such a method since it "may be no more than a reshuffling of prejudices," and Hare complains that the equilibrium reached "is one between forces which might have been generated by prejudice." Moreover, as we have seen, Hare objects to the appeal to our original convictions "for which no ground or argument was given." For Brandt and Hare, the remedy or alternative is to "get outside" our own moral beliefs by appealing to nonmoral beliefs to defend a moral criterion. In their view, we must seek an independent argument for a moral criterion, independent in the sense that it does not presuppose the truth of any of our moral beliefs. Thus, we find Brandt appeals to beliefs about "rational" action and desire and Hare to beliefs about various logical principles, including principles about the logic of moral terms and various empirical, nonmoral premises. Let us consider these objections more closely.

Why should we think it important that we set aside all our moral beliefs in trying to support and assess a moral criterion? One rationale for excluding them might be that moral beliefs and intuitions are epistemically a pretty sorry lot and so it would be better to appeal to epistemically superior nonmoral beliefs, such as beliefs about the rationality of actions and desires and the logic of moral terms. But as a rationale for excluding *all* moral beliefs from the assessment of moral criteria this seems rather poor. No doubt some moral beliefs are epistemically inferior to the nonmoral beliefs on which one might base a moral criterion. But some are not. Consider such moral beliefs as I ought not to be tortured to death now and it would be wrong for me now to torture my parents. Such beliefs are at least as epistemically justified as the nonmoral beliefs to which Brandt and Hare would appeal. For example, in arguing for a utilitarian criterion, Hare asks us to consider the following two propositions: (i) I now prefer with strength S that if I were in that situation x should happen rather than not, and (ii) If I were in that situation, I would prefer with strength S that x should happen rather than not. Hare claims that it is a conceptual truth that to know (ii), (i) must be true.[27] But is this conceptual truth really more evident than the proposition that it would be wrong to torture my parents now? Is that moral proposition really less evident than propositions about what it would be rational for me to do? Since such moral beliefs are not epistemically inferior, this rationale would seem to be a poor one to support their exclusion by Brandt and Hare.

Of course, Hare complains about the appeal to our original convictions, our ordinary moral beliefs, "for which no ground or argument was given." Perhaps the point of this objection is that in the absence of argument or the giving of grounds such ordinary moral beliefs are not epistemically justified. If our ordinary moral beliefs are not justified, then in Hare's view we build our moral theory on sand. However, we should distinguish between the activity of justifying a belief and a belief's being justified. The former is an activity that one engages in, typically, though not always, when one's belief has been challenged; the latter, however, is a state. Justifying a belief usually involves giving an argument for it or producing a ground. But that is not necessary in order for a belief to be justified. We have many justified beliefs for which we have never argued or offered any grounds. Neither foundationalist nor coherentist views require that one give an argument or ground in order for a belief to be justified. As we have seen, the foundationalist may hold that some moral beliefs are basically or immediately justified, either by being self-justified, or through experience, or through being the product of a reliable cognitive process or intellectual virtue. Similarly, the coherentist may hold that belonging to a coherent body of belief is sufficient for justification, and that one need not, in addition, give an argument or produce a ground for that belief.

Still, let us grant that Brandt and Hare are right that even the most prejudiced and vicious moral beliefs can be spun into a coherent web. Of course, that is not a unique feature of our moral beliefs. Wildly defective perceptual beliefs and fanatical epistemic beliefs can with enough ingenuity or stubbornness be spun into a coherent fabric. Let us grant that mere coherence alone does not distinguish reasonable or justified moral belief from mere vicious prejudice. But that much can also be claimed, as noted above, by the foundationalist, since he does not see coherence as sufficient for justification and need not hold that all coherent bodies of belief are epistemically on a par.

Suppose we grant that mere coherence alone does not separate reasonable or justified moral belief from mere prejudice. Why would such a concession imply that we must "get outside" our moral beliefs and should not use them as data to reach knowledge or justified belief about moral criteria? Perhaps the answer may be put in terms of the following argument:

Argument A

1. In order to distinguish moral beliefs that are true from those that are false, we must distinguish between those moral beliefs that are reliably formed from those that aren't.
2. In order to distinguish those moral beliefs that are reliably formed from those that aren't, we can either (a) use our moral beliefs as data or (b) "go outside" our moral beliefs in order to discover a criterion of moral rightness and then see which dispositions lead one to form moral beliefs that accord with this independently established criterion.
3. (a) is viciously circular.
4. Therefore, in order to distinguish moral beliefs that are true from those that are false, we must follow (b).

If this is the line of reasoning for rejecting moral beliefs as data, it does not seem compelling. First consider premise (1). If "distinguishing" between true and false moral beliefs is understood as *knowing* which are true and which are false, then it is not obvious that either a foundationalist or a coherentist would accept the first premise. Each might agree that *knowing* that p requires that one's belief be reliably formed, but why in addition must we require that one know that his belief that p is reliably formed? Neither a foundationalist nor a coherentist is committed to that requirement.

Second, even if we did think that S's knowing that p required that S know that his belief that p was reliably formed, how would going outside our moral beliefs put us in a better position? Consider those nonmoral beliefs from which we might argue for our criterion, beliefs, for example, about what it is rational to do or desire, or beliefs about the logic of moral terms and various empirical premises. Surely, if we are to know our criterion on the basis of these nonmoral beliefs, they too must be known. But if knowing that p requires that one know one's belief is reliably formed *and* if this in turn requires that we "go outside" such beliefs for a noncircular argument, then it seems that any knowledge will be impossible. For S to know that p, S must also know that his belief that p is reliably formed, and let's suppose he knows this on the basis of q and r. But to know q, he must know that his belief that q is reliably formed and to know that he must know it on the basis of s and t, and so on. To insist on the external validation of all our beliefs and the dispositions to form those beliefs is to insist on a requirement that cannot be met.

Let us set aside the claim that S knows that *p* only if S knows that his belief that p is reliably produced. We still might take seriously, with Brandt and Hare, the question about the reliability of our dispositions to form moral beliefs. So even if we reject premise (1) we still might wonder how we are to know that our dispositions to form moral beliefs are reliable. Must we conclude, as Brandt and Hare do, that the only way to know that our dispositions are reliable is by "going outside", by producing an external validation of our dispositions to form moral beliefs? But here again it is not clear how such a move would help. Could we not, as philosophers and reflective thinkers, also wonder about the reliability of the dispositions to produce these nonmoral beliefs on which we would base our criterion? Even if there were widespread agreement about the reliability of these dispositions, why should we insist on an external validation of our dispositions to form moral beliefs and reject or ignore questions about the reliability of these other dispositions? But if we insist on the requirement for external validation of all our belief forming dispositions, then what? How could that demand be satisfied?

But perhaps it will be argued that though we need an external validation of our dispositions to form moral beliefs we do not need an external validation of the reliability of our dispositions to form these nonmoral beliefs upon which we base our moral criterion. One might claim that various facts about the genesis of our moral beliefs require the need for external validation. But what facts are these supposed to be? Suppose that it is claimed that we must seek such a validation of our moral beliefs because they are influenced by our teachers and peers. But surely our beliefs about what it is rational to do, the logic of moral terms, and our empirical beliefs are also influenced by our culture and upbringing, by our teachers and peers. Suppose it is claimed that we must seek such an external validation of our moral beliefs because there is disagreement over which ways of forming moral beliefs are reliable. But is there not also disagreement over the reliability of the way in which we form our nonmoral beliefs? Surely there are skeptical challenges to the reliability of belief forming processes of perception, memory, and even reason itself. Suppose it is claimed that the reliability of our dispositions to form moral beliefs is simply lower than the reliability of our dispositions to form these nonmoral beliefs by which we might validate our dispositions to form moral beliefs. We must thus seek to found our moral criterion on these more reliable dispositions. Such an answer seems tempting, yet if the only way to assess the reliability of a belief forming process is on the basis of an external validation of the sort that Brandt and Hare call for, then how can one know in the absence of such an external validation of perception, memory, and reason that they really are more reliable than our dispositions to form moral beliefs? If the only legitimate way to assess the reliability of some belief forming process is through such an external validation, then in the absence of such validation of particular ways of forming moral and nonmoral beliefs, there is no reason for assuming that a particular way of forming moral beliefs really is less reliable than other sorts of belief-forming dispositions. It is not clear that any of these considerations supports the need for an external validation of our dispositions to form moral beliefs and for giving a free pass to our dispositions to form nonmoral beliefs. Surely as philosophers we can always at least raise the question about the reliability of other dispositions.

The problem of how we can know that our ways of forming beliefs are reliable is certainly not unique to the moral philosopher. The problem of how we know that our ways of forming moral beliefs are reliable may be viewed as a particular instance of that broader issue familiar to epistemology in general. I have suggested that we take Brandt and Hare to hold that we are driven to an external validation of our dispositions to form moral beliefs because the alternative is viciously circular. But is it? Some have thought not. Ernest Sosa, for example, calls our attention to the second paragraph of Descartes's "Third Meditation," where Descartes reasons:

> I am certain that I am a thinking being. Do I not therefore know what is required for my being certain about anything? In this first item of knowledge there is simply a clear and distinct perception of what I am asserting; this would not be enough to make me certain of the truth of the matter if it could ever turn out that something which I perceived with such clarity and distinctness was false. So now I seem to be able to lay down as a general rule that whatever I perceive very clearly and distinctly is true.[28]

Sosa notes that Descartes grants that a very powerful being might lead him astray even with respect to what is most manifest to him. The doubt arising from this possibility must be blocked if one is to attain certainty by intuiting something as clear and distinct, and so Descartes launches on the theological reflection that leads to a nondeceiving God. But Sosa suggests that Descartes takes himself to have attained some positive justification even without the further certainty provided by the proof of a nondeceiving God. Sosa is concerned with the reasoning that leads Descartes to the rule that "whatever I perceive very clearly and distinctly is true." He tentatively suggests that Descartes's reasoning might take the following form:

Argument B

(1) Datum: I know with a high degree of certainty that I think.
(2) I clearly and distinctly perceive that I think, and that is the only, or anyhow the best account of the source of my knowledge that I think.
(3) So my clear and distinct perception that I think is what explains why or how it is that I know I think.

(4) But my clear and distinct perception could not serve as a source of that knowledge if it were not an infallibly reliable faculty.

(5) So, finally, my clear and distinct perception must be an infallibly reliable faculty.

As Sosa notes, the move from 1 and 2 to 3 "is an inference to an explanatory account that one might accept for the coherence it gives to one's view of things in the domain involved."[29] As Sosa construes the argument, it is important to see that in this argument knowledge of the first premise is *not* based on knowledge of the conclusion. It is not as though Descartes's knowledge of the first premise is epistemically based on his knowledge that his clear and distinct perceptions are reliable. Rather, Descartes's justification for accepting the conclusion is the result of this line of explanatory reasoning. So the argument is not epistemically circular in the sense that knowledge of the premises rests upon epistemically prior knowledge of the conclusion.

Sosa goes on to suggest that G. E. Moore might have availed himself of an analogous line of reasoning to the conclusion that his perception that he has a hand is reliable. Let us set aside, however, Moore's concerns and ask if a similar line of reasoning can be adopted concerning moral and evaluative beliefs and the processes that yield them. Let p be the proposition that a life filled with pleasure and morally and intellectually virtuous activity is intrinsically better than one filled with pain, morally vicious activities, and error. Now consider the following argument that a rationalist such as Ross (or a rationalist Russell) might offer:

Argument C

(1) Data: I know that p and I know that p is necessarily true.

(2) I rationally intuit that p and that p is necessarily true, and that is the best account of the source of my knowledge that p and that p is necessarily true.

(3) So my rational intuition that p and that p is necessarily true is what explains why or how I know them.

(4) But my rational intuition could not serve as a source of that degree of justified certainty if it were not a reliable faculty.

(5) So, finally, my rational intuition must be a reliable source or faculty.

Along with knowledge of intrinsic value, Ross might take as his data various principles of *prima facie* duty, holding that rational intuition is the best account of his knowledge of such principles. But note that nothing in this line of reasoning forces Ross, or rationalists in general, to hold that rational intuition is infallible, that it is perfectly reliable. Nothing in this line of argument precludes him from adopting a form of modest foundationalism with respect to the a priori or commits him to infallible Cartesian faculties. Of course, as with any inference to an explanatory account, there is the possibility that one has overlooked better explanations of the data. In this case, some might argue that there are better explanations of the data than that offered by the rationalist; some might hold, for example, that our emotional experiences are better explanations of how we know p (though it seems unclear how such emotional experience would explain our knowing that p is necessarily true.) But let us set such points aside, for the objection that Brandt and Hare would raise to this sort of argument is that it is "viciously circular," not that there are better explanations of the data. Argument C is not, in their view, appropriately independent, since the first premise presupposes the truth of evaluative beliefs.

I suspect that what bothers Hare and Brandt is that someone with conflicting data might reason in the same way to the conclusion that his rational intuitions are reliable. We can imagine someone, Jones, who takes as his data that he knows that *not-p* and knows that *not-p* is necessarily true. Or we can imagine someone, Smith, who claims to know that a life filled with pain, moral viciousness, and error is intrinsically better than one filled with pleasure and acts of moral and intellectual virtue and that this is necessarily true. Jones and Smith might reason in a manner analogous to Argument C and conclude that their rational intuitions are reliable. As Hare says, reasoning in this way would not settle the dispute between them and Ross over whose intuitions are reliable. That much seems right. But why should we conclude that one who knows the premises of Argument C could not come to know the conclusion on the basis of that argument, and why should we assume that the conclusions of Jones and Smith are epistemically on a par? Of course, the beliefs of Jones and Smith might exhibit as much internal coherence as the beliefs of one who accepts Argument C, but we need not think, again, that coherence is the only thing relevant to the epistemic merit of a body of beliefs. What would distinguish Ross from the others is his knowing the data and his knowing that p and that p is necessarily true on the basis of reliable rational intuition. As Sosa writes, "What privileges our position, if anything does, cannot be that it is self-supportive, as we have seen; *but nor can it possibly be that it is ours.* Our position would be privileged rather by deriving from cognitive virtues, from the likes of perception and cogent thought, and not from derangement or superstition or their ilk."[30] The upshot of this is that Sosa would hold that premise 3 of Argument A is false. Though Argument C is not an independent argument for the reliability of our way of forming some moral or evaluative belief, insofar as the first premise presupposes the truth of such a belief, Sosa would hold that it is not *vicious*. Given knowledge of the premises, one can, in virtue of this line of reasoning, know or at least have some positive justification for believing the conclusion. This remains so even if others can offer analogous lines of reasoning for their ways of forming moral and evaluative beliefs.

NOTES

1. J. L. Mackie argues along these lines in *Ethics: Inventing Right and Wrong* (New York: Penguin, 1977), 36.

2. Two noteworthy responses to the argument from disagreement are in Bruce Russell, "Two Forms of Ethical Skepticism," *Ethical Theory*, ed. Louis Pojman (Belmont, Calif.: Wadsworth 1989), and David Brink, *Moral Realism and the Foundations of Ethics* (New York: Cambridge University Press, 1989), 197–209.

3. For a good discussion of these issues that draws a different conclusion than that drawn here see Alan Gewirth's "Positive 'Ethics' and Normative 'Science',￼" *Philosophical Review* 69 (1960).

4. See Gilbert Harman, *The Nature of Morality* (New York: Oxford University Press, 1977), 7.

5. See Nicholas Sturgeon, "Moral Explantions," *Morality, Reason, and Truth*, ed. D. Copp and D. Zimmerman (Totowa, N.J.: Rowman & Littlefield, 1984), and David Brink, *Moral Realism and the Foundations of Ethics*, chap. 7.

6. The explanatory requirement has been challenged by several writers. See Peter Achinstein, "Concepts of Evidence," *Mind* 87 (1978); Warren Quinn, "Truth and Explanation in Ethics," *Ethics* 96 (1986); John Pollock, *Contemporary Theories of Knowledge* (Totowa, N.J.: Rowman & Littlefield, 1986), 42–44. Achinstein, for example, notes that the fact that Jones has a certain chest wound and that all who have had that chest wound will die is a reason to believe that Jones will die. But the fact that Jones will die does not explain the fact that he has that chest wound or the deaths of others similarly wounded.

7. Bruce Russell makes this argument in his fine essay, "Two Forms of Ethical Skepticism," 464.

8. In ethics, the method of wide reflective equilibrium figures prominently in John Rawls's *A Theory of Justice* (Cambridge, Mass.: Harvard University Press, 1971). See also, Norman Daniels, "Wide Reflective Equilibrium and Theory Acceptance in Ethics," *Journal of Philosophy* 76 (1979); Michael DePaul, "Reflective Equilibrium and Foundationalism," *American Philosophical Quarterly* 23 (1986); Stephen Stich, "Reflective Equilibrium, Analytic Epistemology and the Problem of Cognitive Diversity," *Synthese* 71 (1988); Ernest Sosa, "Equilibrium in Coherence?" in *The Current State of the Coherence Theory*, ed. John Bender (Dordrecht: Kluwer, 1989), reprinted in Sosa's *Knowledge in Perspective* (Cambridge: Cambridge University Press, 1991).

9. William Alston, "Two Types of Foundationalism," *Journal of Philosophy* 73 (1976): 170. Richard Hare expresses a similar view concerning our knowledge of goodness in *The Language of Morals* (Oxford: Oxford University Press, 1952), 111. Hare writes, "[I]f we knew all of the descriptive properties which a particular strawberry had . . . and if we knew also the meaning of the word 'good', then what else should we require to know, in order to be able to tell whether a strawberry was a good one? We should require to know, what are the criteria in virtue of which a strawberry is to be called a good one, or what are the characteristics that make a strawberry a good one, or what is the standard of goodness for strawberries. We should be required to be given the major premiss."

10. W. D. Ross, *The Right and the Good* (Oxford: Oxford University Press, 1930), 29–30.

11. Bertrand Russell, *The Problems of Philosophy* (Oxford: Oxford University Press, 1912), 75–76.

12. See for example Laurence BonJour, *The Structure of Empirical Knowledge* (Cambridge, Mass.: Harvard University Press, 1985), 208; Donna Summerfield, "Modest *A Priori* Knowledge," *Philosophy and Phenomenological Research* 51 (1991): 49–50; Tyler Burge, "Content Preservation," *Philosophical Review* 102 (1993), 461; Alvin Plantinga, *Warrant and Proper Function* (Oxford: Oxford University Press, 1993), chap. 6, esp. 112; Jerold Katz, "What Mathematical Knowledge Could Be," *Mind* 104 (1995).

13. Russell writes, "It should be observed that, in all cases of general principles, particular instances dealing with familiar things, are more evident than the general principle. For example, the law of contradiction states that nothing can both have a certain property and not have it. This is evident as soon as it is understood, but it is not so evident as that a particular rose which we see cannot be both red and not red" (*Problems of Philosophy*, 112–113). If the general principle is less evident than the particular instance, then the general principle is not maximally warranted.

14. Ewing writes, "Many philosophers have preferred to limit the term 'intuition' to cases of certain knowledge, but there are many cases where something presents itself to one intuitively as deserving a certain degree of credence but falling short of certainty or where an intuition has some value but is confused and inextricably blended with erroneous assumptions and inferences." A. C. Ewing, *The Fundamental Questions of Philosophy* (London: Routledge and Kegan Paul, 1951), 49. He adds, "Arguments may well be available which without strictly proving either side to be wrong put a disputant in a position in which he can see better for himself whether he is right or wrong or at least cast doubt on the truth of his view" (50–51).

15. Thomas Reid, *Essays on the Intellectual Powers of Man* (Cambridge, Mass.: MIT Press, 1969), essay 6, chap. 4, 610.

16. Reid, essay VI, chap. 4, 603–604.

17. Plantinga, *Warrant and Proper Function*, 110.

18. See for example William Lycan, "Moral Facts and Moral Knowledge," *Southern Journal of Philosophy* 24 Suppl. (1986), 89; John L. Pollock, "A Theory of Moral Reasoning," *Ethics* 96 (1986): 512–515.

19. Franz Brentano, *The Origin of Our Knowledge of Right and Wrong*, trans. Roderick Chisholm and Elizabeth Schneewind (London: Routledge and Kegan Paul, 1969), 24.

20. Alexius Meinong, *On Emotional Presentation*, trans. Marie-Luise Schubert (Evanston: Northwestern University Press, 1972), 28.

21. Max Scheler, *Formalism in Ethics and Non-Formal Ethics of Values*, trans. Manfred S. Frings and Roger L. Funk (Evanston: Northwestern University Press, 1973), 68.

22. This line of objection is presented by Walter Sinnott-Armstrong, "Moral Skepticism and Justification," in *Moral Knowledge?: New Readings in Moral Epistemology*, ed. Walter Sinnott-Armstrong and Mark Timmons (New York: Oxford University Press, 1995), 27–28.

23. Two recent supporters of coherence theories in moral epistemology are David Brink, *Moral Realism and the Foundations of Ethics*, chap. 5, and Geoffrey Sayre-McCord, "Coherentist Epistemology and Moral Theory," in *Moral Knowledge?*, 137–189. For a crit-

ical discussion of coherence theories see Noah Lemos, *Intrinsic Value* (Cambridge: Cambridge University Press, 1994), chap. 9.

24. Richard M. Hare, *Moral Thinking* (Oxford: Oxford University Press, 1981), 12.

25. Richard Brandt, *A Theory of the Good and the Right* (Oxford: Oxford University Press, 1979), 21–22.

26. Hare, *Moral Thinking*, 40.

27. Ibid., 95–96.

28. Rene Descartes, *The Philosophical Writings of Descartes*, ed. J. Cottingham, R. Stoothoff, and D. Murdoch (New York: Cambridge University Press, 1975), vol. 2, 24.

29. Ernest Sosa, "Reflective Knowledge in the Best Circles," *Journal of Philosophy* (1997): 416.

30. Ernest Sosa, "Philosophical Skepticism and Epistemic Circularity," *Empirical Knowledge*, 2d ed., ed. Paul K. Moser (Lanham, Md.: Rowman & Littlefield, 1996), 325.

CHAPTER 18

EPISTEMOLOGY IN PHILOSOPHY OF RELIGION

PHILIP L. QUINN

ALMOST every topic in philosophy of religion gives rise to epistemological questions. Consider, for example, the claim of some political liberals that religious arguments ought to be excluded from the public square of American democracy. Often supporters of this claim back it up with an appeal to the dreadful consequences of religious controversy. Look at what happens, they say, when religion and politics get entangled; recall the conflicts in Northern Ireland, Lebanon, Bosnia, and Kashmir! Their opponents may, however, not be moved by this appeal. Do we have any reasons to believe, they may ask, that similar conflicts would result in America from religious arguments in the public square? This question about reasons to believe is obviously a good epistemological question, and it is clearly relevant to a topic debated by philosophers of religion.

But it is not a question in religious epistemology. Intuitively speaking, I suppose it is a question in the epistemology of the social sciences. It asks about reasons for believing that social conflict of a certain sort is likely to arise from religious disagreement under political conditions that prevail in contemporary America. The considerations that bear on answering it will be drawn from such empirically oriented disciplines as sociology, political science, and history. Quite a few of the epistemological questions of interest to philosophers of religion are of this kind; though they concern fascinating epistemological issues, they are not questions in religious epistemology. To keep this essay within manageable bounds, I shall set aside such questions and focus exclusively on questions in religious epistemology.

What is religious epistemology? It is simple enough to say that it is the epistemology of distinctively religious beliefs, but that will not be helpful in the absence of a definition of religious beliefs. Prospects for an illuminating definition of religious beliefs are bleak because scholars generally agree that religion cannot usefully be defined in terms of necessary and sufficient conditions. The concept of religion is, on the received view, at best a family-resemblance concept and at worst a Western imposition that seriously distorts some of the forms of life to which it has been applied. Fortunately, this definitional issue can be bypassed here in the present context by restricting the discussion to a single belief that is paradigmatically religious. It is belief in the existence of God, where God is understood to be the deity of classical monotheism. In other words, God is, if such a being exists, the omniscient, omnipotent, and perfectly good creator of all contingent reality. This restriction is feasible because the most important questions in recent analytic religious epistemology concern the epistemic status of belief in the existence of God. Is it rational? Is it justified? Can it amount to knowledge? These are the questions I shall address in this essay.

Of course similar questions can be asked about the ultimate religious realities of other traditions. Is belief in the existence of the Tao rational? Is belief in the nirvana of Buddhism justified? Can belief in the Brahman of advaita Hinduism amount to knowledge? It seems plausible to suppose that the resources available for use in evaluating the epistemic status of any of these beliefs will be in some ways similar to and in other ways different from those at our disposal for assessing the epistemic status of belief in God. Answering these questions in nontheistic religious epistemology will therefore be a complicated and delicate matter. I offer two reasons for not even to trying to do so: lack of competence and lack of space. As for the limits of my own expertise, I must confess that I do not know enough about any nontheistic religious tradition to speak with authority about the epistemic status of its core beliefs. This is a task I must leave to others. Moreover, even if I knew more than I do about some nontheistic tradition, I would not be able to do justice to the complexities of issues concerning the epistemic status of core beliefs in both theism and that tradition within the confines of a single essay. So I invite interested readers of this essay to explore the question of whether, or to what extent, points that emerge in my discussion of the epistemic status of belief in the existence of God can be transferred or adapted to belief in the ultimate realities of other religious traditions. I shall be content if I succeed in giving a fairly comprehensive account of the main debates about the epistemic status of belief in the existence of God in recent analytic religious epistemology.

Proving the existence of God has been on the agenda of theistic philosophers for a long time. The enterprise of constructing and criticizing such proofs constitutes the domain within philosophy of religion known as natural theology. Among the historical fruits of natural theology are Anselm's ontological argument and the five ways of Aquinas, as well as Hume's criticism of the cosmological argument and the design argument and Kant's critique of the ontological, cosmological, and teleological arguments. Contemporary philosophers of religion continue to debate the merits of the historical legacy of natural theology and to construct and criticize new arguments for the existence of God. Their discussions often have an epistemological dimension. It is clear that a proof is supposed to be a discursive argument for its conclusion; a proof is also supposed to be a cognitive achievement of some sort. To put the point modestly, perhaps a proof is supposed to raise the epistemic status of its conclusion above what that status would be in the absence of the proof. Or, more ambitiously, if we remind ourselves that the notion of proof has its home in mathematics, maybe a proof is supposed to yield knowledge of its conclusion that would be absent were it not for the proof or to bestow on its conclusion an exalted epistemic status such as certainty. But what sort of epistemic conditions would a discursive argument have to satisfy in order to perform such cognitive functions? And do any arguments for the existence of God succeed in satisfying such conditions? Questions such as these serve as the focus of the first main part of this essay.

Of course hostility to natural theology is also deeply embedded in the historical traditions of theism. Some of it comes from fideists who hold that belief in God is and should be outside the domain of the rational or is even contrary to reason. Pascal and Kierkegaard are often counted among the fideists. But there are also philosophers of religion who are hostile to natural theology but shy away from the irrationalism of the fideists. A group of such philosophers who have made important contributions to recent discussions in religious epistemology have come to be known as Reformed epistemologists because they trace their ancestry back to the Calvinist strand of the Reformation. Reformed epistemologists contend that belief in the existence of God can, in some circumstances, have an epistemic status high enough to render it worthy of acceptance even if it has no support from the arguments of natural theology or from any other beliefs. Indeed, some of them go so far as to suggest that the enterprise of natural theology is somehow misguided and perhaps even a bit impious. But what kinds of circumstances render beliefs worthy of acceptance even when they have no support from other beliefs? And does belief in the existence of God occur in such circumstances in the lives of typical theists? Questions such as these serve as the focus of the second main part of this essay.

My chief aim throughout the essay is to convey to readers a sense of what has been going on in recent years at what I take to be the center of analytic religious epistemology. I have views of my own about these developments. Some of them are critical, and I shall set them forth boldly. But, though I would like to persuade readers to share my views, I am more interested in persuading them that religious epistemology has recently been and continues to be an exciting and fertile part of philosophy and should be of interest to anyone who wishes to achieve a comprehensive view of the whole of epistemology.

I. Epistemology inside Natural Theology

In his elegant little book, *Belief in God: A Study in the Epistemology of Religion*, George I. Mavrodes asks the reader to consider the following argument:

(1) Either nothing exists or God exists.

(2) Something exists.

(3) Therefore, God exists.

This argument is a deductively valid disjunctive syllogism. Its second premise is obviously true. Since its first premise follows deductively from its conclusion, it is a sound argument if God exists. Suppose that God does exist. The argument is then a sound argument for the existence of God. But is it a proof of God's existence? Even philosophers who are theists would be likely to deny that it is. If they are correct, soundness is a necessary but not sufficient condition for deductive proof.

What needs to be added to soundness to yield a sufficient condition? Mavrodes thinks it is an epistemic condition. He suggests that the most prominent feature of our ordinary notion of proof "is the conviction that the discovery or construction of a proof represents some cognitive advance—an epistemic achievement, an event which is internally and necessarily related to some knowledge-gaining project" (Mavrodes 1970, 31). He tries to spell this idea out in two steps.

The first step is to define a technical notion of cogency. An argument is *cogent* for a person S if and only if S knows it to be sound. However, as the following example shows, cogency is not sufficient for proof:

(4) Either Mars has no moons or George W. Bush is a Republican.

(5) Mars has some moons.

(6) Therefore, George W. Bush is a Republican.

This argument is cogent for most of us; we know it to be valid and its premises to be true. Yet it suffers from epistemic circularity for most of us because our knowledge of the truth of its first premise rests on our knowledge of the truth of its conclusion. Hence it does not represent a cognitive advance for us. In order to deal with the problem of epistemic circularity, Mavrodes introduces a second technical notion. An argument is *convincing* for a person S if and only if it is cogent for S, and S knows that each of its premises is true without having to infer any of them from its conclusion or from any other statements S knows only by an inference from that conclusion. He proposes that "we will have proved a statement to S if and only if we succeed in presenting S with an argument that that is convincing for S" (Mavrodes 1970, 35). On this conception of proof, when we present a convincing argument to individuals, we may extend their knowledge by showing them how to derive a further consequence from things they already know that will have epistemic grounds that are just as good as the grounds they have for the knowledge from which that consequence is derived. This surely represents a cognitive or epistemic achievement.

Though refinements in the simple account Mavrodes offers of what it takes to be a proof might be needed, let us accept it for the purposes of the present discussion. We may then ask whether any of the arguments of natural theology are proofs in this sense and, if so, for which individuals or groups they count as proofs. As it turns out, related questions have been raised in important recent treatments of ontological and cosmological arguments for the existence of God by Alvin Plantinga and William L. Rowe. And we may also ask whether such arguments, even if they fall short of being proofs for anyone in this sense, can nevertheless make cognitive or epistemic advances of less impressive sorts. Behind the somewhat technical proposal Mavrodes endorses lies the intuitive idea that, by means of an argument known to be deductively valid, a proof transfers to its conclusion from premises that have it independent of that conclusion the high epistemic status ingredient in knowledge. But suppose an argument for God's existence, known to be deductively valid, transferred to its conclusion from premises that have it independent of that conclusion, not the exalted epistemic status that makes for knowledge, but some weaker positive epistemic status, say, justification or rationality of some kind. Such an argument, though it would not be a proof in the sense delineated by Mavrodes, would nevertheless be a valuable cognitive or epistemic advance for those people for whom it performed this function. It is therefore worth considering whether the arguments discussed by Plantinga and Rowe can perform this function, even if they are not proofs for anyone.

Plantinga's *The Nature of Necessity* contains an ontological argument for the existence of God that improves on arguments constructed by Charles Hartshorne and Norman Malcolm. It has the following premises:

(7)   The property *has maximal greatness* entails the property *has maximal excellence in every possible world.*

(8)   *Maximal excellence* entails *omniscience, omnipotence,* and *moral perfection.*

(9)   *Maximal greatness* is possibly exemplified.

From these premises, Plantinga deduces the conclusion that there actually exists a being, God, who is omniscient, omnipotent, and morally perfect and who exists and has these properties in every possible world. We know that this argument is deductively valid if we make the usual assumption that modal status does not vary from one possible world to another. Moreover, premises (7) and (8) are obviously true in virtue of the way he defines maximal greatness and maximal excellence. So (9) is the controversial premise of the argument. Plantinga reports that he thinks this premise is true, though he does not claim to know it, and so thinks his argument is sound.

Yet he concedes that it is not a successful piece of natural theology. The problem, as he sees it, is not epistemic circularity or, as he puts the point, dialectical deficiency. After considering an argument that fairly clearly suffers from this defect in much the same way that (4)–(6) does for most of us, Plantinga denies that his ontological argument must be flawed in this manner for those who accept it. He notes that it is not obvious that those who accept its controversial premise do so only because they infer it from the conclusion. Of course, if anyone did that, the argument would be dialectically deficient or epistemically circular for such a person. According to Plantinga, however, his ontological argument "need not be thus dialectically deficient for one who accepts it" (Plantinga 1974, 218).

The problem for Plantinga is rather that a successful piece of natural theology typically draws its premises from a body of propositions accepted by nearly every sane or rational person, and the controversial premise of his ontological argument clearly is not accepted by nearly every sane or rational person. Quite a few rational people deny it, while others, who are more cautious, remain agnostic, neither affirming nor denying it. But it does not follow from this, as Plantinga is quick to observe, that it is irrational or improper to accept the controversial premise of his ontological argument. He compares it in this respect to Leibniz's law of the indiscernibility of identicals. There seems to be no argument for it accepted by all philosophers, and some philosophers object to or reject it. In these circumstances, if we carefully consider Leibniz's law and the objections to it, and if we reflect on its connections with other propositions we accept or reject, then if we still find it compelling we are within our epistemic rights, and it is rationally permissible for us to accept it. And the same goes, Plantinga urges, for the controversial premise of his argument, the claim that maximal greatness is possibly exemplified. And so his final verdict on his version of the ontological argument and variants of it is this: "They cannot, perhaps, be said to *prove* or *establish* their conclusion. But since it is rational to accept their central premise, they do show that it is rational to *accept* that conclusion" (Plantinga 1974, 221).

So Plantinga does not argue that his ontological argument transmits from its premises to its conclusion the high epistemic status requisite for knowledge. In other words, he does not claim that it is a proof of the existence of God for anyone in the sense explicated by Mavrodes. However, he does argue that it represents a cognitive or epistemic achievement. He claims that it does transfer from its premises to its conclusion the positive epistemic status of rationality in the sense of rational permission to accept.

I am inclined for skeptical reasons to take issue with Plantinga's claim that it is rationally permissible to accept the premise that maximal greatness is possibly exemplified in a way that is not dialectically deficient. I doubt that we have significant cognitive access to possibilities that is independent of our knowledge of actualities and slight imaginative variations in them. Unless we appeal to God's actual existence for support, which would introduce epistemic circularity, we are rationally required, I tend to think, to withhold on the premise that maximal greatness is possibly exemplified, in which case it is not rationally permissible for us to accept that premise. But I could easily be mistaken on this point. And, in any case, this disagreement does not affect the two main epistemological lessons I wish to draw from Plantinga's discussion. The first is that it is always worthwhile to try to ascertain exactly what positive epistemic status an argument of natural theology that is known to be valid succeeds in transferring from its premises to its conclusion. The second is that an argument of natural theology might represent a cognitive advance by transferring some positive epistemic status from premises to conclusion, even if it did not amount to a proof in the sense elucidated by Mavrodes because it did not transfer the high status requisite for knowledge.

William L. Rowe's *The Cosmological Argument*, which devotes most of its attention to the sort of argument advocated by Samuel Clarke, concludes with a chapter entitled "The Cosmological Argument as a Justification for Belief in God." Like Mavrodes, Rowe insists that an argument must satisfy epistemic conditions if it is to count as a proof for the existence of God. He lists the following five necessary conditions for being a proof of God's existence: "(i) The conclusion asserts or entails (in some fairly obvious way) that God exists. (ii) The conclusion must follow from the premises of the argument. (iii) The premises of the argument must be true. (iv) The premises of the argument are known to be true. (v) The premises are known independently of any knowledge of the conclusion" (Rowe 1975, 254). And, in a footnote in which he expresses doubt about the completeness of this list, he adds that it seems to him that an argument is a proof for a person only if that person knows that its conclusion follows from its premises. Clearly conditions (ii) and (iii) are meant to insure that a proof will be a sound argument, and condition (iv) together with the condition suggested in the footnote will insure that a proof is known to be a sound argument. So satisfaction of these four conditions will guarantee that a proof is a cogent argument for someone in the sense defined by Mavrodes. Condition (v) is meant to rule out the sort of epistemic circularity or dialectical deficiency that concerns Mavrodes and Plantinga. Hence satisfaction of all of these conditions will guarantee that a proof is a convincing argument for someone in the sense specified by Mavrodes. The chief difference between Mavrodes and Rowe on the issue of proof lies in the way they handle the person-relativity of knowledge. As we have seen, Mavrodes builds person-relativity into his definitions of cogency, convincingness, and proof. Rowe distinguishes between being a proof, which requires only that the conditions involving knowledge he enumerates be satisfied by someone, and being a proof for a person, which requires that those conditions be satisfied by that person.

Rowe argues at length that the kind of cosmological argument developed by Clarke is not a proof of God's existence. The problem, as he sees it, is that it includes the principle of sufficient reason among its premises. After arguing for the falsity of one version of that principle, he formulates a cosmological argument using the following principle as its crucial premise:

(10)   Every existing thing has a reason for its existence either in the necessity of its own nature or in the causal efficacy of some other beings.

He tries to show that, though no one has formulated a convincing argument for its falsity, it becomes reasonably clear, when one examines what its supporters say on its behalf, that none of them has knowledge of its truth. Assuming that no one other than its supporters, or at least no one else with the possible exception of God, knows that it is true, we may conclude that the cosmological argument of which it is a premise is not a proof of God's existence for anyone, or at least for anyone other than God, and so is not a proof of the existence of God.

But because this version of the principle of sufficient reason has not been shown to be false, Rowe suggests that the cosmological argument of which it is a premise may have some epistemological value for theism. He reminds us that "there are many deductively valid arguments whose premises we have reasons to believe, thus making it reasonable for us to accept their conclusions, even though none of us can claim to *know* that the premises of these arguments, or their conclusions, are true" (Rowe 1975, 267). He does not claim that the cosmological argument of which (10) is a premise is such an argument. He does, however, conclude the book by directing to the theist the following irenic suggestion: "I am proposing to the theist that in seeking rational justification for his belief in the conclusion of the Cosmological Argument he would do well to abandon the view that the Cosmological Argument is a proof of theism, and, in its place, pursue the possibility that the Cosmological Argument shows the reasonableness of theistic belief, even though it perhaps fails to show that theism is true" (Rowe 1975, 269).

Unfortunately, Rowe does not offer an account of the sense in which his cosmological argument might show theistic belief to be reasonable. If we reflect carefully on the epistemic status of (10), however, I think we should conclude that some reasonable people will deny it and others will remain agnostic about it, neither affirming nor denying it. Thus it seems likely to me that rational permissibility is the strongest sense of reasonableness in which it is plausible to suppose that a cosmological argument might transfer reasonableness from premises that include (10) to its conclusion. Those who share my skeptical turn of mind may, of course, think that we are rationally required to remain agnostic about (10) and hence have no rational permission to accept it. And it is vulnerable to critics who may sooner or later come up with what would be generally regarded as a convincing argument for its falsity.

There are some comparisons of the views of Plantinga and Rowe that are worth spelling out. Plantinga does not claim that he or anyone else knows the central premise of his ontological argument, and he acknowledges that perhaps it is not a proof. By contrast, Rowe does claim that no one, or at least no human, knows the central premise of his cosmological argument, and he concludes that it is not a proof. Plantinga does claim that it is rationally permissible to accept the central premise of his ontological argument and thus also rationally permissible to accept its conclusion. Again, by contrast, Rowe does not claim that it is reasonable to accept the central premise of his cosmological argument and thus also reasonable to accept its conclusion, though he leaves open for theists to pursue, if they wish, the possibility that this is the case. Nevertheless, there is considerable convergence of the views of these two philosophers, and it seems to me to support two theses. First, it is not plausible to suppose that ontological or cosmological arguments, even when they are known to be deductively valid, will be proofs for those acquainted with them in the strong sense that they transfer the high epistemic status requisite for knowledge from their premises to their conclusions. And, second, the view that such arguments are cognitive achievements, because they do for some people who are acquainted with them transfer from their premises to their conclusions some positive epistemic status less than what is requisite for knowledge, is both quite plausible and eminently worthy of further exploration.

My discussion up to this point has focused on Mavrodes, Plantinga, and Rowe because I find them clearer and more explicit than most other philosophers about the epistemological issues that arise within natural theology. But of course similar issues also come up when we think about contributions to natural theology other than ontological or cosmological arguments. Let me briefly survey a couple of them.

The design argument for God's existence has since the time of David Hume often been presented as an inductive argument. It would therefore be appropriate to explore the question of what sort of positive epistemic status a sound inductive argument for the existence of God might bestow on its conclusion. Two obstacles stand in the way of answering this question in a fashion that is both precise and general. First, philosophers disagree about how to explicate for inductive arguments the analogue of deductive validity. And, second, unlike sound deductive arguments, which guarantee the truth of their conclusions, sound inductive arguments, because they are ampliative, will only guarantee that their conclusions are more or less probable but not that they are true, and so the epistemic status of the conclusion of even a sound inductive argument for theism may turn out to be less than the positive epistemic status of any of its premises.

We can, however, gain some insight into the epistemological problems that inductive arguments for the existence of God are likely to encounter by looking at a particular specimen. The most impressive inductive argument for the existence of God constructed recently is the long Bayesian argument formulated in Richard Swinburne's *The Existence of God*. Its ultimate conclusion is that "on our total evidence theism is more probable than not" (Swinburne 1979, 291). Swinburne arrives at this conclusion by an application of Bayesian inference to evidence he finds among the claims that typically serve as premises for cosmological and teleological arguments for theism as well as arguments from consciousness, morality, providence, history, miracles, and religious experience. And he includes the existence of evil in the body of evidence he considers. Though he does not try to assign exact numerical values to the probabilities that feature in his Bayesian inferences, he does make qualitative and comparative judgments, claiming, for example, that one probability is very high and another, though low, is not too low or that one probability is very much lower than another.

To his credit, Swinburne usually supports such judgments with arguments from other philosophical doctrines he endorses. A striking example is his reliance on considerations of simplicity. He contends that the probability of theism on tautological evidence depends mainly on how simple a theory it is and that theism "is an extremely simple theory" in part because it "postulates the existence of the simplest kind of person which there could be" (Swinburne 1979, 282). Another striking feature of Swinburne's discussion is the intermediate conclusion he reaches about the problem of evil. He defines a good C-inductive argument as one that makes its conclusion more probable than it otherwise would be. His claim about the evidential force of evil is this: "For these reasons the existence of the evil which we find *does not count* against the existence of God. There is no good C-inductive argument from the existence of evil to the nonexistence of God" (Swinburne 1979, 220, my emphasis). The strength of this claim deserves emphasis. Swinburne is not merely denying that the nonexistence of God is more probable than not on the evidence of the evil known to us; he is asserting that the existence of God is no less probable on the evidence of the evil known to us than it would be in the absence of that evidence.

So suppose for the sake of discussion that Swinburne's Bayesian argument is known by someone to be inductively valid or can be made so solely by fixing minor technical glitches. We may then ask what sort of positive epistemic status its premises have and what kind of epistemic status it bestows on its ultimate conclusion for such a person. When we reflect on the claims concerning simplicity to which it appeals in order to support some of its qualitative or comparative judgments about probabilities and the claim about the evidential force of evil that is among its intermediate conclusions, I think we should conclude that it is unlikely that Swinburne or any other human knows all its premises to be true. Reasonable philosophers who have thought carefully about such claims disagree about their truth. It thus seems unlikely that Swinburne's argument is for anyone a proof of its ultimate conclusion in any strict sense. Indeed, it seems rational permissibility or something in its neighborhood is likely to be the highest epistemic status its most controversial premises have for Swinburne or anyone else. Its cognitive achievement, if any, is therefore likely at most to be bestowing such a status on its ultimate conclusion for some people.

Though Swinburne does not explicitly frame his argument in these terms, it might be thought of as a cumulative case argument for theism, because it draws on evidence from a variety of sources. Many philosophers consider cumulative case arguments for the existence of God the most promising apologetic strategy currently available to theists, and arguments of this kind raise further epistemological issues. Some of them appear in a simple example. Consider people who know that both Plantinga's ontological argument and Rowe's cosmological argument are deductively valid and are within their epistemic rights in accepting the crucial premises of both arguments. Perhaps, though each argument by itself transfers from its premises to their common conclusion only rational permissibility for such people, the two arguments taken together confer on that conclusion some higher epistemic status such as requirement or even whatever it takes to secure knowledge for them. If we suppose that whatever is transmitted from premises to conclusion by a deductive argument that is known to be valid comes in epistemic quanta, so to speak, then we might imagine that such quanta behave additively in the context of a good cumulative case argument. But even if we are skeptical about the use of quantitative thinking in this context, we might nevertheless believe that good cumulative case arguments exploit a threshold phenomenon. Maybe the ontological and cosmological arguments work together to boost their common conclusion above the threshold requisite for a high epistemic status such as rational requirement despite the fact that the crucial premise of each argument lies below that threshold.

Typically, the operation of cumulative case arguments of the sort portrayed in my example is described in terms of similes or metaphors. For instance, it could be said that the individual arguments that make up a good cumulative case confer epistemic support on its conclusion like the legs of a well-constructed chair support the weight of someone seated upon it. All the legs together support the weight, but none of them by itself could do so. Similarly, all of the arguments in a good cumulative case taken together confer high epistemic status on its conclusion, though none of them by itself confers anything more than a lower status. This seems to be the way medical diagnosis often works: various pieces of evidence that support a diagnostic hypothesis together lend it greater support than that contributed by any one bit of evidence alone. And I think that something of this sort was what William Whewell was getting at in his discussions of the consilience of inductions.

But things may be more complex in a good cumulative case for theism because the various parts of the case are not evidentially independent of one another in a manner similar to the way the legs of a chair bear weight independently of each other. An example is the sort of cumulative case discussed by William P. Alston in his *Perceiving God: The Epistemology of Religious Experience*. Alston's approach to epistemology makes crucial use of the concept of a doxastic practice. A doxastic practice is a way of forming beliefs and evaluating them epistemically in terms of a background system of beliefs that furnish potential overriders. In the case of the particular religious practice he calls Christian Mystical Practice (CMP), the inputs to the practice are religious experiences in which a presentation or appearance to the subject of something the subject identifies as God occurs, and the outputs are beliefs about God's self-manifestations to or actions directed toward the subject at the time of the experience. The deliverances of CMP will contribute to a good cumulative case for Christian theism provided its outputs have a sufficiently high positive epistemic status. However, their epistemic status will depend in part on the epistemic status of the background system of beliefs that is included in CMP, and, according to Alston, its epistemic status will in turn depend, at least in part, on epistemic grounds derived from sources other than CMP itself. He concludes that "we can't suppose that CMP simply adds a completely independent quantum of justification to that provided by the other grounds. The situation is more complicated than that" (Alston 1991, 292).

Alston's book is a detailed defense of the view that CMP is rationally engaged in by its practitioners and therefore its outputs are *prima facie* justified. Only in its final chapter does he offer a sketch of the sort of cumulative case for Christian faith into which he envisages his results being integrated. What epistemic fruits does he hope for from such a cumulative case? On the book's penultimate page, after expressing doubt about the project of seeking infallible, indubitable, or incorrigible foundations for one's faith, he makes the following suggestion: "Perhaps a more reasonable aspiration for the human condition is to have multiple sources of support such that although each can be questioned and none renders any of one's beliefs absolutely certain, they lend support to each other as well as to the beliefs they are invoked to support; so that in the way the whole assemblage fits together we have sufficient reason to take the beliefs to be true" (Alston 1991, 306). The metaphor Alston uses to illustrate this suggestion is that, though each of these sources "can itself be doubted and though no single strand is sufficient to keep the faith secure, when combined into a rope they all together have enough strength to do the job" (Alston 1991, 306). Since I take it that having sufficient reason to take the tenets of Christian faith to be true entails having rational permission to believe them, I think Alston's hope for a good cumulative case argument is that it will keep the tenets of Christian faith secure by conferring on them a positive epistemic status at least as high as rational permissibility. Of course a good cumulative case argument might do more—and so much the better if it does—but it must do at least this much.

I agree with those who think that a cumulative case argument of one sort or another offers the best apologetic strategy currently available to theists and, more specifically, to Christian believers. One might legitimately wonder, however, whether anything so elaborate is needed in order for belief in the existence of God to have positive epistemic status of various kinds. When I was discussing the account of proof Mavrodes proposes, I was careful to claim only that a proof may extend the knowledge of someone to whom it is presented. But it may not. Nothing in his definitions rules out the possibility of proving to someone a conclusion already known to that person. Similarly, a person for whom a certain belief is already rationally permissible might be presented with an argument for it such that the argument transfers rational permissibility for that person from its premises to the belief in question. Presenting an argument of this kind to such a person would have about it an air of carrying coals to Newcastle. One of the central claims of Reformed epistemology is that theistic beliefs, or more precisely, beliefs that obviously entail the existence of God, both can in certain circumstances and are for many theists rationally permissible even in the absence of any arguments or propositional evidence for them. If this claim is correct, then for such theists arguments that do no more than confer rational permissibility on the conclusion that God exists are at best superfluous. But is it correct?

II. REFORMED EPISTEMOLOGY

The views of Alston and Mavrodes are sometimes said to display an affinity with Reformed epistemology, and Nicholas Wolterstorff has made significant contributions to its development (see, for example, Wolterstorff 1976). But Plantinga has clearly been the leading contemporary advocate of this school of thought in religious epistemology, and so my discussion will focus exclusively on his work. Over a period of roughly a quarter of a century, he has published three books and numerous articles on topics in epistemology; naturally his views in religious epistemology have not remained static throughout that period. During the earlier phase of their development, Plantinga concentrated on defending the view that theistic belief can be in certain conditions, and is for many theists, properly basic in the sense that a properly basic belief is justified or rationally held even in the absence of any propositional evidence or supporting argument. The main project of the later phase has been to formulate and defend an account of warrant, where warrant is defined as that epistemic status which, when present in sufficient quantity, converts true belief into knowledge, and to argue that theistic belief and, indeed, a fairly comprehensive package of distinctively Christian beliefs can and probably do, if they are true, have enough warrant to be knowledge even if they are basic.

Plantinga's treatment of warrant fills three volumes (Plantinga 1993a, 1993b, 2000). It would therefore be impossible to do full justice to its complexity and richness in a single essay. So my strategy will be first to discuss at length the somewhat simpler doctrine of proper basicality of Plantinga's earlier phase and some of the criticism it has attracted. My source for this doctrine will be his influential paper, "Reason and Belief in God" (Plantinga 1983). My attempt to criticize this doctrine (Quinn 1985) gave rise to a debate in which Plantinga published a reply (Plantinga 1986) and I published a rejoinder (Quinn 1993). Later William Hasker offered an assessment of the results of this debate (Hasker 1998), and the final volume of Plantinga's trilogy on warrant contains further thoughts on some of the disputed issues (Plantinga 2000). In the present discussion, I shall only consider criticism of the doctrine of Plantinga's earlier phase that seems to me to have survived the debate without losing all its bite and thus to have retained some merit. I shall then briefly address the adjustments to our conception of these matters that are required by the shift to the doctrine of warrant of Plantinga's later phase.

A belief is basic for a person at a time just in case it is not based on any other belief for the person at that time. Basic beliefs are at the foundations of a person's doxastic structure; they do not rest on propositional evidence or argumentative support. It is quite clear that many of our sense-perceptual and memorial beliefs are basic. Propriety is, of course, a normative notion; it brings epistemic evaluation onto the scene. But which positive epistemic status do properly basic beliefs have? Plantinga's answer during his earlier phase was that it is some sort of justification. The sense of proper basicality that was at center stage in "Reason and Belief in God" was, he has recently said, one in which a belief is properly basic for a person just when "it is indeed basic for him (he doesn't accept it on the evidential basis of other propositions) and, furthermore, he is *justified* in holding it in the basic way: he is within his epistemic rights, is not irresponsible, is violating no epistemic or other duties in holding that belief in that way" (Plantinga 2000, 178). Propriety thus understood is obviously akin to the sort of rational permissibility that played a large role in the previous section of this essay. Intuitively speaking, unless we adopt a skeptical stance we seem committed to the view that many of our perceptual and memorial beliefs are properly basic in this sense. Is belief in God, that is, belief that God exists or belief in propositions obviously entailing God's existence, ever properly basic for anyone?

If we set skepticism aside, it seems intuitively clear that the answer to this question is yes. Consider a young girl who is being brought up in an isolated Christian community in rural Kansas. As far back as she can remember, she has believed in God in the basic way. All the adults around her profess to believe in God, and she has encountered no objections to believing that God exists. She has even had a few experiences that she construes as warnings from God not to disobey her elders. Given her circumstances, it would be very harsh of us to judge that she is not within her epistemic rights, is irresponsible, or violates some duty in believing in God in the basic way. Of course, as she grows older and her circumstances change, she may encounter serious objections to her belief in God, and it might even cease to be properly basic for her.

It is important to keep in mind the relativity of proper basicality to conditions in which a belief is held in the basic way. Plantinga thinks there are conditions in which the following beliefs are properly basic:

(11)   God is speaking to me.

(12)   God disapproves of what I have done.

He offers a partial description of such conditions in these remarks: "Upon reading the Bible, one may be impressed with a deep sense that God is speaking to him. Upon having done what I know is cheap, or wrong, or wicked, I may feel guilty in God's sight and form the belief *God disapproves of what I have done*" (Plantinga 1983, 80). In conditions other than these, however, beliefs such as (11) and (12) will not be properly basic. If I have done something I know is admirable or virtuous and feel that God is pleased with me, but I believe in the basic way that God disapproves of what I have done, this belief will not be properly basic for me. And if I read one of those stories in the Hebrew Bible in which God is said to have commanded the Israelites to wage genocidal war on a neighboring tribe and shudder with repugnance, then the belief that God is speaking to me will not be properly basic for me, even if for some reason I cannot help holding it in the basic way.

It is worth noting that the conditions mentioned by Plantinga in which beliefs such as (11) and (12) are properly basic include an experiential component. He even speaks of exploring their phenomenology. So it seems fair to attribute to him the assumption that such beliefs are, when properly basic, grounded in such experiences and are, when basic but not properly so, as in the examples I presented in the previous paragraph, held in the basic way in the face of experiences that do not adequately ground them. If this is correct, the experiences in which properly basic theistic beliefs are grounded are in a sense nonpropositional evidence for them. Seen in this light, Plantinga's view is not that properly basic theistic beliefs always lack evidential support of any kind; it is instead the more modest claim that there are conditions in which theistic beliefs, even when they are basic and so lack evidential support from other beliefs, are nevertheless properly basic.

But should we rest content with ignoring skeptical challenges and sticking with the conviction that theistic belief is properly basic for our naive young theist in Kansas or in conditions of the sort partially described by Plantinga? Initially, the answer to this question is not obvious. We might begin with the hope, as Descartes did, that we could carry out a reconstructive project that would put our revised doxastic structures on foundations so firm that they could withstand rather than ignore skeptical challenges. One way to secure such firm foundations would be to insist on a criterion for proper basicality that is very stringent. This is the tack taken by classical foundationalism. According to Plantinga, the classical foundationalist endorses the following criterion:

(13)   A proposition p is properly basic for a person S at a time t if and only if p is self-evident or incorrigible or evident to the senses for S at t.

It is fairly clear that belief in God's existence does not satisfy this criterion; it is neither self-evident nor incorrigible nor evident to the senses for humans at any time in this life. For the classical foundationalist, then, theistic belief requires support from propositional evidence or argument if it is to be rationally or justifiably held. To be sure, by parity of reasoning, the same goes for ever so many of the sense-perceptual and memorial beliefs we typically hold in the basic way, because they too fail to satisfy the classical foundationalist's criterion for proper basicality. However, this is not by itself a decisive objection if the classical foundationalist is engaged in a reconstructive project of the Cartesian sort. The classical foundationalist can try to base such sense-perceptual and memorial propositions on others that do satisfy the criterion; the customary candidates for this role are propositions about how the subject is being appeared to at a given time. And if this project fails, as a pessimistic induction from the history of modern philosophy would lead us to believe that it will, it is open to the classical foundationalist to conclude that many of the sense-perceptual and memorial beliefs we hold, as well as theistic beliefs, cannot withstand skeptical challenges.

Is there a more conclusive argument against classical foundationalism's criterion? Plantinga has observed that (13) is not properly basic by its own lights for any of us; it is neither self-evident nor incorrigible nor evident to the senses for humans. He seems to have taken it for granted at first that it follows directly from this fact that classical foundationalism is self-referentially incoherent and so must be rejected. I think it does not. The classical foundationalist can concede that (13) is not properly basic and then go on to argue inductively for her criterion from examples that satisfy it. Having recently acknowledged that this move is open to her, Plantinga imagines that "she proposes to develop a criterion of justified belief by assembling samples of justified and samples of unjustified belief and finding a criterion that best fits them" (Plantinga 2000, 95). But he argues that her prospects for carrying this procedure to a successful completion are dim. The main obstacle to success is the existence of examples such as the belief in God of our young Kansas theist. If we keep it firmly in mind that justification and proper basicality are to be understood in terms of being within one's epistemic rights or not violating duties, then we will find it very implausible that our Kansas theist's belief in God is unjustified or fails to be properly basic. We will reach a similar verdict about many of our own basic sense-perceptual and memorial beliefs that do not satisfy (13). So if the classical foundationalist does not rely on biased samples of justified and unjustified beliefs, it is unlikely that the results of her efforts will be inductive support for (13). And if she fails to garner such support for (13), it is hard to see how else she might argue successfully for it. Absent such an argument, (13) will be unjustified for her either because she bases it on propositions that fail to justify it or because she holds it in the basic way though it is not properly basic by its own lights.

I think the upshot is that classical foundationalism's criterion cannot be used to show that belief in God is never properly basic for anyone. But can it be shown that theistic belief is properly basic in certain conditions? If the theist could justify a criterion for proper basicality according to which belief in God is properly basic in certain conditions, thereby succeeding where the classical foundationalist has failed, perhaps this would count as showing theistic belief to be properly basic in those conditions. So we may ask how one would justify a criterion for proper basicality.

Plantinga's answer is that we should use the sort of inductive procedure we have seen he is willing to allow the classical foundationalist to employ. He says:

> We must assemble examples of beliefs and conditions such that the former are
> obviously properly basic in the latter, and examples of beliefs and conditions
> such that the former are obviously *not* properly basic in the latter. We must
> then frame hypotheses as to the necessary and sufficient conditions of proper
> basicality and test these hypotheses by reference to those examples. (Plantinga
> 1983, 76)

Call the set of examples thus assembled the initial data set. Plantinga realizes that the initial data set "should be revisable in the light of theory and under the

pressure of argument" (Plantinga 1983, 76). Just as in science, when we test theoretical hypotheses against empirical data we may sometimes throw away what
are called 'bad data points,' so also in philosophy, when we test criterial hypotheses
against intuitive data we may sometimes eliminate data from the initial set. For
we may discover that the initial data set is internally inconsistent or otherwise
defective. Or we may come up with some hypothesis that accounts for most of
the data in the initial set, though it conflicts with a few of them, and conclude
that its theoretical virtues justify accepting it and rejecting the conflicting data.

Plantinga supposes Christians will hold that belief in God is to be included
in their initial data sets in examples of beliefs that are obviously properly basic in
some conditions. He claims: "The Christian will of course suppose that belief in
God is entirely proper and rational; if he doesn't accept this belief on the basis of
other propositions, he will conclude that it is basic for him and quite properly
so" (Plantinga 1983, 77). I doubt that all Christians will be of one mind about
whether belief in God is ever properly basic. I am willing to grant, however, that
many Christians will regard it as properly basic in various conditions and will
therefore include the relevant examples in their initial data sets. But what follows
from this concession?

Nowhere does Plantinga actually work through the procedure of testing hypotheses about necessary and sufficient conditions for proper basicality against the
examples from initial data sets that include belief in God as properly basic in certain conditions. He seems simply to assume that the result of such an exercise
would be to justify a criterion according to which theistic beliefs are properly basic
in some conditions. I think this assumption is at best premature. Consider a scenario described by Hasker. Someone whose initial data set includes examples of
properly basic theistic beliefs frames a necessary condition for proper basicality
that is satisfied by most data in the initial set but not its theistic beliefs. Upon reflection, this person concludes that theoretical considerations favoring this necessary condition outweigh the intuition that supports including examples of theistic
beliefs among the data and so proceeds to eliminate them from the initial set and
to arrive at a criterion which, though it accounts for everything in the revised data
set, rules that theistic beliefs are never properly basic. The conclusion Hasker
draws is that "it is necessary actually to construct the criteria for proper basicality;
it is not sufficient to specify a few examples and just assume that they will be preserved by the criteria that eventually emerge" (Hasker 1998, 54). I concur. As I had
earlier said, we should pass judgment on the success of the enterprise of justifying
criteria for proper basicality according to which theistic beliefs are properly basic
in some conditions "only after it has been completed" (Quinn 1993, 21).

Hence I think Plantinga has not shown that theistic belief is properly basic
by justifying, or even by describing a procedure that is bound to justify, criteria
according to which it is properly basic in certain conditions. As I see it, intuitions

about particular examples remain the sole grounds for the claim that belief in God is properly basic in some conditions.

Nevertheless, I am firmly convinced that belief in God is properly basic for our youthful Kansas theist. But as I described her situation, she has not encountered any serious objections to theistic belief. Most educated adult theists in our culture have encountered such objections. Does belief in God remain properly basic for them, or do the objections serve to defeat it?

A great deal of effort has recently been expended in exploring the intricacies of the topic of epistemic defeat. For purposes of the present discussion, however, a simple conception will be adequate. A proposition is a potential defeater for properly basic theistic belief for a person just in case the person would not be rational or justified in both accepting theistic belief in the basic way and accepting that proposition. If a person in such a situation of conflict is rational or justified in accepting a potential defeater, then it is not rational or justified for the person to accept theistic belief in the basic way, even if the person does in fact hold belief in God in that way. In this case, the potential defeater is an actual defeater, and properly basic theistic belief is defeated. If, by contrast, the person in such a situation of conflict is rational or justified in accepting theistic belief in the basic way, then it is not rational or justified for the person to accept the potential defeater. In this case, the potential defeater is itself defeated, and theistic belief remains properly basic. Educated adult theists in our culture are aware of potential defeaters for properly basic theistic belief from several sources; the most prominent among them are projective explanations of theistic belief in the social sciences, the evils that infest the world, and the phenomenon of religious diversity. Do such potential defeaters, either individually or collectively, actually serve to defeat properly basic theistic belief?

Clearly, a maximally strong potential defeater for properly basic theistic belief is the following proposition:

(14)   God does not exist.

In our debate, Plantinga and I disagreed sharply about the extent to which considerations involving projective explanations and evils support or justify accepting (14) for those who are aware of them. I think the issues that divide us remain unresolved and thus deserve to be rehearsed in the present discussion.

Consider first evils. I share Plantinga's view that there is no deductive proof of (14) from premises about the existence or amount of evil in the world, but I differ with him about whether there is a grave but unsolved evidential problem of evil. My initial claim was this: "What I know, partly from experience and partly from testimony, about the amount and variety of nonmoral evil in the universe confirms highly for me the proposition expressed by (14)" (Quinn 1985, 481). I am now less confident than I was then that nonmoral evil confirms (14) *highly*, but I remain convinced that it is confirmed by such evil. Plantinga's counter claim was this: "So far as I can see, no atheologian has given a successful or cogent way of working out or developing a probabilistic atheological argument from evil; and I believe there are good reasons for thinking that it can't be done" (Plantinga 1986, 309). But even if it cannot be shown that (14) is highly probable given the amount and variety of nonmoral evil in the world, and, indeed, even if it turns out not to be probable on that evil, it does not follow that (14) is not confirmed by that evil unless it is also assumed that confirmation must be understood probabilistically. I do not accept this assumption. It seems to me that the failure of the Carnapian tradition in philosophy of science to construct a generally acceptable probabilistic confirmation theory gives me sufficient reason not to accept it. What is more, the claim that (14) is confirmed by the nonmoral evil in the world is in my initial data set against which philosophical theories of confirmation are to be tested. And I know of no probabilistic confirmation theory whose other merits are so great that they rationally require me to eliminate it from my initial set. So I continue to think that the nonmoral evil in the world is evidence against the existence of God and has some justificatory force in support of (14). However, I do not claim that (14) is confirmed by my total evidence. Everything I have said so far is consistent with (14) being highly disconfirmed by my total evidence.

Consider next projective accounts of theistic belief of the sort proposed by Feuerbach, Marx, Freud, Durkheim, and their disciples. According to such accounts, there is in human psychology a mechanism, usually hidden from introspective awareness, that under a wide variety of conditions constructs a concept of an idealized human nature, father figure, or social group and then projects it onto the external world by postulating an entity which instantiates the concept. The formation and persistence of theistic belief is explained wholly in terms of the operations of the mechanism; there is no explanatory role for contact or interaction with an entity of the kind postulated by the mechanism to play in accounting for theistic belief. Even if there were by chance an entity of that kind, it would be explanatorily idle. But if projective accounts do explain theistic beliefs in a wide variety of circumstances, leaving unexplained no more anomalies than other good theories, then appeal can be made, in the customary way, to principles of economy in order to support the conclusion that the postulated entity does not exist because it plays no role in the best available scientific explanation of theistic beliefs.

In our debate, Plantinga adopted a very dismissive attitude toward projection theories. He said: "Freud's jejune speculations as to the psychological origin of religion and Marx's careless claims about its social role can't sensibly be taken as providing argument or reason for (14), i.e., for the nonexistence of God; so taken they present textbook cases (which in fact are pretty rare) of the genetic fallacy" (Plantinga 1986, 308). I think his judgment was, at the very least, uncharitable in the extreme. My rejoinder was: "I believe that projection hypotheses have so far achieved a real, but limited, success in explaining religious beliefs of some sorts, and I think this success does give the intellectually sophisticated adult theist in our culture a substantial reason for thinking that (14) is true" (Quinn 1993, 42). This remains my view, though I would now describe the reason provided by the limited success of projective explanations as nontrivial rather than substantial to avoid any hint of rhetorical exaggeration.

It seems fairly clear to me that projective accounts do provide the best explanations of theistic beliefs in some instances. Even traditional theists should find them attractive in cases of two sorts: those in which theistic beliefs portray God as an especially harsh and unloving tyrant; and those in which theistic beliefs are used to rationalize ways of life that are systematically at odds with the command to love the neighbor as oneself. So projective accounts have, as I see it, some inductive support. Moreover, as Hasker has argued, to the extent that they are successful, they undercut "the claim that theistic beliefs are non-inferentially justified by religious experience" (Hasker 1998, 62). For example, if my basic belief that God is speaking to me is grounded solely in some experience I have when reading the Bible, then, to the extent that I have reason to believe that a projective mechanism explains the experience and the belief, I also have reason to believe that the experience is not an adequate ground for the belief and so to conclude that the belief is not properly basic under this condition. Hence I think the success of projective explanations too is evidence against the existence of God and has some justificatory force in support of (14).

Yet a balanced picture must also acknowledge that the success of projective explanations of theistic beliefs is currently limited in several ways. The search for projective accounts has not yielded any theory with the explanatory power of Newtonian mechanics. This is not to be expected in the social sciences, however; and we should heed Aristotle's warning about not asking for more than the subject matter permits. In addition, some projective accounts are embedded in larger theoretical systems that are extremely vulnerable to criticism. Many of Freud's claims to have given scientific explanations, for example, have been discredited by critics such as Adolf Grünbaum. Moreover, projection theorists have not constructed a general or unified account of projective mechanisms and their operations. It may well be that there are several such mechanisms awaiting discovery. And it is now far from clear what the full scope of projective explanations will turn out to be. It certainly has not been shown that projective explanations will successfully cover the entire range of theistic beliefs; in fact, at present it seems intuitively unlikely that they will do so. But, despite these limitations, I remain convinced that projective accounts have had some successes and thus do have real evidential force.

In our debate, Plantinga and I did not exchange views about the problem of religious diversity, but it is clear that we share the view that it is a source of potential defeaters for properly basic theistic belief for those who are sufficiently aware of it. Nontheistic religions such as Theravada Buddhism and Advaita Hinduism seem to be no less well supported than theistic religions by experiential grounds and philosophical arguments. In the absence of independent reasons for thinking one's own theistic religion is epistemically superior to such nontheistic rivals, they remain uneliminated competitors to any theistic religion. Their core nontheistic beliefs are therefore potential defeaters for theistic beliefs.

I consider it significant that Alston regards religious diversity as the most difficult problem for his defense of the rationality of engaging in CMP, the distinctively Christian experiential doxastic practice. If our only respectable basis for a positive epistemic evaluation of CMP were the fact that it is socially established and has not been shown to be unreliable, he tells us, religious diversity would reduce its epistemic status to an alarming degree. Given the epistemic parity of uneliminated competitors with respect to social establishment and lack of an argument that shows unreliability, the most reasonable hypothesis would be that, in each case, social establishment reflects a culturally generated way of reinforcing socially desirable attitudes and practices, in which case "the justificatory efficacy of any of these practices has been dissipated altogether" (Alston 1991, 276). What blocks complete dissipation, according to Alston, is that each of the practices also enjoys significant self-support. Even so, on the assumption that significant independent reasons for epistemically preferring CMP to its rivals are absent, Alston is only prepared to claim that, given religious diversity, "the justificatory efficacy of CMP is by no means dissipated, though it may be significantly weakened" (Alston 1991, 270). And critics have challenged his argument for the conclusion that, despite the significant weakening, continuing to engage in CMP is the rational thing for its practitioners to do.

I think there are parallels to the case of religious experiential doxastic practices, as Alston understands it, in the case of basic theistic beliefs. For those who are sufficiently aware of it, religious diversity that includes nontheistic religions weakens the justification of basic theistic beliefs and strengthens the justification of some of their potential defeaters. I conclude that religious diversity is also evidence against the existence of God and has some justificatory force in support of (14). Of course, by epistemic parity, religious diversity will then be evidence against the absolutes or ultimates of competing nontheistic religions and furnish justificatory force to some of their defeaters too.

It may turn out that, for some people, neither evil, nor projective explanations nor religious diversity by itself makes it rational or justified to accept a defeater of properly basic theistic belief, yet they add up or otherwise cooperate to raise the epistemic status of a potential defeater above the threshold at which it becomes an actual defeater. Like arguments for theistic belief, objections can in principle constitute a cumulative case, and it can result in the defeat of properly basic theistic belief.

It is not likely that we will be able to say anything precise or general about how many educated adult theists in our culture whose belief in God is basic have actual defeaters for properly basic theistic belief. Much will depend on such factors as the kind of experience that grounds their belief in God. The experience Moses had when he heard a voice speaking from the burning bush is apt to make properly basic belief more resistant to defeat than the experience an ordinary theist has when reading a biblical passage and being struck by the sense that God is speaking to him. Yet I think it is possible to say something illuminating about my disagreement with Plantinga. He attributes little if any justificatory force to the individual objections to theistic belief, and he just seems to take it for granted that they seldom if ever combine to defeat properly basic belief in God. I share Hasker's suspicion that "quite a few theists will fail to be satisfied by Plantinga's approach to this problem" (Hasker 1998, 62). I think each of the three objections to theistic belief considered in this essay has significant justificatory force on its own, and I am convinced that they frequently combine to defeat properly basic belief in God. So Plantinga thinks there are many fewer adult educated theists in our culture than I do whose properly basic belief in God is actually defeated. I thus believe that there are many more people than he does whose belief in God will be rational or justified only if it is supported by a cumulative case that includes arguments from natural theology of the sort discussed in the previous section of this essay. Such people need those arguments, or at least need testimony that the experts have such arguments, if their theistic beliefs are to be justified or rational. For them, belief in God will be justified or rational only if it is based in part on such arguments or testimony about them and is therefore not basic and a fortiori not properly basic.

When Plantinga focuses his attention on warrant in his later phase, he distinguishes between proper basicality with respect to justification, which is the sort of proper basicality that has been under consideration up to this point, and proper basicality with respect to warrant. A belief is properly basic with respect to warrant for a person at a time if and only if the person accepts the belief in the basic way at the time and it then has warrant for the person, accepted in that way. He also fleshes out his general concept of warrant as that which, when enough of it is added to true belief, yields knowledge with a specific conception or theory of warrant. According to that theory's core idea, "a belief has warrant for a person S only if that belief is produced in S by cognitive faculties functioning properly (subject to no dysfunction) in a cognitive environment that is appropriate for S's kind of cognitive faculties, according to a design plan that is successfully aimed at truth" (Plantinga 2000, 156). When a belief satisfies these conditions and has warrant, the degree of warrant it enjoys depends, in a way that is directly proportional, on the strength or firmness with which it is held.

Plantinga argues that if theistic belief is true and is held in the basic way, then it probably does have warrant. Sketched out in rough fashion, his argument proceeds in the following way. If theistic belief is true, then God created us and means for us to come to have knowledge of God. If this is the case, it is natural to think that God created us in such a way that we would come to have true theistic beliefs. And if that is so, it is natural to think that God endowed us with faculties and placed us in an environment such that, when the faculties do produce belief in God, they are functioning properly in an appropriate environment and in accord with a design plan successfully aimed at truth. But if that is the case, then our theistic beliefs have warrant. Of course, this argument is not a proof. As Plantinga acknowledges, it is not even deductively valid, and it does not rule out the possibility that our theistic beliefs are produced by cognitive faculties that malfunction on account of damage done by our race's fall into sin. Yet he thinks the more probable thing is that theistic beliefs, even when held in the basic way, do have warrant. And a parallel argument leads him to the conclusion that if theistic belief is false, but is held in the basic way, then it probably has no warrant.

If Plantinga's views on these two points are correct, the dialectical situation assumes the following shape. From within a theistic perspective, there is a very direct argument for the conclusion that basic theistic belief probably has warrant. But if it is addressed to an atheistic naturalist, this argument will be dialectically deficient because it begs the question. By the same token, from within the atheistic naturalist's perspective, there is a very direct argument for the conclusion that basic theistic belief probably has no warrant. But if it is addressed to a theist, this argument will also be dialectically deficient because it begs the question. And both these direct arguments will be dialectically deficient if addressed to anyone who is not antecedently committed either to theism or to atheistic naturalism or to anyone in search of reasons for thinking that basic theistic belief has warrant, or reasons for thinking that basic theistic belief lacks warrant, that are independent of the truth or falsity of theism.

In the preface to the third volume of his trilogy on warrant, Plantinga tells the reader that he is simultaneously engaged in two projects. He says: "The first is addressed to everyone, believer and nonbeliever alike; it is intended as a contribution to an ongoing public discussion of the epistemology of Christian belief; it does not appeal to specifically Christian premises or presuppositions. I shall argue that, from this public point of view, there isn't the faintest reason to think that Christian belief lacks justification, rationality, or warrant—at least no reason that does not presuppose the *falsehood* of Christian belief" (Plantinga 2000, xiii). Within the confines of this public project, it would clearly be illegitimate for Plantinga to make use of the direct argument for the conclusion that basic theistic belief has warrant. The book's other project is an exercise in Christian philosophy, an effort to answer philosophical questions from a Christian perspective. Within the bounds of this project, he could legitimately make use of that argument.

When we focus on Plantinga's public project, we should understand the familiar objections to belief in God as sources of potential defeaters for theistic belief that is properly basic with respect to warrant. Plantinga has taken it upon himself to show, without relying on theistic presuppositions, that there is no reason, apart from those presupposing the falsity of theism, to think that the potential defeaters, either individually or collectively, have enough warrant to defeat theistic belief that is properly basic with respect to warrant. And so he revisits some familiar topics. At the end of a discussion of Freud that is much more nuanced than his earlier remarks, he concludes that Freud's reason for thinking that belief in God lacks warrant "really depends on his atheism" (Plantinga 2000, 198). A chapter devoted to the problem of evil arrives at the conclusion that "the atheologian can properly claim that evil constitutes a defeater for Christian belief, therefore, only if he already assumes that Christian belief is false" (Plantinga 2000, 492). He also explicitly considers the problem of religious diversity. After conceding that awareness of the facts of religious diversity can decrease the warrant of theistic belief by decreasing the strength with which it is held, he concludes that the facts of religious diversity "do not or need not constitute a defeater for Christian belief" (Plantinga 2000, 457). It seems to me the only major gap in Plantinga's treatment of these issues is his failure to consider the possibility that the potential defeaters combine to compose a cumulative case strong enough to defeat theistic belief that would otherwise remain properly basic with respect to warrant. I consider it rather likely that, for some people at least, awareness of particularly horrendous evils, when coupled with awareness of religious diversity, would serve to decrease the firmness with which their theistic beliefs are held, when accepted in the basic way, to such a degree that they cease to be properly basic with respect to warrant. In saying this, am I presupposing the falsity of theism? I think not. I am not claiming that theistic belief never has warrant when it is accepted in the basic way.

Having only recently appeared in print when this essay was being written, Plantinga's book on warranted Christian belief had at that time not yet been much discussed in the published literature. But its public project seems likely to attract critics. Several strategies are available to them. They might contest his theory of warrant, or they might argue that theistic presuppositions are implicit in the book's responses to some of the potential defeaters. However, I think the most promising critical enterprise would be to argue, without presupposing the falsity of theism, that several of the potential defeaters have some warrant individually and enough warrant collectively to defeat in many cases theistic belief that is properly basic with respect to warrant. In such cases, belief in God will have enough warrant to be knowledge only if it is supported by a cumulative case that includes arguments from natural theology, in which case it will be based in part on their premises and so will not be basic and a fortiori will not be properly basic.

But Plantinga's book is more than 500 pages long, and its arguments are quite intricate. It would not be possible in a single essay to give them the detailed attention needed to vindicate the claim that this critical strategy can deliver on the promise I attribute to it. So having guided my readers up to what is currently the cutting edge of debate in religious epistemology, I must conclude by inviting you to examine Plantinga's execution of his public project and to judge for yourselves whether he has brought it to a successful completion.

REFERENCES

Alston, William P. (1991). *Perceiving God: The Epistemology of Religious Experience*. Ithaca, N.Y.: Cornell University Press.

Hasker, William (1998). "The Foundations of Theism: Scoring the Quinn-Plantinga Debate." *Faith and Philosophy* 15, no. 1: 52–67.

Mavrodes, George I. (1970). *Belief in God: A Study in the Epistemology of Religion*. New York: Random House.

Plantinga, Alvin (1974). *The Nature of Necessity*. Oxford: Clarendon.

———. (1983). "Reason and Belief in God." In *Faith and Rationality: Reason and Belief in God*, ed. Alvin Plantinga and Nicholas Wolterstorff. Notre Dame: University of Notre Dame Press. 16–93.

———. (1986). "The Foundations of Theism: A Reply." *Faith and Philosophy* 3, no. 3: 298–313.

———. (1993a). *Warrant: The Current Debate*. New York: Oxford University Press.

———. (1993b). *Warrant and Proper Function*. New York: Oxford University Press.

———. (2000). *Warranted Christian Belief*. New York: Oxford University Press.

Quinn, Philip L. (1985). "In Search of the Foundations of Theism." *Faith and Philosophy* 2, no. 4: 469–486.

———. (1993). "The Foundations of Theism Again: A Rejoinder to Plantinga." In *Rational Faith: Catholic Responses to Reformed Epistemology*, ed. Linda Zagzebski. Notre Dame: University of Notre Dame Press.

Rowe, William L. (1975). *The Cosmological Argument*. Princeton: Princeton University Press.

Swinburne, Richard (1979). *The Existence of God*. Oxford: Clarendon.

Wolterstorff, Nicholas (1976). *Reason within the Bounds of Religion*. Grand Rapids, Mich.: Eerdmans.

CHAPTER 19

FORMAL PROBLEMS ABOUT KNOWLEDGE

ROY SORENSEN

IN one episode of the children's cartoon series "Arthur," Arthur's sister, DW, threatens to tell on him. Arthur replies that if DW tells on him, he will tell that she told on him. DW counters that she would then tell that he told that she told on him. At that stage, Arthur gives up.

But Arthur and DW could have gone on endlessly. Their tattling becomes complex in an orderly way. A longer tattle results from applying the rule that informing on someone for informing is itself informing. This output can become the input for another application of the rule. Just as large crystals can be understood via the repeating patterns that govern their growth, complicated epistemological phenomena can be understood by virtue of their underlying recursive structure.

1. THE INEVITABILITY OF RECURSION

When phenomena are open-ended, there is no alternative to recursion. Consider common knowledge. When you draw my attention to your pierced navel, you know that I know you have a pierced navel. And I know you know that I know you have a pierced navel. And so on indefinitely. Since we only have finite resources for contemplating your naval, we must possess common knowledge in virtue of rules that allow outputs to become inputs.

Englishmen know the meanings of the infinitely many sentences that constitute English because each sentence of English can be generated with a finite primitive vocabulary plus a finite battery of rules for combining those terms into sentences. For instance, one of the rules of English is that if S is a declarative sentence, then 'It is known that S' is a sentence. Applying the rule to this second sentence yields the sentence 'It is known that it is known that S'. Sentences with indefinitely many 'It is known that' clauses can be created by this cycle.

Grammaticality does not suffice for truth. 'S' can be true without 'It is known that S' being true. To obtain rules that always generate true outputs from true inputs, we need a deductive system.

Standard logic (first order predicate logic with identity) is a well-understood deductive system. But it is not strong enough to capture special inferences that 'know' appears to license. For instance, we would like to have the resources to formulate a reservation about Arthur's threat. If his mother has a rule against tattling, then Arthur's mother will know DW has violated the rule as soon as she tattles on Arthur. There would be no need for Arthur to point out his sister's infraction. Indeed, Arthur's protest would be worse than redundant. For it would itself be an easily detectable infraction of the rule and so get Arthur into trouble— maybe even double-trouble for being a hypocrite. DW should foresee that he would lack a reason to carry out his threat. And Arthur should anticipate his sister's foresight and thus not bother with the bootless warning.

Thinkers have attempted to integrate a logic of knowledge into economics and game theory (Bacharach 1997). After all, common knowledge plays a strong role in the formation of strategy, conventions, and social institutions. Epistemic logic has also attracted the attention of computer scientists modeling question–answer systems (Meyer and van der Hoek 1995). Philosophers of language have recently applied epistemic logic to vagueness (Williamson 1994). The breadth of possible applications widens when one considers the precedent of probability theory.

2. THE ANALOGY BETWEEN KNOWLEDGE AND NECESSITY

Our rules for attributing knowledge embody principles that go beyond those sufficient for formulating mathematical proofs. If we wish to validate these patterns of inference, we will need to add extra inference rules to standard logic. The resulting *supplemental* logic will expand the system's set of theorems. (Deviant logics have the reverse effect of shrinking the set of theorems.)

Hundreds of supplemental logics have been proposed. The most impressive are modal logics. And of these, the most successful are logics dealing with necessity and possibility. Logics of necessity date back to Aristotle. After a period of stagnation and skepticism, logicians in the 1950s and 1960s managed to give logics of necessity a rigorous semantics. Although some skeptics remain, most of the doubters have been marginalized by the achievements of these pioneering logicians.

Some of these pioneers (most notably Jaakko Hintikka) scouted for opportunities to expand their conquests. They believed that what had been done for necessity could be done for knowledge. The basis for their optimism is the long appreciated analogy between knowledge and necessity.

Part of the resemblance between knowledge and necessity is at the level of inference rules. At first blush, there is the following parallel: Knowledge and necessity each entail truth. Each distribute and collect over conjunction and material conditionals. Each reiterate. That is, if a proposition is necessary, then it is necessarily necessary. And if a proposition is known, then it is known that it is known. Any logical consequence of a necessary proposition is itself necessary. A restricted form of this closure principle has been long presupposed for knowledge: If one knows that p and knows that p entails q, then one knows that q.

Knowledge and necessity also exhibit syntactic similarities such as the *de dicto/de re* distinction. Consequently, the syntactic equivocations involving necessity forewarn us of epistemic fallacies.

The modal words *might, possible,* and *could* are ambiguous between alethic possibility and epistemic possibility. When a mathematician says that Goldbach's conjecture might be true, he cannot be charitably interpreted as saying it is alethically possible that Goldbach's conjecture is true. Any alethically possible mathematical statement is a necessary truth. But the mathematician does not commit himself to the truth of Goldbach's conjecture. He means something like, 'For all we know, Goldbach's conjecture is true'.

There is an underlying semantic rationale for the similarity between the alethic and epistemic senses of 'possible'. Both knowledge and necessity exclude luck. If I know that p, then it is not an accident that my belief that p is true (Unger 1968). The belief *must* be correct because the alternatives are ruled out by my evidence (or for reliabilists, by the method or process by which the belief originated). If someone can show that my evidence is compatible with p being false, then they have shown that I do not know that p. Skeptics generalize this strategy by constructing clever counterexplanations of my evidence.

A supplemental logic can illuminate epistemological matters without being an epistemic logic. Consider the old argument that contingent truths are unknowable: "Necessarily, knowledge implies truth. A contingent truth is possibly false. Therefore, no contingent truth is known." This argument relies on the inference

□(Kp → p) therefore, (Kp → □p). Thus it fallaciously passes from the necessity of the consequence to the necessity of the consequent. Medieval logicians noted that the same fallacy is committed by those who believe free choice is precluded by foreknowledge. A Scottish waitress can know that an adventuresome tourist will order haggis without this knowledge making 'He will choose haggis' a necessary truth. The logic of necessity does all the work here. Can an epistemic logic teach its own lessons?

3. THE FITCH PROOF AND THE SURPRISE-TEST PARADOX

The ambitions of epistemic logicians can be illustrated against the background of the system KT. This epistemic analogue of the modal system deontic S4 licenses the following inferences:

KI: ⊢p   KDE: K(p → q)   KD&: K(p & q)
—————   —————————   ——————————
Kp   Kp → Kq   Kp & Kq

KEI: Kp   [Where (P & Q) → R   KK: Kp   KE: Kp
—————   ————   ————
Kq   is a truth of logic]   KKp   p
——
Kr

Although there are some controversial principles in this system, the uncontroversial KE ("Knowledge implies truth") and KD ("Knowledge distributes over conjunction") suffice for Frederic Fitch's simple proof that some propositions are unknowable.

1. K(p & Kp)   Assume
2. Kp & KKp   1, KD
3. ~Kp   2, KE (from the second conjunct)
4. Kp & ~Kp 2, 3 by conjunction elimination of the first conjunct and then conjunction introduction
5. ~K(p & ~Kp) 1, 4 *reductio ad absurdum*

Since all the assumptions are discharged, the conclusion is a necessary truth. (Well, a schema for a necessary truth; you can fill in the values of 'p' at your leisure.) Idealism, logical positivism, and other verificationist philosophies imply that all truths are knowable. Astonishingly, they seem refuted by this pinch of epistemic logic. (For a review of efforts to slither out of this simple argument, see chapter 12 of Williamson 2000.)

The 'Kp' notation is felicitously coarse. Sure, this crude symbolization fails to reflect the fact that knowledge requires a knower and that the knower's knowledge varies over time. But since the argument is valid in this less informative notation, it will be valid under any more detailed notation. Introducing irrelevant detail is misleading. The proof is solid as it stands. Coarse sandpaper is better for some modeling projects than fine sandpaper.

Notation of a finer grain is genuinely needed to model the surprise-test paradox: A teacher announces that there will be a surprise test next week. Arthur is a clever student and protests that the surprise test is impossible: "Everybody knows class meets Mondays, Wednesdays, and Fridays. If the test were on Friday, then on Thursday I could predict it. Consequently, a Friday test would not be a surprise. Could the test be given on Wednesday? Since that would now be the last possible day, the previous reasoning for Friday also eliminates Wednesday. This leaves Monday as the only possible test day. All this reasoning would be available to me on Sunday, so a Monday test would also fail to be surprising. Therefore, a surprise test is impossible." What are we to say to Master Arthur? The words of Lady Brute come to mind: "I think, sir, your sophistry has all the effect you can reasonably expect it should have: it puzzles, but don't convince" (from John Vanbrugh's *The Provok'd Wife*). But we still want to know *where* the argument goes wrong.

W. V. Quine (1953) diagnosed the problem as a false premise. The announcement itself does not lead to absurdity—only *knowledge* of the announcement leads to absurdity. Therefore, Quine treats Arthur's argument as a *reductio* of the supposition that Arthur *knows* that the teacher's announcement is true.

But if Arthur cannot trust his teachers, who can he trust? The only way to deny that Arthur knows the announcement is to deny that we gain knowledge by testimony or to deny that we can have knowledge of the future. Since the surprise-test paradox can be formulated in terms of justified belief instead of knowledge, the denial would have to extend to justification as well. And indeed, Quine's later (1969) essay "Epistemology Naturalized" embraces eliminativism. Unlike the skeptic, who admits that knowledge is a coherent notion (for he wants 'Little or nothing is known' to come out true), Quine has no room at all for epistemic normativity. Having Quine on the editorial board of *The Skeptical Inquirer* is like having the feminist Gloria Steinem on the editorial board of *Playboy*.

Those who believe we know much of what we seem to know will prefer to challenge the paradoxical *"reductio"*. But it must be conceded that the announcement contains unknowable elements. To see this, let 'Ka$_1$M' read 'Arthur knows on Sunday that the test is on Monday', 'Ka$_2$W' read 'Arthur knows on Tuesday that the test is on Wednesday', and 'Ka$_3$F' read 'Arthur knows on Wednesday that the test is on Friday'. The teacher's announcement can then be symbolized as a disjunction:

(A): (M & ~Ka$_1$.M) or (W & ~Ka$_2$.W) or (F & ~Ka$_3$.F)

Each of the disjuncts is personally unknowable to Arthur. However, a disjunction of unknowable propositions can itself be knowable. Witness 'Either the stars are even and no one knows it or the number of stars is odd and no one knows it'. Arthur could know this. And he could know the teacher's announcement.

The paradoxical argument assumes that a subject will continue to know the announcement throughout the week. Crispin Wright and Aidan Sudbury formulate this as an inference rule, the "temporal retention principle", which allows one to infer that a proposition is known at one time if it is known at some earlier time. When this principle is inserted into the environment of KT, we can validate Arthur's elimination argument (Sorensen 1988, 289–290).

Given our unwillingness to challenge Arthur's premises, the only way to avoid his paradoxical conclusion is to reject an inference rule. A natural strategy is to challenge the most controversial inference rule employed in the deduction. Arthur's argument involves predictions about what he will know under certain scenarios. These predictions are inferred with the KK principle. There are counter-examples to KK that involve a potpourri of cognitive lapses and imperfections. They may work in practice. But could they work in theory? After all, the surprise-test situation could arise among ideal thinkers.

At first blush, the appeal to ideal thinkers also quashes any challenge to the temporal retention principle. Ideal thinkers never forget. However, there are other ways of losing knowledge. Consider Arthur's predicament on Thursday. At that juncture, Arthur cannot know both that no test has been given and that there will be a surprise test. For that would imply

(B)   The test is on Friday and Arthur does not know it before Friday.

Although (B) is consistent and might be knowable by others, (B) cannot be known by Arthur (recall the Fitch proof above). Hence, the teacher can give a surprise test on Friday because waiting past Wednesday would force the Thursday Arthur to lose his knowledge of the original announcement (A).

Knowledge can be lost without forgetting anything. This is a consequence of the fact that there are propositions which are individually knowable and even co-possible but which are not co-knowable. If one of these relative blindspots becomes known, then its partner is rendered unknown.

Co-knowability issues crop up more expectedly for distinct people. The following petition was printed in the November 1985 *Proceedings of the American Philosophical Association*: "Proposed nominees must be asked to consent to nomination, and before giving a firm answer must be told who the other nominees are to be" (278). Opponents of the motion objected that the proposal was contradictory: if one nominee knows the identities of all other nominees, then the remaining nominees could not know the identity of all other nominees. Keeping one nominee informed conflicts with keeping other nominees informed. Similarly, in the scenario in which a test is given on Friday, the early Arthur can be kept informed only at the expense of a later Arthur.

Actually, the petition to give each nominee foreknowledge of all other nominees is not quite contradictory. The petition merely implies that there are no nominees. An anarchist could consistently endorse the petition. The surprise-test paradox is disanalogous. The teacher's announcement is not that any test that there might be will be a surprise test. The teacher says there will be a surprise test.

Notice that, Arthur's *mother* need not lose *her* knowledge that there will be a surprise test. Since she is not among those who are to be surprised by the test, there is no logical pressure against attributing uninterrupted knowledge of the announcement to her. (B) is a "blindspot" for Arthur but not a blindspot for his mother.

This epistemological asymmetry between Arthur and his mother conflicts with the principle that ideal thinkers must agree if they have the same evidence and inference rules. Their disagreement must be explained in terms of their distinct ranges of rationally believable propositions.

4. KNOWLEDGE BY PROOF

Philosophers have tried to connect the surprise-test paradox to a wide variety of issues: logical fatalism, mixed strategies in game theory, Gödel's incompleteness theorems, the preface paradox, Moore's problem, and especially the liar paradox. Richard Montague and David Kaplan (1960) argue that the teacher's announcement really has a self-referential form, 'Either the test will happen on Friday and you will not know it before Friday or the test will happen on Wednesday and you will not know it before Wednesday or the test will happen on Monday and you will not know it before Monday or *this announcement is known to be false*.'

The number of test days could be decreased or increased—even to infinity

(Sorensen 1999). Perversely, Kaplan and Montague argue that the nerve of the paradox is exposed when the number of alternatives is reduced to *zero*. If the teacher announces 'This announcement is known to be false', then Arthur appears to have a simple rigorous proof of the announcement. Assume the announcement is false. Then it is known. But if known, then it is true. So the announcement cannot be false. Therefore, the announcement is true. Yet the proof cannot give knowledge. For if it did, the announcement would be true and hence false.

The Kaplan–Montague interpretation of the announcement does not seem faithful to the intent of the original posers of the paradox. And it is reckless! Note that the formulation as (A) uses sentences that are subject to Fitch's proof. This locates the paradox safely away from the vicinity of the liar paradox. Kaplan and Montague are artificially repositioning the paradox. By coming so close to the notorious liar paradox, they play with fire.

Many experiments with the liar paradox have resulted in emoliation. Still, it is overly cautious to entirely suppress pyromania. Georg Cantor's diagonal argument, Kurt Godel's incompleteness theorem, and Alan Turing's halting theorem have all been cooked up by reasoning just above the fires of "self-referential paradox". Each of these great thinkers comes close to the flames without getting burnt.

Well, not *badly* burnt. Cantor did get singed by Bertrand Russell's (1918, 260–262) paradox about the set of all sets that do not contain themselves as a member. Godel came so close that he had lingering, neurotic worries that he had been burnt. In any case, let us follow Kaplan and Montague along their trail of embers.

The path may have been blazed before. The knower paradox is closely related to Jean Buridan's sophism 'I do not believe this very sentence'. Believing Buridan's sentence is self-defeating. By inhibiting belief, the sentence ensures its truth. To be aware of a sentence's truth is to believe it. Hence, I am unable to form a stable attitude toward 'I do not believe this very sentence'. I cannot know whether I believe it.

An onlooking psychologist could know whether I believe it because the sentence does not go false when *he* believes the sentence. The sentence is about *my* beliefs, not his. The personal nature of this paradox is not shared by the universal variant 'No one believes this very sentence'.

Is there a personal variant of the knower paradox?

KS: Roy Sorensen knows this very sentence is false.

KA: Tony Anderson knows this very sentence is false.

If I know KS, then it would follow that I did not know it. So I cannot know KS. Can others know KS? It is not directly self-defeating for them to claim knowledge of KS. They appear free to use the preceding proof that I do not know KS to gain knowledge that I do not know KS. Accordingly, Tony Anderson (1983, 349) thinks he knows KS. Tony Anderson also thinks I know KA even though he cannot. So do other commentators on the knower such as Thomas Tymoczko (1984, 443) and Raymond Smullyan (1982, 99–100).

I disagree. True, I do not *directly* defeat myself by claiming to know KA. But I do *indirectly* defeat myself. If I know KA, then Tony Anderson knows KS. For our epistemic situations are symmetrical. But if I know that Tony Anderson knows KS, then I know KS. Since I cannot know KS, I cannot know that Tony Anderson knows KS. Therefore, I cannot know KA. Unlike Buridan's 'I do not believe this sentence', the knower sentence does not generate personal paradoxes.

Commentators on Moore's problem carefully distinguish between two interpretations of 'Human beings have 206 bones but I do not believe it' (Williams 1979). One parsing corresponds to an error of omission, 'p & Bp', while the other parsing corresponds to an error of commission 'p & Bp'. Proofs that one cannot consistently believe 'p & B~p' require less resources than proofs that one cannot consistently believe 'p & Bp'. This makes the 'p & Bp' variation more powerful and interesting. Further differences emerge when the belief operator is iterated (Sorensen 2000). 'Human beings have 206 bones but I believe that I believe that I believe that . . . I believe they do not' is unbelievable. But 'Human beings have 206 bones but it is not the case that I believe that I believe that . . . I believe human beings have 206 bones' is believable.

Attention to the position of the negation sign in the knower paradox is also rewarding. The original knower paradox has the commissive form:

KC: This sentence is known to be false.

However, some commentators (such as Smullyan and Tymockyo) drift into an *omissive* variation of the knower paradox:

KO: No one knows this very sentence.

Their unhistorical placement of the negation improves the paradox by diluting the content of the paradoxical claim. After all, skeptics escape the original KC version by denying that there is any knowledge. But the absence of knowledge would entail the truth of KO.

The most influential solution to the knower paradox imputes a hidden hierarchical structure to knowledge. The idea is based on Charles Parsons's (1974) solution to the liar paradox. The basic idea is that 'true' is an indexical term such as *here, I, now*, and *yesterday*. Just as there is a sense in which 'I' changes meaning with each speaker's use, there is a sense in which 'true' changes meaning with each new use of 'true'. The liar paradox is puzzling because we do not want to affirm L but wish to affirm M:

L: L is not true.

M: L is not true.

This seems inconsistent because L and M are tokens of the same sentence type. They refer to the same sentence. However, if the utterance of L changes the meaning of 'true', then there need be no inconsistency.

Tyler Burge (1984) elaborates the hierarchical approach. He extends it to puzzles involving truth-oriented propositional attitudes. Burge's solution to the knower paradox is that 'know' inherits the indexicality of 'true'. When we appear to echo 'This is not known' in the course of our reasoning about it, we are actually thinking a different thought than we appear to think. In other words, KM does not exactly repeat what KL says:

KL: KL is not known.

KM: KL is not known.

When we deduce KM from the argument which reasons about KL, we subtlely equivocate. Thus we can know$_2$ that 'No one knows$_1$ this sentence'.

Postulations of ambiguities are treated with suspicion by epistemologists. Sense splitters have long claimed that debates with skeptics are verbal disputes (involving a weak and strong sense of 'know'). The splitters resolve the tension between science and religion by claiming 'know' is used differently in 'I know a river made the Grand Canyon' and 'I know a god made the Howe Cavern'. But this simple kind of solution comes at the price of proliferating semantic entities. Semantic theories that minimize the number and variety of readings of 'know' are preferable on grounds of parsimony.

Critics doubt that the hierarchical ambiguities exist. But even if they do exist, what prevents us from univocally formulating the knower by fixing our attention on say, level 1, of the hierarchy? One might answer: "Well that would lead to the contradiction that someone knows$_1$ that 'No one knows$_1$ this sentence'. "But this rejoinder only festoons the original paradox with subscripts. The hierarchical approach must find some independent rationale for banning the sentence. This ban must also cover variations of the knower paradox that use an existential generalization. They must say 'This statement is not known at any level' is ill-formed. Given that we are getting into the business of banning sentences, why not ban the knower sentence itself at the ground level? Why straddle up the burgeoning beanstalk of knowledge$_n$?

Even if the ban can be formulated, it will fail to stop a variant of the knower paradox. This version involves two sentences that are named after the contentious twins in Lewis Carroll's *Through the Looking-Glass*:

Tweedledee: Tweedledum is not known.

Tweedledum: Tweedledee is not known.

We can now reason as follows:

1. It is not the case that Tweedledee and Tweedledum are known because knowledge implies truth and each of these sentences says that the other is unknown.

2. Since the sentences are symmetrical, it cannot be the case that one is known while the other is unknown.

3. Therefore, both are unknown.

If this proof gives anyone knowledge of the conclusion, then someone knows that Tweedledee is true and that Tweedledum is true. But this contradicts the first premise.

In our age of cloning, Tweedledee-Tweedledum can be generalized:

1. Statement 2 is not known.

2. Statement 3 is not known.

.

.

.

n-1.   Statement n is not known.

n.   Statement 1 is not known.

If none of the statements is true, then statement 1 is known and so is true. Contradiction. So at least one of the statements is true. Since the statements are symmetrical, it cannot be the case that some are true and some are false. Therefore, all of the statements are true. But if this reasoning gives me knowledge that all of the statements are true, then statement 1 is false. Contradiction.

Tweedledee-Tweedledum has two advantages over the lonely, self-involved knower KO. First, there is no direct self-reference. This advantage is only minor. There are many innocent self-referential statements in mathematics and ordinary language such as, 'This sentence is in English'. Self-reference is avoided entirely by a version of the knower that uses an infinite sequence of sentences (Sorensen 1998, 150–151). In any case, the effect of self-reference can be emulated by Godel numbering.

The more significant advantage of Tweedledee-Tweedledeum is that the hierarchical approach is inapplicable. Tweedledee and Tweedledum are asserted in parallel. Thus they cannot have a difference in level.

The virtues of Tweedledee-Tweedledum should not dull our appreciation of KO's singular merits. KO brings out a resemblance to the kind of sentence Godel uses in his incompleteness theorems. Roughly, a Gödel sentence says 'This very sentence cannot be proved in this system'. If the sentence were provable, then it would be false. So we can see that the sentence is true in that system even though that sentence lacks a proof for the statement's truth. Therefore, contrary to David Hilbert's program of formalism, there are unprovable mathematical truths. Moreover, we *know* the Godel sentence is true and so have a counterexample to the principle that all mathematical knowledge rests on proof within a single system. (A Gödel sentence of one system can be a theorem of another system.)

Perhaps the knower paradox illustrates the converse. Perhaps 'This is not known' is a proposition that can be proved but not known. A prover can fail to gain knowledge if the conclusion is not believed. Consider Galileo's simple proof that there are as many squares of natural numbers as there are natural numbers. He simply arranged the two sequences into a one to one correspondence:

Natural numbers: 1, 2, 3, 4, . . .

Squares of natural numbers:1, 4, 9, 16, . . .

This is now a standard textbook illustration of how one proves two infinite collections are equal in size. But Galileo only advanced the argument as a curiosity. He found it difficult to believe that the part could be as big as the whole. In 1733 Gerolamo Sacchiri published *Euclides ab Omni Naevo Vindicatus.* He presents deductions of characteristic theorems of non-Euclidean geometry. But Sacchiri took himself to be proving that Euclidean geometry is uniquely correct via the method of *reductio ad absurdum.*

The problem with the knower is not the mere psychological fact that KO is not believed.

KO: No one knows this very sentence.

Even if someone managed to believe KO while also competently following the proof, he would still lack knowledge. We need to consider ways in which a believing and competent prover could fail to know.

Meta-argumentative principles can defeat knowledge by proof. Consider a person who believes the premises and conclusion of a sound argument and also accepts each step of the proof. He could still have a reasonable (but false) worry that there is a mistake *somewhere.*

Meta-argumentative principles can defeat knowledge even if the thinker does not accept them. Consider an average mathematician who discovers a proof of a mildly interesting theorem. The proof is accepted for publication in a middle-level journal. But as this author is going over the final typescript, he receives a late referee report: "There must be something wrong with the author's proof because it entails Fermat's last theorem." The editor has verified the entailment with some experts. Consequently, the editor no longer accepts the author's proof. He requests that the author double-check his work.

The problem is not that the author's conclusion entails an absurdity. The editor and his experts know that Fermat's last theorem is true. After all, Andrew Wiles recently proved the theorem to worldwide acclaim. The editor explains that the real problem is that it is unlikely that the author would have discovered a much simpler proof of Fermat's last theorem.

The author denies the relevance of the editor's inductive considerations. "This is mathematics!" The author grants that he is just an average mathematician. As the editor concedes, the author would not have been challenged had it not been for the late referee report. Therefore, the unvain but confident author respectfully declines to double-check his proof.

To complete the fantasy of the average mathematician, suppose that the experts eventually confirm that author's original proof is indeed sound. Nearly miraculously, the undistinguished mathematician did prove a theorem which is lemma for a much simpler proof of Fermat's last theorem. Question: Did the confident author have knowledge before the mathematical establishment relented?

I contend that when the author stood alone, he failed to obtain knowledge from his proof. Although the author did not have second thoughts about his proof, he ought to have had them. The problem is not so much his conscious refusal to double-check. It is doubtful that the author knew his conclusion even before the referee's letter arrived. Misleading evidence need not be actually possessed to undermine knowledge.

People who go through the proof of KO ought to have worries about there being a mistake somewhere. And they do! Students who are introduced to the knower regard it as a paradox. Experts have the same unease. Witness the impressive technical studies of the proofs (Grim 1988, 1993). Scholars fret just as they ought. But these formal investigations have not yielded any flaws. To the contrary, logical work on the knower paradox has only served to enhance the credentials of the proof. The vexing deduction has become more rigorous, streamlined, and general.

Perhaps this is just what we should expect if there are epistemically sterile proofs. Our frustration would lead us to follow out suspicions that had the by-product of tightening the grip of the frustrating line of reasoning. We are struggling in quicksand. Our struggles increase depth but decrease hope.

There is a hitch to my solution to the knower paradox (that it is a sound but epistemically sterile proof). If this sterility solution were *known* to be true, we would know that there is sound proof of the knower sentence and therefore have knowledge of the knower sentence. Since we have already proven that no one can know 'No one knows this very sentence', we must reject the premise that we know that the sterility solution to the knower paradox is correct.

Perhaps we could at least rationally believe the solution. This fallback position is unavailable for a normative variant of Buridan's sentence:

BR: No one rationally believes this sentence.

Anyone who rationally believes BR would disconfirm B by that very belief. Thus no one rationally believes BR. But then we appear to have a proof of BR. Generally, proof is thought sufficient for rational belief. But here we would have to deny it generates rational belief. As with the knower, one solution is that the proof of B is sound but cannot generate rational belief in BR. This applies to any metaproof that there is a proof of BR.

So there may be a metaparadox on top of the knower paradox. Normally, a solution to a paradox can be known or at least rationally believed. The sterility solution to the knower paradox may itself be unknowable and unbelievable. The problem is not understanding the solution. The proof offers us a simple, rigorous explanation of why we cannot know the proof is sound. The problem is not that our puny minds are not up to the task. The paradox is universal to all possible knowers.

Universal paradoxes are precluded by metaphilosophies that put a biological spin on Immanuel Kant's *Critique of Pure Reason*. Arthur Schopenhaur believed that the human intellect is designed to serve the will. Thus it is "a quite abnormal event if in some man intellect deserts its natural vocation . . . in order to occupy itself purely objectively. But it is precisely this which is the origin of art, poetry and philosophy, which are therefore not produced by an organ intended for that purpose" (*Essays and Aphorisms*, 127). Paradoxes are just symptoms of intellectual perversion. This theme is now backed by constellations of data which indicate that much of the mind has a modular construction. Colin McGinn connects the dots in *Problems in Philosophy: The Limits of Inquiry*. He speculates that philosophical problems arise from species-specific cognitive defects. As such, philosophical problems are not objective problems. However, the knower paradox may resist McGinn's approach.

Just as Galileo offered his proof as an edifying curiosity, I offer the sterility solution to the knower paradox as an edifying curiosity. I do not claim to know the proposal is correct. I am not sure whether it is even rational to believe the sterility solution. Nor do I claim that anyone in the future could ever know it. Indeed, I deny that the sterility solution to the knower paradox can be known. I merely claim to understand the solution and how it could still manage to be inaccessible to me and others. Lastly, I claim the solution is interesting. In addition to suggesting a significant limitation on what can be learned by proof, the knower illuminates the possibility of there being a well-understood but completely intractable philosophical problem.

In personal correspondence, Patrick Grim invites me to deepen my intellectual humility:

U: Statement U is not both true and understood.

If U is false, then it is true. So it must be true. But if true, then U is not understood. Thus Grim appears to have proved a theorem that no one can understand!

A wedge between proof and understanding has some precedents. Computers produce proofs they do not understand. One can imagine zombie mathematicians doing the same. More realistically, one might misunderstand the nature of the activity in which one is engaged. One could be proving a theorem while under the impression that one is merely playing a game.

However, at this stage many will claim to smell smoke. They will say that Grim's sentence and the knower sentence itself are merely disjunctive liar sentences. The liar sentence says 'This is not true' while its attitudinal disjunctions say 'This is either not true or not A-ed,' where 'A' is some propositional attitude such as knowledge or belief or understanding. If the liar sentence fails to express a genuine proposition, then perhaps its disjunctive variants also fail to express genuine propositions. If so, then *poof*—our proofs go up in smoke.

Would the paradox go poof as well? Paradoxes must be composed of propositions. How else are we to get a contradiction? If the knower sentence does not express a proposition, then it does not lead to a paradox. Possibly, all this shows is that whatever drives our interest in paradoxes should motivate healthy interest in pseudoparadoxes.

5. Epistemic Closure

I say we have overestimated the ability of logical demonstration to produce knowledge. For instance, I reject Thomas Tymockzko's (1984, 449) "Completeness Principle": "For any sentence A, (x) (x logically proves 'A' → x knows 'A')". I think the case of the average mathematician is an independent counterexample to even the qualified versions Tymockzko proposes. The sterility solution to the knower paradox denies that proving p always gives the prover knowledge that the premises entail the conclusion.

The sterility solution should be contrasted with Stephen Maitzen's (1998) idea that the knower is solved by denying the epistemic closure principle:

EC: If x knows p and knows p entails q, then x knows q.

Maitzen says that we know premises of the argument for 'No one knows this sentence' and know that those premises entail the conclusion, but still fail to know the conclusion 'No one knows this sentence'.

Maitzen's solution is vulnerable to a formal trick. Axioms can be mimicked by inference rules that allow one to infer the axiom from zero premises. Consider a system of "natural deduction" that employs these surrogates for the premises of the knower paradox. In this system, the knower sentence can be deduced without premises. Hence the closure principle will not be needed.

The artificial flavor of this system can be diminished by restricting it to an a priori variation of the knower:

AP: This sentence is not an a priori truth.

If AP is false, then it is true. So it must be true. But if true, then AP is not a priori. If deducibility from the empty set sufficed for a priority, then AP would be a priori. But since AP entails that it is not a priori, we must reject this deducibility principle (which so appealed to Leibniz and Frege).

The sterility solution to the knower paradox is not affected by the exchange of premises in favor of inference rules. I deny that proving p always gives knowledge that p. This denial extends to zero premise proofs. The sterility solution is neutral with respect to the epistemic closure principle.

6. CHALLENGING THE SKEPTIC'S INFERENCE RULES

The rejection of epistemic closure is associated with a key development in the history of epistemology. Prior to the rise of epistemic logic in the 1960s, skeptical arguments were attacked principally for their premises and occasionally for the commission of generic fallacies. For instance, Rene Descartes rejected the skeptic's premise that nothing is certain by claiming that 'I am thinking' cannot be doubted. He claimed this provided a foundation upon which all of our knowledge could be grounded. Phenomenalists claimed that sense data statements are certain and proceeded to build on this much wider, ever shifting foundation.

After the development of epistemic logic, epistemologists elaborated a new strategy: attacking internal inference rules. The rationale for the strategy is straightforward. The stronger one's inference rules, the more that follows from a proposition. The more that follows, the more risk of error. So skeptics (who characterize knowledge attributions as overly optimistic) gravitate to strong inference rules. For instance, if the KK principle is true, then one can defeat a knowledge claim by showing that the thinker does not know that he knows. Invalidating the KK principle partially disarms the skeptic.

Invalidating the epistemic closure principle promises a much greater antiskeptical impact. Fred Dretske (1970) illustrates with an example of someone at the zoo looking at a zebra in a pen. If the viewer knows that the animal he is viewing is a zebra, then that animal cannot be a mule cleverly painted to look like a zebra. Since the viewer does not know that the animal is not a painted mule, the skeptic concludes the viewer does not know that he is viewing a zebra. Dretske objects to the underlying principle that if one knows then one knows the known logical consequences of what one knows.

Jonathan Vogel (1990) lacks Dretske's intuition that the man at the zoo fails to know the animal is not a painted mule. Zoos are set up to display genuine specimens. This background seems to foreclose the painted mule worry. Many epistemologists would second Vogel's objection.

Epistemologists have been more receptive to examples involving far-out entailments. If the man knows that the animal is a zebra, then he is not dreaming that he is at the zoo. Equally obviously, he is not a brain in a vat that is merely being stimulated to hallucinate that he is at the zoo looking at a zebra. But does the man at the zoo know that he is not dreaming? Does he know that he is not the hallucinating plaything of whimsical scientists? The man at the zoo is not in a position to deny these possibilities. The skeptic and the anticlosure strategist conclude that the man fails to know that these exotic hypotheses are false.

An older antiskeptical strategy is to boldly insist that one does have knowledge of the far-out entailments. Dretske complains that this is dogmatism. Consider how Norman Malcolm wields his knowledge that there is an ink-bottle on his desk. Professor Malcolm denies that any future evidence could indicate that there is no ink-bottle on his desk. In particular, Malcolm denies that he would be justified in treating as contrary evidence any of the following occurrences: his hand seemingly passing through the object, suddenly finding himself under a tree in a garden, being contradicted by other observers, or even being presented with a photograph indicating that there was no ink-bottle on his desk.

> Not only do I not *have* to admit that (those) extraordinary occurrences would be evidence that there is no ink-bottle here: the fact is that I *do not* admit it. There is nothing whatever that could happen in the next moment

that would by me be called *evidence* that there is not an ink-bottle here now.
No future experience or investigation could prove to me that I am mistaken.
(1963, 67–68)

Diluting epistemic principles is certainly preferable to Malcolm's intransigence.

But there is an alternative to denying closure that still preserves the intuition
that the skeptical hypotheses cannot be flatly denied. Knowledge as a whole could
be deductively closed even if salient species of knowledge are not closed. Let us
distinguish between robust knowledge and junk knowledge (Sorensen 1988b). The
normal point of acquiring knowledge is to gain further knowledge through inference. If I know that either my fuses blew or there was a general blackout, then
learning that my neighbors still have their lights on allows me to infer that my
fuses blew. My knowledge of the disjunction survives news that a particular disjunct is false. Junk knowledge does not have this robust quality. If I know that
my fuses blew, then I can pedantically infer that either my fuses blew or all my
electrical appliances failed simultaneously. I know this adulterated proposition
even though I would not use it to make the normal kind of inferences. For instance, if I obtained surprising evidence that my fuses did not blow then I would
not infer that all of my electrical appliances failed simultaneously. I would instead
abandon the adulterated proposition.

Junk knowledge is best known through the Gettier counterexamples. If Smith
knows that Jones owns a Ford, then he can infer 'Either Jones owns a Ford or
Brown is in Barcelona,' even though he hasn't the slightest reason to believe the
second disjunct. But despite the fact that he knows the disjunction, it would be a
misdeed to assert it. For the disjunction is not robust with respect to the negation
of the first disjunct and asserting it suggests otherwise. The unassertibility of these
Gettier knowledge claims helps to explain why epistemologists overlooked them;
they are not the sort of statements we would ordinarily say we know. This also
explains the pedagogical problem in teaching students about the Gettier counterexamples.

Since Malcolm knows there is an ink-bottle on the desk, he (trivially) knows
that any future evidence which goes against the presence of the ink-bottle is
misleading evidence. But knowledge of this conditional does not survive the actual
acquisition of the evidence. True, knowledge of some conditionals about misleading evidence do survive. When the evening weatherman confidently predicts rain
tomorrow afternoon, people infer that if the morning is sunny, then that will be
misleading evidence as to whether there will be rain in the afternoon. People stick
to this conditional even after they learn the morning is sunny. Malcolm, in contrast, derived his conditional trivially. From the mere fact that p is true, it ana-
lytically follows that any evidence against p is misleading evidence. But this is
only "junk knowledge" that cannot be used to obtain new knowledge through a
modus ponens inference.

The point of knowledge is to guide action and produce new knowledge. If one associates knowledge too intimately with these roles, then one will rule our junk knowledge as a contradiction in terms. Epistemologists need to emulate the biologists' flexibility. Genes are defined by their contribution to the organism's phenotype and the formation of new genes. But this does not foreclose the possibility of junk DNA. Biologists have discovered that junk DNA constitutes the overwhelming majority of the genetic matter residing in the nuclei of many organisms. Psychologists might discover that our heads are stuffed with representations that enter into no psychological processes and produce no behavior. Adequate theories of mental content must make room for "junk representations" (Shapiro 1997).

Any knowledge generates a flimsy veneer of "protective" conditionals. If I know that I gave correct change to the cashier, I know that if the cashier objects that I gave incorrect change, then the cashier's objection is erroneous. But if the cashier actually objects, then my knowledge that 'I gave correct change' is undermined. That knowledge was my only basis for inferring that 'If the cashier objects, then her objection is erroneous'. So once I lose knowledge of my correct counting, I also lose knowledge of the conditional.

We are only entitled to assert what we robustly know. This means that we are normally not entitled to deny skeptical hypotheses. For such denials suggest that we have nondegenerate evidence against them. The sort of evidence that we are suggesting we possess can be illustrated by the skeptical hypotheses that have been refuted. Recall the hypothesis that the universe doubled in size last night. The hypothesis successfully neutralizes evidence obtained from rulers and other linear measurements. But it overlooks the evidence from geometrical relationships such as the relationship between surface area and volume. Once you learn the relevant physics, you are in a position to nonmisleadingly deny the hypothesis of nocturnal expansion. Background scientific knowledge is almost always sufficient to refute the novel skeptical hypotheses devised by college students and other amateurs. A well-crafted skeptical hypothesis is rare and almost always the work of a scholar long immersed in philosophical research.

Can these polished gems be substantively refuted? A few philosophers think they can refute dream skepticism by jejune tests such as pinching yourself (Nelson 1966). J. L. Austin (1962, 48–49) maintains that the sheer lucidity of his experience entitled him to deny the hypothesis that he was dreaming. More commonly, the hope of substantive refutation is based on the discovery of a technical obstacle. Consider Daniel Dennett's (1991, 3–10) evidence that he is not a brain in a vat. He concedes neuroscientists may be able to arrange a passive hallucination in which the subject has no control of the course of experience. But active hallucinations are intractable because they involve a combinatorial explosion. Every time Dennett performs an action, he would introduce another branch of events. Thus Dennett thinks the experience of voluntarily wiggling his fingers rules out the hypothesis that he is a brain in a vat. Dennett and other straight-shooters may ultimately be basing their claims on defective evidence. But their denials of the skeptical hypotheses satisfy robustness conditions for assertibility.

Most philosophers think that clever skeptics can devise hypotheses that successfully neutralize our evidence. These well-crafted hypotheses come close to achieving the skeptic's desired effect. No well-informed person can flatly deny them. However, we still have knowledge that the skeptical hypotheses are false and can responsibly deny skeptical hypotheses given the cancellation of some conversational implicatures.

Those who talk of the impotence of skeptical hypotheses are generally suspected of whistling in the graveyard. Very well then, to control for wishful thinking, focus on situations in which knowledge is *unwelcome*. I knew a philosophy professor who received an anonymous phone call. The caller began reading off the questions of tomorrow's examination. The professor now *knew* that someone else knew which questions were on the test. He preferred not to know because this knowledge obligated him to spend the whole night constructing a new test. The professor's knowledge of two thousand years of skeptical hypotheses could not relieve him of this knowledge.

We must labor to keep others ignorant. Diaries are locked. Messages are encrypted. Shades are drawn. Yet our secrecy is fragile. It is wishful thinking to deny that others know much of what we prefer that they do not know. In these circumstances, the impotence of skeptical hypotheses is impartially exposed.

7. Relevant Alternatives and the Completeness Concern

Those who reject closure portray the principle as an overgeneralization. When a subject knows p his evidence must exclude all *relevant* alternatives to p. An alternative to p is just a contrary proposition. A relevant alternative is one that fits the interests of the conversationalists. Thus 'know' has the contextual subtleties of other absolute terms: *flat, empty, sterile, clean*, and so on.

Developers of the relevant alternatives theory have addressed the question of what makes an alternative relevant. They have also addressed the question of how much evidence is needed to exclude an alternative (Is induction sufficient or must the evidence deductively entail the falsehood of the alternative?). I want to raise a third issue: Is it enough that each alternative is eliminated piecemeal by the evidence or must the evidence further insure that *all* the alternatives have been eliminated?

This third issue arises when each alternative is indeed ruled out by the subject's evidence but there is a concern about whether this excludes all the alternatives.

Suppose an amateur geometrician proves that the hexahedron and octahedron are duals (in the sense that if the center of all the adjacent faces on one are connected by straight lines, the lines form the edge of the others). He proves that the dodecahedron and icosahedron are dually related in the same way. And thirdly he proves that tetrahedron is its own dual. The amateur knows that each of these five figures is a Platonic solid (a polyhedron bounded by straight lines, with equal sides and equal interior angles). He is not sure whether there are any further Platonic solids but makes the following enumerative induction:

1. The tetrahedron is a Platonic solid that has a dual.
2. The octahedron is a Platonic solid that has a dual.
3. The hexahedron is a Platonic solid that has a dual.
4. The dodecahedron is a Platonic solid that has a dual.
5. The icosahedron is a Platonic solid that has a dual.
6. Therefore, all Platonic solids have duals.

In Aristotle's language, this is a "perfect induction"—an induction that is based on a complete census of the cases in question. For there are exactly five Platonic solids. Since the amateur does not know that his inventory of Platonic solids is complete, he does not know all Platonic solids have duals. Yet the three proofs supporting his premises eliminate every possible counterexample.

In the era of logical atomism, Bertrand Russell (1918, 235) voiced a completeness concern about Ludwig Wittgenstein's proposal to analyze universal generalizations as long conjunctions. According to Wittgenstein, 'All lesbians are feminists' is equivalent to a list of statements that attribute feminism to each lesbian: 'Andrea is a lesbian and is a feminist and Babette is a lesbian and is a feminist and Cynthia is a lesbian and is a feminist and . . . '. Russell objected that this conjunction would mean as much as 'All lesbians are feminists' only if it contained an added clause saying 'and that is all the lesbians there are'. But that clause is itself a universal generalization so the analysis would be circular.

The completeness concern does not arise for absolute terms such as 'flat' and 'empty'. These privational terms apply simply if there is an absence of Fs. Epistemic absolute terms such as 'know' and 'certain' have an extra requirement. There must also be exclusion of the existential generalization that there are further Fs.

In the case of knowledge, 'There are further alternatives to p' does not itself qualify as an alternative to p. For the existential generalization is not a contrary to p. It is about alternatives but is not itself an alternative. If it were an alternative, then the completeness concern would lead to an infinite regress. Happily, adding 'There are no further Platonic solids' to the above deduction completely slakes our thirst for knowledge of the conclusion.

David Armstrong's (1997, 196–201) truthmaker theory elaborates Bertrand

Russell's (1918, 236–241) suggestion that there are "totality facts" which make universal generalizations true. Armstrong's fellow reliabilists do not think there is any special difficulty detecting whether universal generalizations hold. When Alvin Goldman summarizes the virtues of his relevant alternatives account of knowledge, he notes:

> A correct definition should be able to explain how speakers arrive at the extended uses from the central ones. With this in mind, consider how tempting it is to say of an electric-eye door that it "knows" you are coming (at least that *something* is coming), or "sees" you coming. The attractiveness of the metaphor is easily explained on my theory: the door has a reliable mechanism for discriminating between something being before it and nothing being there. (1976, 790–791)

If mechanical venders, smoke detectors, and dryers can satisfy the completeness concern, then so can animals, children, and scientists.

We can discriminate between animals that satisfy the completeness concern and those that do not. Suppose Fido learns that his master is away by checking each room of the house. A visiting dog, Visitor, tags along with Fido. Visitor knows of each room in the house that it is unoccupied by Fido's master. But since Visitor is unfamiliar with the house, Visitor does not know that all the rooms have been examined. Hence only Fido knows that his master away.

Fido need not have any conscious concern about the completeness with which he is conducting his domestic survey. Dogs are designed to explore new surroundings and this gives them background knowledge for exhaustive searches. When a dog enters a new house, he is guided by the same spontaneous curiosity as we are. We enjoy opening doors and moving about the whole space. This reconnoitering may later prove useful when searching for things in the house even though our introductory survey yielded nothing of positive interest and was not conducted for utilitarian motives. (To avoid concern that the KK principle is involved, assume the dogs lack the concept of knowledge and so *cannot* know that they know.)

Since the completeness concern adds a requirement to knowledge, some may fear that it introduces a new skeptical threat. The old threat, championed by Peter Unger (1975), is that one is rarely in a position to exclude all the alternatives, and so one knows very little. The new threat is that one is rarely in a position to exclude the existential generalization that there are further alternatives. Consequently, even if the old threat is met, the new threat can still defeat the knowledge claim.

Bertrand Russell has trouble containing his skeptical impulses when discussing the epistemology of general propositions. He first argues that we have knowledge of general propositions only if some general propositions are known without inference. For one needs knowledge of a general premise to infer knowledge of a general conclusion. But we cannot acquire all of the primitive knowledge of general propositions from experience. For experience only provides knowledge by inference. Where does this knowledge come from? Russell grows suspicious:

> I think that the sort of way such knowledge—or rather the belief that we have such knowledge—comes into ordinary life is probably very odd. I mean to say that we do habitually assume general propositions which are exceedingly doubtful: as, for instance, one might, if one were counting up the people in this room, assume that one could see all of them, which is a general proposition, and very doubtful as there may be people under the tables. But, apart from that sort of thing, you do have in any empirical verification of general propositions some kind of assumption that amounts to this, that what you do not see is not there. Of course, you would not put it so strongly as that, but you would assume that, with certain limitations and certain qualifications, if a thing does not appear to your senses, it is not there. That is a general proposition, and it is only through such propositions that you arrive at the ordinary empirical results that one obtains in ordinary ways. (1918, 235–236)

I think Russell is underestimating resources afforded by natural selection. The exhaustivity of an organism's sensings increases its reproductive success. So we should expect all perceivers to have innate knowledge of the proposition Russell finds so occult.

The most resilient approach to skeptical threats is close attention to our ordinary patterns of knowledge attributions. This quickly reveals that the completeness concern can often be satisfied without a census. A biologist can know that a species is extinct by knowing that there are no habitats for the species. I can know that my child has a temperature of 101 degrees Fahrenheit without knowing how finely the thermometer is scaled or what the minimum and maximum temperatures are. I do not need to know what the relevant alternatives are to exclude all of them. For exclusions may proceed by kinds rather than by particulars. The reading of 101 excludes all the higher readings and all the lower readings.

8. IMPLICATIONS OF THE DISANALOGY

'Necessary' is a nonepistemic absolute term. Consequently, it simply excludes alternative alethic possibilities. There is no need to exclude the existential generalization that there are further possibilities.

This upsets the analogy between knowledge and necessity. We can illustrate the disruption with the case of epistemic semantics. In epistemic semantics, alethic possibility is explained as a suitably universalized form of epistemic possibility. In particular, a statement is a necessary truth iff it is true in each rational belief system. A rational belief system is an idealization that satisfies certain desiderata such as thoroughness and consistency. (These desiderata take on a life of their own when Brian Ellis (1979, 33–42) defines necessity. Any modal system can be defined in terms of rational belief if one is uninhibited about the antecedent meaning of 'rational belief'. Since the epistemic character of epistemic semantics disappears in the course of this syntactic exercise, these are not *epistemic* explications of necessity. I am restricting attention to epistemic explications.)

Since epistemic necessity has a completeness requirement, we should expect it to be narrower than alethic necessity. Consider the S4 principle that whatever is necessary is necessarily necessary ($\Box p \rightarrow \Box \Box p$). This fails because there can be ignorance of whether one has reviewed all the rational systems. Suppose p is stocked by each belief system and suppose that Harvey has a rational belief system. Each belief system could be known by Harvey to contain p without Harvey knowing that he has surveyed all the belief systems. So although $\Box p$ holds in virtue of p being a member of every rational belief system, $\Box p$ is not part of Harvey's belief system. Consequently, $\Box p$ is true without $\Box \Box p$ being true. And that is contrary to S4.

The completeness concern also affects the flexible term 'determinate'. A proposition is determinate iff it is free of indeterminacies. If the indeterminacies are metaphysical, then 'determinate' will behave like necessity. But if indeterminacies are epistemic, then 'determinate' will behave like knowledge.

This divergence undermines recent efforts to synchronize supervaluational and epistemicist treatments of vagueness.

According to the supervaluationist, a vague statement lacks a truth-value iff it comes out true under some ways of precisifying it and false under other ways of precisifying it. If a vague statement comes out true under all precisifications, then it is simply true. This explains how 'Either John is bald is not' can be true even if John is a borderline case of a bald man. Neither disjunct is true but the whole disjunction is true under all precisifications—and hence true.

According to the epistemicist, vagueness is just a special kind of ignorance concerning which concepts we are using: 12:15 is a borderline case of 'noonish' because there is no way to tell whether 'noonish' includes 12:15. For all anyone can know, our language could be such that '12:15 is noonish' is true and for all anyone can know, our language could be such that '12:15 is noonish' is false. Thus '12:15 is noonish' has a *hidden* truth-value.

Supervaluationism and epistemicism seem as different as communism and capitalism. But the peace-makers have looked for convergences (McGee and McLaughlin 1995). Even the militant epistemicist Timothy Williamson has claimed that the two positions yield isomorphic results for higher order vagueness:

> As a first approximation, for the supervaluationist, definiteness is truth under
> all sharpenings of the language consistent with what speakers have already fixed
> about its semantics ("admissible sharpenings"); for the epistemicist, definiteness

is truth under all sharp interpretations of the language indiscriminable from
the right one. In both cases, we hold everything precise constant as we vary the
interpretation. (Williamson 1999, 128)

The idea is that 'true under all admissible sharpenings' and 'true under all indiscriminable sharpenings' work analogously to necessity. The task is to find a modal
logic that accords with how we use 'definitely true' in contexts of vagueness.
According to Williamson, this search can proceed without raising the divisive
question about what 'definitely true' means. For the underlying semantics are not
structural rivals.

I agree that the supervaluationist's 'true under all admissible precisifications'
behaves like necessity. If there are only ten sharpenings of 'noonish' and '12:10 is
noonish' comes out true under each of them, then (given the supervaluational
gloss on 'definitely') '12:10 is noonish' is definitely true.

But what about 'true under all indiscriminable sharpenings'? If there are only
ten sharpenings of 'noonish' and '12:10 is noonish' comes out knowably true under
all of them, then is '12:10 is noonish' knowably true?

The complication is that no one may be in a position to exclude the existential
generalization that there are further sharpenings of 'noonish'. Each sharpening of
'noonish' may be known to be a sharpening that makes '12:10 is noonish' true.
But if there is no way to know that this set of sharpenings is complete, then no
one can know '12:10 is noonish'. This uncertainty can arise from the vagueness of
'admissible sharpening'. Some interpretations of 'noonish' are clearly admissible,
while others are clearly inadmissible. In between are interpretations that are borderline cases of 'admissible sharpening'.

Supervaluationism and epistemicism diverge when we cannot know (for reasons of vagueness) whether we have exhausted every sharpening but each sharpening can be individually known to make the statement true. In these circumstances, supervaluationism implies that the statement is definitely true while
epistemicism implies the statement is indefinite (though true). So, contrary to
Williamson, epistemicism and supervaluationism give incompatible verdicts for
both first order vagueness and higher order vagueness.

9. RATIONALITY AND INCOMPLETENESS

The completeness concern also affects rationality via Rudolph Carnap's (1950, 211)
requirement of total evidence. The original purpose of the requirement was to
provide a perspective from which one can consistently propound inductive ar-

guments. Suppose 99 percent of long-haired people are female and 99 percent of mechanics are males. Pat is a long-haired mechanic. You could infer that Pat is male from the premise that 99 percent of mechanics are male. You could infer that Pat is female from the premise that 99 percent of long-haired people are not male. But you should not propound either argument. Each fails to reflect available evidence. The requirement of total evidence says that one's judgment should be based on all the available evidence.

Carnap's requirement of total evidence is compelling. But often there is uncertainty as to what the available evidence is. Is a large head evidence of intelligence? Are the blurbs on book jackets evidence about the quality of the book? We are ambivalent about discarding ostensible evidence that is tainted or conflicting or controversial.

Now suppose a person fortunately *does* base his judgment on all the evidence but is not in a position to know that this is all the available evidence. Does his judgment satisfy the requirement of total evidence?

An irrational judgment can be accidentally based on all the available evidence. Consider dogmatists who arbitrarily ignored the counsel of water dowsers. Luckily for the dogmatists, the dowsings are not evidence about the location of water. But the dogmatists are still being irrational.

The completeness concern also spills over to practical reason. Practical syllogisms have the same character as statistical syllogisms. To propound a practical syllogism, one must take a perspective on the body of reasons one will consider. The only perspective that is free of inconsistency is one that considers all available relevant reasons. Donald Davidson calls this the principle of continence (1970, 41). He analyzes weakness of will as violations of this principle. However, a parallel question can be asked. Must a continent agent know that he has considered all the available relevant evidence? Or is it good enough that he happens to have actually considered all the available relevant reasons?

10. THE HEAVENLY BIAS OF IDEALIZATION

Epistemologists divide on the relevance of rationality to knowledge. The recent "bottom-up" epistemologists have played down the role of reasons (Dretske 1991). They favor a conception of knowledge that fits our tendency to ascribe knowledge to pre-rational children and animals. The traditional "top-down" epistemologists take such ascriptions to be metaphorical or peripheral. The top-downer's paradigm of the knower is the scientist.

Epistemic logic has grown top down. Ordinary knowers have been pictured as imperfect approximations of perfectly rational agents. For instance, Jaakko Hintikka uses model theory to develop his epistemic logic. This automatically renders the knowers perfectly consistent, complete, and aware of their own epistemic states.

Critics have complained that the resulting account of knowledge fails to correspond to ordinary usage. For instance, Hintikka's doxastic logic endorses the principle that belief collects over conjunction: $(Bp \ \& \ Bq) \rightarrow B(p \ \& \ q)$. The appeal of this principle fades when applied on a large scale. In D. C. Makinson's (1965) preface paradox, an author believes each of the assertions in his book. But since the author regards himself as fallible, he believes that the conjunction of all his assertions is false. If $(Bp \ \& \ Bq) \rightarrow B(p \ \& \ q)$ held, then the author would both believe and disbelieve the conjunction of all the assertions in his book. At this point many philosophers reject $(Bp \ \& \ Bq) \rightarrow B(p \ \& \ q)$ and conclude that it can be rational to have jointly inconsistent beliefs.

Hintikka's idealization also makes it difficult to explain some of the phenomena that epistemic logic might be expected to illuminate. For instance, why is circular reasoning bad? If the conclusion appears as a premise, then the argument is automatically valid. Thus standard logic cannot explain the defect as invalidity. Indeed, it lacks the resources to fend off Sextus Empiricus' contention that all valid arguments are circular. It seems epistemic logic should have the resources to meet this challenge.

However, Hintikka's epistemic logic leaves us few options. The informativeness of a deduction cannot be explained as the exposure of an inconsistency between the target thinker's belief in the premises and disbelief in the conclusion. For Hintikka's thinkers are perfectly consistent. Nor can the informativeness of deduction be understood as a process of teasing out implications. Hintikka's thinkers believe all the logical consequences of what they believe.

The model-theoretic approach to knowledge is reminiscent of early geometrical theories of vision. These theories treated the eye as a point. Since a point is simple, the eye can have no relevant structure in such a theory. Consequently, none of the early researchers on vision bothered to dissect eyes.

Idealizations tend to rise to the heavens. But this may be a prejudice. Recall that Crispin Wright and Aidan Sudbury suggested that the temporal retention principle ("If you know, you continue to know") is central to the surprise-test paradox. They suggested that the solution to the paradox was to reject this principle. This proposal is incomplete because there are variations of the paradox that side-step commitment to the temporal retention principle (Sorensen 1988, 320–321). But more surprisingly, there is a variation of the surprise-test paradox that saliently depends on the *falsehood* of the principle. Suppose the students have a reunion many years after graduation. The alumni are reminiscing about the class involving the paradoxical surprise test. One alum recalls that the teacher also announced a most recently forgotten test. The test would take place at the latest date which would be forgotten by all the students. The alumni remember the test took place but cannot remember when. One of them concludes that the test must have therefore taken place on the last day of classes. For that would be the most recent forgotten date. But another alum points out that if they are able to reconstruct the test date from memory, then they do indeed remember the date of the test and so it cannot be the date of the most recently forgotten test. Someone suggests that the test date must therefore have been the penultimate day of class. However, the self-defeating nature of this inference is quickly spotted. So the penultimate day is excluded as well. Each alternative is eliminated in a like manner.

This retrospective variation of the surprise test has several instructive features. The alumni variation allays any Aristotelian concern that the paradox turns on the fact that the future is indeterminate (Weiss 1952). Concerns about the practical point of having surprise tests are set aside because this kind of retrospective ignorance is not action-oriented. There is also a lesson about idealization. We cannot picture epistemic logic as a description of *the* ideal thinker. For thinkers can be idealized in different directions for different purposes. In the alumni variation, we cannot idealize the agents by supposing the alumni do not forget. The whole puzzle is generated by a phenomenon of epistemic decay.

Epistemologists generally take a youthful perspective in which they manage the growth of knowledge. However, our internal library faces both loss and gain. Some of the loss is lamentable but other losses are helpful. From medicine, we know that human beings spend only their first seventeen years or so in the process of growth. This is followed by a lifetime of gradual deterioration in performance and well-being. Rational medicine consists in the intelligent management of this inevitable decline. The brain is just another organ, subject to the same melancholy generalizations. An epistemic logician who tried to formalize this wider perspective would use different principles than Professor Hintikka.

Given the relativity of idealization to purposes, we may need to adopt a pluralistic attitude toward epistemic logics. There is also the possibility that there are overwhelmingly many rules for attributing knowledge. The fate of epistemic logic lies partly in the hands of psychologists.

Epistemic logicians could take comfort in the fact that a deductive system can do work besides validating inferences. Even a misconceived epistemic logic could be a tool for reconstructing the reasoning of skeptics and their foes. The doctrine of methodological solipsism says that a thinker can be understood completely in terms of the internal properties of his mind. His environment is psychologically relevant only insofar as it affects his mind. Although logical properties are trivially deducible from anything (and thus degenerately qualify as internal properties of the mind), the *spirit* of methodological solipsism suggests that we ignore the validity of the thinker's inferences along with the truth-value of his beliefs. What matters for interpretative purposes is appearances.

REFERENCES

Anderson, C. Anthony (1983). "The Paradox of the Knower." *Journal of Philosophy* 80: 338–355.

Armstrong, David (1997). *A World of States of Affairs*. Cambridge: Cambridge University Press.

Austin, J. L. (1962). *Sense and Sensibilia*. Oxford: Oxford University Press.

Bacharach, M. O. L. et al. (1997). *Epistemic Logic and the Theory of Games and Decisions*. Boston: Kluwer.

Boh, Ivan (1993). *Epistemic Logic in the Later Middle Ages*. London: Routledge.

Burge, Tyler (1984). "Epistemic Paradox." *Journal of Philosophy* 81, no. 1: 5–29.

———. (1978a). "Buridan and Epistemic Paradox." *Philosophical Studies* 34: 21–35.

Carnap, Rudolph (1950). *The Logical Foundations of Probability*. Chicago: University of Chicago Press.

Davidson, Donald (1970). "How Is Weakness of Will Possible?" In *Moral Concepts*, ed. Joel Feinberg. Oxford Readings in Philosophy. New York: Oxford University Press.

Dennett, Daniel (1991). *Consciousness Explained*. Boston: Little, Brown.

Dretske, Fred (1970). "Epistemic Operators." *Journal of Philosophy* 67: 1007–1023.

———. (1991). "Two Conceptions of Knowledge: Rational vs. Reliable Belief." *Grazer Philosophiche Studien* 4: 15–30.

Ellis, Brian (1979). *Rational Belief Systems*. Totawa, N.J.: Rowman & Littlefield.

Fitch, Frederic (1963). "A Logical Analysis of Some Value Concepts." *Journal of Symbolic Logic* 28, no.2: 135–142.

Goldman, Alvin (1976). "Discrimination and Perceptual Knowledge." *Journal of Philosophy* 1976: 771–791.

Grim, Patrick (1988). "Truth, Omniscience, and the Knower." *Philosophical Studies* 54: 9–41.

———. (1993). "Operators in the Paradox of the Knower." *Synthese* 94, no.3: 409–428.

Hintikka, Jaakko (1962). *Knowledge and Belief*. Ithaca, N.Y.: Cornell University Press.

Hocutt, Max O. (1972). "Is Epistemic Logic Possible?" *Notre Dame Journal of Formal Logic* 13, no. 4: 433–453.

Kaplan, David, and Richard Montague (1960). "A Paradox Regained." *Notre Dame Journal of Formal Logic* 1: 79–90.

Makinson, D. C. (1965). "The Paradox of the Preface." *Analysis* 25: 205–207.

Maitzen, Stephen (1998). "The Knower Paradox and Epistemic Closure." *Synthese* 114: 337–354.

Malcolm, Norman (1963). *Knowledge and Certainty*. Englewood Cliffs, N.J.: Prentice-Hall.

McGee, Vann, and Brian McLaughlin (1995). "Distinctions without a Difference." *Southern Journal of Philosophy* 33 (Suppl): 203–251.

McGinn, Colin (1993). *Problems in Philosophy: The Limits of Inquiry*. Oxford: Blackwell.

Meyer, John-Jules Ch., and W. van der Hoek (1995). *Epistemic Logic for AI and Computer Science*. Cambridge: Cambridge University Press.

Nelson, John (1966). "Can One Tell That He Is Awake by Pinching Himself?" *Philosophical Studies* 17: 81–84.

Nozick, Robert (1981). *Philosophical Explanations*. Cambridge, Mass.: Harvard University Press.

Parsons, Charles (1974). "The Liar Paradox." *Journal of Philosophical Logic* 3: 381–412.

Quine, W. V. (1953). "On a So-called Paradox." *Mind* 62, no. 245: 65–67.

———. (1969). "Epistemology Naturalized." *Ontological Relativity and Other Essays*. New York: Columbia University Press.

Read, Stephen (1995). *Thinking about Logic*. New York: Oxford University Press.

Reicher, G. M. (1969). "Perceptual Recognition as a Function of the Meaningfulness of the Stimulus Material." *Journal of Experimental Psychology* 81: 275–280.

Russell, Bertrand (1918). "The Philosophy of Logical Atomism." In *Logic and Knowledge*, ed. Robert Marsh. London: Great Britain, 1956. 177–281.

Schopenhaur, Arthur (1970). *Essays and Aphorisms*. New York: Penguin.

Smullyan, Raymond (1982). *Alice in Puzzle-Land*. New York: Morrow.

Shapiro, Lawrence (1997). "Junk Representations." *British Journal for the Philosophy of Science* 48, no. 3: 345–361.

Sorensen, Roy (1988a). *Blindspots*. Oxford: Clarendon.

———. (1988b). "Dogmatism, Junk Knowledge, and Conditionals." *Philosophical Quarterly* 38 (Oct.): 433–454.

———. (1996). "Modal Bloopers: Why Believable Impossibilities Are Necessary." *American Philosophical Quarterly* 33, no. 1. (July): 247–261. Repr. in *The Philosopher's Annual 1996*, ed. Patrick Grim, Kenneth Baynes, and Gary Mar. Atascadero, Calif.: Ridgeview, 1998, vol. 19.

———. (1998). "Yablo's Paradox and Kindred Infinite Liars." *Mind* 107 (Jan.): 137–155.

———. (1999). "Infinite 'Backward' Induction Arguments." *Pacific Philosophical Quarterly* 80, no. 3: 278–283.

———. (2001). *Vagueness and Contradiction*. Oxford: Oxford University Press.

Tymoczko, Thomas (1984). "An Unsolved Puzzle about Knowledge." *Philosophical Quarterly* 34: 437–458.

Unger, Peter (1968). "An Analysis of Factual Knowledge." *Journal of Philosophy* 65, no. 6: 157–170.

———. (1975). *Ignorance: A Case for Scepticism*. Oxford: Clarendon.

Vogel, Jonathan (1990). "Are There Counterexamples to the Closure Principle?" In *Doubting: Contemporary Perspectives on Skepticism*, ed. Michael D. Roth and Glenn Ross. Dordrecht: Kluwer. 13–27.

Weiss, Paul (1952). "The Prediction Paradox." *Mind* 61: 265–269.

Wheeler, D. D. (1970). "Processes in Word Recognition." *Cognitive Psychology* 1: 59–85.

Williams, John (1979). "Moore's Problem: One or Two?" *Analysis* 39: 141–142.

Williamson, Timothy (1994). *Vagueness*. London: Routledge.

———. (2000). *Knowledge and Its Limits*. Oxford: Oxford University Press.

BIBLIOGRAPHY ON EPISTEMOLOGY

PAUL K. MOSER

GENERAL WORKS

Achinstein, Peter, ed. *The Concept of Evidence*. Oxford: Oxford University Press, 1983.

Alcoff, Linda, and Elizabeth Potter, eds. *Feminist Epistemologies*. London: Routledge, 1993.

Almeder, Robert. *Blind Realism*. Lanham, Md.: Rowman & Littlefield, 1992.

Alston, William P. *Epistemic Justification*. Ithaca, N.Y.: Cornell University Press, 1989.

———. "Meta-Ethics and Meta-Epistemology." In *Values and Morals*, pp. 275–297. Edited by A. I. Goldman and J. Kim. Dordrecht: Reidel, 1978.

———. *The Reliability of Sense Perception*. Ithaca, N.Y.: Cornell University Press, 1993.

———. "The Role of Reason in the Regulation of Belief." In *Rationality in the Calvinian Tradition*, pp. 135–170. Edited by N. Wolterstorff et al. Lanham, Md.: University Press of America, 1983.

Antony, Louise, and Charlotte Witt, eds. *A Mind of One's Own*. Boulder, Colo.: Westview, 1992.

Armstrong, David M. *Belief, Truth, and Knowledge*. Cambridge: Cambridge University Press, 1973.

Audi, Robert. *The Architecture of Reason*. New York: Oxford University Press, 2001.

———. *Epistemology*. London: Routledge, 1998.

———. *Moral Knowledge and Ethical Character*. New York: Oxford University Press, 1997.

———. *The Structure of Justification*. Cambridge: Cambridge University Press, 1993.

————, ed. *The Cambridge Dictionary of Philosophy*. Cambridge: Cambridge University Press, 1995; 2d ed., 1999.

Aune, Bruce. *Knowledge, Mind, and Nature*. New York: Random House, 1967.

————. *Knowledge of the External World*. London: Routledge, 1991.

Axtell, Guy, ed. *Knowledge, Belief, and Character: Readings in Virtue Epistemology*. Lanham, Md.: Rowman & Littlefield, 2000.

Ayer, A. J. *Probability and Evidence*. New York: Columbia University Press, 1972.

————. *The Problem of Knowledge*. Baltimore: Penguin, 1956.

Baergen, Ralph. *Contemporary Epistemology*. New York: Harcourt Brace, 1995.

BonJour, Laurence. *The Structure of Empirical Knowledge*. Cambridge, Mass.: Harvard University Press, 1985.

Butchvarov, Panayot. *The Concept of Knowledge*. Evanston, Ill.: Northwestern University Press, 1970.

Campbell, Richmond. *Illusions of Paradox: A Feminist Epistemology Naturalized*. Lanham, Md.: Rowman & Littlefield, 1998.

Carruthers, Peter. *Human Knowledge and Human Nature*. Oxford: Oxford University Press, 1992.

Cassam, Quassim, ed. *Self-Knowledge*. Oxford: Oxford University Press, 1994.

Chisholm, Roderick M. *The Foundations of Knowing*. Minneapolis: University of Minnesota Press, 1982.

————. *Perceiving: A Philosophical Study*. Ithaca, N.Y.: Cornell University Press, 1957.

————. *Theory of Knowledge*, 1st ed. Englewood Cliffs, N.J.: Prentice-Hall, 1966; 2d ed., 1977; 3d ed., 1989.

Chisholm, Roderick, and Robert Swartz, eds. *Empirical Knowledge*. Englewood Cliffs, N.J.: Prentice-Hall, 1973.

Clay, Marjorie, and Keith Lehrer, eds. *Knowledge and Skepticism*. Boulder, Colo.: Westview, 1989.

Coady, C. A. J. *Testimony*. Oxford: Oxford University Press, 1992.

Code, Lorraine. *Epistemic Responsibility*. Hanover, N.H.: Brown University Press/University Press of New England, 1987.

Coffa, J. Alberto. *The Semantic Tradition from Kant to Carnap*. Cambridge: Cambridge University Press, 1991.

Cornman, James W. *Perception, Common Sense, and Science*. New Haven, Conn.: Yale University Press, 1975.

Craig, Edward. *Knowledge and the State of Nature*. Oxford: Oxford University Press, 1991.

Dancy, Jonathan. *An Introduction to Contemporary Epistemology*. Oxford: Blackwell, 1985.

————, ed. *Perceptual Knowledge*. Oxford: Oxford University Press, 1988.

Dancy, Jonathan, and Ernest Sosa, eds. *A Companion to Epistemology*. Oxford: Blackwell, 1992.

Danto, Arthur. *Analytical Philosophy of Knowledge*. Cambridge: Cambridge University Press, 1968.

DePaul, Michael, and William Ramsey, eds. *Rethinking Intuition*. Lanham, Md.: Rowman & Littlefield, 1998.

DeVries, Willem, and Timm Triplett. *Knowledge, Mind, and the Given*. Indianapolis: Hackett, 2000.

Dicker, Georges. *Perceptual Knowledge*. Dordrecht: Reidel, 1980.

Dretske, Fred I. *Seeing and Knowing*. Chicago: University of Chicago Press, 1969.

Fairweather, Abrol, and Linda Zagzebski, eds. *Virtue Epistemology*. New York: Oxford University Press, 2001.

Fales, Evan. *A Defense of the Given*. Lanham, Md.: Rowman & Littlefield, 1996.

Feldman, Richard and Earl Conee. "Evidentialism." *Philosophical Studies* 48 (1985): 15–34. Reprinted in P. K. Moser and Arnold vander Nat, eds., *Human Knowledge*, pp. 334–345. Oxford: Oxford University Press, 1987.

Firth, Roderick. *In Defense of Radical Empiricism*. Edited by John Troyer. Lanham, Md.: Rowman & Littlefield, 1998.

Foley, Richard. *Intellectual Trust in Oneself and Others*. New York: Cambridge University Press, 2001.

———. *The Theory of Epistemic Rationality*. Cambridge, Mass.: Harvard University Press, 1987.

———. *Working Without a Net*. New York: Oxford University Press, 1993.

French, Peter, et al., eds. *Midwest Studies in Philosophy*, vol. 5, *Studies in Epistemology*. Minneapolis: University of Minnesota Press, 1980.

Fumerton, Richard. *Metaphysical and Epistemological Problems of Perception*. Lincoln: University of Nebraska Press, 1985.

———. *Metaepistemology and Skepticism*. Lanham, Md.: Rowman & Littlefield, 1995.

Gardner, Howard. *The Mind's New Science*. New York: Basic, 1985; expanded ed., 1987.

Ginet, Carl. "The Justification of Belief: A Primer." In *Knowledge and Mind*. Edited by C. Ginet and S. Shoemaker. Oxford: Oxford University Press, 1983.

———. *Knowledge, Perception, and Memory*. Dordrecht: Reidel, 1975.

Goldman, Alvin I. *Epistemology and Cognition*. Cambridge, Mass.: Harvard University Press, 1986.

———. *Knowledge in a Social World*. New York: Oxford University Press, 1999.

———. *Liaisons*. Cambridge, Mass.: MIT Press, 1992.

———. *Pathways of Knowledge*. New York: Oxford University Press, 2001.

Greco, John. "Two Kinds of Intellectual Virtue." *Philosophy and Phenomenological Research* 60 (2000): 179–184.

———. "Virtue Epistemology and the Relevant Sense of 'Relevant Responsibility'." *Southern Journal of Philosophy* 32 (1993): 61–77.

———. "Virtues and Vices in Virtue Epistemology." *Canadian Journal of Philosophy* 23 (1993): 413–432.

Greco, John, and Ernest Sosa, eds. *The Blackwell Guide to Epistemology*. Malden, Mass.: Blackwell, 1999.

Griffiths, A. P., ed. *Knowledge and Belief*. Oxford: Oxford University Press, 1967.

Grossmann, Reinhardt. *The Fourth Way*. Bloomington: Indiana University Press, 1990.

Haack, Susan. *Evidence and Inquiry*. Oxford: Blackwell, 1994.

———. "Theories of Knowledge: An Analytic Framework." *Proceedings of the Aristotelian Society* 83 (1983): 143–157.

Hamlyn, D. W. *The Theory of Knowledge*. Garden City, N.Y.: Doubleday, 1971.

Harman, Gilbert. *Change In View*. Cambridge, Mass.: MIT Press, 1986.

———. *Thought*. Princeton, N.J.: Princeton University Press, 1973.

Hetherington, Stephen. *Epistemology's Paradox*. Lanham, Md.: Rowman & Littlefield, 1992.

Hill, Thomas. *Contemporary Theories of Knowledge*. New York: Macmillan, 1961.

Hintikka, Jaakko. *Knowledge and Belief*. Ithaca, N.Y.: Cornell University Press, 1962.
———. *Knowledge and the Known*, 2d ed. Dordrecht: Kluwer, 1991.
Hirsch, Eli. *Dividing Reality*. Oxford: Oxford University Press, 1993.
Hirst, R.J., ed. *Perception and the External World*. New York: Macmillan, 1965.
Jeffrey, Richard C. *The Logic of Decision*, 2d ed. Chicago: University of Chicago Press, 1983.
Kaplan, Mark. *Decision Theory as Philosophy*. New York: Cambridge University Press, 1998.
Kitcher, Philip. *The Advancement of Science*. New York: Oxford University Press, 1993.
Kornblith, Hilary, ed. *Epistemology: Internalism and Externalism*. Malden, Mass.: Blackwell, 2001.
Kulp, Christopher, ed. *Realism/Antirealism and Epistemology*. Lanham, Md.: Rowman & Littlefield, 1997.
Kvanvig, Jonathan. *The Intellectual Virtues and the Life of the Mind*. Lanham, Md.: Rowman & Littlefield, 1992.
———, ed. *Warrant in Contemporary Epistemology*. Lanham, Md.: Rowman & Littlefield, 1996.
Lehrer, Keith. *Knowledge*. Oxford: Clarendon, 1974.
———. *Self-Trust*. Oxford: Clarendon, 1997.
———. *Theory of Knowledge*. Boulder, Colo.: Westview, 1990.
Levi, Isaac. *The Enterprise of Knowledge*. Cambridge, Mass.: MIT Press, 1980.
Lewis, C. I. *An Analysis of Knowledge and Valuation*. LaSalle, Ill.: Open Court, 1946.
Lycan, William. *Judgment and Justification*. Cambridge: Cambridge University Press, 1988.
Malcolm, Norman. *Knowledge and Certainty*. Ithaca, N.Y.: Cornell University Press, 1963.
McGinn, Colin. *Knowledge and Reality: Selected Essays*. Oxford: Clarendon, 1999.
Meyers, Robert. *The Likelihood of Knowledge*. Dordrecht: Kluwer, 1988.
Montmarquet, James. *Epistemic Virtue and Doxastic Responsibility*. Lanham, Md.: Rowman & Littlefield, 1993.
Moser, Paul K. *Empirical Justification*. Dordrecht: Reidel, 1985.
———. *Knowledge and Evidence*. New York: Cambridge University Press, 1989.
———. *Philosophy after Objectivity*. New York: Oxford University Press, 1993.
———. "Epistemology (1900–Present)." In John Canfield, ed., *Routledge History of Philosophy*, vol. 10, *Philosophy of the English Speaking World in the 20th Century*. London: Routledge, 1996.
———, ed. *Empirical Knowledge*, 2d ed. Lanham, Md.: Rowman & Littlefield, 1996.
———, ed. *Rationality in Action*. Cambridge: Cambridge University Press, 1990.
Moser, Paul K., J. D. Trout, and D. H. Mulder. *The Theory of Knowledge*. New York: Oxford University Press, 1998.
Moser, Paul K., and Arnold VanderNat, eds. *Human Knowledge: Classical and Contemporary Approaches*. Oxford: Oxford University Press, 1987; 2d ed., 1995; 3d ed., 2002.
Nagel, Ernest, and Richard Brandt, eds. *Meaning and Knowledge*. New York: Harcourt, Brace & World, 1965.
Pappas, G. S., ed. *Justification and Knowledge*. Dordrecht: Reidel, 1979.
Pappas, G. S. and Marshall Swain, eds. *Essays on Knowledge and Justification*. Ithaca, N.Y.: Cornell University Press, 1978.
Plantinga, Alvin. *Warrant: The Current Debate*. Oxford: Oxford University Press, 1993.
———. *Warrant and Proper Function*. Oxford: Oxford University Press, 1993.

Pollock, John L. *Contemporary Theories of Knowledge*. Lanham, Md.: Rowman & Little-field, 1986; 2d ed. (with J. Cruz), 1999.

———. *Knowledge and Justification*. Princeton, N.J.: Princeton University Press, 1974.

Popper, Karl. *Objective Knowledge*. Oxford: Oxford University Press, 1972.

Quine, W. V. *Pursuit of Truth*. Cambridge, Mass.: Harvard University Press, 1990.

Quine, W. V., and J. S. Ullian, *The Web of Belief*, 2d ed. New York: Random House, 1978.

Roth, Michael, and Leon Galis, eds. *Knowing: Essays in the Analysis of Knowledge*. New York: Random House, 1970.

Russell, Bertrand. *Human Knowledge: Its Scope and Limits*. New York: Simon & Schuster, 1948.

Schlesinger, George N. *The Range of Epistemic Logic*. Atlantic Highlands, N.J.: Humanities, 1985.

Schmitt, Frederick. *Knowledge and Belief*. London: Routledge, 1992.

———, ed. *Socializing Epistemology*. Lanham, Md.: Rowman & Littlefield, 1994.

Sellars, Wilfrid. *Science, Perception, and Reality*. Atascadero, Calif.: Ridgeview, 1991.

———. *The Metaphysics of Epistemology*. Atascadero, Calif.: Ridgeview, 1989.

Shope, Robert. "The Conditional Fallacy in Contemporary Philosophy." *Journal of Philosophy* 75 (1978): 397–413.

Sintonen, Matti, ed. *Knowledge and Inquiry: Essays on Jaakko Hintikka's Epistemology and Philosophy of Science*. Amsterdam: Rodopi, 1997.

Sorensen, Roy. *Thought Experiments*. New York: Oxford University Press, 1998.

Sosa, Ernest. *Knowledge in Perspective*. New York: Cambridge University Press, 1991.

———, ed., *Knowledge and Justification*. Aldershot, U.K.: Dartmouth, 1994.

Sosa, Ernest, and Jaegwon Kim, eds. *Epistemology*. Malden, Mass.: Blackwell, 2000.

Stalnaker, Robert C. *Inquiry*. Cambridge, Mass.: MIT Press, 1984.

Steup, Matthias, ed. *Knowledge, Truth, and Duty*. New York: Oxford University Press, 2001.

Stich, Stephen. *The Fragmentation of Reason*. Cambridge, Mass.: MIT Press, 1990.

Stroll, Avrum, ed. *Epistemology*. New York: Harper & Row, 1967.

Stroud, Barry. *Understanding Human Knowledge: Philosophical Essays*. New York: Oxford University Press, 2000.

Swain, Marshall. *Reasons and Knowledge*. Ithaca, N.Y.: Cornell University Press, 1981.

Swartz, R.J., ed. *Perceiving, Sensing, and Knowing*. Garden City, N.Y.: Doubleday, 1965.

Tomberlin, James, ed. *Philosophical Perspectives*, vol. 2, *Epistemology*. Atascadero, Calif.: Ridgeview, 1988.

———, ed. *Philosophical Perspectives*, vol. 13, Epistemology. Cambridge, Mass.: Blackwell, 1999.

Williams, Michael. *Problems of Knowledge*. New York: Oxford University Press, 2001.

A PRIORI KNOWLEDGE

Benacerraf, Paul, and Hilary Putnam, eds. *Philosophy of Mathematics*. Englewood Cliffs, N.J.: Prentice-Hall, 1964.

Bennett, Jonathan. *Kant's Analytic*. Cambridge: Cambridge University Press, 1966.

Blackburn, Simon, ed. *Meaning, Reference, and Necessity*. Cambridge: Cambridge University Press, 1975.

BonJour, Laurence. *In Defense of Pure Reason: A Rationalist Account of "A Priori" Justification*. New York: Cambridge University Press, 1998.

Casullo, Albert, ed. *A Priori Knowledge*. Aldershot, U.K.: Ashgate, 1999.

————. *A Priori Justification*. New York: Oxford University Press, forthcoming.

————. "Actuality and the A Priori". *Australasian Journal of Philosophy* 66 (1988): 390–402.

————. "Necessity, Certainty, and the 'A Priori'." *Canadian Journal of Philosophy* 18 (1988): 43–66.

————. "Revisability, Reliabilism, and A Priori Knowledge." *Philosophy and Phenomenological Research* 49 (1988): 187–213.

Harris, J. F., and R. H. Severens, eds. *Analyticity: Selected Readings*. Chicago: Quadrangle, 1970.

Kitcher, Philip. *The Nature of Mathematical Knowledge*. New York: Oxford University Press, 1983.

————. "A Priori Knowledge." *Philosophical Review* 76 (1980): 3–23.

————. "Apriority and Necessity." *Australasian Journal of Philosophy* 58 (1980): 89–101.

Kripke, Saul A. *Naming and Necessity*. Cambridge, Mass.: Harvard University Press, 1980.

————. "Identity and Necessity." In *Naming, Necessity, and Natural Kinds*, pp. 66–101. Edited by S. P. Schwartz. Ithaca, N.Y.: Cornell University Press, 1977.

————. *Wittgenstein on Rules and Private Language*. Cambridge, Mass.: Harvard University Press, 1982.

Lewis, C. I. *An Analysis of Knowledge and Valuation*, chaps. 3–6. La Salle, Ill.: Open Court, 1946.

————. *Mind and the World Order*, chaps. 7–9. New York: Scribner's, 1929.

————. "A Pragmatic Conception of the A Priori." *Journal of Philosophy* 20 (1923): 169–177. Reprinted in *Collected Papers of Clarence Irving Lewis*, pp. 231–239. Edited by J. D. Goheen and J. L. Mothershead. Stanford: Stanford University Press, 1970.

Moser, Paul K., ed. *A Priori Knowledge*. Oxford: Oxford University Press, 1987.

Pap, Arthur. *The A Priori in Physical Theory*. New York: King's Crown, 1946.

————. *Semantics and Necessary Truth*. New Haven, Conn.: Yale University Press, 1958.

Pasch, Alan. *Experience and the Analytic: A Reconsideration of Empiricism*. Chicago: University of Chicago Press, 1958.

Price, H. H. *Thinking and Experience*, 2d ed. London: Hutchinson, 1969.

Putnam, Hilary. "The Analytic and the Synthetic." In Putnam, *Mind, Language, and Reality, Philosophical Papers*, vol. 2, pp. 33–69. Cambridge: Cambridge University Press, 1975.

————. "Analyticity and Apriority: Beyond Wittgenstein and Quine." In *Midwest Studies in Philosophy*, vol. 4, pp. 423–441. Edited by P. French et al. Minneapolis: University of Minnesota Press, 1979.

————. "There Is at Least One A Priori Truth." *Erkenntnis* 13 (1978): 153–70. Reprinted in Putnam, *Realism and Reason, Philosophical Papers*, Vol. 3, pp. 98–114. Cambridge: Cambridge University Press, 1983.

————. " 'Two Dogmas' Revisited." In Putnam, *Realism and Reason, Philosophical Papers*, vol. 3, pp. 87–97. Cambridge: Cambridge University Press, 1983.

Quine, W. V. "Carnap and Logical Truth." In Quine, *The Ways of Paradox*, pp. 100–125. New York: Random House, 1966.

———. "The Ground of Logical Truth." In Quine, *Philosophy of Logic*, chap. 7. Englewood Cliffs, N.J.: Prentice-Hall, 1970.

———. "Truth by Convention." In Quine, *The Ways of Paradox*, pp. 70–99. New York: Random House, 1966.

———. "Two Dogmas of Empiricism." In Quine, *From a Logical Point of View*, 2d ed. New York: Harper & Row, 1963.

———. "Two Dogmas in Retrospect." *Canadian Journal of Philosophy* 21 (1991): 265–274.

Resnik, M. D. *Frege and the Philosophy of Mathematics*. Ithaca, N.Y.: Cornell University Press, 1980.

Rosenthal, Sandra. *The Pragmatic A Priori: A Study in the Epistemology of C. I. Lewis*. St. Louis, Green, 1976.

Sleigh, R. C., ed. *Necessary Truth*. Englewood Cliffs, N.J.: Prentice-Hall, 1972.

Steiner, Mark. *Mathematical Knowledge*. Ithaca, N.Y.: Cornell University Press, 1975.

Wittgenstein, Ludwig. *Remarks on the Foundations of Mathematics*, 3d ed. Cambridge, Mass.: MIT Press, 1978.

Wright, Crispin. *Wittgenstein on the Foundations of Mathematics*. Cambridge, Mass.: Harvard University Press, 1980.

EPISTEMIC FOUNDATIONALISM

Almeder, Robert F. "Basic Knowledge and Justification." *Canadian Journal of Philosophy* 13 (1983): 115–28.

Alston, William P. *Epistemic Justification*. Ithaca, N.Y.: Cornell University Press, 1989.

———. "Plantinga's Religious Epistemology." In *Alvin Plantinga*, pp. 287–309. Edited by J. E. Tomberlin and P. van Inwagen. Dordrecht: Reidel, 1985.

———. "Some Remarks on Chisholm's Epistemology." *Noûs* 14 (1980): 565–586.

Annis, David B. "Epistemic Foundationalism." *Philosophical Studies* 31 (1977): 345–352.

Armstrong, David M. *Belief, Truth, and Knowledge*. Cambridge: Cambridge University Press, 1973.

Audi, Robert. *The Structure of Justification*. Cambridge: Cambridge University Press, 1993.

Ayer, A. J. "Basic Propositions." In *Philosophical Analysis*, pp. 60–74. Edited by M. Black. Englewood Cliffs, N.J.: Prentice-Hall, 1950. Reprinted in Ayer, *Philosophical Essays*. London: Macmillan, 1965.

———. *The Foundations of Empirical Knowledge*. New York: Macmillan, 1940.

BonJour, Laurence. "Externalist Theories of Empirical Knowledge." In *Midwest Studies in Philosophy*, vol. 5: *Studies in Epistemology*, pp. 53–74. Edited by P. French et al. Minneapolis: University of Minnesota Press, 1980.

———. *The Structure of Empirical Knowledge*. Cambridge, Mass.: Harvard University Press, 1985.

Chisholm, Roderick. "The Directly Evident." In *Justification and Knowledge*, pp. 115–127. Edited by G. S. Pappas. Dordrecht: Reidel, 1979.

———. "On the Nature of Empirical Evidence." In *Essays on Knowledge and Justification*, pp. 253–278. Edited by G. S. Pappas and M. Swain. Ithaca, N.Y.: Cornell University Press, 1978.

———. *Theory of Knowledge*, 1st ed. Englewood Cliffs, N.J.: Prentice-Hall, 1966; 2d ed., 1977; 3d ed., 1989.

———. "Theory of Knowledge in America." In Chisholm, *The Foundations of Knowing*, pp. 109–196. Minneapolis: University of Minnesota Press, 1982.

———. "A Version of Foundationalism." In Chisholm, *The Foundations of Knowing*, pp. 3–32. Minneapolis: University of Minnesota Press, 1982.

Churchland, Paul M. *Scientific Realism and the Plasticity of Mind*, chap. 2. Cambridge: Cambridge University Press, 1979.

Cornman, James W. "Foundational versus Nonfoundational Theories of Empirical Justification." *American Philosophical Quarterly* 14 (1977); 287–297. Reprinted in *Essays on Knowledge and Justification*, pp. 229–252. Edited by G. S. Pappas and M. Swain. Ithaca, N.Y.: Cornell University Press, 1978.

———. *Skepticism, Justification, and Explanation*. Dordrecht: Reidel, 1980.

Dancy, Jonathan. *An Introduction to Contemporary Epistemology*, chaps. 4 and 5. Oxford: Blackwell, 1985.

DePaul Michael, ed. *Resurrecting Old-Fashioned Foundationalism*. Lanham, Md.: Rowman & Littlefield, 2001.

Foley, Richard. *The Theory of Epistemic Rationality*. Cambridge, Mass.: Harvard University Press, 1987.

———. *Working without a Net*. Oxford: Oxford University Press, 1993.

Fumerton, Richard. *Metaepistemology and Skepticism*. Lanham, Md.: Rowman & Littlefield, 1995.

———. *Metaphysical and Epistemological Problems of Perception*, chap. 2. Lincoln: University of Nebraska Press, 1985.

Goldman, Alan H. *Empirical Knowledge*. Berkeley, Calif.: University of California Press, 1988.

———. "Epistemic Foundationalism and the Replaceability of Ordinary Language." *Journal of Philosophy* 79 (1982): 136–154.

Heidelberger, Herbert. "Chisholm's Epistemic Principles." *Noûs* 3 (1969): 73–82.

Heil, John. "Foundationalism and Epistemic Rationality." *Philosophical Studies* 42 (1982): 179–188.

Kornblith, Hilary. "Beyond Foundationalism and the Coherence Theory." *Journal of Philosophy* 72 (1980): 597–612. Reprinted in *Naturalizing Epistemology*, pp. 115–128. Edited by H. Kornblith. Cambridge, Mass.: MIT Press, 1985.

Lehrer, Keith. *Theory of Knowledge*. Boulder, Colo.: Westview, 1990.

Lewis, C. I. *An Analysis of Knowledge and Valuation*, chaps. 7 and 8. LaSalle, Ill.: Open Court, 1946.

———. "The Given Element in Empirical Knowledge." *Philosophical Review* 61 (1952): 168–175.

———. *Mind and the World Order*. New York: Scribner's, 1929.

McGrew, Timothy. *The Foundations of Knowledge*. Lanham, Md.: Littlefield Adams, 1995.

Moser, Paul K. "A Defense of Epistemic Intuitionism." *Metaphilosophy* 15 (1984): 196–209.

———. *Empirical Justification*, chaps. 4 and 5. Dordrecht: Reidel, 1985.

———. *Knowledge and Evidence.* Cambridge: Cambridge University Press, 1989.

———. *Philosophy after Objectivity.* Oxford: Oxford University Press, 1993.

Pastin, Mark. "Lewis' Radical Foundationalism." *Noûs* 9 (1975): 407–420.

———. "Modest Foundationalism and Self-Warrant." In *American Philosophical Quarterly Monograph Series, No. 9: Studies in Epistemology*, pp. 141–149. Edited by N. Rescher. Oxford: Blackwell, 1975. Reprinted in *Essays on Knowledge and Justification*, pp. 279–288. Edited by G. S. Pappas and M. Swain. Ithaca, N.Y.: Cornell University Press, 1978.

Pollock, John. *Contemporary Theories of Knowledge.* Lanham, Md.: Rowman & Littlefield, 1986; 2d ed. (with J. Cruz), 1999.

———. *Knowledge and Justification.* Princeton, N.J.: Princeton University Press, 1974.

———. "A Plethora of Epistemological Theories." In *Justification and Knowledge*, pp. 93–113. Edited by G. S. Pappas. Dordrecht: Reidel, 1979.

Quinton, Anthony. "The Foundations of Knowledge." In *British Analytic Philosophy*, pp. 55–86. Edited by Bernard Williams and Alan Montefiore. London: Routledge & Kegan Paul, 1966.

———. *The Nature of Things*, chap. 8. London: Routledge & Kegan Paul, 1973.

Russell, Bertrand. *Human Knowledge: Its Scope and Limits*, part 2. New York: Simon & Schuster, 1948.

———. *An Inquiry into Meaning and Truth*, chaps. 9 and 10. New York: Norton, 1940.

———. "On Verification." *Proceedings of the Aristotelian Society* 38 (1937–1938), 1–15.

Scheffler, Israel. *Science and Subjectivity*, 2d ed., chaps. 2 and 5. Indianapolis: Hackett, 1982.

Sellars, Wilfrid. "Does Empirical Knowledge Have a Foundation?," in *Empiricism and the Philosophy of Mind. Minnesota Studies in the Philosophy of Science*, vol. 1, pp. 293–300. Edited by H. Feigl and M. Scriven. Minneapolis: University of Minnesota Press, 1956. Reprinted in Sellars, *Science, Perception, and Reality*. London: Routledge & Kegan Paul, 1963.

Sosa, Ernest. *Knowledge in Perspective.* Cambridge: Cambridge University Press, 1991.

Strawson, Peter F. "Does Knowledge Have Foundations?." In *Teorema, Mono. 1: Conocimiento y Creencia*, pp. 99–110. Universidad de Valencia, 1974.

Swain, Marshall. "Cornman's Theory of Justification." *Philosophical Studies* 41 (1982): 129–148.

———. *Reasons and Knowledge.* Ithaca, N.Y.: Cornell University Press, 1981.

Van Cleve, James. "Epistemic Supervenience and the Circle of Belief." *The Monist* 68 (1985): 90–104.

———. "Foundationalism, Epistemic Principles, and the Cartesian Circle." *Philosophical Review* 88 (1979): 55–91.

EPISTEMIC COHERENTISM

Audi, Robert. *The Structure of Justification.* Cambridge: Cambridge University Press, 1993.

Bender, John, ed. *The Current State of the Coherence Theory.* Dordrecht: Kluwer, 1989.

Blanshard, Brand. *The Nature of Thought*, vol. 2, chaps. 25–27. London: Allen & Unwin, 1939.

BonJour, Laurence. "The Coherence Theory of Empirical Knowledge." *Philosophical Studies* 30 (1976): 281–312.

———. *The Structure of Empirical Knowledge*. Cambridge, Mass.: Harvard University Press, 1985.

Dancy, Jonathan. *An Introduction to Contemporary Epistemology*, chaps. 8 and 9. Oxford: Blackwell, 1985.

———. "On Coherence Theories of Justification: Can an Empiricist be a Coherentist?." *American Philosophical Quarterly* 21 (1984): 359–365.

Davidson, Donald. "A Coherence Theory of Truth and Knowledge." In *Kant oder Hegel*, pp. 423–438. Edited by Dieter Henrich. Stuttgart: Klett-Cotta, 1983.

Firth, Roderick. "Coherence, Certainty, and Epistemic Priority." *Journal of Philosophy* 61 (1964), 545–557.

Harman, Gilbert. *Change In View*. Cambridge, Mass.: MIT Press, 1986.

———. "Knowledge, Inference, and Explanation." *American Philosophical Quarterly* 5 (1968): 164–173.

———. "Knowledge, Reasons, and Causes." *Journal of Philosophy* 67 (1970): 841–855.

———. *Thought*, chap. 8. Princeton, N.J.: Princeton University Press, 1973.

Lehrer, Keith. "Justification, Explanation, and Induction." In *Induction, Acceptance, and Rational Belief*, pp. 100–33. Edited by M. Swain. Dordrecht: Reidel, 1970.

———. *Knowledge*, chaps. 7 and 8. Oxford: Clarendon, 1974.

———. "The Knowledge Cycle." *Noûs* 11 (1977): 17–26.

———. "Knowledge, Truth, and Ontology." In *Language and Ontology: Proceedings of the 6th International Wittgenstein Symposium*, pp. 201–211. Edited by W. Leinfellner et al. Vienna: Holder-Pichler-Tempsky, 1982.

———. "Self-Profile." In *Keith Lehrer*, pp. 3–104. Edited by R. J. Bogdan. Dordrecht: Reidel, 1981.

———. *Theory of Knowledge*. Boulder, Colo.: Westview, 1990.

Lehrer, Keith, and Stewart Cohen. "Justification, Truth, and Coherence." *Synthese* 55 (1983): 191–208.

Lemos, Noah. "Coherence and Epistemic Priority." *Philosophical Studies* 41 (1982): 299–316.

Moser, Paul K. *Empirical Justification*, chap. 3. Dordrecht: Reidel, 1985.

———. *Knowledge and Evidence*. Cambridge: Cambridge University Press, 1989.

Pastin, Mark. "Social and Anti-Social Justification: A Study of Lehrer's Epistemology." In *Keith Lehrer*, pp. 205–222. Dordrecht: Reidel, 1981.

Rescher, Nicholas. "Blanshard and the Coherence Theory of Truth." In *The Philosophy of Brand Blanshard*, pp. 574–588. Edited by P. Schilpp. LaSalle, Ill.: Open Court, 1980.

———. *Cognitive Systematization*. Oxford: Blackwell, 1979.

———. *The Coherence Theory of Truth*. Oxford: Clarendon, 1973.

———. "Foundationalism, Coherentism, and the Idea of Cognitive Systematization." *Journal of Philosophy* 71 (1974): 695–708.

———. *A System of Pragmatic Idealism*, 3 vols. Princeton, N.J.: Princeton University Press, 1991–1994.

———. "Truth as Ideal Coherence." *Review of Metaphysics* 38 (1985): 795–806.

Sellars, Wilfrid. "Epistemic Principles." In *Action, Knowledge, and Reality: Critical Studies in Honor of Wilfrid Sellars*, pp. 332–348. Edited by H.-N. Castaneda. Indianapolis: Bobbs-Merrill, 1975.

————. "Givenness and Explanatory Coherence." *Journal of Philosophy* 70 (1973): 612–624.

————. "More on Givenness and Explanatory Coherence." In *Justification and Knowledge*, pp. 169–181. Edited by G. S. Pappas. Dordrecht: Reidel, 1979.

Sosa, Ernest. "Circular Coherence and Absurd Foundations." In *A Companion to Inquiries into Truth and Interpretation*. Edited by E. Lepore. Oxford: Blackwell, 1985.

————. *Knowledge in Perspective*. Cambridge: Cambridge University Press, 1991.

EPISTEMIC CONTEXTUALISM

Airaksinen, Timo. "Contextualism: A New Theory of Epistemic Justification." *Philosophia* 12 (1982): 37–50.

Annis, David. "The Social and Cultural Component of Epistemic Justification: A Reply." *Philosophia* 12 (1982): 51–55.

Morawetz, Thomas. *Wittgenstein and Knowledge*. Amherst: University of Massachusetts Press, 1978.

Moser, Paul K. *Empirical Justification*, chap. 2. Dordrecht: Reidel, 1985.

Rorty, Richard. *Philosophy and the Mirror of Nature*, chap. 7. Princeton, N.J.: Princeton University Press, 1979.

————. "From Epistemology to Hermeneutics." In *Acta Philosophica Fennica*, vol. 30, *The Logic and Epistemology of Scientific Change*. Edited by I. Niiniluoto and R. Tuomela. Amsterdam: North-Holland, 1978.

Schmitt, Frederick, ed. *Socializing Epistemology*. Lanham, Md.: Rowman & Littlefield, 1994.

Shiner, Roger. "Wittgenstein and the Foundations of Knowledge." *Proceedings of the Aristotelian Society* 78 (1977–78): 103–124.

Sosa, Ernest. "On Groundless Belief." *Synthese* 43 (1979): 453–460.

Williams, Michael. "Coherence, Justification, and Truth." *Review of Metaphysics* 34 (1980): 243–272.

————. *Groundless Belief*. Oxford: Blackwell, 1977; 2d ed., Princeton, N.J.: Princeton University Press, 1999.

————. *Unnatural Doubts*. Oxford: Blackwell, 1991.

Wittgenstein, Ludwig. *On Certainty*. Edited by G. E. M. Anscombe and G. H. von Wright. Oxford: Blackwell, 1969.

EPISTEMIC RELIABILISM

Armstrong, David M. *Belief, Truth, and Knowledge*. Cambridge: Cambridge University Press, 1973.

———. "Self-Profile." In *D. M. Armstrong*, pp. 30–37. Edited by R. Bogdan. Dordrecht: Reidel, 1984.

Audi, Robert. *The Structure of Justification*. Cambridge: Cambridge University Press, 1993.

BonJour, Laurence. "Externalist Theories of Empirical Knowledge." In *Midwest Studies in Philosophy*, vol. 5, *Studies in Epistemology*, pp. 53–73. Edited by P. French et al. Minneapolis: University of Minnesota Press, 1980.

Cohen, Stewart. "Justification and Truth." *Philosophical Studies* 46 (1984): 279–295.

Dretske, Fred I. "Conclusive Reasons." *Australasian Journal of Philosophy* 49 (1971): 1–22. Reprinted in *Essays on Knowledge and Justification*, pp. 41–60. Edited by G. S. Pappas and M. Swain. Ithaca, N.Y.: Cornell University Press, 1978.

———. "The Pragmatic Dimension of Knowledge." *Philosophical Studies* 40 (1981): 363–378.

———. *Knowledge and the Flow of Information*, chaps. 4 and 5. Cambridge, Mass.: MIT Press, 1981.

———. "Precis of *Knowledge and the Flow of Information*." *Behavioral and Brain Sciences* 6 (1983): 55–63.

Feldman, Richard. "Reliability and Justification." *The Monist* 68 (1985): 159–174.

Feldman, Richard and Earl Conee. "Evidentialism." *Philosophical Studies* 48 (1985): 15–34.

Firth, Roderick. "Epistemic Merit, Intrinsic and Instrumental." In *Proceedings and Addresses of the American Philosophical Association* 55 (1981): 5–23.

Foley, Richard. "What's Wrong with Reliabilism?" *The Monist* 68 (1985): 188–202.

Friedman, Michael. "Truth and Confirmation." *Journal of Philosophy* 76 (1979): 361–382. Reprinted in *Naturalizing Epistemology*, pp. 147–168. Edited by H. Kornblith. Cambridge, Mass.: MIT Press, 1985.

Ginet, Carl. "*Contra* Reliabilism." *The Monist* 68 (1985): 175–187.

Goldman, Alvin I. "Discrimination and Perceptual Knowledge." *Journal of Philosophy* 73 (1976): 771–791. Reprinted in *Essays on Knowledge and Justification*, pp. 120–145. Edited by G. S. Pappas and M. Swain. Ithaca, N.Y.: Cornell University Press, 1978.

———. *Epistemology and Cognition*. Cambridge, Mass.: Harvard University Press, 1986.

———. "The Internalist Conception of Justification." In *Midwest Studies in Philosophy*, vol. 5, *Studies in Epistemology*, pp. 27–52. Edited by P. French et al. Minneapolis: University of Minnesota Press, 1980.

———. *Liaisons*. Cambridge, Mass.: MIT Press, 1992.

———. "What Is Justified Belief?" In *Justification and Knowledge*, pp. 1–23. Edited by G. S. Pappas. Dordrecht: Reidel, 1979.

Heil, John. "Reliability and Epistemic Merit." *Australasian Journal of Philosophy* 62 (1984): 327–338.

Kornblith, Hilary. "Beyond Foundationalism and the Coherence Theory." *Journal of Philosophy* 72 (1980): 597–612.

———. "Ever Since Descartes." *The Monist* 68 (1985): 264–276.

———. "Justified Belief and Epistemically Responsible Action." *Philosophical Review* 92 (1983): 33–48.

———. "The Psychological Turn." *Australasian Journal of Philosophy* 60 (1982): 238–253.

———, ed. *Naturalizing Epistemology*. Cambridge, Mass.: MIT Press, 1994.

Kvanvig, Johathan. *The Intellectual Virtues and the Life of the Mind*. Lanham, Md.: Rowman & Littlefield, 1992.

Lycan William G. "Armstrong's Theory of Knowing." In *D. M. Armstrong*, pp. 139–160. Edited by R. Bogdan. Dordrecht: Reidel, 1984.

———. *Judgment and Justification*. Cambridge: Cambridge University Press, 1988.

Montmarquet, James. *Epistemic Virtue and Doxastic Responsibility*. Lanham, Md.: Rowman & Littlefield, 1993.

Moser, Paul K. *Empirical Justification*, chap. 4 and appendix. Dordrecht: Reidel, 1985.

———. "Knowledge without Evidence." *Philosophia* 15 (1985): 109–116.

Nozick, Robert. *Philosophical Explanations*, chap. 3. Cambridge, Mass.: Harvard University Press, 1981.

Pappas, George S. "Non-Inferential Knowledge." *Philosophia* 12 (1982): 81–98.

Pastin, Mark. "Knowledge and Reliability: A Critical Study of D. M. Armstrong's *Belief, Truth, and Knowledge.*" *Metaphilosophy* 9 (1978): 150–162.

———. "The Multi-perspectival Theory of Knowledge." In *Midwest Studies in Philosophy*, vol. 5, *Studies in Epistemology*, pp. 97–111. Edited by P. French et al. Minneapolis: University of Minnesota Press, 1980.

Pollock, John. *Contemporary Theories of Knowledge*. Lanham, Md.: Rowman & Littlefield, 1986; 2d ed. (with J. Cruz), 1999.

———. "Reliability and Justified Belief." *Canadian Journal of Philosophy* 14 (1984): 103–114.

Schmitt, Frederick F. "Justification as Reliable Indication or Reliable Process." *Philosophical Studies* 40 (1981): 409–417.

———. *Knowledge and Belief*. London: Routledge, 1992.

———. "Knowledge as Tracking." *Topoi* 4 (1985): 73–80.

———. "Knowledge, Justification, and Reliability." *Synthese* 55 (1983): 209–229.

———. "Reliability, Objectivity, and the Background of Justification." *Australasian Journal of Philosophy* 62 (1984): 1–15.

Shope, Robert K. "Cognitive Abilities, Conditionals, and Knowledge: A Response to Nozick." *Journal of Philosophy* 81 (1984): 29–47.

Sosa, Ernest. *Knowledge in Perspective*. Cambridge: Cambridge University Press, 1991.

Swain, Marshall. "Justification and the Basis of Belief." In *Justification and Knowledge*, pp. 25–49. Edited by G. S. Pappas. Dordrecht: Reidel, 1979.

———. "Justification and Reliable Belief." *Philosophical Studies* 40 (1981): 389–407.

——— "Justification, Reasons, and Reliability." *Synthese* 64 (1985): 69–92.

———. *Reasons and Knowledge*, chap. 4. Ithaca, N.Y.: Cornell University Press, 1981.

Van Cleve, James. "Reliability, Justification, and the Problem of Induction." In *Midwest Studies in Philosophy*, vol. 9, pp. 555–567. Edited by P. French et al. Minneapolis: University of Minnesota Press, 1984.

NATURALIZED EPISTEMOLOGY

Almeder, Robert. *Harmless Naturalism*. Chicago: Open Court, 1998.

———. "On Naturalizing Epistemology." *American Philosophical Quarterly* 27 (1990): 263–279.

Bogen, James. "Traditional Epistemology and Naturalistic Replies to its Skeptical Critics." *Synthese* 64 (1985): 195–223.

Boyd, Richard. "Scientific Realism and Naturalistic Epistemology." In *PSA* 80 (1982), vol. 2. East Lansing, Mich.: Philosophy of Science Association.

Dancy, Jonathan. *An Introduction to Contemporary Epistemology*, chap. 15. Oxford: Blackwell, 1985.

Devitt, Michael. *Realism and Truth*, chap. 5. Princeton, N.J.: Princeton University Press, 1984; 2d ed., 1991.

Goldman, Alvin I. *Epistemology and Cognition*. Cambridge, Mass.: Harvard University Press, 1986.

———. "Epistemology and the Psychology of Belief." *The Monist* 61 (1978): 525–535.

———. "Epistemology and the Theory of Problem Solving." *Synthese* 55 (1983): 21–48.

———. *Liaisons*. Cambridge, Mass.: MIT Press, 1992.

———. "The Relation between Epistemology and Psychology." *Synthese* 64 (1985): 29–68.

———. "Varieties of Cognitive Appraisal." *Noûs* 13 (1979): 23–38.

Haack, Susan. "The Relevance of Psychology to Epistemology." *Metaphilosophy* 6 (1975): 161–176.

Kitcher, Philip. "The Naturalists Return." *Philosophical Review* 101 (1992): 53–114.

Kornblith, Hilary, ed. *Naturalizing Epistemology*. Cambridge, Mass.: MIT Press, 1985; 2d ed., 1994.

Lycan, William G. "Epistemic Value." *Synthese* 64 (1985): 137–164.

Moser, Paul K., and David Yandell. "Against Naturalizing Rationality." In Gerhard Preyer and Georg Peter, eds. *The Contextualization of Rationality*, pp. 81–94. Paderborn: Mentis, 2000.

Putnam, Hilary. "Why Reason Can't Be Naturalized." In Putnam, *Realism and Reason: Philosophical Papers*, vol. 3, pp. 229–247. Cambridge: Cambridge University Press, 1983.

Quine, W. V. "The Nature of Natural Knowledge." In *Mind and Language: Wolfson College Lectures*, pp. 67–81. Edited by S. Guttenplan. Oxford: Oxford University Press, 1975.

Rorty, Richard. *Philosophy and the Mirror of Nature*, chap. 5. Princeton, N.J.: Princeton University Press, 1979.

Siegel, Harvey. "Empirical Psychology, Naturalized Epistemology, and First Philosophy." *Philosophy of Science* 51 (1984): 667–676.

———. "Justification, Discovery, and the Naturalizing of Epistemology." *Philosophy of Science* 47 (1980): 297–321.

———. "Naturalism, Instrumental Rationality, and the Normativity of Epistemology." In Gerhard Preyer and Georg Peter, eds. *The Contextualization of Rationality*, pp. 95–107. Paderborn: Mentis, 2000.

Sosa, Ernest. "Nature Unmirrored, Epistemology Naturalized." *Synthese* 55 (1983): 49–72.

Stroud, Barry. "The Significance of Naturalized Epistemology." In *Midwest Studies in Philosophy*, vol. 6, *Analytic Philosophy*, pp. 455–471. Edited by P. French et al. Minneapolis: University of Minnesota Press, 1981. Reprinted in *Naturalizing Epistemology*, pp. 71–89. Edited by H. Kornblith. Cambridge, Mass.: MIT Press, 1985.

———. *The Significance of Philosophical Scepticism*, chap. 6. Oxford: Clarendon, 1984.

Swain, Marshall. "Epistemics and Epistemology." *Journal of Philosophy* 75 (1978): 523–525.

GETTIER PROBLEM

Audi, Robert. "Defeated Knowledge, Reliability, and Justification." In *Midwest Studies in Philosophy,* vol. 5, *Studies in Epistemology,* pp. 75–95. Edited by P. French et al. Minneapolis: University of Minnesota Press, 1980.

Chisholm, Roderick M. "Knowledge as Justified True Belief." In Chisholm, *The Foundations of Knowing,* pp. 43–49. Minneapolis: University of Minnesota Press, 1982.

Dancy, Jonathan. *An Introduction to Contemporary Epistemology,* chap. 2. Oxford: Blackwell, 1985.

Dretske, Fred I. "Conclusive Reasons." *Australasian Journal of Philosophy* 49 (1971): 1–22.

Feldman, Richard. "An Alleged Defect in Gettier Counter-Examples." *Australasian Journal of Philosophy* 52 (1974): 68–69.

Gettier, Edmund. "Is Justified True Belief Knowledge?." *Analysis* 23 (1963): 121–123.

Goldman, Alvin. "A Causal Theory of Knowing." *Journal of Philosophy* 64 (1967): 357–372. Reprinted in *Essays on Knowledge and Justification,* pp. 67–86. Edited by G. S. Pappas and M. Swain. Ithaca, N.Y.: Cornell University Press, 1978.

———. "Discrimination and Perceptual Knowledge." *Journal of Philosophy* 73 (1976): 771–791. Reprinted in *Essays on Knowledge and Justification,* pp. 120–45.

Harman, Gilbert. "Knowledge, Inference, and Explanation." *American Philosophical Quarterly* 5 (1968): 164–173.

———. "Knowledge, Reasons, and Causes." *Journal of Philosophy* 67 (1970): 841–855.

———. "Reasoning and Evidence One Does Not Possess." In *Midwest Studies in Philosophy,* vol. 5, *Studies in Epistemology,* pp. 163–182. Edited by P. French et al. Minneapolis: University of Minnesota Press, 1980.

———. *Thought,* chaps. 7–9. Princeton, N.J.: Princeton University Press, 1973.

Kaplan, Mark. "It's Not What You Know That Counts." *Journal of Philosophy* 82 (1985): 350–363.

Klein, Peter D. "Knowledge, Causality, and Defeasibility." *Journal of Philosophy* 73 (1976): 792–812.

———. "A Proposed Definition of Propositional Knowledge." *Journal of Philosophy* 68 (1971): 471–482.

———. "Misleading Evidence and the Restoration of Justification." *Philosophical Studies* 37 (1980): 81–89.

———. "Real Knowledge." *Synthese* 55 (1983): 143–164.

Lehrer, Keith. "The Gettier Problem and the Analysis of Knowledge." In *Justification and Knowledge,* pp. 65–78. Edited by G. S. Pappas. Dordrecht: Reidel, 1979.

———. *Knowledge,* chap. 9. Oxford: Clarendon, 1974.

———. "Self-Profile." In *Keith Lehrer,* pp. 3–104. Edited by R. Bogdan. Dordrecht: Reidel, 1981.

———. *Theory of Knowledge.* Boulder, Colo.: Westview, 1990.

Moser, Paul K. *Knowledge and Evidence.* Cambridge: Cambridge University Press, 1989.

———. "Propositional Knowledge." *Philosophical Studies* 52 (1987): 91–114. Reprinted in Ernest Sosa, ed., *Knowledge and Justification,* vol. 1, pp. 99–124. Aldershort, U.K.: Dartmouth, 1994.

Roth, Michael D, and Leon Galis, eds. *Knowing: Essays in the Analysis of Knowledge.* New York: Random House, 1970.

Shope, Robert K. *The Analysis of Knowing.* Princeton, N.J.: Princeton University Press, 1983.

———. "Knowledge and Falsity." *Philosophical Studies* 36 (1979): 389–405.

———. "Knowledge as Justified Belief in a True, Justified Proposition." *Philosophy Research Archives* 5 (1979): 1–36.

Slaght, Ralph. "Is Justified True Belief Knowledge?: A Selective Critical Survey of Recent Work." *Philosophy Research Archives* 3 (1977): 1–135.

Sosa, Ernest. "How Do You Know?." *American Philosophical Quarterly* 11 (1974): 113–122. Reprinted in *Essays on Knowledge and Justification*, pp. 184–205. Edited by G. S. Pappas and M. Swain. Ithaca, N.Y.: Cornell University Press, 1978.

———. "Epistemic Presupposition." In *Justification and Knowledge*, pp. 79–92. Edited by G. S. Pappas. Dordrecht: Reidel, 1979.

Swain, Marshall. "Epistemic Defeasibility." *American Philosophical Quarterly* 11 (1974): 15–25. Reprinted in *Essays on Knowledge and Justification*, pp. 160–183. Edited by G. S. Pappas and M. Swain. Ithaca, N.Y.: Cornell University Press, 1978.

———. "Knowledge, Causality, and Justification." *Journal of Philosophy* 69 (1972): 291–300. Reprinted in *Essays on Knowledge and Justification*, pp. 87–99.

———. *Reasons and Knowledge.* Ithaca, N.Y.: Cornell University Press, 1981.

———. "Reasons, Causes, and Knowledge." *Journal of Philosophy* 75 (1978): 229–249.

Thalberg, Irving. "In Defense of Justified True Belief." *Journal of Philosophy* 66 (1969): 794–803.

Williams, Michael. "Inference, Justification, and the Analysis of Knowledge." *Journal of Philosophy* 75 (1978): 249–263.

EPISTEMOLOGICAL SKEPTICISM

Amico, Robert. *The Problem of the Criterion.* Lanham, Md.: Rowman & Littlefield, 1993.

Brueckner, Anthony L. "Skepticism and Epistemic Closure." *Philosophical Topics* 13 (1985): 89–117.

Burnyeat, Myles, ed. *The Skeptical Tradition.* Berkeley: University of California Press, 1983.

Butchvarov, Panayot. *Skepticism about the External World.* New York: Oxford University Press, 1998.

Chisholm, Roderick M. "The Problem of the Criterion." In Chisholm, *The Foundations of Knowing*, pp. 61–75. Minneapolis: University of Minnesota Press, 1982.

Clay, Marjorie, and Keith Lehrer, eds. *Knowledge and Skepticism.* Boulder, Colo.: Westview, 1989.

Cornman, James W. *Skepticism, Justification, and Explanation.* Dordrecht: Reidel, 1980.

Dancy, Jonathan. *An Introduction to Contemporary Epistemology*, chap. 1. Oxford: Blackwell, 1985.

DeRose, Keith, and Ted Warfield, eds. *Skepticism.* New York: Oxford University Press, 1999.

Floridi, Luciano. *Scepticism and the Foundation of Epistemology*. Leiden: Brill, 1996.

Fogelin, Robert. *Pyrrhonian Reflections on Knowledge and Justification*. Oxford: Oxford University Press, 1994.

Foley, Richard. *Working without a Net*. Oxford: Oxford University Press, 1993.

———. Review of Peter Klein's *Certainty: A Refutation of Scepticism*. *Philosophy & Phenomenological Research* 4 (1984).

Fumerton, Richard. *Metaepistemology and Skepticism*. Lanham, Md.: Rowman & Littlefield, 1995.

Greco, John. *Putting Skeptics in their Place*. New York: Cambridge University Press, 2000.

Hilpinen, Risto. "Skepticism and Justification." *Synthese* 55 (1983): 165–174.

Huemer, Michael. *Skepticism and the Veil of Perception*. Lanham, Md.: Rowman & Littlefield, 2001.

Johnson, Oliver. "Ignorance and Irrationality: A Study in Contemporary Scepticism." *Philosophy Research Archives* 5 (1979): 368–417.

———. *Skepticism and Cognitivism*. Berkeley: University of California Press, 1978.

Klein, Peter D. *Certainty: A Refutation of Scepticism*. Minneapolis: University of Minnesota Press, 1981.

———. "Real Knowledge." *Synthese* 55 (1983): 143–164.

Lehrer, Keith. *Knowledge*, chap. 10. Oxford: Clarendon, 1974.

———. "The Problem of Knowledge and Skepticism." In James Cornman, Keith Lehrer, and George Pappas, *Philosophical Problems and Arguments: An Introduction*, 3d ed., chap. 2. New York: Macmillan, 1982.

———. *Theory of Knowledge*. Boulder, Colo.: Westview, 1990.

———. "Why Not Scepticism?" *Philosophical Forum* 2 (1971): 283–298. Reprinted in *Essays on Knowledge and Justification*, pp. 346–363.

Luper-Foy, Steven, ed. *The Possibility of Knowledge: Nozick and his Critics*. Lanham, Md.: Rowman & Littlefield, 1986.

Moser, Paul K. "Justified Doubt without Certainty." *Pacific Philosophical Quarterly* 65 (1984): 97–104.

———. *Knowledge and Evidence*. Cambridge: Cambridge University Press, 1989.

———. *Philosophy After Objectivity*. Oxford: Oxford University Press, 1993.

———. "Skepticism Undone?" In *The Philosophy of Ernest Sosa*. Edited by John Greco. Cambridge, Mass.: Blackwell, 2002.

Naess, Arne. *Skepticism*. London: Routledge & Kegan Paul, 1969.

Nathan, N. M. L. *The Price of Doubt*. London: Routledge, 2001.

Nozick, Robert. *Philosophical Explanations*, chap. 3. Cambridge, Mass.: Harvard University Press, 1981.

Oakley, I. T. "An Argument for Skepticism Concerning Justified Belief." *American Philosophical Quarterly* 13 (1976): 221–228.

O'Connor, D. J., and Brian Carr. *Introduction to the Theory of Knowledge*, chap. 1. Minneapolis: University of Minnesota Press, 1982.

Odegard, Douglas. "Chisholm's Approach to Scepticism." *Metaphilosophy* 12 (1981): 7–12.

———. *Knowledge and Skepticism*. Totowa, N.J.: Rowman & Littlefield, 1983.

Pappas, George. "Some Forms of Epistemological Scepticism." In *Essays on Knowledge and Justification*, pp. 309–316. Edited by G. Pappas and M. Swain. Ithaca, N.Y.: Cornell University Press, 1978.

Rescher, Nicholas. *Scepticism: A Critical Reappraisal*. Oxford: Blackwell, 1979.

Roth, M. D., and G. Ross, eds. *Doubting*. Dordrecht: Kluwer, 1990.

Slote, Michael. *Reason and Scepticism*. New York: Humanities, 1970.

Sosa, Ernest, and Enrique Villanueva, eds. *Skepticism*. Cambridge, Mass.: Blackwell, 2000.

Strawson, Peter F. *Skepticism and Naturalism*. New York: Columbia University Press, 1985.

Stroud, Barry. *The Significance of Philosophical Scepticism*. Oxford: Clarendon, 1984.

———. "The Significance of Scepticism." In *Transcendental Arguments and Science*. Edited by P. Bieri et al. Dordrecht: Reidel, 1979.

———. "Skepticism and the Possibility of Knowledge." *Journal of Philosophy* 81 (1984): 545–551.

Unger, Peter. "A Defense of Skepticism." *Philosophical Review* 80 (1971): 198–218. Reprinted in *Essays on Knowledge and Justification*, pp. 317–336. Edited by G. Pappas and M. Swain. Ithaca, N.Y.: Cornell University Press, 1978.

———. *Ignorance*. Oxford: Clarendon, 1976.

———. "Two Types of Scepticism." *Philosophical Studies* 25 (1974): 77–96.

Vinci, Thomas. Critical Notice of Peter Klein's *Certainty: A Refutation of Scepticism*. *Canadian Journal of Philosophy* 14 (1984): 125–145.

Watkins, John. *Science and Scepticism*. Princeton, N.J.: Princeton University Press, 1984.

Williams, Michael. *Unnatural Doubts*. Oxford: Blackwell, 1991.

Wittgenstein, Ludwig. *On Certainty*. Edited by G. E. M. Anscombe and G. H. von Wright. Oxford: Blackwell, 1969.

Woods, Michael. "Scepticism and Natural Knowledge." *Proceedings of the Aristotelian Society* 54 (1980): 231–248.

INDEX

....